COOK'S
ILLUSTRATED

~ 2009 ~

$35.00

Published by
America's Test Kitchen
17 Station Street
Brookline, MA 02445

ISBN-13: 978-1-933615-49-3
ISBN-10: 1-933615-49-4
ISSN: 1933-639X

To get home delivery of *Cook's Illustrated,* call 800-526-8442 inside the U.S., or 515-247-7571 if calling from outside the U.S., or subscribe online at www.cooksillustrated.com.

In addition to *Cook's Illustrated* Hardbound Annual Editions available from each year of publication (1993–2009), America's Test Kitchen offers the following cookbooks and DVD sets:

The America's Test Kitchen Family Cookbook
The America's Test Kitchen Family Baking Book

The Best Recipe Series
More Best Recipes
The Best Skillet Recipes
The Best Slow & Easy Recipes
The Best Chicken Recipes
The Best International Recipe
The Best Make-Ahead Recipe
The Best 30-Minute Recipe
The Best Light Recipe
The Cook's Illustrated Guide to Grilling and *Barbecue*
Best American Side Dishes
The Best Cover & Bake Recipes
The New Best Recipe
Steaks, Chops, Roasts, and Ribs
Baking Illustrated
Perfect Vegetables
Italian Classics
The Best American Classics
The Best Soups & Stews

The Cook's Country Series
America's Best Lost Recipes
The Cook's Country Cookbook
Best Grilling Recipes
Best Lost Suppers

Cook's Country Hardbound Annual Editions
2009 Cook's Country Annual Edition
2008 Cook's Country Annual Edition
2007 Cook's Country Annual Edition
2006 Cook's Country Annual Edition
2005 Cook's Country Annual Edition

Additional books from America's Test Kitchen
The Best of America's Test Kitchen 2010
The Best of America's Test Kitchen 2009
The Best of America's Test Kitchen 2008
The Best of America's Test Kitchen 2007
834 Kitchen Quick Tips
Cooking for Two 2009
1993–2009 Cook's Illustrated Master Index

The America's Test Kitchen Series
Companion Cookbooks
The Complete America's Test Kitchen TV Show Cookbook
America's Test Kitchen: The TV Companion Cookbook (2009)
Behind the Scenes with America's Test Kitchen (2008)
Test Kitchen Favorites (2007)
Cooking at Home with America's Test Kitchen (2006)
America's Test Kitchen Live! (2005)
Inside America's Test Kitchen (2004)
Here in America's Test Kitchen (2003)
The America's Test Kitchen Cookbook (2002)

The America's Test Kitchen Series DVD Sets
(from our hit public television series)
The *America's Test Kitchen* 2009 Season (4-DVD set)
The *America's Test Kitchen* 2008 Season (4-DVD set)
The *America's Test Kitchen* 2007 Season (4-DVD set)
The *America's Test Kitchen* 2006 Season (4-DVD set)
The *America's Test Kitchen* 2005 Season (4-DVD set)
The *America's Test Kitchen* 2004 Season (4-DVD set)
The *America's Test Kitchen* 2003 Season (4-DVD set)
The *America's Test Kitchen* 2002 Season (4-DVD set)
The *America's Test Kitchen* 2001 Season (2-DVD set)

To order any of our cookbooks and DVDs listed above, give us a call at 800-611-0759 inside the U.S., or at 515-246-6911 if calling from outside the U.S. You can order subscriptions, gift subscriptions, and any of our books by visiting our online store at www.cooksillustrated.com.

NUMBER NINETY-SIX

JANUARY & FEBRUARY 2009

COOK'S
ILLUSTRATED

Chicken Noodle
Soup
Quick No-Bones Recipe

The Perfect
French Omelet
All-New Foolproof Method

Braised Short Ribs
Taking Out the Fat

Chewy Chocolate
Cookies

Testing 12-Inch
Skillets
Best Buy Saves 50%

Rating Maple Syrups

Tandoori Chicken at Home
Thin and Crisp Pork Cutlets
Best Swedish Meatballs
Better French Toast
Guide to Prepping Vegetables

www.cooksillustrated.com

$5.95 U.S./$6.95 CANADA

0 74470 62805 7

0 2>

CONTENTS

January & February 2009

COOK'S ILLUSTRATED

Founder and Editor Christopher Kimball
Editorial Director Jack Bishop
Executive Editor Amanda Agee
Test Kitchen Director Erin McMurrer
Managing Editor Rebecca Hays
Senior Editors Keith Dresser
Lisa McManus
Features Editor Lisa Glazer
Copy Editor Amy Graves
Associate Editors J. Kenji Alt
Charles Kelsey
David Pazmiño
Production Editor, Special Issues Elizabeth Bomze
Test Cooks Francisco J. Robert
Yvonne Ruperti
Assistant Test Kitchen Director Matthew Herron
Assistant Editors Meredith Butcher
Peggy Chung
Executive Assistant Meredith Smith
Senior Kitchen Assistant Nadia Domeq
Kitchen Assistants Maria Elena Delgado
Ena Gudiel
Edward Tundidor
Producer Melissa Baldino
Contributing Editors Matthew Card
Dawn Yanagihara
Consulting Editors Scott Brueggeman
Guy Crosby
Proofreader Jean Rogers

Online Managing Editor David Tytell
Online Editor Kate Mason
Online Media Producer Peter Tannenbaum
Online Assistant Editor Leaya Lee

Design Director Amy Klee
Art Director, Magazines Julie Bozzo
Senior Designer Christine Vo
Designers Jay Layman
Lindsey Timko
Staff Photographer Daniel J. van Ackere

Vice President Marketing David Mack
Circulation Director Doug Wicinski
Circulation & Fulfillment Manager Carrie Horan
Circulation Assistant Megan Cooley
Partnership Marketing Manager Pamela Putprush
Direct Mail Director Adam Perry
Marketing Database Analyst Ariel Gilbert-Knight
Product Operations Director Steven Browall
Product Promotions Director Randi Lawrence
E-Commerce Marketing Director Hugh Buchan
Associate Marketing Manager Laurel Zeidman
Marketing Copywriter David Goldberg
Customer Service Manager Jacqueline Valerio
Customer Service Representatives Jillian Nannicelli
Kate Sokol

Sponsorship Sales Director Marcy McCreary
Retail Sales & Marketing Manager Emily Logan
Corporate Marketing Associate Bailey Vatalaro

Production Director Guy Rochford
Traffic & Projects Manager Alice Carpenter
Senior Production Manager Jessica L. Quirk
Production & Imaging Specialists Judy Blomquist
Lauren Pettapiece
Imaging & Color Specialist Andrew Mannone

Systems Administrator S. Paddi McHugh
Web Production Coordinator Evan Davis
Support Technician Brandon Lynch

Chief Financial Officer Sharyn Chabot
Human Resources Director Adele Shapiro
Controller Mandy Shito
Senior Accountant Aaron Goranson
Staff Accountant Connie Forbes
Accounts Payable Specialist Steven Kasha
Office Manager Tasha Bere
Receptionist Henrietta Murray
Publicity Deborah Broide

For list rental information, contact: Specialists Marketing Services, Inc., 777 Terrace Ave., 4th Floor, Hasbrouck Heights, NJ 07604; 201-865-5800.

Editorial Office: 17 Station St., Brookline, MA 02445; 617-232-1000; fax 617-232-1572. Subscription inquiries, visit www.americastestkitchen.com/customerservice or call 800-526-8442.

Postmaster: Send all new orders, subscription inquiries, and change-of-address notices to Cook's Illustrated, P.O. Box 7446, Red Oak, IA 51591-0446.

PRINTED IN THE USA

TISANE HERBS AND FLOWERS

Tisanes are herbal infusions brewed from fresh or dried fruits, flowers, seeds, or roots. These aromatic beverages are often used as herbal remedies. Sedating chamomile can be blended or steeped alone to maximize its sweet, apple notes. Lavender is potent, so the flowers, which are said to be calming, are often used as part of a blend. The intoxicating aroma of jasmine flowers has been captured in tea since the fifth century. Fragrant gardenia blossoms are often used to scent black, green, and oolong teas. Nepeta, also known as catnip, has a minty flavor once steeped. Pungent thyme is favored for addressing upper-respiratory ailments. The roots of the purple coneflower, echinacea, are valued for their licorice-like, caramel flavors and are said to boost the immune system. Yellow and white chrysanthemums are often floating in the tea that is served with dim sum. Sweet ground fennel seeds are used in brews meant to aid digestion. The menthol quality of spearmint tea makes it refreshing served hot or cold. Tart, fruity rose hips are often combined with hibiscus flowers. Yarrow flowers produce a warm-flavored tea that is recommended as a fever reducer.

COVER (*Pineapple*): Robert Papp, BACK COVER (*Tisane Herbs and Flowers*): John Burgoyne

America's TEST KITCHEN *America's Test Kitchen* is a very real 2,500-square-foot kitchen located just outside of Boston. It is the home of *Cook's Illustrated* and *Cook's Country* magazines and is the workday destination for more than three dozen test cooks, editors, and cookware specialists. Our mission is to test recipes over and over again until we understand how and why they work and until we arrive at the best version. We also test kitchen equipment and supermarket ingredients in search of brands that offer the best value and performance. You can watch us work by tuning in to *America's Test Kitchen* (www.americastestkitchen.com) on public television.

THE VERMONT CREED

Calvin Coolidge once remarked that Vermonters might be called upon to restore the Union through their free spirit and support of liberty. I might amend that notion by pointing out that the "Vermont Creed," as it were, is shared by millions of working-class folks around the country. It can be summed up in two words: "seen worse," a wry, tough-minded statement of independence, with a streak of macabre humor thrown in for good effect. Here is my version of that creed.

Think Locally: The phrase "think globally" was not coined by a Vermonter. The first question that comes to mind when we hear about a logging accident, a scandal, or someone winning top prize on the buckboard is always, "Did it happen in town?" Vermonters know that what's closest to home matters most. If you don't care about your own backyard, you aren't going to be of much use to the rest of the world.

When You Don't Know What to Do, Do the Work in Front of You: This is an old Coolidge saying. Don't dither. Don't fret. Don't think of the myriad possibilities when faced with a difficult situation. Just do the work in front of you and things will always work themselves out. (And if they don't, at least your chores will be up-to-date.)

Worse Things than Death: Vermonters don't think about death much; they just die when they having nothing left to do. Once you're dead, you are no longer useful. If you are no longer useful, you might as well be dead. That's also true of the living, as any Vermonter will tell you.

Every Day Is a New Day: One of our retired neighbors, John, used to tell me this almost every time I saw him. I'd ask, "What are you up to these days?" and he would say, "Every day in the woods is a new day." He'd have a spark in his eye and a spring in his step and tell me about logging, cutting firewood, maintaining trails, and clearing pastures. That's why he always looked forward to getting up early, even in later years when he was having trouble walking. The trees needed him.

The Early Bird Gets the Worm: Many a year, I have planted the corn too early, before the cold weather was done and before the soil temperature was up to 70 degrees. After two or three hot days

in late April, having hooked up the planter and filled it with seed and fertilizer, off I'd go. Then it would turn cold and wet. The seed would rot in the ground. And Charlie Bentley would turn to me after church and say, "Guess you planted too early. Again." The early bird gets the worm, not the corn.

Look, Aim, Then Shoot: When I first learned to rabbit hunt, I would blast away as soon as I saw a "brownie" moving across the snow or out of a stand of pines. On one particular occasion, after I had unloaded all five shells in my 20-gauge semi-automatic, our neighbor Tom asked me, "Need more ammo?" That afternoon, Tom's dog Bucket pushed out a good-sized rabbit and Tom waited for what seemed a solid minute. Five yards. Ten yards. Twenty yards. Thirty yards. Tom finally shot and brought the rabbit down with just one shell. He didn't say anything. He didn't have to.

Be Useful: Vermonters would answer the old Zen koan about the tree falling in the woods right off the bat. If nobody was there to hear it, it didn't happen. Same thing for people. If you volunteer for rescue squad, set up tables for Old Home Day, or pitch in as zoning administrator, you exist. If you can't be counted on in a pinch, you are like a tree falling unobserved in the woods. It just doesn't matter much. All you're good for is firewood.

Know Your History: A newcomer to our town just built a house in a flood plain, just 100 yards up from the Green River. Now, the field hasn't flooded in over half a century, but most people in town know the story of the last time it happened. And most of us figure that the river is about due for another spring flood. Except, of course, the flatlander. The zoning board never mentioned this when reviewing his application. This brings up another Vermont rule of thumb: "Don't Ask, Don't Tell."

Mind Your Own Business: Last year, one of our selectmen proposed a law restricting the use of four-wheeler ATVs. He was sick and tired of hearing them run up and down logging trails near his house. He got quiet support all over town: at the country store, gassing up his car at ChemClean, and at the odd church

Christopher Kimball

supper. Then he called a town meeting to vote on his proposal and got the bum's rush. Seems that his neighbors didn't mind a bit of gossip but knew better than to seriously interfere with other people's business. That way, they won't interfere with yours.

Waste Not, Want Not: When I was 12 years old, I purchased a lemon meringue pie from Marie, the town baker. When I got home, I shot upstairs to eat it. My mother, being instantly suspicious, came up to my room to check things out. I hid the pie under my patchwork comforter and, in my panic, ended up sitting on it. The next day, Marie asked, "How was the pie?" I told her the truth, including the part about throwing it out afterward. I had never seen her so mad. "You threw it out?" she said quietly. With great restraint, she added, "That pie was still good eating." There is, I learned, a world of difference between real country living and just playing at it.

Life Is Fair, Really! Vermonters don't envy the flatlander with the $2 million house or the fisherman who won the $25,000 salmon tournament up on Lake Ontario. They know that life is fair, which means that the rich flatlander will end up divorced and the lucky fisherman's pickup will run into a bull moose. Life is indeed fair; it always gets even.

Don't Look in the Mirror: As far as I can tell, Vermonters don't use mirrors. That's because they don't care what they look like, and that, in turn, is because they don't care what anyone else thinks of them. No point checking on the three-legged dog to see if he grew an extra leg overnight. Some things in life are just not gonna change.

Check the Weather: Vermonters check the weather first thing in the morning and then two or three times during the day. That way, they can reassure themselves that life is, ultimately, beyond their control, a notion that provides a sense of well-being. Who better than the weatherman to remind us of man's shortcomings?

Make Hay While the Sun Shines: There is never a perfect time for anything, but there is a right time for everything. A real Vermonter knows the difference.

FOR INQUIRIES, ORDERS, OR MORE INFORMATION

www.cooksillustrated.com
At www.cooksillustrated.com, you can order books and subscriptions, sign up for our free e-newsletter, or renew your magazine subscription. Join the website and gain access to 16 years of *Cook's Illustrated* recipes, equipment tests, and ingredient tastings, as well as Cook's Live companion videos for every recipe in this issue.

COOKBOOKS
We sell more than 50 cookbooks by the editors of *Cook's Illustrated*. To order, visit our bookstore at www.cooksillustrated.com or call 800-611-0759 (or 515-246-6911 from outside the U.S.).

COOK'S ILLUSTRATED Magazine
Cook's Illustrated magazine (ISSN 1068-2821), number 96, is published bimonthly by Boston Common Press Limited Partnership, 17 Station St., Brookline, MA 02445. Copyright 2009 Boston Common Press Limited Partnership. Periodicals postage paid at Boston, Mass., and additional mailing offices USPS #012487. Publications Mail Agreement No. 40020778. Return undeliverable Canadian addresses to P.O. Box 875, Station A, Windsor, Ontario N9A 6P2. POSTMASTER: Send address changes to Cook's Illustrated, P.O. Box 7446, Red Oak, IA 51591-0446. For subscription and gift subscription orders, subscription inquiries, or change-of-address notices, call 800-526-8442 in the U.S. or 515-247-7571 from outside the U.S. or write us at Cook's Illustrated, P.O. Box 7446, Red Oak, IA 51591-0446.

NOTES FROM READERS

≥ COMPILED BY DAVID PAZMIÑO ≤

Sturdy Parchment Paper

Your recipe for Almost No-Knead Bread (January/February 2008) has become a weekly favorite in our house. We have just one problem: The parchment paper sling used to transfer the dough into the pot often breaks after cooking, making it hard to remove the bread from the hot Dutch oven. Do you have any suggestions?

MARTI SIMPSON
MUNSTER, IND.

➤In the test kitchen, we use parchment paper for all sorts of tasks. Because this paper is treated with sulfuric acid and then coated with silicone, it is both nonstick and heat-resistant. Previous tests (January/February 2002) had declared Reynolds our favorite retail brand of parchment paper, but since then several other brands have come on the market with claims that they can withstand temperatures up to 450 degrees. To see how our original winner (which claims it can withstand temperatures only up to 420 degrees) would do in our Almost No-Knead Bread recipe, we pitted it against four other brands: Wilton, Homelife, Beyond Gourmet, and Regency. After 45 minutes in a 425-degree oven, a clear winner emerged: Regency. It maintained its shape without tearing and exhibited very little browning. Our previous winner, Reynolds, was the next best; it was a bit more fragile than the Regency, but not nearly as breakable as the other brands. While all the parchment papers performed fine below 400 degrees, we'll choose Regency for high-heat applications, including our Almost No-Knead Bread.

Regency parchment paper can withstand temperatures of up to 450 degrees.

Sweet Onions

I often buy Vidalia onions to use raw in salads because they are less pungent than yellow onions. One day I found myself without yellow onions for cooking. Can I use sweet onions like Vidalias as a substitute for yellow onions?

SUSAN FRANCK
ATLANTA, GA.

➤For starters, onions such as Vidalias, Texas SuperSweets, and Walla Wallas belong to a group labeled "sweet onions." Although they are sweet, they don't contain any more sugar than yellow onions. They do, however, contain lower levels of sulfur compounds—the stuff that makes onions potent. The amount of sulfur is determined not only by the variety of onion but also by the soil and growing conditions. In the case of sweet onions, which mostly grow in low-sulfur soils and are picked before the heat of summer, the plants have little stress and are therefore less sulfurous.

We have already determined that in recipes like French Onion Soup (January/February 2008), sweet onions offer too much sweetness (this recipe uses 4 pounds). To see how they fared in recipes calling for fewer onions, we cooked up German Potato Salad (September/October 2003), Simple Beef Chili (March/April 2003), Grilled Sausages and Onions (July/August 2008), and Basic Risotto (March/April 1994). Although some tasters noted that the dishes made with Vidalia onions were slightly less "pungent" and "sharp," most tasters noticed little to no difference. While we wouldn't go out and stock our pantry with sweet onions (they usually cost significantly more than yellow onions), they're fine to use in recipes where onions aren't the main ingredient.

Freezing Ricotta

I often make fresh ravioli or manicotti and find myself with leftover ricotta cheese. I hate to see it go to waste. Is it possible to freeze the leftovers for later use?

JILL RICHLOVSKY
CLEVELAND, OHIO

➤Ricotta is a fresh cheese that contains a lot of water, so our suspicion was that freezing would cause the extra water to leach out when thawed, giving the cheese a gritty texture and chalky taste. To find out for sure, we froze a few previously opened containers of ricotta for two months. We then defrosted them to make two batches each of Baked Manicotti (January/February 2007), ricotta cheesecake, and Pasta with Sun-Dried Tomatoes, Ricotta, and Peas (January/February 2004), one with the previously frozen ricotta and one with fresh ricotta. We also tasted both ricottas plain.

When the ricotta was sampled plain, most tasters preferred the never-frozen version for its smooth, clean taste. The frozen ricotta was more granular, looser in texture, and slightly watery. Few tasters could detect any differences when the ricotta was baked in the manicotti. The cheesecake made with the frozen ricotta was slightly firmer and not quite as moist, but the difference was negligible. But the frozen ricotta tossed with pasta was objectionable. In this recipe, the ricotta does not get cooked, and its texture was noticeably granular. So go ahead and freeze extra ricotta—just make sure to use it in an application such as manicotti or cheesecake where you are actually cooking the ricotta. Avoid applications in which it is served raw or barely cooked.

Sugar Substitutes

I try to avoid using all types of white and brown sugar in my recipes. I have tried using substitutes like honey or rice bran syrup, but these often change the texture of the recipe completely. Do you know of any ingredients that might swap easily with sugar?

KRISTINA DRINKWINE
DENVER, COLO.

➤After a bit of research, we narrowed our focus to two alternatives that mimic the dry, crystallized nature of white and brown sugar: maple and date sugar. Maple sugar is made by boiling maple syrup until it crystallizes. Date sugar is made by grinding dates and then processing them into a powder.

First, we selected recipes that call for brown sugar. We chose Brown Sugar Cookies (March/April 2007), Oatmeal Cake (May/June 2008), and Glazed Pork Chops (March/April 2006). The date sugar bombed the tests. The cookie dough did not spread as it baked, resulting in hard, round cookies; the cake was quite dry; and the glaze on the pork chops was gloppy and grainy. On the other hand, the maple sugar won near-universal approval in all three recipes.

MADE WITH DATE SUGAR

MADE WITH MAPLE SUGAR
Brown Sugar Cookies made with date sugar failed to spread during baking. Maple sugar performed well.

The real test was to see how the maple sugar would fare in recipes that call for white sugar. To test this, we made our Classic Pound Cake (January/February 2007) and Sugar Cookies (November/December 2002). The maple sugar performed just as well as white sugar, creaming well with the butter and making a perfectly domed pound cake and pleasantly chewy cookies. The only distraction was that the maple sugar turned the cake and cookies light brown. As for flavor, some tasters enjoyed the maple notes, while others thought they were a bit too intense. If you don't mind the intense taste of maple sugar, it's a good substitute for white and brown sugar.

Rosemary Overload

I recently made a recipe that called for one sprig of rosemary. Not knowing what that meant, I tossed in a bushy 10-inch stem. The resulting dish tasted like a pine forest. How long is one sprig?

PATRICIA FRY
HARWICH, MASS.

➤ When cooking with herbs that have a low essential oil content (such as parsley), adding a little extra won't ruin a soup or stew. When it comes to stronger herbs such as rosemary, however, using too much can ruin a recipe, and there's no way to repair this mistake. In the test kitchen, we consider an herb sprig to be medium-sized (about 6 inches long)—neither a large, bushy branch nor a wispy tendril.

To demonstrate the effect of using large and medium sprigs of rosemary in our Tuscan White Bean Soup (January/February 2001), we made two batches. The first soup was made with a bushy sprig measuring 12 inches. After the beans were soaked with this sprig, they were nearly inedible. The strong oils in the rosemary overwhelmed all other flavors. When using a less bushy 6-inch stem, the flavors were just right. When in doubt, use a small amount of rosemary and taste the dish. You can always add a bit more of this potent herb.

TOO BUSHY

JUST RIGHT
A 6-inch sprig of rosemary will add the right amount of flavor, but a 12-inch sprig will be overwhelming.

Sharpening Steels

I recently bought a set of good chef's knives. What type of steel should I buy to sharpen them? Stores seem to stock three kinds: regular cut, fine cut, and polished cut.

LARRY CASEY
SHELTON, CONN.

➤ If the metal rod that goes by the name of sharpening steel were called a honing steel, it would save a lot of confusion. This tool does not actually sharpen knives but merely readjusts the angle of the cutting edge. As a knife is used, the cutting edge tends to bend and fold slightly, giving the perception of a less sharp knife. By running the edge of a knife across a steel, the small folds and burrs that form are straightened, or honed, making the knife perform better. A knife sharpener, on the other hand, actually removes metal from both sides of the blade's edge, creating a new surface for cutting.

The three types of steels on the market—regular, fine, and polished cut—all accomplish the same task to a lesser or greater degree. The rough, filed lines of the regular-cut steel are best for home cooks who only occasionally hone the edge of a knife. For professional chefs and meat cutters who use their knives for hours

on end (and steel them dozens of times per day), the fine and polished cuts are a better choice, as constant contact with the rougher surface of a regular-cut steel could wear away their knives' edges.

Cornichon Substitute

I often see cornichons listed in recipes but have a hard time finding them in the supermarket. Is there something else I can use instead?

SHANNON PLANK
WATERTOWN, MASS.

➤ *Cornichon* is the French word for a pickled gherkin cucumber. They are most often served as a condiment to rich foods such as pâtés and cured meats. Although they look like the sweet gherkins found in the supermarket, the similarities end there. Cornichons are pickled in vinegar and flavored with onions, mustard, and aromatics. Sweet gherkins, on the other hand, contain a fair amount of sugar or corn syrup along with spices such as cloves and allspice.

To find an acceptable substitute, we tasted plain cornichons, sweet gherkins, and chopped dill pickles straight up and in our French Potato Salad (July/August 2002) and Tartar Sauce (January/February 2005). In the end, tasters felt that chopped dill pickles came the closest to the tart and briny flavors of true cornichons. Sweet gherkins tasted too "candylike," and their spices upset the balance of flavors. There is no substitute for the real thing, but if you need something in a pinch, a dill pickle is a good stand-in.

Cooking with Sherry

I often see recipes that call for dry sherry. Is it OK to substitute cream sherry?

JULIA GRIMALDI
EVERETT, MASS.

➤ Sherry is a fortified wine that originated in the Andalusia region of southern Spain. Dry sherry is made from Palomino grapes, and cream (also called sweet) sherry comes from Pedro Ximénez grapes. To find out if cream sherry could be a viable substitute in recipes that call for dry, we cooked up our Pan-Roasted Chicken Breasts with Garlic-Sherry Sauce (March/April 2003) and Stir-Fried Beef with Snap Peas and Red Peppers (November/December 2007) with the sweet wine. To our surprise, only a few tasters objected to the sweetness of the cream sherry in either dish. In both cases, we were able to address these concerns with a squeeze of lemon juice that helped balance out the flavors.

One final note: While cream sherry may be a fine stand-in for dry sherry in most instances, always avoid cooking sherry. Loaded with salt and artificial caramel flavoring, this sherry will ruin the flavor of most dishes.

SEND US YOUR QUESTIONS We will provide a complimentary one-year subscription for each letter we print. Send your inquiry, name, address, and daytime telephone number to Notes from Readers, Cook's Illustrated, P.O. Box 470589, Brookline, MA 02447, or to notesfromreaders@americastest kitchen.com.

Quick Tips

⇒ COMPILED BY YVONNE RUPERTI & FRANCISCO J. ROBERT ⇐

Neater Egg Slicing

Slicing hard-cooked eggs can be messy because the yolk tends to crumble and stick to the blade of the knife.

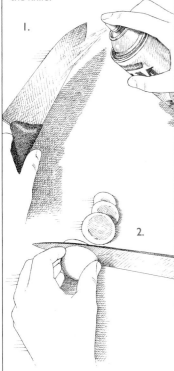

1.

2.

1. Casey O'Hearn of Norfolk, Va., solves the problem by spraying the knife with nonstick cooking spray.
2. The eggs can now be neatly sliced. Respray the knife blade as needed.

Keeping Avocado Green

Avocado flesh turns brown very quickly once it is exposed to air. Lauren Coroy of Houston, Texas, has found a solution for preserving the color of extra avocado halves.

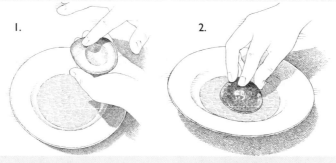

1.   2.

1. Rub 1 tablespoon of olive oil on all of the exposed avocado flesh.
2. Allow the excess oil to drip into a shallow bowl, then place the avocado half cut-side down in the center of the oil puddle, creating a "seal." Store the avocado in the refrigerator.

Easier Zesting

Licia Jaccard of Culver City, Calif., found that when she zested fruit over her Microplane grater onto a cutting board, she couldn't see how much zest was accumulating. She decided to hold the fruit in her hand and run the zester over the fruit instead. This method allows the zest to collect in the grater's chute, neatly and in full view.

Disposable Spoon Rest

For a quick, impromptu spoon rest, Cindy Johnston of Lakewood, Wash., uses recycled lids from plastic containers of sour cream, cottage cheese, or yogurt.

Keeping Maple Syrup Warm

There's nothing like pouring warm maple syrup over hot French toast or pancakes. To keep the syrup from getting cold during breakfast, Holly Hetherington of New York, N.Y., pours the freshly warmed syrup into an insulated thermos.

Rescuing Overwhipped Cream

When whipping cream, it's always wise to pay careful attention so that the cream doesn't become too stiff. But if it's been whipped just a bit too much, Dartagnan Brown of Everett, Mass., has a trick to ensure all is not lost.

1.

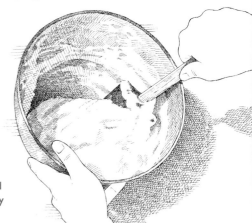

2.

1. Add unwhipped cream into the over-whipped mixture 1 tablespoon at a time.
2. Gently fold the mixture, adding more unwhipped cream until the desired consistency is reached.

Send Us Your Tip We will provide a complimentary one-year subscription for each tip we print. Send your tip, name, and address to Quick Tips, Cook's Illustrated, P.O. Box 470589, Brookline, MA 02447, or to quicktips@americastestkitchen.com.

Mixing Small Quantities

Jayashree Chava of San Jose, Calif., found herself in a bind when she wanted to use her hand-held mixer to whip just a few egg whites for a recipe. The volume of whites was too shallow for the beaters to work. She solved this dilemma by transferring the whites to a smaller bowl and then removing one of the beaters from the mixer. The single beater was a perfect fit for the smaller bowl, and she was able to whip the whites easily.

Split and Freeze

When freezing English muffins or bagels, Michael Miller of Tampa, Fla., finds that they often fuse together, becoming difficult to separate when he is ready to toast them. To expedite breakfast preparation, he now uses this method.

1. Split each English muffin or bagel in half.
2. Place the halves back together. Wrap with plastic wrap and freeze.

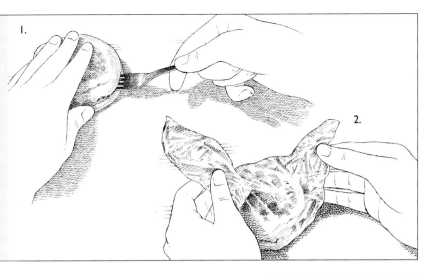

A Clean Stream

Some liquid measuring cups have itsy-bitsy pourer spouts that can make a big mess if you pour too quickly—the liquid will leak and run down the cup, not into your bowl. For a mess-free pour, Maia Miller of Brooklyn, N.Y., follows this easy procedure. As you pour, hold a butter knife (blade up) in the spout and at an angle. The liquid will follow the knife and stay in a steady stream.

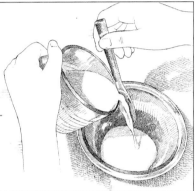

From Lumpy to Smooth

If a pudding or pastry cream has become lumpy during cooking, Patricia Williams of Houston, Texas, uses this restaurant trick to whip it back into shape.

Easier Muffin Removal

Just-baked muffins can be tricky to dislodge from the pan; they can stick or, if they are top heavy, break in half. Elizabeth Hurwitz of Brookline, Mass., recommends tilting the muffin pan on its side and then slowly removing the muffins. They will slide out more easily and in one piece.

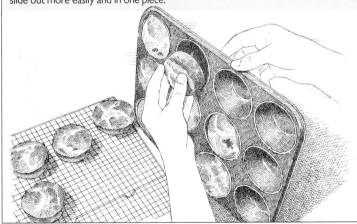

No More Soggy Cheesecake

Most cheesecake recipes call for wrapping a springform pan with foil before placing the cake in a water bath. The foil is meant to keep the water out, but sometimes water leaks in anyway and you wind up with an unappetizing, soggy crust. Arlene Gunter of Berkeley Lake, Ga., offers an easy solution. She simply places the filled springform pan in a large oven bag (the kind used for baking ham) and pulls the bag up the sides of the pan, leaving the top surface of the cake exposed. When the pan is placed in a water bath, it is sure to stay dry.

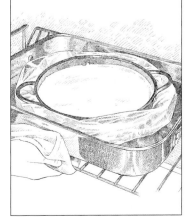

1. Using an immersion blender, quickly blend the pudding until smooth.
2. Pass the pudding through a fine-mesh strainer to remove any remaining solid bits.

Keeping Chives in Check

When prepping a bunch of chives, the slender herbs can roll all over the cutting board, making them difficult to chop. Angela Helman of Somerville, Mass., secures the chives with a rubber band to keep the leaves together.

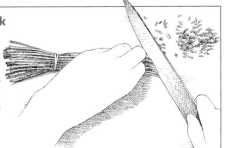

Tandoori Chicken, Reworked

We weren't going to let a 24-hour marinade or the lack of a 900-degree oven keep us from turning this great Indian classic into an easy weeknight dinner.

≥ BY FRANCISCO J. ROBERT ≤

When I'm craving the taste of a good piece of chicken and another plain, boring breast or thigh just won't cut it, there's no better balm than tandoori chicken. The best renditions of this famous Indian specialty feature lightly charred pieces of juicy chicken infused with smoke, garlic, ginger, and spices for a dish that manages to be exotic and homey at the same time.

Authentic versions call for a 24-hour marinade and a tandoor, the traditional beehive-shaped clay oven that fires up to 900 degrees—requirements that keep the dish mainly in the realm of restaurants, even in India. As much as I love the dish, I've often wondered: Do you really need either of these things to create great-tasting chicken full of the same robust flavors?

I decided to take on the challenge of reinventing this Indian classic. But instead of an adaptation geared for the grill—the most obvious means to approximate the tandoor's fierce heat—I wanted a recipe I could make year-round. My tandoori-less chicken would have to be cooked in the oven.

Tandoori Pyrotechnics

Searching through Indian cookbooks, I found that traditional recipes for the dish are all fairly similar. They start with skinless pieces of bone-in chicken marinated in yogurt flavored with ginger, garlic, and garam masala, a mix of spices that typically includes ground cumin, cardamom, coriander, cinnamon, and black pepper. Many call for food coloring to give the meat its characteristic orange cast. And almost all call for a 24-hour soak.

Test-Driving a Tandoor

How would our recipe for Tandoori Chicken—which forgoes the typical daylong marinade and searing heat for a low oven and a quick pass under the broiler—stand up to the real thing?

To find out, I hauled back a tandoor from an Indian specialty store and fired it up in the test kitchen's outdoor grilling area. When its temperature reached 780 degrees (the highest reading my laser thermometer would record), I skewered chicken pieces I'd marinated for 24 hours the traditional way and placed them inside. Fifteen minutes later, I pulled them out and tasted them alongside a batch of chicken baked in the oven according to our recipe. Other than finding the tandoor-cooked chicken smokier, tasters could detect few differences. Given the convenience of cooking in a conventional oven (not to mention the fact that a 140-pound tandoor will set you back $600), we're sticking with our method. –F.J.R.

Our chicken gets its crisp char from just a brief stint under the broiler.

Before I started meddling with the marinating time and the cooking method, I needed to get a better handle on how the traditional approach worked. I prepped some chicken pieces according to a standard recipe and placed them in the refrigerator to marinate for a day. While I waited, I did some research on the tandoor. This simple clay vessel originated thousands of years ago as a means to bake bread. The clay is capable of maintaining extraordinarily high temperatures from the burning charcoal or wood spread over its bottom, while the oblong shape ensures that heat radiates evenly.

WHO NEEDS IT?
This tandoor costs $600 and weighs 140 pounds. We did fine without it.

When meat encounters this fierce heat, the protein molecules on its surface cross-link and contract, trapping moisture inside. Any juices that escape fall to the coals along with rendered fat, creating smoke that flavors the food inside.

Oven Heat: The Highs and Lows

Since the tandoor cooks through ambient versus direct heat, my first thought was to simply crank my oven as high as it would go. I took out my long-marinated chicken pieces, placed them on a wire rack set inside a baking sheet (to prevent the chicken from braising in its own juices), and slid them into a 500-degree oven. The chicken that emerged 30 minutes later was a big disappointment: pasty and hopelessly dry.

Maybe the direct heat of the broiler would work better. This approach proved to be an even greater failure: The placement of the broiler coils gave me some chicken pieces that were browned, some that were undercooked, and others that were dry to the bone. Even worse, each broiler in the test kitchen performed differently. (See "When Older Is Better: Oven Broilers," page 7.) I then tried baking the chicken first at 500 degrees, switching to the broiler just at the end, but the results were still dry.

Maybe it was time to stop mimicking a tandoor and go for something radically different. In the test kitchen, we've preserved the juiciness of thick-cut steaks by starting them in a low oven and searing them at the end. Following this approach, I baked the chicken until almost done in a 325-degree oven, then gave it a quick broil to char the exterior.

This was the winning method—but only if I treated the chicken with extreme care. After several tests, I found it best to remove the chicken pieces just before they were fully cooked (an internal temperature of 125 degrees for the white meat and 130 for the dark meat). I let them rest while the broiler reached temperature, then slid them back into the oven to broil for 10 minutes. Success! The meat was nicely charred on the outside and succulent within.

But two problems remained: The dish took more than 24 hours to make and though the meat was juicy, some tasters thought its texture was too tender, even mushy.

Going for a Dip

Could the mushiness have something to do with the marinade? Not only did most of the recipes I consulted call for a 24-hour soak, many even insisted that longer marinating meant better flavor. Testing this advice, I marinated the chicken for different lengths of time, from 72 hours down to just a brief dip. Surprisingly, my colleagues strongly preferred the chicken that had been dipped versus soaked for any length of time—even just 30 minutes. This outcome actually made sense. Yogurt contains acid, which breaks down proteins to "tenderize" meat. But the longer meat is exposed to acid, the more its proteins break down, to the point where they can actually become soluble. This leads to a texture some might call tender, but my tasters found mushy.

I didn't want to abandon the yogurt altogether, as it adds a distinctive tang. To avoid mushiness, I would stick with just a dip. But now I had a new problem: Without a lengthy soak, how was I going to get the other flavors into the meat? I first tried brining the chicken in a solution of salt and spices, but not enough of the spice flavor made it into the cooked meat. Then a fellow test cook suggested trying a salt-spice rub. The idea seemed promising: Salt draws juices out of the meat, then the reverse happens and the salt, along with the spices and moisture, flows back in, bringing flavor deep into the meat.

I created a rub with the same spices I'd used in the marinade—garam masala, ground cumin, and a little chili powder—then cooked them in oil with ginger and garlic to amplify their flavor. I added a couple of teaspoons of salt and some lime juice to the mix, massaged the rub into the chicken pieces, and then left them to sit for half an hour. After a dunk

STEP-BY-STEP | TANDOORI CHICKEN WITHOUT THE TANDOOR

1. SALT RUB Massage chicken pieces with salt-spice rub to lock in juices and infuse flavor.

2. YOGURT COATING Toss chicken in spiced yogurt for another layer of flavor.

3. LOW OVEN To ensure juicy meat, bake chicken slowly in 325-degree oven until not quite cooked through.

4. BROILER For smoky flavor, briefly broil chicken until lightly charred and fully cooked.

in yogurt flavored with the same spice mixture, the chicken was ready for the oven. The results were terrific: juicy, lightly charred, well-seasoned meat with concentrated flavor and just the right degree of tenderness. That clay oven and 24-hour marinade were finally history. But for the fact that my tandoori-less chicken wasn't orange (I opted not to use food coloring), I'd be willing to bet that few people would notice the difference.

TANDOORI CHICKEN
SERVES 4

We prefer this dish with whole-milk yogurt, but low-fat yogurt can be substituted. If garam masala is unavailable, substitute 2 teaspoons ground coriander, ¼ teaspoon ground cardamom, ¼ teaspoon ground cinnamon, and ½ teaspoon ground black pepper. It is important to remove the chicken from the oven before switching to the broiler setting to allow the broiler element to come up to temperature. Serve with basmati rice and a few chutneys or relishes. Our free recipes for Basmati Rice, Pilaf-Style; Cilantro-Mint Chutney; Onion Relish; and Raita are available at www.cooks illustrated.com/feb09.

- 2 tablespoons vegetable oil
- 6 medium garlic cloves, minced or pressed through garlic press (about 2 tablespoons)
- 2 tablespoons grated fresh ginger
- 1 tablespoon garam masala (see note)
- 2 teaspoons ground cumin
- 2 teaspoons chili powder
- 1 cup plain whole-milk yogurt (see note)
- 4 tablespoons juice from 2 limes, plus 1 lime, cut into wedges
- 2 teaspoons table salt
- 3 pounds bone-in, skin-on chicken parts (breasts, thighs, drumsticks, or mix with breasts cut in half), skin removed and trimmed of excess fat

1. Heat oil in small skillet over medium heat until shimmering. Add garlic and ginger and cook until fragrant, about 1 minute. Add garam masala, cumin, and chili powder; continue to cook until fragrant, 30 to 60 seconds longer. Transfer half of garlic-spice mixture to medium bowl; stir in yogurt and 2 tablespoons lime juice and set aside.

2. In large bowl, combine remaining garlic-spice mixture, remaining 2 tablespoons lime juice, and salt. Using sharp knife, lightly score skinned side of each piece of chicken, making 2 or 3 shallow cuts about 1 inch apart and about ⅛ inch deep; transfer to bowl. Using hands, gently massage salt-spice mixture into chicken until all pieces are evenly coated; let stand at room temperature 30 minutes.

3. Adjust oven rack to upper-middle position (about 6 inches from heating element) and heat oven to 325 degrees. Pour yogurt mixture over chicken and toss until chicken is evenly coated with thick layer. Arrange chicken pieces, scored-side down, on wire rack set in foil-lined, rimmed baking sheet or broiler pan. Discard excess yogurt mixture. Bake chicken until instant-read thermometer inserted into thickest part of chicken registers 125 degrees for breasts and 130 for legs and thighs, 15 to 25 minutes. (Smaller pieces may cook faster than larger pieces. Transfer chicken pieces to plate as they reach correct temperature.)

4. After removing chicken from oven, turn oven to broil and heat 10 minutes. Once broiler is heated, flip chicken pieces over and broil until chicken is lightly charred in spots and instant-read thermometer inserted into thickest part of chicken registers 165 degrees for breasts and 175 for legs and thighs, 8 to 15 minutes. Transfer chicken to large plate, tent loosely with foil, and rest 5 minutes. Serve with chutney or relish, passing lime wedges separately.

COOK'S VIDEOS Original Test Kitchen Videos
www.cooksillustrated.com/feb09
HOW TO MAKE
• Tandoori Chicken
BEHIND THE SCENES
• How we developed our Tandoori Chicken recipe
VIDEO TIP
• Getting to know your broiler

Rethinking Braised Short Ribs

Rich, fork-tender short ribs usually need an overnight rest to get rid of the grease.
We wanted the fat gone by dinnertime—no bones about it.

⇒ BY DAVID PAZMIÑO ⇐

There may be no cut of meat better suited for braising than the rich, beefy short rib. Thanks to copious amounts of fat and gnarly sinews of connective tissue, these "short" portions cut from a cow's ribs start out tough and chewy but are transformed into soft, succulent morsels through hours of braising.

I love eating short ribs in restaurants, but I think long and hard before making them at home. The cooking isn't a challenge: Browning the ribs, then placing them in the oven with plenty of liquid until tender, is about as hands-off as it gets. It's what happens next that can be maddening. Since so much fat is rendered during the ribs' three- or four-hour stint in the oven, most recipes (including ours) call for resting the ribs in the braising liquid overnight, so that the fat solidifies into an easy-to-remove layer.

Recognizing that most people don't plan their dinners days in advance, those same recipes usually offer home cooks an out: ". . . or just skim the fat with a spoon and serve," they say. That method may work fine for leaner cuts. But short ribs simply give off too much fat, and the meat and sauce come out greasy, no matter how diligent one's spoon-wielding.

Was I in for either a greasy mess or a two-day affair? There had to be a better way.

Bon(e) Voyage

My first task was to choose the right rib. Butchers typically divide the ribs into sections about 10 inches square and 3 to 5 inches thick. Cutting the ribs between the bones and into lengths between 2 and 6 inches yields what butchers call "English" style, a cut typically found in European braises. Cutting the meat across the bone yields the "flanken" cut, more typically found in Asian cuisines.

Since English-style short ribs are more widely available, I focused my attention there. I quickly discovered that the smallest, about 2 inches in length, were too short; once braised, they shrank into pieces resembling stew meat. At the other extreme, the 6- to 8-inchers were fairly unwieldy to brown in the pan. I split the difference and settled on 4-inch-long ribs.

Don't let the carrots deceive you—our braised short ribs have far more flavor than a pot roast.

The first step in most braises is browning the meat. Searing adds color and flavor, but in this case it also presents an opportunity to rid the ribs of some of their excess fat. But why not get rid of the fat before they even went into the pan? I took out my chef's knife and trimmed the hard, waxy surface fat from each rib, leaving only a thin layer. I then browned the meat and proceeded with the usual protocol.

This first test provided an important clue as to how to reduce the fat further. Short ribs contain a layer of fat and connective tissue between the meat and the bone. Once fully cooked, this layer shrinks into a tough, chewy strip called "strap meat." While some short-rib fans in the kitchen loved the strap meat, most found it unsightly and, frankly, inedible. To get rid of that strip would mean cutting the meat off the bone and serving the ribs boneless.

Come to think of it, every time I'd ordered braised short ribs in a restaurant, the meat was served off the bone, leaving the connective tissue and bones behind in the kitchen. Calling around to a few local chefs, I found out that most restaurant kitchens cook the meat on the bone, but since they cool the braising liquid overnight, they don't have to worry about removing all the fat on the meat. When it's time to serve the ribs, they remove the bones and excess connective tissue before reheating the meat in the defatted and reduced braising liquid.

What if I followed suit but in reverse, removing the bones before cooking? For my next batch, I simply lopped the meat from the bone in one easy cut and then trimmed the fat on both sides of the meat. As an added benefit, I now had more brownable surface area.

Conducting a side-by-side test of this boneless method versus bone-in, I was shocked by the difference in the amount of fat I ended up with. The bone-in batch rendered nearly 1½ cups of hardened fat. The boneless? A mere ¼ cup. Talk about lean and mean! The results were so shocking that I repeated the test. The outcome was the same. Removing the bones (and the fat between the bones and meat) nearly solved the greasy sauce problem.

To further streamline the recipe, why not just buy boneless short ribs? Boneless short ribs generally cost about $1 more per pound than bone-in ribs, but are actually cheaper in the end. To get the 3 pounds of meat I wanted required 7 pounds of bone-in ribs. With boneless, I needed to buy just 3½ pounds of meat.

Going Boneless

The good news about the bones in short ribs is that they contain marrow, which contributes flavor and body to a braise. The bad news is that they contain lots of fat. Bones also have connective tissue attached to them that looks unsightly when the meat is cooked. We eliminated these problems by using boneless short ribs in our braise. Surprisingly, we didn't miss much flavor from the bones, and adding a half teaspoon of gelatin to the sauce restored any missing suppleness.

BONE REPLACEMENT

A Real Melting Pot

Although we expected that bone-in short ribs would exude more fat than their boneless counterparts, we were shocked by the dramatic difference—a quarter-cup versus 1½ cups (six times as much)! No wonder most short rib recipes call for letting the fat solidify overnight in the fridge.

BONE-IN = LOTS OF FAT

BONELESS = MANAGEABLE FAT

Braised and Infused

Using boneless ribs cut time, money, and fat, but conventional wisdom holds that bones equal flavor. I wondered if this was really the case. So I saved some bones after removing and trimming the meat and placed them into the pot along with the braising liquid. At the same time, I made a batch with only the boneless ribs. They tasted almost the same. (And at this point the flavor was more like pot roast, not nearly intense enough.) But the dish with cooked bones did come out differently in other ways: It had significantly more body, which came from the connective tissue attached to the bone that had broken down into gelatin over time.

If I wanted to spend another few hours in the kitchen, I could have added back the bones and gone through another degreasing. But if it was only gelatin that I needed, well, that wasn't hard to come by. Experimenting with various increments of powdered gelatin—sprinkled into the sauce a few minutes before serving—I found that just half a teaspoon provided a similar supple texture.

Now that I knew I could work with boneless ribs without dramatically reducing flavor and body, I wanted to ramp up the richness of the sauce a bit. After searing the meat in a pan over relatively high heat, most recipes call for cooking aromatics such as onions, shallots, celery, and carrots in the pan drippings before returning the meat to the pot with several cups of stock and some wine. After a few hours, meat cooked this way was certainly tender, but the liquid was thin and not very bold. Reducing the liquid improved matters somewhat, but the sauce tasted acidic and lacked balance.

In our recipe for French-Style Pot Roast (November/December 2007), we jump-started the flavor by reducing the wine before using it to cook the meat. This worked with the ribs, but it also added a step, not to mention an extra saucepan. Simplifying matters, I tried pouring 2 cups of wine right over the browned aromatics and reducing it in the pan. This added just the right intensity, but I didn't end up with enough liquid to keep the meat half-submerged (the right level for braises). I needed another cup of liquid. More wine yielded too much wine flavor; tested against water and chicken broth, beef broth won out for its intensity.

But what about the ¼ cup of excess fat—much more manageable than the 2 cups I'd ended up with using bone-in ribs, but excess all the same? I found that straining and defatting the liquid in a fat separator was all I needed to produce a silky, grease-free sauce. Reducing the degreased cooking liquid to 1 cup concentrated the flavors, making a rich, luxurious sauce—the perfect complement to the fork-tender short-rib meat. And all in a few hours' work.

BRAISED BEEF SHORT RIBS
SERVES 6

Make sure that the ribs are at least 4 inches long and 1 inch thick. If boneless ribs are unavailable, substitute 7 pounds of bone-in beef short ribs at least 4 inches long with 1 inch of meat above the bone. To remove the meat from the bone, see the illustrations above. We recommend a bold red wine such as Cabernet Sauvignon or Côtes du Rhône. The test kitchen's preferred brand of beef broth is Pacific. Serve with egg noodles, mashed potatoes, or roasted potatoes.

3½ pounds boneless short ribs, trimmed of excess fat (see "Boning Short Ribs," above) (see note)
Kosher salt and ground black pepper
2 tablespoons vegetable oil
2 large onions, peeled and sliced thin from pole to pole (about 4 cups)
1 tablespoon tomato paste
6 medium garlic cloves, peeled
2 cups red wine (see note)
1 cup beef broth (see note)
4 large carrots, peeled and cut crosswise into 2-inch pieces
4 sprigs fresh thyme
1 bay leaf
¼ cup cold water
½ teaspoon powdered gelatin

1. Adjust oven rack to lower-middle position and heat oven to 300 degrees. Pat beef dry with paper towels and season with 2 teaspoons salt and 1 teaspoon pepper. Heat 1 tablespoon oil in large heavy-bottomed Dutch oven over medium-high heat until smoking. Add half of beef and cook, without moving, until well browned, 4 to 6 minutes. Turn beef and continue to cook on second side until well browned, 4 to 6 minutes longer, reducing heat if fat begins to smoke. Transfer beef to medium bowl. Repeat with remaining tablespoon oil and meat.

2. Reduce heat to medium, add onions, and cook, stirring occasionally, until softened and beginning to brown, 12 to 15 minutes. (If onions begin to darken too quickly, add 1 to 2 tablespoons water to pan.) Add tomato paste and cook, stirring constantly, until it browns on sides and bottom of pan, about 2 minutes. Add garlic and cook until aromatic, about 30 seconds. Increase heat to medium-high, add wine and simmer, scraping bottom of pan with wooden spoon to loosen browned bits, until reduced by half, 8 to 10 minutes. Add broth, carrots, thyme, and bay leaf. Add beef and any accumulated juices to pot; cover and bring to simmer. Transfer pot to oven and cook, using tongs to turn meat twice during cooking, until fork slips easily in and out of meat, 2 to 2½ hours.

3. Place water in small bowl and sprinkle gelatin on top; let stand at least 5 minutes. Using tongs, transfer meat and carrots to serving platter and tent with foil. Strain cooking liquid through fine-mesh strainer into fat separator or bowl, pressing on solids to extract as much liquid as possible; discard solids. Allow liquid to settle about 5 minutes and strain off fat. Return cooking liquid to Dutch oven and cook over medium heat until reduced to 1 cup, 5 to 10 minutes. Remove from heat and stir in gelatin mixture; season with salt and pepper. Pour sauce over meat and serve.

BRAISED BEEF SHORT RIBS WITH GUINNESS AND PRUNES

Follow recipe for Braised Beef Short Ribs, substituting 1 cup Guinness (or other full-flavored porter or stout) for red wine and omitting 8- to 10-minute reduction time in step 2. Add ⅓ cup pitted prunes to pot along with broth.

🎥 COOK'S VIDEOS Original Test Kitchen Videos
www.cooksillustrated.com/feb09
HOW TO MAKE
• Braised Beef Short Ribs
VIDEO TIP
• Choosing boneless short ribs

TECHNIQUE | BONING SHORT RIBS

1. With the chef's knife as close as possible to the bone, carefully remove the meat.

2. Trim the excess hard fat and silver skin from both sides of the meat.

Thin and Crisp Pork Cutlets

The hallmark of wiener schnitzel is its light, puffy bread-crumb coating. So why is it typically so soggy and greasy?

⇒ BY KEITH DRESSER ⇐

Wiener schnitzel or Viennese cutlet (named for Wien, or Vienna, the capital of Austria) features a thin, tender veal cutlet coated in ultra-fine bread crumbs and then fried until puffy and golden brown. What separates wiener schnitzel from ordinary breaded cutlets is the coating's rumpled appearance. In fact, one German cookbook I consulted advises that with good wiener schnitzel you should be able to slide a knife between the meat and the crisp coating. But my experience with this dish has been quite different. Not only have I never been able to slide a knife between the meat and coating, I usually just feel lucky to get my knife to pass through the cutlet.

To avoid this toughness, not to mention the high price of veal, many recipes substitute pork. Though it may save a couple of bucks, pork doesn't usually improve the dish much. After sampling a number of recipes that yielded dry, tough pork cutlets with greasy coatings, I wondered whether I could put the puff into this reinterpreted classic.

Pounding the Pork

Focusing on the pork first, I found that most recipes call for boneless pork chops, pounded thin. However, pork chops have very compact muscle fibers, which means that pounding them into thin cutlets is laborious. It also means that once cooked, the pork has a dry, mealy texture. Another option is

Properly cooked, these crisp cutlets absorb very little oil.

prepackaged pork cutlets, but when I managed to find these at the supermarket, they were sinewy and fatty. The other option is pork tenderloin. Pounded thin and fried, cutlets made from tenderloin were far superior to the others. They were remarkably tender and had a mild flavor that was similar to veal.

The only drawback to the tenderloin was its long, cylindrical shape. When I sliced it into thin cutlets, I ended up with a dozen small pieces—nothing like the dinner-plate-sized veal cutlets of authentic wiener schnitzel. Cutting the tenderloin crosswise into four equal chunks (each two to three inches long) and then pounding them increased the size of the cutlets, but these were so large I could cook only one at a time. I tried again with just a slight variation, cutting at an angle to get four chunks of meat (see "Cutting Pork Tenderloin for Cutlets," left). I ended up with oblong pieces that, when pounded, were twice as long as they were wide. Two fit perfectly in a pan.

Crumb Trail

The standard breading method for wiener schnitzel is no different than for most other breaded cutlets. The meat is dredged in flour, then egg, and finally bread crumbs. The final element struck me as the most important, so I started exploring options.

I tried seasoned store-bought bread crumbs, panko, ground Melba toasts, ground stuffing mix, and ground saltine crackers, with results ranging from dry and pasty to gritty and greasy—all unappealing, with no puff in sight. Next, I tried making my own bread crumbs, tossing fresh slices of firm white sandwich bread into the food processor. When I used these crumbs for coating, they took so long to crisp that the pork was overcooked. Plus, their texture was too coarse. Then I dried the bread in a low-temperature oven before processing it. This created extra-dry, extra-fine bread crumbs, but the drying took almost an hour. Worse, the bread turned brown, and my crumbs tasted too much like toast.

I then remembered all the times I've thawed bread too long in the microwave, only to find that its edges had become brittle and dry. Perhaps I could use the microwave to dry pieces of bread without developing a toasted flavor. After incinerating a couple of loaves, I discovered an easy technique. Cubing slices and microwaving them, first on high power and then on medium, stopping occasionally to stir, produced ultra-parched bread. After 45 seconds in the food processor, I had super-fine, super-dry bread crumbs that fried up extra-crisp. The total time for homemade bread crumbs? Ten minutes.

Despite this little breakthrough, I was still missing puff. Maybe I could find it by reconsidering the other parts of the coating—the flour and egg wash. I tried adding baking powder and baking soda to the flour, hoping to chemically induce puffiness, but instead I got off-putting flavors. I also experimented with cornstarch, expecting its lightness to be an asset, but it made the coating stick like glue to the meat. My next efforts involved adding melted butter, mayonnaise, and milk to the egg wash in an attempt to create a soufflé effect, but these ingredients made for chewy, greasy coatings that expanded like rubber balloons. The only addition that furthered my cause was a small amount of vegetable oil. Whisked

📹 **COOK'S VIDEOS** Original Test Kitchen Videos
www.cooksillustrated.com/feb09
HOW TO MAKE
• Breaded Pork Cutlets (Pork Schnitzel)
VIDEO TIP
• Disposing of used oil

TECHNIQUE | CUTTING PORK TENDERLOIN FOR CUTLETS

Cutting pork tenderloin on an angle yields pounded cutlets that fit easily in the pan. Cut the tenderloin in half at about a 20-degree angle. Using the same angle, cut each half in half again, cutting the tapered tail pieces slightly thicker than the middle medallions.

1. MICROWAVING dries bread cubes quickly without adding toasted flavor.

2. PROCESSING dried bread in food processor creates ultra-fine crumbs.

3. ADDING oil to eggs keeps coating from fusing with meat.

4. FRYING in 2 cups of oil allows egg to set quickly and trap steam, creating puff.

5. SHAKING the pan bathes each cutlet in hot oil, helping egg to set faster, enhancing puff.

into the egg, a tablespoon of oil made the coating crisper and helped it slide free of the meat, making it puff—but just slightly.

Puff Pieces

I had spent several days doing tests, but really hadn't made anything more than plain old breaded pork cutlets. Admittedly, they were crisp and tender, but I had not achieved the wrinkled, puffy exterior that is wiener schnitzel's signature. Frustrated, I decided to do some more research and soon found a video clip of a chubby German chef cooking wiener schnitzel in his kitchen. Most of what he was doing was very similar to what I had discovered (even adding a little oil to the egg). But I was surprised when he cooked his cutlets. While I had been using a skillet, he used a shallow pot similar to a Dutch oven and cooked the cutlets in an inch of oil—a very generous amount—shaking the pot the entire time.

I went to the kitchen, got out a Dutch oven, and poured in an inch of vegetable oil. After heating the oil, I cooked the cutlets, shaking the pan like the German chef. I was astounded by the difference. The coating resembled a Shar-Pei (one of those wrinkly Chinese dogs) and was beautifully browned.

What was the secret to this success? Learning about the structure of my ingredients and how they interacted offered some answers. With a lot of hot oil in the pan, I was heating the eggs in the coating very quickly and solidifying the protein. This created

RECIPE TESTING: The Real Schnitzel

AUTHENTICALLY THIN AND PUFFY
When properly cooked in an abundance of oil, the thin schnitzel coating will puff away from the meat.

GREASY AND THICK
Cooked in a small amount of oil, a traditional coating becomes greasy, never puffs, and fuses to the meat.

a barrier, trapping the moisture on the surface of the pork so that it formed steam. As the steam tried to escape, it created puff. Having an ample volume of oil was key. Too little and the temperature cooled, causing a shortage of steam; this made the coating absorb oil so that it became greasy. (Ultimately I decided that 2 cups was the perfect amount of oil.) As for the shaking, I was dubious about whether it really did anything, but when I skipped this part, the results were not as good. Looking more closely, I realized that shaking sent the hot oil over the top of the cutlets, speeding up the setting process for the egg protein and ultimately enhancing the Shar-Pei effect.

Now that my cutlets were finally crisp, rumpled, and properly puffed, all they needed was a spritz of lemon, a sprinkling of parsley, and some capers (and for truly authentic flavor, a sieved hard-boiled egg). The result: a cutlet so tender I could cut it with a fork.

BREADED PORK CUTLETS (PORK SCHNITZEL)

SERVES 4

The two cups of oil called for in this recipe may seem like a lot—but they're necessary to achieve a wrinkled texture on the finished cutlets. When properly cooked, the cutlets absorb very little oil. To ensure ample cooking space, a large Dutch oven is essential. In lieu of an instant-read thermometer to gauge the oil's temperature, place a fresh (not dry) bread cube in the oil and start heating; when the bread is deep golden brown, the oil is ready.

- 7 large slices high-quality white sandwich bread, crusts removed, cut into ¾-inch cubes (about 4 cups)
- ½ cup unbleached all-purpose flour
- 2 large eggs
- 2 cups plus 1 tablespoon vegetable oil (see note)
- 1 pork tenderloin (1¼ pounds), trimmed of fat and silver skin and cut on angle into 4 equal pieces (see illustration on page 10)
  Table salt and ground black pepper

Garnishes
- 1 lemon, cut into wedges
- 2 tablespoons chopped fresh parsley leaves

- 2 tablespoons capers, rinsed
- 1 large hard-cooked egg, yolk and white separated and passed separately through fine-mesh strainer (optional)

1. Place bread cubes on large microwave-safe plate. Microwave on high power for 4 minutes, stirring well halfway through cooking time. Microwave on medium power until bread is dry and few pieces start to lightly brown, 3 to 5 minutes longer, stirring every minute. Process dry bread in food processor to very fine crumbs, about 45 seconds. Transfer bread crumbs to shallow dish (you should have about 1¼ cups crumbs). Spread flour in second shallow dish. Beat eggs with 1 tablespoon oil in third shallow dish.

2. Place pork, with 1 cut-side down, between 2 sheets of parchment paper or plastic wrap and pound to even thickness between ⅛ and ¼ inch. Season cutlets with salt and pepper. Working with 1 cutlet at a time, dredge cutlets thoroughly in flour, shaking off excess, then coat with egg mixture, allowing excess to drip back into dish to ensure very thin coating, and coat evenly with bread crumbs, pressing on crumbs to adhere. Place breaded cutlets in single layer on wire rack set over baking sheet; let coating dry 5 minutes.

3. Heat remaining 2 cups oil in large Dutch oven over medium-high heat until it registers 375 degrees on instant-read thermometer. Lay 2 cutlets, without overlapping, in pan and cook, shaking pan continuously and gently, until cutlets are wrinkled and light golden brown on both sides, 1 to 2 minutes per side. Transfer cutlets to paper towel–lined plate and flip cutlets several times to blot excess oil. Repeat with remaining cutlets. Serve immediately with garnishes.

TASTING: Capers

Capers are the sun-dried, pickled flower buds from the spiny shrub *Capparis spinosa*. We tasted six supermarket brands, evaluating them on sharpness, saltiness, and overall appeal. The winner, Reese Non Pareil Capers ($2.39 for 3.5 ounces), had it all: crunchy texture, an acidic punch, and a lingering sweetness. For complete tasting results, go to www.cooksillustrated.com/feb09.

—Meredith Butcher

CRUNCHY AND PUNCHY

A Better French Omelet

Could we defy 100 years of French culinary tradition and create an omelet you could get right the first time?

⇒ BY CHARLES KELSEY ⇐

Give a chef an old chicken, a bottle of wine, and a Dutch oven and she will easily whip up a robust, glossy stew. But give that same chef a few eggs, a pat of butter, and a hot skillet—and the challenge of creating the perfect French omelet—and watch her toque tremble.

In contrast to lacy brown half-moon omelets stuffed to the seams with filling that any short-order cook can get right, the French omelet is a pristine affair. The ideal specimen is unblemished golden yellow with an ultra-creamy texture and minimal filling. The method for making it, penned more than a century ago by legendary chef Auguste Escoffier, sounds simple enough: Melt butter in a blazing hot omelet pan, add beaten eggs, scramble vigorously with a fork until the omelet starts to set, roll it out onto a plate, and—voilà!—breakfast.

That's the idea, at any rate. In reality, success with these steps is maddeningly elusive. The temperature of the pan must be just right, the eggs beaten just so, and your hand movements as swift as your ability to gauge the exact second the omelet is done. With everything happening at lightning speed, even a few extra seconds of cooking can spell disaster. In an attempt to unscramble things for chefs and home cooks alike, Julia Child devoted 11 pages to omelet-making in *Mastering the Art of French Cooking*, concluding that success takes a lot of practice—and, no surprise—a lot of flubs.

I'm all in favor of tradition—when it works. But surely it was high time to figure out a different approach to making this creamy style of omelet, one that even an inexperienced cook could get right the first time around.

Stirring Conclusions

I began by examining the equipment. The classic method calls for an omelet pan made of high-quality black carbon steel—preferably reserved exclusively for eggs and seasoned over a period of years—and a fork. Modern concessions allow for a nonstick skillet and a heatproof spatula. Certainly, an 8-inch nonstick pan seemed like a fine idea. I wasn't so sure about a bulky spatula.

Unlike diner-style omelets bursting with cheese, meat, and veggies, French omelets are rolled, not folded, over minimal filling.

In the kitchen, I first tested two omelets side by side: one using a spatula, the other using a fork. (Forks usually scratch nonstick pans, but I figured I could sacrifice one pan for testing.) We used three eggs per omelet, along with salt and pepper and butter as the cooking fat. I started as instructed by many classic tomes: I preheated the pan for several minutes over high heat to get it good and hot, added the butter and waited for it to melt, then poured in the seasoned egg mixture and got busy stirring. The difference was clear: The fork did a better job than the spatula, scrambling the eggs into smaller curds with silkier texture. And I eventually achieved the same results using bamboo skewers and wooden chopsticks—without scraping my pan.

But there was a problem. The omelets were turning out brown and splotchy instead of evenly golden. This was due to hot spots over the pan's bottom, which I was able to eliminate when I preheated the pan for a full 10 minutes over low heat (see "Preheat

Your Omelet Pan Slowly," page 31).

Next up: creamy texture. Typically, to achieve a creamy omelet, you pull the eggs off the heat at just the right moment, but it's nearly impossible to know when that occurs. What if I cheated and used creamy ingredients instead? In my next tests, I made omelets with heavy cream and half-and-half. The results were richer, but tougher.

I recalled an intriguing recipe I'd found in my research: It called for adding diced butter (about 1 tablespoon) to the beaten eggs right before cooking. I heated up a pan and in went the butter-studded egg

📹 **COOK'S VIDEOS** Original Test Kitchen Videos
www.cooksillustrated.com/feb09
HOW TO MAKE
• Perfect French Omelets
VIDEO TIPS
• How we developed our omelet-folding technique
• Why to preheat the pan slowly

1. Preheat skillet on low heat at least 10 minutes to heat it thoroughly and evenly.

2. Stir frozen cubed butter into beaten eggs to ensure creaminess.

3. Add eggs to skillet and stir with chopsticks to produce small curds for silkier texture.

4. Turn off heat while eggs are still runny; smooth with spatula into even layer.

5. Sprinkle with cheese and chives. Cover so residual heat gently finishes cooking omelet.

6. Slide omelet onto paper towel–lined plate. Use paper towel to lift omelet and roll it up.

mixture. As I stirred the eggs, I observed the butter melting. At first I thought the excess butter was going to yield a greasy, overly rich omelet. But then I noticed the creamy fat fusing with eggs. Sure enough, the butter made the omelet richer and creamier! I couldn't believe it, so I made another dozen omelets using the technique, and those were creamy too. As it turned out, very cold butter (I popped it into the freezer for a few minutes before cooking) melted less quickly than merely chilled butter, allowing it to disperse more thoroughly throughout the eggs (melted butter clumped in one place), producing the creamiest results. (For more on this topic, see "Does Butter Make It Better?" on page 12.) There was one hitch: Some tasters thought the butter made the omelet a little too rich. I removed some

Julia & Company: Omelets for Experts?

Julia Child did more to make classic French cooking accessible to ordinary cooks than anyone. But, like the omelet advice of the culinary giants that preceded her, her omelet-making instructions (though marvelously thorough and precise) aren't exactly for the unskilled. They take up 11 pages of *Mastering the Art of French Cooking.*

protein—1 egg white—and cut the butter to just half a tablespoon, which satisfied everyone.

I had creaminess. Now what about lightness? I knew that the way I beat the raw eggs would be a big factor. A little air helps, but excessive beating with a whisk unravels the egg proteins, causing them to cross-link, leading to denser eggs. After some arm-numbing testing, I concluded that 80 strokes with a fork was enough to achieve a viscous, emulsified consistency for the lightest eggs.

Heat of the Matter

At this point, I was still using high heat, which gave me only a tiny window for perfection. I tried a range of different heat levels but found that anything lower than medium-high heat wouldn't trigger the rapid vaporization of the eggs' water that causes them to puff up with steam before solidifying. But even at medium heat, the omelet cooked so quickly it was still vexingly difficult to judge when it was done on both sides. To solve this problem, I turned to a test kitchen technique we've used in the past. I cooked an omelet until just formed but slightly runny on top, took it off the heat, smoothed the egg into an even layer, covered the pan, and let it sit for a minute or two. The skillet's gentle residual heat finished cooking the omelet without turning it tough, a brilliant solution.

Now I just needed to get the darn thing out of the pan. The traditional way is to give the skillet a quick jerk to fold the omelet over. You then slide it out of the pan, tilting the skillet so that the remaining flap of eggs rolls over neatly—or not. I've spent hours

cleaning dried egg off my stove trying to master this "jerk" technique. For an easier approach, I tried slipping the omelet onto a plate, then using my fingers to roll it. Too hot. I tried again, this time sliding the omelet onto a paper towel and using the towel to help roll the omelet into the sought-after cylinder. Voilà! Not only did I have a perfect French omelet, it was perfectly easy to make.

PERFECT FRENCH OMELETS
MAKES 2

Because making omelets is such a quick process, make sure to have all your ingredients and equipment at the ready. If you don't have skewers or chopsticks to stir the eggs in step 3, use the handle of a wooden spoon. Warm the plates in a 200-degree oven.

- 2 tablespoons unsalted butter, cut into 2 pieces
- 6 large eggs, cold
    Table salt and ground black pepper
- ½ teaspoon vegetable oil
- 2 tablespoons shredded Gruyère cheese
- 4 teaspoons minced fresh chives

1. Cut 1 tablespoon butter in half again. Cube remaining tablespoon butter into small dice, transfer to small bowl, and place in freezer while preparing eggs and skillet, at least 10 minutes. Meanwhile, place oil in 8-inch nonstick skillet and heat over low heat 10 minutes.

2. Crack 2 eggs into medium bowl and separate third egg; reserve white for another use and add yolk to bowl. Add ⅛ teaspoon salt and pinch of pepper. Break yolks with fork, then beat eggs at moderate pace, about 80 strokes, until yolks and whites are well combined. Stir in half of frozen butter cubes.

3. When skillet is fully heated, use paper towels to wipe out oil, leaving thin film on bottom and sides of skillet. Add ½ tablespoon reserved butter piece to skillet and heat until foaming subsides, 45 to 90 seconds. Swirl butter to coat skillet, add egg mixture, and increase heat to medium-high. Following photos above, use 2 chopsticks or wooden skewers to scramble eggs using quick circular motion to move around skillet, scraping cooked egg from side of skillet as you go, until eggs are almost cooked but still slightly runny, 45 to 90 seconds. Turn off heat (remove skillet from heat if using electric burner) and smooth eggs into even layer using rubber spatula. Sprinkle omelet with 1 tablespoon cheese and 2 teaspoons chives. Cover skillet with tight-fitting lid and let sit 1 minute for runnier omelet and 2 minutes for firmer omelet.

4. Heat skillet over low heat 20 seconds, uncover, and, using rubber spatula, loosen edges of omelet from skillet. Place folded square of paper towel onto warmed plate and slide omelet out of skillet onto paper towel so that omelet lies flat on plate and hangs about 1 inch off paper towel. Roll omelet into neat cylinder and set aside. Return skillet to low heat and heat 2 minutes before repeating instructions for second omelet starting with step 2. Serve.

Real Swedish Meatballs

Meatballs have to be Sweden's national dish for a reason. What's the secret to making them light, springy, and flavorful?

⋛ BY J. KENJI ALT ⋚

Most of us know Swedish meatballs as lumps of flavorless ground beef or pork covered in heavy gravy that congeals as it all sits, untouched, on the buffet table. After countless years enduring the sinkers that a relative inflicts on my family at reunions, I made a resolution: Meatballs had to be Sweden's national dish for a reason, and I was going to find out why.

The answer came when I visited Aquavit, Swedish chef Marcus Samuelsson's high-end New York restaurant, where I found meatballs that tasted as they were meant to taste. Unlike Italian meatballs, which are melt-in-your-mouth tender, these main-course meatballs were substantial yet delicate. Biting into them, I noticed the springiness and satisfying snap you get from a good sausage or hot dog. Even better, the heavy brown gravy had been replaced by a light cream sauce. The meal was perfectly complemented by a spoonful of sweet and sour lingonberry preserves and a dish of pickled cucumbers.

I came back to the test kitchen with a lofty goal: discovering the secret to standout Swedish meatballs. Served simply with potatoes and some Swedish condiments for extra authenticity, these meatballs would be the proud centerpiece of my meal.

Getting the Ball Rolling

An initial testing of five meatball recipes quickly revealed why this dish has such a bad reputation. With little exception, these recipes produced flavorless balls with thick, grainy sauces. The most successful used two Italian meatball tricks: a combination of meats (usually beef and pork) and a panade (a paste of bread and liquid that is mixed into the meat). Although these tricks yielded a moist finished product, the meatballs were too tender—they practically fell apart. While this trait is desirable in Italian meatballs, I wanted springy, Swedish-style

Our meatballs are good enough to serve as a main course, Swedish-style.

meatballs to rival those at Aquavit.

My working recipe started with two slices of bread soaked in ½ cup of cream and then mixed by hand with ¾ pound ground beef, ¼ pound pork, an egg, and a few basic flavorings: onions, nutmeg, and allspice. The balls were cooked to a golden brown color before being simmered in the gravy. Thinking that less panade might make my meatballs more cohesive, I made three batches and compared them side by side: my working recipe using two slices of bread, one slice of bread, and no bread at all. The results?

As I reduced the amount of panade, the meatballs gained substance, but they also became progressively drier and tougher. To understand why, I was going to have to take a closer look at their structure.

Meat is made of long strands of protein that run parallel to each other, producing long fibers. When meat is ground and mixed, these proteins get tangled up, producing a weblike matrix that gives meatballs a cohesive structure. Without anything to break up this web, however, the proteins wrap together tightly and squeeze out moisture, making the meatballs dry and tough. A panade works in two ways: Its liquid adds moisture, and the bread starch gets in the way of the proteins, preventing them from interconnecting too strongly. But it can also take things too far, resulting in meatballs that barely hold together. I needed to find just the right balance.

Thinking of other ingredients used to lighten food, I turned to baking powder. Could it leaven a meatball the same way it leavens bread? Indeed. Replacing the panade with 2 teaspoons of baking powder produced meatballs that were solid yet light. But without the panade, the meatballs were too dry. In the end, combining both approaches—a single teaspoon of baking powder and a slice of bread mixed with cream—provided the ideal moistness, substance, and lightness.

The next step in perfecting my meatballs was adding a bit of sausagelike springiness. To figure out how to do this, I scanned our library for books on sausage-making, which turned up an interesting technique: When making a smooth sausage, the meat, fat, salt, and flavorings are whipped together using a stand mixer with a paddle attachment until the mixture forms a homogeneous paste. This accomplishes two things. First, it very finely distributes the fat into the lean meat, trapping the fat within the structure of the sausage, thus guaranteeing a juicy finished product. (Without this

📹 **COOK'S VIDEOS** Original Test Kitchen Videos
www.cooksillustrated.com/feb09
HOW TO MAKE
• Swedish Meatballs
VIDEO TIP
• Testing for seasoning in a raw-meat mixture

Three Tricks for Better Texture

ADD BAKING POWDER
Baking powder provides lift to lighten texture.

USE A PANADE
Mixing in a panade made with bread and cream adds moistness.

WHIP IT UP
Whipping the pork mixture distributes fat and creates springiness.

emulsification, fat tends to escape from the sausage during cooking.) Second, whipping causes the meat proteins to stretch out and link up end to end. This creates tension in the sausage that breaks when you bite into it—hence the snap.

What if I were to apply this technique to my meatballs? I made a new batch, this time dumping all the ingredients directly into a stand mixer and whipping them into a homogeneous mass. It was a disaster. These meatballs were more like mini hot-dog nuggets than Swedish meatballs. Since everything I read about sausage-making indicated that this technique worked best with pork, which has a higher fat content and less robust muscle structure than beef, what if I were to separate the meats? Starting with a new meat ratio of equal parts beef and pork, I whipped the pork with the salt, baking powder, and seasonings until an emulsified paste formed, added the panade, and then gently folded in the ground beef. The results were exactly what I wanted: The panade and baking powder kept the meatballs delicate and juicy, the whipped pork provided just enough spring, and the barely mixed beef offered heartiness.

Sugar and Spice

Now that I'd mastered texture, all the meatballs needed was a little flavor adjustment. Swedish meatballs invariably contain some form of sweetener. White sugar proved too one-dimensional, and tasters didn't like the distinct flavor of honey, but a teaspoon of brown sugar added complexity without being cloying. Tasters liked pinches of nutmeg and allspice, but felt that diced onions detracted from the meatballs' otherwise smooth texture. Grated onions, however, dispersed easily and evenly in the meat mixture.

As for the cooking technique, baking turned out meatballs that overcooked before they had browned properly, while sautéing in oil resulted in spotty browning. My solution: shallow frying, which browned the meatballs evenly and cooked them through.

The final step was perfecting the gravy. Most recipes call for a flour-thickened blend of stock and cream in roughly equal proportions, but this was too rich for my taste. Using mostly stock and just a touch of cream was a big improvement. I had already added sugar to the meatballs, but adding more to the sauce helped balance flavors. Finally, a splash of lemon juice added just before serving contributed brightness.

After cooking more than a thousand Swedish meatballs, I finally had my ideal recipe. I couldn't avoid the occasional lead ball at family reunions, but in my own home I would serve Swedish meatballs as they're meant to be—light and juicy, bursting with sweetness and meaty flavor.

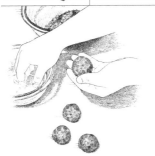 

USE WET HANDS
Keep a bowl of water nearby and dip your fingers after every two or three meatballs to prevent the meat from sticking as you form the balls.

KEEP ORGANIZED
Starting near the skillet handle, arrange the meatballs in a clockwise spiral to keep track of when each one needs to be flipped.

SWEDISH MEATBALLS
SERVES 4 TO 6

The traditional accompaniments for Swedish meatballs are lingonberry preserves and Swedish Pickled Cucumbers (recipe follows). If you can't find lingonberry preserves, cranberry preserves may be used. For a slightly less sweet dish, omit the brown sugar in the meatballs and reduce the brown sugar in the sauce to 2 teaspoons. A 12-inch slope-sided skillet can be used in place of the sauté pan—use 1½ cups of oil to fry instead of 1¼ cups. The meatballs can be fried and then frozen for up to 2 weeks. To continue with the recipe, thaw the meatballs in the refrigerator overnight and proceed from step 3, using a clean pan. Serve the meatballs with mashed potatoes, boiled red potatoes, or egg noodles.

Meatballs

1	large egg
¼	cup heavy cream
1	large slice high-quality white sandwich bread, crusts removed and bread torn into 1-inch pieces
8	ounces ground pork
1	small onion, grated on large holes of box grater (about ¼ cup)
⅛	teaspoon freshly grated nutmeg
⅛	teaspoon ground allspice
⅛	teaspoon ground black pepper
1	teaspoon packed brown sugar (see note)
1½	teaspoons table salt
1	teaspoon baking powder
8	ounces 85 percent lean ground beef
1¼	cups vegetable oil

Sauce

1	tablespoon unsalted butter
1	tablespoon unbleached all-purpose flour
1½	cups low-sodium chicken broth
1	tablespoon packed brown sugar (see note)
½	cup heavy cream
2	teaspoons juice from 1 lemon
	Table salt and ground black pepper

1. **FOR THE MEATBALLS:** Whisk egg and cream together in medium bowl. Stir in bread and set aside. Meanwhile, in stand mixer fitted with paddle attachment, beat pork, onion, nutmeg, allspice, pepper, brown sugar, salt, and baking powder on high speed until smooth and pale, about 2 minutes, scraping bowl as necessary. Using fork, mash bread mixture until no large dry bread chunks remain; add mixture to mixer bowl and beat on high speed until smooth and homogeneous, about 1 minute, scraping bowl as necessary. Add beef and mix on medium-low speed until just incorporated, about 30 seconds, scraping bowl as necessary. Using moistened hands, form generous tablespoon of meat mixture into 1-inch round meatball; repeat with remaining mixture to form 25 to 30 meatballs.

2. Heat oil in 10-inch straight-sided sauté pan over medium-high heat until edge of meatball dipped in oil sizzles (oil should register 350 degrees on instant-read thermometer), 3 to 5 minutes. Add meatballs in single layer and fry, flipping once halfway through cooking, until lightly browned all over and cooked through, 7 to 10 minutes. (Adjust heat as needed to keep oil sizzling but not smoking.) Using slotted spoon, transfer browned meatballs to paper towel–lined plate.

3. **FOR THE SAUCE:** Pour off and discard oil in pan, leaving any fond (browned bits) behind. Return pan to medium-high heat and add butter. When foaming subsides, add flour and cook, whisking constantly, until flour is light brown, about 30 seconds. Slowly whisk in broth, scraping pan bottom to loosen browned bits. Add brown sugar and bring to simmer. Reduce heat to medium and cook until sauce is reduced to about 1 cup, about 5 minutes. Stir in cream and return to simmer.

4. Add meatballs to sauce and simmer, turning occasionally, until heated through, about 5 minutes. Stir in lemon juice, season with salt and pepper, and serve.

SWEDISH PICKLED CUCUMBERS
MAKES 3 CUPS

Kirby cucumbers are also called pickling cucumbers. If these small cucumbers are unavailable, substitute 1 large American cucumber. Serve the pickles chilled or at room temperature.

1	pound Kirby cucumbers (3 small), sliced into ⅛- to ¼-inch-thick rounds (see note)
1½	cups white vinegar
1½	cups sugar
1	teaspoon table salt
12	whole allspice berries

Place cucumber slices in medium heatproof bowl. Bring vinegar, sugar, salt, and allspice to simmer in small saucepan over high heat, stirring occasionally to dissolve sugar. Pour vinegar mixture over cucumbers and stir to separate slices. Cover bowl with plastic wrap and let sit for 15 minutes. Uncover and cool to room temperature, about 15 minutes. Pickles can be refrigerated in their liquid in airtight container for up to 2 weeks.

Basic Vegetable Prep

You peel, slice, and chop common vegetables like garlic, onions, and carrots every day. But are you doing it right? BY CHARLES KELSEY

The six indispensable vegetables in any cook's arsenal are onions, garlic, leeks, carrots, celery, and shallots. These so-called aromatics provide the flavor base for virtually everything you cook, from soups and stews to sauces and salad dressings. Here's how to avoid common mistakes in buying, storing, and prepping them to ensure you're making the most of these staples.

ONIONS

Storing

➤ **DO** store onions at cool room temperature and away from light.

➤ **DON'T** store onions in the refrigerator, where their odors can permeate other foods.

Dicing and Mincing

A sharp knife and a good technique make chopping onions quick, easy, and even tear-free.

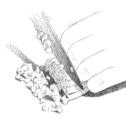

1. Using a chef's knife, halve the onion pole to pole. Lop off the tops of each half, leaving the root end intact, and peel the onion.

2. Make horizontal cuts, starting with the heel of the blade and carefully pulling the knife toward you, without cutting through the root end.

3. Using the tip of the knife, make several vertical cuts, dragging the knife toward you and making sure to keep the tip against the board.

4. Slice across the lengthwise cuts, using your knuckles as a guide for the knife while holding the onion with your fingertips.

Slice It Right

The way in which onions are sliced makes no difference to flavor, but we find it does affect appearance, especially in soups, stews, and braises. Cooked in liquid, onions sliced against the grain (parallel with the root end) turn lifeless and wormy-looking. Sliced with the grain (pole to pole), onions retain more shape and become a more significant component of a dish.

What's the Yield?

MINCED GARLIC	
Medium head (about 2½ inches across)	2 Tbs.
Small clove	½ tsp.
Medium clove	I tsp.
Large clove	2 tsp.
Extra-large clove	I Tbs.
CHOPPED ONION	
Small (about 2 inches in diameter)	½ cup
Medium (about 2½ to 3 inches in diameter)	I cup
Large (about 4 inches in diameter)	2 cups
MINCED SHALLOT	
Medium	3 Tbs.
CHOPPED CARROT/CELERY	
Medium	½ cup
CHOPPED LEEK	
Medium	I ½ cups

GARLIC

Buying

➤ **DO** buy loose garlic, not the heads sold packaged in little cellophane-wrapped boxes that don't allow for close inspection.

➤ **DON'T** buy heads that feel spongy or have skins where cloves used to reside. Also avoid garlic that smells fermented or unusually fragrant or has spots of mold—all signs of spoilage.

Storing

➤ **DO** keep unpeeled garlic heads and cloves in a cool, dry, pantry space away from direct sunlight.

➤ **DON'T** store garlic in the refrigerator. In tests, we've found this causes it to soften and deteriorate far more quickly.

➤ **NEVER** store raw garlic cloves in oil; this can result in botulism.

Prepping

➤ **DO** remove any green sprout from the center of the clove before cooking. It contains strong-tasting compounds that can add bitterness to food.

➤ **DO** use a garlic press to mince cloves. In the test kitchen, we've found that a good press can break down the cloves more finely and evenly (and far faster) than the average cook wielding a knife, which means better distribution of garlic flavor throughout a dish.

The Only Way to Skin a Clove

Forget trying to painstakingly peel skin off garlic. Crush the clove with the side of a chef's knife. The skin will loosen for easy removal.

Make (Garlic) Paste

Here's an easy way to turn minced garlic into a smooth puree for applications such as aioli or pesto, where you want the garlic texture to be as unobtrusive as possible.

1. Sprinkle minced garlic with a coarse salt such as kosher.

2. Repeatedly drag the side of a chef's knife over the mixture until all the garlic turns into a smooth paste.

Know Your Cuts

MINCED	⅛-inch pieces or smaller
CHOPPED FINE	⅛- to ¼-inch pieces
CHOPPED MEDIUM	¼- to ½-inch pieces
CHOPPED COARSE	½- to ¾-inch pieces
CUT INTO CHUNKS	¾-inch pieces or larger
SLICED	Cut into flat, thin pieces
DICED	Cut into uniform cubes
CUT ON THE BIAS	Cut at an angle

LEEKS

Buying

➤**DO** buy leeks with sprightly, unblemished leaves and long white stems, as the white and light green parts are the only edible portions. In tests, we found the size of the leek has no impact on taste or texture.

➤**DON'T** buy leeks pretrimmed down to the lighter base—the purpose of this procedure is to trim away aging leaves and make old leeks look fresher.

When to Use

We turn to leeks in place of onions when we want a milder, sweeter flavor and a texture that turns tender and silky when cooked. We love leeks in soups, but they're also delicious braised and served hot or cold with a vinaigrette.

Storing

Store leeks in a partially open plastic bag in your refrigerator's crisper. The crisper provides a humid environment that helps keep the leeks—which have a high water content—from shriveling and rotting.

Cleaning

Because leeks are often quite gritty, thorough cleaning is a must. Trim off the dark green leaves (discard or save to flavor a stock), then trim the root end, keeping the base intact. Halve lengthwise, still keeping the base intact, and rinse under cool running water, pulling apart the layers to expose any clinging dirt.

Slice It Right

Cut the leek in half through the base, then lay each cleaned half cut-side down on a board and slice crosswise into thin strips.

CARROTS

Buying

➤**DO** look for sturdy, hard carrots—a sign of freshness.

➤**DON'T** buy extra-large carrots, which are often woody and bitter.

Storing

To prevent carrots from shriveling, store them in the crisper, wrapped in their original plastic bag or in a partially open plastic bag.

Dicing

Trying to cut wobbly, tapered carrots can be a dangerous proposition. Start by creating a stable edge.

1. Remove a thin slice from one side of the carrot to form a flat edge.

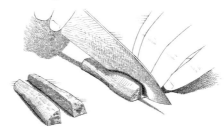

2. Place the carrot on that edge and slice it lengthwise into strips of even thickness.

3. Turn the strips 90 degrees and cut horizontally to complete the dice.

Best Equipment for the Job

Fast, precise slicing, chopping, and mincing begins with the right tools. Here are our test kitchen winners:

CHEF'S KNIFE: Victorinox Fibrox 8-inch Chef's Knife ($24.95)
PARING KNIFE: Victorinox 4-inch Paring Knife ($12.95)
PEELER: Prepara Trio Three Blade Peeler ($14.95)
CUTTING BOARD: Totally Bamboo Congo Board ($49.99)

CELERY

Buying

➤**DO** look for tightly packed, crisp green stalks.

➤**DON'T** buy bunches with brown spots or blemishes or stalks that have begun to shrivel from age.

Storing

Like carrots, celery should be stored in the crisper in its original plastic wrapping or a partially open plastic bag. Note: In a pinch, you can revive wayward celery stalks by trimming off an inch from each end and submerging the stalks in a bowl of ice water for 30 minutes.

Dicing

To yield even dice, start by slicing a rib of celery in half crosswise. Then, cut each half lengthwise into strips of equal width. Cut across the strips to form even dice.

SHALLOTS

When to Use

Shallots have a more mild and delicate flavor than onions—a difference accentuated by cooking. A finely minced shallot will also melt away during cooking until its texture is all but indiscernible. Choose shallots when you want silky texture and onion flavor to meld into the mix.

Substitutes

Scallions (white part only) or red onion

Mincing

1. Place the peeled shallot flat-side down on a work surface and make closely spaced vertical cuts through it, leaving the root end intact.

2. Make 2 or 3 horizontal cuts through the shallot.

3. Thinly slice the shallot crosswise, creating a fine mince.

Pasta with Butternut Squash and Sage

The blandness of butternut squash usually gets camouflaged inside ravioli. Our goal was to bump up its flavor to bring it out of hiding.

> BY FRANCISCO J. ROBERT

Butternut squash needs heavy-duty coaxing to draw out its inherent charms. Long on silky texture, this watery vegetable is woefully short on flavor. No wonder it's usually pureed and hidden away inside ravioli, not featured prominently in simpler pasta dishes. To make butternut squash worthy of an "outside job" (one that didn't require hours of rolling, then filling, fresh pasta), I needed to amplify its mild flavor.

First, I tried roasting the squash in the oven. The high, dry heat did a nice job evaporating the excess water (the enemy of deep flavor), but it took too long, about 45 minutes. Next, I tried sautéing peeled and diced squash in a hot pan with olive oil. Stirred constantly, the squash cooked consistently—but browning was another story. I repeated the test, this time without stirring. Much better. After about five minutes, enough moisture had evaporated from the squash to begin browning, producing nice, flavorful caramelization.

I tossed the cooked squash with boiled pasta (choosing short, tubular penne), along with some chopped fresh sage and a little olive oil, hoping to call it a day. Not so fast. The flavor of the squash was still too delicate—especially with so potent an herb as sage—and it didn't really meld with the pasta.

This dish clearly needed some sort of sauce, but what? I tried making a basic broth by boiling squash scraps (the seeds and fibers) in a little water. Though more flavorful, it wasn't transformative enough to justify the extra effort. Next, I tried removing half the sautéed squash and making a puree with chicken broth, then introducing this back into the mix. Not bad, but—once again—too many steps (and too many pots) to justify the modest improvement.

The sauce idea was a step in the right direction, however. That's when it hit me: a short braise. Too much liquid—or too long a simmer—would surely yield soggy squash. But if I used just enough to deglaze the pan, and then simmered the squash briefly, it might yield just the texture I was looking for. I sautéed the squash over high heat until caramelized, added two cups of chicken broth, then braised it for a few minutes. Success: Not only did

📹 COOK'S VIDEOS Original Test Kitchen Videos
www.cooksillustrated.com/feb09
HOW TO MAKE
• Pasta with Butternut Squash and Sage
VIDEO TIP
• How to prepare and dice squash

A short, tubular pasta works best in this recipe.

this method produce silky squash, but the sauce was just the right consistency to cling to the penne.

My pasta was coming along nicely, but I was having herb issues. Too much sage yielded pockets of sharp, strident flavor that some tasters called "medicinal." Too little and you could barely taste it at all. Either way, it was hard to control. Taking a cue from countless test kitchen recipes that tame strong flavors—garlic, herbs, chiles—by making an infused oil, I cooked some fresh sage leaves in olive oil, then used the herb-infused oil to sauté the squash. Close, but too subtle. I repeated the experiment, also adding a tablespoon of minced fresh sage to the squash as it cooked. This time, the sage infused the entire dish.

When some tasters still weren't wowed by the overall flavor of the dish, I knew it was time to break out the big guns: smoky bacon. A classic companion for butternut squash and sage, bacon also adds heft to a meal. Could I use bacon as my starting point, using the rendered fat instead of olive oil to cook the sage and the squash? Sure enough, it worked like a charm.

To fine-tune the sauce, I added a tablespoon of butter and a teaspoon of sugar, which brought out the sweet, nutty notes of the butternut squash. Sautéing scallions in the butter added brightness and a dash of nutmeg contributed earthiness. Just before serving, I tossed the squash and sauce with the pasta and the crisped bacon, then rounded out the dish with grated Parmesan and bracing lemon. Toasted sliced almonds were the final touch to a satisfying meal—easily cooked in under an hour.

PASTA WITH BUTTERNUT SQUASH AND SAGE
SERVES 4 TO 6

Don't be tempted to use dried sage in this recipe.

- 4 slices bacon, halved lengthwise, then cut crosswise into ¼-inch pieces
- 8 large fresh sage leaves, plus I tablespoon minced (see note)
- I medium butternut squash (about 2 pounds), peeled, seeded, and cut into ½-inch dice
- I tablespoon unsalted butter
- 6 scallions, sliced thin (about I cup)
- ¼ teaspoon freshly grated nutmeg
- I teaspoon sugar
  Table salt and ground black pepper
- 2 cups low-sodium chicken broth
- I pound penne or other short, tubular pasta
- 2 tablespoons grated Parmesan cheese, plus extra for serving
- 4 teaspoons juice from I lemon
- ⅓ cup sliced almonds, toasted

1. Cook bacon in 12-inch skillet over medium heat until crisp, about 8 minutes. Add whole sage leaves and cook until fragrant, about 1 minute. Strain mixture through fine-mesh strainer into small bowl, reserving bacon fat and bacon-sage mixture separately.

2. Return skillet to high heat, add 2 tablespoons reserved bacon fat (adding olive oil if necessary) and heat until shimmering. Add squash in even layer and cook, without stirring, until beginning to caramelize, 4 to 5 minutes. Continue cooking, stirring occasionally until spotty brown, 3 to 4 minutes longer. Add butter and allow to melt, about 30 seconds. Add scallions, nutmeg, sugar, ½ teaspoon salt, ¾ teaspoon pepper, and minced sage; cook, stirring occasionally, until scallions are softened, about 3 minutes. Add broth and bring to simmer; continue to cook until squash is tender, 1 to 3 minutes longer.

3. Meanwhile, bring 4 quarts water to boil in large Dutch oven over high heat. Add 1 tablespoon salt and pasta. Cook until just al dente, then drain pasta, reserving ½ cup cooking water, and transfer back to Dutch oven.

4. Add squash mixture to pasta; stir in 2 tablespoons Parmesan cheese, lemon juice, and reserved bacon-sage mixture, adjusting consistency with reserved pasta liquid. Serve, passing almonds and Parmesan separately.

How to Cook Hearty Greens

We wanted a one-pot approach to turning meaty winter greens like kale and collards tender—without spending hours or leaving them awash in liquid.

⇒ BY YVONNE RUPERTI ⇐

The traditional approach to tackling meaty, assertively flavored greens like kale and collards is to do as Southerners do: Throw them into a pot of water with a ham hock and cook the life out of 'em. Newfangled methods call for first blanching and then sautéing the greens, with the goal of retaining more of their deep color, fleshy texture, and earthy flavor.

Neither of these methods has ever entirely satisfied me. While its pot "likker" tastes great, the Southern-style braise is an hours-long project that doesn't meet my craving for greens that are at least a little al dente. (Besides, a soupy mess o' greens just doesn't work with most of the food I serve.) The blanching-then-sautéing route is quicker and yields greens that still have chew, but blanching, draining, squeezing—and then sautéing? Forget it. Plus, even a brief dip in boiling water can rob the greens of flavor that gets tossed down the drain. I wanted a one-pot recipe that wouldn't require parcooking or take hours of time and would highlight the greens' cabbagelike flavor and firm texture.

Because the large, dense leaves of collards are more of a challenge to cook than kale, I began my testing with them. As for most greens, what looks like a mountain cooks down to a minuscule amount, so I prepped 2 pounds, removing the tough center ribs and chopping the leaves into rough pieces. My first thought was to treat them as I do tender greens like spinach and chard: Skip blanching and go directly to sautéing. I heated 2 tablespoons of oil in a Dutch oven, added garlic and onion, and began tossing in the collards.

I'd only added about half of the greens when it became clear that sautéing alone wasn't going to work: The collards took so long to soften that the leaves on the bottom of the pot started to scorch, while the leaves on top remained virtually raw. Adding half a cup of liquid helped—but not enough. While I managed to wilt down the greens enough to fit all 24 cups into the pot, the water still evaporated well before they were tender.

There was no getting around the fact that if I wasn't going to parcook the greens, I couldn't be stingy with the liquid I added to the pot. I didn't want to resort to a traditional braise in which liquid covers the greens (I'd wind up with exactly the soupy greens I was trying to avoid), but what if I used just a couple of cups? That way, once the greens were softened, I could cook off any liquid that remained so that flavor released from the greens would go right back in.

In my next test, I sautéed half of the collards with the onions and garlic, then poured in 2 cups of water and added the rest of the greens. After about 45 minutes, the greens were almost the tender-firm texture I wanted, and I removed the lid to allow the liquid to cook off. When I tasted the greens, I knew I was almost there: The texture was perfect, but the flavor was a little one-dimensional. This was quickly resolved. I added a dash of red pepper flakes when I sautéed the garlic and onions and replaced 1 cup of water with chicken broth. As finishing touches, I tossed the cooked collards with lemon juice just before serving to balance out the flavors, along with a tablespoon of olive oil for extra richness.

The collards tamed, I checked my method with more-tender kale and was pleased to find that it translated almost seamlessly; all I needed to do was shave 10 minutes off the braising time. Back-burner, Southern-style braised greens have their place, but I'll be turning to my faster-paced Northern approach that keeps all the flavor in the greens—not the likker—a lot more often.

BRAISED WINTER GREENS
SERVES 4

For best results, be sure your greens are fully cooked and tender in step 1 before moving on to step 2.

- 3 tablespoons olive oil
- 1 medium onion, minced (about 1 cup)
- 5 medium garlic cloves, minced or pressed through garlic press (about 5 teaspoons)
- ⅛ teaspoon red pepper flakes
- 2 pounds kale or collard greens, ribs removed, leaves chopped into 3-inch pieces and rinsed (about 24 loosely packed cups; see "Removing the Stem from Greens" on page 31)
- 1 cup low-sodium chicken broth
- 1 cup water
-   Table salt
- 2–3 teaspoons juice from 1 lemon
-   Ground black pepper

1. Heat 2 tablespoons oil in Dutch oven over medium heat until shimmering. Add onion and cook, stirring frequently, until softened and beginning to brown, 4 to 5 minutes. Add garlic and pepper flakes; cook until garlic is fragrant, about 1 minute. Add half of greens and stir until beginning to wilt, about 1 minute. Add remaining greens, broth, water, and ¼ teaspoon salt; quickly cover pot and reduce heat to medium-low. Cook, stirring occasionally, until greens are tender, 25 to 35 minutes for kale and 35 to 45 minutes for collards.

2. Remove lid and increase heat to medium-high. Cook, stirring occasionally, until most of liquid has evaporated (bottom of pot will be almost dry and greens will begin to sizzle), 8 to 12 minutes. Remove pot from heat; stir in 2 teaspoons lemon juice and remaining tablespoon olive oil. Season with salt, pepper, and remaining teaspoon lemon juice. Serve.

BRAISED WINTER GREENS WITH BACON AND ONION

Cut 6 slices bacon into ¼-inch-wide pieces and cook over medium heat until crisp, 8 to 10 minutes. Using slotted spoon, transfer bacon to paper towel–lined plate and discard all but 2 tablespoons fat. Proceed with recipe as directed, using rendered fat in place of 2 tablespoons olive oil and substituting 1 medium red onion, halved and sliced pole to pole into ¼-inch slices, for diced onion, and 3 to 4 teaspoons cider vinegar for lemon juice. Stir reserved bacon into greens before serving.

BRAISED WINTER GREENS WITH COCONUT AND CURRY

Follow recipe for Braised Winter Greens, substituting 2 teaspoons grated fresh ginger and 1 teaspoon curry powder for red pepper flakes and 1 (14-ounce) can coconut milk for water. Substitute 1 tablespoon lime juice for lemon juice and sprinkle greens with ⅓ cup toasted cashews before serving.

BRAISED WINTER GREENS WITH CHORIZO

Cut 8 ounces chorizo sausage into ¼-inch-thick half moons. Follow recipe for Braised Winter Greens, cooking chorizo in oil until lightly browned, 4 to 6 minutes. Using slotted spoon, transfer chorizo to paper towel–lined plate. Proceed with recipe, cooking onion and garlic in remaining oil and substituting 1½ teaspoons ground cumin for red pepper flakes. Stir reserved chorizo into greens before serving.

◾ COOK'S VIDEOS Original Test Kitchen Videos
www.cooksillustrated.com/feb09
HOW TO MAKE
• Braised Winter Greens

Updating Chicken Noodle Soup

Why should any modern cook spend all day eking out flavorful stock from mere scraps and bones?

⇒ BY J. KENJI ALT ⇐

If I wanted to make chicken soup the old-fashioned way, I'd scrupulously freeze the scraps every time I butchered a whole chicken. Once I had saved enough, I would simmer the collected backs, ribs, and wing tips for hours, hovering over the pot with a skimmer in hand, until I had intensely flavored stock, to which I'd add vegetables, shredded chicken, and noodles.

But is this time-honored method really the best way to make stock? Sure, it made sense in the past as an economical way to get a second meal from the carcass of a spent bird. These days, however, spending hours to make a pot of soup from scraps and bones just isn't practical. I wanted deeply flavorful chicken soup, full of vegetables, tender meat, and soft noodles, but I also wanted to find a faster, more convenient way to make it.

Scrapping Scraps

I figured that making my stock with a mixture of canned chicken broth and water would jump-start its flavor. The trick would be to add enough real chicken flavor to the broth so that tasters wouldn't be able to detect its canned origins. Instead of blindly accepting conventional wisdom about how to do that, I decided to take a scientific approach, isolating the variables and testing each one.

Using a ratio of 2 quarts of canned broth to 1 quart of water, I made six different stocks, using 1 pound each of various chicken parts (bone-in breasts, boneless breasts, bone-in dark meat, boneless dark meat, wings, and just bones and scraps) to analyze the flavor that each lent to the finished stock. To my surprise, the stock made from bones and scraps—the traditional choice—was the weakest-tasting of all. Clearly, these parts are traditional on account of frugality, not flavor. Wings produced flavorless, fatty stock, and bone-in dark meat produced dishwater-colored stock with a mineral flavor (caused by the blood around the joints of the thighs and drumsticks). Boneless breasts and dark meat, which had the cleanest chicken flavor, were the best choices.

My stock now had decent flavor, but I wanted it to be much more intense. In restaurants, stocks

This rich-tasting soup—full of potato chunks, Swiss chard, and silky egg noodles—can be on the table in just over an hour.

are cooked at a bare simmer for hours to keep them crystal clear. But I discovered that letting the stock cook at a medium boil emulsified some of the chicken fat, turning the stock slightly cloudy but greatly enhancing its taste. A few more quick tests determined that a bay leaf plus the usual trio of vegetables—onion, carrot, and celery—added desirable complexity. But the flavor still needed greater depth. The easy solution was to add more chicken. A full 3 pounds created a wonderfully rich stock, but spending money on a large quantity of chicken that would eventually be discarded (once simmered in stock, chicken is bland and lifeless) seemed a bit absurd. I was at a dead end. I decided to get out of the kitchen and into the library.

The Ground Rules

Chicken Stock 101: Extract as much flavor as possible from the chicken. Many stock recipes advise starting with raw chicken parts, but I wondered if the chicken would benefit from sautéing before it was simmered in water and broth. I cooked the chicken pieces in a tablespoon of oil along with the aromatics just until the meat lost its pink color. The direct heat encouraged the release of flavorful juices from the chicken and vegetables, contributing additional layers of complexity to the stock. Conclusion: The sautéing step was well worth a few minutes of extra time.

Another fact: Flavor extraction happens quickly on the surface of meat, but the molecules deeper inside (say, at the center of a chicken breast) take more time to travel to the surface. So, in order to increase the rate at which the chicken's flavor is extracted, I would need to increase the surface area of the meat. For my next stock, I chopped a pound of boneless breasts and dark meat into 1-inch pieces. Tasters found this stock to be far more flavorful than one made with whole chicken pieces. Cutting the meat into ½-inch pieces was better still. Could I take this notion to the extreme?

I got out a food processor and pulsed the chicken pieces until they were very finely chopped. Tasters claimed that the stock I made from this pulverized meat had the richest flavor of any I'd made yet. Just to preclude any second-guessing, I sent samples to a lab to determine what quantity of dissolved solids had been extracted from the ground meat versus from the whole chicken pieces. The results confirmed what I already knew: Ground chicken releases a lot more flavor than whole chicken pieces. (For more information on the topic, see "Boosting Soup Flavor" on page 31.)

But why bother with the food processor when ground chicken is available at the supermarket? Good question. A pound of store-bought ground chicken gave up its flavor so readily that, in just about an hour, I had an intense, golden, chickeny stock.

Soup's On

Though my stock now had great flavor, it lacked the body of stock made with bones, which contain connective tissue that converts to gelatin when heated, thus thickening the liquid. I tested various thickeners and finally settled on 1 tablespoon of cornstarch per quart of liquid. (Cornstarch is cleaner-tasting and makes a more translucent stock than flour, and it's easier to incorporate into stock than gelatin.)

I also needed to introduce a second form of chicken to the soup—there was no way I was going to serve the spent ground chicken. Tasters preferred white meat to dark meat, and two bone-in breast halves provided just the right amount. Leaving the skin on protected the chicken from drying out, and adding it to the pot when I added the water allowed it to cook gently and evenly, ensuring that the meat remained moist (I removed it during the last 20 minutes to let it cool before shredding).

Finally, the vegetables that I had used to make the stock were now limp and lifeless. After discarding them, I added fresh onion, carrots, and celery to the stock, cooking them until they were just tender. Rich egg noodles were a prerequisite, but in order for the soup to be deemed "hearty," tasters demanded another starch, and potato was the obvious choice. I put a diced russet potato into the pot at the same time as the fresh vegetables. For a final burst of color

Bag the Bones

Instead of waiting hours to extract flavor from a chicken carcass, we short-cut the process using ground chicken meat, which releases flavor far more quickly.

OLD-FASHIONED APPROACH

MODERN METHOD

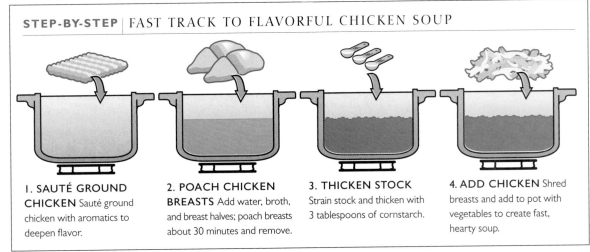

STEP-BY-STEP | FAST TRACK TO FLAVORFUL CHICKEN SOUP

1. SAUTÉ GROUND CHICKEN Sauté ground chicken with aromatics to deepen flavor.

2. POACH CHICKEN BREASTS Add water, broth, and breast halves; poach breasts about 30 minutes and remove.

3. THICKEN STOCK Strain stock and thicken with 3 tablespoons of cornstarch.

4. ADD CHICKEN Shred breasts and add to pot with vegetables to create fast, hearty soup.

---

and flavor, I added a few handfuls of torn Swiss chard leaves right at the end of cooking, along with the shredded chicken and some minced parsley.

Though it had taken a month of testing, I had finally ushered chicken noodle soup into the 21st century. But how would it compare to a slow-cooked, old-fashioned recipe? One last round of tasting proved that my modern technique was not only faster than the traditional method—it also yielded a soup that was every bit as satisfying.

HEARTY CHICKEN NOODLE SOUP
SERVES 4 TO 6

When skimming the fat off the stock, we prefer to leave a little bit on the surface to enhance the soup's flavor. The soup can be prepared through the end of step 2 and refrigerated for up to 2 days or frozen for up to 3 months. Store the chicken breasts in a zipper-lock bag with the air squeezed out and the stock in an airtight container.

Stock
- 1 tablespoon vegetable oil
- 1 pound ground chicken
- 1 small onion, chopped medium (about 1 cup)
- 1 medium carrot, peeled and chopped medium (about ½ cup)
- 1 medium celery rib, chopped medium (about ½ cup)
- 1 quart water
- 2 quarts low-sodium chicken broth
- 2 bay leaves
- 2 teaspoons table salt
- 2 bone-in, skin-on chicken breast halves (about 12 ounces each), cut in half crosswise

Soup
- 3 tablespoons cornstarch
- ¼ cup cold water
- 1 small onion, halved and sliced thin (about 1 cup)
- 2 medium carrots, peeled, halved lengthwise, and cut crosswise into ¾-inch pieces (about 1 cup)
- 1 medium celery rib, halved lengthwise and cut crosswise into ½-inch pieces (about ½ cup)

- 1 medium russet potato (about 8 ounces), peeled and cut into ¾-inch cubes (about 1½ cups)
- 4 ounces egg noodles (about 1 cup)
- 4–6 Swiss chard leaves, ribs removed, torn into 1-inch pieces (about 2 cups) (optional)
- 1 tablespoon minced fresh parsley leaves
  Table salt and ground black pepper

1. **FOR THE STOCK:** Heat oil in large Dutch oven over medium-high heat until shimmering. Add ground chicken, onion, carrot, and celery. Cook, stirring frequently, until chicken is no longer pink, 5 to 10 minutes (do not brown chicken).

2. Reduce heat to medium-low. Add water, broth, bay leaves, salt, and chicken breasts; cover and cook for 30 minutes. Remove lid, increase heat to high, and bring to boil. (If liquid is already boiling when lid is removed, remove chicken breasts immediately and continue with recipe.) Transfer chicken breasts to large plate and set aside. Continue to cook stock for 20 minutes, adjusting heat to maintain gentle boil. Strain stock through fine-mesh strainer into large pot or container, pressing on solids to extract as much liquid as possible. Allow liquid to settle about 5 minutes and skim off fat (see note).

3. **FOR THE SOUP:** Return stock to Dutch oven set over medium-high heat. In small bowl, combine cornstarch and water until smooth slurry forms; stir into stock and bring to gentle boil. Add onion, carrots, celery, and potato and cook until potato pieces are almost tender, 10 to 15 minutes, adjusting heat as necessary to maintain gentle boil. Add egg noodles and continue to cook until all vegetables and noodles are tender, about 5 minutes longer.

4. Meanwhile, remove skin and bones from reserved cooked chicken and discard. Shred meat with fingers or 2 forks. Add shredded chicken, Swiss chard (if using), and parsley to soup and cook until heated through, about 2 minutes. Season with salt and pepper; serve.

🎥 **COOK'S VIDEOS** Original Test Kitchen Videos
www.cooksillustrated.com/feb09
HOW TO MAKE
• Hearty Chicken Noodle Soup

Chewy Chocolate Cookies

"Death-by-chocolate" cookies usually claim texture as their first victim—but not ours.

≥ BY YVONNE RUPERTI ≤

Whenever a cookie recipe trumpets its extreme chocolate flavor, I'm always a bit suspicious. It's not the flavor I doubt, it's the texture. Cookies with names like Death by Chocolate, Super-Duper Chocolate, and Thick and Chewy Triple Chocolate (full disclosure: that's one of ours) provide plenty of intensity. But these over-the-top confections also tend to be delicate and crumbly, more like cakey brownies than cookies. I wanted an exceptionally rich chocolate cookie I could really sink my teeth into—without having it fall apart in my hand.

Surveying the options, I soon discovered that no recipe offered it all. Chocolate butter cookies were rich and crisp and not particularly chocolaty. Chocolate sugar cookies were soft and moist, but without the chewiness I wanted. Chocolate "crinkle" cookies looked the part—the sturdy exterior mottled with sugary cracks offering hints of the molten center within—but they were so delicate they collapsed on impact. Clearly, for the kind of cookie I had in mind, I was going to have to build it myself.

What's Cookin' in Cookies

Baking is all about how ingredients interact, with even the smallest changes transforming flavor and texture. So before I began my quest for rich chocolate flavor and chewiness, I needed to review my main ingredients. Most chocolate cookie recipes call for flour, butter, eggs, sugar, chocolate or cocoa powder (or both), leavener, salt, and vanilla. Flour builds structure; when mixed with liquid, it forms gluten, the protein that gives baked goods their chew. Butter

These cookies combine deep chocolate flavor with the satisfying chewiness of molasses cookies.

adds flavor and tender texture, while eggs contribute richness and lift. Sugar not only offers sweetness but, when melted, also brings more chewiness to the final product—think caramel. Chocolate can challenge even the most experienced baker. The cocoa butter

it contains coats the proteins in flour, preventing it from forming gluten and thereby tenderizing dough, making it very difficult to develop solid structure.

Looking for Cutbacks

Using one of the extreme-chocolate cookie recipes as a starting point, I creamed 12 tablespoons of butter with a cup of sugar in a stand mixer, whipped in two eggs, then blended in half a pound of melted semisweet chocolate (that's two full bars of chocolate—more than our Classic Brownie recipe [March/April 2004] calls for!), followed by a dry mixture of 1¾ cups flour, ½ cup cocoa powder, and some baking soda and salt. Scooped onto a parchment-lined baking sheet, these cookies baked up rich and fudgy. But for my purposes, they were overly tender and much too cakey.

The melted chocolate was an obvious culprit for my tenderness trouble: All its fat was softening up my dough. But before I made cutbacks there, I decided to try decreasing the butter. When I knocked off a few tablespoons, I found the cookies didn't spread as well (besides, 12 tablespoons of butter was fairly modest for an entire batch of cookies). Though I was loath to do it, I looked to the melted chocolate, scaling back by increments over the course of several batches. Sure enough, the less chocolate I used, the progressively less cakey and tender (and thus more like a cookie) the texture became. When I eliminated melted chocolate entirely, they were finally sturdy, but—no surprise!—not very chocolaty despite some cocoa powder in the mix.

To restore the lost chocolate flavor without adding too much in the way of fat, I replaced some of the flour with more cocoa powder—in particular, Dutch-processed cocoa (which the test kitchen has found delivers fuller chocolate flavor than the "natural" variety). As I tinkered with proportions, I found that replacing too much of the flour with cocoa powder compromised the texture. (Less flour means less production of gluten—the backbone of the cookie's structure.) Persevering, I found that increasing the cocoa by ¼ cup and reducing the flour by the same amount yielded both decent chocolate flavor and reasonably sturdy texture.

But how to get the texture sturdier still? Eggs were another prime suspect for fat, and I zeroed

Keys to Chewy Cookies

ELIMINATE THE YOLK
Reducing the egg to a single white cuts down on excess fat, which can make cookies too tender.

INCORPORATE COCOA
Using cocoa powder instead of melted chocolate in the batter keeps tenderness in check.

USE LESS WHITE SUGAR
Replacing some white sugar with dark corn syrup and dark brown sugar boosts chewiness.

The Right-Sized Chunk

TOO SMALL
Tiny chocolate pieces will melt and disappear into the dough when baked.

JUST RIGHT
Half-inch chunks contribute chocolate flavor while staying intact.

in on them, decreasing from two to just one. The reduction improved matters—could I take it further? In my next test, I eliminated the yolk. With just an egg white, the cookies finally had the stalwart structure I was looking for.

Chew's Clues

At this point, I had cookies with fine chocolate flavor and good structure—but they simply weren't chewy enough. One baker's trick for increasing a cookie's chewiness is to use melted butter in the dough; the liquid released from the melted butter (butter is 20 percent water) encourages gluten formation in the flour. When I tried using melted butter, however, the increase in chewiness was woefully modest, and the wetter dough was harder to shape.

Another weapon in the cookie baker's arsenal is brown sugar, which is hygroscopic—meaning that it attracts and retains water. I found that replacing some of the white sugar with dark brown sugar resulted in distinctly moister cookies with a better flavor and slightly more chew. But they still weren't chewy enough.

Determined to solve the need for chewiness once and for all, I tried to remember where I'd experienced the ultimate chewy cookie. Of course: It was the molasses cookie—the chewiest cookie in the modern world! Could molasses—that syrupy, dark brown sweetener—hold the key to the chocolate cookie of my dreams?

For texture, it was absolutely perfect. The cookies came out almost as chewy as molasses cookies, with a moist, cohesive crumb. And the flavor? As I might have expected, not so perfect. The assertive molasses was clearly the wrong companion for chocolate. Simple enough to fix, however: Swapping out the molasses for dark corn syrup yielded an incredibly moist and chewy cookie. What's more, it offered an agreeable hint of caramel flavor that enhanced the chocolate taste without overwhelming it.

Still, some tasters wanted more chocolate flavor, but I hated to risk ruining all my hard work getting the dough just so. Then it occurred to me: What if I simply added some chocolate at the end of mixing, à la chocolate chip cookies? The structure of the dough would be unaffected. I folded in 4 ounces of chopped Callebaut dark chocolate (the test kitchen's favorite bittersweet chocolate,

which has far better flavor than the typical packaged chips). The half-inch chunks stayed intact, adding intense flavor—and gooey bites of pure chocolate satisfaction.

Another pleasing textural improvement came from rolling the dough into balls and dipping them in granulated sugar, giving the finished cookies a slightly sweet crunch and an attractive crackled appearance. An oven temperature of 375 baked the cookies quickly without drying them, so that their exteriors were firm and crisp while their interiors remained delectably moist and chewy.

CHEWY CHOCOLATE COOKIES
MAKES 16 COOKIES

We recommend using the test kitchen's favorite baking chocolate, Callebaut Intense Dark L-60-40NV, but any high-quality dark, bittersweet, or semisweet chocolate will work. Light brown sugar can be substituted for the dark, as can light corn syrup for the dark, but with some sacrifice in flavor. A spring-loaded ice cream scoop (size #30) can be used to portion the dough.

⅓ cup granulated sugar (about 2½ ounces), plus ½ cup for coating
1½ cups (7½ ounces) unbleached all-purpose flour
¾ cup (3 ounces) Dutch-processed cocoa powder
½ teaspoon baking soda
¼ teaspoon plus ⅛ teaspoon table salt
½ cup dark corn syrup (see note)
1 large egg white
1 teaspoon vanilla extract
12 tablespoons (1½ sticks) unsalted butter, softened (70 degrees)
⅓ cup (about 2½ ounces) packed dark brown sugar (see note)
4 ounces bittersweet chocolate, chopped into ½-inch pieces (see note)

1. Adjust oven racks to upper- and lower-middle positions and heat oven to 375 degrees. Line 2 large (18- by 12-inch) baking sheets with parchment paper. Place ½ cup granulated sugar in shallow baking dish or pie plate. Whisk flour, cocoa powder, baking soda, and salt together in medium bowl. Whisk corn syrup, egg white, and vanilla together in small bowl.

2. In stand mixer fitted with paddle attachment, beat butter, brown sugar, and remaining ⅓ cup granulated sugar at medium-high speed until light and fluffy, about 2 minutes. Reduce speed to medium-low, add corn syrup mixture, and beat until fully incorporated, about 20 seconds, scraping bowl once with rubber spatula. With mixer running at low speed, add flour mixture and chopped chocolate; mix until just incorporated, about 30 seconds, scraping bowl once. Give dough final stir with rubber spatula to ensure that no pockets of flour remain at bottom. Chill dough 30 minutes to firm slightly (do not chill longer than 30 minutes).

TECHNIQUE | WHEN ARE COOKIES COOKED?

When the cookies have cracked but still look wet between the fissures, take them out of the oven. This ensures a moist, chewy texture.

3. Divide dough into 16 equal portions; roll between hands into balls about 1½ inches in diameter. Working in batches, drop 8 dough balls into baking dish with sugar and toss to coat. Set dough balls on prepared baking sheet, spacing about 2 inches apart; repeat with second batch of 8. Bake, reversing position of the baking sheets halfway through baking (from top to bottom and front to back), until cookies are puffed and cracked and edges have begun to set but centers are still soft (cookies will look raw between cracks and seem underdone), 10 to 11 minutes. Do not overbake.

4. Cool cookies on baking sheet 5 minutes, then use wide metal spatula to transfer cookies to wire rack; cool cookies to room temperature.

EQUIPMENT TESTING:
Chocolate Chippers

We hate clogging our kitchen drawers with unnecessary equipment, but chipping chocolate into the right-sized pieces with a chef's knife is so tiresome that we wondered: Could a tool designed for the task make things easier? We found two models, both shaped like mini pitchforks with tiny tines. The top chipper, Lehman's Porcelain-Handled Chocolate Chipper ($6.95), was comfortable to hold, didn't damage our cutting board, and broke uniform pieces of chocolate without excess force. Given its modest price tag, we're happy to add this handy tool to our drawer. For complete testing results, go to www.cooksillustrated.com/feb09.
                                        –Meredith Butcher

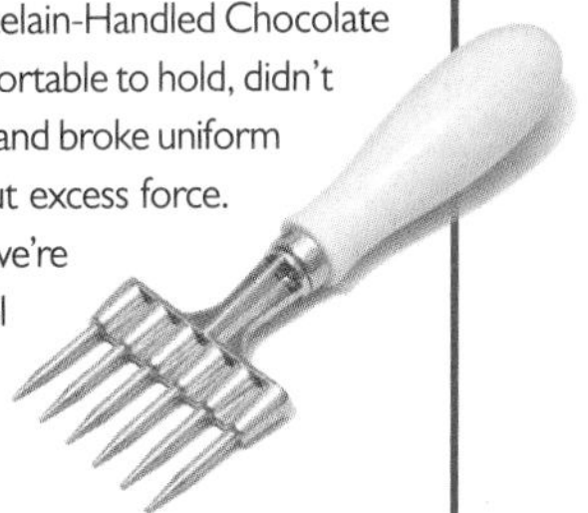

CHOICE CHIPPER

◼◄ **COOK'S VIDEOS** Original Test Kitchen Videos
www.cooksillustrated.com/feb09
HOW TO MAKE
• Chewy Chocolate Cookies

Really Good French Toast

For French toast that's crisp on the outside and soft—not soggy—on the inside, you need to do more than just throw milk, eggs, and bread into a bowl.

⇒ BY DAVID PAZMIÑO ⇐

As breakfast foods go, French toast falls in the same category as scrambled eggs—why bother with a recipe for something so simple? Most people merely whisk together milk and eggs, dunk in the bread, then throw the slices into the skillet. The results are rarely worth the trouble. The bread is soggy, too eggy, or just plain bland. With just a little extra effort, I figured I could solve these problems and come up with a really good French toast that's crisp on the outside, soft and puffy on the inside, with rich, custardlike flavor every time.

Since Sliced Bread

People all around the world soak and cook bread and have done so for centuries, all the way back to the Romans. Whatever the name or national origin, battering has always been a way to transform old bread into something new and flavorful. The French version is *pain perdu*, the Germans have *arme ritter*, and in Spain the dish is *torrijas*. American cookbooks in the 19th century typically called battered bread arme ritter, but after World War I the German name lost favor and the dish went Gallic—which explains why we call it French toast.

Reviewing American and European recipes, I saw many that called for rich breads such as French brioche or Jewish challah, made with eggs and butter. I would definitely test these richer styles, but first I wanted to try ordinary bread from the supermarket, the kind I would more likely have on hand on any given morning. I gathered a dozen brands of white presliced sandwich breads, along with loaves of French and Italian bread that are also widely available at grocery stores. Which would fare best in a typical batter made with 1 part milk and 3 parts eggs?

Though their tougher crust and more substantial crumb seemed promising, tasters quickly eliminated the French and Italian bread for being chewy. I then turned my attention to sandwich breads, which come in two kinds: regular and hearty. The regular bread was hopelessly gloppy both inside and out, triggering memories of the mediocre French toast of my youth. The hearty bread crisped up nicely on the outside, but still had more mushiness inside than I wanted, even when I dipped it just long enough to soak it through.

Our French toast recipe works just as well with challah as it does with white sandwich bread.

What could I do to make that last bit of sogginess go away? Turning to a pain perdu technique, I tried soaking the bread in milk before dipping it separately in beaten eggs. This technique produced a light, puffy interior, but the exterior was overpoweringly eggy—a definite deal-breaker. Some recipes called for letting the bread go stale overnight, but these days, is such a thing even possible? Normally, exposing bread to air causes its starch molecules to bond and recrystallize, leading to a harder texture, but most breads now include stabilizers in the form of mono- and diglycerides that slow down this process. In the test kitchen, we've determined that leaving bread out to stale isn't nearly as effective as drying it in the oven, which hardens it by actually removing moisture. I checked this conclusion, testing French toast made with hearty white bread dried in a low oven side by side with the same bread left out overnight. I soaked the bread in each batch for about 20 seconds per side to help ensure thorough saturation without contributing to soggy texture. At last, success! The oven-dried version won hands-down, producing French toast that was browned and crisp on the outside and tender and velvety on the inside, with no trace of sogginess.

White-Out Formula

Though I had nailed the texture, tasters complained that the toast still tasted more like scrambled eggs than buttery fried bread. I tried reducing the eggs from three to two and increasing the milk, only to have the sogginess return. At a loss for anything else to try, I remembered a recipe that called for dipping the bread in milk mixed with just yolks, versus whole eggs. Though I wasn't sure how this would help, I decided to give it a shot. I stirred 1½ cups of milk (increased from 1 cup to compensate for the lack of whites) together with three egg yolks and dipped in the bread. To my surprise, the yolks-only soaking liquid made a huge difference, turning the taste from eggy to rich and custardlike.

So why would eliminating the whites—the bland part of the egg by anyone's standards—reduce an unpleasantly strong egg flavor? Research revealed that most of the flavor in eggs comes not from the yolk but from the sulfur compounds in the whites. These are the same compounds that lead to the offensive odors of an overdone hard-cooked egg. With French toast, the more the egg whites interact with heat, the more sulfur compounds are released, which in turn leads to eggier-tasting toast. The whites can also contribute an unappealing ropy texture, especially if they're not well-combined with the milk, giving the toast a speckled white appearance.

Soaking Solution

With texture and egginess resolved, it was time to do some fine-tuning. Dunking multiple bread slices in a bowl of soaking liquid sometimes led to uneven saturation, resulting in the occasional slice that still cooked up soggy or even dry in places. The simple solution: Switching to a 13- by 9-inch baking dish in which up to three slices could fit flat and soak up liquid evenly.

As for flavorings, I settled on ½ teaspoon of cinnamon and 1 tablespoon of vanilla, and a little light brown sugar for sweetness. To bump up the nutty flavor of butter throughout the toast, I borrowed a trick from pancake recipes, incorporating melted butter right into the soaking liquid, warming the milk first to prevent the butter from solidifying.

One question remained: Would my method work equally well with challah (a little more available than brioche)? I cooked up another batch to find out—and tasters polished it off faster than I could say maple syrup.

TASTING MAPLE AND PANCAKE SYRUPS

Twenty-two *Cook's Illustrated* staff members tasted nine top-selling national brands identified by the Chicago-based market research firm Information Resources, Inc.: four genuine maple syrups and five pancake syrups made from corn syrup. We also included our favorite mail-order maple syrup from a previous tasting. We sampled the syrups with waffles and in our Maple-Pecan Pie (November/December 1995) in blind tastings and rated them on maple flavor, complexity, sweetness, texture, and overall appeal. The results were averaged, and the syrups are listed in order of preference. Prices were paid at Boston-area supermarkets.

RECOMMENDED

MAPLE GROVE FARMS Pure Maple Syrup
Grade A Dark Amber (Product of U.S. and Canada)
Price: $5.29 for 8.5 ounces (62 cents per ounce)
Sugar Content: 62.9g/100g
Comments: "A good balance of maple and sweetness," "potent," "clean," and "intense," with "good earthy, mapley notes." "Lovely," "very sweet and natural," with a "perfect consistency, not too thick or thin" and "a rich, mapley aftertaste." In pie, it was "very mild, but tasted real and satisfying."

HIGHLAND SUGARWORKS
Grade B Cooking Maple (Product of Vermont)
Price: $16.95 per pint ($1.06 per ounce)
by mail order plus shipping
Sugar Content: 63.3g/100g
Comments: While tasters agreed on our favorite mail-order syrup's "excellent maple flavor," described as "intense and complex, well-balanced," with notes of "whiskey" or "molasses," a few found it "a bit much" when tasted plain. But this dark syrup shone in pie, earning praise for "very rich, deep" maple flavor.

CAMP Maple Syrup
Grade A Dark Amber (Product of Canada)
Price: $12.49 for 12.5 ounces ($1 per ounce)
Sugar Content: 61.8g/100g
Comments: Tasters found this syrup "clean" and "mild," with "light maple flavor" that was "pleasantly thin and sweet." Some described notes of "wood and coffee"; one said it "tastes like trees and mountains." In pie, it was "mild" and "barely there."

RECOMMENDED WITH RESERVATIONS

SPRING TREE Pure Maple Syrup
Grade A Dark Amber (Product of Canada)
Price: $9.49 for 12.5 ounces (76 cents per ounce)
Sugar Content: 65.4g/100g
Comments: "A good maple flavor, with thin consistency," almost "like it wasn't reduced," this syrup had a "light body and a slight burned taste," though it was also deemed "sweet, natural," and "clearly maple." A few tasters detected a "slightly acidic" off-note.

MAPLE GOLD Syrup
Grade A Dark Amber (Product of Canada)
Price: $5.29 for 8.5 ounces (62 cents per ounce)
Sugar Content: 64.9g/100g
Comments: Tasters enjoyed the "solid maple flavor" of this contender, but also noted that it was "thin," "achingly sweet," and "slightly off-tasting," with an "astringent" initial flavor and "citrusy" aftertaste.

NOT RECOMMENDED

KELLOGG'S EGGO Original Syrup
Price: $3.49 for 23 ounces (15 cents per ounce)
Comments: "Very sugary. Slightly plastic. Maple aftertaste, but weak." In pie, while a minority of tasters liked its "nice, toasted sweetness," many complained: "Where's the maple?" and "Yuck. I can taste the chemicals." In sum: "What's the point of being the best of the worst?"

AUNT JEMIMA Original Syrup
Price: $3.59 for 24 ounces (15 cents per ounce)
Comments: A few tasters liked this syrup's "honey and vanilla" notes; one fondly quipped: "The taste I grew up with. Straightforward corn syrup laced with maple." But most comments were less forgiving: "Fake, viscous corn syrup," with a "fake maple smell" and "fake butter flavor."

MRS. BUTTERWORTH'S Original Syrup
Price: $3.49 for 24 ounces (15 cents per ounce)
Comments: Tasters likened this syrup to "melted candy," "cheap butterscotch," and "what a maple-flavored Life Saver would taste like." One summed it up: "Sweet, thick, vile." In pie, it was "saccharine sweet," with "no off-flavors, but not very mapley either."

LOG CABIN Pancake Syrup
Price: $3.59 for 24 ounces (15 cents per ounce)
Comments: The "smooth," "melted caramel" sweetness of this syrup was inoffensive, but tasters found its "salty, strong artificial butter flavor—like movie-theater popcorn" thoroughly off-putting. In pie, it fared better, but most agreed it was "cloyingly sweet."

HUNGRY JACK Original Syrup
Price: $3.99 for 27.6 ounces (14 cents per ounce)
Comments: Tasters described this syrup as "super sweet and sloppy, with a vanilla flavor." They also said it was "thick and buttery, but tastes like corn syrup" and "more sweet than maple." Its texture was decried as "so thick you could stand a spoon in it," "like tar," and "gloppy."

---

least favorite syrup had a high level of sugar and weak maple flavor, while our winner embodied a balance of the two.

Any number of environmental factors, including changes in soil, weather, and growing conditions, can account for variations in maple flavor. But why are some maple syrups sweeter than others, when all must fall within a few percentage points of federal standards for sugar density? Density reflects the percentage of all dissolved solids in the syrup; these are mainly sugars, but also include trace amounts of minerals. Experts told us that minute differences in manufacturing—such as boiling the syrup too long, not long enough, or at too high a temperature—can affect the amount of sugar in the final product. The sugar content only needed to vary by a percentage point or two for our tasters to notice the difference.

Low Price, Top Taste
In the end, tasters agreed that one real maple syrup stood out. The Maple Grove Farms Grade A Dark Amber syrup—one of the lowest-priced, at 62 cents per ounce—had everything we sought: "potent, clean, intense" maple flavor, moderate sweetness, a consistency that was neither too thick nor too thin, and no off-flavors. We'll be happy to pour it over our next batch of pancakes and cook with it, too.

The Best All-Purpose Skillet

A 12-inch skillet should last a lifetime and cook almost anything. But does quality construction have to cost top dollar?

⇒ BY LISA McMANUS ⇐

If I were going to be stranded on that proverbial desert island with just one pan, I'd grab my 12-inch skillet. I can cook almost anything in it, whether I want to sauté, shallow-fry, pan-roast, or even stir-fry. In the test kitchen, we prefer a skillet with a traditional, rather than nonstick, surface precisely because we want the food to adhere slightly, in order to create the caramelized, browned bits called fond that are the foundation for great flavor. What's more, while even the best nonstick surface will wear off eventually, a well-made traditional skillet should last a lifetime.

Skillets are simply frying pans with low, flared sides. Their shape encourages evaporation, which is why skillets excel at searing, browning, and sauce reduction. Traditional versions come in three main materials: stainless steel, anodized aluminum, and cast iron. We're not big fans of the dark surface of anodized aluminum, as it makes it hard to judge the color of fond. And while cast-iron skillets have their uses, they are cumbersome and can react with acidic sauces.

We prefer traditional skillets made of stainless steel sandwiched around a core of aluminum. Aluminum is one of the fastest conductors of heat, but it reacts with acidic foods and is overly responsive to temperature fluctuations, making cooking harder to control. Stainless steel is nonreactive, but it's a poor conductor of heat (indeed, handles made of stainless generally won't get hot on the stovetop). But a marriage of the two metals makes the ideal composition for a skillet.

One of the most common stainless-aluminum formulations is a style known as "clad," where the entire pan is made of three or more layers ("tri-ply") of metal. Manufacturers also sell skillets composed of up to seven layers, or with copper cores (the best heat conductor used in cookware), but these high-quality pans usually cost well over $200—more than most of us want to spend on a single pan. We chose seven skillets from leading manufacturers with a price range of $49 to $135. Four were tri-ply; one was a five-ply pan that offered extra layers of aluminum. The last two, the least expensive of the lot, had disk bottoms, where the aluminum core is confined to a thick plate attached to the bottom of an otherwise

📹 **COOK'S VIDEOS** Original Test Kitchen Videos
www.cooksillustrated.com/feb09
BEHIND THE SCENES
• Testing Traditional Skillets

stainless steel pan. From prior testing, we knew that disk-bottom pans can sometimes perform as well as fully clad pans. Which style is best, and how much do you need to spend to get a top-notch skillet?

Required Elements

A great skillet will transmit heat evenly across its cooking surface. This helps you produce uniformly cooked food, with no under- or overcooked spots. It should never leave you struggling with the heat suddenly surging out of control and scorching your dinner—or stall out instead of sizzling when food is added.

To test our lineup, we seared steaks, made pan sauces, pan-roasted chicken pieces, sautéed onions, and flipped crêpes. With steaks, it was immediately clear which pans transmit heat steadily and evenly across their surface, allowing them to easily achieve a deeply seared crust on both sides, and which ones didn't. (And all this time you thought it was your cooking skills.) One pan browned the first side of the steaks well—but after we flipped them, the pan temperature continued to surge, blackening the second side in just over a minute. Another pan lost its heat when we added the steaks, leaving the meat with a soft "steamed" exterior instead of a flavorful crust.

What made good steak go bad? The two worst performers in this test were the disk-bottom pans. The pan that lacked sizzle when we added steaks had the thickest cooking surface in the lineup, with a 5.5-mm bottom—but only 0.5mm was heat-conducting aluminum. With so much slow-responding stainless steel, no wonder it was sluggish. And how about the pan that raced ahead, scorching our steaks? Its construction was just the opposite—a full 3mm of its 4-mm-thick bottom was composed of aluminum, with just a thin layer of steel to temper heat. A few of the fully clad pans suffered from similar problems, but they weren't nearly as severe.

A great skillet has a steady, moderate sauté speed and will not require endless fiddling with the temperature dial to balance any shortcomings. To test this, we sautéed chopped onions in each pan for 15 minutes over medium heat. Some skillets turned out soft, uniformly golden onions without us ever touching the dial, others cooked pieces that were too light and too dark in the same pan, while still others forced us to constantly turn the heat down to prevent the onions from burning.

To confirm how quickly each skillet came up to temperature, we tested with solder, choosing a tin-lead alloy with a melting point of exactly 361 degrees.

We placed six small rings of solder wire in a circle an inch from the edge of each pan, placed the pan on a burner set to medium, and recorded the time it took for the solder to melt. Times ranged from just under three minutes to just over six. Our top two pans finished at a moderate pace of just over four minutes.

A great skillet will have a generous cooking surface. Almost all the pans were advertised as 12 inches (measured across the top), but actual cooking surfaces were often two or three inches smaller, depending on how the sides were angled. We preferred roomy pans; pans that crowded steaks or crammed together chicken pieces steamed the food instead of browning it. Top performers had lower sides, which made it easier to turn a crêpe without tearing. They had a well-calibrated distribution of weight between handle and pan for easy maneuvering.

Winning Style

Six years ago, we chose the All-Clad Stainless 12-Inch Fry Pan ($135) as our favorite. After going up against six new rivals, it is still our top choice. One of the lightest pans in the lineup, it also offers one of the thickest bottoms of the fully clad pans, which made it easy to maneuver while providing steady heat and even browning. Its well-balanced weight made it comfortable to lift while spreading crêpe batter or spooning out sauce, and its nearly 10 inches of cooking surface gave it an edge over smaller competitors.

At $135, our favorite is not cheap, but it is built to last. Perhaps not coincidentally, the two cheapest pans in the lineup, both with disk bottoms—the MIU Stainless Steel 12-Inch Open Fry Pan ($48.99) and the Cuisinart Chef's Classic Stainless 12-Inch Skillet ($49.95)—rated the worst.

Don't Buy This

Manufacturers often use labels like "omelet pan," "fry pan," "sauté pan," and "skillet" interchangeably, but there are important differences. We define a skillet as having low, flared sides and curved corners, while a sauté pan has high, L-shaped sides to keep liquids from evaporating. Sauté pans are best for braising, and skillets are used for everything else. Buy your skillet by its shape, not its name.

NOT A SKILLET

TESTING TRADITIONAL SKILLETS

We tested seven traditional skillets; five were fully clad with layers of aluminum and stainless steel covering the entire pan, while two had aluminum-steel disk bottoms. With one exception, we chose 12-inch skillets (measured across the top; the diameter of the actual cooking surface is indicated below). The pans are listed in order of preference. Sources for the winner and Best Buy appear on page 32.

PERFORMANCE: Using a KitchenAid stove with 15,000-BTU-per-hour gas burners, we seared steaks, made pan sauce, and cooked crêpes to look for hot and cool spots. We also pan-roasted chicken pieces, starting on the stovetop and finishing in the oven. Additionally, we measured the time for rings of solder (with a melting point of 361 degrees) to melt in each pan. Scores of good, fair, or poor were assigned in each test, and a composite of these scores constitutes the overall performance rating for each pan.

SAUTÉ SPEED: We sautéed chopped onions in vegetable oil over medium heat for 15 minutes, rating pans highly if the onions turned soft and uniformly golden. Pans that produced onions that were overly dark or cooked unevenly rated fair; pans that burned or crisped onions rated poor.

USER-FRIENDLINESS: We evaluated factors including whether the pan accommodates eight pieces of chicken without overlap, how the weight and handle shape influenced maneuverability, and whether the handle remained cool and comfortable.

DURABILITY: To see if pans warped when exposed to thermal shock, we heated them to 500 degrees on the stovetop, then plunged each into ice water. We also held each pan by the handle and whacked it three times on a towel-covered concrete platform to check solidity of construction. Pans that showed the least damage rated highest. (See "Inside Story: Getting Whacked," page 30.)

HIGHLY RECOMMENDED

ALL-CLAD Stainless 12-Inch Fry Pan Model 5112
Price: $135 **Weight:** 2.75 lbs
Bottom thickness: 3.18mm
Cooking surface diameter: 9¾ inches
Height of sides: 1⅞ inches

RATINGS
Performance: ★★★
Sauté Speed: ★★★
User-Friendliness: ★★★
Durability: ★★★

TESTERS' COMMENTS
Testers praised this pan for having "everything you need in a skillet and nothing you don't," with enough cooking surface for sautéing eight chicken pieces without crowding; steady, controlled heat for excellent browning; and a good shape with low sides. The weight balance was outstanding; it was easy to manipulate and lift. In the durability test, it sustained the least damage, with barely visible dents.

RECOMMENDED

GOURMET Standard Tri-Ply 12-Inch Skillet Model AS11135
Price: $64.99 **Weight:** 3.25 lbs
Bottom thickness: 2.59mm
Cooking surface diameter: 9 inches
Height of sides: 2¼ inches

BEST BUY

RATINGS
Performance: ★★★
Sauté Speed: ★★★
User-Friendliness: ★★
Durability: ★★

TESTERS' COMMENTS
At half the price of our winner, this skillet browned foods "perfectly well"—though the crêpe test revealed a slightly uneven heat pattern. While its cooking surface is smaller, testers observed that the gentle slope of the sides let food spread out nicely. The balance was slightly off, with weight overly concentrated in the pan. When whacked, the body dented.

CALPHALON Contemporary Stainless 12-Inch Omelette Pan Model LR 1392
Price: $119.95 **Weight:** 2.9 lbs
Bottom thickness: 2.44mm
Cooking surface diameter: 9¾ inches
Height of sides: 2¼ inches

RATINGS
Performance: ★★★
Sauté Speed: ★★
User-Friendliness: ★★★
Durability: ★★

TESTERS' COMMENTS
This handle-heavy skillet struck testers as "lightweight, almost flimsy." This pan is the thinnest of the lineup, which made it hard to control: We had to keep reducing the flame, but once we did, the results were excellent. In our solder test, the heat distribution was especially fast and even. The pan's handle loosened during the durability test, and the body dented.

WEIL by Spring, The Healthy Kitchen 12-Inch Fry Pan Model 1812
Price: $120 **Weight:** 3.95 lbs
Bottom thickness: 3.5mm
Cooking surface diameter: 9 inches
Height of sides: 1⅞ inches

RATINGS
Performance: ★★
Sauté Speed: ★★★
User-Friendliness: ★★
Durability: ★★

TESTERS' COMMENTS
This "five-ply" pan with extra layers of aluminum alloy around an aluminum core (manufactured under the name of healthy living guru Dr. Andrew Weil) had slow and steady heat. Its smaller cooking surface left steaks slightly crowded and chicken unevenly browned. It is heavier than we prefer but handled well despite its weight, though it dented when whacked.

ALL-CLAD 13-Inch Stainless French Skillet Model 5113
Price: $99.95 **Weight:** 3.6 lbs
Bottom thickness: 3.42mm
Cooking surface diameter: 11 inches
Height of sides: 2⅛ inches

RATINGS
Performance: ★★
Sauté Speed: ★★
User-Friendliness: ★★
Durability: ★★

TESTERS' COMMENTS
Testers loved the generous 11-inch span of this pan's cooking surface, but it was heavy and awkward to manipulate, with a fast sauté speed that required vigilance. The pan's corners are not as sloped as we like, making it harder to blend pan sauce. It dented and the handle loosened in our abuse test. (We asked All-Clad what made it "French." The reply? It's just a name.)

NOT RECOMMENDED

MIU Stainless Steel 12-Inch Open Fry Pan Model 95039
Price: $48.99 **Weight:** 2.65 lbs
Bottom thickness: 5.5mm
Cooking surface diameter: 9 inches
Height of sides: 2⅛ inches

RATINGS
Performance: ★
Sauté Speed: ★★
User-Friendliness: ★★★
Durability: ★

TESTERS' COMMENTS
While comfortable and easy to maneuver, this disk-bottom pan is small—two steaks were a tight fit, and they steamed rather than browned. Mostly thick stainless steel, it had trouble recovering lost heat, and tall sides increased the potential for steaming. In the durability test, the handle tore partly away, and the body warped.

CUISINART Chef's Classic Stainless 12-Inch Skillet Model 722-30H
Price: $49.95 **Weight:** 3.05 lbs
Bottom thickness: 4.0mm
Cooking surface diameter: 10½ inches
Height of sides: 2 inches

RATINGS
Performance: ★
Sauté Speed: ★
User-Friendliness: ★★
Durability: ★

TESTERS' COMMENTS
This disk-bottom pan offers a generous cooking surface, but testers called it "flighty." Heat built up in the thick aluminum disk and transmitted abundantly through the cooking surface, making the temperature climb precipitously. Steaks browned well on the first side, but got too dark on the second. Onions scorched and smoked, even when we lowered the heat. In the durability test, the disk bottom fell off.

KITCHEN NOTES

≥ BY J. KENJI ALT ≤

TASTING: A Good Egg

Here's the latest from the henhouse: eggs with a high level of omega-3 fatty acids. This unsaturated fat, also found in fish oil, is said to reduce blood pressure and the risk of coronary disease as well as relieve stress and depression. That's all well and good, but how do the eggs taste? We set up a blind tasting of eggs containing levels of omega-3 from around 50 mg per egg (the standard amount in ordinary supermarket eggs) up to 310 mg per egg. Our finding: The more omega-3's, the richer the egg flavor and the deeper the yolk color. Why? Commercially raised chickens usually peck on corn and soy, while chickens on the omega-3-enriched diet have supplements of greens, flax seed, and algae, which also add flavor, complexity, and color.

When shopping for a good egg, buyer beware: Brands may claim a high level of omega-3's, but the fine print sometimes reveals that the number refers to the level present in two eggs, not one. Look for brands that guarantee at least 200 mg per egg.

READ CLOSELY
A good dose of omega-3's is 200 mg per egg.

TEST KITCHEN TIP: Avoid Advance Prep for Garlic

We're always looking for ways to make our kitchen work more efficient and will often prep recipes a day in advance if we know we're going to be busy. But noticing that garlic can develop a particularly strong odor if minced too far in advance, we decided to run a quick test. We used garlic in three different applications: lightly cooked in Spaghetti with Garlic and Olive Oil (March/April 1999), raw in a garlicky Aïoli (July/August 2005), and as a more subtle flavoring in our Best Caesar Salad (September/October 1997). For each recipe, we used freshly minced garlic, garlic that had been minced 6 hours in advance, and garlic that had been minced the day before. Both the 6-hour- and 1-day-old minced garlic were so power-ful, they overwhelmed the other flavors in the dish.

Turns out, garlic flavor comes from a compound called allicin, which is not formed until after the garlic's cells are ruptured. As soon as you cut into garlic, the allicin will start to build and build until its flavor becomes overwhelmingly strong. So if you're going to prep a recipe in advance, make sure to leave the garlic cloves whole until the last minute.

FRESH CRUSH
Garlic minced too early can develop an overly powerful flavor and aroma. Keep your cloves whole until just before using.

SHOPPING: Sizing Up Squash

Making batch upon batch of our Pasta with Butternut Squash and Sage (page 18), we noticed a lot of inconsistency: Sometimes the cooked squash tasted slightly sweet, other times it tasted muddy or dull. Could the size of the squash influence flavor? We bought squash ranging from small 1½ pounders all the way up to 5 pound-plus behemoths and tasted them sautéed in bacon fat per our recipe, as well as boiled and pureed. Tasters overwhelmingly found that the smaller the squash, the more concentrated the flavor and the finer the texture. Larger squash not only had a more washed-out, "dirty" flavor, but also tended to be more fibrous and spongy when cooked. So when a recipe calls for a large amount of squash, it's better to buy a few smaller squashes than one big one. We recommend avoiding squash weighing more than 2½ pounds.

SMALL SIZE, BIG FLAVOR
Our blind tasting showed that the smaller the squash, the bigger the flavor.

INSIDE STORY: Getting Whacked

A great skillet should last a lifetime, withstanding decades of normal wear and tear in the kitchen. To evaluate the durability of the seven traditional stainless-steel skillets we tested in "The Best All-Purpose Skillet," page 28, we heated the pans to 500 degrees on the stovetop, then plunged them into a bucket of ice water to see if they warped. Thermal shock can cause metal to distort—similar to when you rinse a very hot pan under cold water—but in this case, none did. We then whacked each skillet three times on a dish towel–covered concrete platform, trying to use the same moderate amount of force with each. While our top-rated skillet, the All-Clad Stainless 12-Inch Fry Pan, survived with barely a ding, most of the other pans sustained pronounced dents and damage. The handle on one pan loosened; another nearly came off. The worst of the bunch was

NOT SO DURABLE
The Cuisinart Chef's Classic Stainless 12-Inch Skillet collapsed under abuse.

the Cuisinart Chef's Classic Stainless 12-Inch Skillet: After only two whacks, it crumpled like a tin can and completely fell apart, with the disk bottom separating from the rest of the pan. –Lisa McManus

Whipping Egg Whites

When whipping egg whites into a foamy meringue, the usual approach is to start slow and build up speed for better volume. But does volume always matter? We wanted to find recipes in which you can simply flip the switch to high.

EXPERIMENT
We made meringue cookies, meringue frosting, chocolate mousse, and chiffon cakes, each with two different batches of whipped egg whites. In one batch, we whipped the whites slowly until foamy, about one minute, and finished on high. In another, we beat the whites at high speed the entire time.

RESULTS
The egg whites with the slow start produced a meringue that was about 10 percent more volumi-nous than the high-speed-only whites, resulting in meringue cookies and frosting that were lighter and airier (the cookies were also larger). Both batches of mousse and chiffon cake, on the other hand, were indistinguishable from one another.

SLOW START
Egg whites whipped first at low speed until frothy and then at high speed produce about 10 percent more meringue than egg whites whipped only at high speed.

EXPLANATION
Beating egg whites slowly at the beginning causes their proteins to loosen up. Like stretching a balloon before trying to inflate it, the improved elasticity allows the proteins to take on air more easily and eventually gain more volume. This extra volume makes a difference when meringue is the main element in a recipe, such as in meringue cookies or frosting. But when meringue is just a minor player that gets folded into a heavier batter or mousse, you can save time by whipping full speed ahead—tasters won't notice the difference.

TASTING: Regular versus Petite Peas

We've always been big fans of frozen peas. Individually frozen right after being shucked from the pod, they are often sweeter and fresher-tasting than the shuck-'em-yourself "fresh" peas that may have spent days in storage, slowly losing sweetness and gaining starchiness. We've seen two varieties in the freezer aisle: regular frozen peas, and bags labeled "petite peas" (or sometimes "petit pois" or "baby sweet peas"). To see if there is a difference, we tasted each type with butter. Tasters unanimously favored the smaller peas for their sweeter flavor and creamier texture. Regular peas were by no means unacceptable but had tougher skins and mealier interiors. Since both varieties are available for the same price, we're going with the petite peas from now on.

SWEET AND PETITE
Petite peas are less starchy with a sweeter flavor than their "regular" counterparts.

SCIENCE: Boosting Soup Flavor

The usual method for making chicken soup is to cover chicken parts with water and bring it to a boil. In our Hearty Chicken Noodle Soup recipe (page 21), we found that using ground chicken rather than parts gave our soup significantly more flavor. Could we back up these subjective results with empirical evidence?

EXPERIMENT

We made two stocks: one with chicken parts and water and one with ground chicken and water. We sent these stocks to a laboratory to measure the total amount of dissolved solids—an indication of how much flavor was extracted from the chicken—in each.

RESULTS

The stock made with chicken parts and tap water had 3.32 grams of dissolved solids per 100 grams of stock. The stock made with ground chicken and tap water had 5.6 grams—an increase of nearly 70 percent.

EXPLANATION

Small pieces of chicken give up flavor much more readily than large pieces of chicken. Using ground chicken maximizes the amount of flavor extraction in the shortest period of time.

TEST KITCHEN TIP: Tender Time Limit for Chicken

According to the May 2008 issue of the *Journal of Food Science*, storing chicken breasts in the freezer for longer than two months negatively affects tenderness. Ever the skeptics, we wanted to double-check the results. So we bought six whole chicken breasts and split each one down the center. We immediately tested one breast from each chicken using a Warner-Bratzler shear device that measures tenderness by quantifying the force required to cut meat. We wrapped and froze the other breasts at 0 degrees (the temperature of the average home freezer). We tested three of the previously frozen breasts for tenderness after two months and the remaining three after three months. Our results confirmed the study's findings: Two-month-old chicken was nearly as tender as fresh chicken, while three-month-old chicken was about 15 percent tougher. We recommend freezing chicken wrapped and sealed in an airtight zipper-lock bag for no longer than two months.

TEST KITCHEN TIP: Preheat Your Omelet Pan Slowly

While developing the recipe for our Perfect French Omelets (page 13), we found that the way we preheated the pan before adding the eggs was critical to achieving a perfectly creamy omelet with a uniformly golden exterior. Instead of preheating over medium-high for 2 or 3 minutes (the most common approach), we preheated the pan over low heat for a full 10 minutes.

On a gas stove, a high flame licks up the sides of the pan, creating hot spots at the outer edges of the pan bottom. These hot spots, in turn, can lead to brown splotches on your omelet. Preheating the low-and-slow way ensures that the heat is more evenly distributed.

Preheating over low heat has another advantage: It gives you a wider window for adding your eggs. Over high heat, it takes just 30 seconds for the pan to go from an acceptable 250 degrees to an egg-toughening 350 degrees. (Note: Preheating an omelet pan is one situation in which electric stoves show an edge over gas. Because of their wide, flat heating element, electric stoves did not produce hot spots in the pan, even over a high setting. However, we still recommend preheating over low heat to allow plenty of time for adding your eggs.)

MEDIUM-HIGH = SPOTTY   **LOW = UNIFORM**

To demonstrate the importance of preheating over the correct (low) temperature, we spread a layer of grated Parmesan cheese over the bottoms of two pans, then heated one over medium-high heat and the other over low heat. Cheese heated over medium-high heat browned on the edges, while the cheese heated over low heat melted to an even, uniform color.

TECHNIQUE | REMOVING THE STEM FROM GREENS

When prepping hearty greens like collards or kale for our Braised Winter Greens (page 19), cutting out the central rib from each leaf individually can be tedious and time-consuming. Here's a way to speed up the process.

 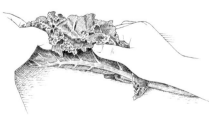  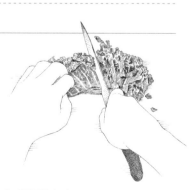

1. STACK three or four leaves on top of each other, large to small, aligning their central ribs.

2. FOLD the stack of greens in half along the central rib.

3. TRIM the central rib using one knife stroke. Repeat with the remaining leaves.

4. CHOP the leaves crosswise into 3-inch pieces.

≥ BY MEREDITH BUTCHER AND PEGGY CHUNG ≤

NEW PRODUCT Cut-Resistant Glove

Cut-resistant gloves are designed to protect fingers when you grate, slice, or chop, but do they really work? We bought four brands and asked for volunteers—but wary test cooks made themselves scarce. So we fit hot dogs into the fingers and ran a sharp knife five times over each one. After every dog emerged unscathed, our testers came back and agreed to wear the gloves to grate and slice carrots and onions on a box grater and mandoline. With the glove (sold one per package; the fabric molds to fit either hand), we could comfortably change the mandoline blades and grip its hand guard. (We don't recommend skipping the hand guard; the gloves

BYE-BYE BAND-AIDS
The Microplane Specialty Series Cut Resistant Glove helps keep your hands safe.

are not infallible.) While all four brands are made of Spectra fiber, a material used in bullet-resistant vests, the tightness of the weave made a difference: Looser-woven fibers on two brands began to shred and pull apart as we worked. In the end, we preferred the snug weave and stretchy fabric of the Microplane Specialty Series Cut Resistant Glove ($24.95), which proved both comfortable and durable.

EQUIPMENT TESTING
Omelet Pans

What's the best pan for making an omelet? Most brands of cookware offer an 8-Inch nonstick "omelet" pan, but these are usually just small versions of their skillets, with upright sides that make it difficult to turn and roll out a perfect omelet. The All-Clad 8-Inch Stainless Nonstick Fry Pan is an exception—its shallow-sloped sides make turning a breeze—but it costs a hefty $90. We tested four other pans with gently sloped sides, all under $25, and found a great buy: the KitchenAid Gourmet Essentials Hard Anodized Nonstick Open

LUXE MODEL
Designed by Julia Child, this Original French Chef Omelette Pan's high-grade performance has a price to match.

BARGAIN PERFORMER
This omelet pan from KitchenAid's Gourmet Essentials line is effective and inexpensive.

French Skillet ($19.99). Although this pan does not have quite the steady, long-lasting heat of heavier pans, its hard anodized material heated quickly and evenly, and the gently sloped sides allowed easy rolling. For fun, we also tested a deluxe model, the Original French Chef Omelette Pan, designed by Julia Child. Its thick, heavy cast aluminum, curving shape, and gently sloped sides churned out perfect omelets, but the price ($139.95) made us balk. For complete testing results, go to www.cooksillustrated.com/feb09.

NEW PRODUCT
Spatula Mixer Blade

Stopping your stand mixer every few minutes to scrape down the sides of the bowl can be tedious, but two new products promise to do it for you (and mix ingredients at the same time): the SideSwipe Spatula Mixer Blade ($24.95) and the BeaterBlade+ ($24.95).The BeaterBlade+ offers a single beating-and-scraping "wing"; the SideSwipe has several angled silicone fins that beat, scrape, and push batter down in the bowl. While both models blended cake batters well and creamed butter in half the time of a traditional paddle (you may need to adjust recipes), it wasn't until we mixed Spritz Cookies that

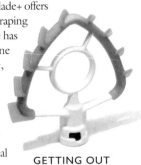

GETTING OUT OF SCRAPES
With the SideSwipe paddle, you won't have to stop and scrape when mixing.

we noticed the major advantage of the SideSwipe: Our recipe recommends stopping three times to scrape the bowl, but with the SideSwipe, we could add ingredients without stopping until the dough came together, leaving completely clean sides in the bowl. Meanwhile, the BeaterBlade+ left smears behind. SideSwipe makes attachments to fit KitchenAid stand mixers and a few other brands (check www.sideswipeblade.com to match your model to a specific blade before buying).

EQUIPMENT TESTING
Milk Frother

For making purees and soups, we turn to our trusty handheld immersion blender (KitchenAid, $49.99). But for smaller tasks, such as frothing milk for coffee drinks or whipping up hot chocolate, cream, or salad dressing for two, we found the Aerolatte Milk Frother ($12.99) quite handy. The lightweight 8¼-inch battery-operated wand works like a mini immersion blender, and it's a snap to use, clean, and store.

Sources

The following are sources for items recommended in this issue. Prices were current at press time and do not include shipping. Contact companies to confirm information or visit www.cooksillustrated.com for updates.

Page 23: CHOCOLATE CHIPPER
- Lehman's Ice Pick/Chocolate Chipper: $6.95, item #1065405, Lehman's (877-438-5346, www.lehmans.com).

Page 25: ELECTRIC GRIDDLES
- BroilKing Professional Griddle: $99.99, item #RP780-3006FB, JCPenney (800-222-6161, www.jcpenney.com).
- West Bend Cool-Touch Nonstick Electric Griddle: $51.95, item #216390, Cooking.com (800-663-8810, www.cooking.com).

Page 29: TRADITIONAL SKILLETS
- All-Clad Stainless 12" Fry Pan: $135, item #100064, Cooking.com.
- Gourmet Standard 12" Skillet: $64.99, item #GST1152, Cookware.com (888-478-4606, www.cookware.com).

Page 32: CUT-RESISTANT GLOVE
- Microplane Specialty Series Cut Resistant Glove: $24.95, item #34007, Microplane (866-968-6665, www.microplane.com).

Page 32: OMELET PAN
- KitchenAid Gourmet Essentials Hard Anodized Nonstick Open French Skillet, $19.99, item #75820, KitchenAid, (800-541-6390, www.shopkitchenaid.com).

PAGE 32: SPATULA MIXER BLADE
- SideSwipe Spatula Mixer Blade: $24.95, Fruit LLC (www.sideswipeblade.com).

Page 32: MILK FROTHER
- Aerolatte Milk Frother: $12.99, item #B0002KZUNK, Amazon.com.

U.S. POSTAL SERVICE STATEMENT OF OWNERSHIP, MANAGEMENT AND CIRCULATION

1. Publication Title: Cook's Illustrated; 2. Publication No. 1068-2821; 3. Filing Date: 9/28/08; 4. Issue Frequency: Jan/Feb, Mar/Apr, May/Jun, Jul/Aug, Sep/Oct, Nov/Dec; 5. No. of Issues Published Annually: 6; 6. Annual Subscription Price: $35.70; 7. Complete Mailing Address of Known Office of Publication: 17 Station Street, Brookline, MA 02445; 8. Complete Mailing Address of Headquarters or General Business Office of Publisher: 17 Station Street, Brookline, MA 02445; 9. Full Names and Complete Mailing Address of Publisher, Editor and Managing Editor: Publisher: Christopher Kimball, 17 Station Street, Brookline, MA 02445; Editor: Christopher Kimball, 17 Station Street, Brookline, MA 02445; Managing Editor: Jack Bishop, 17 Station Street, Brookline, MA 02445; 10. Owner: Boston Common Press Limited Partnership, Christopher Kimball, 17 Station Street, Brookline, MA 02445; 11. Known Bondholders, Mortgagees, and Other Securities: None; 12. Tax Status: Has Not Changed During Preceding 12 Months; 13. Publication Title: Cook's Illustrated; 14. Issue Date for Circulation Data Below: September/October 2008; 15a. Total Number of Copies: 1,190,487 (Sep/Oct 2008: 1,185,827); b. Paid Circulation: (1) Mailed Outside-County Paid Subscriptions Stated on PS Form 3541: 915,035 (Sep/Oct 2008: 907,622); (2) Mailed In-County Paid Subscriptions Stated on PS Form 3541: 0 (Sep/Oct 2008: 0); (3) Paid Distribution Outside the Mails Including Sales Through Dealers and Carriers, Street Vendors, Counter Sales, and Other Paid Distribution Outside the USPS: 105,213 (Sep/Oct 2008: 99,127); (4) Paid Distribution by Other Classes of Mail Through the USPS: 0 (Sep/Oct 2008: 0); c. Total Paid Distribution: 1,025,268 (Sep/Oct 2008: 1,011,671); d. Free or Nominal Rate Distribution: (1) Free or Nominal Rate Outside-County Copies Included on PS Form 3541: 4,955 (Sep/Oct 2008: 4,857); (2) Free or Nominal Rate In-County Copies Included on Form PS 3541: 0 (Sep/Oct 2008: 0); (3) Free or Nominal Rate Copies Mailed at Other Classes Through the USPS: 0 (Sep/Oct 2008: 0); (4) Free or Nominal Rate Distribution Outside the Mail: 65 (Sep/Oct 2008: 65); e. Total Free or Nominal Rate Distribution: 5,020 (Sep/Oct 2008: 4,922); f. Total Distribution: 1,025,268 (Sep/Oct 2008: 1,011,671); g. Copies Not Distributed: 165,219 (Sep/Oct 2008: 174,156); h. Total: 1,190,487 (Sep/Oct 2008: 1,185,827); i. Percent Paid: 99.51% (Sep/Oct 2008: 99.51%).

INDEX
January & February 2009

RECIPES

🎥 COOK'S VIDEOS Original Test Kitchen Videos www.cooksillustrated.com

MAIN DISHES
- **How to Make Braised Beef Short Ribs**
- Choosing boneless short ribs

- **How to Make Breaded Pork Cutlets (Pork Schnitzel)**
- Disposing of used oil

- **How to Make Hearty Chicken Noodle Soup**

- **How to Make Pasta with Butternut Squash and Sage**
- How to prepare and dice squash

- **How to Make Swedish Meatballs**
- Testing for seasoning in a raw-meat mixture

- **How to Make Tandoori Chicken**
- Behind the Scenes: How we developed our Tandoori Chicken recipe
- Getting to know your broiler

SIDE DISH
- **How to Make Braised Winter Greens**

BREAKFAST
- **How to Make French Toast**
- Testing Electric Griddles

- **How to Make Perfect French Omelets**
- How we developed our omelet-folding technique
- Why to preheat the pan slowly

DESSERT
- **How to Make Chewy Chocolate Cookies**

TESTING
- Behind the Scenes: Testing Traditional Skillets

AMERICA'S TEST KITCHEN
Public television's most popular cooking show

Join the millions of home cooks who watch our show, *America's Test Kitchen*, on public television every week. For more information, including recipes and program times, visit www.americastestkitchen.com.

Braised Beef Short Ribs, 9

Hearty Chicken Noodle Soup, 21

Pasta with Butternut Squash and Sage, 18

French Toast, 25

Breaded Pork Cutlets, 11

Swedish Meatballs, 15

Tandoori Chicken, 7

Perfect French Omelets, 13

Braised Winter Greens, 19

Chewy Chocolate Cookies, 23

PHOTOGRAPHY: CARL TREMBLAY, STYLING: MARIE PIRAINO

Chamomile

Nepeta

Thyme

Lavender

Echinacea

Chrysanthemum

Jasmine

Fennel

Rose Hip

Gardenia

Spearmint

Yarrow

TISANE HERBS AND FLOWERS

NUMBER NINETY-SEVEN

MARCH & APRIL 2009

COOK'S
ILLUSTRATED

Best Beef Tenderloin
Forgo Classic Approach

Glazed Roast Chicken
Barbecue Trick Ensures Even Coating

Reviving Baked Ziti
Two Sauces to the Rescue

Rating Blenders
It's All about the Blades

Keeping Pantry Staples Fresh

French Mashed Potatoes
Rich, Cheesy, Garlicky

Real vs. Fake Vanilla

Easiest-Ever Chocolate Cake

Pan-Seared Pork Chops

Chicken Cutlets
with Porcini Sauce

Cod Baked in Foil

Rustic Ciabatta Bread

www.cooksillustrated.com

$5.95 U.S./$6.95 CANADA

0 74470 62805 7

CONTENTS

March & April 2009

COOK'S ILLUSTRATED
www.cooksillustrated.com

HOME OF AMERICA'S TEST KITCHEN

Founder and Editor Christopher Kimball
Editorial Director Jack Bishop
Executive Editor Amanda Agee
Test Kitchen Director Erin McMurrer
Managing Editor Rebecca Hays
Senior Editors Keith Dresser
Lisa McManus
Features Editor Lisa Glazer
Copy Editor Amy Graves
Associate Editors J. Kenji Alt
Charles Kelsey
David Pazmiño
Bryan Roof
Production Editor, Special Issues Elizabeth Bomze
Test Cooks Francisco J. Robert
Yvonne Ruperti
Assistant Test Kitchen Director Matthew Herron
Assistant Editors Meredith Butcher
Peggy Chung Collier
Assistant Test Cook Marcus Walser
Executive Assistant Meredith Smith
Editorial Assistant Abbey Becker
Senior Kitchen Assistant Nadia Domeq
Kitchen Assistants Maria Elena Delgado
Ena Gudiel
Edward Tundidor
Producer Melissa Baldino
Contributing Editors Matthew Card
Dawn Yanagihara
Consulting Editors Scott Brueggeman
Guy Crosby
Proofreader Jean Rogers

Online Managing Editor David Tytell
Online Editor Kate Mason
Online Media Producer Peter Tannenbaum
Online Assistant Editor Leaya Lee
Online Editorial Assistant Mari Levine

Design Director Amy Klee
Art Director, Magazines Julie Bozzo
Senior Designer Christine Vo
Designers Jay Layman
Lindsey Timko
Staff Photographer Daniel J. van Ackere

Vice President Marketing David Mack
Circulation Director Doug Wicinski
Circulation & Fulfillment Manager Carrie Horan
Circulation Assistant Megan Cooley
Partnership Marketing Manager Pamela Putprush
Direct Mail Director Adam Perry
Marketing Database Analyst Ariel Gilbert-Knight
Product Operations Director Steven Browall
Product Promotions Director Randi Lawrence
E-Commerce Marketing Director Hugh Buchan
Associate Marketing Manager Laurel Zeidman
Marketing Copywriter David Goldberg
Customer Service Manager Jacqueline Valerio
Customer Service Representatives Jillian Nannicelli
Kate Sokol

Sponsorship Sales Director Marcy McCreary
Retail Sales & Marketing Manager Emily Logan
Corporate Marketing Associate Bailey Vatalaro

Production Director Guy Rochford
Traffic & Projects Manager Alice Carpenter
Senior Production Manager Jessica L. Quirk
Production & Imaging Specialists Judy Blomquist
Lauren Pettapiece
Imaging & Color Specialist Andrew Mannone

Systems Administrator S. Paddi McHugh
Web Production Coordinator Evan Davis
Support Technician Brandon Lynch

Chief Financial Officer Sharyn Chabot
Human Resources Director Adele Shapiro
Controller Mandy Shito
Senior Accountant Aaron Goranson
Staff Accountant Connie Forbes
Accounts Payable Specialist Steven Kasha
Office Manager Tasha Bere
Receptionist Henrietta Murray
Publicity Deborah Broide

For list rental information, contact: Specialists Marketing Services, Inc., 777 Terrace Ave., 4th Floor, Hasbrouck Heights, NJ 07604; 201-865-5800.

Editorial Office: 17 Station St., Brookline, MA 02445; 617-232-1000; fax 617-232-1572. Subscription inquiries, visit www.americastestkitchen.com/customerservice or call 800-526-8442.

Postmaster: Send all new orders, subscription inquiries, and change-of-address notices to Cook's Illustrated, P.O. Box 7446, Red Oak, IA 51591-0446.

PRINTED IN THE USA

CARROTS
The cultivation of new carrot varieties like Purple Haze and Cosmic Purple (both display purple exteriors) demonstrates a renewed interest in this everyday vegetable. Lighter-skinned carrots, such as Yellowstone and White Satin, tend to be sweeter and crisper than darker varieties. Atomic Reds have a more assertive flavor than most carrots and intensify in color as they cook. As their name implies, Sugar Snacks are quite sweet, making them ideal snacking carrots. Tapered Imperators have enjoyed commercial success in North America as a good storage root, one durable enough to be whittled into pseudo baby carrots. Young, tender, and squat Chantenay carrots are the variety sold as true baby carrots. Cigar-shaped Nantes are preferred in Europe for their sweet, mild taste. Kamaran carrots, used primarily by commercial food manufacturers, fall between Nantes and Imperators in shape and sweetness. Round carrots are dependable growers; their stout, bulbous roots make an attractive addition to plates.

COVER (*Fennel*): Robert Papp, BACK COVER (*Carrots*): John Burgoyne

America's Test Kitchen is a very real 2,500-square-foot kitchen located just outside of Boston. It is the home of *Cook's Illustrated* and *Cook's Country* magazines and is the workday destination for more than three dozen test cooks, editors, and cookware specialists. Our mission is to test recipes over and over again until we understand how and why they work and until we arrive at the best version. We also test kitchen equipment and supermarket ingredients in search of brands that offer the best value and performance. You can watch us work by tuning in to *America's Test Kitchen* (www.americastestkitchen.com) on public television.

THE SKY COMES NOVEMBER

The president of the Old Rabbit Hunters Association likes to take his time on a dark morning in deer season. I pull up at his garage at precisely 5:15 a.m., a snout full of the unusually warm (for November), ripe air (the thermometer read a balmy 35 degrees when I left the farm) and feeling better for it. On the first day of the season, every hunter imagines a stand of pine in early light, a large rack emerging above the undergrowth, the crosshairs of the Bushnell scope sighting in, and then an echoing boom down and out of the valley. So I'm in a hurry to get up the mountain and into my stand, one that puts me almost 20 feet up a tree, a stripped-down model without arm or gun rests. You can feel the stand shudder during a blast of wind, the tree dancing with you helpless in its arms.

But, as I said, Mr. President is not one to be rushed. He is puttering about, making coffee, laying the cups neatly and upside down on a sheet of patterned paper towels, looking for his blue bottle of liquid nondairy creamer in the small refrigerator he keeps in his well-stocked garage. The torpedo-shaped kerosene heater is backwashing like a jet engine; the four-wheeler is already on his pickup bed and strapped in; and Mr. President is about half-dressed, an old-fashioned men's hat squarely aloft above his brow, a strip of orange hunting tape festooning its circumference. "Now, just sit down and have a cup of coffee," he demands. "The deer can wait."

His son Nate shows up and we joke around a bit as I check my watch over a second cup of coffee. We talk about the benefits of silk socks for keeping one's feet warm, the pros and cons of lined hunting jackets, whether open sights are better than a scope, and then, of course, where each of us is going to spend the morning. Nate is headed for the top of the gut behind our pond; Mr. President has a stand set up in a small clearing where there were a few good hookings (where bucks have rubbed the bark off of saplings), and I am headed for the top of it, a spot Nate has used for years with a wide view of a hollow.

"Well," says Mr. President, "I'm going to warm up my truck and I'll see you boys in a few minutes." Then he adds, "Leave the gate open for me." He isn't in much of a rush as I eagerly head out to my pickup.

I start up the mountain, unlock the gate, and move slowly through the darkness, negotiating a road slick with wet leaves and thick mud. I park, punch the clip into my .308, turn on my walkie-talkie, and take out a small flashlight to find my way. I'd tapped a few lightning bug–sized reflectors into trees so I'll know where to turn. I move through the damp woods, cross a downed sheep fence, and then the laddered stand looms ahead. I'm up and seated, as if waiting for the start of a first-run movie.

High up in a tree on a dark November morning, I watch the details come into focus. The trees grow bark, the pattern of leaves on the ground takes shape, the woods awaken with the rustling of a field mouse just below the stand, and the aggressive nattering of a small, red squirrel calls out an alarm when he discovers the large, orange-vested trespasser staring down at him. The big, old trees, veterans, also start to show themselves, their shorn limbs choppy, their dead branches making sad, ragged profiles.

A rhythmic walking sound starts and stops behind the stand toward the road. I listen. Then silence. Then a regular hoofbeat, a quick-footed, light padding through the woods, and a coyote appears, loping directly across the gray hollow. Then more rustling, something bigger than a squirrel, and a small flock of turkeys emerges about 200 yards away. I watch intently, although the season is now over. They prance about, moving forward in stops and starts, a few hens in the lead with the small chicks close behind.

Then I'm startled by a noise over my right shoulder. I turn and there stands, to my great surprise, a grand buck, thick-muscled through the shoulders. He's just 20 feet away and almost directly behind me. I stop breathing. I'm too excited to count the points on the wide, forward-leaning rack, but I can see he's big and doesn't see me looking down from my perch. This buck is wild and powerful, and for a split second I wonder about his secret life of finding does, surviving the lean winters, knowing where the scrub oaks are (the only ones producing acorns this year), and which sunny southern slope he prefers on a cold afternoon in January, where he can nestle down in the thick brush and stay warm and hidden. A hunter

Christopher Kimball

can spend a lifetime in the woods and never come face to face with a buck as fine as this. It is so startling that you forget what you think you know, as if the earth no longer revolved around the sun.

A poet might end this story with a stanza to the divine, with the laying down of arms, but I disappoint. I stand, swivel, and sight in the buck zigzagging through the woods, now 50 yards away in the weak, early morning light. I fire three times, chambering new shells with a Winchester-style lever, and then he stops far off, behind a thicket of trees, taunting me with the only part visible, a white tail flicking casually. With one shot left I wait, but he takes off in an explosion of forward movement, and I make a poor, halfhearted shot through the trees. He wins the encounter hands down.

November had come again with heavy, pewter skies and dawns that develop thoughtfully, reluctantly; with quick snow showers that crystallize the forest carpet, making the woods impressionable, with gusts and gamy scent from days spent in the woods, predawn to sunset, looking for the object of our desire. And I kept coming back to the stand at that wee hour, sitting and looking over my right shoulder, to refresh my memory. A hunter sits in a tree, a buck stands behind him, and the world stops to consider.

If we meet again, I won't hesitate to shoot. I've always been a hunter (but not a great one). The woods are full of life and death, of neighbors who still make it through the winter on a freezer full of venison or moose meat. There is no reprieve in nature, no intercession, just necessity. I came out of the woods at sunset that day with an empty truck bed but with something wild in my heart.

That evening, sitting in front of the fire, Mr. President asked about the shots, and said, "Yup, I thought it was you." Then he added, "You ought to have moved over a bit in the stand—that old buck might have climbed up and joined you for a visit!" Then he sat back and closed his eyes, remembering, I guess, all the proud-footed bucks that he has missed over the years, and a deep contented smile slowly took shape, just at the corners of his mouth.

FOR INQUIRIES, ORDERS, OR MORE INFORMATION

www.cooksillustrated.com

At www.cooksillustrated.com, you can order books and subscriptions, sign up for our free e-newsletter, or renew your magazine subscription. Join the website and gain access to 16 years of *Cook's Illustrated* recipes, equipment tests, and ingredient tastings, as well as Cook's Live companion videos for every recipe in this issue.

COOKBOOKS

We sell more than 50 cookbooks by the editors of *Cook's Illustrated*. To order, visit our bookstore at www.cooksillustrated.com or call 800-611-0759 (or 515-246-6911 from outside the U.S.).

COOK'S ILLUSTRATED Magazine

Cook's Illustrated magazine (ISSN 1068-2821), number 97, is published bimonthly by Boston Common Press Limited Partnership, 17 Station St., Brookline, MA 02445. Copyright 2009 Boston Common Press Limited Partnership. Periodicals postage paid at Boston, Mass., and additional mailing offices USPS #012487. Publications Mail Agreement No. 40020778. Return undeliverable Canadian addresses to P.O. Box 875, Station A, Windsor, ON N9A 6P2. POSTMASTER: Send address changes to Cook's Illustrated, P.O. Box 7446, Red Oak, IA 51591-0446. For subscription and gift subscription orders, subscription inquiries, or change-of-address notices, call 800-526-8442 in the U.S. or 515-247-7571 from outside the U.S. or write us at Cook's Illustrated, P.O. Box 7446, Red Oak, IA 51591-0446.

White Anchovies?

I recently saw a package of white anchovies in the refrigerator section of my supermarket. Is there any difference between these and the regular canned variety?

AYA ALT
ITHACA, N.Y.

➤ Anchovies of any type come from the same variety of small fish related to herring. The only difference is in how they're cured. Tinned anchovies are normally filleted and packed in salt for up to 10 months before being canned, usually in oil. During the lengthy salting, the white flesh turns brown. White anchovies are only briefly salted before being packed in a pickling solution of vinegar and oil. To evaluate flavor differences, we tasted each variety alone and in Caesar salad. Aficionados preferred the fuller, more intense flavor of canned anchovies, while those

WHITE FISH
White anchovies taste milder than tinned.

less enthusiastic about these small, oily fish preferred white anchovies for their milder, less fishy taste. If you buy the white variety, make sure to keep them refrigerated. Use the same amount to substitute them for the canned.

Pitted versus Unpitted Olives

Are there any differences in flavor or texture among pitted and unpitted brine-cured olives?

MELISSA REED
DURHAM, N.C.

➤ To evaluate any differences between pitted and unpitted olives, we gathered both green and black brine-cured olives from deli sections at supermarkets, as well as olives packed in plastic and glass containers. After tasting many samples, it became clear that the pitted olives suffered on two counts: They tasted saltier and their flesh was mushier. They also lacked the complex, fruity flavors of the unpitted kind. Here's why: Before being packed for sale, fresh-picked olives are soaked in brine for periods of up to a year to remove bitterness and develop flavor. Once pitted, the olives are returned to the brine for packing, which can penetrate the inside of the olive and turn it mushy and pasty, as well as increase the absorption of salt. That saltier taste can mask subtler flavors. If you have the time, it makes sense to buy unpitted olives and pit them yourself.

Vinegar Sediment

I have several jars of vinegar in my cabinet with a cloudy, slimy sediment at the bottom. Should I throw them away?

SHERI POWELL
ENCINITAS, CALIF.

➤ Nearly all commercially made vinegar will last indefinitely in an unopened bottle. Once opened and exposed to air, however, harmless "vinegar bacteria" may start to grow. This bacteria causes the formation of a cloudy sediment that is nothing more than harmless cellulose, a complex carbohydrate that does not affect the quality of the vinegar or its flavor. We confirmed this with a side-by-side comparison of freshly opened bottles of vinegar and those with sediment (strained before tasting).

The Vinegar Institute carried out storage studies of vinegar and determined that the shelf life of opened vinegar stored in a dark cabinet at room temperature is "almost indefinite." To deal with the unsightly sediment, simply strain the vinegar through a coffee filter set inside a fine-mesh strainer before using it.

Shiitake Substitute

Fresh shiitake mushrooms often cost three to four times as much as fresh cremini mushrooms. Do I need to adjust the cooking time if I make a substitution?

CECELIA BAYLIS THOMAS
DALLAS, TEX.

➤ The goal of cooking mushrooms is to evaporate their liquid so they can brown and their flavor can intensify. To identify any difference in water weight between cremini and shiitake mushrooms that would affect cooking times, we chopped 8 ounces of each and placed them in separate pots with no liquid or oil. We covered the pots and cooked each batch for 10 minutes over medium-low heat. We then removed the mushrooms from the pans and weighed them again. The shiitakes lost 1.1 ounces of water, or about 14 percent of their weight, while the cremini mushrooms lost 4.8 ounces, or about 60 percent of their weight. The higher water content of the creminis was confirmed when we sautéed a batch of each mushroom. The creminis took nearly five minutes longer than the shiitakes to release their liquid and begin to brown. In the end, we decided that it's fine to make a substitution, keeping in mind that the creminis will have a slightly softer texture and a bit less intense flavor. Just remember to sauté or stir-fry creminis for a few extra minutes until their excess liquid completely evaporates.

Swanson Cooking Stock

I follow your recommendations and buy your favorite brand of chicken broth: Swanson Certified Organic Free Range Broth. I recently noticed that Swanson has a new product called Cooking Stock. What is the difference between the broth and the stock?

LARISA HULNICK
NEWTON, MASS.

BEST FOR GRAVY

WELL-SUITED FOR SOUP
Swanson's new cooking stock fares best in recipes that call for reducing the stock. For soup-making, stick with broth.

➤ Technically speaking, home-made broth is made from meat, bones, and vegetables, while stock is made strictly from bones and vegetables. In commercial products, however, the distinction is less clear.

Swanson claims its new chicken stock is best suited for gravies and pan sauces in which the stock is reduced; the broth is intended for soup. Its website says the stock has a "robust, less-seasoned, meaty" flavor while the broth has a "finished, highly seasoned" flavor. Heated and tasted plain, the chicken broth was the most seasoned (it contains 550 mg of sodium per cup versus the stock's 510 mg per cup), but we also found it to have "bolder" chicken flavor than the stock. However, when we used both broth and stock to make gravy and pan sauce, Swanson's claims rang true: Tasters found the less-seasoned stock had richer chicken flavor after it was reduced during cooking. If you tend to use a canned product mainly to make pan sauces, gravies, risotto, or other applications in which the liquid is reduced, it makes sense to buy the stock. If you are more likely to use a commercial product to make soup, keep the original broth in your cupboard.

Roux Replacements

I know that roux is often made with butter. Is it OK to substitute oil for the butter?

MICHAEL DISHAROOL
NORFOLK, VA.

➤ *Larousse Gastronomique* defines roux as "a cooked mixture of equal amounts of flour and butter, used to thicken sauces." Nevertheless, some recipes that borrow from classic French technique specifically call for making roux with oil (gumbo, for example). To find out if oil can be successfully used in a roux that calls for butter, we made a classic béchamel, or white sauce, with butter and compared it to béchamel made with neutral-tasting canola oil (we knew the distinctive flavor of olive oil would prevent it from being a viable substitute).

Tasters found the texture of the sauces identical. The sauces also tasted remarkably similar, though a few astute tasters thought the sauce made with butter was the richer of the two.

Next, we used these same sauces as part of a more complex dish, lasagna Bolognese. Here the flavor differences faded away, with the meaty tomato sauce overpowering the béchamel. Our recommendation: If the roux will be used in a dish that involves multiple flavors, go ahead and substitute canola oil for butter. If the roux will be used to thicken a simple sauce, it's best to stick with butter.

Sorting Out Sea Salt

I am confused by the variety of international sea salts available at the supermarket. They vary in price, color, and coarseness. Can you provide guidelines on how to use them?

SUE KILLION
ROTONDA WEST, FLA.

MALDON SEA SALT
Use regular table salt for cooking and choose a flaky, coarse sea salt for sprinkling.

➤Natural sea salt is simply sodium chloride and in its pure form is no different from everyday table salt. However, depending on where the salt is harvested (a *terroir* can be as exotic as Hawaiian black lava or Australian red algae), trace mineral elements such as potassium, magnesium, and calcium can be found. These elements cause variation in the flavor and color of the salt. And depending on how the salt crystals are harvested, their texture can range from sandlike and powdery to crystalline and flaky.

But can these characteristics be detected when the salts are used for cooking? To find out, we bought an array of salts: Fleur de Sel de Camargue ($17.27 per pound), Esprit du Sel de Ile de Ré ($35.68 per pound), La Baleine ($2.15 per pound), Grey Celtic ($28 per pound), Morton's Coarse Kosher Salt ($.35 per pound), and Maldon Sea Salt ($12.24 per pound). We used the salts in simple applications, including seasoning chicken stock and salting cooking water for pasta. The results were definitive: Tasters couldn't tell one salt from another in cooked applications. Only when the salts were sprinkled over slices of beef tenderloin could tasters detect subtle flavor nuances. But it was the texture that really distinguished some salts: Samples with large, flaky crystals such as Maldon Sea Salt had a crunch we particularly enjoyed. Our advice? Save your money and use fancy sea salts only for garnishing.

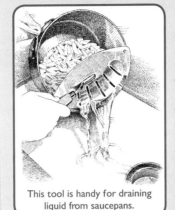
Cloudy Olive Oil

I often store oils in my refrigerator to prevent them from going bad. Why is it that certain oils (like olive) become solid and others (like canola) don't?

ED PELLICCIOTTI
ENDICOTT, N.Y.

➤Some oils become thick and viscous at cold temperatures due to fats and compounds called polyphenols suspended in their midst. Because olive oil is minimally processed, it contains more polyphenols than other oils. (Canola oil is usually processed to the point where very few of these compounds remain.) Polyphenols are soluble in oil only at room temperature. As the temperature decreases, they begin to separate out, making the oil cloudy. (For olive oil, this separation occurs at 43 degrees.) Returned to room temperature, the polyphenols will dissolve once again and the oil will look normal. Even so, olive oil takes a few hours to "melt" back into its liquid form once it has been refrigerated, so we recommend storing it at room temperature in a cool, dark place. Once opened, olive oil has a shelf life of about three months.

Sleuthing Scallions

Some recipes call for using only the green or white part of a scallion. Color aside, is there really a difference between the two sections?

CAROLYN HERRON
GALLUP, N. MEX.

➤To answer your question, we started by tasting raw scallions. Tasters described distinctly different flavor profiles for the white and green parts. The white section has a delicate, sweet taste similar to shallots, while the green portion has grassy notes and a peppery bite. When we used the raw scallions in salsa, tasters were still able to identify the same distinguishing characteristics; which worked better depended on individual taste. Finally, we cooked scallions in a pork stir-fry. Tasters didn't notice major flavor differences, but the textures varied: The whites softened nicely while the greens wilted, taking on a limp texture that some tasters didn't like.

So, if texture is an issue, cook only the white part and reserve the green portion to use as a garnish. When it comes to using the scallions raw, choose the white part for mild flavor and add the green for a strong, peppery taste.

Rye Bread Choices

The rye bread for sale in my supermarket includes light, dark, and pumpernickel. How do they differ?

ELLEN CAIN
AUBURN, NEB.

➤All three types of bread are made from flour milled from rye grass. Light rye flour is produced by removing the coarse outer layer of the rye berry (like a wheat berry, this is the "fruit" of the grain), exposing its relatively light interior. This kernel is then ground to a fine powder that is typically blended with white wheat flour to produce light rye bread. Dark rye flour includes some of the outer layers of the rye berry, while pumpernickel flour is ground from the whole rye berry and left rather coarse instead of fine.

We tasted all three types of bread plain and in Reuben sandwiches. There was no clear winner; any preference boiled down to personal taste. Some liked the mild taste of the lighter rye bread, while others preferred the stronger flavors of dark rye and pumpernickel. If you have trouble choosing, consider marbled rye, the swirled bread made with light rye dough and either dark rye or pumpernickel dough.

SEND US YOUR QUESTIONS We will provide a complimentary one-year subscription for each letter we print. Send your inquiry, name, address, and daytime telephone number to Notes from Readers, Cook's Illustrated, P.O. Box 470589, Brookline, MA 02447, or to notesfromreaders@americastestkitchen.com.

Quick Tips

⇒ COMPILED BY YVONNE RUPERTI & FRANCISCO J. ROBERT ⇐

Cool Decorating

Many frostings, such as buttercream and ganache, soften as they warm up. This means that when piping designs with a pastry bag, warm hands can cause sloppy-looking decorations. To keep her rosettes and borders perky, Cathy Durso of Denver, Colo., wears latex gloves while piping. The gloves help to insulate her hands and thereby prevent her body heat from softening the frosting.

Easier Meat Defrosting

Freezing a large portion of ground meat is problematic when it comes time to cook and you only need to use a small quantity. Jane Wright of Weston, Conn., solves this problem by transferring the ground meat to a large zipper-lock bag. Using her fingers, she presses through the bag to divide the mass into 4 equal portions, and then places the bag flat in the freezer. When it's time to cook, she simply breaks off the amount of meat that she needs.

Rice at the Ready

Whenever she makes rice, Donna Clarke of Bartlett, Ill., prepares a double batch and freezes the leftovers. Later, they can be reheated in the microwave, used to make fried rice, or added to soups and stews. Here's how she does it.

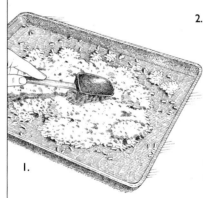

1. Spread the hot rice out on a baking sheet to cool. Break up any large clumps.
2. Place the cooled rice in a zipper-lock bag and freeze until needed.

A Long Reach

When making recipes such as hummus in a food processor, Gregory Welch of Union, N.J., found that it was impractical to remove the lid every time he wanted to do a taste test. Instead, he takes out a long-handled iced-tea spoon, which is the perfect length to reach down the feed tube. (Be sure to turn off the processor before tasting.)

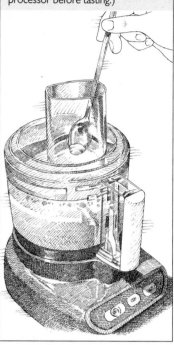

Single-Serving Whipped Cream

Fresh whipped cream is an ideal topping for a mug of hot chocolate. For just one serving, however, it's too much hassle to drag out a hand mixer to whip the cream. Instead, Frank Barrett of Seattle, Wash., employs a tiny, hand-held milk frother, the kind used to whip milk for cappuccino. Just pour 2 tablespoons of cold heavy cream into a mug, add a pinch of sugar, and whirl until the cream holds soft peaks.

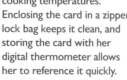

Handy Temperature Guide

Tired of fumbling through recipe books every time she cooked fish, meat, or poultry, Alice Pruce of Edmonds, Wash., created an index card with a list of final internal cooking temperatures. Enclosing the card in a zipper-lock bag keeps it clean, and storing the card with her digital thermometer allows her to reference it quickly.

Waffle Maker Double Duty

Kristofer Robert of Peachtree City, Ga., finds that her waffle maker comes in handy at lunch as well as at breakfast: She uses it to make grilled cheese and panini sandwiches. A bonus is that the deep grooves in the waffle maker yield extra-crisp crusts.

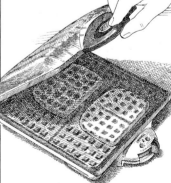

Assemble the sandwiches with buttered bread and then place them in a preheated waffle maker, checking often for doneness.

Send Us Your Tip We will provide a complimentary one-year subscription for each tip we print. Send your tip, name, and address to Quick Tips, Cook's Illustrated, P.O. Box 470589, Brookline, MA 02447, or to quicktips@americastestkitchen.com.

ILLUSTRATION: JOHN BURGOYNE

Disposable Ice Packs

Julia Hurwitz of Dunwoody, Ga., wanted to find a way to keep snacks destined for lunch boxes chilled as long as possible. She came up with this easy solution.

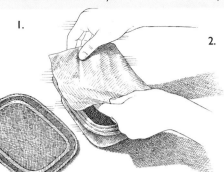
1.

2.

3.

1. Fold a paper towel in thirds, saturate it with water, and then fit it inside the bottom of a storage container.
2. Put the container in the freezer.
3. When it's time to pack lunch, place the food in a zipper-lock bag, set the bag in the frozen plastic container, and put on the lid. The food will stay cool until lunchtime.

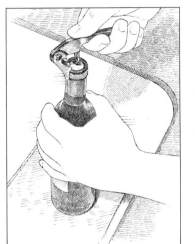

Easy-Open Wine

Whenever she needs to open a bottle of wine, Joan Worley of Maryville, Tenn., sets the bottle on a folded dish towel placed in the kitchen sink. Having the bottle at a lower level provides extra leverage for uncorking, making the task a snap.

No More Fruit Flies

Many fruits, such as tomatoes and bananas, are best stored at room temperature. During the warmer months, however, fruit flies find ripening produce irresistible. Kendra Grady of Newburgh, N.Y., entices the pests with this trick. She places ¼ cup of orange juice in a small drinking glass and then tops it with a funnel. Placed next to a fruit bowl, the juice lures the tiny flies into the funnel, where they are unable to escape.

Making Flavored Salt

Peter Thompson of Arlington, Mass., found a great use for small amounts of fresh herbs or citrus zest: flavored salt. To make citrus salt, mix 2 teaspoons of freshly grated lemon, lime, grapefruit, or orange zest with ½ cup of kosher salt. For herb salt, mix 1 tablespoon chopped fresh rosemary, thyme, or mint leaves with ½ cup of kosher salt. Transfer the salt to an airtight container and store at room temperature. The citrus salts can be stored indefinitely, and the herb salts can be stored for up to 3 weeks.

Neater Lemon Wedges

The thick strand of white pith along the center ridge of a lemon wedge can cause the juice to squirt out in all directions during squeezing.

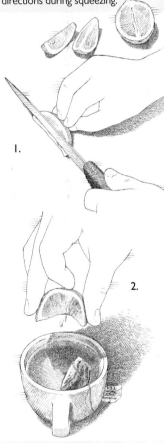
1.

2.

1. For juice that lands in her teacup (and not in her eye), Lois Jacobson of Memphis, Tenn., uses a paring knife to remove the tough pith from wedges.
2. The resulting wedges will squeeze neatly into food and drinks.

Removing the "Eyes" from Pineapple

After removing the rind from a pineapple, the hard, dark bits, or "eyes," remain attached to the flesh. Using a paring knife to trim the eyes is time-consuming and can result in a good deal of waste.

1. Janet Mercuri of North Royalton, Ohio, trims the rind from the fruit.
2. Then she uses a small melon baller to quickly and neatly scoop out the "eyes."

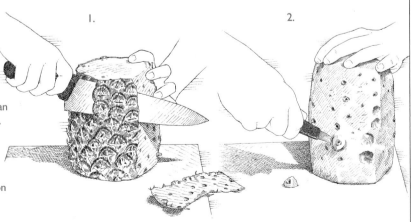
1.   2.

The Best Beef Tenderloin

The classic approach to roasting this prime cut sacrifices juiciness for crust. Why settle for anything less than perfection?

⇒ BY CHARLES KELSEY ⇐

Nothing beats the extravagantly buttery texture of beef tenderloin. It may not be the most intensely flavored cut, but that is easily overcome by a rich sauce or accompaniment. The challenge is in expertly cooking the meat. The moist, delicate texture of tenderloin can easily be compromised by the oven's harsh heat. And considering its steep price, overcooking this special-occasion roast is not an option (my preferred cut rings up at about $18 per pound).

Yet when I tried a handful of recipes and techniques, all of which gave fairly vague instructions, the tenderloins emerged from the oven with one of two problems. Some cooked evenly but didn't have the dark, caramelized crust that gives meat a deep roasted flavor. Others had optimal flavor and an appealing brown crust, but were marred by a thick, gray band of overdone meat near the edge. I wanted a technique that produced perfectly cooked and deeply flavored meat—ideally without too much fuss.

Getting Even

With only two options, whole and center-cut, choosing the style of tenderloin roast was straightforward but critical to my success. Whole tenderloin is huge—the typical roast is 5 or 6 pounds, serving up to 16 people. It often comes covered in a thick layer of fat and sinew that is time-consuming to trim and peel. Plus its long, tapered shape is a challenge to cook evenly. Over the years, we've become fond of the smaller center-cut roast, known in industry argot as the Châteaubriand,

For perfect tenderloin, sear last, not first, and rub with flavored butter.

Tenderloin Troubles

CRUSTY BUT OVERCOOKED
Tenderloin with a good flavorful crust is often marred by a band of gray, overcooked meat near the edge.

EVENLY COOKED BUT NO CRUST
Tenderloin that is rosy from edge to edge typically lacks a good crust and meaty flavor.

after the 19th century French author and statesman François-René de Châteaubriand (who is said to have particularly enjoyed this prized meat). Some butchers charge significantly more for center-cut versus whole tenderloin, but it comes already trimmed (so there's no waste) and its cylindrical shape practically guarantees that both ends cook to the same degree of doneness. What you're getting is the best of the best—the centerpiece of the most exquisitely tender part of the cow (see "Locating the Châteaubriand," page 7).

To achieve a good crust on the meat, I could either sear it first in a skillet or simply crank up the oven as high as it would go, at the beginning or end of cooking. As oven-searing wouldn't require splattering grease on my stovetop or dirtying an extra pan, I started there. I tied the meat crosswise with twine at intervals to make it more compact and help form an even crust, then placed the meat in a roasting pan that I'd preheated to further encourage browning. But no matter what I tried—starting out high (at 500 degrees) and dropping down much

lower (400 degrees), or the reverse—the meat would not brown adequately. My best results came from simply cooking the tenderloin at 425 degrees for half an hour and turning it after 15 minutes. The roast that emerged from the oven looked promising, with a somewhat dark crust. But any hopes I had were dashed when I cut into the meat: The slices were a nice deep pink at the center but marred by a pesky band of gray, overcooked meat at the edge.

Pan-searing it would have to be. I heated a few tablespoons of vegetable oil over medium-high heat in a large skillet and then added my roast, browning it on all sides before transferring it to the oven. This time, with browning already done, I placed it on a rack set inside a rimmed baking sheet to promote air circulation and more even cooking. I prepared several roasts this way, and experimented with different oven temperatures, from 500 degrees on down to 350. Naturally, each of these roasts had a good-looking crust, but each also had an overdone "ring around the collar." The best of the bunch was the tenderloin roasted at 350, but there was still plenty of room for improvement. Tinkering around, I decided to try reversing the cooking order, roasting first, then searing, a technique we've used successfully in other meat recipes. The switch worked wonders here as well. Because the roast started out warm and dry, it could reach the 310 degrees necessary for browning to occur a lot faster than searing when it was raw, cold, and wet. (Until the moisture burns off, the surface of the meat can't rise above 212 degrees, the boiling point of water.) Less searing time, in turn, minimized the overcooked layer of gray.

Could I get rid of the gray band altogether by taking the oven temperature down further? In the past, the test kitchen has roasted meat at even lower temperatures with great success, transforming tough, inexpensive cuts into meltingly tender meat ("Slow-Roasted Beef," January/February 2008). I hadn't initially thought to try slow roasting because tenderloin is so soft to begin with. Now I reconsidered. After tying several more roasts, I put them in the oven and began dialing back the temperature from 350 degrees. As it turned out, I didn't have that far to go: 300 degrees proved the magic temperature for yielding consistent ruby coloring from edge to edge.

Locating the Châteaubriand

CHÂTEAUBRIAND

The center-cut tenderloin, or Châteaubriand, comes from the middle of the whole tenderloin. The meat sits beneath the spine of the cow and gets no exercise at all, making it exceptionally tender. Furthermore, its cylindrical shape is an advantage for even cooking.

Beefing Up Flavor

Despite decent progress, I still hadn't coaxed deep beefy flavor from my mild-mannered tenderloin. The issue was the meat itself: With so little fat, it was lacking ideal flavor, even after searing to create a crust and carefully calibrating the cooking. I knew I could lean on a rich sauce like a béarnaise or an intense wine reduction—indeed, I was planning to add an accompaniment of some sort—but I was also set on intensifying the flavor of the meat itself.

First I was curious to explore some of the offbeat techniques I'd come across in my research. The most appealing involved roasting the meat wrapped in a couple slices of bacon, which then get discarded and the meat seared. I had high hopes; after all, what doesn't taste better with bacon? Tenderloin, as it turned out; the bacon caused the meat to steam and didn't really add or detract flavor. Shrouding the tenderloin in butter-soaked cheesecloth produced similarly uninspiring results. And soaking the meat in a soy-Worcestershire mix—ingredients often used to accentuate beef flavor—was just plain overpowering, more teriyaki than tenderloin.

In the end, a tried-and-true test kitchen method proved best—sprinkling all sides of the meat with salt, covering it with plastic wrap, and then letting it sit at room temperature. After sitting for an hour, the roast cooked up with significantly more flavor. Here's why: The salt draws juices out of the meat, then the reverse happens and the salt and moisture flow back in, drawing flavor deep into the meat.

I got the best results of all when, after salting the meat, I rubbed it with a couple of tablespoons of softened butter before cooking, which added surprisingly satisfying richness. In fact, this technique was so effective that I decided against a rich, complex sauce and instead created some easy compound butters, combining shallot with parsley and chipotle chile with garlic and cilantro. The wafting aroma of the flavored butter melting into the crevices of the meat proved irresistible to tasters. I had spent $1,200 on more than 25 tenderloins, but that satisfaction made it worth every penny.

ROAST BEEF TENDERLOIN
SERVES 4 TO 6

If using table salt, reduce the amount to 1 teaspoon. Ask your butcher to prepare a trimmed, center-cut Châteaubriand from the whole tenderloin, as this cut is not usually available without special ordering. If you are cooking for a crowd, this recipe can be doubled to make two roasts. Sear the roasts one after the other, wiping out the pan and adding new oil after searing the first roast. Both pieces of meat can be roasted on the same rack. For our free recipe for Blue Cheese and Chive Butter, go to www.cooksillustrated.com/apr09.

- 1 beef tenderloin center-cut Châteaubriand (about 2 pounds), trimmed of fat and silver skin (see note)
- 2 teaspoons kosher salt (see note)
- 1 teaspoon coarsely ground black pepper
- 2 tablespoons unsalted butter, softened
- 1 tablespoon vegetable oil
- 1 recipe flavored butter (recipes follow)

1. Using 12-inch lengths of twine, tie roast crosswise at 1½-inch intervals. Sprinkle roast evenly with salt, cover loosely with plastic wrap, and let stand at room temperature 1 hour. Meanwhile, adjust oven rack to middle position and heat oven to 300 degrees.

2. Pat roast dry with paper towels. Sprinkle roast evenly with pepper and spread unsalted butter evenly over surface. Transfer roast to wire rack set in rimmed baking sheet. Roast until instant-read thermometer inserted into center of roast registers 125 degrees for medium-rare, 40 to 55 minutes, or 135 degrees for medium, 55 to 70 minutes, flipping roast halfway through cooking.

3. Heat oil in 12-inch heavy-bottomed skillet over medium-high heat until just smoking. Place roast in skillet and sear until well browned on four sides, 1 to 2 minutes per side (total of 4 to 8 minutes). Transfer roast to carving board and spread 2 tablespoons flavored butter evenly over top of roast; let rest 15 minutes. Remove twine and cut meat crosswise into ½-inch-thick slices. Serve, passing remaining flavored butter separately.

SHALLOT AND PARSLEY BUTTER
MAKES ABOUT 8 TABLESPOONS

- 4 tablespoons unsalted butter, softened
- ½ medium shallot, minced (about 2 tablespoons)
- 1 medium garlic clove, minced or pressed through garlic press (about 1 teaspoon)
- 1 tablespoon finely chopped fresh parsley leaves
- ¼ teaspoon table salt
- ¼ teaspoon ground black pepper

Combine all ingredients in medium bowl.

CHIPOTLE AND GARLIC BUTTER WITH LIME AND CILANTRO
MAKES ABOUT 8 TABLESPOONS

- 5 tablespoons unsalted butter, softened
- 1 medium chipotle chile in adobo sauce, seeded and minced, with 1 teaspoon adobo sauce
- 1 medium garlic clove, minced or pressed through garlic press (about 1 teaspoon)
- 1 teaspoon honey
- 1 teaspoon grated zest from 1 lime
- 1 tablespoon minced fresh cilantro leaves
- ½ teaspoon table salt

Combine all ingredients in medium bowl.

COOK'S VIDEOS Original Test Kitchen Videos
www.cooksillustrated.com/apr09
HOW TO MAKE
- Roast Beef Tenderloin

STEP-BY-STEP | A BETTER WAY TO ROAST BEEF TENDERLOIN

1. SALT meat and let stand 1 hour to intensify flavor.

2. RUB roast with small amount of softened butter to further boost flavor.

3. ROAST ON LOW to ensure evenly cooked meat throughout.

4. SEAR ON STOVETOP after roasting to create well-caramelized crust with deep meaty flavor.

5. TOP WITH HERB BUTTER before meat rests to bring extra layer of bright, rich flavor.

Better Glazed Roast Chicken

Applying a glaze to a whole chicken can land you in a sweet mess. To resolve this sticky situation, we brought an outdoor method indoors.

⇒ BY DAVID PAZMIÑO ⇐

Roasting chicken on a beer can is the perfect way to achieve crisp skin and an even glaze all over.

Most glazed roast chicken recipes offer some variation on these instructions: Roast a chicken as you would normally, painting on a sweet glaze 15 to 30 minutes before the bird is done. It sounds simple, but following these recipes actually turns up a host of troubles, as the problems inherent in roasting chicken (dry breast meat, flabby skin, big deposits of fat under the skin) are compounded by the problems of a glaze (won't stick to the meat, burns in patches, introduces moisture to already flabby skin).

Yet I know that great glazed chicken is possible. Barbecued rotisserie chicken turns slowly as it cooks, making it a cinch to apply sauce to every nook and cranny while also ensuring even cooking. Likewise, Chinese chefs glaze whole ducks that roast while suspended from hooks, turning out perfectly lacquered, crisp-skinned birds. With these techniques as my inspiration, I set out to develop a method for evenly glazed roast chicken with crisp skin and moist, tender meat.

Chicken on a Rack

I chose a large roaster chicken (6 to 7 pounds), enough to feed four to six people, and started with an approach we developed for Crisp Roast Chicken (March/April 2008). I separated the skin from the meat and pricked holes in the fat deposits (to allow rendering fat to escape, resulting in crisper skin), then rubbed it with salt and baking soda (to dehydrate the skin and help it to crisp) and let the chicken rest. I then roasted the chicken breast-side down on a V-rack at 450 degrees for 30 minutes, flipped it over, and roasted it another 30 minutes. Then, with the chicken nearly done, I brushed it with a simple glaze of maple syrup, marmalade, vinegar, and Dijon mustard, and finished it with a blast of 500-degree heat.

While the meat was moist and evenly cooked, the glaze was disappointing. The top of the bird was a lacquered mahogany, while the bottom was merely golden brown—a good color for roast chicken, but not the deep, even tone I expected with a glaze. And although the precautions I'd taken helped the fat render from beneath the skin, 15 minutes of steaming under a moist glaze left the skin woefully soggy.

Chicken on a Can

With one side of the chicken facing down during the entire glazing process, I could never hope to glaze the whole bird evenly. Short of installing meat hooks or a rotisserie in my oven, what could I do? A vertical roaster, which cooks chicken standing up, was possible, but did I really want yet another gadget in the kitchen? (See "Vertical Roasters," page 9.) Then I remembered a simpler alternative, found right in my fridge: a beer can. We've had great success placing a beer can in the chicken cavity and standing it upright on the grill, which allows heat to circulate freely so that the bird cooks evenly from all sides. Why not bring this popular technique from the barbecue circuit into my oven?

I prepared the chicken and applied a rub as before. After allowing the chicken to rest for an hour, I grabbed a 16-ounce can of beer (the large bird didn't fit on anything smaller), took a few sips to prevent spills, and straddled the chicken on top. I then placed it in a roasting pan (the helper handles on the pan make it the best choice for transporting the bird), and slid it into the oven. The technique seemed like a winner—no awkward flipping, glazing every nook and cranny was easy, and fat dripped freely out of the bird. But cutting into the chicken revealed that the breast, now exposed to the high oven heat for the entire cooking time, was dry and tough. Scaling back the oven temperature to a gentler 325 degrees resolved this issue, but even without steaming under a glaze, the skin was far from crisp.

TECHNIQUE | PRIMING CHICKEN FOR CRISPER SKIN

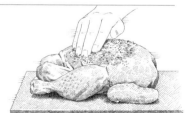

1. CUT CHANNELS in the skin along the chicken's back to create openings for fat to escape.

2. LOOSEN THE SKIN from the thighs and breast to allow rendering fat to trickle out.

3. POKE HOLES in the skin of the breast and thighs to create additional channels for fat and juices to escape.

4. APPLY A RUB of salt and baking powder; air-dry in the refrigerator before roasting for crisper skin.

1. Start in low oven.

2. Reduce glaze on stovetop.

3. Remove chicken, increase oven heat.

4. Return rested chicken to 500-degree oven.

5. Brush with glaze (twice).

A Glaze of Glory

To develop a crisp skin, the chicken needs to finish roasting at a very high heat (around 500 degrees) for about 30 minutes. But in the time it takes the oven to heat from 325 to 500 degrees, the delicate breast meat overcooks. With regular roast chicken, we've solved this problem by letting it rest at room temperature for about 20 minutes while the oven heats up for its final blast. Would that work with a vertically roasted chicken? Though the rested-before-blasted chicken came out much crisper than before and the breast meat was perfectly cooked, the glaze was still robbing my chicken of optimum skin quality.

This was the problem: Most recipes call for a watery glaze that slowly reduces and thickens as the bird cooks—a hindrance when you're trying to crisp the skin. What if I reduced the glaze on the stovetop before I applied it? That way, I could wait to brush on the glaze only at the very end, when it wouldn't ruin the texture of the skin. I made another glaze, this time thickening it with cornstarch. I reduced it to a syrupy consistency and applied it before the final 5 minutes of roasting. This chicken emerged from the oven with a burnished sheen of deep brown, and its rendered skin crackled as I cut into it, revealing moist, tender meat. For good measure, I brushed more glaze on the chicken and made extra to pass tableside. Now when I hanker for perfect glazed chicken, I'll forget about the rotisserie—all I need is a beer can to get the job done right.

GLAZED ROAST CHICKEN
SERVES 4 TO 6

If using table salt, reduce the amount to 2½ teaspoons. For best results, use a 16-ounce can of beer. A larger can will work, but avoid using a 12-ounce can, as it will not support the weight of the chicken. A vertical roaster can be used in place of the beer can, but we recommend only using a model that can be placed in a roasting pan. Taste your marmalade before using it; if it is overly sweet, reduce the amount of maple syrup in the glaze by 2 tablespoons. Trappist Seville Orange Marmalade is the test kitchen's preferred brand.

📹 **COOK'S VIDEOS** Original Test Kitchen Videos
www.cooksillustrated.com/apr09
HOW TO MAKE
• Glazed Roast Chicken

Chicken

- 1 whole chicken (6 to 7 pounds), giblets removed and discarded
- 5 teaspoons kosher salt (see note)
- 1 teaspoon baking powder
- 1 teaspoon ground black pepper
- 1 (16-ounce) can beer (see note)

Glaze

- 1 teaspoon cornstarch
- 1 tablespoon water
- ½ cup maple syrup
- ½ cup orange marmalade (see note)
- ¼ cup cider vinegar
- 2 tablespoons unsalted butter
- 2 tablespoons Dijon mustard
- 1 teaspoon ground black pepper

1. **FOR THE CHICKEN:** Place chicken breast-side down on work surface. Following illustrations on page 8, use tip of sharp knife to make 1-inch incisions below each thigh and breast along back of chicken (four incisions total). Using fingers or handle of wooden spoon, carefully separate skin from thighs and breast. Using metal skewer, poke 15 to 20 holes in fat deposits on top of breasts and thighs. Tuck wingtips underneath chicken.

2. Combine salt, baking powder, and pepper in small bowl. Pat chicken dry with paper towels and sprinkle evenly all over with salt mixture. Rub in mixture with hands, coating entire surface evenly. Set chicken, breast-side up, on rimmed baking sheet and refrigerate, uncovered, 30 to 60 minutes. Meanwhile, adjust oven rack to lowest position and heat oven to 325 degrees.

3. Open beer can and pour out (or drink) about half of liquid. Spray can lightly with nonstick cooking spray and place in middle of roasting pan. Slide chicken over can so drumsticks reach down to bottom of can, chicken stands upright, and breast is perpendicular to bottom of pan. Roast until skin starts to turn golden and instant-read thermometer inserted in thickest part of breast registers 140 degrees, 75 to 90 minutes. Carefully remove chicken and pan from oven and increase oven temperature to 500 degrees.

4. **FOR THE GLAZE:** While chicken cooks, stir cornstarch and water together in small bowl until no lumps remain; set aside. Bring remaining glaze ingredients to simmer in medium saucepan over

medium-high heat. Cook, stirring occasionally, until reduced to ¾ cup, 6 to 8 minutes. Slowly whisk cornstarch mixture into glaze. Return to simmer and cook 1 minute. Remove pan from heat.

5. When oven is heated to 500 degrees, place 1½ cups water in bottom of roasting pan and return to oven. Roast until entire chicken skin is browned and crisp and instant-read thermometer registers 160 degrees inserted in thickest part of breast and 175 degrees in thickest part of thigh, 24 to 30 minutes. Check chicken halfway through roasting; if top is becoming too dark, place 7-inch square piece of foil over neck and wingtips of chicken and continue to roast (if pan begins to smoke and sizzle, add additional ½ cup water to roasting pan).

6. Brush chicken with ¼ cup glaze and continue to roast until browned and sticky, about 5 minutes. (If glaze has become stiff, return to low heat to soften.) Carefully remove chicken from oven, transfer chicken, still on can, to carving board and brush with another ¼ cup glaze. Let rest 20 minutes.

7. While chicken rests, strain juices from pan through fine-mesh strainer into fat separator; allow liquid to settle 5 minutes. Whisk ½ cup juices into remaining ¼ cup glaze in saucepan and set over low heat. Using kitchen towel, carefully lift chicken off can and onto platter or cutting board. Carve chicken, adding any accumulated juices to sauce. Serve, passing sauce separately.

Rethinking Thick-Cut Pork Chops

Thick pork chops may boast a juicy interior or a nicely caramelized exterior—but rarely both. We wanted it all, in one recipe.

⇒ BY FRANCISCO J. ROBERT ⇐

Most recipes offer one of two scenarios for cooking thick, bone-in pork chops: searing them in a smoking skillet or roasting them in a blazing hot oven. Both methods are woefully outdated. Thanks to genetic manipulation, today's pork has about 30 percent less fat than it did just a few decades ago, and less fat means blander, drier meat. The exposure to high heat required to cook thick chops through—recipes call for up to 475 degrees—can help form a nice crust, but also turns already dry meat into pork jerky. Pork chop perfection, by contrast, means not only a rich, brown crust but also plump, juicy meat that's full of flavor down to the last gnaw of the bone.

Salt 'Em Up

You can generally find four different cuts of pork chops: sirloin, blade, center-cut, and rib loin. I immediately ruled out sirloin. These chops, cut from the hip end of the pig, are tough, dry, and bland. I also decided against blade chops (cut from near the shoulder), which contain a portion of the loin muscle and some shoulder muscle as well as a fair amount of connective tissue and fat. Although the fat promises a juicy, flavorful chop, the connective tissue requires a long, moist cooking method to become tender. After comparing center-cut chops (cut from the center of the loin) and rib loin chops (cut from the rib section), I decided on the latter, preferring their meaty texture and slightly higher fat content. I opted to leave the bone in, knowing that it acts as an insulator and helps the chops cook gently; fat in the nooks and crannies of a bone also helps to baste the meat as it cooks.

Many of the test kitchen's pork chop recipes call for brining—a soak in a saltwater solution before cooking. Brining tenderizes the meat and increases the muscle cells' capacity to hold water, yielding juicier chops. (While you can buy "enhanced" pork that's been injected with saltwater and sodium phosphate, we prefer the clean flavor of natural pork.) I went ahead and brined a couple of bone-in, 1½-inch-thick chops for an hour. Knowing that an oven- or stovetop-only technique wouldn't work, I tried an approach popular in restaurant kitchens: starting the chops in a skillet and then finishing them in a hot

These chops are cooked in the oven—and then on the stovetop.

oven. As I expected, the meat was pleasingly juicy. But there wasn't much browning, and many tasters complained that these chops lacked the roasted quality that gives meat deep flavor. I suspected that the moisture in the brine had hindered browning.

What if I skipped the liquid part of the brine and simply salted the chops? Although salt initially draws moisture out of protein, the reverse happens soon afterward, as salt and juices flow back in. I got out a box of kosher salt, sprinkled the chops (about ½ teaspoon per side), and let them sit for 45 minutes. (Any less and the salt would not have enough time to penetrate the meat.) After 45 minutes, I seared the chops and finished them in a 475-degree oven. These chops were wonderfully juicy—the salt had done its job—but they were also on the tough side, and the crust was still meager.

Flip-Flopping Tradition

For my next test, I seared the chops and then transferred them to a much cooler oven (a mere 275 degrees) to finish cooking. Forty minutes later, the chops were cooked through and notably more tender than chops cooked in a hot oven. Evidently, I was on to something. Our science editor explained

that enzymes called cathepsins break down proteins such as collagen, helping to tenderize meat, but these enzymes are only active at temperatures below 122 degrees. If I wanted optimally tender chops, it would be in my interest to keep the pork at a low temperature for as long as possible.

Boldly, I decided to turn my method upside down: I would begin by cooking the salted chops in a gentle 275-degree oven until their internal temperature reached 120 degrees, and then sear them in a smoking pan, until they reached an ideal serving temperature of 145 to 150 degrees. How did my topsy-turvy technique pan out, so to speak? Like a charm. The chops were supremely tender and beautifully caramelized, simply because I had kept them below 122 degrees for about 20 minutes longer than the conventional 475-degree method could do. The advantages of this were twofold: First, the meat cooked slowly, allowing ample time for the enzymes to do their work; second, the gentle roasting dried the exterior of the meat, creating a thin, arid layer. When the chop was seared, this layer turned into a gratifyingly crisp crust. (As a bonus, if you can't find anything other than enhanced pork, the method will help to ensure that this salt water–injected meat also dries out in the oven before searing and can actually brown in the pan.)

While the chops rested, I created a quick white wine pan sauce. As an alternative, I also developed a Thai-inspired sauce made with coconut milk, ginger, cilantro, and lime. As I cut into the perfectly cooked meat, I knew it was time to say so long to tradition.

TECHNIQUE

AVOIDING BUCKLED CHOPS

Meat often comes covered in a thin membrane called silver skin. This membrane contracts faster than the rest of the meat, causing buckling and leading to unevenly cooked chops. Cutting slits in the silver skin prevents the problem.

Cut slits about 2 inches apart into the fat and underlying silver skin, opposite the bone of the chop.

PAN-SEARED THICK-CUT PORK CHOPS
SERVES 4

Buy chops of similar thickness so that they cook at the same rate. If using table salt, sprinkle each chop with ½ teaspoon salt. We prefer the flavor of natural chops over that of enhanced chops (which have been injected with a salt solution and sodium phosphate to increase moistness and flavor), but if processed pork is all you can find, skip the salting step below. Serve the chops with one of our sauces or with applesauce.

- 4   bone-in rib loin pork chops, 1½ inches thick (about 12 ounces each) (see note)
     Kosher salt and ground black pepper (see note)
- 1–2   tablespoons vegetable oil
- 1   recipe sauce (recipes follow)

1. Adjust oven rack to middle position and heat oven to 275 degrees. Pat chops dry with paper towels. Using sharp knife, cut 2 slits, about 2 inches apart, through outer layer of fat and silver skin (see "Avoiding Buckled Chops," page 10). Sprinkle entire surface of each chop with 1 teaspoon salt. Place chops on wire rack set in rimmed baking sheet and let stand at room temperature 45 minutes.

2. Season chops liberally with pepper; transfer baking sheet to oven. Cook until instant-read thermometer inserted into centers of chops and away from bones registers 120 to 125 degrees, 30 to 45 minutes.

3. Heat 1 tablespoon oil in 12-inch heavy-bottomed skillet over high heat until smoking. Place 2 chops in skillet and sear until well browned and crusty, 1½ to 3 minutes, lifting once halfway through to redistribute fat underneath each chop. (Reduce heat if browned bits in pan bottom start to burn.) Using tongs, turn chops and cook until well browned on second side, 2 to 3 minutes. Transfer chops to plate and repeat with remaining 2 chops, adding extra tablespoon oil if pan is dry.

4. Reduce heat to medium. Use tongs to stand 2 pork chops on their sides. Holding chops together with tongs, return to skillet and sear sides of chops (with exception of bone side) until browned and instant-read thermometer inserted into center of chop and away from bone registers 140 to 145 degrees, about 1½ minutes. Repeat with remaining 2 chops. Let chops rest, loosely tented with foil, for 10 minutes while preparing sauce.

GARLIC AND THYME PAN SAUCE
MAKES ½ CUP

- 1   large shallot, minced (about ¼ cup)
- 2   medium garlic cloves, minced or pressed through garlic press (about 2 teaspoons)
- ½   cup dry white wine
- ¾   cup low-sodium chicken broth
- 1   teaspoon minced fresh thyme leaves
- ¼   teaspoon white wine vinegar

STEP-BY-STEP | JUICY, CRISP-CRUSTED THICK-CUT PORK CHOPS

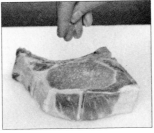

1. SALTING pork chops draws out moisture that, 45 minutes later, is pulled back in, producing juicy, well-seasoned meat.

2. SLOW-ROASTING increases enzymatic activity that breaks down connective tissue, leading to more tender chops.

3. SEARING the chops after roasting them at a low temperature ensures a crisp crust, as the meat now has a drier surface.

- 3   tablespoons cold unsalted butter, cut into 3 pieces
     Table salt and ground black pepper

Pour off all but 1 teaspoon oil from pan used to cook chops and return pan to medium heat. Add shallot and garlic and cook, stirring constantly, until softened, about 1 minute. Add wine and broth, scraping pan bottom to loosen browned bits. Simmer until reduced to ½ cup, 6 to 7 minutes. Off heat, stir in thyme and vinegar, then whisk in butter, 1 tablespoon at a time. Season with salt and pepper and serve with chops.

CILANTRO AND COCONUT PAN SAUCE
MAKES ½ CUP

- 1   large shallot, minced (about ¼ cup)
- 2   medium garlic cloves, minced or pressed through garlic press (about 2 teaspoons)
- 1   tablespoon grated fresh ginger
- ¼   cup low-sodium chicken broth
- ¾   cup coconut milk
- 1   teaspoon sugar
- ¼   cup chopped fresh cilantro leaves
- 2   teaspoons juice from 1 lime
- 1   tablespoon unsalted butter
     Table salt and ground black pepper

Pour off all but 1 teaspoon oil from pan used to cook chops and return pan to medium heat. Add shallot, garlic, and ginger and cook, stirring constantly, until softened, about 1 minute. Add broth, coconut milk, and sugar, scraping pan bottom to loosen browned bits. Simmer until reduced to ½ cup, 6 to 7 minutes. Off heat, stir in cilantro and lime juice, then whisk in butter. Season with salt and pepper and serve with chops.

📹 **COOK'S VIDEOS** Original Test Kitchen Videos
www.cooksillustrated.com/apr09
HOW TO MAKE
• Pan-Seared Thick-Cut Pork Chops
VIDEO TIPS
• How do I check the temperature of a bone-in chop?
• Why do I score the fat?

TASTING: **Applesauce**

Few things seem more wholesome than applesauce. So imagine our surprise when we tasted seven brands—and found that our runaway favorite contains sucralose, the very same artificial sweetener found in Splenda. A minute amount was enough to boost the applesauce's sweetness without overpowering its fresh, bright apple flavor. An artificial sweetener with 600 times the potency of sugar, sucralose turned out to have another benefit: It doesn't contribute to the slimy consistency our tasters noticed in applesauce sweetened with corn syrup (the preferred sweetener in applesauce). According to an expert in applesauce processing at Cornell University, a thick but somewhat mucilaginous texture can be created when the sugars in corn syrup bond with the pectin and fructose in apples. Still, the absence of added sugars was not a good thing: With one exception, these unsweetened renditions tasted bland and washed-up with a watery consistency. The other key ingredient in our top applesauce? A pinch of flavor-boosting salt. For complete tasting results, go to www.cooksillustrated.com/apr09.

–Meredith Butcher

FRESH 'N' LITE
MUSSELMAN'S Lite Apple Sauce
Price: $2.35 for 23 ounces
Comments: Much to our surprise, tasters raved about the "fresh," "bright," even "excellent" apple flavor of this sucralose-sweetened applesauce, preferring it by a wide margin to all the other brands.

SUGAR BOOST
MUSSELMAN'S Apple Sauce, Home Style
Price: $2.35 for 24 ounces
Comments: Though it is one of the better options out there, this corn syrup–sweetened applesauce came in a distant second.

Fish en Papillote?

Unless you're a whiz at origami, parchment-baked fish can be long on labor and short on flavor. Here's how we foiled these problems.

⇒ BY KEITH DRESSER ⇐

Cooking *en papillote*—where the food is baked in a tightly sealed, artfully folded parchment package to essentially steam in its own juices—may seem as outdated as Beef Wellington and Pheasant under Glass. But there's a reason the technique has held its own through countless culinary fads and fashions. It's an easy, mess-free way to enhance delicate flavor, particularly that of fish, leaving no odors to linger in the kitchen. The fish cooks quickly in such a moist environment, and because there's no water added to dilute flavors, it's a more flavorful method than ordinary poaching. It requires little additional fat and, if you throw in vegetables, adds up to a light but satisfying "one-pouch" meal.

When done correctly, that is. Without the right blend of flavorings, the fish can taste so lean and bland, you might as well be dining on diet food. Not all vegetables pair well with fish, and careful consideration must be given to their size and whether precooking is necessary, or you can wind up with overcooked fish surrounded by undercooked vegetables. I wanted to create an approach worthy of this technique's haute roots, with moist, flaky fish and tender-firm vegetables flavored by the rich, aromatic goodness of their mingled juices.

Foiled Again

All the classic recipes call for cutting parchment paper into attractive shapes such as teardrops, hearts, and butterflies, then creasing the seams into painstakingly precise little folds. But just looking at the illustrations made my thumbs throb. I wanted to get dinner on the table as quickly as possible—not create origami. I went directly to aluminum foil, sandwiching the fish between two 12-inch squares, then crimping the edges to create an airtight seal that would lock in steam. This was admittedly not as glamorous as an intricately folded parchment packet, but definitely serviceable.

My next step was to figure out what type of fish worked best in this dish and how long it would take to cook. After trying a variety of fish fillets, I quickly determined that tasters favored flaky, mild fish like haddock and cod over more assertively flavored fish like salmon or tuna. In the moist atmosphere of the

We use foil, not parchment paper, and the right blend of flavorings to create a satisfying one-pouch meal.

foil pouch, these oilier fish had a tendency to overpower the flavors of the vegetables (for the moment I was simply placing the fish on a bed of sliced zucchini); better to save them for sautéing or searing.

Since the goal of cooking en papillote is to create enough steam from the food's own juices, most recipes recommended cranking the heat way up, even as high as 500 degrees. Though a wet method like this one is more forgiving than a dry approach like roasting, 500 degrees seemed excessive. And it was. When I opened the foil after just 15 minutes for a "nick and peek," my 1-inch fillets were chalky white and well-done (and the zucchini was slightly underdone). Cooking at this temperature for less time didn't work either—the food was barely in the oven long enough for steam to form, leaving both fish and vegetable undercooked. After more experimentation, I arrived at 450 degrees for 15 minutes as the ideal temperature and cooking time—hot enough to produce steam relatively quickly but not so hot that the food overcooked. Placing the packets on the lower-middle rack of the oven, close

to the heat source, helped concentrate the exuded liquid and deepen its flavor.

Veggin' Out

With the cooking time and temperature nailed down, I could now turn my attention to selecting the vegetables. I quickly winnowed my options. Dense vegetables like potatoes, even when parcooked, failed to cook evenly in the foil packets. Vegetables with an absorbent structure, like eggplant, simply cooked into mush in all the moisture. Others, such as broccoli, overpowered the delicate fish flavor. Beyond these considerations, the most important aspect was how the vegetables were prepared before they went into the packets. I found that carrots and leeks could be added to the packets raw, provided they were cut into matchsticks. Fennel was another vegetable that paired well with fish, but it needed to be wilted slightly in the microwave to become tender within the brief cooking time. The zucchini was much improved—and the juices in the packet less diluted—if I salted it first to get rid of excess moisture.

While tasters liked these fish and vegetable pairings, many felt that the components lacked harmony and overall the dish tasted a little too lean. A dash of vermouth, which was absorbed by the fish and vegetables, boosted flavor

TECHNIQUE | EVENLY COOKING UNEVEN FILLETS

If your fish has a thin tailpiece, tuck it under so it cooks at the same rate as the rest of the fillet: Cut halfway through the flesh crosswise, 2 to 3 inches from the tail end, then fold the tail end under the cut seam to create a fillet of even thickness.

STEP-BY-STEP | ASSEMBLING FOIL PACKETS

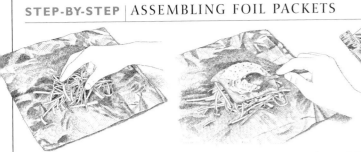

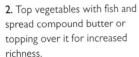

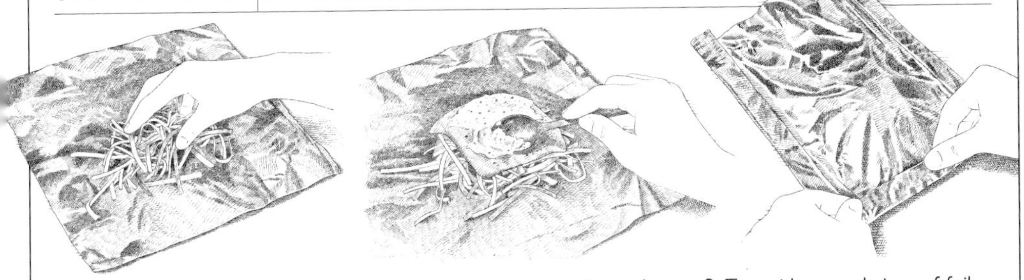

1. Arrange vegetables on foil first so they will be closest to heat source; drizzle with vermouth to deepen flavor.

2. Top vegetables with fish and spread compound butter or topping over it for increased richness.

3. Top with second piece of foil and crimp edges together in ½-inch fold, then fold over three more times to create airtight packet.

but not quite enough. What if I created a topping to flavor the fish as it cooked? A tomato, garlic, and olive oil "salsa" added kick to my zucchini variation, while compound butters flavored with garlic, herbs, and zest enlivened the others. These toppings basted the fish as it cooked and mingled with the wine and juices given off by the vegetables, leaving behind an aromatic, full-flavored sauce that perfectly complemented the fish. Each recipe was so light, fresh, and easy to prepare, it couldn't be more contemporary.

COD BAKED IN FOIL WITH LEEKS AND CARROTS

SERVES 4

Haddock, red snapper, halibut, and sea bass also work well in this recipe and those that follow as long as the fillets are 1 to 1¼ inches thick. The packets may be assembled several hours ahead of time and refrigerated until ready to cook. If the packets have been refrigerated for more than 30 minutes, increase the cooking time by 2 minutes. Open each packet promptly after baking to prevent overcooking. Zest the lemon before cutting it into wedges. See page 31 for tips on cutting the carrots and leeks.

- 4 tablespoons unsalted butter, softened
- 1¼ teaspoons finely grated zest from 1 lemon; lemon cut into wedges (see note)
- 2 medium garlic cloves, minced or pressed through garlic press (about 2 teaspoons)
- 1 teaspoon minced fresh thyme leaves
- Table salt and ground black pepper
- 2 tablespoons minced fresh parsley leaves
- 2 medium carrots, peeled and cut into matchsticks (about 1½ cups) (see note)
- 2 medium leeks, white and light green parts halved lengthwise, washed, and cut into matchsticks (about 2 cups) (see note)
- 4 tablespoons vermouth or dry white wine
- 4 skinless cod fillets, 1 to 1¼ inches thick (about 6 ounces each) (see note and illustration on page 12)

1. Combine butter, ¼ teaspoon zest, 1 teaspoon garlic, thyme, ¼ teaspoon salt, and ⅛ teaspoon pepper in small bowl. Combine parsley, remaining teaspoon zest, and remaining teaspoon garlic in another small bowl; set aside. Place carrots and leeks in medium bowl, season with salt and pepper, and toss together.

2. Adjust oven rack to lower-middle position and heat oven to 450 degrees. Cut eight 12-inch sheets of foil; arrange four flat on counter. Divide carrot and leek mixture among foil sheets, mounding in center of each. Pour 1 tablespoon vermouth over each mound of vegetables. Pat fish dry with paper towels; season with salt and pepper and place one fillet on top of each vegetable mound. Spread quarter of butter mixture on top of each fillet. Place second square of foil on top of fish; crimp edges together in ½-inch fold, then fold over three more times to create a packet about 7 inches square (see illustrations, above). Place packets on rimmed baking sheet (overlapping slightly if necessary).

3. Bake packets 15 minutes. Carefully open foil, allowing steam to escape away from you. Using thin metal spatula, gently slide fish and vegetables onto plate with any accumulated juices; sprinkle with parsley mixture. Serve immediately, passing lemon wedges separately.

COD BAKED IN FOIL WITH ZUCCHINI AND TOMATOES

SERVES 4

- 1 pound zucchini (2 medium), ends trimmed and sliced crosswise into ¼-inch-thick rounds
- Table salt
- ½ pound plum tomatoes (2 medium), cored, seeded, and chopped into ½-inch pieces (about 1 cup)
- 2 tablespoons extra-virgin olive oil
- 2 medium garlic cloves, minced or pressed through garlic press (about 2 teaspoons)
- 1 teaspoon minced fresh oregano leaves
- ⅛ teaspoon red pepper flakes
- Ground black pepper
- 4 tablespoons vermouth or dry white wine
- 4 skinless cod fillets, 1 to 1¼ inches thick (about 6 ounces each)
- ¼ cup minced fresh basil leaves
- 1 lemon, cut into wedges

1. Toss zucchini with ½ teaspoon salt in large bowl; transfer to colander set over bowl. Let stand until zucchini releases 1 to 2 tablespoons liquid, about 30 minutes. Arrange zucchini on triple layer paper towels; cover with another triple layer paper towels. Firmly press each slice to remove as much liquid as possible. Meanwhile, combine tomatoes, oil, garlic, oregano, red pepper flakes, ¼ teaspoon salt, and ⅛ teaspoon pepper in medium bowl.

2. Follow recipe for Cod Baked in Foil with Leeks and Carrots from step 2, mounding salted zucchini in center of foil, drizzling with vermouth, placing fish on top, then spooning quarter of tomato mixture over each fillet. Bake and arrange on plates as directed in step 3, sprinkling basil over fish and passing lemon wedges separately.

COD BAKED IN FOIL WITH FENNEL AND SHALLOTS

SERVES 4

Zest the orange before it is peeled and quartered.

- 1 large fennel bulb (about 1 pound), trimmed, halved, cored, and sliced into ¼-inch strips (about 4 cups)
- 2 medium shallots, sliced thin (about ½ cup)
- 4 tablespoons unsalted butter, softened
- 2 medium oranges, ¼ teaspoon finely grated zest removed from one; both peeled, quartered, and cut crosswise into ¼-inch-thick pieces (see note)
- 1 medium garlic clove, minced or pressed through garlic press (about 1 teaspoon)
- 2 teaspoons minced fresh tarragon leaves
- Table salt and ground black pepper
- 4 tablespoons vermouth or dry white wine
- 4 skinless cod fillets, 1 to 1¼ inches thick (about 6 ounces each)

1. Combine fennel and shallots in large microwave-safe bowl; cover tightly with plastic wrap. Microwave on high power until fennel has started to wilt, 3 to 4 minutes, stirring once halfway through cooking. Combine butter, zest, garlic, 1 teaspoon tarragon, ¼ teaspoon salt, and ⅛ teaspoon pepper in small bowl. Combine orange pieces and remaining teaspoon tarragon in another small bowl; set aside.

2. Follow recipe for Cod Baked in Foil with Leeks and Carrots from step 2, mounding fennel mixture in center of foil, drizzling with vermouth, placing fish on top, then spreading quarter of butter mixture over each fillet. Bake and arrange on plates as directed in step 3, spooning orange and tarragon mixture over fish before serving.

COOK'S VIDEOS Original Test Kitchen Videos
www.cooksillustrated.com/apr09

HOW TO MAKE
- Cod Baked in Foil with Leeks and Carrots

VIDEO TIP
- How do I make a parchment pouch?

Rescuing Baked Ziti

Transforming this tired Italian-American classic into a dish worth making took more than swapping out the ricotta.

⇛ BY DAVID PAZMIÑO ⇚

Many cooks, myself included, don't mind lavishing time and tender loving care on lasagna or stuffed manicotti—the outcome speaks for itself. Baked ziti, however, is another matter. It's supposed to be simple: just pasta and a robust tomato sauce baked under a cover of bubbling, gooey cheese. But over time the dish has devolved from simple to merely lazy. Most versions seem like they went directly from the pantry into the oven, calling for little more than cooked pasta, jarred tomato sauce, a container of ricotta, and some preshredded cheese. The results—overcooked ziti in a dull, grainy sauce topped with a rubbery mass of mozzarella—more than earn the dish its reputation as mediocre church-supper fare.

Without turning baked ziti into a weekend project, I wanted to get the same rewarding outcome from ziti that I've come to expect from any other baked pasta.

The Special Sauce

The first problem to tackle was the sauce. I didn't want to spend all day hovering over a pot of stewing tomatoes, so I needed a sauce that was big on flavor and light on prep. Most "quick" tomato sauces call for sweating garlic in olive oil before adding some type of tomato product. (I'd deal with the dairy question later; for now, I'd finish my sauce by mixing in ricotta cheese.) Whole canned tomatoes and crushed tomatoes both had good flavor but took a long time to cook down. To speed things up, what

Our baked ziti boasts flavorful sauce and cheese in every bite.

if I used a tomato product that was already concentrated? Canned sauce provided the viscous texture I wanted but lacked bright tomato flavor. Doctoring the sauce with a little tomato paste wasn't the answer; it merely reinforced the cooked flavor of the sauce. Ultimately, I struck an ideal balance by adding a can of diced tomatoes.

Now it was time to layer flavors. Fresh basil added rich, aromatic savor, but more herbs were essential. In the test kitchen, we usually opt for fresh herbs, but after simmering my sauce with both fresh and dried oregano, tasters were divided. This is not as odd as it might sound. Some herbs that grow in hot, arid environments, including oregano, bay leaves, and rosemary, contain exceptionally stable flavor compounds that survive drying quite well—leaving plenty of flavor to release when simmered. For convenience, I chose dried oregano.

Introducing Secret Weapons

Just when my tomato sauce seemed perfect, I added the ricotta, and a familiar problem reared its head: Rather than baking up creamy and rich, the ricotta was grainy and dulled the sauce. Maybe a different dairy product was in order? Straight-up heavy cream added lushness but dulled the flavor just as much as ricotta. I needed something creamy yet bright.

A colleague suggested I try her mother's baked ziti recipe, which called for two unorthodox ingredients: cottage cheese and jarred Alfredo sauce. I was skeptical, but I tried the cottage cheese. To my surprise, it was a smashing success. Its pillowy curds have a texture similar to ricotta, but it possesses a much creamier consistency and a more distinct, tangy flavor. And since cottage curds are bigger, it bakes up with none of ricotta's graininess.

Alfredo sauce sounded intriguing—what could be wrong with taking a rich sauce made of reduced cream and Parmesan cheese and pouring it over ziti, even if it was meant for fettuccine? But why go with jarred? A quick scan of the jar's label revealed that commercial Alfredo sauce also contains eggs and thickener. Plain heavy cream didn't work in my previous tests, but maybe thickening it and enriching it with eggs would help. For my next batch, I combined cottage cheese with eggs, Parmesan, and heavy cream thickened with a bit of cornstarch. Combining this milky, tangy mixture with the bright tomato sauce won instant converts. I now had a sauce that was bright, rich, and creamy—all at the same time.

Diced for Success

The pasta presented its own challenges. Most recipes cook the ziti in boiling water until al dente before tossing it with the sauce and baking. But pasta continues to absorb sauce as it bakes, with two unfortunate consequences: overcooked pasta and sauce that has been robbed of moisture. Covering

---

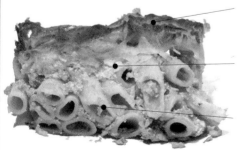

RECIPE DIAGNOSIS: Baked Ziti Gone Bad

RUBBERY CHEESE
Preshredded mozzarella melts into an unappetizing rubbery crust.

DRY, GRAINY SAUCE
Ziti absorbs liquid as it cooks, leaving the sauce dry and the ricotta grainy and broken.

MUSHY PASTA
Starting the casserole with al dente pasta leads to overcooked, mushy ziti by the time it emerges from the oven.

Keys to Better Flavor and Texture

NOT RICOTTA
Our recipe swaps ricotta for cottage cheese, which maintains its creamy texture even when hot.

TWO SAUCES
We combine traditional tomato sauce with nontraditional Alfredo sauce to achieve a perfect balance of brightness and richness.

DICEY SOLUTION
Diced mozzarella, stirred into the sauce and sprinkled on top of the dish, leads to melted cheese in every bite.

the casserole with aluminum foil as it baked helped to retain moisture and keep the top from drying out, but I needed more drastic measures. I ran a series of tests, finding that cooking the pasta for roughly five minutes and using more than 8 cups of sauce—about half the cooking time that most recipes call for and nearly twice the amount of sauce—yielded perfectly al dente pasta in the baked dish with plenty of sauce left to keep the whole thing moist.

The only remaining question was how to deal with the cheese. Grated cheese congeals into a mass that makes the dish not only unappetizing but difficult to portion, as some pieces get more than their share of cheese while others get none. Instead of shredding the mozzarella, I tried cutting it into small cubes—reasoning that they would melt into distinct but delectable little pockets of cheese—but they ended up flowing into each other and, like the shredded cheese, forming a heavy crust on top. Using only half of the cheese worked—sort of; the cubes stayed separate from each other, but now the dish lacked richness. What if I mixed half of the cheese with the sauce just before adding it to the pasta, and then sprinkled the rest over the top? This strategy yielded a hot, bubbly success. The cubes on top remained perfectly distributed, and the casserole below was dotted with gooey bits of cheese.

TECHNIQUE | THE RIGHT
DEGREE OF AL DENTE

To ensure perfectly al dente pasta in the finished dish, we boil ziti just until it begins to soften but is not yet cooked through, 5 to 7 minutes—half the time most recipes call for. The pasta continues to cook in the oven, where it absorbs the flavorful sauce. To compensate, we add nearly twice the amount of sauce as in most recipes.

While second-rate red-sauce restaurants continue to make "lazy-man's" baked ziti, my family will have this dish the way it's meant to be—with perfectly al dente pasta, a rich and flavorful sauce, and melted cheese in every bite.

BAKED ZITI
SERVES 8 TO 10

The test kitchen prefers baked ziti made with heavy cream, but whole milk can be substituted by increasing the amount of cornstarch to 2 teaspoons and increasing the cooking time in step 3 by 1 to 2 minutes. Our preferred brand of mozzarella is Dragone Whole Milk Mozzarella. Part-skim mozzarella can also be used, but avoid preshredded cheese, as it does not melt well. For tips on cooking with cottage cheese, see page 31.

- 1 pound whole milk or 1 percent cottage cheese (see note)
- 2 large eggs, lightly beaten
- 3 ounces grated Parmesan (about 1½ cups)
  Table salt
- 1 pound ziti or other short, tubular pasta
- 2 tablespoons extra-virgin olive oil
- 5 medium garlic cloves, minced or pressed through garlic press (about 5 teaspoons)
- 1 (28-ounce) can tomato sauce
- 1 (14.5-ounce) can diced tomatoes
- 1 teaspoon dried oregano
- ½ cup plus 2 tablespoons chopped fresh basil leaves
- 1 teaspoon sugar
  Ground black pepper
- ¾ teaspoon cornstarch
- 1 cup heavy cream (see note)
- 8 ounces low-moisture mozzarella cheese, cut into ¼-inch pieces (about 1½ cups) (see note)

1. Adjust oven rack to middle position and heat oven to 350 degrees. Whisk cottage cheese, eggs, and 1 cup Parmesan together in medium bowl; set aside. Bring 4 quarts of water to boil in large Dutch oven over high heat. Stir in 1 tablespoon salt and pasta; cook, stirring occasionally, until pasta begins to soften but is not yet cooked through, 5 to 7 minutes. Drain pasta and leave in colander (do not wash Dutch oven).

2. Meanwhile, heat oil and garlic in 12-inch skillet over medium heat until garlic is fragrant but not brown, about 2 minutes. Stir in tomato sauce, diced tomatoes, and oregano; simmer until thickened, about 10 minutes. Off heat, stir in ½ cup basil and sugar, then season with salt and pepper.

3. Stir cornstarch into heavy cream in small bowl; transfer mixture to now-empty Dutch oven set over medium heat. Bring to simmer and cook until thickened, 3 to 4 minutes. Remove pot from heat and add cottage cheese mixture, 1 cup tomato sauce, and ¾ cup mozzarella, then stir to combine. Add pasta and stir to coat thoroughly with sauce.

4. Transfer pasta mixture to 13- by 9-inch baking dish and spread remaining tomato sauce evenly over pasta. Sprinkle remaining ¾ cup mozzarella and remaining ½ cup Parmesan over top. Cover baking dish tightly with foil and bake for 30 minutes.

5. Remove foil and continue to cook until cheese is bubbling and beginning to brown, about 30 minutes longer. Cool for 20 minutes. Sprinkle with remaining 2 tablespoons basil and serve.

COOK'S VIDEOS Original Test Kitchen Videos
www.cooksillustrated.com/apr09
HOW TO MAKE
• Baked Ziti

Keeping Kitchen Staples Fresher Longer

Moving your olive oil, vinegar, and spices off the kitchen counter is only the first step. Here's how to prolong the life of essential kitchen ingredients. BY CHARLES KELSEY

Few things last forever—including some of the pantry staples you might think are fine to squirrel away for years. And even if you do observe expiration and sell-by dates, we've found they can't always be trusted. Here's how to preserve the freshness of pantry items—and how to know when it's time to restock.

SPICES & DRIED HERBS

➤ SHELF LIFE:
Whole Spices: 2 years
Ground Spices and Dried Herbs: 1 year

➤ DO buy spices whole, versus ground, whenever possible and grind them just before using. Grinding releases the volatile compounds that give a spice its flavor and aroma. The longer the spice sits around (or is stored), the more compounds disappear.

➤ DON'T store spices and herbs on the counter close to the stove. Heat, light, and moisture shorten their shelf life.

CHECKING FOR FRESHNESS

Crumble a small amount of the dried herb between your fingers and take a whiff. If it releases a lively aroma, it's still good to go. If the aroma and color of a spice have faded, it's time to restock.

Other Oils

Here's a quick guide to storing open bottles of oil in your kitchen. For optimal flavor, replace these oils 6 months after opening.

STORE IN PANTRY	STORE IN FRIDGE
Canola	Sesame
Corn	Walnut
Peanut	
Vegetable	

VINEGARS

➤ SHELF LIFE: Long-lasting

➤ DON'T toss old vinegar. Most vinegars contain about 5 percent acetic acid, which (along with pasteurization) prevents the growth of harmful bacteria, and will last indefinitely.

➤ DO ignore any sediment in your vinegar. The sediment is a harmless cellulose that our testing has shown doesn't affect taste; it can be easily strained out (see "Vinegar Sediment," page 2).

OLIVE OIL

➤ SHELF LIFE:
Unopened: 1 year
Open: 3 months

➤ DO check the harvest date printed on the label of high-end oils to ensure the freshest bottle possible. (Some labels cite an expiration date, which producers typically calculate as 18 months from harvesting. We think unopened olive oil can go rancid 1 year after the harvest date.)

➤ DO move olive oil from the countertop or windowsill to a dark pantry or cupboard. Strong sunlight will oxidize the chlorophyll in the oil, producing stale, harsh flavors.

➤ DON'T buy olive oil in bulk. Once opened, it has a very short shelf life.

CHECKING FOR FRESHNESS

Heat a little olive oil in a skillet. If it smells rancid, throw out the bottle. (This test works for all vegetable oils.)

Beyond the Pantry

While not pantry staples per se, eggs and butter are essential to everyday cooking.

BUTTER

➤ Butter can pick up off-flavors and turn rancid if kept in the refrigerator for longer than a month. If you don't use a lot, store butter in the freezer for up to 4 months in a zipper-lock bag and thaw sticks as needed.

EGGS

➤ NEVER put eggs in the egg tray on the refrigerator door, which is too warm. Keep them in the carton, which holds in moisture and protects against odor absorption.

CHECKING FOR FRESHNESS

Legally, eggs may already be up to two months old by the end of the "sell by" date, so it's best to check for freshness yourself. If an egg has an unpleasant odor, discard it. Store eggs in the refrigerator for 3 to 5 weeks.

SOY SAUCE

➤ SHELF LIFE: 1 year

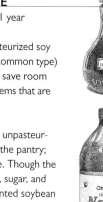

➤ DO store pasteurized soy sauce (the most common type) in the pantry and save room in the fridge for items that are more perishable.

➤ DON'T store unpasteurized soy sauce in the pantry; put it in the fridge. Though the high levels of salt, sugar, and acid in this fermented soybean liquid protect against rapid spoilage, in tests we found it took on a fishy flavor after a few months in the cupboard.

SWEETENERS

➤ **SHELF LIFE:**
Granulated Sugar, Honey, and Molasses: Long-lasting
Maple Syrup: 2 years unopened, 1 year open

➤ **DO** store granulated sugar in an airtight container to protect it from heat, moisture, and critters.

➤ **DO** keep molasses and honey in the pantry (in the fridge, molasses temporarily turns into a thick, unpourable sludge, and honey crystallizes).

➤ **DO** store unopened maple syrup in the pantry, but move the opened syrup to the refrigerator. Because of its high moisture level and lack of preservatives, maple syrup is susceptible to the growth of yeast, mold, and bacteria.

REVIVING CRYSTALLIZED HONEY

To remove the crystals, open a glass honey jar, put it in a saucepan filled with 1 inch of water, and heat until it reaches 160 degrees.

SOFTENING BROWN SUGAR

When brown sugar comes into contact with air, the moisture in the sugar evaporates, and the sugar turns rock-hard. Here are two easy methods to soften it.

Quick Fix: Place the hardened brown sugar in a bowl with a slice of sandwich bread. Cover with plastic wrap and microwave for 10 to 20 seconds.

Ongoing Remedy: Store brown sugar in a sealed container with a terra cotta Brown Sugar Bear ($3.25), which gets a brief soak in water before being added to the sugar.

Chill Out

These items stay fresher in the freezer:

➤ **Bay leaves**
➤ **Flours with heavy germ content** (such as whole wheat) **and cornmeal**
➤ **Nuts and seeds**
➤ **Yeast**

LEAVENERS

➤ **SHELF LIFE:**
Baking Powder and Baking Soda: 6 months
Instant or Active Dry Yeast: 4 months (in freezer)

➤ **DO** replace baking powder and soda regularly. Despite most manufacturer claims of a shelf life of 1 year, our tests have proven they lose potency far sooner (see below).

➤ **DON'T** keep yeast in the pantry—put it in the freezer to slow deterioration. And because yeast is a living organism, the expiration date on the package should be observed.

WHEN BAKING POWDER LOSES PUNCH

Over time, baking powder (comprised of baking soda, acid salt, and cornstarch) loses its ability to produce carbon dioxide and give baked goods their lift—sooner than many producers claim. We compared biscuits made with a newly opened can of baking powder to biscuits made with cans opened and stored for 1 month all the way up to a year. The rise of the biscuits began to decrease with the 6-month-old powder and continued to decline to half the height of fresh at the 10-month-old mark. For best results, replace your baking powder (and soda) every 6 months.

FLOUR

➤ **SHELF LIFE:**
All-Purpose Flour: 1 year
Whole Wheat Flour and Cornmeal: 1 year (in freezer)

➤ **DO** transfer all-purpose flour out of its paper bag and into an airtight container to protect it from humidity.

➤ **DON'T** leave whole wheat flour or cornmeal in the pantry; they contain natural oils that will go rancid in as little as 3 months.

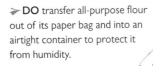

➤ **DO** enclose whole wheat flour and cornmeal in zipper-lock bags and store them in the freezer.

Dry Storage Containers

Airtight containers keep moisture at bay and make scooping and measuring easier. Our preferred storage choice for flour and sugar is a container that easily accommodates an entire 5-pound bag, with an opening wide enough to dip in a measuring cup and level off the excess right back into the container. Our favorite, the Rubbermaid 4-Quart Carb-X Commercial Food Storage container ($5.78), stands out because of the measurement marks along the sides, its sturdy handles, and its clear plastic for visibility.

OUR WINNING CONTAINER

CHOCOLATE

➤ **SHELF LIFE:**
Unsweetened and Dark Chocolate: 2 years
Milk and White Chocolate: 6 months

➤ **DO** wrap open bars of chocolate tightly in plastic and store in a cool pantry to ensure optimum freshness. If chocolate is exposed to rapid changes in humidity or temperature, sugar or fat may soften and migrate, discoloring the surface. This cosmetic condition, called bloom, doesn't affect the flavor of the chocolate.

➤ **DON'T** store chocolate in the refrigerator or freezer, as cocoa butter easily absorbs off-flavors from other foods and changes its crystal structure.

➤ **DO** keep in mind that the milk solids in milk and white chocolate give them a shorter shelf life than unsweetened and dark chocolate.

VANILLA

➤ **SHELF LIFE:** Long-lasting

➤ **DO** keep vanilla in a tightly sealed container away from light and heat.

➤ **DON'T** get rid of old vanilla. Vanilla's high alcohol content makes it extremely shelf-stable. In tests, we've found that even 10-year-old vanilla is indistinguishable from fresh.

Mashed Potatoes, French-Style

French cookery's intensely rich, cheesy take on mashed potatoes flouts the rules.
To Americanize the dish, we ignored a few more. Vive la résistance!

⋟ BY CHARLES KELSEY ⋞

Leave it to the French to take a concept as simple as throwing cheese and garlic into mashed potatoes and elevate it into something far more interesting than, well, mashed potatoes with cheese and garlic. The dish, called *aligot*, comes from the Auvergne region of south-central France, where it is so revered, an entire festival is devoted each year to celebrating it.

I first encountered aligot at a Boston bistro, where the taciturn waiter billed it merely as "French" mashed potatoes. That didn't prepare me for the dish that arrived at my table. Instead of a fluffy mound of spuds, this mash pooled on the plate. And when I lifted my fork to take a bite, the potatoes stretched and pulled like taffy. Was that a good thing? One intensely garlicky, cheesy bite and I knew it was a superb thing.

I did a little research when I got home and learned that aligot gets this uniquely elastic, satiny texture through prolonged, vigorous stirring. Now I was really intrigued. Here in the test kitchen, we've confirmed time and again that a light touch is the secret to great mashed potatoes. How could a heavy-handed technique create such a velvety puree without any trace of glueyness or stickiness?

Going for Gold

In the test kitchen's cookbook library, I learned that most aligot recipes combine pureed boiled potatoes with butter and crème fraîche (a matured, thickened cream with tangy flavor), then energetically beat in handfuls of cheese until the mixture achieves its signature stretch and lifts in long, elastic ribbons. This hearty side dish is traditionally served with equally rib-sticking fare such as sausages or grilled meat.

When I looked closely at a few of the recipes, two things became clear. First, aligot calls for so much butter, cheese, and crème fraîche that if I planned to serve it for anything but a really special meal, a little lightening up would be in order. Second, I was going to have to improvise with the cheese. The traditional choice is *tomme fraîche,* a soft, mild cheese made from fresh curds. Given the U.S.

Two kinds of cheese (both nontraditional) and vigorous stirring give our mash the same creamy stretch as the French original.

government ban on the sale of raw (unpasteurized) cow's milk cheese aged less than 60 days, this cheese would be out of reach for most Americans. For the time being I settled on Cantal, an aged, semihard version of tomme fraîche with a flavor similar to mild cheddar.

The next pressing issue: choosing a potato. The three obvious contenders were russet, Yukon Gold, and Red Bliss. I mixed up batches of aligot with each kind and then tasted them side by side. The Red Bliss were ruled out on two counts. In regular mashed potatoes, we've found that they are the

enemy of light and fluffy; in aligot, their density was still apparent. Furthermore, tasters found the flavor of Red Bliss all but undetectable. Russets did far better on flavor, lending a nice earthiness, but their high starch content produced a palate-sticking tackiness that surfaced through the cheese. The medium-starch Yukon Golds were the clear winner, yielding a puree with a mild, buttery flavor and a light, creamy consistency.

Lift and Stretch

Now I was ready to consider cooking technique. In the test kitchen, we've found that how you cook the potatoes for a regular mash is critical to their final texture. To avoid glueyness, we've gone so far as to steam as well as rinse the spuds midway through cooking to rid them of excess amylose, the "bad" starch in potatoes that turns them tacky. But if the potatoes were to be stirred so vigorously later (rough handling also bursts the granules that contain amylose, releasing the starch into the mix), would such treatment even matter? As it turned out, no. When I compared a batch of aligot made with steamed and rinsed potatoes to one made with simple boiled potatoes (the method advocated by virtually every recipe I came across), tasters could detect no difference.

Now what about mashing? The French turn to a tool called a *tamis,* a metal sieve mounted over a shallow drum. Food is pressed through the screen to create a super-smooth puree free of even the tiniest lumps. Both a ricer and a food mill seemed like close cousins to the tamis, but neither gave me the velvety texture I was looking for. Normally I wouldn't dream of "mashing" potatoes in a food processor—its metal blade would surely burst every starch granule in the mix. But since glueyness wasn't an issue in aligot, I brought the processor out, and found it worked beautifully.

Next up: creaminess. Traditional aligot uses butter and crème fraîche to add flavor and loosen the potato puree's texture before mixing in the cheese. Since crème fraîche isn't always easy to find, I decided to try making aligot with sour cream (a common substitute) as well as heavy cream

Tuber Testing

RED POTATO
Red Bliss potatoes were
overly dense.

RUSSET
Russet potatoes yielded
a tacky texture.

YUKON GOLD
Yukon Golds had winning flavor
and a lighter, creamier texture.

and milk. Sour cream produced results that were certainly creamy but also way too rich. Ditto on the version made with cream, which sated tasters with a single bite. In the end, whole milk proved best, providing depth without going overboard. I found that the amount of milk it took to loosen the texture varied from batch to batch, depending on the moisture content of the potatoes. As for butter, after testing various amounts, I settled on 6 tablespoons for 2 pounds of potatoes. (Some recipes called for as much as two sticks for the same quantity of spuds, but with the cheese still to come, that was overkill.)

At last, I could concentrate on selecting the cheese. For testing purposes, I'd been using Cantal—which seemed like a good bet, given that it's an older cousin of the authentic choice, tomme fraîche. But adding handfuls of the shredded cheese thickened my potatoes so much that I needed brute force to stir them. Plus, the dish lacked the stretchiness I remembered from my bistro meal. Searching for a more elastic substitute, I tried cheddar and then Swiss, with similarly unsatisfactory results. Grabbing a quick piece of pizza one day and watching how ribbons of gooey mozzarella stretched between two slices, it came to me: Why not try typical pizza cheese, the prepackaged mozzarella from the supermarket dairy section? If it worked, who would care that this cheese was about as far as you could get from aligot's French farmhouse origins?

This was a stretch in the very best way—after adding a generous 3 cups, I could lift my wooden spoon and entertain my colleagues with the aligot's incredible expansion. Yet its taste fell flat: The mozzarella was just too mild. Stirring and lifting, I tested versions in which I replaced some of the mozzarella with slightly stronger tasting Cantal (in smaller portions, it didn't lessen elasticity), sharp cheddar, and nutty Gruyère. Gruyère turned out to be the top choice. Still there were complaints: With 3 cups of cheese and 2 pounds of potatoes (a lesser proportion of cheese than most recipes called for), tasters thought the aligot was still overly rich. Cutting back to just a cup of mozzarella and a cup of Gruyère reduced the stretch slightly, but kept richness in check.

As for the stirring, at this point my arm was going around in circles in my sleep. Testing proved that stirring was key to the aligot equation: Too much and the aligot turned so rubbery that it reminded me of chewing gum; too little and the cheese didn't truly marry with the potatoes for that essential elasticity. I eventually surmised that five minutes was the right workout. But I still didn't understand why the stirring worked so well, since the vigorous motion (like that of the food processor) releases amylose, the pesky starch molecule that turns good potatoes gluey. After consulting with our science editor, I learned that in this case, amylose was an asset—the sticky molecules were binding with the proteins from the melted cheese,

enhancing its stretch without causing glueyness (see "The Science of Stretch: Rough 'Em Up," below).

Thus informed, I could focus on the remaining element: garlic. Adding two minced cloves to the potatoes as I pureed them in the food processor yielded just the right amount of garlic punch.

At last my aligot was so rich, garlicky, and stretchy, I was willing to bet it would even pass muster in Auvergne.

FRENCH MASHED POTATOES WITH CHEESE AND GARLIC (ALIGOT)
SERVES 6

The finished potatoes should have a smooth and slightly elastic texture. White cheddar can be substituted for the Gruyère. For richer, stretchier aligot, double the mozzarella.

- 2 pounds Yukon Gold potatoes (4 to 6 medium), peeled, cut into ½-inch-thick slices, rinsed well, and drained
  Table salt
- 6 tablespoons unsalted butter
- 2 medium garlic cloves, minced or pressed through garlic press (about 2 teaspoons)
- 1–1½ cups whole milk
- 4 ounces mozzarella cheese, shredded (about 1 cup) (see note)
- 4 ounces Gruyère cheese, shredded (about 1 cup) (see note)
  Ground black pepper

1. Place potatoes in large saucepan; add water to cover by 1 inch and add 1 tablespoon salt. Partially cover saucepan with lid and bring potatoes to boil over high heat. Reduce heat to medium-low and simmer until potatoes are tender and just break apart when poked with fork, 12 to 17 minutes. Drain potatoes and dry saucepan.

2. Transfer potatoes to food processor; add butter, garlic, and 1½ teaspoons salt. Pulse until butter is melted and incorporated into potatoes, about ten 1-second pulses. Add 1 cup milk and continue to process until potatoes are smooth and creamy, about 20 seconds, scraping down sides halfway through.

3. Return potato mixture to saucepan and set over medium heat. Stir in cheeses, 1 cup at a time, until incorporated. Continue to cook potatoes, stirring vigorously, until cheese is fully melted and mixture is smooth and elastic, 3 to 5 minutes. If mixture is difficult to stir and seems thick, stir in 2 tablespoons milk at a time (up to ½ cup) until potatoes are loose and creamy. Season with salt and pepper. Serve immediately.

COOK'S VIDEOS Original Test Kitchen Videos
www.cooksillustrated.com/apr09
HOW TO MAKE
• French Mashed Potatoes with Cheese and Garlic (Aligot)

The Science of Stretch: Rough 'Em Up

Normally we wouldn't dream of mashing potatoes in a food processor, let alone whipping them by hand for a protracted period—two techniques called for in our aligot recipe. Such rough handling causes the release of amylose, the tacky gel-like starch found in potatoes that spells the end of light, fluffy texture. But in these cheesy, garlicky French mashed potatoes, the release of amylose is actually a good thing. When combined with the cheese in the recipe, it helps produce aligot's signature stretch.

Here's how it works: When cheese is stirred vigorously into the hot boiled potatoes, this rough treatment causes the waterlogged starch granules in the spuds to burst, releasing sticky, gluey amylose. At the same time, the protein molecules in the melting cheese are uncoiling and stretching out like curly hair straightened by a flat iron. When amylose released from the potatoes comes into contact with the uncoiled proteins, it links them together into long, elastic fibers that give aligot its stretch. –C.K.

WHIP INTO SHAPE
For smooth, elastic texture, stir
potatoes three to five minutes.

Easy Chicken Cutlets with Porcini Sauce

Italians braise chicken for hours in a rich wine and mushroom sauce. We wanted to keep the flavor but cut the cooking time.

⊰ BY J. KENJI ALT ⊱

On the surface, *pollo ai funghi porcini* isn't the likeliest candidate for a quick weeknight dinner. This classic Northern Italian dish simmers fresh porcini, white wine, tomato, and a whole chicken until the chicken is fall-off-the-bone tender and the broth rich and satisfying. But with deeply flavored porcini mushrooms on my side, maybe I could distill the essence of this braise into a complex-tasting pan sauce served over simple sautéed chicken cutlets. My goal was dinner on the table in no more than 30 minutes, start to finish.

I started the countdown by sautéing eight thinly pounded cutlets in two speedy batches (each batch only required 2½ minutes). I transferred the chicken to a plate and added fresh porcini and a minced shallot to the pan, sautéing them briefly. Then I deglazed the pan with white wine, tomato paste, and chicken stock, finishing with butter. Even with the earthy savor of porcini in the mix, the sauce tasted weak; plus its consistency was thin, barely clinging to the chicken. Clearly I needed to bump up flavor. But first, I had to get the sauce to coat the chicken. Adding flour as I sautéed the mushrooms and the shallot made the sauce thicker, but it still slid off the cutlets. The solution was to also dredge the cutlets in flour before sautéing, which not only improved browning but also added a rough surface to capture the sauce.

Now, what to do about flavor? When a wine-based liquid simmers for a long time, flavor compounds in the wine break down and recombine to form new compounds known as esters, which bring fruity depth to the mix. A pan sauce reduced for 5 minutes doesn't cook long enough for this reaction to happen. But what if I were to swap wine for vermouth—which has many of the qualities of a good dry white wine but more concentrated flavor? While vermouth helped, tasters still missed the subtle sweetness contributed by long-simmered wine. The answer proved as simple as adding half a teaspoon of sugar.

It was time to take a step back and consider my choice of fresh porcini. Their rich, woodsy flavor is superior to the dried kind, but as they're so hard to find, I knew I had to at least try substituting dried. A half-ounce of dried porcini soaked in chicken stock, then strained and chopped, was all my tasters could handle before protesting about too many soggy mushroom bits in the sauce. Yet this wasn't enough to deliver the same degree of flavor as 4

ounces of fresh. Trying to add flavor by browning the reconstituted porcini was fruitless—they were too wet to caramelize properly. Then I remembered a test kitchen trick to increase savory flavor: adding a dash of soy sauce. The natural glutamates found in soy sauce (the compound that gives food umami, or savory flavor) are the same compounds that make mushrooms taste meaty. I was afraid tasters might complain about an Asian condiment in an Italian-inspired dish, but all they noticed was deeper porcini flavor—exactly what I wanted.

To perfect the sauce, all I needed was fresh thyme and a shot of lemon juice stirred in before serving. Ready in just 30 minutes, I had a new chicken dish that was so full of flavor, it tasted like it had been slow-cooked in a traditional Italian kitchen.

SAUTÉED CHICKEN CUTLETS WITH PORCINI SAUCE
SERVES 4

For even more intense mushroom flavor, grind an additional half-ounce of dried porcini mushrooms in a spice grinder until it is reduced to fine dust. Sift the dust through a fine-mesh strainer and then stir it into the flour before dredging the chicken. Look for dried mushrooms that are smooth and have small pores; shriveled porcini with large holes will retain dirt and grit even after rinsing (see page 31 for more information). The chicken breasts will be easier to slice in half if you freeze them for 15 minutes. To slice a breast in half, place one hand on top of the breast to secure it, hold a chef's knife parallel to the cutting board, and slice through the middle of the breast horizontally.

½ ounce (about ¾ cup) dried porcini mushrooms (see note)
1 cup low-sodium chicken broth
¼ cup plus 1 teaspoon unbleached all-purpose flour
   Table salt and ground black pepper
4 boneless, skinless chicken breasts (6 to 8 ounces each), tenderloins removed and breasts trimmed of excess fat, halved horizontally, and pounded ¼ inch thick (see note)
2 tablespoons plus 1 teaspoon vegetable oil
1 small shallot, minced (about 2 tablespoons)
¼ cup dry vermouth
1 teaspoon tomato paste
1 teaspoon soy sauce
½ teaspoon sugar

2 tablespoons cold unsalted butter
½ teaspoon minced fresh thyme leaves
½ teaspoon juice from 1 lemon

1. Rinse porcini in large bowl of cold water, agitating them with hands to release dirt and sand. Allow dirt and sand to settle to bottom of bowl, then lift porcini from water and transfer to microwave-safe 2-cup measuring cup. Add chicken broth, submerging porcini beneath surface of liquid. Microwave on high power 1 minute, until broth is steaming. Let stand 10 minutes. Using tongs, gently lift porcini out of broth and transfer to cutting board, reserving broth. Chop porcini into ¾-inch pieces and transfer to medium bowl. Strain broth through fine-mesh strainer lined with large coffee filter into bowl with chopped porcini.

2. Combine ¼ cup flour, 1 teaspoon salt, and ½ teaspoon pepper in pie plate. Working one piece at a time, dredge chicken in flour, shaking gently to remove excess. Set aside on plate.

3. Heat 1 tablespoon oil in 12-inch skillet over medium-high heat until smoking. Place 4 cutlets in skillet and cook without moving until browned, about 2 minutes. Flip cutlets and continue to cook until second sides are opaque, 15 to 20 seconds. Transfer to large plate. Add 1 tablespoon oil to now-empty skillet and repeat to cook remaining cutlets. Tent plate loosely with foil.

4. Add remaining teaspoon oil to now-empty skillet and return pan to medium heat. Add shallot and cook, stirring often, until softened, about 30 seconds. Add remaining teaspoon flour and cook, whisking constantly, 30 seconds. Increase heat to medium-high and whisk in vermouth, soaked porcini and their liquid, tomato paste, soy sauce, and sugar. Simmer until reduced to 1 cup, 3 to 5 minutes.

5. Transfer cutlets and any accumulated juices to skillet. Cover and simmer until cutlets are heated through, about 1 minute. Remove skillet from heat and transfer cutlets to serving platter. Whisk butter, thyme, and lemon juice into sauce and season with salt and pepper. Spoon sauce over chicken and serve immediately.

■◀ COOK'S VIDEOS Original Test Kitchen Videos
www.cooksillustrated.com/apr09
HOW TO MAKE
• Sautéed Chicken Cutlets with Porcini Sauce
VIDEO TIP
• Buying and cooking with dried porcini mushrooms

COOK'S ILLUSTRATED
20

Dressing Up Brown Rice

We've already solved the cooking problems that plague brown rice. Now, what to do about jazzing up its taste?

≥ BY YVONNE RUPERTI ≤

Let's face it: Brown rice has issues. It takes almost an hour to cook and can be devilishly hard to get right. With such a long stay over the direct heat of the stovetop, the bottom layer typically turns dry and crusty, leaving you with far less edible rice than you expected. Sure, you can speed up the process by cooking it in the microwave, but that just creates new problems: One batch will be dry and brittle, another too sticky. If you appreciate the mildly nutty taste and chewy texture of plain brown rice, you can address these shortcomings, but many people view the grain with suspicion. How could such a wholesome hippie-era holdover actually taste good?

Cooks who take the trouble know that rice cookers can deliver excellent results, but not everyone wants another appliance in the house. In the test kitchen, we've licked brown rice's cooking problems another way: We bake it in the oven, where the consistent, indirect heat actually simulates the environment of a rice cooker, eliminating scorching and creating perfect, evenly cooked rice every time. Armed with this method, I set out to win converts to this nutritious grain by bumping up its flavor and complementing its chewy texture with a few easy additions.

To get my bearings, I cooked a batch of oven-baked brown rice using our method: I boiled 2⅓ cups water, stirred it into 1½ cups of brown rice in a glass baking dish, covered the dish tightly with foil, then slid it into the oven to bake for an hour. I knew once I added other ingredients, the 8-inch-square baking dish would get a little tight. Of course, I could bake it in a bigger dish, but since I was sure to be adding at least a few sautéed vegetables like onion and garlic, I would also be using a skillet. Why not streamline things by cooking everything in just one vessel? A roomy Dutch oven seemed like the best bet—plus its lid would mean I could eliminate the foil step. Putting the additions on hold until I perfected the cooking method, I prepped a new batch, stirring rice into water I boiled in a Dutch oven, which I then covered and placed in the oven.

To my surprise, when I lifted the lid an hour later, the rice looked brittle and bone-dry—the liquid had evaporated before the rice was cooked. The big culprit—literally—turned out to be the pot itself. Because the Dutch oven had a greater surface area than the 8-inch baking dish, more liquid was exposed to the heat of the oven, so more of it evaporated before the rice had a chance to cook. After some tinkering, I was able to achieve perfectly chewy brown rice in a Dutch oven by increasing the liquid to 3¼ cups and the cooking time to 65 to 70 minutes.

It was finally time to dress up this dish. Incorporating some chicken broth into the cooking liquid was an obvious first step toward bolstering flavor. My next move was to determine when other additions should go into the pot—with the rice as it cooked, or after? It was a given that onions would go into the pot with the uncooked rice, but first I caramelized them for deeper flavor. I did the same with green peppers. Other ingredients like peas and black beans did best with a gentle warming, stirred into the rice after it was removed from the oven. Just before serving, I brightened the flavors of each variation with a sprinkle of fresh herbs and a squeeze of citrus.

These few ingredients transformed my plain grain into something so fresh, bright, and interesting, the naysayers would never believe it was still wholesome.

A few simple additions dress up this plain grain.

BROWN RICE WITH ONIONS AND ROASTED RED PEPPERS
SERVES 4 TO 6

Short-grain brown rice (see page 31) can also be used. For our free recipe for Brown Rice with Andouille, Corn, and Red Peppers, go to www.cooksillustrated.com/apr09.

- 4 teaspoons olive oil
- 2 medium onions, chopped fine (about 2 cups)
- 1 cup low-sodium chicken broth
- 2¼ cups water
- 1½ cups long-grain brown rice (see note)
- 1 teaspoon table salt
- ¾ cup roasted red peppers, chopped
- ½ cup chopped fresh parsley leaves
- ¼ teaspoon ground black pepper
- 1 ounce Parmesan, grated (½ cup)
- 1 lemon, cut into wedges

1. Adjust oven rack to middle position; heat oven to 375 degrees. Heat oil in large Dutch oven over medium heat until shimmering. Add onion and cook, stirring occasionally, until well browned, 12 to 14 minutes.

2. Add broth and water; cover and bring to boil. Remove pot from heat; stir in rice and salt. Cover and bake rice until tender, 65 to 70 minutes.

3. Remove pot from oven, uncover, fluff rice with fork, stir in roasted red peppers, and replace lid; let stand 5 minutes. Stir in parsley and black pepper. Serve, passing Parmesan and lemon wedges separately.

BROWN RICE WITH PEAS, FETA, AND MINT
SERVES 4 TO 6

Follow recipe for Brown Rice with Onions and Roasted Red Peppers through step 2, decreasing oil to 1 tablespoon and omitting 1 onion. In step 3, substitute 1 cup thawed frozen peas for roasted red peppers, ¼ cup chopped fresh mint leaves for parsley, ½ teaspoon grated lemon zest for black pepper, and 2 ounces (½ cup) crumbled feta for Parmesan. Serve with lemon wedges.

BROWN RICE WITH BLACK BEANS AND CILANTRO
SERVES 4 TO 6

Follow recipe for Brown Rice with Onions and Roasted Red Peppers through step 2, substituting 1 green bell pepper, chopped fine, for 1 onion. Once vegetables are well browned, stir in 3 minced garlic cloves and cook until fragrant, 30 seconds. In step 3, substitute 1 can (15½ ounces) drained and rinsed black beans for roasted red peppers and ¼ cup chopped fresh cilantro leaves for parsley; omit Parmesan. Substitute lime wedges for lemon.

🎥 COOK'S VIDEOS Original Test Kitchen Videos
www.cooksillustrated.com/apr09
HOW TO MAKE
• Brown Rice with Onions and Roasted Red Peppers

Discovering Authentic Ciabatta

This Italian loaf boasts a crisp, flavorful crust and a chewy, open crumb—in the hands of a master. Where does that leave the rest of us?

> BY KEITH DRESSER

A secret ingredient and a few good turns give this bread just the right amount of air and lift.

I'm an armchair baker. I love looking at a gorgeous, perfectly formed loaf and imagining all the artistry that went into it—but when it comes to actually baking one, I'll usually leave it to the masters. Especially when the bread is ciabatta.

In the right hands, this low-rising, rustic Italian loaf boasts a flour-streaked crust and tangy, open crumb with so much flavor, you can eat it straight up without any toppings (though just as often the bread is cut horizontally, stuffed, and grilled for panini). As much as I admire ciabatta's taste and form, it's the need to set aside time for the starter that keeps me from rolling up my sleeves and baking it myself. Most bread starters need at least 12 hours to ferment, and at an ideal temperature for best flavor, before you even get to the fun part of mixing and kneading.

With ciabatta available everywhere these days—even Blimpie sandwich outlets—why would anyone bother to make it? Because unless your source is an artisanal bakery, most of the loaves you find just aren't any good. Some lack flavor, others are too flat, still others have holes so big there's hardly any bread. Uninterested in yet another lackluster loaf from the supermarket, I decided get out of my armchair and head into the kitchen to learn how it's done.

Bread Basics

As a first step, I reviewed the mechanics of making bread. Reduced to its essence, all bread making is simple. First you create dough out of flour, water, yeast, and salt. Then you knead the dough, let it rise, and bake it into bread. The catalyst for the transformation from dough to risen loaf is fermentation, the process whereby the starches and sugars in the flour break down to feed the yeast, which then releases carbon dioxide. As the carbon dioxide bubbles up and attempts to escape, this gas gets trapped by elastic gluten (the network of proteins that gives bread structure and chew), and the dough rises.

Ciabatta follows this basic formula, with some twists. First, instead of mixing all of the ingredients together at once, it begins with that inconvenient bread starter, also known as a sponge, or in Italian as a *biga*. Like stock in soup, the biga provides a strong foundation for flavor. The biga is made with a little flour and water along with a scant amount of yeast. The mixture ferments for several hours before being added to more of the same ingredients.

Second, unlike most bread dough, ciabatta dough is extremely wet. Its hydration is a whopping 80 percent, which means there are 8 ounces of water for every 10 ounces of flour (compared to the hydration of standard sandwich bread, which can be as low as 60 percent). So much water was certain to make the dough unwieldy, but it's essential for the final texture. Not only does water reinforce gluten development, it also develops the bread's signature holes. As the water turns to steam during baking, the moisture rushes out, filling the existing bubbles created by the carbon dioxide and then enlarging them.

Biga Deal

The first thing to decide on was the flour—bread or all-purpose? By name alone, bread flour seemed the obvious choice, but I found I preferred all-purpose. Bread flour is made from hard wheat, which has a high protein content that leads to lots of gluten development, but in ciabatta it proved too much of a good thing: These loaves were tough and overly chewy. All-purpose flour, on the other hand, is made from both hard and soft wheat and has slightly less protein. It produced loaves with a more open, springy texture. (They were still a bit flat, but I would deal with that later.)

The next step was to build flavor through the biga. As it ferments, the yeast in the biga produces a byproduct of lactic and acetic acids, which give the bread its characteristic sourness. Most recipes called for a ratio of 25 percent biga to 75 percent dough, but after trying this and finding it lacked character, I changed the proportions to half biga and half dough. Bad move—the bread became boozy-tasting from the yeast. Cutting back, I settled on 30 percent sponge and 70 percent dough as the ideal proportion for nonalcoholic tang.

Following standard protocol, I combined the biga ingredients in a bowl, covered the bowl, and left it out on the counter overnight. About 12 hours later,

The best way to remove sticky bread dough or runny batter from a bowl is with a bowl scraper—a hand-held spatula that fits in your palm. We tested five models to find a curved scraper with enough grip to scrape the bowl clean and enough rigidity to move heavy dough easily. We tried scrapers made of plastic, metal, silicone, and combinations of these materials, zeroing in on contoured silicone covering a metal insert as our favorite. For complete testing results, go to www.cooksillustrated.com/apr09. –Peggy Chung Collier

CLEAN CONTOURS
iSi BASICS Silicone Scraper Spatula
Price: $5.99
Comments: The rigidity and generous surface area of this winning scraper left no dough or batter behind. Another plus: a straight edge that doubles as a bench scraper

LIMITED FLEXIBILITY
ATECO Bowl Scraper
Price: 80 cents
Comments: This rectangular plastic scraper (the cheapest of the lot) was stiff enough to efficiently move large quantities of dough, but it couldn't match the iSi scraper when it came to sweeping up batter trails.

THICK AND FLIMSY
TRUDEAU Silicone Bowl Scraper
Price: $6.95
Comments: This thick, floppy silicone scraper lacked the metal insert that made our winner so effective. It left trails of batter behind and was awkward to hold.

---

it bubbled and had a pleasant, sour aroma. Some recipes were very particular about the temperature of the room where the biga ferments, but I found that as long as it was between 60 and 70 degrees—typical ambient room temperature—the biga turned out fine. (At higher room temperatures, however, the biga overfermented and produced bread that was too sour and poorly leavened, while biga left in a chilly room fermented too slowly and yielded bland loaves.)

After combining the biga with the dough ingredients, the next step was kneading. The dough was simply too wet to knead by hand, so I turned to a stand mixer. Most of the recipes I consulted kneaded the dough for only a few minutes—just long enough to activate the gluten in the flour. But when I put these loaves in the oven, they spread out instead of rising. Clearly, I needed better gluten development, so I increased the kneading time to 10 minutes at medium speed. Alas, the bread baked from this dough still barely rose. But anything beyond 10 minutes of kneading and the loaves turned out tough.

In our recipe for Rustic Dinner Rolls (November/December 2008), we used a gentler approach to coaxing out gluten: turning. This involves using a rubber spatula or bowl scraper to fold the dough over itself several times in movements similar to folding egg whites into batter, and then letting it rest to rise. Ten minutes of kneading augmented by one series of turns was helpful, but repeating the process for a total of 16 turns was the perfect pick-me-up, producing loaves that rose about 2 inches.

Milky Way

As it stood, my recipe now yielded ciabatta with good flavor and just the right domed shape, but when I cut into it, I got lost in its gigantic holes. My kneading and turning had encouraged strong strands of gluten, which are good for structure but also sup-

port oversized holes. I retraced my kneading times, flour choice, sponge and water ratios, and turning steps, but every time I altered the recipe, I upset the delicate balance and the dough either lacked structure or lost flavor. I wondered if olive oil, an optional ingredient in one of the original recipes I consulted, would weaken the gluten strands enough to yield smaller holes. I tried my recipe with varying amounts, but the oil had no impact until I reached 3 tablespoons. At that point the bread's sour flavor was overwhelmed by the oil's taste—better to save it for dipping.

Another ingredient mentioned in a few recipes I found was milk. I initially thought the milk was added solely for flavor, but when I tried it in my recipe, the results surprised me. Cutting into this ciabatta revealed a uniform crumb pockmarked with medium-sized bubbles. Success at last! Curious about why this addition worked, I did a little digging and learned that milk contains a protein fragment called glutathione, which acts to slightly weaken the gluten strands. A mere ¼ cup of milk was enough to moderately reduce the size of the bubbles. (For more information, see "Ridding Bread of Oversized Air Holes," above.)

With the crumb issues resolved, I could turn to shaping. I hoped to use the simplest method: stretching portions of dough into loaves. Unfortunately, this produced homely, unevenly baked bread. Trying another common approach, I shaped a portion of dough into a rectangle, then folded the shorter ends over each other like a business letter to form a stubby rectangle. Much better. To avoid extra handling of the dough, I simply formed the loaves on parchment paper and then slid the parchment onto the baking surface.

Now it was time to refine the actual baking of the bread. Most recipes I consulted recommended using a baking stone set in a 500-degree oven. After

some testing, I found that while the baking stone was key to developing a good crust (a preheated, overturned baking sheet was also an option), baking the bread at 500 degrees was excessive. At this temperature, the crust became too dark before the inside was fully cooked. Reducing the oven temperature to 450 degrees and baking the bread for a little longer solved the problem. My final enhancement was to spray the loaves with water in the first minutes of baking. This produced a crisper crust and loaves that rose a bit higher (steam delays crust formation and promotes a higher spring in the oven).

Finally, I had ciabatta with such airy texture, full, tangy flavor, and perfect lift, you might even say I'd mastered the form.

🎥 **COOK'S VIDEOS** Original Test Kitchen Videos
www.cooksillustrated.com/apr09
HOW TO MAKE
• Ciabatta
VIDEO TIP
• How to handle a wet dough

CIABATTA

MAKES 2 LOAVES

Two tablespoons of nonfat milk powder can be used in place of the liquid milk; increase the amount of water in the dough to 1 cup. As you make this bread, keep in mind that the dough is wet and very sticky. The key to manipulating it is working quickly and gently; rough handling will result in flat, tough loaves. When possible, use a large rubber spatula or bowl scraper to move the dough. If you have to use your hands, make sure they are well floured. Because the dough is so sticky, it must be prepared in a stand mixer. If you don't have a baking stone, bake the bread on an overturned and preheated rimmed baking sheet set on the lowest oven rack. The bread will keep for up to 2 days, well wrapped and stored at room temperature. To recrisp the crust, place the unwrapped bread in a 450-degree oven for 6 to 8 minutes. The bread will keep frozen for several months wrapped in foil and placed in a large zipper-lock bag. Thaw the bread at room temperature and recrisp using the instructions above.

Biga
1 cup (5 ounces) unbleached all-purpose flour
⅛ teaspoon instant or rapid-rise yeast
½ cup (4 ounces) water, at room temperature

Dough
2 cups (10 ounces) unbleached all-purpose flour
½ teaspoon instant or rapid-rise yeast
1½ teaspoons table salt
¾ cup (6 ounces) water, at room temperature
¼ cup (2 ounces) milk, at room temperature (see note)

1. **FOR THE BIGA:** Combine flour, yeast, and water in medium bowl and stir with wooden spoon until uniform mass forms, about 1 minute. Cover bowl tightly with plastic wrap and let stand at room temperature (about 70 degrees) overnight (at least 8 hours and up to 24 hours).

2. **FOR THE DOUGH:** Place biga and dough ingredients in bowl of stand mixer fitted with paddle attachment. Mix on lowest speed until roughly combined and shaggy dough forms, about 1 minute; scrape down sides of bowl as necessary. Continue mixing on medium-low speed until dough becomes uniform mass that collects on paddle and pulls away from sides of bowl, 4 to 6 minutes. Change to dough hook and knead bread on medium speed until smooth and shiny (dough will be very sticky), about 10 minutes. Transfer dough to large bowl and cover tightly with plastic wrap. Let dough rise at room temperature until doubled in volume, about 1 hour.

3. Spray rubber spatula or bowl scraper with non-stick cooking spray; fold partially risen dough over itself by gently lifting and folding edge of dough toward middle. Turn bowl 90 degrees; fold again. Turn bowl and fold dough six more times (total of eight turns). Cover with plastic wrap and let rise for 30 minutes. Repeat folding, replace plastic wrap, and

1. MAKE BIGA Combine yeast with small amounts of flour and water; let rest overnight to build flavor.

2. MAKE DOUGH, KNEAD Add biga to remaining dough ingredients; knead in stand mixer.

3. LET RISE Allow dough to rise at room temperature until doubled, about 1 hour.

4. TURN 8 TIMES Turn partially risen dough by folding it in on itself to gently encourage more gluten development. Let rise 30 minutes.

5. REPEAT STEP 4 More turning and rising ensure a loaf with just enough lift.

6. DIVIDE DOUGH Transfer dough to floured surface and halve with bench scraper.

7. PRESS Press each half into rough 12- by 6-inch rectangle.

8. SHAPE Fold each dough half like business letter into 7- by 4-inch loaf and let rest 30 minutes.

9. PRESS, SPRAY, BAKE Press out dough into 10- by 6-inch rectangles, spray with water, and bake.

let rise until doubled in volume, about 30 minutes longer. Meanwhile, adjust oven rack to lower-middle position, place baking stone on rack, and heat oven to 450 degrees at least 30 minutes before baking.

4. Cut two 12- by 6-inch pieces of parchment paper and liberally dust with flour. Transfer dough to liberally floured counter, being careful not to deflate completely. Following photos 6 through 9 above, liberally flour top of dough and divide in half. Turn 1 piece of dough so cut side is facing up and dust with flour. With well-floured hands, press dough into rough 12- by 6-inch shape. Fold shorter sides of dough toward center, overlapping them like business letter to form 7- by 4-inch loaf. Repeat with second dough piece. Gently transfer each loaf seam-side down to parchment sheets, dust with flour,

and cover with plastic wrap. Let loaves sit at room temperature for 30 minutes (surfaces of loaves will develop small bubbles).

5. Slide parchment with loaves onto inverted, rimmed baking sheet or pizza peel. Using floured fingertips, evenly poke entire surface of each loaf to form 10- by 6-inch rectangle; spray loaves lightly with water. Carefully slide parchment with loaves onto baking stone using jerking motion. Bake, spraying loaves with water twice more during first 5 minutes of baking time, until crust is deep golden brown and instant-read thermometer inserted into centers of loaves registers 210 degrees, 22 to 27 minutes. Transfer to wire rack, discard parchment, and cool loaves to room temperature, about 1 hour, before slicing and serving.

Emergency Chocolate Cake

This easy wartime cake made with mayonnaise has a lot of good things going for it. Chocolate flavor isn't one of them.

≽ BY KEITH DRESSER ≼

When ingredients like butter and fresh eggs were scarce during World War II, cooks came up with cakes that worked without them. Homemakers found these wartime recipes so convenient (the cakes could be whipped up with ingredients on hand), they continued to bake them long after rationing was over. I recently came across a classic from this era in a collection of family recipes: my grandmother's Emergency Chocolate Cake. Of course I had to try it. The recipe called for water and ingredients straight from the pantry: flour, sugar, cocoa powder, baking soda, vanilla, and the real kicker—mayonnaise, a stand-in for butter and eggs.

I followed her instructions, mixing the water with the mayonnaise, combining this liquid with the dry ingredients, pouring the batter into an 8-inch-square pan, and then baking the whole thing at 350 degrees. The dark, shiny cake I took out of the oven a half hour later was remarkably moist and tender, with no trace of a mayonnaise taste. But a dessert this easy had to have at least one hitch, and it did: The chocolate flavor, while decent, was far from decadent. I didn't want to turn this snack cake into a pan of brownies, but if I did a little tinkering, could I ramp up the chocolate flavor enough to take the cake from good to great?

Increasing the cocoa powder was an obvious first step, and I quickly discovered that my grandmother knew what she was doing when she arrived at ½ cup. Cocoa powder is composed mainly of cocoa solids; any more than that turned the cake dry and chalky. Good-quality bar chocolate has deeper flavor than cocoa powder, but swapping one for the other wasn't a solution either. Solid chocolate contains lots of cocoa butter. To get the intense flavor I wanted, I needed to use so much that the cake became greasy and soft. I got the best results supplementing the cocoa powder with 2 ounces of melted bittersweet chocolate. But before I was done with the chocolate, I had a trick I wanted to try: In other recipes calling for cocoa powder, we've intensified its flavor by "blooming" it in hot water first. Cocoa powder contains solid particles of fat and protein with tiny flavor molecules trapped inside. The hot water causes these flavor molecules, which would otherwise remain imprisoned, to burst forth, amplifying overall flavor.

These measures helped, but could I take things further? We've also had success getting deeper chocolate flavor by combining chocolate with coffee.

A cake this moist, tender, and chocolaty isn't just for emergencies.

Instead of blooming the cocoa in hot water, I used a hot cup of coffee to great effect: The chocolate flavor became richer with coffee a silent partner. I also found that if the dark chocolate was chopped fine enough, I could add it to the cocoa to melt while the cocoa was blooming—no need to melt it separately in the microwave or double boiler.

Now it was time to think about the oddball ingredient in the mix: mayonnaise. I wondered if I could make my cake richer by replacing the mayo with eggs and butter or even eggs and oil. I made two more cakes: one with melted butter and an egg and one with vegetable oil and an egg. While perfectly fine specimens, these cakes weren't quite as moist and velvety as the mayonnaise version. How could this be? Research revealed that oil, butter, and mayo each interact a little differently with flour. While all three coat the protein particles and reduce gluten development, creating a tender crumb, commercially prepared mayonnaise contains lecithin, an emulsifier that helps keep the oil suspended in micro-droplets. These small droplets greatly aid the oil's ability to coat the flour's protein particles, leading to a supremely tender cake.

While butter and oil were out, the egg was a keeper. When I compared a cake made with mayo only to one with both the sandwich spread and an egg, the cake with egg had richer flavor and a springier texture.

With only a little more work, I now had a super-easy cake with such velvety texture and deep chocolate flavor, it was good enough for special occasions as well as emergencies.

THE BEST EASY CHOCOLATE CAKE
MAKES ONE 8-INCH-SQUARE CAKE

We recommend using one of the test kitchen's favorite baking chocolates, Callebaut Intense Dark L-60-40NV, or Ghirardelli Bittersweet Chocolate Baking Bar for this recipe, but any high-quality dark, bittersweet, or semisweet chocolate will work. Instead of confectioners' sugar, the cake can also be served with sweetened whipped cream.

- 1½ cups (7½ ounces) unbleached all-purpose flour
- 1 cup (7 ounces) sugar
- ½ teaspoon baking soda
- ¼ teaspoon table salt
- ½ cup (2 ounces) Dutch-processed cocoa powder
- 2 ounces bittersweet chocolate, chopped fine (see note)
- 1 cup hot coffee
- ⅔ cup mayonnaise
- 1 large egg
- 2 teaspoons vanilla extract
- Confectioners' sugar (for serving; optional)

1. Adjust oven rack to middle position and heat oven to 350 degrees. Lightly spray 8-inch-square baking dish with nonstick cooking spray.

2. Whisk flour, sugar, baking soda, and salt together in large bowl. In separate bowl, combine cocoa and chocolate; pour hot coffee over cocoa mixture and whisk until smooth; let cool slightly. Whisk in mayonnaise, egg, and vanilla. Stir mayonnaise mixture into flour mixture until combined.

3. Scrape batter into prepared pan and smooth top. Bake until wooden skewer inserted into center of cake comes out with few crumbs attached, 30 to 35 minutes.

4. Let cake cool in pan on wire rack, 1 to 2 hours. Dust with confectioners' sugar, cut into squares, and serve straight from the pan; or turn cake out onto serving platter and dust with confectioners' sugar.

What's the Real Deal with Vanilla?

Still shocked by past results, we had to do another tasting. In the battle between pure and imitation extracts, could we declare a winner?

≥ BY LISA McMANUS ≤

In two past tastings of vanilla extract, we reached a conclusion that still amazes us: It matters not a whit whether you use real or imitation vanilla, because you can't tell the difference when you bake. But at a recent editorial meeting, we took a poll: Did that mean anyone had stopped buying the real thing? No. Our test cooks held firmly to the belief that natural vanilla is the best choice. So we returned to the test kitchen for a definitive tasting.

In our newest quest for great vanilla, we sampled 12 of the country's top-selling supermarket brands of vanilla extract, both fake and pure, this time stirring them into milk and pudding before trying a few choices in cake and cookies. Searching broadly for the best vanilla flavor, we also compared extract to vanilla beans, vanilla paste, and vanilla powder (see "Beans, Paste, and Powder" at right).

The Real Deal

Vanilla is a powerful "flavor potentiator," meaning it enhances our ability to taste other foods, including chocolate, coffee, fruit, and nuts, and boosts our perception of sweetness. While this is true for both pure and imitation vanilla, the two choices are far from identical. Scientists have identified around 250 flavor and aroma compounds in real vanilla, while the artificial version has just one: vanillin, the predominant flavor in natural vanilla. Pure vanilla is made by steeping vanilla beans in water and ethyl alcohol, with the exact proportions of each mandated by the government. The beans are expensive, grown on flowering orchid vines in only a handful of tropical countries. They take much time and painstaking labor to grow, process, and ship, even before they are converted to extract.

Imitation vanilla, on the other hand, is a byproduct of paper production or a derivative of coal tar, chemically manufactured through fairly simple and inexpensive processes. Because it's so cheap, annual global demand for imitation vastly outstrips that for natural vanilla, at 16,000 metric tons to just 40 metric tons for natural vanilla.

In our supermarket lineup, imitation vanillas cost as little as 18 cents per ounce, compared with up to $4.50 per ounce for natural. In another strike against natural vanilla, most of those 250 flavor and aroma compounds are driven off by high heat during baking or cooking. So if that complex, natural vanilla flavor really can't be detected, what's the point of ever buying it?

VANILLA VARIATIONS: Beans, Paste, and Powder

Grabbing vanilla extract in the baking aisle is far cheaper and easier than special-ordering vanilla beans, paste, or powder. But do these other options deliver better flavor?

Vanilla beans are the original source of the extract we all know, while vanilla paste is actually a sugar syrup flavored with vanilla extract, ground vanilla beans, and tiny seeds from the beans. As for vanilla powder, it's dried pure vanilla extract on a cornstarch base. To determine which we liked best, we held a blind four-way tasting, pitting desserts made with beans, paste, and powder against those made with our winning pure vanilla extract.

In crème anglaise, a velvety custard, vanilla beans won by a landslide. Tasters preferred the beans' "rich," "natural," "big vanilla" flavor over any other form—and nearly 2 to 1 over vanilla extract, which came in third after vanilla paste. Powder, which was clumpy and difficult to blend into the milk, lacked flavor and trailed in a distant last place. Because this custard is cooked at a low temperature, never exceeding 180 degrees, the beans' flavor remained intact.

But when we baked these four forms of vanilla into yellow cake, vanilla extract shone. Tasters found it sweeter, with more vanilla flavor, while beans landed in last place in this application. The only form of vanilla that did well in both tests was vanilla paste, our tasters' second choice.

Our conclusion: When you're baking cake or cookies, extract is the top choice. In creamy puddings and sauces, beans are best. –L.M.

WORTH BUYING
Vanilla beans add complex flavor to custards and ice cream, but stick with extract for baking.

PASTE PALES
Vanilla paste is a slightly less flavorful stand-in for beans or extract.

DON'T BOTHER
Vanilla powder has weak flavor no matter how you use it.

To answer these questions, we tested vanilla in a variety of cooked and uncooked preparations. First, we stripped away competing flavors to taste the extracts themselves. Vanilla experts do this by mixing them in milk; we used an 8–1 ratio of milk to vanilla. Tasted this way, real vanilla extracts clearly won the day. Their greater complexity shone through, with testers detecting everything from notes of honey and maple to licorice and prune.

In this case, imitation vanillas all fell to the bottom half of the rankings. Tasters said they had a strong, pleasing aroma, "like vanilla cookies that have already been baked," but little vanilla flavor and a taste that was bitter and medicinal. More research revealed that imitation vanilla is known to taste harsh if too much is used—which helps explain our tasters' reaction.

But you would never use vanilla extract in such a heavy concentration. So we sampled them again, in vanilla pudding. Now the ratio of dairy to vanilla was a whopping 56 to 1. Our recipe adds vanilla extract at the end of cooking, off the stove, to help preserve its flavor. Despite this precaution, many of those distinctions we had noted among vanillas in the milk tasting were dimmed. Some aroma and flavor still may have been driven off by the warmth of the cooked pudding and muted by the eggs, butter, and sugar. Our results shuffled, but only slightly—except for one imitation extract that shot from seventh place up to the top of the ranking.

One of the most striking differences between pure and fake vanilla involved alcohol flavor. While federal guidelines demand 35 percent alcohol in pure vanilla extract, there's no minimum for alcohol in imitation vanilla, and manufacturers have an incentive to use as little as possible to make synthetic vanillin soluble: If they use more, it costs more to make. This explains why tasters kept describing real vanilla as "boozy," an adjective rarely applied to fake vanilla. But they also found the real stuff nutty, spicy, and more complex.

The Heat Is On

Real vanilla's good performance in milk and pudding was clear, but the vast majority of time, we're using vanilla extract in cookies and cakes. To help our tasters focus, we limited our baked-goods tasting to just three samples. After averaging the scores from the milk and pudding tastings, we chose the top-ranked pure vanilla, the highest-ranked imitation, and the bottom-ranked

TASTING VANILLA EXTRACT

Twenty-one members of the *Cook's Illustrated* staff tasted 12 vanilla extracts, both imitation and pure, from top-selling supermarket brands compiled by the Chicago-based market research firm Information Resources, Inc. We sampled them mixed in whole milk (using an 8–1 ratio of milk to extract) and vanilla pudding. Results were averaged, and brands appear below in order of preference. We also tested three of the vanilla extracts in baked goods: our top-ranked real vanilla, McCormick Pure Vanilla Extract; the highest-ranked imitation, Gold Medal; and the bottom-ranked performer, Durkee Imitation Vanilla Flavor. Here, the results were split: McCormick Pure Vanilla ranked highest in cakes, while Gold Medal was the winner in cookies.

RECOMMENDED

McCORMICK Pure Vanilla Extract
Price: $7.99 for 2 ounces ($4 per ounce)
Comments: This vanilla won top praise for being "strong," "rich," and "spicy," with a "sweet undertone." It had "clear vanilla flavor with nice balance" and notes of "dried fruit," "caramel," and "chocolate," "like Kahlúa or Bailey's." In pudding, it was deemed "a step above," with an extremely "pleasing finish."

RODELLE Pure Vanilla Extract
Price: $7.99 for 4 ounces ($2 per ounce)
Comments: "Smoky" and "earthy," with "caramel," "prune," and "chocolate" notes, it was praised for offering "deeper, richer 'bass tones' of flavor." Prepared in pudding, it was "subtle," a "gentlemanly vanilla: well-balanced, mature, a suggestion of alcohol and smoke."

NIELSEN-MASSEY Madagascar Bourbon Pure Vanilla Extract
Price: $9.99 for 4 ounces ($2.50 per ounce)
Comments: "Sweeter and more pleasant" than other vanillas, it lacked the "boozy burn" of some of the pure extracts and offered a "sweet floral flavor," with "honey" and "maple" notes. In pudding, it was "like burnt marshmallows," with a "nutty" finish.

GOLD MEDAL Imitation Vanilla Extract **BEST BUY**
Price: $2.25 for 8 ounces (28 cents per ounce)
Comments: Tasters felt that this imitation vanilla ranked with the pure extracts. "Lovely, seemed like pure vanilla," said one; another described it as "mild and gentle; maybe it's not real, but it tastes good." Others said it was "perfumy," with notes of "toasted rice" and "buttered popcorn."

SAUER'S Pure Vanilla Extract
Price: $5.25 for 2 ounces ($2.62 per ounce)
Comments: "Sweet," with "a nice depth" was a common reaction to this extract. Some noted that it had "elements of tea," "chocolate," and "a little caramel" and was "clovey," with "assertive vanilla" flavor. But the alcohol struck many as "overpowering."

SPICE ISLANDS Pure Vanilla Extract
Price: $7.43 for 2 ounces ($3.72 per ounce)
Comments: "Sweet," but with a "harsh, boozy finish" and a "peaty, almost smoky flavor," it "smells great, but tastes blah." In pudding, it was "much too smoky and heavy," though some found it "potent" and "complex."

RECOMMENDED *(continued)*

DURKEE Pure Vanilla Extract
Price: $27.87 for 16 ounces ($1.74 per ounce)
Comments: The ingredient list shows "vanilla bean extractives" in last place, after corn syrup. "Good aroma, but flavor is straightforward and somewhat lacking," said one taster; others called it "mild," with a "malted flavor." In pudding, it was "subtle." In sum: "decent but unremarkable."

RECOMMENDED WITH RESERVATIONS

MORTON & BASSETT Pure Vanilla Extract
Price: $9.09 for 4 ounces ($2.27 per ounce)
Comments: Has a "sharp scent, followed by a sharp and unforgiving flavor"; "heavy on the alcohol," it was "slightly herbaceous, a mix of floral and earthy." In pudding, tastes "like melted Breyers vanilla ice cream," but with a "harsh" aftertaste that "hits sharply in the back of the throat," leaving "a little burn."

McCORMICK Premium Imitation Vanilla Extract
Price: $3.69 for 2 ounces ($1.85 per ounce)
Comments: Includes cocoa and tea extractives "and other artificial flavorings" to mimic the complexity of pure vanilla. Tasters detected "some vanilla, but that dissipates, and tastes almost fruity," with "nuts," "cherry cola," and "coffee" notes. In pudding, it was "bright," like a "girly cocktail."

McCORMICK Gourmet Collection Organic Pure Madagascar Vanilla Extract
Price: $10.55 for 2 ounces ($5.28 per ounce)
Comments: With a "barely there aroma and flavor" that came across as "faint, but otherwise fine," this gourmet line from McCormick is not worth its high price. In pudding, tasters said there was "not much vanilla coming through."

ADAMS Pure Vanilla Extract
Price: $7.88 for 4 ounces ($1.97 per ounce)
Comments: "Mild," "thin," "sharp," and "weak," this came across as "all nose, no flavor," with an aftertaste of "bitterness at the back of the throat like Robitussin." In pudding, it was "bland" and "medicinal," though a few tasters found it "floral."

DURKEE Imitation Vanilla Flavor
Price: $2.84 for 16 ounces (18 cents per ounce)
Comments: Tasters liked its "sweet" aroma, but complained that this imitation had "virtually no" vanilla taste, and what there was seemed "way too mild," like "Carnation Instant Breakfast." In pudding, tasters described it as "soft-serve vanilla" and "commercial-tasting."

imitation. If tasters couldn't tell these three vanillas apart in baked goods, we knew the game was up; it really didn't matter. We baked three yellow cakes and three batches of vanilla cookies—and waited.

To our surprise, each application showed two distinct outcomes. In cake, the pure vanilla came out on top but just a hair ahead of the high-ranking imitation. In cookies, the pure vanilla dropped to last place, and that high-ranking imitation soared to first place. As it turns out, flavor and aroma compounds in vanilla begin to bake off at around 280 to 300 degrees. Most cakes' internal temperatures do not rise above 210 degrees, while cookies become much hotter as they bake. As a result, pure vanilla kept a slight flavor advantage in the cake—but not in the cookies.

Tasters' Choice

So what's our conclusion? If you're only buying one bottle of vanilla for cooking, baking, and making cold and creamy desserts, our top choice is a real extract. If you only use vanilla for baking, we have to admit there's not much difference between a well-made synthetic vanilla and the real thing. Speaking to pastry chefs, we learned that many buy an arsenal of vanilla extracts, using cheaper imitation for baking and pure for confections made with moderate or no heat, such as puddings, pastry cream, and buttercream frosting.

In the test kitchen, we go through so much vanilla extract that we buy it in bulk. From now on, we'll be ordering our winner, McCormick Pure Vanilla Extract, by the case. We also recommend our top-rated imitation vanilla, Gold Medal, for its "mild and gentle" vanilla flavor and its budget-friendly price. At just 28 cents an ounce, it's the second-cheapest choice in our lineup.

In Search of a Better Blender

All we ask of a blender is that it can crush ice and produce a smooth purée. So why can't more models deliver?

⇒ BY MEREDITH BUTCHER ⇐

We've long been skeptical of souped-up blenders with dizzyingly high horsepower, a slew of buttons promising minute gradations in speed, and functions for grating cheese, pulverizing nuts into butter, and other specialized tasks. When you come right down to it, a blender has one basic job—to blend food into a uniform consistency, whether it's crushing ice or producing lump-free purees for smoothies, soups, or hummus. (We leave other ingredient-altering tasks, like grinding, shredding, and chopping, to our food processor.) Past testing has taught us that just two things matter for success at this basic job: the configuration of the blender blades and a V-shaped jar that keeps food close to the blade edges.

Still, with the latest generation of blenders claiming such innovations in blade design as "dual wave action," "reversible motion," and serrated edges, we couldn't help but take notice. Would any of these enhanced models offer blending that was fast and effective enough to make them worth price tags that are often well over $100? To find out, we gathered 10 models, including basic machines as well as those that boasted fancy new features.

Crushing Concerns

We began by testing a function that no food processor can duplicate—crushing ice. There's no way to sugarcoat the results: Faced with the challenge of pulverizing 15 ice cubes, most blenders failed miserably, breaking down only some of the ice before the blade wedged the remainder against the side of the jar. While some models boasted an "ice crushing" button, unless there was enough power to keep the ice cubes moving, this function worked no better than a pulse button or a simple on/off setting. As for innovative design, the reversible blade model, which whirled first in one direction and then the other, couldn't free trapped ice to pulverize it. On the other hand, our top performer in this area was the "dual wave" model, which has twin blades set side by side. With the ice bouncing from blade to blade in a game of toss, it was quickly chipped down.

When it comes to turning solids into liquids, blenders have a natural edge over food processors. A tall jar and short, rotating blades allow a blender to swirl food into a vortex, potentially making swift work of purées, soups, and icy cocktails. To test this function, we made smoothies with rock-hard frozen berries and fibrous mango, then poured each one through a sieve to examine texture. While most blenders performed reasonably well in this test (liquid kept the food moving), lots of pulp and frozen-fruit nuggets did turn up in our sieve, and only a few models achieved the perfectly smooth, frothy texture we wanted. We noticed that flutes, or vertical ribs inside the blender jar, helped make the difference. These provide "push back," preventing food from being plastered to the jar walls by centrifugal force. Yet a little fluting goes a long way—some models had big flutes that bulged inward and got in the way of overall circulation.

Next test: whirling chickpeas, olive oil, and tahini into hummus. Here we confirmed that tapered, V-shaped jars are best at keeping food in contact with the whirling blades. Wide-based jars left food too far from the cutting action, resulting in grainy, greasy hummus. The blender with twin side-by-side blades, which excelled at blending smoothies and crushing ice, actually did poorly in this test. It was just too powerful for more-solid food preparation; even at the lowest setting, we wound up with hummus so frothy it was more smoothie than dip.

Going Green

From past testing, we knew that manufacturers' listings of horsepower and wattage have little bearing on performance. (The data measure only the power consumed.) Similarly, when we used a laser tachometer a few years ago to record the revolutions per minute (rpm) of each blender blade, we found that a high rpm had little or no connection to kitchen success. This time, we measured speed and efficiency by putting plain yogurt in each blender and adding drops of yellow and blue food coloring to opposite sides of the jar. To get a good look at the action, we turned each blender on at its lowest speed, set a timer, and watched. While all the blenders took less than 2 minutes to turn the yogurt bright green, two blenders proved their superior efficiency by managing it in under 30 seconds.

All of this testing took place in a corner of the test kitchen, where we had been banished for making a ruckus. The noise piqued our interest in finding the quietest blender. Using a computer program, we compared the sound output of each blender on high speed. The scores varied widely. Not surprisingly, the blender with twin side-by-side blades was the loudest. The quietest blenders turned out to be our overall winners, perhaps a testament to the efficiency of their motors.

We considered other characteristics: material (one thick polycarbonate jar was incredibly tough), weight (too-light models rattled across the countertop), capacity (we prefer larger jars), buttons (we prefer dials, but touch pads are a close second), and cleanup (we like blenders that come apart for easy washing). While these characteristics are important, we valued performance above all—if a blender couldn't crush and purée, none of the other features mattered.

Cutting Edges

Wondering what, exactly, about the blade design resulted in such dramatic differences in performance, we detached the blades from each machine (in one case literally sawing off the blades from the base) and examined them closely. Models with blades that merely reached up or down like a pair of matching arms—two up, two straight out—had a much harder time moving and chopping food than blenders with asymmetrical blades in varying positions. Among the better blenders, some blades curved upward, acting as an escalator, lifting and rotating foods into a vortex, while other blades leaned down to skim the floor of the jar. We also noticed that the blades that tapered the most or were serrated performed better overall.

In the end, we recommended only two blenders out of the 10 we tested. Our top performer was the KitchenAid 5-Speed Blender ($149.99), which impressed us with its brute strength and efficiency. Each of its four blades was positioned at a different angle, maximizing its ability to pulverize food. Ice was demolished in just five bursts of power, smoothies were quickly lump-free, and hummus came out perfectly consistent.

For a less expensive alternative, consider our Best Buy, the Kalorik BL Blender ($49.99). Although noticeably slower than our top performer, this model's six blades (including two that were serrated) were positioned at different angles (see "Sharp Differences," page 29), allowing it to excel at crushing ice and making hummus. It was also the quietest blender overall.

▇ **COOK'S VIDEOS** Original Test Kitchen Videos
www.cooksillustrated.com/apr09
BEHIND THE SCENES
• Testing Blenders

TESTING BLENDERS

KEY
GOOD: ★★★
FAIR: ★★
POOR: ★

Prices for the 10 blenders we tested were paid in Boston-area retail stores or online. Blenders are listed in order of preference. Sources for the winner and Best Buy appear on page 32.

ICE CRUSHING: We pulsed 15 ice cubes. Models that produced uniform "snow" rated highest.

SMOOTHIE: We blended frozen fruit, juice, and yogurt for 1 minute on high (or on the "puree" or "liquefy" setting). Blenders that produced a lump-free puree won top marks.

HUMMUS: We processed chickpeas, olive oil, and tahini on high for 1 minute. Blenders that emulsified to smoothness ranked highest.

SPEED: We added three drops of yellow and blue food coloring to either side of the jar atop 16 ounces of plain yogurt and timed how long it took with the blender on low until the yogurt turned uniformly green.

SOUND LEVEL: Using ProLogic 8 software, we recorded sound levels with each blender on high. Blenders that made the least noise ranked highest.

Sharp Differences

A blender is only as good as its blades. Our Best Buy, the Kalorik BL (left), excelled thanks to an innovative six-blade design that hit food at differing angles. A losing design, the Hamilton Beach Liquid Blu 5-Speed (right), has four blades divided into pairs that only hit food vertically and horizontally, making it far less effective at crushing and pureeing.

SMASHING SUCCESS   POOR PERFORMER

HIGHLY RECOMMENDED — PERFORMANCE — TESTERS' COMMENTS

KITCHENAID 5-Speed Blender
Model: KSB580
Price: $149.99
Jar material and capacity:
Polycarbonate, 56 ounces

Ice crushing: ★★★
Smoothie: ★★★
Hummus: ★★★
Speed: ★★★
Sound level: ★★★

A large, powerful machine that aced our three key performance tests. Ice was quickly pulverized into snow, smoothies were lump-free, and hummus was perfectly consistent. Although the blades could not be removed, the entire jar is dishwasher-safe.

RECOMMENDED — PERFORMANCE — TESTERS' COMMENTS

KALORIK BL Blender
Model: 16909
Price: $49.99
Jar material and capacity:
Glass, 50 ounces

Ice crushing: ★★★
Smoothie: ★★
Hummus: ★★★
Speed: ★★
Sound level: ★★★

Excelled at ice crushing and hummus mixing but left pulp in the smoothie. This ultra-quiet blender had six blades—two serrated—and a steeply tapered glass jar that helped keep the contents moving. The removable base and blades made cleaning a breeze.

RECOMMENDED WITH RESERVATIONS — PERFORMANCE — TESTERS' COMMENTS

L'EQUIP RPM Blender
Model: 228
Price: $165.99
Jar material and capacity:
Plastic, 56 ounces

Ice crushing: ★
Smoothie: ★★★
Hummus: ★★★
Speed: ★★★
Sound level: ★

Our past winner sailed through the smoothie and hummus tests but fell seriously short when it came to crushing ice, leaving lots of solid chunks stuck to the walls beyond reach of the blades. This model also lost points for noise.

HAMILTON BEACH Dual Wave Blender
Model: 52147H
Price: $69.99
Jar material and capacity:
Plastic, 80 ounces

Ice crushing: ★★★
Smoothie: ★★★
Hummus: ★
Speed: ★★
Sound level: ★

A huge jar and side-by-side "dual-action" blades. With ice and smoothies, the two blades tag-teamed to pulverize ingredients, but they turned hummus into a frothy drink instead of a purée. Excellent for frozen drinks, but not a good all-purpose blender.

WARING Professional Bar Blender
Model: MBB518
Price: $129.95
Jar material and capacity:
Glass, 40 ounces

Ice crushing: ★
Smoothie: ★★
Hummus: ★★
Speed: ★★
Sound level: ★★★

Struggled to crush ice efficiently; only a middling performer with smoothies and hummus. The clover-leaf-shaped jar was extremely narrow, which made it difficult to remove the hummus.

CUISINART SmartPower Premiere 600-Watt Blender
Model: CBT-500
Price: $99.95
Jar material and capacity:
Glass, 50 ounces

Ice crushing: ★★★
Smoothie: ★★
Hummus: ★
Speed: ★★
Sound level: ★★

Crushed ice with ease, but its bulky, square jar didn't push food to the center, leaving hummus grainy. Unlike standard blenders, to remove this jar you must lift without twisting. If you twist, as some testers mistakenly did, the jar's contents pour out the bottom.

VIKING Professional Blender
Model: VBLG01
Price: $149.95
Jar material and capacity:
Glass, 40 ounces

Ice crushing: ★
Smoothie: ★★
Hummus: ★★
Speed: ★★
Sound level: ★★

Not powerful enough to crush ice, and it left small chunks of mango in the smoothies. The base stands so tall that the model felt unsteady during blending. Jar comes apart for easy cleaning.

NOT RECOMMENDED — PERFORMANCE — TESTERS' COMMENTS

HAMILTON BEACH Liquid Blu 5-Speed Blender
Model: 59207
Price: $59.99
Jar material and capacity:
Glass, 48 ounces

Ice crushing: ★
Smoothie: ★★
Hummus: ★
Speed: ★★
Sound level: ★★

Looked more like a spaceship than a blender—but failed liftoff, performing poorly in both our ice-crushing and hummus tests. Did better with smoothies, but took extra time to fully break down the fruit.

OSTER Counterforms 2-in-1 Appliance
Model: BVLB07-L
Price: $89.99
Jar material and capacity:
Glass, 48 ounces

Ice crushing: ★
Smoothie: ★
Hummus: ★★
Speed: ★
Sound level: ★★

The only blender in the lineup with reversible blades designed to draw food back down into the base. Unfortunately, this feature was ineffective at ice-crushing, and testers had to run the cycle twice to get fruit to break down into smoothies.

BLACK & DECKER Cyclone 12-Speed Blender
Model: BLC12650HB
Price: $29.88
Jar material and capacity:
Glass, 48 ounces

Ice crushing: ★
Smoothie: ★
Hummus: ★★
Speed: ★
Sound level: ★★

Ice jammed the blades, leaving large chunks on top; fruit fibers and seeds clogged the smoothie, and the hummus was grainy. Has 12 push buttons, which were flimsy and difficult to clean, and there wasn't much difference among the speeds.

≥ BY J. KENJI ALT ≤

SCIENCE: Testing Olive Oil's Bitter End

Over the years, we've noticed that when we blend mayonnaise or vinaigrette with extra-virgin olive oil in a food processor or blender, they end up tasting bitter. Did we use over-the-hill olive oil in these cases, or was something else going on?

To verify our observations, we made two batches of aïoli using olive oil from the same freshly opened bottle. We emulsified one batch in a food processor, adding the oil in a slow stream to minced garlic, egg yolks, and lemon juice and processing until creamy. In the second batch, we whisked the olive oil into the other ingredients in a bowl by hand.

RESULTS

Tasters found the batch emulsified in the food processor to be markedly bitter.

EXPLANATION

Extra-virgin olive oil contains bitter-tasting compounds called polyphenols that are normally coated by fatty acids, which prevent them from dispersing in the presence of liquid. When olive oil is broken into droplets in an emulsion, the polyphenols get squeezed out and will disperse in any liquid in the mix, so that their flavor becomes evident. The blades of a food processor break olive oil into much smaller droplets than those created from whisking. The smaller the droplets, the more polyphenols that break free and disperse, and the more bitter an emulsion will taste. (Note: In recipes such as pesto, which contain lots of other robust flavors from herbs, nuts, and cheese, we found that any bitter taste went unnoticed.)

BOTTOM LINE

You can whisk your mayo or dressing entirely by hand—but it's hard to whisk fast enough to form a stable emulsion. To capitalize on the convenience of a food processor, you have two options: Use pure, versus extra-virgin, olive oil, as it has fewer polyphenols (but you'll lose some flavor). Or, process your aïoli or vinaigrette ingredients with vegetable oil just until an emulsion forms, then whisk in extra-virgin olive oil by hand.

SUBSTITUTION: Better Bean Soup from a Can

We find there's a real difference in flavor and texture between dried beans you cook yourself and those out of a can. Dried beans can take on the flavors of the garlic, bay leaves, and other flavorings you add to the water, while canned beans taste of salt and not much else. We all need to take shortcuts sometimes—but when it comes to substituting canned beans for dried in soup, don't be tempted to merely dump them in the pot and think you're done.

We prepared Tuscan white bean soup and black bean soup with canned beans, adding them to the sautéed aromatics and cooking liquid in each recipe and simmering just until they were heated through, about 5 minutes. Not surprisingly, both soups had flat, disappointing flavor. Next, we made another batch of each soup, this time simmering the canned beans for 30 minutes (any longer and the beans began to disintegrate and fall apart). Although these soups could not compare with the rich flavor of soups made with dried beans simmered for hours, they were worlds apart from the first batches.

The bottom line: If you're going to substitute canned beans for dried in soup, make sure you simmer them for 30 minutes so they have enough time to take on the flavor of the other ingredients. If a recipe calls for a pound of dried beans, you'll need 58 ounces of drained, rinsed, canned beans—depending on can size, that's three or four cans.

CANNED SOLUTION
To substitute canned beans for dried in soup, make sure to simmer for 30 minutes.

TEST KITCHEN TIP: Extra-Old Extract

Some people bake enough cookies and cakes to blow through a whole bottle of vanilla extract in just a month, while less enthusiastic bakers may keep the same bottle for years. Does vanilla extract ever go bad or lose potency?

We located 3-year-old and 10-year-old bottles of vanilla extract and compared them with a fresh bottle of the same brand in three of our recipes: yellow cupcakes, vanilla frosting, and chocolate chip cookies. Although the older bottles took a bit of effort to open, once the extract was incorporated into recipes, tasters could detect no difference between the old and the new.

Vanilla extract has a minimum alcohol content of 35 percent, which, according to Matt Nielsen of vanilla manufacturer Nielsen-Massey, makes it the most shelf-stable form of vanilla (beans and paste can lose flavor quickly). It will last indefinitely if stored in a sealed container away from heat and light.

WELL-PRESERVED
This bottle may look old on the ouside, but the extract inside will stay fresh indefinitely.

TECHNIQUE: Two Ways to Melt Chocolate

Melting chocolate can be a dangerous game—let it get too hot and it will break, becoming irretrievably grainy. A heavy-bottomed skillet over a very low flame does the trick, but not every burner is capable of maintaining a low enough heat. Here are two melting techniques we've tested again and again and found to be foolproof.

DOUBLE-BOILER METHOD

1. Bring a pot of water to a near simmer over low heat; set a large heatproof bowl (the edges should overhang the pot for easier removal) over it, making sure that the water does not touch the bottom of the bowl (to avoid overheating the chocolate).

2. Add 8 ounces chocolate chips (or bar chocolate chopped into ½-inch pieces) and heat, stirring occasionally with a rubber spatula, until uniformly smooth and glossy, about 10 minutes (adjust the cooking time as necessary for larger or smaller amounts of chocolate). If the recipe calls for melting the chocolate with butter, add both to the bowl at the same time.

MICROWAVE METHOD

1. Put 8 ounces chocolate chips (or bar chocolate chopped into ½-inch pieces) in a large microwave-safe bowl. Microwave at high power for 45 seconds.

2. Stir with a rubber spatula, scraping down the sides of the bowl, then heat 30 seconds more. Continue heating and stirring for 15-second intervals until the chocolate is uniformly smooth and glossy. (To melt smaller or larger amounts, decrease or increase the initial microwaving time by 10 seconds for every 2 ounces of chocolate.) If the recipe calls for melting the chocolate with butter, do not add the butter until the chocolate is almost completely melted. (Adding the butter earlier will cause it to splatter.)

Best Vanilla Practices

Does it matter when you add vanilla extract as you make baked goods and other sweets? As we researched vanilla for our tasting (see page 26), manufacturers told us that to maximize flavor, the extract should be added while creaming the butter and sugar for cakes and cookies. Their theory: If you add vanilla with butter, much of its flavor gets captured by the butterfat instead of evaporating during baking. We tested this claim by comparing two batches of sugar cookies and yellow layer cake, one made with the vanilla added after creaming the butter and sugar and the other with the extract added as the butter and sugar creamed. As much as we love small tweaks that lead to big differences, tasters could detect no difference between the finished baked goods.

On the other hand, when we repeated a similar experiment with pudding, crème brûlée, and flan, timing did make a difference: Stirring the extract into the cold custard base before cooking not only gave the volatile vanilla compounds too much time to evaporate, the prolonged exposure to heat also drove off flavor. Adding the extract after the custard base was removed from the heat yielded more intense vanilla flavor.

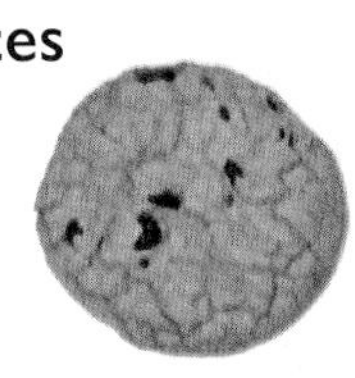

ADD VANILLA ANYTIME
When you add vanilla to cookie or cake batter doesn't impact flavor.

SAVE VANILLA FOR LAST
For more intense vanilla flavor in custard-based desserts, add it after cooking.

Pre- vs. Fresh-Grated Parmesan

We've never been tempted by the tasteless powdered Parmesan that comes in a green can—and in tests, we've found that the higher-grade pregrated cheese in the refrigerator section of the supermarket is uneven in quality. But what about pregrating or grinding your own Parmesan to always have at the ready? Do you sacrifice any flavor for convenience? To find out, we divided a block of Parmigiano-Reggiano in two, reducing one half to a powder in a food processor and leaving the other whole. We stored both the solid and grated cheese in the refrigerator for two weeks, then compared them side by side mixed into polenta, added to breading for chicken Milanese, and on their own. After two weeks of storage, tasters were hard-pressed to detect a difference between the cheeses, even in the side-by-side tasting. But after a full month of storage, tasters found a noticeable drop-off in flavor.

The bottom line: Pregrating is fine, as long as you don't store the cheese longer than two to three weeks. To grind Parmesan, cut a block into 1-inch chunks. Place the chunks in a food processor (no more than 1 pound at a time) and process until ground into coarse particles, about 20 seconds. Refrigerate in an airtight container until ready to use.

TASTING: **Brown Rice Varieties**

Brown rice is nothing more than white rice with the bran layer left intact. Like white rice, it comes in different varieties. After cooking our way through the four most common types (see the chart below), we discovered that the cooking times and liquid-to-rice ratios were comparable for each—they cooked in about 65 minutes, using our oven-baked method and 3¼ cups of liquid per 1½ cups of rice. Texture and flavor, however, varied considerably.

BROWN RICE TYPE		TEXTURE	FLAVOR
Basmati	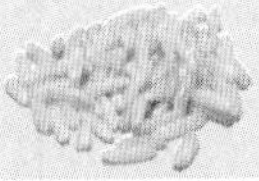	Distinctly separate grains with an elastic, almost spongy texture	Mildly sweet with clean nut and barley flavors
Short Grain		Soft and creamy with a starchiness similar to that of risotto	Very sweet and malty-tasting
Long Grain	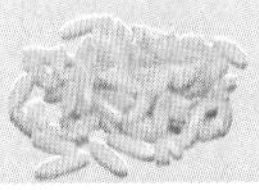	Very firm, separate grains with almost no elasticity	Earthy-tasting with a slightly chalky finish
Jasmine		Moderately firm, separate grains	Nutty, buttery, and rich-tasting

Picking Proper Porcini

Our recipe for Sautéed Chicken Cutlets with Porcini Sauce (page 20) served as a reminder that, like fresh fruits and vegetables, the quality of dried porcini mushrooms can vary dramatically from package to package and brand to brand. Always inspect the mushrooms before you buy.

PREVIOUSLY OCCUPIED
Small holes indicate that the mushroom was maybe home to pinworms.

CLEAN & CLEAR
Look for large, smooth porcini, free of worm holes, dust, and grit.

TECHNIQUE

HOW TO JULIENNE CARROTS AND LEEKS

Our recipe for Cod Baked in Foil with Leeks and Carrots (page 13) relies on vegetables cut into thin matchsticks that are just the right size—too thick and they won't cook through; too thin and they'll turn mushy. Here's an easy way to achieve uniform ⅛-inch pieces.

CARROTS
1. Peel, then cut carrot into 2-inch segments. Cut thin slice from each segment to create flat base.

2. Using knuckles of non-knife hand to steady carrot, cut each segment into ⅛-inch-thick planks.

3. Working with 3 planks at a time, stack planks and cut into ⅛-inch-thick matchsticks.

LEEKS 
1. Trim dark green top and bottom ¼ inch of root end from leek, then cut into 2-inch segments.

2. Halve each segment lengthwise and rinse under cold water to remove sediment.

3. Working with 3 to 4 layers at a time, stack layers, then fold in half crosswise and cut into ⅛-inch-thick matchsticks.

Cooking with Cottage Cheese

Our Baked Ziti recipe (page 15) calls for whole-milk cottage cheese, which tasters preferred over the more traditional choice, ricotta. If all you have on hand is 1 percent or nonfat cottage cheese, does it make a difference in this or other cooked applications?

We prepared three different batches of three recipes—our Baked Ziti; spinach lasagna bound with a cottage cheese-and-egg mixture; and low-fat cheesecake made with a blend of cream cheese and cottage cheese—using whole-milk, 1 percent, and nonfat cottage cheese. Tasters detected almost no difference in the cheesecakes, though the lower-fat cakes tended to set a little more firmly. Ziti and lasagna were a different story. Both the whole-milk and 1 percent cottage cheeses produced acceptable results, but the nonfat cottage cheese broke as the pasta baked, leaving a grainy, watery slick at the bottom of the dish. Our advice? When cooking with cottage cheese, skip the nonfat variety.

EQUIPMENT CORNER

≥ BY PEGGY CHUNG COLLIER ≤

EQUIPMENT UPDATE Garlic Press

Last year, we named Kuhn Rikon's Epicurean Garlic Press ($34.95) our favorite for producing uniform minced garlic with minimal effort and an easy-to-clean hopper. Since then, the company has introduced its Easy-Squeeze Garlic Press ($20), which claims to require 60 percent less effort than the original model. Taking the challenge, we pressed peeled and unpeeled garlic in new and old models. The new model came out the champ. Simple physics explains why: A longer handle and a shorter distance between the pivot point and the plunger help make pressing less work. The curving plastic handles are also much easier to squeeze together than the straighter metal handles of the old model. One flaw: Garlic sometimes oozed out of the sides, whereas the old model pushed through perfectly minced garlic every time. Nevertheless, we like the Easy-Squeeze's ergonomic features and friendly price enough to name it our new favorite.

GARLIC'S NEW MAIN SQUEEZE
The Kuhn Rikon Easy-Squeeze Garlic Press is cheaper and easier to use than its predecessor.

EQUIPMENT TESTING
Electric Egg Cookers

It doesn't take an expert to boil or poach eggs, but it does take good timing. Like rice cookers, electric egg cookers eliminate the need to watch the clock by controlling the heat and turning off automatically. The amount of water added determines the consistency of the egg—hard-, medium-, soft-boiled, or poached. We tested six models. All boiled eggs without creating a green ring around the yolk (a sign of overcooking). But the similarities ended there. One model could boil just four eggs at a time—and leaked; two others boiled perfectly, but poached eggs came out spongy or overcooked; a fourth had a too-tight lid that nearly burned our tester as she tried to remove it; the fifth cooked too slowly. Our favorite was the West Bend Automatic Egg Cooker ($24.99). It produces a maximum of either seven perfectly boiled eggs in 17 minutes or four perfectly poached eggs in 7.5 minutes, has a pleasantly audible timer, and is easy to use.

EGGS-PRESS
The West Bend Automatic Egg Cooker quickly poaches and hard-cooks eggs to perfection.

EQUIPMENT TESTING Funnels

In the test kitchen, we use funnels to transfer liquids and oils, fill pepper mills, and refill spice bottles. But poorly designed funnels can back up or wobble when filled, and they are often bulky to store. We tested seven brands, including funnel sets, collapsible and flexible silicone models, and one that offers a spout that opens and closes. Our favorite was the Progressive Collapsible Funnel ($6.49). It has a generous 1-cup capacity, smooth and sturdy walls to let liquid and dried herbs slide down easily, and a 1-centimeter-wide spout that is narrow enough to fit into most small-necked bottles, yet wide enough to prevent backup of thicker liquids. It collapses from 5 inches to 1¾ inches, making storage easy.

FUNNELING INNOVATION
The Progressive Collapsible Funnel transfers liquids and spices without mess, then collapses to fit in a drawer.

EQUIPMENT TESTING
Innovative Teapots

We tested four small teapots with unusual strainers and dispensing mechanisms that promised to make dealing with loose tea mess-free. In each case, we used the same tea and a four-minute steeping time. The glass Bodum Assam Teapot ($24.95), which makes 2 cups per pot, presses tea like a French coffee press—but it traps the strongest tea inside the solid, closed bottom of the press insert, producing weaker tea than the other pots. The BonJour Smart Brewer ($19.95) was fussy; if the lid of this 1-cup brewer didn't click perfectly into place, tea leaked out the bottom valve. The Easy Pot by Northwest Glass Designs ($16.50) couldn't brew even 1 full cup and didn't contain loose leaves well. Our favorite, the inge-nuiTEA by Adagio Teas ($14.95), met all criteria. It brewed 2 cups of good, strong tea and kept loose leaves in check with its ultra-fine-mesh strainer. To use, add tea leaves and water, let steep, and then place the pot over a cup to automatically open a bottom valve—brewed tea will flow into the cup below.

NOT YOUR GRANDMOTHER'S TEAPOT
The ingenuiTEA by Adagio Teas makes tea dregs a thing of the past.

EQUIPMENT TESTING
Counter Protectors

Do you really need an extra piece of equipment to protect your countertop, or will a heavy cloth suffice? Using a hot Dutch oven, a large rimmed baking sheet, and a 12-inch skillet, we tested eight counter protectors (some were raised trivets, others had a flat design) in materials that ranged from old-fashioned braided cloth to wood, cast iron, and silicone. Our finding: Models made with silicone perform best. They resisted skidding and kept the pan from sliding, cleaned up easily, prevented a buildup of condensation on the counter (a problem with braided cloth), and even doubled as potholders. Magnetic counter protectors were our least favorite, as they stuck to cookware too well—a tester nearly burned her hand trying to remove one that had attached itself to the edge of the pan instead of the bottom. Our favorite was the Big HotSpot Silicone Counter Cover ($15), a large silicone pad that withstood the heat of a 500-degree pot.

Sources

The following are mail-order sources for items recommended in this issue. Prices were current at press time and do not include shipping and handling. Contact companies to confirm information or visit www.cooksillustrated.com for updates.

PAGE 9: VERTICAL ROASTER
- Norpro Vertical Roaster with Infuser: $27.95, item #303876, Cooking.com (800-663-8810, www.cooking.com).

PAGE 23: BOWL SCRAPER
- iSi Basics Silicone Scraper Spatula: $5.99, item #B10002, iSi Store (800-211-9608, www.isi-store.com).

PAGE 29: BLENDERS
- KitchenAid 5-Speed Blender: $149.99, item #23244, Chef's Catalog (800-338-3232, www.chefscatalog.com).
- Kalorik BL Blender: $49.99, item #rik1027, Cookware.com (888-478-4606, www.cookware.com).

PAGE 32: GARLIC PRESS
- Kuhn Rikon Easy-Squeeze Garlic Press: $20, item #592527, Sur La Table (800-243-0852, www.surlatable.com).

PAGE 32: EGG COOKER
- West Bend Automatic Egg Cooker: $24.99, item #86628, Target.com (800-591-3869, www.target.com).

PAGE 32: FUNNEL
- Progressive Collapsible Funnel: $6.49, item #793011, Cooking.com.

PAGE 32: TEAPOT
- Adagio Teas ingenuiTEA Dispensing Teapot: $14.95, item #500261, Cooking.com.

PAGE 32: COUNTER PROTECTOR
- Big HotSpot Silicone Counter Cover: $15, item #07088, Lamson & Goodnow (800-872-6564, www.lamsonsharp.com).

INDEX
March & April 2009

RECIPES

🎥 **COOK'S LIVE** Original Test Kitchen Videos **www.cooksillustrated.com**

AMERICA'S TEST KITCHEN
Public television's most popular cooking show
Join the millions of home cooks who watch our show,
America's Test Kitchen, on public television every week.
For more information, including recipes and program
times, visit www.americastestkitchen.com.

French Mashed Potatoes, 19

Roast Beef Tenderloin, 7

Ciabatta, 24

The Best Easy Chocolate Cake, 25

Pan-Seared Thick-Cut Pork Chops, 11

Sautéed Chicken Cutlets with Porcini Sauce, 20

Baked Ziti, 15

Glazed Roast Chicken, 9

Cod Baked in Foil, 13

Brown Rice with Onions and Red Peppers, 21

PHOTOGRAPHY: CARL TREMBLAY, STYLING: MARIE PIRAINO

Purple Haze

Round

Nantes

White Satin

Kamaran

Imperator

Sugar Snack

Cosmic Purple

Yellowstone

Atomic Red

Chantenay

CARROTS

NUMBER NINETY-EIGHT

MAY & JUNE 2009

COOK'S
ILLUSTRATED

Italian Grilled
Chicken

Quick Tomato Sauce
Big, Fresh Flavor in 15 Minutes

Foolproof Grilled
Salmon
Nonstick Method Superheats Grill

Cookware Sets
Is $700 Better than $145?

Blueberry Muffins

Chocolate Chip
Cookies, Reinvented
We Retool the Toll House Recipe

Complete Guide to
Marinating

Chocolate Chip Taste Test
Ultra-Crisp Shrimp Tempura
Grilled Beef Teriyaki
Maple-Glazed Pork Tenderloin

www.cooksillustrated.com

$5.95 U.S./$6.95 CANADA

0 6>

0 74470 62805 7

CONTENTS

May & June 2009

COOK'S ILLUSTRATED

www.cooksillustrated.com

Founder and Editor	Christopher Kimball
Editorial Director	Jack Bishop
Executive Editor	Amanda Agee
Test Kitchen Director	Erin McMurrer
Managing Editor	Rebecca Hays
Senior Editors	Keith Dresser
	Lisa McManus
Features Editor	Lisa Glazer
Copy Editor	Amy Graves
Associate Editors	J. Kenji Alt
	Bryan Roof
Test Cooks	Francisco J. Robert
	Yvonne Ruperti
Assistant Test Kitchen Director	Matthew Herron
Assistant Editors	Meredith Butcher
	Peggy Chung Collier
Assistant Test Cook	Marcus Walser
Executive Assistant	Meredith Smith
Editorial Assistant	Abbey Becker
Senior Kitchen Assistant	Nadia Domeq
Kitchen Assistants	Maria Elena Delgado
	Ena Gudiel
	Edward Tundidor
Producer	Melissa Baldino
Contributing Editors	Matthew Card
	Dawn Yanagihara
Consulting Editor	Scott Brueggeman
Science Editor	Guy Crosby, Ph.D.
Proofreader	Holly Hartman
Managing Editor, Special Issues	Todd Meier
Production Editor, Special Issues	Elizabeth Bomze
Online Managing Editor	David Tytell
Online Editor	Kate Mason
Online Media Producer	Peter Tannenbaum
Online Associate Editor	Leaya Lee
Online Editorial Assistant	Mari Levine
Design Director	Amy Klee
Art Director, Magazines	Julie Bozzo
Designers	Jay Layman
	Lindsey Timko
Deputy Art Director, Marketing/Web	Christine Vo
Staff Photographer	Daniel J. van Ackere
Vice President Marketing	David Mack
Circulation Director	Doug Wicinski
Circulation & Fulfillment Manager	Carrie Horan
Circulation Assistant	Megan Cooley
Partnership Marketing Manager	Pamela Putprush
Direct Mail Director	Adam Perry
Product Operations Director	Steven Browall
Product Promotions Director	Randi Lawrence
E-Commerce Marketing Director	Hugh Buchan
E-Commerce Marketing Manager	Laurel Zeidman
Marketing Copywriter	David Goldberg
Customer Service Manager	Jacqueline Valerio
Customer Service Representatives	Jillian Nannicelli
	Kate Sokol
Sponsorship Sales Director	Marcy McCreary
Retail Sales & Marketing Manager	Emily Logan
Corporate Marketing Associate	Bailey Vatalaro
Production Director	Guy Rochford
Traffic & Projects Manager	Alice Carpenter
Senior Production Manager	Jessica L. Quirk
Production & Imaging Specialists	Judy Blomquist
	Lauren Pettapiece
Imaging & Color Specialist	Andrew Mannone
Technology Director	Rocco Lombardo
Systems Administrator	S. Paddi McHugh
Web Production Coordinator	Evan Davis
Support Technician	Brandon Lynch
Chief Financial Officer	Sharyn Chabot
Human Resources Director	Adele Shapiro
Controller	Mandy Shito
Senior Accountant	Aaron Goranson
Staff Accountant	Connie Forbes
Accounts Payable Specialist	Steven Kasha
Office Manager	Tasha Bere
Receptionist	Henrietta Murray
Publicity	Deborah Broide

For list rental information, contact: Specialists Marketing Services, Inc., 777 Terrace Ave., 4th Floor, Hasbrouck Heights, NJ 07604; 201-865-5800.

Editorial Office: 17 Station St., Brookline, MA 02445; 617-232-1000; fax 617-232-1572. Subscription inquiries, visit www.americas testkitchen.com/customerservice or call 800-526-8442.

Postmaster: Send all new orders, subscription inquiries, and change-of-address notices to Cook's Illustrated, P.O. Box 7446, Red Oak, IA 51591-0446.

PRINTED IN THE USA

MESCLUN GREENS Once relegated to specialty markets, young, small mesclun greens now populate grocery shelves. The pale ivory center of frisée, or curly endive, is great for eating raw, but the bitter, green tangle of outer leaves is best cooked. Peppery notes prevail in watercress, though leggy examples sometimes have mineral or soapy qualities. The young, tender leaves of the common dandelion make a great addition to salads. A hint of celery characterizes baby red chard leaves. Tatsoi, or rosette bok choy, gets its name from its growth pattern of concentric circles, like rose petals. The coral-like ruffles of baby lola rosa, much like the crimps of baby red oak leaf lettuce, make optimal dressing-catchers. Sorrel bursts with sharp citrus notes. Salads brighten with the herbaceous addition of mizuna. Ultra-tender mâche is mild and clean-tasting, but must not be dressed too early, or it will wilt. Though milder, baby red romaine has the same slightly mineral flavor of mature romaine.

COVER (Strawberries): Robert Papp, BACK COVER (Mesclun Greens): John Burgoyne

America's Test Kitchen is a very real 2,500-square-foot kitchen located just outside of Boston. It is the home of *Cook's Illustrated* and *Cook's Country* magazines and is the workday destination for more than three dozen test cooks, editors, and cookware specialists. Our mission is to test recipes over and over again until we understand how and why they work and until we arrive at the best version. We also test kitchen equipment and supermarket ingredients in search of brands that offer the best value and performance. You can watch us work by tuning in to *America's Test Kitchen* (www.americastestkitchen.com) on public television.

VOLUNTEERS OF AMERICA

My sister-in-law is married to Scott Taylor, who grew up in Gaysville, Vermont. When he was in the sixth grade, he watched the three-story Track and Trail building—it had served in previous incarnations as the town hall and the schoolhouse—burn to the ground next door to his home. Neighbors helped to evacuate the contents of the house in minutes, and he watched awestruck as his dad strapped the refrigerator to his back with a rope and walked it outside. Then, from across the street, he saw something that changed his life. In the 8-foot gap between the burning building and his house, firefighters standing in harm's way used pike poles to push a collapsing wall away to save his home.

Today, in addition to working at the factory in Bethel Mills, Scott is Assistant Fire Chief. The work is hard, especially in winter when his coat and helmet often get so frozen that when he takes them off, they can stand upright in the road, the helmet fused to the coat. A few weeks ago, one of his firefighter friends tried to get into a burning house through a locked sliding-glass door by throwing lawn furniture at it. The glass had been so tempered by the fire that the furniture broke with barely a crack in the glass. But there are lighter moments too: a bit of slapstick, pranks played on the fire chief, a snowball fight, the humor found in the odd comment that keeps their minds off the long hours of waiting until sunup when they often begin the search for bodies.

In America, most of us are just a generation away from the idyll that life can be in a small town. Scott spent summers at the Twin Bridges swimming hole, jumping off rocks 35 feet above the clear, cold water. Clarence Guy, his grandfather, rang the church bell every Sunday, and Halloween was spent mostly at the schoolhouse where they dunked for apples and drank Morris Thompson's homemade cider (there were few houses in town so the "take" was on the low side). The great flood of 1927 took out the hydroelectric dam, the local factory (buttons, then lightbulbs, then clothing) and the 19-mile Peavine Railroad, which started at Bethel and ran through town, meandering up to Rochester like a pea vine. (Or, as a Yankee of few words once said, "Sir, where the railway was, the river is.") Scott's grandmother took the train to school as a kid.

Adrienne and I attend the annual firemen's dinner in our town, and last year at the event I ran into Tiger Skidmore, a neighbor who volunteers for fire departments in three different towns. He has the volunteer bug so bad that on his wedding day, just as he was about to walk down the aisle, his pager went off and his friends watched in awe as he started over toward his pickup to respond. They quickly got him turned around. (he still doesn't see what all the fuss was about).

Firehouses have to raise funds continually, so in Scott's town they hold the annual Haw Hee talent show with stand-up routines and stocky men in funny costumes, including Ed Bean, the fire chief, dressed in a straw hat and denim overalls in imitation of Grandpa Bean. In our village, the firehouse still puts on chicken dinners, barbecues, bingo, and the annual Old Home Day parade and carnival, complete with the "Win a Cake!" contest (bet 25 cents on the spinning wheel); "Win a Goldfish!" featuring yellow rubber ducks (almost everybody wins and then you have to buy the goldfish bowl); plenty of homemade "fast" food including fried dough, hand-cut French fries, maple syrup milkshakes, and cotton candy; and a country and western band featuring a cowgirl playing the fiddle and a drum set with a Wyoming landscape. You can bet good money that the first song will be "Okie from Muscogee." Older folks look on, seated in collapsible lawn chairs, much like distinguished visitors at an inauguration.

In small towns across America, most of the municipal offices are volunteer or pretty close to it, considering the short money: the select board, the zoning administrator (the worst job in town), the town clerk, the rescue squad, constable, etc. In

Christopher Kimball

our town, volunteers organize the Town Hall Christmas Party, the annual tag sale for the church, last-minute pancake breakfasts to help with a neighbor's medical bills, and the annual clean-up day, to say nothing of helping to get in the hay, especially last summer when it threatened rain almost every day.

In the country, it's how you spend your time, not your money, that counts, whether you are completing the 180-hour firefighter training course or cooking for the church dinner, the one that offers roast pork, Jell-O salad as a vegetable, and pineapple fluff cake for dessert. Being poor, hungry, sick, or short a paycheck never stopped Scott's parents or grandparents from getting up early and doing what needed to be done. When his grandmother was stranded seven miles away in the next town after the '27 flood, she simply walked home. Somebody had to feed the kids.

I once heard a story about a call that came in from a firebox on a street corner, and two fire stations were dispatched. When the first company pulled up, they saw a little boy standing at the firebox on the seat of his tricycle. When they went up to him, they quickly realized that he was the son of one of the firefighters on the other truck. When asked what was wrong, he replied, "I just wanted to see my daddy!" *

That boy knew his dad was both a volunteer and a hero—not heroic in the grand scheme of things, perhaps, but where it really matters: in a small town, in a small state. In an age when we think that we can simply buy our way out of trouble, Scott and others remind us that Americans once built something out of nothing, that kids grew up proud, and that if you called in a fire, you would soon see some folks you know showing up in a big red truck, and one of them, riding shotgun, would probably be your daddy.

* Story courtesy of Roland LaFrance, Redford, N.Y.

FOR INQUIRIES, ORDERS, OR MORE INFORMATION

www.cooksillustrated.com

At www.cooksillustrated.com, you can order books and subscriptions, sign up for our free e-newsletter, or renew your magazine subscription. Join the website and gain access to 16 years of *Cook's Illustrated* recipes, equipment tests, and ingredient tastings, as well as Cook's Live companion videos for every recipe in this issue.

COOKBOOKS

We sell more than 50 cookbooks by the editors of *Cook's Illustrated*. To order, visit our bookstore at www.cooksillustrated.com or call 800-611-0759 (or 515-246-6911 from outside the U.S.).

COOK'S ILLUSTRATED Magazine

Cook's Illustrated magazine (ISSN 1068-2821), number 98, is published bimonthly by Boston Common Press Limited Partnership, 17 Station St., Brookline, MA 02445. Copyright 2009 Boston Common Press Limited Partnership. Periodicals postage paid at Boston, Mass., and additional mailing offices USPS #012487. Publications Mail Agreement No. 40020778. Return undeliverable Canadian addresses to P.O. Box 875, Station A, Windsor, ON N9A 6P2. POSTMASTER: Send address changes to Cook's Illustrated, P.O. Box 7446, Red Oak, IA 51591-0446. For subscription and gift subscription orders, subscription inquiries, or change-of-address notices, call 800-526-8442 in the U.S. or 515-247-7571 from outside the U.S. or write us at Cook's Illustrated, P.O. Box 7446, Red Oak, IA 51591-0446.

Salted versus Unsalted Butter

Is it OK to replace unsalted (sweet cream) butter with salted butter if I reduce the total amount of salt in the recipe?

JOYCE CLUTTER
STREETSBORO, OHIO

➤ We advise against cooking with salted butter for three reasons. First, the amount of salt in salted butter varies from brand to brand—it can range from 1.25 percent to 1.75 percent of the total weight, making it impossible to offer conversion amounts that will work with all brands. Second, because salt masks some of the flavor nuances found in butter, salted butter tastes different from unsalted butter. Finally, salted butter almost always contains more water than unsalted butter. The water in butter ranges from 10 to 18 percent. In baking, butter with a low water content is preferred, since excess water can interfere with the development of gluten. In fact, when we used the same brand of both salted and unsalted butter to make brownies and drop biscuits, tasters noticed that samples made with salted butter were a little mushy and pasty; they preferred the texture of baked goods made with unsalted butter.

Apple Cider versus Apple Juice

What is the difference between apple cider and apple juice? Can I use them interchangeably?

EDITH LI
HOUSTON, TEXAS

➤ To make cider, apples are simply cored, chopped, mashed, and then pressed to extract their liquid. Most cider is pasteurized before sale, though unpasteurized cider is also available. To make apple juice, manufacturers follow the same steps used to make cider, but they also filter the extracted liquid to remove pulp and sediment. Apple juice is then pasteurized, and potassium sorbate (a preservative) is often mixed in to prevent fermentation. Finally, apple juice is sometimes sweetened with sugar or corn syrup.

We tried using unsweetened apple juice in recipes for pork chops and glazed ham that call for cider. Tasters were turned off by excessive sweetness in the dishes made with apple juice, unanimously preferring those made with cider. This made sense: The filtration process used in making juice removes some of the complex, tart, and bitter flavors that are still present in cider. (When we tested the pH level of both liquids, the cider had a lower pH than the apple juice, confirming its higher level of acidity.) The bottom line: When it comes to cooking, don't swap apple juice for cider.

Xanthan Gum

What is xanthan gum, and why is it used in recipes?

PEG SCOTT
BROOKLYN, N.Y.

XANTHAN GUM
A few teaspoons add lift and elasticity to gluten-free baked goods.

➤ Xanthan gum is a polysaccharide—a chain of complex carbohydrates produced during the fermentation of corn syrup by the bacterium *Xanthomonas campestris*. Lately, it has been turning up at fine-dining restaurants in foams, gels, and other creative applications. However, it has also long been used as a thickener, emulsifier, and stabilizer in the commercial production of foods ranging from ketchup to salad dressing and ice cream.

In home kitchens, this powdery substance is most commonly used in gluten-free recipes for its supposed ability to add lift and glutenlike elasticity to baked goods. When we added xanthan gum to zucchini and banana breads made with gluten-free rice flour, we weren't crazy about the finished products, but the loaves weren't nearly as dense and heavy as the same breads made without it. Xanthan gum can be purchased at some supermarkets and at natural foods stores.

Blanching Vegetables

I have heard that when you blanch green vegetables, you should not cover the pot. Is this true, or is it just an old wives' tale?

HILLARY FEMAL
TAMPA, FLA.

➤ Blanching involves briefly dunking fruits or vegetables in boiling water to set color, flavor, and texture. Some sources say that to successfully blanch green vegetables, the lid must be kept off of the pot to allow the acids they contain to evaporate, rather than trapping them in the cooking water and turning the vegetables brown.

To examine the validity of this claim, we blanched batches of broccoli, green beans, and broccoli rabe in both covered and uncovered pots. After blanching, the pH (acid) level of the water in both pots was identical for each vegetable. Moreover, all of the vegetables were bright green, and the covered and uncovered batches tasted exactly the same. The bottom line: When it comes to blanching, it makes not a whit of difference whether you cover the pot or not.

Cooking with Savory

What is savory and what does it taste like? If I can't find it at the supermarket, what would be a good substitute?

ANUSUYA BABN
LANSING, MICH.

➤ Native to the Mediterranean region, savory is an aromatic herb found in two varieties: winter and summer. The types are quite similar, though the flavor of the latter is slightly more delicate, and the former has a coarser texture. To find a substitute, we started by asking a panel of tasters to release the scent of the herb (we chose the more widely available summer savory) by rubbing the leaves between their fingers to draw out essential oils. Then they tasted the herb. Although savory is in the mint family, most tasters detected a stronger resemblance to thyme and sage.

To find out if a combination of thyme and sage could substitute for savory, we made batches of sausage stuffing and chicken soup with that combination and with the real thing. We replaced the 3 teaspoons of chopped fresh summer savory leaves in each recipe with 2 teaspoons of chopped fresh thyme leaves and 1 teaspoon of chopped fresh sage leaves. Sampled side by side, tasters approved of the substitution, claiming that the thyme-sage combination was nearly identical to savory.

SAVORY SUBSTITUTE
Replace summer savory with 2 parts fresh thyme to 1 part fresh sage.

Better-Tasting Leftovers

In your September/October 2008 issue, you addressed the fact that soups and stews often taste better after they are cooled and reheated. In a similar vein, I've puzzled over "seasoning" soups and stews or "ripening" quick breads before freezing. I often make extra batches to freeze and use at a later time and have always wondered: Is it better to wait a few days before freezing them?

CAROLYN JACOBSEN
LOS GATOS, CALIF.

➤ We previously determined that the flavor of soups and stews improves over time because many chemical reactions that produce flavor enhancers continue to take place during the cooling process. According to our science editor, however, those reactions slow way down once the food is cold and stop completely when it is frozen.

To test his claim, we made two batches each of chili and banana bread, then froze one batch right after cooling it and refrigerated the other for three days before freezing. Despite the ability of food to continue to build some flavor in the refrigerator, most of the changes happen during the initial cooling period, and a tasting revealed no noticeable differences among the samples. In addition, foods like banana bread will stale somewhat after just a day or two, so it's better not to wait before freezing. Finally, bacteria develop as foods sit in the refrigerator, so the safest course of action is not to delay: Freeze foods as soon as they have cooled to room temperature.

Cold Brew Iced Tea

In the summer, I make iced tea almost every day. I have seen Lipton Cold Brew tea in the supermarket and wondered if it could save me some time. Do you recommend this product?

CHRIS DANKULICH
BEDFORD, MASS.

➤Our go-to method for making iced tea is to brew an extra-strong batch of regular tea and then stir in ice, which simultaneously cools the tea and dilutes it to just the right strength. But what if we could skip the cumbersome heating and cooling steps? Lipton Cold Brew tea promises just that—full-strength iced tea brewed in just 3 minutes, using cold water.

We held a blind tasting with Lipton Cold Brew tea, brewed according to package directions, versus Lipton Yellow Label tea and Twinings English Breakfast tea (our winning brand for drinking hot without milk), brewed via our go-to method. Both the Twinings and Lipton Yellow Label had fans, but tasters unanimously deemed the Lipton Cold Brew their least favorite, complaining of "lots of sediment" and "no flavor at all." Cold brewing may be a nice idea, but we'll choose flavor over convenience any day.

COLD BREW LEFT US COLD

Baking Soda as Odor Absorber

Can baking soda really remove unpleasant odors from the refrigerator or freezer?

ENRIQUE CARLO
SAN ANTONIO, TEXAS

➤Baking soda is sodium bicarbonate, an alkali used as a leavening agent in baking. To test whether it can also absorb or neutralize odors from the refrigerator or freezer, we placed equal amounts of sour milk, stinky cheese, and spoiled fish into two airtight containers, then added an open box of baking soda to one container and left the second alone. We sealed the samples and let them sit overnight at room temperature. Finally, we asked a panel of "sniffers" to

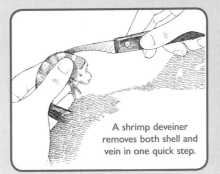
smell each container after 24 hours and again after 48 hours, removing the boxes of baking soda each time. The results were inconclusive, with some sniffers claiming they couldn't detect much difference and others swearing they could.

As it turns out, food scientists, including *Washington Post* columnist Robert Wolke, dismiss the notion that baking soda has deodorizing power in the fridge. In his book *What Einstein Told His Cook 2*, Wolke writes that while baking soda does neutralize acids, the likelihood of gaseous molecules from acidic sour milk migrating through the refrigerator and interacting with the baking soda is slight. He also concludes that no single chemical has the ability to deactivate all of the complex, gaseous chemicals that smell bad.

ODOR EATER?
Baking soda is ineffective at removing odors in the fridge.

But don't rule out baking soda altogether. When this alkaline powder comes into direct contact with smells, it can make a difference. We recently tested different approaches to removing garlic and onion smells from a cutting board (July/August 2007) and found scrubbing with a paste of 1 tablespoon baking soda and 1 teaspoon water to be the most effective.

Bleached versus Unbleached Flour

What is the difference between bleached and unbleached flour, and should I buy one over the other?

MICHAEL JURLANDO
PROSPECT, KY.

➤When flour is first milled, it has a yellowish cast that some consumers find unappealing. Within a few months of milling, however, these carotenoids, or pigments, in all-purpose flour naturally whiten. Because it is expensive to naturally "age" flour, some producers expedite the process chemically. In flours labeled "bleached," benzoyl peroxide has likely been used to fade the yellow color. In baking tests, bleached flour was criticized for tasting flat or having "off" flavors (texturally, the flours behaved the same). These characteristics, however, were much harder to detect in recipes with a high proportion of ingredients other than flour, such as cornbread or oatmeal cookies.

To find out if bleached flour would compromise the flavor or texture of a savory sauce, we made batches of basic white sauce (béchamel) using 1 tablespoon of bleached or unbleached flour per cup of milk. We tasted the sauces plain as well as in lasagna Bolognese. In both instances, tasters pronounced the sauces identical in flavor and texture. Our conclusion: It's fine to use small amounts of bleached flour to thicken sauces, but avoid using it for baking.

The Science of Staling

When baked goods go stale, why does bread turn hard, while crackers soften?

JOSEBA ENCABO
MARLBORO, N.Y.

➤According to our science editor, crackers are manufactured to be very dry to make them shelf-stable. Once the package is opened and the crackers are exposed to air, their sugars and starches start to absorb ambient moisture. After a few days, the once-crisp crackers will be soft and soggy.

When bread turns stale, an entirely different process takes place. Once exposed to air, bread starch undergoes a process called retrogradation: The starch molecules in the bread begin to crystallize and absorb moisture, turning the bread hard and crumbly.

SEND US YOUR QUESTIONS We will provide a complimentary one-year subscription for each letter we print. Send your inquiry, name, address, and daytime telephone number to Notes from Readers, Cook's Illustrated, P.O. Box 470589, Brookline, MA 02447 or to notesfromreaders@americastest kitchen.com.

Quick Tips

⇒ COMPILED BY FRANCISCO J. ROBERT AND YVONNE RUPERTI ⇐

Using Up Leftover Meat

Instead of tossing out scraps of cured meat such as dry sausage or prosciutto, Jeffrey Held of Spokane, Wash., places leftovers in a zipper-lock bag and stores them in the freezer. When making tomato sauce, soups, or stews, he adds the meat to the simmering pot for extra flavor.

Reminder to Turn Off the Grill

MaryAnn Grecco of El Paso, Texas, often found herself in a hot spot whenever she forgot to turn off the gas tank after grilling. She now jogs her memory by slipping a rubber band around the knob of the gas tank. When she turns the tank on, she places the rubber band around her wrist, only removing it when she turns the tank off. As long as she's wearing the rubber band, she knows that the tank is on.

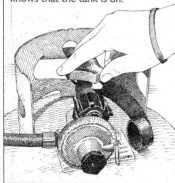

Lighting a Charcoal Fire

Kenneth Mora of Buffalo, N.Y., offers a method for lighting a charcoal fire that also happens to be a great way to use up stale potato chips.

Arrange 2 cups of plain potato chips in a coffee filter and place the filter in the bottom of a charcoal grill. Place a chimney starter on top of the chips, fill the chimney with charcoal, and light the chips. The greasy chips burn slowly, igniting the charcoal with ease.

Easier Steaming

Many vegetable steamer baskets have short legs that allow only a small amount of water to be added beneath its base. For vegetables that take awhile to cook through, Matthew Gitano of Hartford, Conn., came up with this ingenious tip that eliminates the need for replenishing the water during steaming. He places three crumpled balls of aluminum foil in the pot and then places the steamer basket on top of the foil. The foil elevates the steamer basket, creating room for extra water.

Stabilizing a Mixing Bowl

When scooping cake frosting or cookie dough out of a bowl, Carly Anderson of New York, N.Y., finds that if the bowl is angled, it is much easier to dig into. To do this, she places the mixing bowl in a pot lined with a dish towel. The now-secure bowl can be tilted in any direction.

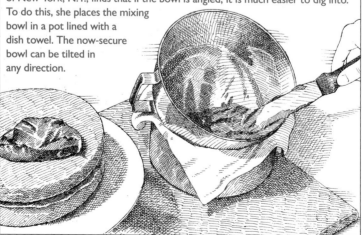

Easier Apple Coring

Linda Brown of Chicago, Ill., found that every time she used an apple corer, the apple wobbled, making it tricky to cut directly through its center. To keep the apple from rolling around, she uses this trick.

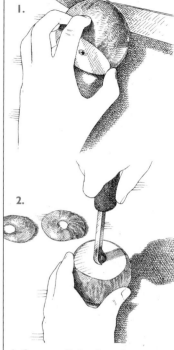

1. Cut a small slice from the top and bottom of the apple.
2. Holding the apple steady on its bottom side, push the corer through.

Steadier Bottle Drying

Tall items such as vases and water bottles are awkward to stand upside down on a dish-drying rack after washing. Michelle Armstrong of Rupert, Vt., holds such items steady by anchoring a wooden spoon in the rack, handle-end up. The dishware fits easily over the handle so it can drain properly.

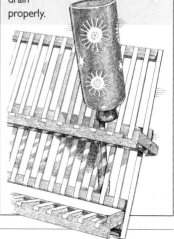

Send Us Your Tip We will provide a complimentary one-year subscription for each tip we print. Send your tip, name, and address to Quick Tips, Cook's Illustrated, P.O. Box 470589, Brookline, MA 02447 or to quicktips@americastestkitchen.com.

Keeping Grill Platters Warm

Andrew Sloan of San Francisco, Calif., was barbecuing a meal on his gas grill when he realized that the flat lid of the grill was an ideal spot to warm a serving platter. The heated platter can be used for serving foods right away or for keeping meat warm as it rests before carving. Make sure to handle the platter with potholders.

Rejuvenating Leftover Polenta

Freshly cooked polenta has a terrific creamy texture, but leftovers cooled in the refrigerator turn thick and stiff. To restore its original creamy state, Kelly Roberts of Los Angeles, Calif., uses the following technique.

1.

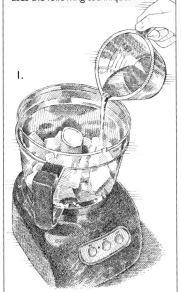

2.

1. Using quick pulses, process the cold polenta in a food processor, adding a few tablespoons of warm water for every cup of cooked polenta, until the mixture is creamy.
2. Transfer the polenta to a microwave-safe bowl, cover with plastic wrap, and heat on high power until warm.

No More Sticky Hands

Washing your hands after working with sticky dough can be a difficult task. Aya Alt of Ithaca, N.Y., has a solution. She keeps a small bowl of cornmeal next to her work station. When she's ready to clean up, she rubs her hands in the cornmeal to help scrape off much of the dough before she goes to the sink.

Impromptu Potato Ricer

While making mashed potatoes at a friend's house, Peter Stein of Philadelphia, Pa., found himself without a potato ricer. Thinking quickly, he grabbed a sturdy metal colander with fine perforations and pressed the potatoes through with a stiff rubber spatula.

Fume-Free Oven Cleaning

Spraying oven cleaner in the oven to remove grime from the racks can fill the kitchen with harsh fumes. Ron Purvis of Everett, Wash., takes the process outdoors.

1.

2.

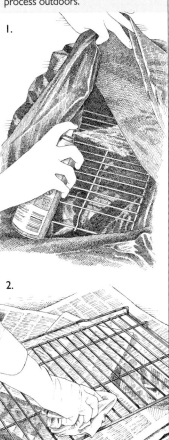

1. Place the dirty oven rack in a large garbage bag. Take the bag outside and, keeping the rack in the bag, spray it with oven cleaner. Close the bag and let it sit outside overnight.
2. Wearing rubber gloves, remove the rack from the bag and place it on several sheets of newspaper. Wipe the rack clean with a damp kitchen towel before returning it to the oven.

Extra Dish-Drying Space

Yolanda Coroy of Houston, Texas, keeps her dish-drying rack underneath a cabinet. For those times when the rack is overflowing with dishes and utensils, she uses hooks attached to the underside of the cabinet. Extra wet items can be suspended from the hooks to drip dry.

Keeping Salads Cold

To help keep salads cool and fresh on her buffet table, Julia Faulk of Grand Rapids, Mich., uses this method.

1.

2.

3.

1. Fill 1 or 2 large zipper-lock bags with ice cubes and a few table-spoons of salt. (The salt helps to keep the ice cold longer.)
2. Place the sealed bags in the bottom of a large serving bowl and cover them with lettuce leaves.
3. Spoon the salad onto the lettuce leaves. The salad will stay cold for at least 1 hour.

Italian Grilled Chicken

What do a pair of bricks have to do with juicy, crisp-skinned chicken?

⇒ BY MATTHEW CARD ⇐

Almost every cuisine that cooks over a live fire has developed a method for overcoming the stiff challenge of grilling a whole chicken. Americans spike their chickens on tallboys of Schlitz and bathe them in low, smoky heat. Brits "spatchcock" their birds, or chop out the backbones and squash them flat. Italians take the British approach one step further by grilling butterflied poultry *al mattone,* or literally, "under a brick." The weight squishing the chicken coal-ward is supposed to accomplish two goals: Compressing the bird for even, quick cooking, and producing perfectly crisp skin by maximizing contact with the grill.

Intrigued? I was, but the recipes I tried nearly dissuaded me. The photos of grill-bronzed chickens in the cookbooks were alluring, but the recipes turned out either greasy, pink, and charred birds or dry, tough, and blackened ones. However, I saw potential: Each chicken had a few edible bits of juicy, browned meat and crisp, crackly skin.

Getting Salty

Most classic Italian recipes do little more than apply salt, pepper, and a liberal wash of olive oil to the meat. Italian chickens might all be juicy and flavorful, but American supermarket chickens—even "natural" or "organic" birds—need more help.

Through the years, the test kitchen has typically brined poultry destined for the grill. A soak in salted water floods the meat with moisture to prevent overcooking and seasons it to the bone. But in this case, all that moisture proved problematic. The brined, butterflied birds emerged from the grill not just charred but burned to black. Risking singed eyebrows, I got level with the grill grate, where I watched torrents of greasy liquid spurt from the seams between chicken and skin and onto the coals beneath, generating flames. All that purged liquid also apparently soaked the skin and prevented it from effectively crisping, even after I cut slits in the skin to provide more channels for moisture to escape. Bricks and brining just don't mix.

We've also discovered that salting can accomplish nearly the same results as brining. Salt, liberally applied beneath the skin, first draws out moisture from inside the bird that, over time, gets reabsorbed with the

Following Italian tradition, we butterfly our chicken to ensure that it cooks evenly under the bricks.

salt, helping the meat retain its juices during cooking. A quick test proved that a salted bird could be grilled under a brick with none of the problems of brining. While an hour of salting sufficed, double that was better yet.

Salting requires loosening the chicken's skin from the meat, which increases its crispness because of improved airflow. As for the olive oil applied by most recipes, I thought it added little flavor, prevented the skin from crisping, and promoted smoky flare-ups. Tradition aside, it had to go.

Double Flipping

Most recipes for chicken under a brick place the bird skin-side down over a moderate fire, drop the bricks on top, and grill the bird until cooked through. Simple, yes, but far from successful: The breast meat was done well in advance of the inner thigh meat, plus there were those flare-ups to fight. I preheated my bricks to provide heat from above as well as below, but this slight improvement did nothing to reduce charring. It became clear that I needed to first render some of the juices and fat over cooler temperatures before the chicken could be set directly over the hot fire.

To that end, a modified two-level fire made sense. I spread coals over half of the grill bottom and left the other half empty. I plopped the chicken skin-side down over the side without coals, balanced the preheated bricks on top, covered the grill, and grilled the bird long enough to firm the flesh, about 20 minutes. I then slid the chicken—bricks and all—to the hot side of the grill to brown and crisp. (Not once, out of the 20 chickens I cooked, did the skin stick.) The differences were pronounced: The meat was juicier thanks to the slower cooking method, and flare-ups were virtually eliminated. As for even cooking, turning the slower-cooking legs toward the coals (and the breast away from them) was a better position for the first stage of grilling.

However, the nooks and crannies of meat closest to the bone remained a bit undercooked. Revisiting previous tests, I remembered one recipe in which the chicken was flipped and cooked skin-side up for a portion of the time. I'd ruled this out as cum-

---

STEP-BY-STEP | **PREPPING CHICKEN FOR THE GRILL**

1. BUTTERFLY Cut through bones on either side of backbone, then discard backbone.

2. PRESS Flip chicken over, then flatten breastbone and tuck wings behind back.

3. SEPARATE Loosen skin over breast and thighs and remove any excess fat.

4. SALT Spread salt-garlic mixture under skin of breast and thighs. Spread salt mixture on meat of bone side.

bersome—it meant removing the bricks, turning the bird, then replacing the bricks—but I decided it was worth another try. Starting over, I cooked the chicken skin-side down over the cooler side of the grill for about 20 minutes, flipped it, and then moved it to the hot side of the grill to cook skin-side up over direct heat for about 15 minutes. The interior was just what I wanted: chicken that was evenly cooked in all parts, from wings to breast, thighs, and drumsticks. Could the skin be even crisper with one final flip? Absolutely. All it took was an extra 5 to 10 minutes on the hot side of the grill. Up until now, the brick had been pressing the bird to the grate to evenly cook and crisp the skin, but at this point I took off the brick to avoid last-minute flare-ups.

Rub It In

Simply seasoned with salt, you would never know this chicken was "Italian." It clearly needed lashings of bold Mediterranean flavor. A couple of the recipes that I had collected rubbed raw garlic, herbs, red pepper flakes, and lemon zest under the chicken's skin, but this approach steamed the flavorings in the chicken's juices and tasted awful.

Some tasters suggested that the seasonings might not taste steamed if they were briefly sautéed before I slid them under the skin. I sizzled minced garlic, zest, red pepper flakes, and herbs (thyme and rosemary tasted best) in olive oil, strained them to remove the oil, and cooled the mixture before spreading it over the salted meat beneath the skin. This infused the chicken with rich flavor without reducing the skin's crispness. It took me a couple of tests before I realized I could simply combine the paste with the salt and thereby eliminate a step.

So what about that olive oil strained from the garlic? Redolent of garlic, zest, and herbs, it was a resource. I had a denuded lemon and plenty of herbs left on my cutting board, so I made a quick vinaigrette to serve with the cooked bird. This chicken would have its olive oil after all.

ITALIAN-STYLE CHARCOAL-GRILLED CHICKEN

SERVES 4

Note: For the best flavor, use a high-quality chicken, such as Bell & Evans. Use an oven mitt or dish towel to safely grip and maneuver the hot bricks. If you're using table salt, reduce the amount to 1½ teaspoons in step 2. You will need two standard-sized bricks for this recipe. Placing the bricks on the chicken while it cooks ensures that the skin will be evenly browned and well rendered—don't skip this step. A cast-iron skillet or other heavy pan can be used in place of the bricks.

COOK'S LIVE Original Test Kitchen Videos

www.cooksillustrated.com/jun09

HOW TO MAKE

- Italian-Style Grilled Chicken

VIDEO TIP

- Do I need to use bricks for Italian-Style Grilled Chicken?

⅓ cup extra-virgin olive oil
8 medium garlic cloves, minced or pressed through garlic press (about 2½ tablespoons)
1 teaspoon finely grated zest plus 2 tablespoons juice from 1 lemon
Pinch crushed red pepper flakes
4 teaspoons chopped fresh thyme leaves
3 teaspoons chopped fresh rosemary leaves
Kosher salt (see note)
Ground black pepper
1 (3¾- to 4¼-pound) whole chicken (see note)
Vegetable oil for cooking grate

1. Combine oil, garlic, lemon zest, and pepper flakes in small saucepan. Bring to simmer, stirring frequently, over medium-low heat, about 3 minutes. Once simmering, add 3 teaspoons thyme and 2 teaspoons rosemary and cook 30 seconds longer. Strain mixture through fine-mesh strainer set over small bowl, pushing on solids to extract oil. Transfer solids to small bowl and cool; set oil and solids aside.

2. Following illustrations on page 6, butterfly chicken, flatten breastbone, and tuck wings behind back. Using hands or handle of wooden spoon, loosen skin over breast and thighs and remove any excess fat. Combine 1 tablespoon salt and 1 teaspoon pepper in small bowl. Mix 3 teaspoons salt mixture with cooled garlic solids. Spread salt-garlic mixture evenly under skin over chicken breast and thighs. Sprinkle remaining teaspoon salt mixture on exposed meat of bone side. Place chicken skin-side up on wire rack set in rimmed baking sheet and refrigerate 1 to 2 hours.

3. Wrap 2 bricks tightly in aluminum foil. Light large chimney starter filled three-quarters with charcoal (4½ quarts, or about 75 briquettes) and burn until coals are covered with layer of fine gray ash, about 20 minutes. Build modified two-level fire by arranging all coals over half of grill, leaving other half empty. Position cooking grate over coals, place bricks on grate over coals, cover grill, and heat about 5 minutes. Scrape cooking grate clean with grill brush. Lightly dip wad of paper towels in vegetable oil; holding wad with tongs, wipe cooking grate. Grill is ready when side with coals is medium-hot (you can hold your hand 5 inches above grate for 3 to 4 seconds).

4. Place chicken skin-side down over cooler side of grill with legs facing fire, place hot bricks lengthwise over each breast half, cover grill, and cook until skin is lightly browned and faint grill marks appear, 22 to 25 minutes. Remove bricks from chicken. Using tongs or towel, grip legs and flip chicken (chicken should release freely from grill; use thin metal spatula to loosen if stuck) and transfer to hot side of grill, skin-side up, with breast facing center of grill. Place bricks over breast, cover grill, and cook until chicken is well browned, 12 to 15 minutes.

5. Remove bricks, flip chicken skin-side down over hot coals, and cook until chicken skin is well crisped and instant-read thermometer inserted into thickest part of thigh registers 165 degrees, 5 to 10 minutes, moving chicken as necessary to prevent flare-ups. Transfer chicken to cutting board and let rest 10 minutes. Whisk lemon juice and remaining thyme and rosemary into reserved oil; season with salt and pepper. Carve chicken and serve, passing sauce separately.

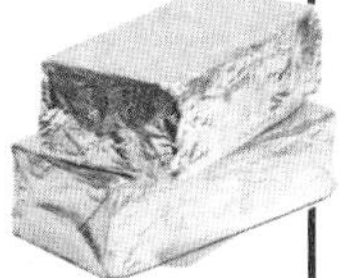

ITALIAN-STYLE GAS-GRILLED CHICKEN

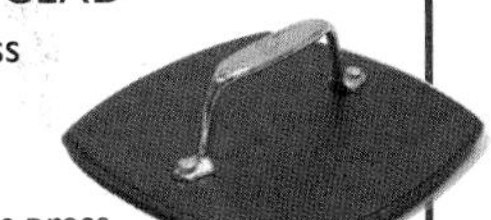

Follow instructions for Italian-Style Charcoal-Grilled Chicken through step 2. Turn all burners to high, place bricks on cooking grate, and heat with lid down until very hot, about 15 minutes. Scrape cooking grate clean. Leave primary burner on high and turn off other burner(s). Proceed with recipe from step 4, cooking with lid down.

EQUIPMENT TESTING

Grill Presses

The key to preparing the Italian classic *pollo al mattone*—chicken under a brick—is the brick itself. The weight (we used two 6-pounders wrapped in foil) holds the bird flat on the grill, helping the chicken to cook faster and the fat to render for crisp, golden skin. Do cast-iron grill presses do the job any better? We tested four brands priced from $14.99 to a whopping $70. Presses that were too light or small left the skin flabby and prolonged the cooking time. We preferred the heftiest model for its comfortable handle and nearly five pounds of chicken-pressing weight. But at $27.95, we can't recommend it over two bricks, which weigh more, press better, and cost far, far less. For complete testing results, go to www.cooksillustrated.com/jun09. –Meredith Butcher

BARGAIN BEAUTIES
BRICKS
Price: 70 cents (35 cents each)
Comments: Two foil-wrapped bricks, each 6 pounds, do the best job of pressing chicken against the grill for crisp skin and quick cooking.

SOLID CHOICE
EMERILWARE BY ALL-CLAD
Cast-Iron Square Grill Press
Price: $27.95
Comments: Weighing in at 4 pounds and 10 ounces, this press yields deep grill marks, rendered skin, and relatively evenly cooked chicken.

LIGHTWEIGHT LOSER
LE CREUSET Grill Press
Price: $69.95
Comments: Too lightweight (just over 3 pounds) to properly press the chicken. At such a high price, it should at least weigh as much as a brick.

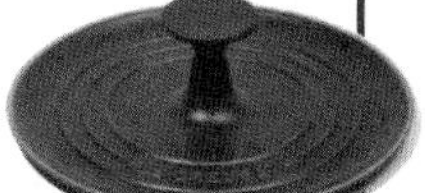

Rescuing Grilled Beef Teriyaki

This Japanese-American standard is synonymous with chewy, flavorless meat shellacked with saccharine-sweet sauce. To beef things up, we turned to a trick from the grill.

⇒ BY KEITH DRESSER ⇐

True Japanese teriyaki is as simple as it is restrained: Take a glossy, salty-sweet glaze made with soy sauce, sake, and mirin (a sweet Japanese rice wine) and paint it over char-grilled fish to accent its delicately smoky flavor. (In Japanese, *teri* means "shine," while *yaki* means "to grill.") After Japanese immigrants introduced this dish to Hawaii in the 19th century, beef and chicken all but replaced the fish, and additions such as sugar and garlic became standard in the sauce. Over time, these perfectly reasonable adaptations morphed into the tired renditions of teriyaki now found at many Japanese-American restaurants: chewy, flavorless slivers of meat daubed with a thick, overly sweet sauce.

I wanted to see this translated dish fulfill its potential, with a juicy, charred steak embellished by a well-balanced, sweet and savory glaze that would be robust enough to stand up to the beef.

Going Against the Grain

All but the most authentic teriyaki recipes that turned up in my research call for at least some sugar. To start, however, I decided to forgo it and stick with tradition, combining equal parts sake, mirin, and soy sauce and simmering the mixture

Marinating the meat before grilling and glazing deepens its flavor.

on the stovetop for an hour until it reduced to a syrupy glaze.

My next decision concerned the beef. I reasoned that a premium cut such as rib eye, tenderloin, or top loin would be an improvement over the cheap cuts used in most restaurants—but why mess with $20-per-pound beef that tastes great on its own? Reaching for less-expensive options, I tried top blade, top sirloin, skirt steak, flank steak, and sirloin tips (also known as flap meat). Tasters quickly ruled out the top blade (gristly) and the top sirloin (bland), but the three remaining cuts all boasted good beefy flavor—steak tips in particular. This cut's marbling melted into the coarse muscle fibers of the beef as it cooked, adding flavor and making it seem more tender than other cheap steaks.

As for the meat's preparation, thin pieces on skewers were a nonstarter: The restaurant and recipe versions I tried were uniformly dry and leathery.

The other end of the spectrum—cooking a whole steak, glazing it with sauce, and slicing before serving—also had its issues. Although a thin teriyaki glaze can cling well to grilled fish, steaks are far juicier, causing the glaze to wash off as soon as I sliced the meat, no matter how long I let it rest.

What if I sliced the steak before it went onto the grill? Butterflying the meat gave me thinner pieces, but tasters found that the long muscle fibers created by cutting the meat with the grain made the steak seem tough. A better idea was to slice the meat into cutlets across the grain at a 45-degree angle, much as I would do for veal scallopini. This shortened the muscle fibers so that the texture was more yielding, and the ½-inch-thick cutlets provided plenty of surface area for charring on the grill. Applied to the browned, caramelized exterior of each slice, the glaze adhered firmly.

The Joy of a (Soy) Marinade

I was making progress, but the meat was still a little dry for my liking. Tasters also complained that my traditional sugarless sauce, while fine for fish, was too understated for beef. Maybe adding a modest amount of sugar wouldn't be such a bad thing. I experimented with various proportions until I was adding as much sugar as the other ingredients. Tasters liked this new balance of flavors, but overall the dish was a little one-dimensional. More sugar wasn't the answer—but what about addressing the taste of the meat itself? To boost flavor, we often marinate meat before putting it on the grill (see "Marinating Done Right" on page 16). I tried soaking the strips of meat for 30 minutes in just enough soy sauce to moisten them (⅓ cup), and it worked beautifully. Not only did the soy promote browning on the grill, but the beef was also juicier. A few tasters complained that it was now a tad salty, but I easily remedied this by adding a tablespoon of sugar and ¼ cup of mirin to the mix. I also reduced the soy sauce in the glaze.

🎥 **COOK'S LIVE** Original Test Kitchen Videos
www.cooksillustrated.com/jun09
HOW TO MAKE
• Grilled Beef Teriyaki
VIDEO TIP
• What is the best way to marinate meat?

SHOPPING **Finding Flap Meat**

Beef labeled "steak tips" can be cut from various muscles of the cow into cubes, strips, or steaks. Our favorite kind is cut into a steak that boasts a coarse, longitudinal grain. Butchers call this form of steak tips "flap meat" or "sirloin tips." Look for pieces that range from 1 to 1½ inches thick.

SKIP THE STRIPS
Don't buy meat that's been cut into strips or cubes.

GO FOR WHOLE
Look for whole steak with a coarse, longitudinal grain labeled "sirloin tips" or "flap meat."

Teriyaki is often served with a garnish of sliced scallions and ginger. I decided to add them directly to the marinade (along with a few cloves of garlic) for an aromatic boost; a small amount of orange zest, while not authentic, contributed freshness that tasters appreciated. Although the sugar in the marinade at first made the meat stick to the grill, a few teaspoons of oil solved the problem.

I was nearly there, but thought that the beef could be smokier and more charred. My single-level fire—a full chimney of charcoal spread over the entire surface of the grill—was not concentrating the heat enough, so I banked all the coals to one side of the grill for a modified two-level fire. Positioned over this higher mound of coals, the steak came out well charred and juicy.

Finessing the Sauce

I had perfectly cooked steak with robust flavors and just the right complement of a spare, salty-sweet sauce. The only remaining problem? The sauce took an hour of simmering to reach the perfect consistency. Spending time to reduce a sauce may make sense at a restaurant, where a large batch can be used for days (in fact, many traditional teriyaki houses never discard it, instead adding fresh sauce to the old batch—the flavor becomes increasingly complex over time), but not for steak at home. Turning up the heat to reduce the sauce more rapidly did not work; vigorous boiling destroyed the subtle flavors of sake and mirin.

If I couldn't thicken the sauce via the traditional low-and-slow reduction, I decided to try the obvious shortcut: cornstarch. A teaspoon was all it took to achieve a nice syrupy consistency, and a mere 15 minutes on the stovetop softened the raw alcohol edge. I now had a sauce that was perfect for both glazing the meat in its final minutes on the grill and passing at the table. This beef teriyaki wasn't true to any tradition, hybrid or otherwise, but it was very, very good.

CHARCOAL-GRILLED BEEF TERIYAKI
SERVES 4

Note: If you can't find flap meat, flank steak is a good alternative. We prefer sake in the sauce, but vermouth may be substituted in a pinch. Mirin, a sweet Japanese rice wine, is a key component of teriyaki; it can be found in Asian markets and the international section of most supermarkets. Alternatively, substitute ¼ cup vermouth or sake and 2 teaspoons sugar for every ¼ cup mirin. If desired, low-sodium soy sauce can be used in place of regular soy. Serve the beef with steamed rice, preferably short-grain.

Steak

- 2 pounds sirloin steak tips (flap meat), trimmed of excess fat (see note)
- ⅓ cup soy sauce (see note)
- ¼ cup mirin (see note)
- 2 tablespoons vegetable oil, plus extra for cooking grate
- 3 medium garlic cloves, minced or pressed through garlic press (about 1 tablespoon)
- 1 tablespoon grated fresh ginger
- 1 tablespoon sugar
- 1 teaspoon finely grated zest from 1 orange
- 2 medium scallions, white parts minced and green parts sliced thin on bias, separated

Sauce

- ⅓ cup soy sauce (see note)
- ½ cup sugar
- ½ cup sake (see note)
- ½ cup mirin (see note)
- 1 teaspoon grated fresh ginger
- 1 teaspoon cornstarch

1. **FOR THE STEAK:** Following photos below, cut steak with grain into 2 to 3 even pieces. (If total length of steak is 12 inches or less, cut into 2 pieces. If over 12 inches, cut into 3 pieces.) Holding knife at 45-degree angle, slice each piece against grain into 4 to 5 slices about ½ inch thick. Combine remaining ingredients, except scallion greens, in gallon-sized zipper-lock bag and toss to combine. Place meat in bag, press out as much air as possible, and seal. Refrigerate 30 minutes or up to 1 hour, flipping bag every 15 minutes to ensure that meat marinates evenly.

2. Light large chimney starter filled with charcoal (6 quarts, about 100 briquettes) and allow to burn until coals are fully ignited and partially covered with thin layer of ash, about 20 minutes. Build modified two-level fire by arranging all coals over half of grill, leaving other half empty. Position cooking grate over coals, cover grill, and heat about 5 minutes; scrape grate clean with grill brush. Dip wad of paper towels in oil; holding wad with tongs, wipe cooking grate. Grill is ready when side with coals is medium-hot (you can hold your hand 5 inches above grate for 3 to 4 seconds).

3. **FOR THE SAUCE:** While grill is heating, whisk sauce ingredients together in small saucepan until combined. Bring sauce to boil over medium-high heat, stirring occasionally. Reduce heat to medium-low and simmer, stirring occasionally, until sauce is syrupy and reduced to 1 cup, 12 to 15 minutes. Transfer ¾ cup sauce to small bowl and set aside to serve with cooked meat.

4. Remove meat from marinade and pat dry with paper towels. Grill over hot coals, uncovered, until well seared and dark brown on first side, 3 to 4 minutes. Using tongs, flip steak and grill until second side is well seared and dark brown, 3 to 4 minutes. Brush top of meat with 2 tablespoons sauce; flip and cook 30 seconds. Brush meat with remaining 2 tablespoons sauce; flip and cook 30 seconds longer.

5. Transfer meat to serving platter and let rest 5 minutes. Sprinkle with scallion greens and serve, passing reserved sauce separately.

GAS-GRILLED BEEF TERIYAKI

Follow instructions for Charcoal-Grilled Beef Teriyaki through step 1. Turn all burners to high and heat with lid down until very hot, about 15 minutes. Scrape and oil grate. Proceed with recipe from step 3, leaving burners on high and cooking meat with lid down.

TECHNIQUE | CUTTING SIRLOIN STEAK TIPS FOR GRILLING

1. Cut the steak with the grain into 2 or 3 even pieces.

2. Hold the knife at a 45-degree angle and cut ½-inch-thick slices.

3. Each piece of steak should yield 4 to 5 slices.

Great Glazed Pork Tenderloin

A glaze is the perfect way to enhance this bland cut—if you can get it to stick. For help, we borrowed a technique used by professional painters.

⇒ BY J. KENJI ALT ⇐

Pork tenderloin is the boneless, skinless chicken breast of the pork world: Even when it's moist, tender, and perfectly cooked, it's still sorely lacking in flavor. For richer taste, there's always the fattier and more forgiving blade-end loin roast, cut from the shoulder end of the loin. But at twice the size of a typical tenderloin, it takes twice as long to cook. With a tenderloin, you can put dinner on the table in less than 30 minutes. And when done right, nothing can match its fine-grained, buttery-smooth texture. It might be the ideal cut—if only there was a way to improve the flavor.

Enter New England's signature ingredient: maple syrup. Its rich, sweet flavor and subtle aroma complement pork beautifully—plus, it's an ingredient I always have on hand. We discovered with our Maple-Glazed Pork Roast (March/April 2003) that the best way to glaze a blade-end loin roast is to sear the pork in a skillet, add the syrup and spices, and then place the meat in the oven—skillet and all—rotating the roast occasionally as the syrup reduces to a thick, fragrant glaze.

With less fat and less flavor, tenderloin has even greater need of such sweet assistance. But when I tried to glaze this faster-cooking and much more delicate cut using the same method, the pork was done long before the syrup had time to reduce, and its exterior was marred by a sheath of dry, stringy meat. To get lean yet tender meat coated with subtle spice and inviting sweetness, I would need to make some major adjustments.

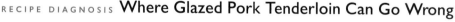

A rough surface helps the bourbon glaze stick, but we didn't use sandpaper to achieve it.

Try a Little Tenderloin

I couldn't hope to produce great glazed pork tenderloin without first producing great plain pork tenderloin, so my first step was to nail down the basic cooking technique. I wanted enough meat for six people, so I chose two tenderloins in a commonly available size, 1¼ pounds. The stovetop-to-oven technique was still under consideration—but only if I could use it without drying out my pork. I seared the tenderloins in a skillet as before, then experimented by placing the pan in the oven at increasingly lower temperatures. But even when I dialed all the way down to a mere 250 degrees, the tenderloins still came out dry and overcooked. The problem was this: The superior heat retention of a skillet is a boon for cuts like the blade-end roast, which boasts an outer layer of fat that protects it from drying out. But the sizzling hot surface was too much for my vulnerable, nearly fat-free tenderloins, causing their exterior to overcook.

I decided to forgo the skillet and stovetop altogether. Instead, I put the tenderloins in a roasting pan and placed them directly in the oven. This approach also proved fruitless. Even at 500 degrees, the pork barely browned and ended up mealy and dry. At lower oven temperatures, it was moist and tender on the inside, but had no outer color or caramelized flavor at all.

Clearly, for the rich taste I was seeking, I would need to sear the meat. I was right back at square one. Or was I? If the skillet was the problem, why not use it to sear the meat, but then transfer the pork to a surface that wouldn't damage its exterior? This line of thinking led me to a two-step: I first seared the tenderloins in the skillet to develop a deep brown crust, then transferred them to a rack set inside a rimmed baking sheet to finish in a gentle 375-degree oven. (Any higher and the meat dried out, while lower temperatures simply took too long.) The rack was essential: It elevated the meat away from the hot surface of the pan and prevented it from overcooking.

With pork that was succulent and tender throughout, I was ready to tackle the glaze.

Stick It to 'Em

Maple syrup would be my base, but tasters deemed the pure stuff overwhelmingly sweet for bland tenderloin. To counter the sweetness, I swapped ¼ cup

---

of the syrup for the same amount of mildly bitter molasses and added a tablespoon of mustard. For more complex flavor, I stirred in a shot of bourbon, which brought notes of smoke and vanilla. With pinches of cinnamon, cloves, and cayenne pepper, the glaze was good to go. But the question of how to apply it still lingered.

Our blade-end loin roast recipe from a few years back relies on a long stay in the oven to thicken the glaze to the right consistency and help it cling to the pork. As you rotate the loin in the glaze, layer after layer of flavorful coating slowly builds up. But with my tenderloins raised on a rack, I didn't have the option of repeatedly turning them as they cooked in a pool of gradually reducing glaze. And even after reducing the glaze to the proper consistency on the stovetop (making sure to scrape up the flavorful, browned bits stuck in the pan), it ended up dripping through the rack, resulting in a perfectly glazed baking sheet and nearly bare tenderloins. I needed to find a way to make it stick.

I noticed while painting the glaze onto the pork that the slick surface of the seared tenderloin was doing nothing to help the syrup stick. Brush in hand, it occurred to me that glazing a tenderloin might be not unlike painting a wall. To ensure that the paint adheres properly, you must prepare the surface with a coat of primer. I wondered: Would the secret to great glazed tenderloins be found, likewise, by "priming" their surface with some coating? Flour and cornstarch seemed like good options. I tried them both, rolling one tenderloin in flour and the other in cornstarch before searing. The cornstarch-encrusted tenderloin did a better job of grabbing the glaze, but too much was still slipping away. What if I added sugar, an ingredient rarely used for seared meat? Mixed with cornstarch, the sugar melted and caramelized as the meat seared, creating a deep brown crust with the texture of sandpaper—perfect for holding a glaze.

I now had a surefire way of making my glaze stick to the meat, but the final coating simply wasn't thick enough. No matter how much glaze I slathered on, just a thin layer was left by the time the tenderloins came out of the oven. I thought back to my painting analogy. With wall paint, one key to good coverage is waiting between coats to allow time for each to dry. Would this be true for glazed tenderloins as well? After applying my first coat of glaze, I let the meat roast in the oven until it was nearly done. Then I applied a second coat. When the tenderloins were done cooking, I painted a third coat on top of the now-dry second coat. Finally, after letting the tenderloins rest, I glazed them one last time.

Key to Good Coverage

LAYER IT ON
Four layers of glaze add up to a thick and flavorful coating.

Slicing into this roast revealed lustrous success—a thick maple glaze coating the meat. And tasting these burnished beauties disproved that old adage: Sometimes it *is* what's on the outside that counts.

MAPLE-GLAZED PORK TENDERLOIN
SERVES 6

Note: This recipe will work with either natural pork or enhanced pork (injected with a salty solution). If your tenderloins are smaller than 1¼ pounds, reduce the cooking time in step 3 (and use an instant-read thermometer for best results). If the tenderloins don't fit in the skillet initially, let their ends curve toward each other; the meat will eventually shrink as it cooks. Make sure to cook the tenderloins until they turn deep golden brown in step 2 or they will appear pale after glazing. We prefer grade B maple syrup in this recipe. (Don't be tempted to substitute imitation maple syrup—it will be too sweet.) Be sure to pat off the cornstarch mixture thoroughly in step 1, as any excess will leave gummy spots on the tenderloins.

¾	cup maple syrup (see note)
¼	cup light or mild molasses
2	tablespoons bourbon or brandy
⅛	teaspoon ground cinnamon
	Pinch ground cloves
	Pinch cayenne pepper
¼	cup cornstarch
2	tablespoons sugar
1	tablespoon table salt
2	teaspoons ground black pepper
2	pork tenderloins (1¼ to 1½ pounds each) (see note)
2	tablespoons vegetable oil
1	tablespoon whole-grain mustard

1. Adjust oven rack to middle position and heat oven to 375 degrees. Stir ½ cup maple syrup, molasses, bourbon, cinnamon, cloves, and cayenne together in 2-cup liquid measure; set aside. Whisk cornstarch, sugar, salt, and black pepper in small bowl until combined. Transfer cornstarch mixture to rimmed baking sheet. Pat tenderloins dry with paper towels, then roll in cornstarch mixture until evenly coated on all sides. Thoroughly pat off excess cornstarch mixture.

2. Heat oil in 12-inch heavy-bottomed nonstick skillet over medium-high heat until just beginning to smoke. Reduce heat to medium and place both tenderloins in skillet, leaving at least 1 inch in between. Cook until well browned on all sides, 8 to 12 minutes. Transfer tenderloins to wire rack set in rimmed baking sheet.

3. Pour off excess fat from skillet and return to medium heat. Add syrup mixture to skillet, scraping up browned bits with wooden spoon, and cook until reduced to ½ cup, about 2 minutes. Transfer 2 tablespoons glaze to small bowl and set aside.

Using remaining glaze, brush each tenderloin with approximately 1 tablespoon glaze. Roast until instant-read thermometer inserted in thickest part of tenderloins registers 130 degrees, 12 to 20 minutes. Brush each tenderloin with another tablespoon glaze and continue to roast until instant-read thermometer inserted in thickest part of tenderloins registers 135 to 140 degrees, 2 to 4 minutes longer. Remove tenderloins from oven and brush each with remaining glaze; let rest, uncovered, 10 minutes.

4. While tenderloins rest, stir remaining ¼ cup maple syrup and mustard into reserved 2 tablespoons glaze. Brush each tenderloin with 1 tablespoon mustard glaze. Transfer meat to cutting board and slice into ¼-inch-thick pieces. Serve, passing extra mustard glaze at table.

MAPLE-GLAZED PORK TENDERLOIN WITH SMOKED PAPRIKA AND GINGER

Follow recipe for Maple-Glazed Pork Tenderloin, substituting dry sherry for bourbon and ¼ teaspoon smoked paprika and 1 teaspoon grated fresh ginger for cinnamon, cloves, and cayenne pepper. Omit mustard in step 4.

MAPLE-GLAZED PORK TENDERLOIN WITH ORANGE AND CHIPOTLE

Follow recipe for Maple-Glazed Pork Tenderloin, substituting 2 tablespoons frozen orange juice concentrate for 2 tablespoons molasses. Omit cinnamon, cloves, and cayenne pepper and add 2 small, finely minced chipotle chiles plus 2 teaspoons adobo sauce to maple syrup mixture in step 1. Omit mustard in step 4.

COOK'S VIDEOS Original Test Kitchen Videos
www.cooksillustrated.com/jun09
HOW TO MAKE
• Maple-Glazed Pork Tenderloin

To create a rough, sandpapery surface on the tenderloin that would hold the glaze, we rolled the meat in a mixture of cornstarch and sugar before browning it in the pan and then roasting and glazing it.

Improving Grilled Vegetables

Most grilled veggies turn out one of two ways: pale and crunchy or blackened and mushy. Maybe it was time to turn down the heat.

 ⋺ BY YVONNE RUPERTI ⋹

What's not to love about fresh veggies combined with the heat and smoke of the grill? I can think of two things. There's the challenge of grilling them to just the right point—gently charred on the outside and tender within (versus pale and crunchy or blackened and mushy). But the big issue is flavor—there's just not enough of it. If I'm serving a juicy steak or tangy barbecued chicken, plain grilled zucchini or onions are sure to play second fiddle. With summer just around the corner, I vowed to find a new approach.

My first idea was to combine some of my favorite vegetables into pairs to double up on flavor. Mindful of complementary cooking times, I matched zucchini with sweet red onion, hearty portobellos with shallots, and eggplant with red peppers. For the grilling itself, most recipes I found suggested a total of 10 minutes for both sides over a hot fire. But when I tried this method, too many samples were incinerated on the exterior and raw on the interior. Trying again, I built a more moderate, medium-heat fire. Ten minutes later, my vegetables remained pale and crunchy. But after 20 minutes, it was clear that what I lost in speed, I gained in taste: All of the vegetables were perfectly tender and full of smoky flavor.

Now, how to boost the taste further still? I considered marinating but didn't want to add extra time to the recipes. Instead, I tried brushing the vegetables with garlic oil, but the garlic bits burned, and the flavor advantage was minimal. Why not forget any precooking treatment and bump up flavor after the vegetables came off the fire? If plain garlic oil was boring, maybe the livelier flavors of a dressing or vinaigrette would do the trick. Tasters complained that my first few tries were too sharp, but after some minor adjustments, I whisked up some winners. Drizzled with dressing while still warm, my vegetables had enough flavor to be the meal's star attraction—never mind the meat.

GRILLED ZUCCHINI AND RED ONION WITH LEMON-BASIL VINAIGRETTE
SERVES 4 TO 6

Note: The vegetables can be served hot, warm, or at room temperature. After about five minutes, faint grill marks should begin to appear on the undersides of the vegetables; if necessary, adjust their position on the grill or adjust the heat level.

- 1 large red onion, peeled and cut crosswise into four ½-inch-thick rounds
- 3 medium zucchini (about 1 pound), ends trimmed, sliced lengthwise into ¾-inch-thick planks
- ¼ cup plus 2 tablespoons extra-virgin olive oil
  Kosher salt and ground black pepper
- 1 small garlic clove, minced or pressed through garlic press (about ½ teaspoon)
- 1 teaspoon finely grated zest plus 1 tablespoon juice from 1 lemon
- ¼ teaspoon Dijon mustard
- 1 tablespoon chopped fresh basil leaves

1. Thread onion rounds, from side to side, onto 2 metal skewers. Brush onion and zucchini evenly with ¼ cup olive oil and season with 2 teaspoons kosher salt (or 1 teaspoon table salt) and pepper to taste.

2. Whisk remaining 2 tablespoons olive oil, garlic, lemon zest and juice, mustard, and ½ teaspoon kosher salt (or ¼ teaspoon table salt) together in small bowl; set aside.

3. Grill vegetables over medium heat, turning once, until tender and caramelized, 18 to 22 minutes (move vegetables as needed to ensure even cooking). Transfer vegetables to platter; remove skewers from onion and discard any charred outer rings. Rewhisk vinaigrette and pour over vegetables. Sprinkle with basil and serve.

GRILLED PORTOBELLOS AND SHALLOTS WITH ROSEMARY-DIJON VINAIGRETTE
SERVES 4 TO 6

- 8 medium shallots, peeled
- 6 portobello mushrooms, each 5 inches in diameter (about 4 ounces each), stems removed and discarded, caps wiped clean
- ¼ cup plus 2 tablespoons extra-virgin olive oil
  Kosher salt and ground black pepper
- 1 small garlic clove, minced or pressed through garlic press (about ½ teaspoon)
- 2 teaspoons juice from 1 lemon
- 1 teaspoon Dijon mustard
- 1 teaspoon finely chopped fresh rosemary leaves

1. Thread shallots through roots and stem ends onto 2 metal skewers. Using sharp knife, cut ¼-inch slits, spaced ½ inch apart, in crosshatch pattern on non-gill side of mushrooms. Brush shallots and mushrooms evenly with ¼ cup olive oil and season with 2 teaspoons kosher salt (or 1 teaspoon table salt) and pepper to taste.

2. Whisk remaining 2 tablespoons olive oil, garlic, lemon juice, mustard, rosemary, and ½ teaspoon kosher salt (or ¼ teaspoon table salt) together in small bowl; set aside.

3. Grill vegetables over medium heat, turning once, until tender and caramelized, 16 to 18 minutes (move vegetables as needed to ensure even cooking). Transfer vegetables to platter; remove skewers from shallots and discard any charred outer layers. Rewhisk vinaigrette, pour over vegetables, and serve.

GRILLED EGGPLANT AND RED PEPPERS WITH MINT-CUMIN DRESSING
SERVES 4 TO 6

- 1 medium eggplant (about 1 pound), ends trimmed, cut crosswise into ½-inch-thick rounds
- 2 red bell peppers, cored, seeded, and cut into 2-inch planks
- ¼ cup plus 1 tablespoon extra-virgin olive oil
  Kosher salt and ground black pepper
- 1 small garlic clove, minced or pressed through garlic press (about ½ teaspoon)
- 1 tablespoon juice from 1 lemon
- ½ teaspoon ground coriander
- ½ teaspoon ground cumin
- 2 tablespoons plain yogurt
- 1 tablespoon chopped fresh mint leaves

1. Brush eggplant and bell peppers evenly with ¼ cup olive oil and season with 2 teaspoons kosher salt (or 1 teaspoon table salt) and pepper to taste.

2. Whisk remaining tablespoon olive oil, garlic, lemon juice, coriander, cumin, yogurt, mint, and ½ teaspoon kosher salt (or ¼ teaspoon table salt) together in small bowl; set aside.

3. Grill vegetables over medium heat, turning once, until tender and caramelized, 16 to 18 minutes (move vegetables as needed to ensure even cooking). Transfer vegetables to platter, rewhisk dressing, pour over vegetables, and serve.

🎥 COOK'S VIDEOS Original Test Kitchen Videos
www.cooksillustrated.com/jun09
HOW TO MAKE
• Grilled Vegetables
VIDEO TIP
• How do I prepare vegetables for grilling?

Best Quick Tomato Sauce

Is it possible to transform canned tomatoes into a bright, fresh-tasting sauce?

⇒ BY KEITH DRESSER ⇐

In a perfect world, when you set out to make a quick tomato sauce, you'd simply reach for a few fresh, garden-ripe tomatoes to get started. But that isn't a realistic option for most of the year. Canned tomatoes far surpass the bland, rock-hard offerings in the produce aisle, but they have their own disadvantages. First, great tomato flavor is as much about taste as it is about smell, and the canning process cooks off many of the key aromatic compounds (16 in all) that food scientists have identified as prime contributors to full, fruity tomato taste. Second, researchers know that people perceive tomatoes to have the best flavor when sweetness and acidity are in balance (for optimal flavor, both should be high). The addition of citric acid as a preservative throws off that delicate but crucial equation.

I wanted to create a complex, brightly flavored sauce, one that tasted first and foremost of tomatoes, in the time it takes to boil pasta. I could never hope to restore the exact flavor of fresh tomatoes—but with the right ingredients, maybe I could come close.

Starting with the right can of tomatoes should greatly improve the odds of success. Of the four major types of canned tomato products (whole, diced, crushed, and pureed), whole and diced tend to be the least cooked and have the freshest flavor. But I wanted a quick recipe, and crushed tomatoes would save me the step of pureeing them myself. Fortunately, in brands such as Tuttorosso or Muir Glen (winners of our taste tests), crushed tomatoes are also minimally processed. I had another reason to choose one of these high-quality producers. While all brands heat their tomatoes to kill off any harmful microorganisms, these two producers use a lower temperature (between 160 and 185 degrees) to preserve an enzyme called lipoxygenase. Lipoxygenase oxidizes two of the pigments found in ripe tomatoes (lycopene and beta-carotene), creating new aromatic compounds that can make a canned tomato literally taste fresh.

Adding sugar to the tomatoes seemed a given, and it helped—in small amounts. Any more than ¼ teaspoon per 28-ounce can of tomatoes, and tasters complained that the sauce was tipping too far to the sweet side. A couple cloves of garlic instantly boosted flavor, as did ¼ teaspoon of dried oregano (as long as I sautéed it before adding the tomatoes, tasters didn't notice its dry texture). But my tasters wanted more depth. I tried a range of other ingredients commonly added to tomato sauce, with little success. Tasters quickly outlawed tomato paste for tasting tinny and overcooked. Red wine—I chose a fruity Côtes du Rhône—brought too much

Our full-flavored tomato sauce takes only 15 minutes to prepare.

of its own distinct profile. Ditto on carrots (too earthy) and lemon zest (too citrusy).

Conversations with several tomato industry specialists provided a clue as to why none of these "enhancers" was in fact enhancing the sauce: A good canned tomato will retain at least some of the fresh fruit's volatile components, but contact with other foods can alter their makeup, turning them into compounds that lack the aromas tasters recognize as tomatolike. If I wanted a sauce to taste primarily of tomatoes, I'd have to single out ingredients that didn't take me too far from their flavor.

One ingredient I hadn't tried was onion, for no other reason than cooking it down to the melting sweetness required by a good sauce takes time, and I wanted a streamlined recipe. Onions contain long chains of fructose molecules linked together in compounds known as inulin. Breaking down inulin releases the fructose, causing onions to become sweet, a reaction I could intensify if I caramelized them. I shredded a small amount of onion on a box grater, which would make it cook faster and release fructose more efficiently.

I started to sauté the onion in olive oil, but then thought better of it. Why not use butter, which also caramelizes in the presence of heat, creating its own new flavor compounds that would hopefully enhance, rather than detract from, my sauce? After about five

minutes, when the onions were lightly browned, I added two cloves of minced garlic, the sugar, and the crushed tomatoes, then allowed the sauce to simmer 10 minutes. (In previous tests, I found cooking times under 15 minutes produced fresher, brighter flavor.)

This was definitely the best sauce I had made yet. But I had one last tweak. To make up for the lost fragrance of fresh tomatoes, I added two highly aromatic ingredients: chopped fresh basil and extra-virgin olive oil. Swirled in just before serving, these ingredients perfumed the sauce with bright, grassy notes.

This sauce, to which I'd done so little, was a huge hit with my tasters, who praised it over and over for a bright, well-balanced flavor that tasted like it had come straight from the garden, not the pantry.

QUICK TOMATO SAUCE
MAKES ABOUT 3 CUPS, ENOUGH FOR 1 POUND OF PASTA

Note: High-quality canned tomatoes will make a big difference in this sauce. Our preferred brands of crushed tomatoes are Tuttorosso and Muir Glen. Grate the onion on the large holes of a box grater.

- 2 tablespoons unsalted butter
- ¼ cup grated onion, from 1 medium onion (see note)
- ¼ teaspoon dried oregano
  Table salt
- 2 medium garlic cloves, minced or pressed through garlic press (about 2 teaspoons)
- 1 (28-ounce) can crushed tomatoes (see note)
- ¼ teaspoon sugar
- 2 tablespoons coarsely chopped fresh basil leaves
- 1 tablespoon extra-virgin olive oil
  Ground black pepper

Heat butter in medium saucepan over medium heat until melted. Add onion, oregano, and ½ teaspoon salt; cook, stirring occasionally, until liquid has evaporated and onion is golden brown, about 5 minutes. Add garlic and cook until fragrant, about 30 seconds. Stir in tomatoes and sugar; increase heat to high and bring to simmer. Lower heat to medium-low and simmer until thickened slightly, about 10 minutes. Off heat, stir in basil and oil; season with salt and pepper. Serve.

📹 **COOK'S VIDEOS** Original Test Kitchen Videos
www.cooksillustrated.com/jun09
HOW TO MAKE
• Quick Tomato Sauce

Foolproof Grilled Salmon Fillets

It's not the seasoning or the cooking that's confounding— it's getting the fish off the grill in one piece.

⪴ BY J. KENJI ALT ⪵

Cooking delicate salmon can be tricky. Even in a nonstick skillet, I still end up breaking the occasional fillet, which requires a patch job on the plate. Introduce the same fillet to a grill, and you've got a real challenge. If the cooking grate on your charcoal grill is encrusted with gunk, things get even messier. And the situation isn't much better on a gas grill: When it's time to flip the fish, the skin invariably gets stuck and the flesh mangled.

So how is it that any halfway decent chophouse or pub manages to serve char-grilled salmon with a tender interior and crisp skin, the fillet perfectly intact? There had to be a secret behind the swinging doors.

Sizing Up Salmon

In truth, part of the solution was already behind the test kitchen's back door, in a protocol we developed to clean the grill thoroughly: Place an overturned disposable aluminum pan over the grate as the grill warms up, trapping hot air and superheating the grate to temperatures that exceed 800 degrees. Just like in a self-cleaning oven, the high heat causes grease and debris to disintegrate. By swapping the disposable pan for aluminum foil pressed flush against the grate (with spaces left on each side for ventilation), I was able to bump this temperature up to nearly 900 degrees, making the technique even more effective. I also decided

RECIPE DIAGNOSIS
A Sticking Situation

BAD BREAKUP
Without intervention, fish fillets bond to the grill, making removal in one piece impossible.

A bright vinaigrette tops off the perfectly grilled fish.

to use salmon fillets with a thickness of ¾ inch to 1 inch, which can stand the heat of the grill for a little while longer before the first turn.

With a clean grill and fish at the ready, I reviewed dozens of recipes that claimed to solve the sticking quandary. Many books (including one of our own) advise using a foil boat to keep the fish from ever touching the grill. This trick works, but it creates a new problem: The fish never picks up true char-grilled flavor. Elevating the salmon on fennel fronds, citrus slices, and other foods created steam that made the fish taste more poached than grilled—definitely not the result I wanted. Other recipes suggest boosting the flame. Thanks to the preheating-with-foil technique, however, my grill was already nearly 900 degrees, yet the salmon still stuck to the grate.

Stumped, I did a bit of research and discovered the cause of my problem. Unlike the superficial stickiness caused by, say, barbecue sauce or a sweet glaze, the bond between proteins and grill is a molecule-to-molecule fusion. Since this reaction happens almost the instant the fish hits the grill, trying to separate them

is an exercise in futility. To prevent sticking, I had two options: altering the proteins on the surface of the fish so they wouldn't bond with the metal grate, or creating a barrier between fish and grill.

The most obvious way to alter proteins is to cook them. Since even a grill as hot as 900 degrees wasn't cooking the salmon fast enough to prevent bonding, I theorized that perhaps the moisture on and just underneath the surface of the fish was slowing things down. (When wet food is placed on a grill, much of the fire's energy is at first used to convert that moisture to steam.) Drying the fish's exterior by wrapping it in kitchen towels and putting it in the refrigerator before grilling helped, but not enough. What if I parcooked the fish just until its exterior was set and then placed it on the grill? I quickly learned there was no efficient way to parcook it. Poaching took too long, microwaving proved uneven, and sautéing seemed silly—if I started it in a pan, after all, I might as well finish it there.

Since altering the proteins didn't seem to be the solution, I was left wondering how I might create a barrier between fish and grill. Scores of recipes advise oiling both the cooking grate and the fish. I found this method only moderately effective at reducing sticking, but it did make me realize that when oil is applied to a hot cooking grate, it vaporizes almost instantly, leaving a black, weblike residue. Here's what happens: As oil heats up, its fatty-acid chains form polymers (that is, they stick together), creating that crisscross pattern over the surface of the metal.

I had observed this reaction while seasoning a cast-iron pan. A single layer of these polymers won't prevent sticking, but applying and heating oil repeatedly will build up a thick layer of them. Eventually, this will mean that proteins can no longer come into direct contact with the metal and therefore cannot bond with it. It was suddenly clear to me why restaurant cooks rarely have the same sticking problems as home grillers: With a grill in use throughout the day, there must be a hefty buildup of polymers. Could I speed the process and "season" my cooking grate in one session?

Teflon Effect

Instead of brushing the cooking grate with a single coat of oil, I decided to try brushing it over and

I. DRYING fillets prevents moisture on their surface from cooling cooking grate, which can lead to sticking.

2. SUPER-HEATING grill by covering it with aluminum foil ensures that all stuck-on debris disintegrates.

3. SEASONING cooking grate with multiple layers of oil builds nonstick surface.

4. POSITIONING fish diagonally on cooking grate creates attractive grill marks and makes flipping easier.

5. DOUBLING UP on spatulas supports fish from two sides while it's being flipped.

over again, until it had developed a dark, shiny coating, and then lay the fillets on the grate. With the help of two spatulas—one in each hand—I easily flipped each fillet without even the tiniest bit of sticking.

Finally, I could focus on the grilling. From experience, I expected that preheating the grill to high and then turning it down to medium once I added the fish would achieve optimum charring without overcooking, and my salmon was no exception.

As for flavor, I ultimately preferred just a sprinkle of salt and pepper or, with just a little more work, a tangy almond vinaigrette. The char-grilled taste I'd worked so hard to achieve didn't need anything more.

EQUIPMENT TESTING
Grill Baskets

Our Gas-Grilled Salmon Fillets recipe solves the biggest challenge in grilling fish: sticking. Could grill baskets, the solution proffered by barbecue-gear manufacturers, also do the trick? We gathered three models, priced from $19 to $28.99, and headed outdoors. Even as skeptics, we were startled that each had serious design flaws: too-deep compartments that let fillets flop and tear, barriers that lifted fish too far from the flame, and nonremovable handles that made it impossible to close the grill lid, leaving fish undercooked. Until manufacturers figure out how to make a better basket, we'll stick to our method of grilling fish. For complete testing results, go to www.cooksillustrated.com/jun09. –Meredith Butcher

BEST OF THE WORST
STEVEN RAICHLEN Rectangular
4 Compartment Nonstick
Grilling Basket
Price: $24.95
Comments: This model was the least flawed of the baskets we tested, but still caused salmon fillets to tear when flipped.

GAS-GRILLED SALMON FILLETS
SERVES 4

Note: This recipe works best with salmon fillets but can also be used with any thick, firm-fleshed white fish, including red snapper, grouper, halibut, and sea bass (cook white fish to 140 degrees, up to 2 minutes longer per side). If you are using skinless fillets, treat the skinned side of each as if it were the skin side. If your fillets are thicker than 1 inch, increase the cooking time on the second side in step 3 until the center of the fillet registers 125 degrees (or 140 degrees for white fish). Serve with Almond Vinaigrette, if desired (recipe follows). For our free recipes for Rouille and Olive Vinaigrette, go to www.cooksillustrated.com/jun09.

4 skin-on salmon fillets, ¾ to 1 inch thick
   (6 to 8 ounces each) (see note)
   Vegetable oil
   Kosher salt and ground black pepper
   Lemon wedges

1. Place fillets skin-side up on rimmed baking sheet or large plate lined with clean kitchen towel. Place second clean kitchen towel on top of fillets and press down to blot liquid. Refrigerate fish, wrapped in towels, while preparing grill, at least 20 minutes.

2. Meanwhile, following photo 2 above, loosely cover cooking grate with large piece of heavy-duty aluminum foil. Turn all burners to high, cover, and heat grill until very hot, about 15 minutes. Remove foil with tongs and discard. Use grill brush to scrape cooking grate clean. Lightly dip wad of paper towels in oil; holding wad with tongs, wipe grate. Continue to wipe grate with oiled paper towels, re-dipping towels in oil between applications, until grate is black and glossy, 5 to 10 times (photo 3).

3. Brush both sides of fish with thin coat of oil and season with salt and pepper. Place fish skin-side down on grill diagonal to grate (photo 4), reduce heat to medium, cover grill, and cook without moving until skin side is brown, well marked, and crisp, 3 to 5 minutes. (Try lifting fish gently with spatula after 3 minutes; if it doesn't cleanly lift off grill, continue to cook, checking at 30-second intervals until it releases.)

Using 2 spatulas, flip fish to second side (photo 5) and cook, covered, until centers of fillets are opaque and register 125 degrees on instant-read thermometer, 2 to 6 minutes longer. Serve immediately with lemon wedges or Almond Vinaigrette.

CHARCOAL-GRILLED SALMON FILLETS

Follow recipe for Gas-Grilled Salmon Fillets through step 1. While fish dries, light large chimney starter filled two-thirds with charcoal (4 quarts, about 65 briquettes) and allow to burn until coals are fully ignited and partially covered with thin layer of ash, 15 to 20 minutes. Build modified two-level fire by arranging coals to cover half of grill, leaving other half empty. Prepare grill as directed in step 2. Proceed with recipe from step 3, cooking fish, covered, directly over coals.

ALMOND VINAIGRETTE
MAKES ABOUT ½ CUP

⅓ cup almonds, toasted
2 teaspoons honey
1 teaspoon Dijon mustard
4 teaspoons white wine vinegar
1 medium shallot, minced (about 2 tablespoons)
⅓ cup extra-virgin olive oil
1 tablespoon cold water
1 tablespoon chopped fresh tarragon leaves
   Table salt and ground black pepper

Place almonds in zipper-lock bag and, using rolling pin, pound until no pieces larger than ½ inch remain. Combine pounded almonds, honey, mustard, vinegar, and shallot in medium bowl. Whisking constantly, drizzle in olive oil until emulsion forms. Add water and tarragon and whisk to combine, then season with salt and pepper. Serve.

📹 **COOK'S VIDEOS** Original Test Kitchen Videos
www.cooksillustrated.com/jun09
HOW TO MAKE
• Gas-Grilled Salmon Fillets
VIDEO TIP
• How can I keep food from sticking to the grill?

Marinating Done Right

Marinating is often regarded as a cure-all for bland, chewy meat. Years of testing have taught us that while it can bump up flavor, it will never turn a tough cut tender. But with the right ingredients in the mix, marinating can enhance juiciness and add complexity to steak, chicken, and pork. BY CHARLES KELSEY

A Better Way to Marinate: Brinerate

Successful marinating is all about getting as much of the soaking liquid flavors into (and on) the meat as possible. Brining in a saltwater solution is a way to create more juiciness. To pump up flavor as well as juiciness, our marinades combine both approaches, with soaking liquids that not only contain lots of seasonings and flavorings but so much salt, you might even call them "brinerades." (In fact, our marinades typically have two to three times more salt than our brines.) As in a brine, salt in a marinade affects meat in two ways. Through osmotic pressure, it pulls moisture from a place of higher water concentration (the marinade) into a place with a lower one (the meat). In addition, it restructures the protein molecules in the meat, creating gaps that fill with water to further increase juiciness. It also seasons the meat, enhancing its inherent flavors.

BUSTING THE MYTHS

MYTH: Marinades Penetrate Meat Deeply
FACT: Most Impact Is Superficial

Contrary to popular belief, marinades do most of their work on the surface of meat or just below. Some ingredients in a marinade do penetrate the meat—but only by a few millimeters (and oil-soluble herbs and spices in the mix merely add flavor to the exterior). To prove the point, we soaked beef short ribs in red wine for intervals from one hour to 18, then measured the band of purple created by the wine. Our finding? Even after 18 hours of soaking, the wine penetrated less than 1 millimeter. Additional testing with marinated boneless chicken breasts confirmed that the flavors of other kinds of soaking liquids do not penetrate to the center of the meat. (See "The Short Journey of a Marinade," page 17.)

MYTH: Acids Tenderize Meat
FACT: Acids Turn Meat Mushy

To tenderize meat, you have to break down muscle fiber and collagen, the connective tissue that makes meat tough, thus increasing the meat's ability to retain moisture. While acidic ingredients like citrus juice, vinegar, yogurt, buttermilk, and wine do weaken collagen, their impact is confined to the meat's surface. We find that if left too long, acids turn the outermost layer of meat mushy, not tender. To minimize mushiness, we use acidic components sparingly (or cut them out entirely) and only for short marinating times.

USE WITH DISCRETION

MYTH: The Longer the Soak, the Better
FACT: A Long Soak Is Pointless—Even Detrimental

Because marinades don't penetrate deeply, a lengthy soak is pointless. Furthermore, too long a soak in an acidic (or enzymatic) marinade can weaken the protein bonds near the surface so that they turn mushy—or worse, can no longer hold moisture and dry out.

MYTH: Marinades Add Flavor to Any Meat
FACT: Marinades Are Best for Thin Cuts

With their influence limited mostly to the surface of meat, we reserve marinades for relatively thin cuts like chicken breasts, pork chops, steaks, cutlets, and meat cut into chunks or slices for kebabs and stir-fries. A large roast or turkey breast is never a good bet; a spice paste that will adhere to the meat is a better option.

THICK: PROBLEMATIC

THIN: OPTIMAL

MYTH: Enzymes Tenderize Meat
FACT: Enzymes Make Meat Mushy

The enzymes in many plants—such as papain in papaya and bromelain in pineapple, to name two—can break down collagen in meat. But as with acids, their impact is limited to the meat's surface, where we find they likewise turn the texture mushy, not tender.

Marinade Must-Haves

Both salt and oil are critical to a successful marinade; soy, sugar, and honey are great flavor boosters.

SALT: NOT JUST SEASONING

To increase the meat's juiciness, our marinades usually include a high concentration of salt (typically about 1½ teaspoons per 3 tablespoons of liquid), and thus serve as "brinerades" that combine the benefits of both marinating and brining.

OIL: FLAVOR FACILITATOR

Most of the herbs and spices we add to marinades are oil-soluble, which means they only release their full flavor when mixed in oil. So, to get the most out of a marinade, always include oil. But note: These flavors will merely coat, not penetrate, the meat. Meat proteins are saturated with water, so they won't absorb the oil or its flavors.

SOY: FLAVOR ENHANCER

For more complex flavor, use soy sauce instead of salt—besides being salty, it contains glutamic acid, which boosts meaty flavor.

SUGAR/HONEY: BROWNING BOOSTERS

Sweeteners like sugar and honey not only add complexity, they also help foods brown during cooking, further developing flavor.

MYTH: Bottled Dressing Is a Great Time-Saver
FACT: Bottled Dressing Makes Mediocre Marinade

Due to high levels of acidity, salad dressings don't add complex flavor and only make meat mushy. Plus, they are laden with sweeteners, stabilizers, and gums, which add a gelatinous consistency and unnatural flavor.

BAN THE BOTTLE

TIPS FOR SUCCESS

Use Lots of Flavorings and Seasonings
➤ In tests, we've found that a high concentration of salt in a marinade (and we use plenty) can inhibit meat from absorbing the flavors of other ingredients, unless they're included in copious quantities (i.e., 3 or 4 cloves of garlic and at least a tablespoon of chopped herbs, if using).

Score Meat before Marinating
➤ To help the marinade penetrate as deeply as possible (especially thicker cuts like flank steak), prick the surface of the meat with a fork or score it with a knife.

Flip or Stir
➤ Place meat in a zipper-lock bag with the air squeezed out or use a large baking dish covered with plastic wrap. Flip the bag or stir the meat halfway through the soaking time to ensure that the meat is thoroughly coated.

Refrigerate while Marinating
➤ To eliminate the risk of microorganisms spreading in raw meat, don't leave meat on the counter—refrigerate it. This keeps it out of the temperature danger zone of 40 to 140 degrees, within which bacteria spread rapidly.

Remove Marinade before Cooking
➤ To prevent flare-ups on the grill and ensure properly browned meat when sautéing or stir-frying, wipe off most of the excess marinade before cooking. Keep just a little marinade on the meat surface to maximize flavor.

Don't Recycle Used Marinade
➤ Used marinade is contaminated with raw meat juice and is therefore unsafe. If you want sauce to serve with the cooked meat, just make a little extra marinade and set it aside before adding the bulk of the marinade to the raw meat.

The Short Journey of a Marinade
To determine how far flavors in different marinades might penetrate into meat, we placed boneless, skinless chicken breasts in four different soaking liquids (variously made with soy sauce, yogurt, wine, and lemon juice and garlic). We soaked all four batches a full 18 hours, then cooked them in a 300-degree oven until the internal temperature registered 160 degrees. We then cut off 3 millimeters from the exterior of each breast (a good 2 millimeters beyond where it was clear the soy and wine marinades had penetrated). Finally, we tasted the trimmed chicken side by side with breasts we baked at 300 degrees without marinating. Tasters could find no distinguishable flavor differences among any of the batches. Our conclusion: Marinade flavors do not penetrate meat beyond the first few millimeters, no matter what is in the mix.

BETTER THAN A-1 STEAK MARINADE
MAKES ENOUGH FOR 2 POUNDS OF STEAK

⅓ cup vegetable oil
½ cup soy sauce
2 tablespoons dark brown sugar
¼ cup Worcestershire sauce
4 medium garlic cloves, minced or pressed through garlic press (about 4 teaspoons)
2 tablespoons minced fresh chives
1½ teaspoons ground black pepper

Whisk together ingredients in medium bowl. Place marinade and steak in gallon-sized zipper-lock bag; press out as much air as possible and seal bag. Refrigerate 1 hour and up to 90 minutes, flipping bag halfway through to ensure that steaks marinate evenly.

HERB-LEMON MARINADE FOR CHICKEN
MAKES ENOUGH FOR 2 POUNDS OF CHICKEN

Note: Boneless, skinless chicken breasts should be marinated for no less than 30 minutes and no more than 1 hour. Skin-on, bone-in chicken should be marinated for at least 45 minutes and no longer than 90 minutes.

3 tablespoons olive oil
1 tablespoon minced fresh herbs, such as tarragon, chives, basil, or parsley
1 tablespoon juice from 1 lemon
3 medium garlic cloves, minced or pressed through garlic press (about 1 tablespoon)
1 teaspoon sugar
1½ teaspoons table salt
½ teaspoon ground black pepper
2 tablespoons water

Whisk together ingredients in medium bowl. Place marinade and chicken in gallon-sized zipper-lock bag; press out as much air as possible and seal bag. Depending on chicken type, refrigerate 30 to 90 minutes (see note), flipping bag halfway through to ensure that chicken marinates evenly.

HONEY-MUSTARD MARINADE FOR PORK
MAKES ENOUGH FOR 2 POUNDS OF PORK

⅓ cup vegetable oil
½ cup soy sauce
4 teaspoons honey
3 tablespoons Dijon mustard
2 tablespoons chopped fresh tarragon leaves
4 medium garlic cloves, minced or pressed through garlic press (about 4 teaspoons)
1½ teaspoons ground black pepper

Whisk together ingredients in medium bowl. Place marinade and pork in gallon-sized zipper-lock bag; press out as much air as possible and seal bag. Refrigerate 1 hour and up to 90 minutes, flipping bag halfway through to ensure that pork marinates evenly.

Better Shrimp Tempura

Japanese chefs spend years learning how to create a light, crisp coating on these quick-fried fritters. We turned to a different secret weapon: the liquor cabinet.

⇒ BY FRANCISCO J. ROBERT ⇐

y anybody's standards, a perfectly cooked piece of shrimp tempura is a beautiful thing—a fried food so light, crisp, and fresh-tasting that it barely seems fried. Done properly, the essence of sweet, tender shrimp defines its taste. Portuguese missionaries introduced quick-fried seafood to Japan in the 16th century (the name is believed to refer to the day of abstinence when missionaries avoided meat), but over the course of the next few centuries, Japanese cooks made this technique their own.

The approach sounds simple enough: Stir together a batter of flour, egg, and water; dip in shrimp (or other ingredients); drop into hot oil; and fry just until crisp and light golden. But a few preliminary attempts at making tempura in the test kitchen made me see why some Japanese chefs devote their careers to this one technique. Success hinges almost entirely on the batter—which is maddeningly hard to get right. Under-mix by just a hair and the batter remains thin, barely providing a barrier against the hot oil and allowing the shrimp to overcook. Overmix by a similarly small degree and you wind up with a coating so thick and doughy that it seems more at home on a corn dog than shrimp.

Short of apprenticing with a tempura master, if I ever wanted to enjoy this specialty outside a restaurant, I needed to make the method foolproof.

Batch Processing

I started with the batter formula found in most traditional recipes: one egg and equal parts ice water and flour. To make dinner for four, I'd need 1½ pounds of shrimp. Since it's all too easy to overcook small shrimp, I chose the largest available (8–12 per pound). Instead of a wok, I substituted the test kitchen's preferred vessel for deep-frying, a large Dutch oven.

I heated 3 quarts of oil to 400 degrees—a little hotter than most recipes called for, but a higher temperature would help the shrimp cook quickly, limiting the absorption of oil. Since tempura tastes best served immediately, I first tried cooking the batter-soaked shrimp in one batch. Total failure: With all 1½ pounds in the pot at once, the oil

Cooking the tempura in 400-degree oil helps limit grease absorption and yields lighter, crisper results.

temperature plunged to 300 degrees, and the shrimp needed to stay so long in the pot that their coating was practically dripping with grease. But cooking in two batches (I kept the first batch warm in the oven while I cooked the second) immediately brought the problems of batter consistency to the fore: Even when my first batch achieved just the right crisp

and delicate texture, the second batch still turned out thick and doughy. Why?

When water and flour are mixed, the proteins in the flour form gluten, giving structure to the coating. Protein from the egg buttresses this structure and adds flavor and color. As it hits the hot oil, the water in the batter rapidly expands into steam, creating small bubbles. At the same time, the egg and gluten coagulate and stiffen, strengthening the bubbles. This chain of reactions is what gives tempura its intricate, lacy-crisp texture—and also what makes the batter so persnickety. As I'd already seen, too little mixing led to too little gluten and a limp coating. Too much mixing led to too much gluten, which made it difficult for water to escape. The result: a greasy, breadlike coating. And there was one more problem. Gluten develops even without stirring; as my batter sat untouched on the counter between batches, it was thickening with every second that passed.

Better Batter

Many chefs claim to make the batter failsafe with "secret" ingredients or novel techniques. It couldn't hurt to try a few. One idea—adding whipped egg white to the batter—led to shrimp encased in a coating so voluminous it resembled a balloon. Other sources recommended adding baking soda to the batter. The coating was crisp, all right, but it was also so crumbly that it fell right off the shrimp. As a last shot, I replaced the flour with cornstarch, which develops no gluten at all. The coating looked delicate and crisp, but turned out to be as tough as Styrofoam.

RECIPE TESTING Batter Up

TOO THICK
Overmixed batter fries into a thick, breadlike coating.

TOO PUFFY
Whisking whipped egg white into the batter creates a balloonlike coating.

TOO THIN
Undermixed batter remains thin, contributing to overcooked shrimp.

JUST RIGHT
A surprise ingredient and the right technique keep our coating crisp and airy.

How to Make Vegetable Tempura

To use leftover batter to make vegetable fritters, dip 2 cups of vegetables in the batter and fry 2 to 3 minutes, following the same instructions for the shrimp.

VEGETABLE	PREP REQUIRED
Green beans	Trim ends
Snow peas	Remove strings
Scallions	Trim ends
Asparagus	Remove woody bottoms and split large spears lengthwise
Shiitake mushrooms	Remove stems
Button mushrooms	Leave small mushrooms whole; halve medium mushrooms; quarter large mushrooms
Portobello mushrooms	Cut into ½-inch slices
Eggplant	Slice into ½-inch rounds or half moons
Onion	Cut into ½-inch rings

Back at square one, I reviewed my batter ingredients one at a time, starting with the flour. Replacing all the flour with cornstarch hadn't worked, but what if I just reduced the amount of gluten instead of eliminating it? Starting with 2 cups of flour and 1 tablespoon of cornstarch, I gradually increased the ratio until I arrived at a mixture of 1½ cups of flour and ½ cup of cornstarch. This significantly improved the structure and lightness in the first batch, but did nothing to address consistency.

Moving on to the egg, I tried adjusting the number of yolks and whites; a single egg produced the best results in every test. Then I considered the final ingredient: water. I was using ice water, which slows down gluten development—until the water warms up. Searching for an alternative, I recalled a recipe that used seltzer. I swapped out the ice water for 2 cups of effervescent seltzer, hoping that its multitude of bubbles would make my batter even more delicate and lacy. Seltzer produced the desired effect—and then some. It turns out that seltzer, with a pH of four, is slightly more acidic than regular tap water, enough to slow down gluten development (a pH of five to six is optimal for gluten formation). My batter now fried up into a wonderfully airy coating—but it was still too easy to overmix, and it turned thicker yet as it sat.

Then it hit me: A couple of years ago, a fellow test cook faced the same conundrum trying to master pie crust. To ensure a perfectly tender crust, he had to minimize gluten development in the dough. His solution? Eighty-proof vodka, which consists of about 60 percent water and 40 percent alcohol.

◄ COOK'S VIDEOS Original Test Kitchen Videos
www.cooksillustrated.com/jun09
HOW TO MAKE
• Shrimp Tempura
VIDEO TIPS
• How do I know what size shrimp to buy?
• How do I prepare vegetables for tempura?

While water contributes to gluten, alcohol doesn't. I fried two batches of shrimp made with 1 cup of seltzer and 1 cup of vodka, and the shrimp I pulled out of the hot oil were not only consistent from the first batch to the second, but also the lightest and crispest I'd made yet.

With a foolproof batter at last, I could now fine-tune the details. Even though the batter was perfectly light and lacy, it still clumped on the inside curl of the shrimp. To set that straight, I made two shallow cuts on the underside of its flesh. The traditional sauce uses *dashi*, a Japanese stock made from dried kelp and bonito (tuna) flakes. I streamlined it and came up with a sweet ginger-soy dip.

My recipe was quite a departure from tradition, but you would never know it from the featherweight coating and supremely tender shrimp on my plate.

SHRIMP TEMPURA
SERVES 4

Note: Do not omit the vodka; it is critical for a crisp coating. For safety, use a Dutch oven with a capacity of at least 7 quarts. Be sure to begin mixing the batter when the oil reaches 385 degrees (the final temperature should reach 400 degrees). It is important to maintain a high oil temperature throughout cooking. If you are unable to find colossal shrimp (8–12 per pound), jumbo (16–20) or extra-large (21–25) may be substituted. Fry smaller shrimp in three batches, reducing the cooking time to 1½ to 2 minutes per batch. See page 30 for tips on preventing the shrimp from curling. For our free recipes for Chile Aïoli Dipping Sauce and Teppanyaki Mustard Dipping Sauce, go to www.cooksillustrated.com/jun09.

- 3 quarts vegetable oil
- 1½ pounds colossal shrimp (8 to 12 per pound), peeled and deveined, tails left on (see note)
- 1½ cups unbleached all-purpose flour
- ½ cup cornstarch
- 1 large egg
- 1 cup vodka (see note)
- 1 cup seltzer water
-    Kosher salt
- 1 recipe Ginger-Soy Dipping Sauce (recipe follows)

1. Adjust oven rack to upper-middle position and heat oven to 200 degrees. In large, heavy Dutch oven fitted with clip-on candy thermometer, heat oil over high heat to 385 degrees, 18 to 22 minutes.

2. While oil heats, make 2 shallow cuts about ¼ inch deep and 1 inch apart on underside of each shrimp. Whisk flour and cornstarch together in large bowl. Whisk egg and vodka together in second large bowl. Whisk seltzer water into egg mixture.

3. When oil reaches 385 degrees, pour liquid mixture into bowl with flour mixture and whisk gently until just combined (it is OK if small lumps remain). Submerge half of shrimp in batter. Using tongs, remove shrimp from batter 1 at a time, allowing excess batter to drip off, and carefully place in oil

(temperature should now be at 400 degrees). Fry, stirring with chopstick or wooden skewer to prevent sticking, until light brown, 2 to 3 minutes. Using slotted spoon, transfer shrimp to paper towel–lined plate and sprinkle with salt. Once paper towels absorb excess oil, place shrimp on wire rack set in rimmed baking sheet and place in oven.

4. Return oil to 400 degrees, about 4 minutes, and repeat with remaining shrimp. Serve immediately with Ginger-Soy Dipping Sauce.

GINGER-SOY DIPPING SAUCE
MAKES ABOUT ¾ CUP

- ¼ cup soy sauce
- 3 tablespoons mirin
- 1 teaspoon sugar
- 1 teaspoon toasted sesame oil
- 1 garlic clove, minced or pressed through garlic press (about 1 teaspoon)
- 2 teaspoons grated fresh ginger
- 1 scallion, finely chopped

Whisk all ingredients together in medium bowl.

Best Blueberry Muffins

The best guarantee of a great blueberry muffin is to start with great blueberries. We wanted a recipe that would work even with the watery supermarket kind.

≥ BY YVONNE RUPERTI ≤

Years ago, I owned a small bakery in rural upstate New York with a seasonal claim to fame: my blueberry muffins. Whenever I could get my hands on locally grown, freshly picked wild blueberries, the word would spread like wildfire in our little town, and patrons would deplete my bakery case of every single muffin before they even had a chance to cool. I'd like to take all the credit for the muffins, but the truth is, the intense fruitiness of the berries was what made these aromatic, sweet-tart gems so special.

Now that I've moved on from the bakery, I can't help turning up my nose at muffins made with supermarket blueberries. Sure, pints of plump blueberries always look appealing, but pop one into your mouth, and its lackluster, watery taste has nowhere to hide. It's really no surprise: Despite the fact that blueberries are indigenous to North America (particularly the Northeast), they can come from as far away as Chile. Fruit picked before it is ripe and shipped thousands of miles away simply can't match the quality of local, wild berries. I wanted to make blueberry muffins that would taste great with any blueberries, regardless of origin. They would be packed with blueberry flavor and have a moist crumb, one sturdy enough to hold up under the weight of a substantial helping of fruit.

Jam Session

Without a doubt, intense, fruity flavor was my top priority. I decided to use the muffin recipe from my bakery to see how many supermarket berries the batter could hold, and then I'd try to work some magic on their flavor. My recipe called for the creaming method, which incorporates a lot of air into the batter by beating butter and sugar, adding eggs and then milk, and finally folding in flour, salt, and baking powder. I did a test run by folding 1 cup of blueberries into this creamed batter before baking the muffins. As soon as I broke into the first one, I could see that 1 cup of fruit wasn't enough. Doubling the amount of berries only weighed the crumb down with heavy pockets of weak, watery fruit. I moved on, scouring the test kitchen pantry for ingredients to bolster the blueberry flavor. The two most promising were dried blueberries and blueberry jam.

Fresh and cooked berries intensify the fruity flavor of our muffins.

I started by swapping out the fresh berries for dried, only to find that they yielded muffins with chewy, raisinlike blueberry bits. And the dehydrated blueberries greedily soaked up moisture from the muffins, making the crumb dry. Rehydrating the berries before incorporating them into the batter wasn't the answer; while the dried berries did plump up and lend a likable zing, they still weren't juicy or fresh-tasting.

Next, I cracked open a jar of blueberry jam. After dividing up the batter, I swirled a spoonful of jam into each filled cup. The muffins baked up with a pretty blue filling, but tasters unanimously agreed that the sugary jam had made them too sweet. On the verge of a muffin meltdown, I suddenly found hope. What if I made my own fresh, low-sugar berry jam to swirl into the muffins? I simmered 1 cup of fresh blueberries on the stovetop to concentrate flavor and evaporate excess juices, adding a mere teaspoon of sugar for a touch of sweetness. After about six minutes, I had ¼ cup of thick, potent, deep-indigo jam that was chock-full of moist, tart blueberries. After my homemade jam cooled, I used a chopstick to swirl a teaspoon of it into each of the batter-filled cups, then baked. Success! The flavor was pure blueberry, reminding me of my wild-berry muffins from long ago.

There was just one thing missing: the juicy texture of fresh berries. This was easily solved; I just added 1 cup of fresh, uncooked berries to the batter before swirling in the jam. The muffins now contained the best of both worlds: intense blueberry flavor and the liquid burst that only fresh berries can provide.

Cake Walk

At this point, I had conquered blueberry flavor. Now all I needed was a great muffin base to show it off. The creaming method had always worked fine for my muffins filled with tiny wild blueberries. But it yielded a texture that was too cakelike and tender to properly support the heavy jam and plump berries in my new muffins. I decided to give the quick-bread method a shot, hoping it would generate a sturdier crumb. This method calls for whisking together the eggs and sugar, adding milk and melted butter, and then gently folding in flour, baking powder, and salt. I was careful to not overmix. (As with pancake batter, overly strenuous mixing encourages the proteins in flour to cross-link and form gluten, toughening the final product.) Tasters agreed that this method was ideal, producing a hearty, substantial crumb that could support a generous amount of fruit.

To achieve the unctuously moist muffins I sought, I examined the fat in the recipe. While the butter was contributing tons of flavor, I knew that oil has a propensity for making baked goods moist and tender. Unlike butter, oil contains no water and is able to completely coat flour proteins and restrict them from absorbing liquid to develop gluten. It made sense to try swapping out some of the butter for vegetable oil. Using small increments, I gradually replaced some of the butter with oil and found that an equal amount of each (4 tablespoons melted butter, 4 tablespoons oil) produced just the right combination of buttery flavor and moist, tender texture.

Almost there, I wondered if I could make the

RECIPE TESTING
When More Isn't Better

To boost berry flavor in a muffin, simply adding more blueberries isn't the answer. With too many in the mix, the berries sink to the bottom, weighing the muffin down.

WEIGHED DOWN

1. MAKE BERRY JAM
Cook half of fresh blueberries into thick jam to concentrate their flavor and eliminate excess moisture.

2. ADD FRESH BERRIES
Stir 1 cup of fresh blueberries into batter to provide juicy bursts in every bite.

3. PORTION BATTER
Scoop batter into muffin pans, completely filling cups.

4. ADD JAM TO BATTER
Place 1 teaspoon of cooled berry jam in center of each batter-filled cup, pushing it below surface.

5. SWIRL INTO BATTER
Using chopstick or skewer, swirl jam to spread berry flavor throughout.

---

muffins even richer. I felt confident that something other than the whole milk I'd been using could deliver more flavor. Rich and tangy sour cream, a popular choice for quick-bread batters, made these muffins somewhat dense and heavy. Buttermilk, however, was just the ticket. It provided appealing richness but was light enough to keep the muffins from turning into heavyweights. As a bonus, its slight tang also nicely complemented the blueberries.

Baking the muffins at 425 degrees on the upper-middle rack gave them a golden brown crust. And as a crowning jewel, I sprinkled lemon-scented sugar on top of the batter just before baking. The oven melted the sugar slightly, which then hardened as it baked to create an irresistibly crunchy shell. I now had muffins to rival the ones I'd so proudly offered at my bakery, and I could make them at any time of the year.

BEST BLUEBERRY MUFFINS
MAKES 12 MUFFINS

Note: If buttermilk is unavailable, substitute ¾ cup plain whole-milk or low-fat yogurt thinned with ¼ cup milk.

Lemon-Sugar Topping
- ⅓ cup (2⅓ ounces) sugar
- 1½ teaspoons finely grated zest from 1 lemon

Muffins
- 2 cups (about 10 ounces) fresh blueberries, picked over
- 1⅛ cups (8 ounces) plus 1 teaspoon sugar
- 2½ cups (12½ ounces) unbleached all-purpose flour
- 2½ teaspoons baking powder
- 1 teaspoon table salt
- 2 large eggs
- 4 tablespoons (½ stick) unsalted butter, melted and cooled slightly
- ¼ cup vegetable oil
- 1 cup buttermilk (see note)
- 1½ teaspoons vanilla extract

1. **FOR THE TOPPING:** Stir together sugar and lemon zest in small bowl until combined; set aside.

2. **FOR THE MUFFINS:** Adjust oven rack to upper-middle position and heat oven to 425 degrees. Spray standard muffin tin with nonstick cooking spray. Bring 1 cup blueberries and 1 teaspoon sugar to simmer in small saucepan over medium heat. Cook, mashing berries with spoon several times and stirring frequently, until berries have broken down and mixture is thickened and reduced to ¼ cup, about 6 minutes. Transfer to small bowl and cool to room temperature, 10 to 15 minutes.

3. Whisk flour, baking powder, and salt together in large bowl. Whisk remaining 1⅛ cups sugar and eggs together in medium bowl until thick and homogeneous, about 45 seconds. Slowly whisk in butter and oil until combined. Whisk in buttermilk and vanilla until combined. Using rubber spatula, fold egg mixture and remaining cup blueberries into flour mixture until just moistened. (Batter will be very lumpy with few spots of dry flour; do not overmix.)

4. Following photos above, use ice cream scoop or large spoon to divide batter equally among prepared muffin cups (batter should completely fill cups and mound slightly). Spoon teaspoon of cooked berry mixture into center of each mound of batter. Using chopstick or skewer, gently swirl berry filling into batter using figure-eight motion. Sprinkle lemon sugar evenly over muffins.

5. Bake until muffin tops are golden and just firm, 17 to 19 minutes, rotating muffin tin from front to back halfway through baking time. Cool muffins in muffin tin for 5 minutes, then transfer to wire rack and cool 5 minutes before serving.

BEST BLUEBERRY MUFFINS
WITH FROZEN BLUEBERRIES

Note: Our preferred brands of frozen blueberries are Wyman's and Cascadian Farm.

Follow recipe for Best Blueberry Muffins, substituting 2 cups frozen berries for fresh. Cook 1 cup berries as directed in step 2. Rinse remaining cup berries under cold water and dry well. In step 3, toss dried berries in flour mixture before adding egg mixture. Proceed with recipe from step 4 as directed.

BEST BLUEBERRY MUFFINS
WITH STREUSEL TOPPING

Follow recipe for Best Blueberry Muffins, omitting Lemon-Sugar Topping. Prepare streusel by combining 3 tablespoons granulated sugar, 3 tablespoons dark brown sugar, pinch table salt, and ½ cup plus 3 tablespoons (3½ ounces) unbleached all-purpose flour in small bowl. Drizzle with 5 tablespoons warm, melted unsalted butter and toss with fork until evenly moistened and mixture forms large chunks with some pea-sized pieces throughout. Proceed with recipe as directed, sprinkling streusel topping over muffins before baking.

BEST BLUEBERRY MUFFINS
WITH ORANGE GLAZE

Follow recipe for Best Blueberry Muffins, omitting Lemon-Sugar Topping. Add 2 teaspoons finely grated orange zest to egg mixture in step 3. Proceed with recipe as directed, sprinkling 4 teaspoons turbinado sugar over muffins before baking. While muffins cool, whisk together 1 cup confectioners' sugar and 1½ tablespoons orange juice until smooth. Drizzle each cooled muffin with 2 teaspoons glaze before serving.

BEST BLUEBERRY MUFFINS
WITH ALMOND CRUNCH TOPPING

Follow recipe for Best Blueberry Muffins, omitting Lemon-Sugar Topping. In step 1, combine ⅓ cup finely ground almonds and 4 teaspoons turbinado sugar; set aside. In step 3, add ⅓ cup finely ground almonds to flour mixture. Proceed with recipe as directed, adding 1 teaspoon almond extract with vanilla extract in step 3 and sprinkling almond topping over muffins before baking.

🎥 **COOK'S VIDEOS** Original Test Kitchen Videos
www.cooksillustrated.com/jun09
HOW TO MAKE
• Best Blueberry Muffins
VIDEO TIP
• Muffin pans 101

The Perfect Chocolate Chip Cookie

We set out to perfect the back-of-the-bag classic with a cookie that was crisp
at the edges, chewy in the middle, and full of rich toffee flavor.

⇒ BY CHARLES KELSEY ⇐

Since Nestlé first began printing the recipe for Toll House cookies on the back of chocolate chip bags in 1939, generations of cooks have packed them into lunches, taken them to bake sales, and kept them on hand for snacking—arguably more so than any other kind of cookie. I've made countless batches myself over the years. The recipe is so easy: Cream butter and sugar (half white and half brown), add two eggs and vanilla, then mix in all-purpose flour, salt, baking soda, some chopped nuts, and the chips. Drop tablespoons of dough on a cookie sheet, bake at 350 for 10 minutes, and you're done.

The Toll House cookie's cakey texture and buttery flavor certainly have their appeal. But is it really the best that a chocolate chip cookie can be? In my opinion, a truly great cookie offers real complexity, not just a one-note sweet taste and uniform texture. My ideal has always been this: a chocolate chip cookie that's moist and chewy on the inside and crisp at the edges, with deep notes of toffee and butterscotch to balance its sweetness. What would it take to achieve the perfect specimen?

Our cookie's crackly exterior helps set it apart from Toll House.

Not-So-Cookie-Cutter Techniques

I'm not the first to think the Toll House cookie could stand improvement.

Not too long ago, *The New York Times* published a recipe inspired by famed New York City pastry chef Jacques Torres trumpeting an unusual tactic for creating more complex flavor in a chocolate chip cookie: resting the dough a full 24 hours before baking. The rest enables the flour to fully absorb moisture from the eggs, leading to drier dough that caramelizes more quickly in the oven and achieves richer flavor. Or at least that's the theory. When I tried the recipe, tasters found it did have a slightly deeper toffee taste than the Toll House cookie—but not nearly enough to warrant the inconvenience of a 24-hour rest.

Several Boston-area bakeries employ their own dough-resting techniques, some of them even more drastic: At Flour Bakery in the South End, chef Joanne Chang swears by a rest of two or even three days. Clear Flour Bread, near our offices in Brookline, portions the dough and freezes it before baking, a trick that helps prevent the dough from spreading too much (and that keeps the center of the cookie moist and chewy). Fine ideas for professional kitchens—but who at home wants to wait two days to bake or try jamming even one cookie sheet into the freezer?

Other chefs endorse "pet" ingredients to get better results. Following the lead of pastry chef Christina Tosi at Manhattan's Momofuku Bakery and Milk Bar, I added milk powder to the Toll House dough. Tosi finds it brings depth to her baked goods; I found it just made the cookies taste milky. I also experimented with a slew of even less likely additives, including tapioca powder, brown rice flour, and xanthan gum—all suggestions for ensuring chewier texture. In each case, tasters were unanimous: No, thanks.

I wasn't having luck on the flavor or chewiness fronts, but an approach for increasing crispness from the Toll House creator herself, Ruth Wakefield, seemed worth trying: In a variation on her chocolate chip cookie recipe published in *Toll House Tried and True Recipes* (1940), Wakefield swaps all-purpose flour for cake flour. But the swap yielded a cookie so crumbly that it practically disintegrated after one bite. I wasn't exactly surprised. Cake flour has less protein (6 to 8 percent) than all-purpose flour (10 to 12 percent). Protein is one of the building blocks of gluten, which gives baked goods their structure. The less protein, the less structure, and the more crumbly the end product.

Examining the Elements

It was time to come up with my own ideas. Since small tweaks in a baking recipe can translate to big differences, I would break down the Toll House recipe into its main components and see what changes I could invoke by playing around with ingredients and proportions.

TECHNIQUE | MEASURE IT RIGHT

Even a tablespoon too much or too little flour can have an impact on cookies. Here's how to measure accurately.

PREFERRED: WEIGH FLOUR

For the greatest accuracy, weigh flour before using it. Put a bowl on a scale, hit the "tare" button to set the scale to zero, and scoop the flour into the bowl.

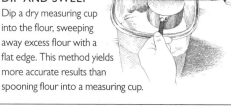

SECOND-BEST: DIP AND SWEEP

Dip a dry measuring cup into the flour, sweeping away excess flour with a flat edge. This method yields more accurate results than spooning flour into a measuring cup.

Creating a New Classic

Here's how we improved on the Toll House classic to create an even better cookie.

TOLL HOUSE RECIPE	OUR RECIPE
Equal Amounts Brown and White Sugar A 1–1 ratio of brown to white sugar creates a cookie that's neither crisp nor chewy.	**More Brown Sugar** Using more brown sugar than white makes for a chewier cookie.
Creamed Solid Butter Creaming butter creates a cakier texture in cookies.	**Browned, Melted Butter** Melting butter contributes to chewiness; browning it enhances flavor.
2 Whole Eggs Whole eggs contribute to a drier texture.	**I Whole Egg, I Yolk** Eliminating one egg white also boosts chewiness.
Beat and Bake Baking the dough immediately after mixing doesn't allow the sugar to dissolve as fully as possible.	**Whisk and Wait** Whisking sugar into the liquid ingredients and then waiting 10 minutes allows more of it to dissolve, setting up better flavor and texture.
Less Dough The smaller the cookie, the more uniform its texture.	**More Dough** Three tablespoons of dough per cookie increases its crisp-chewy contrast.

I decided to start by tackling texture, first zeroing in on the impact of the fat. I already knew I wanted to stick with butter—vegetable shortening and oil could never compete with its rich flavor. The Toll House recipe calls for creaming the butter with the sugar, which creates tiny air bubbles that bring a cakey lift to cookies. Developing a recipe for Brown Sugar Cookies (March/April 2007), I discovered that melting the butter before combining it with the other ingredients led to a chewier texture. Here's why: Butter contains up to 18 percent water. When butter melts, the water separates from the fat and can then interact with the proteins in flour to create more structure-enhancing gluten. Melting the two sticks of butter called for in the Toll House recipe created a relative abundance of water (more than 3 tablespoons), for cookies that tasters found noticeably chewier.

Since I was melting butter, I saw an opportunity to brown it, a technique we often use in the test kitchen to add nutty flavors to food. Sure enough, it worked here as well. But since browning burns off some of the butter's moisture, I made sure not to brown all of it.

Next ingredient under the microscope: sugar. Besides adding sweetness, sugar affects texture. White sugar granules lend crispness, while brown sugar, which is hygroscopic (meaning it attracts and retains water, mainly from the air), enhances chewiness. All that moisture sounded like a good thing—too good, in fact. Cookies from the all-brown-sugar batch I baked were beyond chewy; they were so moist, they were nearly floppy. The Toll House recipe calls for an equal amount of white and brown sugar; I got the best results when I simply upped the brown sugar (tasters preferred dark for its deeper flavor) to 60 percent and knocked the granulated down to 40 percent.

Next came flour. I had already seen how cake flour, with its low protein content, yields a crunchy, crumbly cookie. What if I took the opposite tack and tried bread flour, with its higher protein content of 12 to 14 percent? Again, this was going too far: The cookies were so dense and chewy that they were breadlike. In the end, just cutting back on the all-purpose flour by ½ cup increased moistness in the cookies and allowed the chewiness contributed by the brown sugar to come to the fore. The only problem: With less flour, the cookies were a little greasy. To resolve the issue, I decreased the butter by 2 tablespoons.

Finally, I was ready to evaluate the role of eggs in my batter. I knew from experience that egg whites, which contain much of the protein in the egg, tend to create cakey texture in baked goods—not what I wanted in my cookies. What's more, as the cookies bake, any white that isn't fully absorbed in the batter readily dries out, which can leave a cookie crumbly. Eliminating one egg white was the right way to go, resulting in cookies that were supremely moist and chewy.

📹 **COOK'S VIDEOS** Original Test Kitchen Videos
www.cooksillustrated.com/jun09
HOW TO MAKE
• Perfect Chocolate Chip Cookies
VIDEO TIP
• What is the best cookie sheet?

SCIENCE EXPERIMENT
For Perfect Cookies, Look to Sugar

Crunchy edges, chewy centers, and big butterscotch flavors—that chocolate chip cookie framework sounded pretty sweet to us. As it turns out, perfect cookies have a lot to do with sugar and how it's treated. Sugar that is dissolved in liquid before baking caramelizes more readily than sugar that simply melts when exposed to the same amount of heat. What would happen if we rested our cookie batter after we added the sugar to allow more of it to dissolve before going into the oven?

EXPERIMENT

We prepared two batches of our Perfect Chocolate Chip Cookies. Dough from the first batch went straight from the mixing bowl onto the baking sheet; the other batch rested for 10 minutes (with occasional whisking) after we combined the sugar with the recipe's liquids.

RESULTS

Cookies baked from the rested batter boasted not only richer, deeper flavor but also crisper edges.

EXPLANATION

Dissolving the sugar in liquid provided by the melted butter, vanilla, and egg (accelerated by whisking and resting) affects both flavor and texture. Dissolved sugar breaks down more quickly from crystalline sucrose into glucose and fructose, which caramelize at a lower temperature to form many rich, new flavor compounds. As the dissolved, caramelized sugar cools, it takes on a brittle structure. In our cookies, this brittle texture is more evident at the edges. Why? As the oven burns off moisture from the cookie perimeter, the remaining moisture gets pulled into the center, keeping it chewy. –C.K.

RECIPE TESTING
Don't Bake in Batches

TOP RACK

BOTTOM RACK

Baking two trays at a time may be convenient, but it leads to uneven cooking. The cookies on the top tray are often browner around the edges than those on the bottom, even when rotated halfway through cooking.

Waiting for Better Flavor

I had achieved chewiness, but what about my other goals? The crisp edges and deep toffee flavor were still missing, and short of melting candy into the dough, I was stumped on how to create these effects. That's when batch number 43 came along.

In the middle of stirring together the butter, sugar, and eggs, I stopped to take a phone call. Ten minutes later, I found the sugars had dissolved and the mixture had turned thick and shiny, like frosting. I didn't think much of it until I pulled the finished cookies from the oven. Instead of the smooth, matte surface of the previous batches, these cookies emerged with a slightly glossy sheen and an alluring surface of cracks and crags. One bite revealed a rush of deep, toffeelike flavor. Mysteriously, these cookies finally had just the texture I was aiming for: crisp on the outside and chewy within. When I made the cookies bigger (3 tablespoons versus the rounded tablespoon called for in the Toll House recipe), the contrast was even greater.

I knew it wasn't just luck, so I pulled our science editor onto the case. His theory was that by allowing the sugar to rest in the liquids, more of it dissolved in the small amount of moisture before baking. The dissolved sugar caramelizes more easily, creating a spectrum of toffee flavors and influencing texture. When sugar dissolved in water is heated, the moisture burns off and its molecules break apart, creating a brittle, amorphous structure that translates to crisper texture. But that effect occurs mainly at the cookie's outer edges. Just like an evaporating lake, as moisture on the perimeter disappears, the remaining moisture becomes concentrated in the center (see "For Perfect Cookies, Look to Sugar" on page 23).

Now all that was left was finessing the baking time and temperature. With caramelization in mind, I

kept the temperature hot, 375 degrees—the same as for Toll House cookies. Watching carefully, I left the cookies in the oven until they were golden brown, just set at the edges, and soft in the center, between 10 and 14 minutes.

I sat down with a tall glass of milk and a sample from my weeks of labor and more than 700 cookies baked. My cookie was crisp and chewy, gooey with chocolate, with a complex medley of sweet, buttery, caramel, and toffee flavors. Perfection is a subjective judgment at best, so I held one more blind tasting, pitting my cookie against the Toll House classic. The verdict? My cookies weren't just better—they were perfect.

PERFECT CHOCOLATE CHIP COOKIES
MAKES 16 COOKIES

Note: Avoid using a nonstick skillet to brown the butter; the dark color of the nonstick coating makes it difficult to gauge when the butter is browned. Use fresh, moist brown sugar instead of hardened brown sugar, which will make the cookies dry. This recipe works with light brown sugar, but the cookies will be less full-flavored. For our winning brand of chocolate chips, see page 29.

1¾	cups (8¾ ounces) unbleached all-purpose flour
½	teaspoon baking soda
14	tablespoons (1¾ sticks) unsalted butter
½	cup (3½ ounces) granulated sugar
¾	cup (5¼ ounces) packed dark brown sugar (see note)
1	teaspoon table salt
2	teaspoons vanilla extract
1	large egg
1	large egg yolk
1¼	cups semisweet chocolate chips or chunks (see note)
¾	cup chopped pecans or walnuts, toasted (optional)

1. Adjust oven rack to middle position and heat oven to 375 degrees. Line 2 large (18- by 12-inch) baking sheets with parchment paper. Whisk flour and baking soda together in medium bowl; set aside.

2. Heat 10 tablespoons butter in 10-inch skillet over medium-high heat until melted, about 2 minutes. Continue cooking, swirling pan constantly until butter is dark golden brown and has nutty aroma, 1 to 3 minutes. Remove skillet from heat and, using heatproof spatula, transfer browned butter to large heatproof bowl. Stir remaining 4 tablespoons butter into hot butter until completely melted.

3. Add both sugars, salt, and vanilla to bowl with butter and whisk until fully incorporated. Add egg and yolk and whisk until mixture is smooth with no sugar lumps remaining, about 30 seconds. Let mixture stand 3 minutes, then whisk for 30 seconds. Repeat process of resting and whisking 2 more times until mixture is thick, smooth, and shiny. Using rubber spatula or wooden spoon, stir in flour mixture

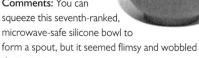
until just combined, about 1 minute. Stir in chocolate chips and nuts (if using), giving dough final stir to ensure no flour pockets remain.

4. Divide dough into 16 portions, each about 3 tablespoons (or use #24 cookie scoop). Arrange 2 inches apart on prepared baking sheets, 8 dough balls per sheet. (Smaller baking sheets can be used, but will require 3 batches.)

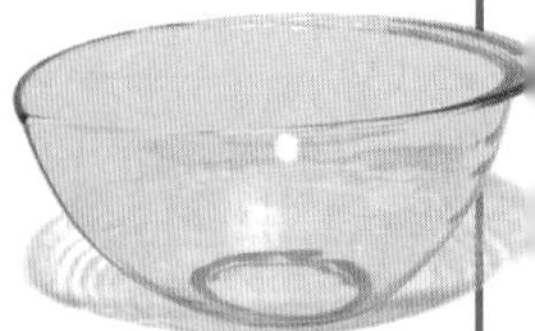

5. Bake cookies 1 tray at a time until cookies are golden brown and still puffy, and edges have begun to set but centers are still soft, 10 to 14 minutes, rotating baking sheet halfway through baking. Transfer baking sheet to wire rack; cool cookies completely before serving.

Should You Buy a Cookware Set?

Does buying a set of cookware get you a bargain—or a bunch of pans you don't really need?

⇒ BY LISA McMANUS ⇐

We've never liked cookware sets. Most bundle together a lot of pans we don't need and not enough of the ones we do—the five or six hardworking multi-taskers that we turn to every day. Besides pans in impractical sizes (1-quart saucepans good for little more than melting butter or 8-inch skillets that are only useful if you're cooking for one), these sets typically boast limited-use "specialty" cookware. Why clog your cabinets with sauté pans (skillets with high, straight sides), sauciers (rounded saucepans with wide rims), or "chef's" pans (saucepans shaped like woks with domed lids) if you've already got a Dutch oven and other basic pans that can do anything they can do and more? And if you think you've found an incredible deal on a "14-piece" assortment, beware: Manufacturers count each lid and anything else that isn't riveted on as a separate piece.

That said, buying pieces one by one gets expensive—particularly with high-end brands. If we could find a set that was a truly good value for the money, offering durable, high-quality construction and a selection on a par with our needs, we'd happily recommend it.

Seeking Out the Sets

Our natural starting point was All-Clad, a brand that has consistently topped our ratings over the years. We like its line in fully clad, stainless steel "tri-ply," a style boasting three layers of metal fused together and extending from the bottom of the pan all the way up to the rim. Such construction helps to ensure pots that cook evenly and transfer heat steadily (see "Go for Triple Metal," right). Our ideal set would include a roomy 12-inch traditional skillet (or fry pan—we use the terms interchangeably) that's big enough to fit four chicken breasts; a 10-inch nonstick skillet for cooking delicate omelets and fish; a 12-inch cast-iron skillet for frying and searing; a 4-quart covered saucepan good for vegetables and other dishes; a 2-quart covered saucepan for heating soup or cooking oatmeal; a 6- or 7-quart enameled cast-iron Dutch oven for braising, deep-frying, and even baking bread; and a large covered stockpot that can double as a pot for pasta, lobster, and corn on the cob.

The downside of All-Clad, of course, is its price: It's one of the most expensive brands on the market. A cursory search unearthed a 14-piece assortment boasting four of the pans on our list, along with four others that definitely were not. This excess of nonessential pieces brought the set's price to an outrageous $1,899.95. Digging deeper, we found a 10-piece All-Clad set (offered exclusively by a single retailer—an irksome trend with sets) with four of the pans we wanted (the 12-inch skillet, the 2- and 4-quart saucepans, and a reasonably large 8-quart stockpot) and just one that we didn't (a 4-quart sauté pan). This was a definite improvement, but we were still stuck with the sauté pan and a total cost of $699.95. Could we do better?

A fully clad, tri-ply set from Calphalon offered eight pieces that were mostly undersized (8- and 10-inch skillets, 1½- and 2½-quart saucepans, and a 6-quart stockpot), but sold for a much more reasonable $299.99. We put it in our lineup. More searching revealed an amazing find: a fully clad 8-piece tri-ply set made by Tramontina costing just a hair under $145. Its assorted sizes were less ideal than the Calphalon combo (8- and 10-inch fry pans, 1-quart saucepan with lid, 2-quart saucepan with lid, and 5-quart Dutch oven with lid)—but given its attractive price, we had to test it.

To get other sets priced under $200, like Tramontina, we'd have to abandon our desire for fully clad tri-ply and go for the next best thing:

Go for Triple Metal

Stainless steel is nonreactive. Aluminum is an efficient conductor of heat. The winning sets in our lineup boasted both metals in a triple ("tri-ply") layer (steel/aluminum/steel) throughout, for pans that transferred heat steadily and cooked evenly. Cheaper sets with "disk" or "encapsulated" bottoms, where the triple layer was confined to the underside, performed less well.

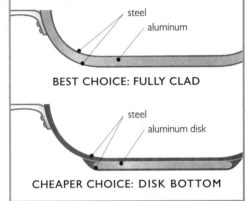

BEST CHOICE: FULLY CLAD
steel
aluminum

CHEAPER CHOICE: DISK BOTTOM
steel
aluminum disk

disk-bottom pans. Here, manufacturers duplicate the three-layer effect, but only on the pan bottom, by attaching a disk of aluminum to the underside of a stainless steel pan, then covering the disk in stainless steel. We found three sets worth considering. A 10-piece set from KitchenAid Gourmet Reserved had the usual too-small pans (8- and 10-inch fry pans, 1- and 2-quart saucepans with lids), but it did offer an 8-quart stockpot, and its price ($179.99) was reasonable. For just a bit more ($189.95), a similarly composed 10-piece set by Rachael Ray caught our eye with its bright orange silicone handle grips and unusual convex design. And finally, a 10-piece Kenmore set (8- and 10-inch fry pans, 1- and 2-quart saucepans with lids, 6-quart stockpot with lid, plus a 3-quart sauté pan and a steamer insert for the 2-quart saucepan) seemed worth a look at $159.99.

Into the Fire

Not surprisingly, the disk-bottom pans performed the worst in each of our cooking tests—and fell to the bottom half of our rankings. Their biggest downfall? Confining the heat-controlling layers to the very bottom of the pan allowed heat to blaze around the perimeter and up the sides; onions, fond (browned bits for pan sauce), and caramel all scorched.

The Inside Story: Tramontina vs. All-Clad

Tramontina cookware is significantly less expensive than All-Clad but performed comparably to this winning brand. To see if we could detect any differences in construction between the two lines, we cut a 2-quart saucepan from each set in half. Our finding? Their differences are minor, as evident in the cross-section photos at right. The All-Clad pan boasts a more squared-off bottom, which allows slightly more surface area to be in direct contact with the heat; it is also infinitesimally thicker (less than ¼ millimeter) than the Tramontina. By all appearances, the three "tri-ply" layers in both pans are equally well-fused.

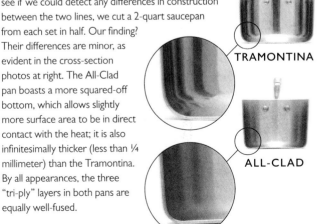

TRAMONTINA

ALL-CLAD

Particularly problematic were the pear-shaped pieces of the Rachael Ray cookware. Bulging sides made it that much easier for heat to bypass the thick, heat-regulating bottom to singe food along the thin, overhanging edges. While the pans suffered from other problems (overheating handles and too-deep skillets that made food steam before browning), this design flaw put the Rachael Ray set in last place.

But the heftless KitchenAid pans were hot on its heels. The lightweight stockpot not only scooted around the stove as we stirred a batch of chili, but it ran so hot that the mixture boiled (even after we turned down the heat). Meanwhile, a skillet singed, rather than sautéed, a piece of sole. Protruding handle rivets in the skillets got sticky with sauce, needing extra elbow grease to scrub clean.

As for the Kenmore set, it fell victim to the same uneven heating as the other disk-bottom sets and felt nearly as lightweight as the KitchenAid set. Its low, open saucepans were a plus, but we didn't like its high-sided skillets. Its handles became very hot, despite silicone grips that tricked us into skipping the potholder. (Plain stainless steel handles on the other cookware sets actually stayed cooler to the touch.)

An Astonishing Bargain

And what of the fully clad cookware? As we might have predicted, the All-Clad set aced every test, earning a perfect score. Its pans are well designed. Skillets have generous cooking surfaces and low, flaring sides that prevent steaming for better browning; its stockpot and saucepans are solid enough to maintain a gentle simmer, but light enough to be maneuverable. Even with the unwanted sauté pan in the mix, this set was still a great bargain over its open stock price (for items sold individually), saving more than $300.

Despite its small pan sizes, the Calphalon set performed very well, passing each of our cooking tests with ease. The pans are well shaped, with low-sided skillets and low, wide saucepans that aced delicate tasks like stirring pastry cream and finicky caramel. Our only real complaint? The tempered glass lids. The supposedly helpful clear windows into the pan's contents steamed up and blocked our view (the glass lids in the KitchenAid and Rachael Ray sets behaved similarly). What's more, the glass is only heatproof up to 450 degrees. But at $299— less than half the price of the All-Clad set—it's not a bad deal.

But at the end of the day, the cheapest set of the entire lineup—the 8-piece Tramontina 18/10 Stainless Steel TriPly-Clad Cookware Set—landed remarkably close behind the vaunted All-Clad. Priced at just $144.97, it is an astonishing bargain.

Remarkably similar in weight, shape, and design to the All-Clad pans (See "The Inside Story: Tramontina vs. All-Clad," page 25), Tramontina's cookware transferred heat evenly, was well balanced and maneuverable, and ranked so close to the performance of the All-Clad pans that we enthusiastically recommend it. Its highly polished skillets released

both fish and frittatas with even golden color and no sticking, earning comments of "Perfect!" from testers. Its rounded handles are even slightly more comfortable than the sharper edges of the All-Clad handles. The 5-quart Dutch oven, while on the small side, was big enough to cook chili, and its handles were easy to grip.

The only slight difference between the two brands: The cooking surfaces of the Tramontina pans are a little smaller in diameter than the All-Clad pieces (Tramontina's 10-inch skillet, for example, measures 7 inches across the bottom, versus the 10-inch All-Clad skillet's 7⅝ inches). A smaller cooking surface may explain why we needed to stir onions in both the Tramontina 2-quart saucepan and 10-inch skillet

a little more frequently than in the comparably sized All-Clad pans to ensure even cooking.

This set comes with a few disadvantages, however. Its pans are those tiny "starter" sizes. Unlike the All-Clad cookware in our test kitchen, it hasn't endured years of daily use, so we can't predict how it will fare over time. And only one store carries the set at this price: Wal-Mart, which is known for dictating a low price to manufacturers and then deciding on a quarterly basis whether it will continue to carry the product. While Wal-Mart has assured us that this cookware set will be available for the time being, there are no guarantees. But for barely $145—a mere $10 more than the cost of one 12-inch stainless tri-ply skillet from All-Clad—this deal is hard to pass up.

The Ideal Cookware Set, à la Carte

While we found a few reasonable options for cookware sets (see the chart on page 27), none provides all the pans essential to a fully equipped kitchen. We've identified seven core pieces that we believe every kitchen should have; at best, the cookware sets we tested included just four of these pans (and none had the mix of different materials that is also key). We highly recommend the lineup below of our favorite winning brands—these are the very pans we use every day in the test kitchen. Their total cost is not insignificant, but for less than two hundred dollars more than our top-rated All-Clad cookware set ($699.95), you'll have every pan that you need—and none that you don't.

12-inch Traditional Skillet
ALL-CLAD Stainless
12-inch Skillet, $134.95
A kitchen workhorse large enough to sear, roast, or sauté a family-sized meal. The traditional finish allows food to stick slightly, developing the crusty brown bits, known as *fond*, that contribute to great flavor.

10-inch Nonstick Skillet
WEAREVER Premium
Hard Anodized 10-inch
Nonstick Sauté Pan, $21.99
* this is actually a skillet in shape, if not in name
Nonstick is terrific for delicate, quick-cooking foods such as omelets, flaky fish fillets, and stir-fries—but don't spend big bucks, since the coating wears off within a few years. The best nonstick pans boast a thick base that distributes heat evenly.

12-inch Cast-Iron Skillet
LODGE LOGIC 12-inch
Cast-Iron Skillet, $33.95
Nothing can top cast iron when it comes to creating a thick, deeply browned crust on steaks and other foods. Also our first choice for cornbread and fried chicken.

2-quart Saucepan (with lid)
ALL-CLAD Stainless
2-quart Saucepan, $139.95
A 2-quart saucepan is just the right size for smaller jobs like heating milk, melting butter, or warming soup.

4-quart Saucepan (with lid)
ALL-CLAD Stainless
4-quart Saucepan, $199.95
In the test kitchen, we use our 4-quart saucepans for making rice and oatmeal, blanching vegetables, and cooking small amounts of pasta, soup, and stew. Since we also use it for making sauces, a traditional finish that allows fond to develop is essential. A stay-cool handle is a must.

Large Enameled Cast-Iron Dutch Oven (with lid)
LE CREUSET 7¼-quart
Round French Oven, $269.95
If we had to single out the pot we use more than any other, it would be our Dutch oven. This incredibly versatile vessel is thicker and heavier than a saucepan or stockpot, and it conducts heat more efficiently. It is ideal for soups, stews, stocks, braises, and even deep-frying and baking.

Large Stockpot (with lid)
CUISINART Chef's Classic
12-quart Stockpot, $69.95
Most home kitchens have room for a single stockpot, so it must handle a variety of big jobs, from steaming lobsters to boiling bushels of corn and cooking pounds of pasta; 12 quarts is the most useful size. Since we use our stockpot mainly for these simple operations, we prefer a good but inexpensive brand.

TOTAL COST OF IDEAL SET: $870.69

TESTING COOKWARE SETS

We tested all pieces in six cookware sets to assess construction, cooking speed, and design. Sets appear in the order of their ranking. All were purchased at Boston-area retail stores or online; sources for winners are on page 32. **COOKING:** To evaluate performance, we prepared chili in the stockpots; made Swedish meatballs in the sauté pans (or 10-inch fry pans); sautéed onions and made frittatas in the 10-inch fry pans; cooked pastry cream and sautéed more onions in the 2-quart saucepans; sautéed sole in the 8-inch fry pans; and made caramel sauce in the 1-quart saucepans (or closest equivalents). **DESIGN:** Handles and the shape, weight, and size of the cooking surfaces were assessed for utility and comfort. **PAN SIZES:** We rated sets according to perceived usefulness of the sizes of included pans.

RECOMMENDED

ALL-CLAD Stainless Steel Cookware Set, 10-piece

Price: $699.95
Material: Fully clad, stainless steel with aluminum core; stainless steel lids
Pieces: 10- and 12-inch stainless fry pans, 2-qt. and 4-qt. saucepans with lids, 4-qt. sauté pan with lid, 8-qt. stockpot with lid

Cooking: ★★★
Design: ★★★
Pan Sizes: ★★★

Comments: This set came closest to our ideal and includes winning pans from previous testings in sizes we've identified as the most useful. The fry pans have low, flaring sides and broad cooking surfaces; the saucepans are sturdy and hefty for slow, steady cooking; the stockpot is roomy enough for most big cooking jobs.

Pros: Superb construction; proven winner; plenty of pans to add
Cons: Expensive; available only at Williams-Sonoma

TRAMONTINA 18/10 Stainless Steel TriPly-Clad Cookware Set, 8-piece

BEST BUY

Price: $144.97
Material: Fully clad, stainless steel with aluminum core; stainless steel lids
Pieces: 8- and 10-inch fry pans, 1-qt. and 2-qt. saucepans with lids, 5-qt. Dutch oven with lid

Cooking: ★★★
Design: ★★★
Pan Sizes: ★

Comments: This fully clad cookware set is an amazing bargain, with performance, design, and construction comparable to All-Clad cookware (though cooking surfaces are slightly smaller). Sturdy and moderately heavy, with riveted handles and slow, steady heating.

Pros: Well designed; performance comparable to All-Clad
Cons: Small pans; limited supply; available only at Wal-Mart

CALPHALON Tri-Ply Stainless Steel Cookware Set, 8-piece, Model LS 8

Price: $299.99
Material: Fully clad, stainless steel with aluminum core; tempered glass lids safe to 450 degrees
Pieces: 8- and 10-inch fry pans, 1.5-qt. and 2.5-qt. saucepans with lids, 6-qt. stockpot with lid

Cooking: ★★★
Design: ★★
Pan Sizes: ★★

Comments: A strong performer at less than half the price of the top-ranked All-Clad set. Wide, low saucepans made it easy to see the food inside; fry pans with low, angled sides encouraged evaporation during simmering. We only wish that instead of glass, the lids were stainless steel, which is more durable and heatproof at any temperature.

Pros: Solid performers; stable supply of additional pans
Cons: Stockpot and fry pans are small; glass lids

RECOMMENDED WITH RESERVATIONS

KITCHENAID Gourmet Reserved Brushed Stainless Steel Cookware Set, 10-piece Model 71984

Price: $179.99
Material: Stainless steel with aluminum disk bottom; break-resistant glass lids
Pieces: 8- and 10-inch fry pans, 1-qt. and 2-qt. saucepans with lids, 3-qt. sauté pan with lid, 8-qt. stockpot with lid

Cooking: ★★
Design: ★★
Pan Sizes: ★★

Comments: Pans are less solidly constructed than we prefer and were the lightest of all the sets we tested. The stockpot shifted as we stirred our chili, and its handles didn't protrude as far as we like for a good grip. The disk bottoms tended to heat up a little too quickly so that chili boiled instead of simmered. Sauces stuck to the raised handle rivets inside the sauté pan, making them harder to clean. Handles became quite hot.

Pro: Decent performer
Cons: Disk bottoms; glass lids; light weight; racing heat

KENMORE Stainless Steel Cookware Set, 10-piece Model 71787-T

Price: $159.99
Material: Stainless steel sides with aluminum disk bottom; stainless steel lids; silicone handle grips
Pieces: 8- and 10-inch fry pans, 1-qt. saucepan with lid, 2-qt. saucepan with lid and steamer insert, 3-qt. sauté pan (shares lid with stock pot), 6-qt. stockpot with lid

Cooking: ★★
Design: ★★
Pan Sizes: ★

Comments: This set was adequate, if underwhelming. We liked the low, open shape of the saucepans, but the silicone handles, while comfortable, got very hot. Pans were all on the lightweight side, and flames tended to darken meatballs, onions, and pan sauce along the perimeter where the heat bypassed the disk bottom. The fry pan heated oil too fast, forcing us to throw out a batch we were using for a frittata, and its sides were a little too high.

Pro: Stainless lids
Cons: Disk bottoms; light weight; overheating handles

NOT RECOMMENDED

RACHAEL RAY Stainless Steel Cookware Set, 10-piece Model 76081

Price: $189.95
Material: Stainless steel with aluminum disk bottom; silicone handle grips safe to 400 degrees; tempered glass lids
Pieces: 8- and 10-inch fry pans, 1.5-qt. and 3-qt. saucepans with lids, 3-qt. sauté pan with lid, 8-qt. stockpot with lid

Cooking: ★★
Design: ★
Pan Sizes: ★★

Comments: Bulging pan sides set atop a comparatively small disk bottoms guaranteed that flames would reach past its protective three layers to scorch food touching the thin metal of the overhanging sides. In fry pans, high sides made it harder to reach under delicate food with a spatula and encouraged steaming rather than browning. Pans were lightweight, and handles became very hot despite silicone grips.

Pro: None
Cons: Disk bottoms; hot handles; light weight; bulging shape

Where the (Chocolate) Chips Fall

Do Nestlé Toll House morsels still deserve to be the nation's top-selling chips?

⇒ BY PEGGY CHUNG COLLIER ⇐

In the 1930s, Ruth Wakefield, owner of the Toll House Inn in Whitman, Mass., famously cut up a bar of Nestlé semisweet chocolate and mixed it into her batter for Butter Drop Do cookies. Soon newspapers around New England were printing her recipe for chocolate chip cookies, and sales of Nestlé semisweet chocolate bars soared. Nestlé made a deal with Wakefield: In exchange for permission to print what became known as the Toll House recipe on its candy bar wrappers, she would receive a lifetime supply of chocolate. By 1939, Nestlé had begun selling packages of small pieces of chocolate, named "Toll House morsels" after the inn where they were invented.

Decades later, Toll House morsels are synonymous with chocolate chips. But with other familiar chocolate names like Hershey's and Baker's in the chip game—along with upscale brands claiming to offer richer flavor and better texture—does Nestlé still deserve to be the nation's best-selling morsel? In a recent tasting of dark chocolate bars (January/February 2008), we found the complex flavor of gourmet brands trounced ordinary supermarket chocolate. To see if the same might hold true for chips, we rounded up eight high-end and middle-market brands (including two from Nestlé, the original morsels and semisweet chunks), all of which are widely available at supermarkets. We then sampled them plain and in nearly 300 cookies.

True Grit

Chip or bar, chocolate has just three basic ingredients: cocoa butter, cocoa solids, and sugar. The "cacao percentage" you hear so much about in bar chocolate refers to the total amount of cocoa butter and cocoa solids contributed by ground-up cacao beans. Sugar accounts for the rest of the content, along with minute amounts (typically less than 2 percent) of emulsifiers, vanilla flavoring, salt, and sometimes milk fat.

The U.S. Food and Drug Administration (FDA) states that dark chocolate, whether labeled bittersweet, semisweet, or dark, must be at least 35 percent cacao.

Chip Shape

WIDENED OUT
The winning Ghirardelli chip's wide, flat shape melts into thin layers in a cookie.

STANDING TALLER
Second-to-last Nestlé morsels retain their firm texture and upright shape during baking.

As a general rule, the higher the cacao percentage, the darker and more intense the chocolate. Since many chocolate makers are secretive about their proprietary methods and formulas, we sent the chips to an independent lab to analyze their cacao percentages. While bars of dark chocolate typically boast cacao amounts starting at about 60 percent, most of the chips we tasted contained far less, 42 to 47 percent.

Why are chips and bars so different? Less cacao means less cocoa butter, which means the chocolate will be less fluid when melted, making it easier for chips to hold that classic teardrop shape on the production line. More significantly, because cocoa butter is expensive, using less of it makes chips cheaper to produce than the average bar (ounce for ounce, the chips in our lineup cost about half as much as bar chocolate from the same brand).

The absence of cocoa butter was immediately clear when we tasted chips right out of the bag. With just one exception, tasters found the chips gritty and grainy instead of creamy and smooth like bar chocolate. The brand that stood apart distinguished itself further when we baked the chips in cookies. Unlike the other chips, which retained their morsel shape during baking, this chip melted into thin layers that spread throughout the cookie, ensuring gooey chocolate in every bite. Furthermore, when we examined its ingredient list, we found that this chip had the highest percentage of cacao in the lineup—60 percent, comparable to bar chocolate—and the most cocoa butter by far (44 percent, minus a tiny amount of milk fat). It was also wider and flatter than standard chips, which enhanced its ability to melt into thin strata throughout the cookie.

Going Dutch

Sugar was another consideration—and more wasn't better. Our favorite chip had the least sugar in the lineup. By contrast, the chip with the most sugar was panned for tasting like "cheap Halloween candy." But a relatively high sugar content wasn't a deal-breaker, as we learned from our second-favorite contender, Hershey's Special Dark Mildly Sweet Chocolate Chips.

This chip had us stumped. Even with a hefty 53 percent sugar (and just 45 percent cacao), its chocolate flavor was unexpectedly potent. The label revealed that this chip contained Dutch-processed cocoa powder (cocoa solids treated with an alkali to neutralize acidity). Chocolate makers grind shelled cacao beans, known as nibs, to create the thick paste called chocolate liquor, which contains both cocoa solids and cocoa butter. Manufacturers frequently bump up chocolate flavor by adding cocoa powder (often made from cheaper, poorly fermented cacao beans, which tend to be very acidic). In the Hershey's chips, Dutch processing tamed the cocoa's acidity, deepening its chocolate punch.

Quality Bean, Quality Chip

Still, good chocolate is not just about a high cacao percentage and plenty of cocoa butter. For complex flavor, a manufacturer must start with good-quality beans that have been grown and harvested under optimal conditions. The beans must then be properly fermented and roasted to bring out traces of flavors such as smoke, caramel, and fruit. Upscale chocolate makers claim that every detail is critical—and are loath to reveal their methods. Other manufacturers cut costs by using poorly fermented beans and then over-roasting and over-conching (a process of beating and turning the chocolate for 24 to 72 hours) to mask bitterness and off-flavors. The result may be acceptable, but, as we found in many of the lower-ranking chips, the flavor is one-dimensional.

Only our winner, Ghirardelli 60% Cacao Bittersweet Chocolate Chips, delivered the intense, complex flavors we expect from superior chocolate. They were so good that we found ourselves sneaking handfuls straight from the bag. This premium chip, it turns out, has the same cacao percentage as the brand's dark chocolate bar, Ghirardelli Bittersweet Chocolate Baking Bar, the runner-up in our dark chocolate tasting. It also has the same smoky, fruity, and winelike flavors. A Ghirardelli spokesperson confirmed that the chocolate is identical in the bar and the chips—the beans undergo the same harvesting, fermenting, and roasting processes for each. The only difference is in how they're manufactured: The bar is tempered to deliver a smooth finish and crisp snap. Curious how the chip would fare against the significantly more expensive chopped-up bar in cookies, we held a side-by-side tasting. Tasters preferred the silkier texture of the bar, but were divided on which form of chocolate tasted better. Given that the bar costs 75 cents an ounce, and the chips cost just 30 cents an ounce (and need no chopping), we'll stick with the chips for cookies—and maybe even for eating out of hand.

As for America's favorite chip, Nestlé Toll House Real Semi-Sweet Chocolate Morsels? They landed in second-to-last place, alongside the brand's semisweet chocolate chunks. With a low cacao percentage and the highest sugar level, these were the very same chips tasters likened to "cheap Halloween candy," and they belong at the bottom of our lineup.

TASTING CHOCOLATE CHIPS

Twenty-one *Cook's Illustrated* staff members tasted eight samples of dark chocolate chips sold at supermarkets nationwide. The chips were tasted plain and in our Perfect Chocolate Chip Cookies (page 24). Data on fat, sugar, and cacao are approximate, with sugar calculated from the package labels and fat and cacao analyzed by an independent laboratory where manufacturer information was not available. Chips appear below in order of preference. Prices were paid in Boston-area supermarkets.

HIGHLY RECOMMENDED

GHIRARDELLI 60% Cacao Bittersweet Chocolate Chips
Price: $3.50 for an 11.5-ounce bag (30 cents per ounce)
Sugar: 40%
Cacao: 60%
Fat (included in cacao percentage): 44%

Comments: Distinct "wine," "fruit," and "smoke" flavors made this "adult chocolate" a clear winner. Low sugar content allowed the chocolate flavor to shine. In cookies, a wider, flatter shape and high percentage of fat helped the chips melt into thin layers for a pleasing balance of cookie and chocolate in every bite.

RECOMMENDED

HERSHEY'S Special Dark Mildly Sweet Chocolate Chips
Price: $2.39 for a 12-ounce bag (20 cents per ounce)
Sugar: 53%
Cacao: 45%
Fat (included in cacao percentage): 38%

Comments: Tasters liked the "simple yet strong cocoa flavor," which stood up to the sweetness of cookies. This chip was the only one that contained Dutch-processed cocoa powder, resulting in a "bold" though "not complex" chocolate flavor. A higher fat percentage gave it a creamier texture in cookies.

GUITTARD Real Semisweet Chocolate Chips
Price: $3.29 for a 12-ounce bag (27 cents per ounce)
Sugar: 53%
Cacao: 43%
Fat (included in cacao percentage): 29%

Comments: A "smoky," "complex" chip with cinnamon and caramel undertones. Some tasters felt it needed a bolder chocolate presence to stand up to other flavors when baked in cookies. This lack of chocolate flavor also made its sweetness more pronounced.

HERSHEY'S Semi-Sweet Chocolate Chips
Price: $2.29 for a 12-ounce bag (19 cents per ounce)
Sugar: 53%
Cacao: 42%
Fat (included in cacao percentage): 30%

Comments: Though praised for "good cocoa" flavor in cookies, this "too sweet" chip didn't have enough chocolate flavor to balance out the high sugar content. This chip also had a distinct "milky" flavor that tasters found more similar to milk chocolate than semisweet chocolate.

GHIRARDELLI Semi-Sweet Chips
Price: $3.50 for a 12-ounce bag (29 cents per ounce)
Sugar: 53%
Cacao: 46%
Fat (included in cacao percentage): 34%

Comments: The unique "tangy, fruity" chocolate flavor of this chip rated well when baked in cookies. But tasters commented that it was "a bit too sweet," lacking the "strong chocolate flavor" of its 60 percent cacao sister chip.

RECOMMENDED WITH RESERVATIONS

BAKER'S Real Semi-Sweet Chocolate Chunks
Price: $2.69 for a 12-ounce bag (22 cents per ounce)
Sugar: 53%
Cacao: 47%
Fat (included in cacao percentage): 35%

Comments: Tasters detected "pleasant coffee and cinnamon tones" in this chip but also an "off, coconut-like" flavor. Overall, tasters noticed "more sweetness than chocolate flavor."

NOT RECOMMENDED

NESTLÉ Toll House Real Semi-Sweet Chocolate Morsels
Price: $2.50 for a 12-ounce bag (20 cents per ounce)
Sugar: 57%
Cacao: 47%
Fat (included in cacao percentage): 30%

Comments: With the highest sugar content in the lineup, tasters agreed this best-selling chip was "unpleasantly sweet" and compared its "fleeting" chocolate flavor to "cheap Halloween candy." Tasters noted a strong "fake" taste, which could be attributed to artificial vanilla.

NESTLÉ Toll House Real Semi-Sweet Chocolate Chunk Morsels
Price: $2.50 for an 11.5-ounce bag (22 cents per ounce)
Sugar: 50%
Cacao: 45%
Fat (included in cacao percentage): 27%

Comments: Tasters panned this chip's "odd, woodlike" flavor, also variously described as "grassy," "like dirt," "vegetal," and "oily." Others noticed that the chunks, which are heavier than the classic morsels, didn't melt enough.

The Milky Way

If intense chocolate flavor, moderate sugar, and a goodly amount of cocoa butter make for a superior dark chip, what factors contribute to the best milk chocolate morsel? Surprisingly, the same three characteristics. Milk chocolate, by definition, contains enough milk solids and milk fat to give the candy a distinctly milky flavor, but when we compared the four top-selling brands of milk chocolate chips (plain and in cookies), tasters still overwhelmingly preferred the chip with bolder chocolate flavor, higher fat content, and lower sugar content.

In this tasting, our winning dark chip brand, Ghirardelli, tanked because tasters disliked the "saccharine" sweetness and Styrofoam-like texture of its milk chocolate chips. For complete tasting results, go to www.cooksillustrated.com/jun09. –P.C.C.

MILK CHOCOLATE CHAMP
Hershey's Milk Chocolate Chips stood out for bold chocolate flavor and creamy texture.

SHOPPING **How the Cheese Crumbles**

How do the precrumbled cheeses found in the deli section of the supermarket stack up to the same brands sold in solid block or log form? We tasted blue cheese, goat cheese, feta, and gorgonzola side by side in their crumbled and solid forms (comparing the same brand of each type) both plain and added to various recipes, including blue cheese dressing, polenta with gorgonzola, spinach dip with feta, and stuffed portobellos. Tasters found the precrumbled versions acceptable in all cases. What we found unacceptable, however, were the price differences. Stella blue cheese that sells for around $8 a pound in block form, for example, is $3.99 for a 5-ounce package in a precrumbled state. That's a price increase of over 160 percent! At prices like that, we'll gladly take 30 extra seconds to crumble our own cheese.

BLOCK CHEESE
$8/pound

PRECRUMBLED CHEESE
$12.77/pound

Where to Store Cut Tomatoes

We never store tomatoes in the refrigerator. Cold damages tomatoes in two ways: It destroys an enzyme that produces flavorful compounds, and it makes water in the tomato expand, rupturing cells and turning the flesh mealy. But what about storing a partially used tomato? We cut a dozen ripe tomatoes in two, stored half of each in the fridge, and kept the other half at room temperature (both were wrapped tightly in plastic). After a few days, the halves at room temperature had begun to soften, while the refrigerated halves were still as firm as the day they were cut. Upon tasting, however, we found the refrigerated halves were bland and mealy compared with the never-refrigerated halves.

Our advice? Keep cut tomatoes tightly wrapped at room temperature and consume them within a few days. The shelf life gained by refrigeration doesn't make up for the loss in flavor and texture.

TECHNIQUE

STRAIGHTEN OUT YOUR SHRIMP

When cooking shrimp for tempura (page 19), the underside tends to shrink more than the top, causing the shrimp to curl tightly and the batter to clump up and cook unevenly inside the curl. Here's a way to alleviate that problem.

After peeling and deveining a shrimp, hold it on its back on the cutting board. Use the tip of a paring knife to make two ¼-inch-deep incisions on the underside about ½ inch apart.

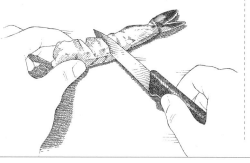

SCIENCE EXPERIMENT **Used Fryer Oil**

In deep-frying, the first batch is never the best. Food writer Russ Parsons explains in *How to Read a French Fry* that fry oil has five stages: break-in (too fresh to fry well), fresh, optimum, degrading (on the way to spoiling), and runaway (dark, smelly, and prone to smoking). Food fried in optimum oil is golden and crisp. Break-in and fresh oil yield paler, less crisp food. Degrading and runaway oil produce dark, greasy food with rancid odors. Could we create optimum oil by mixing used and new?

EXPERIMENT

We fried shrimp, fish, and French fries in fresh oil and in a mixture of fresh oil and oil that had been used once to make French fries (and then strained through a coffee filter to remove any solids).

RESULTS

Food fried in the mix of new and used oil was crisper and more uniformly golden than food fried in fresh oil.

EXPLANATION

Oil that is too fresh can't penetrate the barrier of moisture that surrounds food as it fries. Over time, as the oil continues to be exposed to heat, it breaks down, producing slippery, soaplike compounds that can penetrate the water barrier. This increased contact between oil and food promotes browning and crispness.

BOTTOM LINE

Save a cup or two of used oil to mix with fresh the next time you fry (we found that a ratio of 1 cup of used oil to 5 cups of fresh oil worked best). Just make sure that you don't save oil used to fry fish—the smell will permeate the new oil.

TEST KITCHEN TIP **The Right Time to Sift**

Does it really matter if you sift your flour before you measure it or after? In a word: Yes. When a recipe calls for "1 cup sifted flour," the flour should be sifted before measuring; whereas "1 cup flour, sifted" should be sifted after measuring. Here's why: A cup of flour sifted before measuring will weigh 20 to 30 percent less than a cup of flour sifted after measuring—a difference that can make a huge impact on the texture of finished baked goods. The best way to make sure you've got the right amount of flour? Weigh it.

Here's what various types of flour weigh, both sifted and unsifted:

TYPE OF FLOUR	WEIGHT OF 1 CUP UNSIFTED	WEIGHT OF 1 CUP SIFTED
All-Purpose	5 ounces	4 ounces
Cake	4 ounces	3.25 ounces
Bread	5.5 ounces	4.5 ounces

JUST RIGHT **TOO LITTLE FLOUR**

The cake on the left was made by measuring flour by weight before sifting, as the recipe directed. The one on the right was made by measuring flour by volume after sifting, causing us to use 25 percent less flour by weight, resulting in an overly wet, dense texture.

TEST KITCHEN TIP Sharper Shallot Shopping

When shopping, avoid shallots packaged in cardboard and cellophane boxes, which prevent you from checking out each shallot. Instead, go for loose shallots or the ones packed in plastic netting. They should feel firm and heavy and have no soft spots. Since most of our recipes call for less than 3 tablespoons of minced shallots, in the test kitchen we use only medium shallots (which yield about 3 tablespoons minced) or small shallots (which yield 2 tablespoons or less). A medium shallot should be about 1½ to 2 inches wide.

| I MEDIUM SHALLOT | = | 3 TBS. MINCED |

Out of Circulation

What's the best way to get a two-layer cake to cook evenly? We baked our Classic White Layer Cake in three placements: side by side on one rack; on two racks with one pan directly above the other; and on two racks with one pan on the top left of the oven and the other on the lower right. Only the cakes on the same rack baked evenly.

The reason is convection—the hot air currents moving around the oven. In bottom-heating ovens, when cakes are stacked, the bottom one acts as a barrier, creating hot air currents that flow up and over the top cake. The result is an overcooked top cake and an undercooked bottom cake. Results are also uneven in rear-heating ovens or those with top and bottom elements. But when cakes are baked side by side, hot air circulates evenly no matter how your oven heats. If you need to cook three cakes at a time, place two on the bottom rack, spaced apart, and one on the rack above and in between the other two. Move the cakes twice during cooking so that each cake spends an equal amount of time in each position.

TOP = PALE	SIDE BY SIDE = EVEN
Cakes stacked above each other disrupt heat flow in the oven.	Cakes kept side by side bake up evenly.

TEST KITCHEN TIP Ripening Avocados

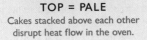

Avocados have a notoriously small window of perfect ripeness. To see if we could broaden this time frame, we bought a case of unripe avocados and ripened them at room temperature and in the refrigerator three ways: on the counter (or refrigerator shelf), enclosed in a paper bag, and enclosed in a paper bag with pieces of green apple (fruit gives off ethylene gas, which helps many fruits and vegetables ripen more quickly). We also tried two more esoteric techniques: burying the avocados at room temperature in flour and in rice. In the end, the only thing that mattered was the temperature at which the avocados were stored.

At room temperature, rock-hard avocados ripened within two days, but many of them ended up ripening unevenly, developing soft spots and air pockets on one side just as the other side was ripening. After completely ripening, they lasted two days on average if kept at room temperature (stored in the fridge after ripening, they lasted five days). Avocados ripened in the refrigerator, whether in a bag or out in the open, took around four days to soften, but did so evenly. Stored in the fridge, they lasted a full five days before starting to show signs of over-ripening.

The bottom line: If you need your avocados to ripen sooner rather than later, keep them on the counter. Otherwise, for better quality, you're better off putting them in the fridge and allowing them to ripen slowly. In either case, store the ripened fruit in the fridge to extend shelf life.

SHOPPING Prepeeled Garlic

We've never met a garlic product we like better than a fresh clove. Recently, we've noticed many supermarkets carrying jars or deli containers of prepeeled garlic cloves and wondered how they compare to fresh garlic bought by the head. We tasted both kinds of garlic raw in aïoli, sautéed in spaghetti with garlic and olive oil, and lightly cooked in stuffed rolled flank steak. In all cases, results were mixed, with neither freshly peeled nor prepeeled garlic claiming victory.

However, we did notice a difference in shelf life: A whole head of garlic stored in a cool, dry place will last for at least a few weeks, while prepeeled garlic in a jar (which must be kept refrigerated) lasts for only about two weeks before turning yellowish and developing an overly pungent aroma, even if kept unopened in its original packaging. (In fact, in several instances we found containers of garlic that had started to develop this odor and color on the supermarket shelf.) But if you go through a lot of garlic, prepeeled cloves can be an acceptable alternative. Just make sure they look firm and white with a matte finish when you purchase them.

TEST KITCHEN TIP Make-Ahead Cookies

These methods will allow you to prep a batch of dough, store it, and bake smaller batches of cookies as you need them.

Type of Cookie	How to Store	How to Bake
ROLL AND CUT • shortbread • gingerbread • jam sandwich	Roll and cut cookies as directed in recipe. Freeze on parchment-lined baking sheet until solid, about 1 hour. Transfer frozen cookies to zipper-lock bag, seal, and return to freezer for up to 2 weeks.	Space frozen cookies on parchment-lined baking sheet as directed in recipe, thaw at room temperature 10 minutes, and bake as directed.
SLICE AND BAKE • butter cookies • sandies	Form dough into logs; wrap in parchment and freeze 30 minutes or until firm. Wrap logs in double layer of plastic wrap (with parchment paper still on) and freeze for up to 2 weeks. If recipe calls for rolling logs in sugar, do so just before baking.	Thaw logs in refrigerator at least 2 hours; remove parchment and plastic wrap, slice, and bake as directed.
SCOOP AND BAKE • oatmeal • chocolate chip • sugar cookies	Portion dough and freeze on parchment-lined baking sheet until completely frozen, about 1 hour. Transfer frozen dough balls to zipper-lock bag, seal, and return to freezer for up to 2 weeks. If recipe calls for rolling cookies in sugar, do so just before baking.	Space frozen cookies on parchment-lined baking sheet as directed in recipe. Thaw at room temperature at least 1 hour, then bake as directed. To bake frozen cookies, add a minute or two to baking time.

Meat, Meet Marmite

Glutamate is part of a naturally occurring amino acid that contributes a savory quality to food. When making stews, soups, sauces, and braises, we often include glutamate-rich ingredients such as soy sauce, mushrooms, and Parmesan cheese to bump up flavor. However, another foodstuff has nearly twice as many glutamates as any of these: Marmite. A yeast extract from the byproducts of beer brewing, Marmite is made in Britain and marketed as a pungent spread for toast. We wondered, though, if it would be equally useful as a flavor enhancer.

We added ¼ teaspoon per serving to beef stew and a quick meat sauce (at the beginning of cooking) and stirred it into a marinade for steak. The Marmite noticeably enhanced the meat sauce and steak, making them significantly more savory. However, the long-cooking beef stew had such concentrated flavors that the Marmite added little.

Look for Marmite (or its similar-tasting Australian cousin, Vegemite) in the international section of the supermarket.

MIGHTY MEATY
Add ¼ teaspoon of Marmite per serving to quick soups, stews, sauces, or marinades for a shot of meaty "long-simmered" flavor.

⇒ BY MEREDITH BUTCHER AND PEGGY CHUNG COLLIER ⇐

DO YOU REALLY NEED THIS?
Electric Wine Openers

It sounds like something that Q would give James Bond: Press a button, and presto, the wine uncorks. But are electric wine openers really handy or just another gimmicky gadget? We placed three cordless, rechargeable models atop bottles with natural as well as synthetic corks. A push of the button on each model sent the corkscrew spiraling down into the cork, then pulled it out—a process that took 12 seconds or less, depending on the brand. The opener with the fastest-moving corkscrew wasn't sturdy enough to drill straight into the cork. It entered at an angle, rattling and jerking and making it difficult to maintain a firm grip on the bottle. Our favorite, the Waring Pro Professional Cordless Wine Opener ($39.95), has a broader base that helps the device rest firmly on the bottle, and its sturdy, quieter corkscrew minimized wobbling. The Waring Pro works just as well as our Best Buy manual tool, the Wine Enthusiast Quicksilver Corkscrew ($29.99), and with far less effort—making it great for opening multiple bottles for a party.

EASY DOES IT
The Waring Pro Professional Cordless Wine Opener removes a cork with the press of a button.

EQUIPMENT UPDATE Salad Spinners

Could any of the new or updated models of salad spinners outspin our favorite, the OXO Good Grips Salad Spinner ($29.95)? Zyliss replaced the pull-cord on its older model with a spring-loaded lever that resembles the center hand pump on the OXO. But in testing, the lever didn't pump smoothly, and the colander struggled to stop spinning when we pressed the brake. Worse, when we released the leverlike pump, it snapped up like a jack-in-the-box. The Chef'n Large Salad Spinner ($24.99) uses the same style of pump more effectively (and with a gentler lever release), but it is smaller and spins more slowly than the OXO, which remains our favorite.

EQUIPMENT TESTING
Electric Deep Fryers

Electric deep fryers seem doubly appealing: Not only are they safer than stovetop frying (because of their enclosed heating elements), but they also have lids and filters to reduce mess and smell. Could any top our usual method of deep frying in a Dutch oven with a candy thermometer clipped on? We made French fries in six fryers priced from $49.95 to $135.95 to find out. Every one had a

problem reaching and maintaining the correct temperature. When set to the maximum temperature, 375 degrees, most could only reach 350 degrees (a few not even that), resulting in limp, greasy fries. Two models overshot the top temperature and got too hot but did produce crisp fries. The best of the lot was the Waring Pro Professional Digital Deep Fryer ($139.95), which has a wide, shallow basket big enough to cook a full batch (four potatoes, serving four people) of fries that were uniformly crisp on the outside and tender on the inside. It works—but not well enough to replace our Dutch oven.

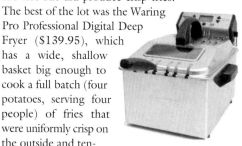

OFF THE MARK
The Waring Pro Professional Digital Deep Fryer produced crisp fries but overshot the top temperature on the gauge.

EQUIPMENT TESTING
Meat Handlers and Insulated Gloves

Meat that's too hot to handle can make shredding barbecued beef a tricky task. Two products, insulated gloves and so-called "meat handlers," promise protection with markedly different approaches. We lifted and shredded beef with Steven Raichlen's Best of Barbecue Insulated Gloves ($14.99) and Bear Paws Meat Handlers ($11.86). The fleece-lined rubber gloves were too large to give medium-sized hands a good grip on the meat and too stiff to let us easily pull beef into even-sized bits. The fat, sharp, widely spaced tines of the plastic bear paws readily pierced the meat, and the handles stayed cool, helping us comfortably lift a heavy cut of beef. They also shredded beef more quickly than the alternative—pulling with two forks—because the meat didn't get stuck between the tines.

PERFECT PULL
Bear Paws Meat Handlers are handy for lifting and shredding hot meat.

EQUIPMENT UPDATE Jar Openers

Manufacturers keep trying to offer new ways to open stubborn jars. We rounded up five new openers plus the Swing-A-Way Comfort Grip Jar Opener, our favorite, and tested them on big jars of spaghetti sauce as well as tiny bottles of vanilla extract. One opener was so cumbersome it was worse than struggling bare-handed with a jar. Two others

couldn't be sized down to grip vanilla lids. Another mangled lids as they were opened. We liked a rubbery disk from Le Creuset that also works as a trivet and potholder, but it couldn't outperform our old standby. For its low price and ability to adjust quickly to any size jar without a single slip, our favorite is still the Swing-A-Way ($6.95). Although it takes a few tries to learn to adjust the clamp, this tool is handy in the stickiest of situations.

NO STRUGGLE
The Swing-A-Way Comfort Grip Jar Opener is still best at removing stubborn lids.

For complete testing results on each item, go to www.cooksillustrated.com/jun09.

Sources

The following are mail-order sources for items recommended in this issue. Prices were current at press time and do not include shipping. Contact companies to confirm or visit www. cooksillustrated.com for updates.

Page 7: GRILL PRESS
- Emerilware by All-Clad Cast-Iron Square Grill Press: $27.95, item #580680, Cooking.com (800-663-8810, www.cooking.com).

Page 24: MIXING BOWL
- Pyrex Grip-Rite 5-Quart Teardrop Mixing Bowl: $16.99, item #1078616, World Kitchen (800-999-3436, www.shopworld kitchen.com).

Page 27: COOKWARE SETS
- All-Clad Stainless Steel Cookware Set, 10-piece: $699.95, item #6461396, Williams-Sonoma (877-812-6235, www.williams-sonoma.com).
- Tramontina 18/10 Stainless Steel Cookware Set, 8-piece: $144.97, item #001480610, Wal-Mart (www.walmart.com).

Page 32: ELECTRIC WINE OPENER
- Waring Pro Professional Cordless Wine Opener: $39.95, item #WO50, Chef's Corner (877-372-4535, www.chefscorner.com).

Page 32: SALAD SPINNER
- OXO Good Grips Salad Spinner: $29.95, item #102038, Cooking.com.

PAGE 32: DEEP FRYER
- Waring Pro Professional Digital Deep Fryer: $139.95, item #59-5787650, Williams-Sonoma.

Page 32: MEAT HANDLERS
- Bear Paws Meat Handlers: $11.86, item #1001-BR, The Barbecue Store (888-789-0650 www.barbecue-store.com).

Page 32: JAR OPENER
- Swing-A-Way Comfort Grip Jar Opener: $6.95, item #711BK, CutleryAndMore (800-650-9866, www.cutleryandmore.com).

INDEX
May & June 2009

◣ COOK'S LIVE Original Test Kitchen Videos **www.cooksillustrated.com**

MAIN DISHES
- **How to Make Grilled Beef Teriyaki**
- What is the best way to marinate meat?

- **How to Make Gas-Grilled Salmon Fillets**
- How can I keep food from sticking to the grill?

- **How to Make Italian-Style Grilled Chicken**
- Do I need to use bricks for Italian-Style Grilled Chicken?

- **How to Make Maple-Glazed Pork Tenderloin**

- **How to Make Quick Tomato Sauce**

- **How to Make Shrimp Tempura**
- How do I know what size shrimp to buy?
- How do I prepare vegetables for tempura?

SIDE DISH
- **How to Make Grilled Vegetables**
- How do I prepare vegetables for grilling?

BREAKFAST
- **How to Make Best Blueberry Muffins**
- Muffin pans 101

DESSERT
- **How to Make Perfect Chocolate Chip Cookies**
- What is the best cookie sheet?

AMERICA'S TEST KITCHEN
Public television's most popular cooking show

Join the millions of home cooks who watch our show, *America's Test Kitchen*, on public television every week. For more information, including recipes and program times, visit www.americastestkitchen.com.

Italian-Style Grilled Chicken, 7

Quick Tomato Sauce, 13

Grilled Salmon Fillets, 15

Perfect Chocolate Chip Cookies, 24

Maple-Glazed Pork Tenderloin, 11

Shrimp Tempura, 19

Grilled Vegetables, 12

Grilled Beef Teriyaki, 9

Best Blueberry Muffins, 21

PHOTOGRAPHY: CARL TREMBLAY, STYLING: MARIE PIRAINO

Watercress

Frisée

Dandelion
Greens

Baby Red
Chard

Tatsoi

Baby Lola
Rosa

Sorrel

Baby Red
Oak

Mizuna

Mâche

Baby Red
Romaine

MESCLUN GREENS

NUMBER NINETY-NINE

JULY & AUGUST 2009

COOK'S
ILLUSTRATED

Grill-Roasted
Turkey Breast
Juicy Meat, Crisp Skin

Easy French Fries
New Cold Oil Method

Kitchen Equipment
Buying Guide

Smoked BBQ
Pork Chops

Best Buttermilk
Pancakes

Fresh Berry Gratin

Rating Grill Cookware

Taste-Testing Oats
Grilled Stuffed Flank Steak
Great Chopped Salads
Tomato-Almond Pesto
Spanish Potato Omelet
Pasta with Eggplant and Tomatoes

www.cooksillustrated.com
$5.95 U.S./$6.95 CANADA

0 74470 62805 7

CONTENTS

July & August 2009

COOK'S ILLUSTRATED

www.cooksillustrated.com

Founder and Editor — Christopher Kimball
Editorial Director — Jack Bishop
Executive Editor — Amanda Agee
Test Kitchen Director — Erin McMurrer
Managing Editor — Rebecca Hays
Senior Editors — Keith Dresser
Lisa McManus
Features Editor — Lisa Glazer
Copy Editor — Amy Graves
Associate Editors — J. Kenji Alt
Bryan Roof
Test Cooks — Francisco J. Robert
Yvonne Ruperti
Assistant Test Kitchen Director — Matthew Herron
Assistant Editors — Meredith Butcher
Peggy Chung Collier
Assistant Test Cook — Marcus Walser
Executive Assistant — Meredith Smith
Editorial Assistant — Abbey Becker
Senior Kitchen Assistant — Nadia Domeq
Kitchen Assistants — Maria Elena Delgado
Ena Gudiel
Edward Tundidor
Producer — Melissa Baldino
Contributing Editors — Matthew Card
Dawn Yanagihara
Consulting Editor — Scott Brueggeman
Science Editor — Guy Crosby, Ph.D.
Proofreader — Jean Rogers

Managing Editor, Special Issues — Todd Meier
Production Editor, Special Issues — Elizabeth Bomze

Online Managing Editor — David Tytell
Online Editor — Kate Mason
Online Media Producer — Peter Tannenbaum
Online Associate Editor — Leaya Lee
Online Editorial Assistant — Mari Levine

Design Director — Amy Klee
Art Director, Magazines — Julie Bozzo
Designers — Jay Layman
Lindsey Timko
Deputy Art Director, Marketing/Web — Christine Vo
Staff Photographer — Daniel J. van Ackere

Vice President Marketing — David Mack
Circulation Director — Doug Wicinski
Circulation & Fulfillment Manager — Carrie Horan
Circulation Assistant — Megan Cooley
Partnership Marketing Manager — Pamela Putprush
Direct Mail Director — Adam Perry
Senior Marketing Database Analyst — Marina Sakharova
Product Operations Director — Steven Browall
Product Promotions Director — Randi Lawrence
E-Commerce Marketing Director — Hugh Buchan
E-Commerce Marketing Manager — Laurel Zeidman
Marketing Copywriter — David Goldberg
Customer Service Manager — Jacqueline Valerio
Customer Service Representatives — Jillian Nannicelli
Kate Sokol

Sponsorship Sales Director — Marcy McCreary
Retail Sales & Marketing Manager — Emily Logan
Corporate Marketing Associate — Bailey Vatalaro

Production Director — Guy Rochford
Traffic & Projects Manager — Alice Carpenter
Senior Production Manager — Jessica L. Quirk
Production & Imaging Specialists — Judy Blomquist
Lauren Pettapiece
Imaging & Color Specialist — Andrew Mannone

Technology Director — Rocco Lombardo
Systems Administrator — S. Paddi McHugh
Web Production Coordinator — Evan Davis
Support Technician — Brandon Lynch

Chief Financial Officer — Sharyn Chabot
Human Resources Director — Adele Shapiro
Controller — Mandy Shito
Senior Accountant — Aaron Goranson
Staff Accountant — Connie Forbes
Accounts Payable Specialist — Steven Kasha
Office Manager — Tasha Bere
Receptionist — Henrietta Murray
Publicity — Deborah Broide

For list rental information, contact: Specialists Marketing Services, Inc., 777 Terrace Ave., 4th Floor, Hasbrouck Heights, NJ 07604; 201-865-5800.

Editorial Office: 17 Station St., Brookline, MA 02445; 617-232-1000; fax 617-232-1572. Subscription inquiries, visit www.americas testkitchen.com/customerservice or call 800-526-8442.

Postmaster: Send all new orders, subscription inquiries, and change-of-address notices to Cook's Illustrated, P.O. Box 7446, Red Oak, IA 51591-0446.

PRINTED IN THE USA

HEIRLOOM CORN For millennia, corn was the staple crop of Mesoamerica. Today, the many hues of heirloom corn make it popular for ornamental use, though many varieties (available mainly through seed catalogs) are also edible. Rainbow Inca, a new cultivar developed from heirloom varieties, is sweet enough to be eaten from the cob. Cherokee White, Hopi Blue, and Bloody Butcher are commonly milled into flour or meal. Like any sweet corn, Guarijio Sweet (named after a Native American tribe of northern Mexico) is well suited for eating fresh. Seneca Blue Bear Dance, once given by shamans to the sick, has multicolored ears of violet, gray, blue, mauve, and cream kernels. Garland, which can be red or yellow, is of a type known as "flint corn," because its kernels have a hard outer shell. Striped is generally used for popping. A soft corn used mainly for flour, Navajo Robin's Egg features blue, white, and speckled kernels.

COVER (Plums): Robert Papp, BACK COVER (Heirloom Corn): John Burgoyne

America's Test Kitchen is a very real 2,500-square-foot kitchen located just outside of Boston. It is the home of *Cook's Illustrated* and *Cook's Country* magazines and is the workday destination for more than three dozen test cooks, editors, and cookware specialists. Our mission is to test recipes over and over again until we understand how and why they work and until we arrive at the best version. We also test kitchen equipment and supermarket ingredients in search of brands that offer the best value and performance. You can watch us work by tuning in to *America's Test Kitchen* (www.americastestkitchen.com) on public television.

PROMISES TO KEEP

In the 1960s, Sonny Skidmore did a lot of work for my mother at the controls of his backhoe: digging ponds, water bars, and septic tanks; grading the driveway; even towing our Army surplus Jeep out of a snowbank just below Charlie Bentley's farm. Sonny's mother, Jenny, maintained the tradition of the Saturday night sauna (a welcome event for those in town who did not have hot running water, plus a great spot, as it turned out, to meet a future spouse). Meanwhile, Harry, his father, was constantly bothered by the influx of hippies from New York and liked to make trouble just to entertain himself. But Sonny was a quiet, gentle man, despite his oversized hands and hogshead build. His penmanship was refined, almost girlish, yet nobody was better at the controls of a backhoe. You knew this because other men would jump down into a foundation hole while he was still digging, unafraid that they would get smacked in the head with the bucket.

I also knew Sonny as a man who kept his word. If he said that he would drop by to dig a new garden, he might not show up soon, but he always got the job done. This, I think, is part and parcel of growing up in the country, where neighbors count on each other to get by. We buy our hay from Dale Aines, who shows up with 2,000 bales every June without having to be reminded. Last fall, I asked Axel Blomberg if I could buy two cords of wood for our sugarhouse, and a month later, without further discussion, two cords were delivered and stacked, just as promised. This fidelity applies to a host of other activities as well: running sap lines, delivering composted manure, spreading lime, transporting pigs and cattle, welding a feeder, and blowing out irrigation lines for the winter. Two years ago, Nate Darrow offered to come over and show me how to prune apple trees. He finally showed up this March

with his farm manager, his wife, and two gas-powered pole saws. Even after two years, his word was good (and he pruned all of our trees to boot).

In summer, I make lots of small promises that I don't keep. I promise to take Emily fishing for bass at the upper pond. I have the best of intentions to saddle up the horses and take the family for a ride over Egg Mountain. I tell the kids that this is going to be the year we make the family movie. I have let them down with promises to explore the cave in Beartown. We don't always make it to all the county fairs we want to or take regular walks after dinner, returning home at twilight through a drifting sea of off-and-on lightning bugs to dish up bowls of homemade caramel ice cream. Every summer, as the nights grow colder, these broken promises are catalogued and recounted by our children in an effort to make sure that the future runs closer to plan.

Despite my shortcomings, I do believe that every life has one promise of note, one that cannot be broken without consequence. Mine is to pass on what I learned as a child on a small mountain farm, in the hay barns and pastures, at the noontime table, in the front seat of a farmer's dusty pickup, and when leading the horses down to the brook for a drink. These were not simply lessons of hard work and personal responsibility. They represent the gift of knowing all that can be done between sunrise and sunset, with two bare hands, a few tools, and a childlike enthusiasm for the world around us.

Last summer, during an afternoon of haying, there was a moment when I felt transported back to the 1960s. Standing in a windrow, I sniffed the hot

Christopher Kimball

breath of wild sage and spearmint, the sweet scent of ferns, and the blast of heat from the tractor and watched the leaves at the edge of the field turn milky silver as they twisted on their stems. In an instant, I was back in Charlie Bentley's hayfield, side-by-side with two farmhands, Herbie and Onie, and Dave Trachte, a local boy. We were haying down by the Green River, and I remembered the orange paintbrushes and tiny buttercups, a flat green snake coiling through a bale, and bumblebees as thick as my thumb, lazy and unsteady in the wind. We had it all back then, a place so intimate that an incense of yeast hung in the parlor, the rivers ran virgin and cold, and the woods were haunted by fiddle tunes from dance halls now sunken down into the weeds. Everything on that mountain farm had a past and a purpose, but even back then, I knew that America was starting to forget.

So I promised myself that I would grow up to build a root cellar, wear boots that have trod through manure, enjoy a sunrise cup of coffee in the barn, and, above all, raise kids who can throw hay, feed pigs, bridle a horse, and put the chickens away at night. I promised that in my family, the America I grew up with would be passed from parent to child, so that our grandchildren will learn how to cast a tight line, hitch up a team, and make a respectable skillet cornbread before the sun washes over the south side of Walnut Mountain. To some, these things may seem trivial, but teaching the next generation how to be useful, how to make the most of what lies between the bookends of a summer day or even a life, is a promise I know I will keep.

FOR INQUIRIES, ORDERS, OR MORE INFORMATION

www.cooksillustrated.com

At www.cooksillustrated.com, you can order books and subscriptions, sign up for our free e-newsletter, or renew your magazine subscription. Join the website and gain access to 16 years of *Cook's Illustrated* recipes, equipment tests, and ingredient tastings, as well as companion videos for every recipe in this issue.

COOKBOOKS

We sell more than 50 cookbooks by the editors of *Cook's Illustrated*. To order, visit our bookstore at www.cooksillustrated.com or call 800-611-0759 (or 515-246-6911 from outside the U.S.).

COOK'S ILLUSTRATED Magazine

Cook's Illustrated magazine (ISSN 1068-2821), number 99, is published bimonthly by Boston Common Press Limited Partnership, 17 Station St., Brookline, MA 02445. Copyright 2009 Boston Common Press Limited Partnership. Periodicals postage paid at Boston, Mass., and additional mailing offices USPS #012487. Publications Mail Agreement No. 40020778. Return undeliverable Canadian addresses to P.O. Box 875, Station A, Windsor, ON N9A 6P2. POSTMASTER: Send address changes to Cook's Illustrated, P.O. Box 7446, Red Oak, IA 51591-0446. For subscription and gift subscription orders, subscription inquiries, or change-of-address notices, call 800-526-8442 in the U.S. or 515-247-7571 from outside the U.S. or write us at Cook's Illustrated, P.O. Box 7446, Red Oak, IA 51591-0446.

Defrosting Sandwich Bread

I often freeze sandwich bread to prevent it from going stale. What is the best way to defrost the bread? My mother tells me I should zap it in the microwave, but my grandmother says it's best to leave it out at room temperature. Who is right?

MARIA ASENJO
BIRMINGHAM, ALA.

➤ We thought that removing slices of bread from the freezer and letting them thaw at room temperature would be the best approach, but our assumption was wrong. After having a conversation with our science editor and performing a few experiments, we realized that by leaving the bread at room temperature, we would be submitting it to an environment that would actually stale it.

As frozen bread warms, its starch molecules begin to form crystalline regions, which absorb the water in bread. The process, called retrogradation, will eventually produce a dry, stale texture. The best way to thaw frozen bread is to place the slices on a plate (uncovered) and microwave them on high power for 15 to 25 seconds. This will get the starch and water molecules to break down the crystalline regions, producing soft, ready-to-eat bread.

Panade Variations

Many of your recipes call for a panade made with white bread. Can a panade also be made with whole wheat bread or store-bought bread crumbs?

MARK SLOAN
SIMSBURY, CONN.

➤ A panade is a paste, typically made of milk and bread. It is often used in recipes calling for ground meat, such as hamburgers and meatballs, to help the formed meat hold its shape and retain moisture during cooking. We usually call for white sandwich bread in our panades because many cooks keep it on hand; plus, its neutral flavor incorporates easily into the meat mixture and doesn't interfere with other flavors in a recipe.

To find out if we could substitute whole wheat sandwich bread or store-bought bread crumbs for the white bread, we tested each in our recipes for Swedish meatballs and hamburgers. Tasters immediately picked up on a distracting wheat flavor from the whole wheat panade in both the meatballs and the burgers; plus, its high fiber content turned out dry meat. Meatballs and burgers made with the packaged bread crumbs tasted fine but lacked the tenderness of those made with white bread. Our conclusion? When it comes to panade, stick with white sandwich bread (unless the recipe says otherwise).

Lite Corn Syrup

I noticed that Karo has introduced a new Lite Corn Syrup into the market. How will it affect my baked goods?

KAREN GLAESEMANN
RICHLAND, WASH.

➤ To answer your question, we chose a few recipes from our repertoire and compared versions made with the original Karo Light Corn Syrup containing a combination of glucose and fructose and the new Karo Lite Corn Syrup, which contains glucose and sucralose (aka Splenda) but no fructose. We made our pecan bars, chewy chocolate cookies, and two kinds of chocolate frosting (bittersweet and milk chocolate) for our experiments.

It took just a few nibbles for tasters to detect an unpleasant aftertaste in the recipes made with lite syrup. Worse, in the bittersweet chocolate frosting, the Splenda-sweetened syrup created a consistency so elastic, it was almost rubbery. Things went further downhill when we made the frosting with milk chocolate: This sample was full of clumps. Why the texture problems? According to our science editor, the culprit was the cellulose gum present in the lite corn syrup, which reacted with the calcium in the milk chocolate; more milk led to the formation of an insoluble calcium salt. The bottom line: We recommend avoiding lite corn syrup in cooking and baking.

LIGHT TRUMPS LITE

Karo Light Syrup is a better choice than the brand's Lite version, which is not worth the calorie savings.

Onion Flavor Differences

When your recipes call for onions, I usually reach for the yellow kind, as it's the variety I normally keep on hand. Can Spanish or white onions also be used?

ROLAND GERHARDT
MEMPHIS, TENN.

➤ These onion varieties have subtle flavor differences, mostly due to the sulfur content of the soil in which each is grown. Different levels of sulfur in the soil contribute to varying levels of sulfur compounds within each onion type, resulting in greater or lesser pungency. White onions tend to have the least amount of sulfur compounds and the sweetest flavor; Spanish tend to have the most, for a far more pungent taste.

To see how much their flavor differences actually matter in recipes, we tasted all three onions raw in salsa, sautéed in oil, and simmered in French onion soup. In salsa, tasters found low-sulfur white onions to be mild and well-balanced, high-sulfur yellow onions notably stronger but still balanced, and Spanish onions decidedly strong, with a lingering harshness. When briefly sautéed, the sweetness of white onions intensified to a caramel flavor, Spanish onions retained their pungency, and yellow onions turned earthy and sweet. In French onion soup (a recipe that calls for deeply caramelized onions), white onions became too sweet for many tasters and Spanish onions left a slight astringent aftertaste, while yellow onions offered just the right balance of sweet and savory.

While such flavor differences may not ruin a recipe, we recommend mild white onions for raw applications and Spanish onions for cooked applications in which a heartier onion flavor is desired. If you want to stock just one type of onion in your pantry, make it yellow onions, which fall somewhere in between these two on the pungency scale.

Garlic Substitutes

What is the difference between dehydrated garlic and garlic powder? Are they ever an acceptable replacement for fresh garlic?

MARC ZIMMERMAN
AGOURA HILLS, CALIF.

➤ Dehydrated garlic is simply minced fresh garlic that is dehydrated before packaging. Garlic powder is made from dehydrated garlic that's been pulverized and, unless you buy a high-quality brand, often includes a slew of artificial ingredients and flavorings meant to improve flavor and extend shelf life.

We compared garlic powder and dehydrated minced garlic to the real thing in our recipes for pasta with garlic and oil, Caesar salad, and garlic bread. In the Caesar dressing, flavor differences were minimal; the assertive flavors of lemon, anchovies, and Worcestershire sauce masked any processed garlic taste. In the pasta and garlic bread, however, tasters preferred the unmistakable bite of real garlic.

Our opinion? In most instances, nothing compares to fresh cloves, especially when garlic is the predominant flavor in the recipe. We don't recommend dehydrated garlic, which takes a while to rehydrate and is quite mild. However, there are a few cases in which garlic powder makes sense. We like its mild roasted flavor in spice rubs for meat or in dishes such as roasted potatoes. (Unlike minced fresh garlic, garlic powder will not burn in the oven.) Substitute ¼ teaspoon of garlic powder for each clove of fresh garlic.

Lobster Tales

When I butcher a live lobster to remove the tail for grilling or sautéing, is it important to cook it right away, or can I keep it in the refrigerator a few hours?

ROB SNOW
QUINCY, MASS.

➤When any animal is killed, rigor mortis, or the stiffening of muscle tissue after death, begins to set in quickly. Over time, the phenomenon is reversed, when enzymes known as proteases break down the contracted muscle fibers to return the meat to a soft, pliable (and edible) state.

With large animals such as cows, pigs, and lambs, there are no adverse effects to the meat contracting and then softening—in fact, resting or aging beef after slaughter results in a more tender texture. With lobsters, however, conventional wisdom holds that a rest after death toughens the flesh. To see for ourselves, we bought a number of live lobsters and butchered them to remove the tails. We cooked some of the tails immediately, then waited intervals of one, two, four, six, and 12 hours before cooking the remainder. The lobster tails that were cooked immediately after butchering (before rigor mortis set in) had an ideal firm and meaty texture. The tails cooked after a rest of one or two hours were dense and rubbery; those cooked four, six, and 12 hours after butchering were mushy.

Our science editor explained why: Unlike in mammals, rigor mortis in lobsters begins to set in within minutes. With a wait of one or two hours after death, lobster meat will be tough and rubbery. However, as the flesh begins to soften again (sometime after two hours), a phenomenon occurs that doesn't happen in pork, beef, or lamb: The tissues loosen and start to come apart, resulting in a mushy, broken-down texture. The bottom line? Cook tails just after removing them from fresh-killed lobsters. If you're dealing with a whole lobster, plunge it live into boiling water or cook it immediately after killing it.

Fortified Substitution

Some of your recipes call for fortified wines, such as port or sherry. What exactly makes a wine fortified, and can I substitute ordinary red or white wine if I don't have any on hand?

SUSAN KUNDA
MALVERN, PA.

➤Fortified wines such as port and sherry start off like any other wine, but are then boosted with additional spirits (usually brandy) to achieve an 18 to 20 percent alcohol level. Traditionally, these wines were fortified to avoid spoilage during long ship voyages. Stylewise, they run the gamut; some are very sweet while others are more dry and savory. Moreover, due to the different manufacturing styles, their flavor profiles can vary dramatically. Sherry, which tasters described as "nutty" and "musky," is traditionally made with white wine, while port, with heavy notes of dried fruit, is developed with red.

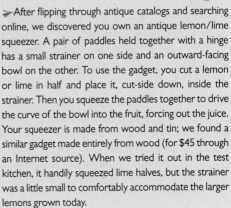

This gadget is still a useful way to extract juice from a lime—but today's larger lemons are a tight fit.

➤After flipping through antique catalogs and searching online, we discovered you own an antique lemon/lime squeezer. A pair of paddles held together with a hinge has a small strainer on one side and an outward-facing bowl on the other. To use the gadget, you cut a lemon or lime in half and place it, cut-side down, inside the strainer. Then you squeeze the paddles together to drive the curve of the bowl into the fruit, forcing out the juice. Your squeezer is made from wood and tin; we found a similar gadget made entirely from wood (for $45 through an Internet source). When we tried it out in the test kitchen, it handily squeezed lime halves, but the strainer was a little small to comfortably accommodate the larger lemons grown today.

To answer your question, we tried adapting recipes for sherry-cream sauce with leftover Chardonnay and a port-cherry reduction with leftover Merlot. In each application, the regular wine's sharper alcohol flavor stood out immediately; adding a sweetener seemed like the next step. We experimented with granulated sugar, light brown sugar, and honey, adding each to different batches of the recipes in ¼-teaspoon increments. Tasters picked up on honey's distinctive taste immediately, but deemed both granulated and brown sugars acceptable, noting that the latter's caramel/molasses flavors best resembled that of the aged fortified wines. Because every bottle of wine is different (even within a certain varietal), a universal substitution formula is nearly impossible. In a pinch, however, the test kitchen's suggestion is to substitute port with red wine and sherry with white, adding light brown sugar in increments of ¼ teaspoon until the boozy wine aftertaste is masked by the sweetness of the added sugar.

Sweetening with Stevia

I've seen a natural low-calorie sugar substitute at the supermarket called Truvia made from the stevia plant. Is this product really an acceptable stand-in for sugar in beverages and cooking?

MARY JO NELSON
ST. PAUL, MINN.

➤The stevia plant, a member of the sunflower family, is native to South and Central America and Mexico. The plant contains stevioside and rebaudioside, compounds that are up to 300 times sweeter than granulated sugar. Some people complain that stevia imparts a bitter taste to foods and beverages. When we sweetened iced tea with Truvia, which is made from the leaves of the stevia plant, we had to agree. Tasters quickly picked up on a disagreeable aftertaste.

For further evaluation, we replaced granulated sugar with Truvia in our recipes for sugar cookies and teriyaki sauce, following the conversion chart on the package, which recommends using about ⅓ cup of Truvia for every cup of sugar. As we mixed the cookie dough, problems became apparent even before the cookies made it into the oven. The Truvia dough was much drier than the dough made with granulated sugar. Once baked, the cookies made with Truvia had not spread nearly as much as the true sugar cookies. And forget about eating these impostors. Tasters complained of a chalky texture and a mouth-puckering bitterness that lingered long after samples were gone.

The Truvia teriyaki sauce didn't fare much better. While the sauce made with granulated sugar had reduced down to a beautifully thick glaze, easily able to coat and stick to chicken, the sauce made with Truvia was thin, lacking the cling of its competitor. The Truvia also imparted a bitter aftertaste to the sauce, albeit more subdued than it was in the cookies. In summary, we don't recommend Truvia as a sugar substitute—for the best results, stick with the real thing.

BITTERSWEET SUBSTITUTE
Recipes made with this stevia-based sweetener had an unacceptable bitter aftertaste.

SEND US YOUR QUESTIONS We will provide a complimentary one-year subscription for each letter we print. Send your inquiry, name, address, and daytime telephone number to Notes from Readers, Cook's Illustrated, P.O. Box 470589, Brookline, MA 02447, or to notesfromreaders@americastest kitchen.com.

Quick Tips

⇒ COMPILED BY YVONNE RUPERTI & FRANCISCO J. ROBERT ⇐

Keeping Cake Moist

To keep leftover cake moist as long as possible, Katie Fisher of Boston, Mass., stores the remaining portion under a cake dome along with a whole peeled apple. The moisture from the apple helps to keep the air under the dome humid and thus discourages the cake and frosting from drying out.

Foolproof Chimney Starter Lighting

It can be tricky to light a chimney starter on a blustery day if the wind extinguishes the paper kindling before it has a chance to ignite the charcoal. Barry Rico of Vacaville, Calif., devised this method to safeguard the process.

1. Place wads of crumpled newspaper underneath the chimney starter and set the chimney starter on the grill grate. Hold an empty paper towel roll in the center of the chimney starter and surround it with briquettes.
2. Light the newspaper. The paper towel roll encourages air to flow up through the briquettes, carrying the flames upward for efficient ignition.

Recycling Leftover Pickle Juice

Instead of tossing out a jar of pickle juice after finishing the last pickle, Diane Talts of Goodyear, Ariz., uses the tangy liquid to make a new condiment. She adds thinly sliced onions to the juice and lets them marinate in the refrigerator for a few days. The drained pickled onions can be used as a topping for hot dogs or hamburgers or in salads. This method also works well with the spicy packing juice from vinegar peppers.

Good to the Last Drop

The last few drops of mustard in a nearly empty jar can be difficult to scrape out. Rachel Mazor of Brooklyn, N.Y., found a great way to use up every last bit: She makes a quick mustard vinaigrette.

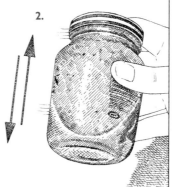

1. Add 3 parts extra-virgin olive oil and 1 part vinegar to the jar, along with salt and pepper to taste. Add garlic, herbs (just before serving), or other seasonings, if desired.
2. Shake the jar well to blend the dressing, then serve.

Homemade Pita Chips

Pam Foreman of Midlothian, Va., discovered that stale pita bread need not be discarded. She transforms the bread into a tasty snack by making it into chips.

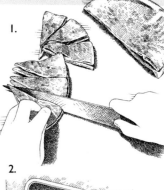

1. Cut two 8-inch pita breads into wedges and arrange them on a baking sheet. Brush the wedges with 2 tablespoons olive oil, then sprinkle with ½ teaspoon table salt and ¼ teaspoon dried herbs.
2. Place the baking sheet on the lower-middle rack of a 350-degree oven and bake until crisp, about 8 minutes. Flip the chips and continue to bake until fully toasted, about 8 minutes longer.

Rescuing a Broken Sauce

Sometimes a finicky sauce, such as beurre blanc, can separate and break if it gets too hot. Trudy Barkas of Davenport, N.Y., says that all is not lost. Simply remove the pan from the heat and whisk an ice cube into the sauce until it comes back together.

Send Us Your Tip We will provide a complimentary one-year subscription for each tip we print. Send your tip, name, and address to Quick Tips, Cook's Illustrated, P.O. Box 470589, Brookline, MA 02447, or to quicktips@americastestkitchen.com.

ILLUSTRATION: JOHN BURGOYNE

Level Measuring

To measure dry ingredients accurately, teaspoons and tablespoons should be leveled off with a straight edge. Tanya Farrow of Philadelphia, Pa., finds the flat spout of a baking powder canister ideal for accomplishing this task, eliminating the need to drag out a leveling tool such as a butter knife.

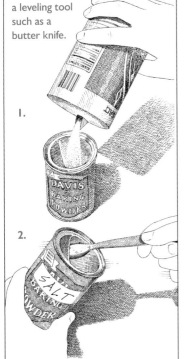

1. Store a frequently used ingredient, such as salt, in a clean baking powder canister.
2. When measuring, scrape the spoon against the level edge of the opening.

No-Drip Ice Cream Cones

When eating ice cream in a cone, the melting ice cream often drips through the bottom of the cone and onto your hands or clothing. Jeanie Lerner of Orinda, Calif., came up with this tasty solution.

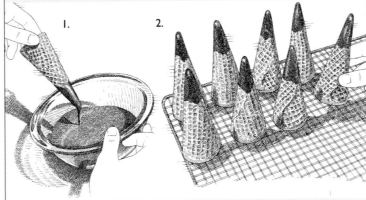

1. Dip the bottom of the cone (at least ½ inch) into the melted chocolate of your choice (dark, milk, or white).
2. Place the cone upside down on a cooling rack until the chocolate sets, fill it with ice cream, and serve. (Hold the cone above the chocolate so it won't melt.)

Stabilizing Whipped Cream

Heavy cream begins to break down and weep soon after whipping. When Nick Lettiere of Staten Island, N.Y., wants to prepare whipped cream in advance, he adds Marshmallow Fluff to help keep it stable. Whip 6 tablespoons of Fluff into every cup of heavy cream, along with ½ teaspoon of rum extract or vanilla extract. Cover and refrigerate. The Fluff not only helps to keep the cream from deflating for up to a day, it also adds a pleasantly sweet marshmallow flavor.

Mess-Free Coffee

Sharon Weissman of Kew Gardens, N.Y., hates the messy chore of cleaning damp coffee grounds out of the plastic basket of her coffee percolator. Here's how she makes cleanup easier.

1. Snip a small hole in the center of a small (4- to 6-cup) basket-style coffee filter.
2. Fit the filter over the percolator tube and into the basket. Fill the filter-lined basket with ground coffee and brew as directed.
3. When it's time to clean up, just dump out the filter with the grounds.

Protecting Drained Pasta

Sarah Strauss of Portland, Ore., noticed that every time she drained pasta into her shallow colander, the hot water would back up into the pasta before it had a chance to empty down the drain, creating a risk of contamination if her sink wasn't perfectly clean. She now steadies the colander on an upside-down cake pan before draining. The pan elevates the colander—and, most important, the pasta—above the basin.

Spooning Off the Fat

After sautéing sausage or bacon, it's often necessary to spoon off the fat before proceeding with the recipe. To get rid of the fat without removing the meat from the pan, Andrea King of Quincy, Mass., uses a pair of metal tongs to prop up one side of the skillet. She pushes the meat to the elevated part of the skillet and lets it sit for a few moments so that the fat collects in the lower portion, where it can be easily spooned away.

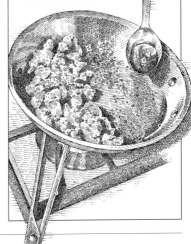

Rethinking Grill-Roasted Turkey Breast

Cooking a lean, delicate turkey breast over the intense heat of a grill is asking for trouble.
Could an old-fashioned restaurant technique save the day?

> BY FRANCISCO J. ROBERT ≤

Introducing mild-mannered turkey to the smoky fire of a grill is a surefire way to add great flavor. For Thanksgiving, I normally grill-roast a whole bird, but in the summer months, turkey breast can be just the ticket. The problem is that unlike fatty pork butt or brisket, which turn moist and tender after a stint on the grill, ultra-lean turkey breast easily dries out. Plus there's the matter of its irregular shape (thick on one end and tapered on the other) that can lead to uneven cooking. I was determined to get around these issues with a recipe that would deliver a grill-roasted breast with all the richness and juiciness I associate with the thighs and legs, along with crisp, well-rendered skin and meat moist all the way through.

Surefire Solution

Grill-roasting involves cooking over indirect heat at a fairly constant temperature, mimicking the environment of an oven. But caution is essential: The fiery heat will quickly turn low-fat meat such as turkey breast chalky and dry. To alleviate this problem, the test kitchen often turns to either salting or brining (a soak in a saltwater solution). Since the latter could interfere with my goal of crisp skin, I opted for salting. When meat is salted, its juices are initially drawn out of the flesh and beads of liquid pool on its surface. Eventually, the salty liquid slowly migrates back into the meat, keeping it moist as it cooks. These moisture-retaining properties are pronounced at the surface of the meat, the area most prone to overcooking. Salting a whole bone-in skin-on turkey breast took about an hour to work and was a good first step in improving the meat's flavor and texture.

On to the grill setup. Grill-roasting typically requires an arrangement that the test kitchen refers to as a modified two-level fire, in which all the coals are pushed to one side of the grill to create two temperature zones. I placed the salted breast on the hotter side of the grill first to crisp the skin, then moved it to the cooler side to cook through. After a few bites, my colleagues agreed that while I had made some progress, the supremely lean meat still had spots that were dry as a bone.

I knew that breast meat starts to dry out when it reaches temperatures above 165 degrees, so I'd have

Boning a whole turkey breast and tying the two halves together created a uniform shape that cooked and sliced evenly.

to find a way to keep as much of the meat as possible below this critical point. In the test kitchen, we recently demonstrated that low heat helps meat cook evenly. We roasted turkey breasts in 400- and 275-degree ovens and then recorded their temperatures with an instant-read thermometer, reading temperatures at ¼-inch intervals from the centers to the very exteriors. In the turkey cooked in a 400-degree oven, over 50 percent of the breast registered higher than 165 degrees (with the very surface reaching over 200 degrees). In the turkey cooked in a 275-degree oven, 80 percent of the breast remained under 165 degrees, with the surface temperature only reaching 176 degrees.

These findings shaped my next grill experiment. Rather than risking parched meat by placing the breast over high heat first, I started by cooking it slowly on the cooler side of the grill until its internal temperature reached 150 degrees. By this time, the meat was moist, and though its skin was not yet crisp, most of its fat had rendered. A quick sear on the hotter side of the grill took care of the skin, and after resting, the breast had reached the ideal serving temperature of 165 degrees.

Back indoors, I sliced into the meat. The skin

was crackling crisp and most of the flesh was moist and juicy. I was about to call it a day until one taster pointed out that the tapered ends were overcooked and dry. Since one side of the breast was over 5 inches thick and the tapered end was only 1 to 2 inches thick, it seemed impossible to avoid overcooking. Repositioning the tapered ends away from the hot side of the grill helped a little, but not enough. Back to the drawing board.

Cut and Tied

Inspiration struck when I started thinking about the myriad ways I've prepared chicken breasts in restaurants. One of the fancier approaches is a roulade. The method involves stuffing a butterflied boneless breast with a flavorful filling, then rolling it into a tight cylinder. The roulade is first browned, then braised or baked. After slicing, it makes an elegant presentation, and its uniform width leads to even cooking. Could I modify this technique for a turkey breast?

For the next go-round, I bought a boneless, skinless turkey breast, butterflied it, salted it, rolled it into a neat cylinder (I'd consider fillings later), and grilled it using my low/high heat method. The meat was evenly cooked, but without its protective skin, the exterior developed a tough, leathery crust. Returning to a whole bone-in, skin-on breast, I removed the breasts from the bone and sprinkled them with salt. Next, I arranged the flesh of the breasts so that the thick end of one was pressed against the tapered end of the other, creating an even thickness throughout. I secured the meat and skin with butcher's twine and grill-roasted the meat with my dual-temperature method.

I was definitely on to something. The only setback was that the skin did not cover the meat well, creating a few desiccated patches where the flesh was exposed during grilling. To solve the problem, I pulled the skin off the breasts before removing the bone. After arranging the breasts thick end to thin end, I strategically draped the large piece of skin around the meat, leaving no areas uncovered save for a narrow seam on the underside. I secured the package with twine, coated the skin lightly with vegetable oil, and proceeded with my grill-roasting

■◀ **COOK'S VIDEOS** Original Test Kitchen Videos
www.cooksillustrated.com/aug09
HOW TO MAKE
• Charcoal Grill-Roasted Boneless Turkey Breast
VIDEO TIP
• How do I bone a turkey breast?

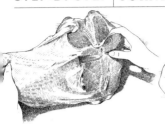

1. REMOVE SKIN Starting at one side of breast and using fingers to separate skin from meat, peel skin off breast meat and reserve.

2. REMOVE BONE Using tip of knife, cut along rib cage to remove each breast half completely.

3. ASSEMBLE Arrange one breast, cut-side up; top with second breast, cut-side down, thick end over tapered end. Drape skin over breasts and tuck ends under.

4. TIE LENGTHWISE Tie one 36-inch piece of twine lengthwise around roast.

5. TIE CROSSWISE Tie five to seven pieces of twine at 1-inch intervals crosswise along roast, starting at its center, then at either end, and then filling in the rest.

---

technique. The roast held its shape beautifully, and when I brought the turkey inside to my colleagues, they finally praised it as moist, evenly cooked, and crisp all around.

With my basic recipe established, I played around with flavorings. Sprinkling wood chips over the hot coals while the turkey roasted lent a touch of smokiness to the mild meat. I also came up with a fresh herb butter to slather onto the breasts before tying. While it may not be the most conventional-looking turkey that's ever come off my grill, it was certainly the best—and my satisfied tasters agreed.

CHARCOAL GRILL-ROASTED BONELESS TURKEY BREAST
SERVES 6 TO 8

NOTE: We prefer either a natural (unbrined) or kosher turkey breast for this recipe. Using a kosher turkey breast (rubbed with salt and rinsed during processing) or self-basting turkey breast (injected with salt and water) eliminates the need for salting in step 2. If the breast has a pop-up timer, remove it before cooking. For our free recipe for Grill-Roasted Boneless Turkey Breast with Olives and Sun-Dried Tomatoes, go to www.cooksillustrated.com/aug09.

- 1 whole bone-in, skin-on turkey breast (5 to 7 pounds) (see note)
- 4 teaspoons kosher salt or 2 teaspoons table salt
- ½ cup wood chips, soaked in water at least 30 minutes (optional)
- 1 teaspoon vegetable oil, plus extra for cooking grate
  Ground black pepper

1. Following illustrations 1 and 2 above, remove skin from breast meat and then remove breasts from bone structure (discard bones or save for stock).

2. Sprinkle entire surface of each breast with 2 teaspoons kosher salt (or 1 teaspoon table salt). Following illustrations 3 through 5 above, assemble and tie turkey breasts. Place roast on wire rack set in rimmed baking sheet and refrigerate, uncovered, 1 hour.

3. Meanwhile, light large chimney starter filled with charcoal (6 quarts, about 100 briquettes) and allow to burn until coals are fully ignited and partially covered with thin layer of ash, about 20 minutes. Build modified two-level fire by arranging all coals over half of grill, leaving other half empty. Sprinkle soaked wood chips (if using) over coals. Position cooking grate over coals, cover grill, and heat rack until hot, about 5 minutes; scrape grate clean with grill brush. Dip wad of paper towels in oil; holding wad with tongs, wipe cooking grate. Grill is ready when side with coals is medium-hot (you can hold your hand 5 inches above grate for 3 to 4 seconds).

4. Rub surface of roast with 1 teaspoon oil and season with pepper. Place roast on grate over cooler side of grill. Cover grill and grill-roast until instant-read thermometer inserted into thickest part of roast registers 150 degrees, 40 to 60 minutes, turning roast 180 degrees halfway through cooking time.

5. Slide roast to hot side of grill and cook, uncovered, until roast is browned and skin is crisp on all sides, 2 to 2½ minutes per side (8 to 10 minutes total). Transfer roast to cutting board and let rest 20 minutes. Cut into ½-inch-thick slices, removing twine as you cut. Serve immediately.

GAS GRILL-ROASTED BONELESS TURKEY BREAST

Follow recipe for Charcoal Grill-Roasted Boneless Turkey Breast through step 2. If using wood chips, place them in shallow aluminum pie plate and place plate on primary burner (burner that will remain on during cooking) and reposition cooking grate(s). Turn all burners to high, close lid, and heat grill until hot, about 15 minutes. Scrape cooking grate clean with grill brush. Dip wad of paper towels in oil; holding wad with tongs, wipe cooking grate. Leave primary burner on high and turn off other burner(s). Continue with recipe from step 4, placing roast on side opposite primary burner and cooking with lid down in step 5.

GRILL-ROASTED BONELESS TURKEY BREAST WITH HERB BUTTER

Place ¼ cup tarragon leaves, 1 tablespoon thyme leaves, 2 medium minced garlic cloves, and ¼ teaspoon black pepper on cutting board; mince to fine paste.

Combine herb paste and 4 tablespoons softened unsalted butter in medium bowl. Follow recipe for Charcoal Grill-Roasted Boneless Turkey Breast through step 1. After salting each breast, place cut-side up on work surface. Lift tenderloin away from each breast, leaving it partially attached, and spread butter evenly over cut side of each breast. Replace tenderloin and proceed with recipe as directed.

Bringing Home Spanish Tortilla

This tapas bar favorite boasting meltingly tender potatoes in a dense, creamy omelet would be the perfect simple supper—if it didn't cook in an entire quart of olive oil.

≥ BY J. KENJI ALT ≤

Potatoes are a must in this Spanish suppertime omelet, but ingredients like sausage, red pepper, and peas are also common.

Americans love everything-but-the-kitchen-sink, diner-style omelets; the French swear by delicate rolled omelets; the Italians make cheese- and herb-stuffed frittatas; and the Spanish serve *tortilla española*. A Spanish tortilla (no relation to Mexican flour and corn tortillas) is an egg-and-potato omelet made by slow-cooking sliced potatoes and onions in olive oil until meltingly tender, mixing them with beaten eggs, and frying the mix into a golden-brown cake. Its intensely rich flavor and velvety, melt-in-your-mouth texture distinguishes it from the omelets of other countries.

If you travel to Spain, you'll discover tortillas in tapas bars, restaurants, and home kitchens, usually served with a garlicky mayonnaise, as an evening snack or light supper alongside a glass of sherry. This savory omelet is immensely appealing—but only if someone else is doing the cooking. The typical recipe calls for simmering the potatoes in 3 to 4 cups of extra-virgin olive oil. This amount is not as taxing on the wallet if you're straining and reusing the oil to make several tortillas a week, as many Spaniards do, but using so much oil for a single, somewhat humble meal seemed excessive. I wanted to keep the satisfying flavor and unctuous texture but lose the quart of oil.

Flipping Out

Heading into the test kitchen, I decided to stick with the traditional volume of olive oil until I could determine the proper type and ratio of ingredients. I wanted a dish that was just as hearty as an American

omelet, so I started by cooking a generous amount of potatoes in 4 cups of oil. Waxy Red Bliss potatoes and new potatoes were out—no matter how long they were cooked, they remained firm instead of becoming creamy. Yukon Golds worked better, but starchy russets were best of all, turning soft and creamy in their oil bath. One and a half pounds of russets yielded a 1½-inch-thick tortilla that just fit inside a 10-inch skillet—perfect for four people as a light dinner.

After hours of slicing and dicing, I found that ⅛-inch-thick slices of quartered potatoes yielded the best distribution of egg and potato. For the onion, tasters favored the mellow flavor of standard yellow onions over shallots, Spanish onions, and sweet Vidalias.

Recipes varied wildly in the ratio of eggs to potatoes. One egg per pound of potatoes was clearly too little; there simply wasn't enough egg for the tortilla to set. But with 10 eggs per pound, my potato cake was overwhelmingly eggy. Five eggs per pound (or 8 eggs per 1½ pounds) of potatoes was just enough to let the tortilla set firm but tender, with the eggs and potatoes melding into one another instead of competing for dominance in flavor and texture.

Up to this point, I had been cooking the potatoes and onions in oil until soft, mixing them with eggs in a bowl, then pouring the mix back into the skillet, shaking it gently to keep the eggs from sticking. Traditional recipes call for flipping the tortilla with the help of a single plate when the bottom is set but the top is still liquid. This might be old hat for Spanish cooks, but for an occasional tortilla-maker, the result was an egg-splattered floor. I tried skipping the flip and finishing the tortilla by browning the second side under a hot broiler, but this puffed up the eggs like a soufflé—not bad, but not the authentic dense and creamy texture I wanted. What if I just trapped the heat inside the pan to set the top? I cooked another tortilla, this time placing a lid on the pan as soon as the bottom of the egg-and-potato mixture was set. Two minutes later, the top was cooked just enough to make flipping less risky—but not easy. Fed up, I fudged tradition and grabbed another plate. By sliding the tortilla out of the pan and onto one plate, then placing another upside-down over the tortilla, I could easily flip the whole thing and slide the tortilla back in the pan, making a once-messy task foolproof.

Oil Embargo

With ingredients and technique settled, I could finally set my sights on scaling down the oil, ideally to a much more reasonable ½ cup. Unfortunately, with this little oil, the potatoes on the bottom of the pan browned and overcooked before the potatoes on the top even began to soften. Perhaps I could learn from my egg technique and try cooking the potatoes with

The Wide World of Omelets

A Spanish tortilla is as much about the potatoes as it is the eggs. Its density and lack of cheese set it apart from other omelet styles.

AMERICAN OMELET
This homely diner staple features a thin layer of egg folded over a loose pile of filling that can include veggies, cheese, plus you-name-it.

FRENCH OMELET
Creamy, cigar-shaped French omelets are too delicate to hold anything more than a small amount of filling.

ITALIAN FRITTATA
Like tortillas, frittatas are not folded. Instead, they're finished in the oven for a dry, lightly souffléed texture, with fillings from sausage to herbs.

1. SLIDE After browning first side, loosen tortilla with rubber spatula and slide onto large plate.

2. FLIP Place second plate face-down over tortilla; invert browned-side up on second plate.

3. SLIDE Slide tortilla back into pan, browned-side up, and tuck edges into pan with rubber spatula.

the lid on? I tossed the potatoes and onions in ¼ cup of olive oil, heated another ¼ cup oil in a hot skillet, then added the potatoes and onions and covered it, stirring the mixture once every five minutes to ensure even cooking. Better, but still not great—even with the stirring, the potatoes on the hot bottom of the pan developed tough brown spots. Turning the heat all the way down to medium-low and extending the cooking time to over 20 minutes prevented these spots from forming, but now the potatoes were turning mushy.

The problem was that with a deep pan of oil, it's easy to cook a large volume of potatoes without disturbing them. The potatoes slowly soften, and as they cook, the starch on their exterior hardens, forming a sheath that keeps their shape intact (just like a French fry, but not browned quite as much). In less oil, however, the potatoes were half frying, half steaming—and without sheath formation, they were disintegrating at the slightest touch. Then I realized that I'd made my potato choice while I was still using the traditional cooking method. With less oil, did russets still make sense?

I started a new tortilla using the slightly firmer, less starchy Yukon Golds that I had initially rejected. With less oil in the skillet, they were clearly a winner: starchy enough to become meltingly tender as they cooked, but sturdy enough to stir and flip halfway through cooking with fewer breaks. In fact, the new approach worked so well that I found I could reduce the oil to a mere 6 tablespoons. The rich flavor was still present as long as I relied on a high-quality extra-virgin olive oil, a much more appealing prospect since I was now using only a moderate amount.

By this point my tortillas were nearing perfection, but my colleagues were curious to see how they might taste with additional ingredients. This was a cinch, since Spanish tortillas are like American diner omelets in one important way: While perfectly good plain, they can also take on an infinite variety of fillings. I prepared two tortillas with typical additions (roasted red peppers and peas, and Spanish chorizo) and served them with a batch of garlicky mayonnaise. Tasters quickly finished their slices and came back for seconds, praising the exceptionally creamy potatoes and eggs studded with salty sausage or sweet vegetables. I had strayed from tradition, but my tortillas still delivered true Spanish flavor.

SPANISH TORTILLA
WITH ROASTED RED PEPPERS AND PEAS
SERVES 4 AS A LIGHT ENTRÉE AND 6 AS AN APPETIZER

NOTE: Spanish tortillas are often served warm or at room temperature with olives, pickles, and Garlic Mayonnaise (recipe follows) as an appetizer. They may also be served with a salad as a light entrée. For the most traditional tortilla, omit the roasted red peppers and peas. We recommend using our winning brand of extra-virgin olive oil, Columela.

- 6 tablespoons plus 1 teaspoon extra-virgin olive oil (see note)
- 1½ pounds Yukon Gold potatoes (3 to 4 medium), peeled, quartered lengthwise, and cut crosswise into ⅛-inch-thick slices
- 1 small onion, halved and sliced thin
- 1 teaspoon table salt
- ¼ teaspoon ground black pepper
- 8 large eggs
- ½ cup jarred roasted red peppers, rinsed, dried, and cut into ½-inch pieces
- ½ cup frozen peas, thawed
  Garlic Mayonnaise (recipe follows) (optional)

1. Toss 4 tablespoons oil, potatoes, onion, ½ teaspoon salt, and pepper in large bowl until potato slices are thoroughly separated and coated in oil. Heat 2 tablespoons oil in 10-inch nonstick skillet over medium-high heat until shimmering. Reduce heat to medium-low, add potato mixture to skillet, and set bowl aside without washing. Cover and cook, stirring with rubber spatula every 5 minutes, until potatoes offer no resistance when poked with tip of paring knife, 22 to 28 minutes (it's OK if some potato slices break into smaller pieces).

2. Meanwhile, whisk eggs and remaining ½ teaspoon salt in reserved bowl until just combined. Using rubber spatula, fold hot potato mixture, red peppers, and peas into eggs until combined, making sure to scrape all potato mixture out of skillet. Return skillet to medium-high heat, add remaining teaspoon oil, and heat until just beginning to smoke. Add egg-potato mixture and cook, shaking pan and folding mixture constantly for 15 seconds. Smooth

top of mixture with rubber spatula. Reduce heat to medium, cover, and cook, gently shaking pan every 30 seconds until bottom is golden brown and top is lightly set, about 2 minutes.

3. Using rubber spatula, loosen tortilla from pan, shaking back and forth until tortilla slides around freely in pan. Following photos at left, slide tortilla onto large plate. Invert tortilla onto second large plate and slide it browned-side up back into skillet. Tuck edges of tortilla into skillet with rubber spatula. Return pan to medium heat and continue to cook, gently shaking pan every 30 seconds, until second side is golden brown, about 2 minutes longer. Slide tortilla onto cutting board or serving plate and allow to cool at least 15 minutes. Cut tortilla into cubes or wedges and serve with Garlic Mayonnaise, if desired.

SPANISH TORTILLA
WITH CHORIZO AND SCALLIONS

NOTE: Use a cured, Spanish-style chorizo for this recipe. Portuguese linguiça is a suitable substitute.

Follow recipe for Spanish Tortilla with Roasted Red Peppers and Peas, omitting roasted red peppers and peas. In step 1, heat 4 ounces Spanish-style chorizo cut into medium dice with 1 tablespoon oil (reduced from 2 tablespoons) in 10-inch nonstick skillet over medium-high heat, stirring occasionally, until chorizo is browned and fat has rendered, about 5 minutes. Once chorizo is browned, proceed with recipe as directed, adding potato mixture to skillet with chorizo and rendered fat and folding 4 thinly sliced scallions (green and white parts) into eggs in step 2.

GARLIC MAYONNAISE
MAKES ABOUT 1¼ CUPS

- 2 large egg yolks
- 2 teaspoons Dijon mustard
- 2 teaspoons juice from 1 lemon
- 1 medium garlic clove, minced or pressed through garlic press (about 1 teaspoon)
- ¾ cup vegetable oil
- 1 tablespoon water
- ¼ cup extra-virgin olive oil
- ½ teaspoon table salt
- ¼ teaspoon ground black pepper

Process yolks, mustard, lemon juice, and garlic in food processor until combined, about 10 seconds. With machine running, slowly drizzle in vegetable oil, about 1 minute. Transfer mixture to medium bowl and whisk in water. Whisking constantly, slowly drizzle in olive oil, about 30 seconds. Whisk in salt and pepper. Refrigerate in airtight container for up to 4 days.

📹 **COOK'S VIDEOS** Original Test Kitchen Videos
www.cooksillustrated.com/aug09
HOW TO MAKE
• Spanish Tortilla
• Garlic Mayonnaise

Really Good Grill-Smoked Pork Chops

To achieve juicy glazed pork infused with deep smoky flavor without a smoker, we couldn't let the chops lie down on the job.

⇒ BY FRANCISCO J. ROBERT ⇐

As a Southerner, to me the term "barbecued" doesn't mean grilled meat with some sauce brushed over it. To be worthy of the term, the meat—pork especially—has to be infused to the core with deep smoke flavor. But I also like my barbecued chops to have a well-browned crust. These two goals are at odds. Good smoke flavor generally requires a lengthy exposure to a slow fire to give the smoke time to penetrate, while a charred crust requires a blast of high heat to quickly sear the exterior of the meat before the interior turns dry and leathery. For juicy chops covered in a crusty glaze full of real smoke flavor, I needed an approach that would somehow reconcile these two extremes.

Chop Choices

My first task was choosing the chops. Since I recently perfected a recipe for Pan-Seared Thick-Cut Pork Chops (March/April 2009), I was well aware of my options, all cut from the loin of the pig. Blade chops, from the shoulder end of the loin, have a lot of connective tissue and require long, moist cooking methods to render them tender. I wanted a fast weeknight dinner, so they were out of the running. I also avoided sirloin chops, which I knew from experience to be irredeemably dry and tough. That left center-cut chops and rib chops. The center-cut chops were good—but the rib chops, which have slightly more fat, were even better. The size of the chop, however, proved critical. Anything less than a 1½-inch thickness and the chops turned leathery and dry before the smoke had a chance to infuse the meat. For the sauce, I kept things simple, briefly simmering ketchup, molasses, onion, Worcestershire sauce, Dijon mustard, cider vinegar, and brown sugar until thickened.

Armed with the right cut of meat and a tasty sauce, I headed outside to fire up the grill. To reap the benefits of both high and low heat, my best bet

📹 **COOK'S VIDEOS** Original Test Kitchen Videos
www.cooksillustrated.com/aug09
HOW TO MAKE
• Best Grill-Smoked Pork Chops
VIDEO TIP
• Working with wood chips

A novel technique prevented these chops from overcooking and deepened smoky flavor.

was a two-level fire, in which all the coals are banked on one side of the grill to create a hot side and cooler side. For smoke flavor, I added a handful of soaked wood chips to the coals. I placed the chops on the hot side first and cooked them uncovered for about three minutes per side to create a good sear. I then moved the chops onto the cooler side, replaced the grill lid to trap smoke, and cooked them until they reached 140 degrees, about nine minutes longer. To prevent burning, I slathered on the barbecue sauce in the last few minutes of cooking.

When I brought the chops inside, tasters deemed them good—but not great. The chops had a decent crust, but they were also dry inside, and the smoke flavor was weak. The only way I was going to get more smokiness was by extending the cooking time. But how could I do that without further overcooking the meat? A larger cut might help, so I hunted down some extra-thick 2-inch chops to try. Their greater girth allowed me to keep them on the grill for about 40 minutes longer, leading to better smoke

flavor, but these Goliaths were ridiculously huge for individual servings. If I was cooking pork this thick, I might as well just put an entire roast on the fire.

Low, Slow Solution

Then my thoughts turned to the barbecued pork chops I grew up eating in Alabama. While they lacked any crust to speak of, they were incredibly smoky thanks to hours of low, slow cooking under the watchful eye of a pit master. Could I reverse the cooking, starting low and finishing with a quick sear? This was exactly the solution I'd come up with for my pan-seared chops, which start in a low-temperature oven. As I'd discovered, enzymes called cathepsins break down proteins such as collagen, helping to tenderize meat, but these enzymes are only active at temperatures below 122 degrees. By cooking my pork slowly, I'd be giving these enzymes more time to work their tenderizing magic on my meat.

This time I started my chops under cover on the cooler side of the grill, allowing the smoke to do its job for about 25 minutes. I then applied a few coats of sauce and finished by searing them, uncovered, over hot coals. The result was almost everything I'd hoped for: my smokiest, most tender chops yet.

The only hitch? With four chops to cook, and only half a grill to work on at a time, things were getting pretty crowded and my chops were cooking unevenly. Rotating the chops throughout the cooking time helped but required me to open the cover every few minutes, allowing that valuable smoke to escape. My answer was reorganizing the coals. Banking the coals on either side of the grill with a disposable aluminum pan in the center created a cooler zone large enough for all four chops to cook more evenly. Still, the edges of the chops closest to the coals were cooking too fast. Using fewer coals was not an option—that kept the fire from getting hot enough at the end to give my chops a good sear. I had done all I could with the grill, so I turned my attention to the chops themselves.

Stand-Up Routine

In the test kitchen we generally opt for bone-in chops. The bones add flavor to the meat as it cooks and contain connective tissues and fat that break

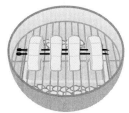

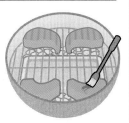

1. BUILD SPLIT FIRE
Place aluminum pan between two mounds of coals to create cooler center flanked by two hot areas.

2. SKEWER CHOPS
Pass two skewers through loin muscle of each chop to provide stability when standing on grill.

3. STAND ON GRILL
Stand skewered chops, bone-side down on cooking grate, in center of grill so smoke can reach all sides.

4. SAUCE & SEAR
Brush chops with sauce and transfer to hot sides of grill to sear on both sides (brushing top of each chop again before flipping).

down to lend suppleness. What's more, the hollow structure of a bone means it acts as an insulator, slowing down heat penetration. Could I use this fact to my advantage and rest each chop on its bone instead of laying it flat? To keep the chops from toppling over on each other, I speared them together with skewers, making sure to leave a good inch between each one to allow smoke to circulate, then stood them upright in the center of the grill. With bone, not meat, touching the grill, I was able to keep the chops over the fire a full 30 minutes. When the meat reached an internal temperature of 120 degrees, I removed the skewers, applied the glaze, and finished the chops, meat-side down, over the hot coals. As I opened the grill, I noticed that standing the chops upright allowed the smoke to freely circulate around all their surfaces. It was easy to take this same method and apply it to a gas grill, with slight adjustments.

These chops had it all: charred crust; rosy-pink, ultra-moist meat; and true smoke flavor throughout. I may have skewered tradition, but I had perfectly barbecued pork chops on the table in about an hour.

BEST CHARCOAL GRILL-SMOKED PORK CHOPS

NOTE: Buy chops of the same thickness so they will cook uniformly. We prefer the flavor of natural pork, but enhanced pork (injected with a solution of water, salt, and sodium phosphate to prevent the meat from drying out) can also be used, but don't sprinkle with salt in step 3. Use the large holes on a box grater to grate the onions. Although we prefer hickory wood chips, any variety of chip will work, except mesquite.

Sauce
½ cup ketchup
¼ cup light or mild molasses
2 tablespoons grated onion (see note)
2 tablespoons Worcestershire sauce
2 tablespoons Dijon mustard
2 tablespoons cider vinegar
1 tablespoon brown sugar

Chops
2 cups wood chips, soaked in water at least 30 minutes (see note)
4 bone-in rib loin pork chops (12 ounces each), 1½ inches thick (see note)
4 teaspoons kosher salt or 2 teaspoons table salt
2 teaspoons ground black pepper
Disposable 13- by 9-inch aluminum cake pan

1. **FOR THE SAUCE:** Bring all ingredients to simmer in small saucepan over medium heat; cook, stirring occasionally, until sauce reaches ketchuplike consistency and is reduced to about 1 cup, 5 to 7 minutes. Transfer ½ cup sauce to small bowl and set aside to serve with cooked chops.

2. **FOR THE CHOPS:** Light large chimney starter filled with charcoal (6 quarts, about 100 briquettes) and allow to burn until coals are fully ignited and partially covered with thin layer of ash, about 20 minutes. Place aluminum cake pan in center of grill. Empty coals into grill, creating equal-sized piles on each side of pan. Sprinkle 1 cup soaked wood chips on each charcoal pile, position cooking grate over coals, cover grill, and heat until grate is hot and chips are smoking, about 5 minutes. Scrape grate clean with grill brush.

3. While grill is heating, pat chops dry with paper towels. Using sharp knife, cut 2 slits about 1 inch apart through outer layer of fat and connective tissue to prevent buckling. Sprinkle entire surface of each chop with 1 teaspoon salt and ½ teaspoon pepper. Place chops side by side, facing in same direction, on cutting board with curved rib bone facing down. Pass 2 skewers through loin muscle of each chop, close to bone, about 1 inch from each end. Once chops have been threaded onto skewers, pull apart to create 1-inch space between each.

4. Place skewered chops, bone-side down, in center of grill on cooking grate, over aluminum pan. Cover grill and cook until instant-read thermometer inserted into center of pork chop, but away from any bone, registers 120 degrees, 28 to 32 minutes.

5. Remove skewers from chops; tip chops onto flat side and brush surface with 1 tablespoon sauce. Transfer chops, sauce-side down, to hotter parts of grill (2 on each side) and cook, uncovered, until browned, 2 to 4 minutes. Brush top of each chop with 1 tablespoon sauce; flip and continue to cook on second side until browned and instant-read thermometer inserted into center of pork chop, but away from any bone, registers 140 to 145 degrees, 2 to 4 minutes longer. Remove chops from grill and allow to rest, tented with foil, 5 minutes. Serve, passing ½ cup reserved sauce separately.

BEST GAS GRILL-SMOKED PORK CHOPS

Follow recipe for Best Charcoal Grill-Smoked Pork Chops, through step 1. Place soaked wood chips in shallow disposable aluminum pie plate and place plate on primary burner (burner that will remain on during barbecuing) and reposition cooking grate(s). Turn all burners to high, close lid, and heat until hot and chips are smoking, about 15 minutes. (If chips ignite, use water-filled spray bottle to extinguish.) Scrape cooking grate clean with grill brush. Proceed with recipe from step 3, leaving primary burner on high, turning off other burner(s), and cooking with lid down. Cook chops on cooler side of grill to internal temperature of 110 degrees, 20 to 25 minutes, and increase browning time on hotter side of grill to 4 to 7 minutes per side.

Rescuing Pasta alla Norma

Meaty eggplant meets bold tomato sauce for a satisfying weeknight meal,
Sicilian-style—but the tale turns tragic if it's dense and greasy.

⇒ BY DAWN YANAGIHARA ⇐

Pasta alla Norma is a lively combination of tender eggplant and robust tomato sauce, seasoned with herbs, mixed with al dente pasta, and finished with shreds of salty, milky ricotta salata (salted and pressed ricotta cheese made from sheep's milk). The textures and flavors have much more nuance than the typical pasta with tomato sauce, and the eggplant lends pasta alla Norma a heartiness—a virtual meatiness—that makes it superbly satisfying.

Although not widely known outside Italy, this pasta is a classic in Sicily, where it was named for a 19th-century opera in which a druid priestess, Norma, perishes alongside her Roman lover. As the story goes, the opera was such a sensation, it inspired a Sicilian chef to create this dish in tribute to the opera and its composer, Vincenzo Bellini, a native son.

But even a classic faces pitfalls. After cooking a slew of different pasta alla Norma versions, I began to know them all too well. The eggplant is a big production to prepare, usually requiring salting before frying, and often ends up soggy and slick with oil. The tomatoes tend to coagulate into a heavy, overwhelming sauce, or they're so few they don't form an adequate foundation. The flavors in the dish can easily drown out the subtle essence of the eggplant.

Determined to do better, I went into the kitchen to develop a bold, complex pasta. I wanted a weeknight meal with rich tomato and eggplant flavors and smooth, silky texture—without an excessive amount of work.

A Steamy Setup

Most pasta alla Norma recipes advise salting cubed eggplant to draw out its excess moisture, usually for about an hour. Since I was keen to streamline at every opportunity, this was the place to start. To determine if I could skip or at least shorten salting, I prepared batches with eggplant I had salted for an hour, a half hour, 15 minutes, and not at all. After tasting these different versions side by side, I had to conclude that salting for an hour was best: It drew out the most moisture, which helped the eggplant brown better and cook faster.

Next, I considered how to cook the eggplant. One of the first recipes I tried called for frying two

Eggplant that's caramelized but not oily brings richness to the pasta, while salty ricotta salata, lots of basil, and a good dose of red pepper add complexity.

eggplants, cut into strips, in 3 inches of oil. The eggplant soaked up about half its weight in oil, turning silky and very rich. But it made for a heavy, greasy sauce—not to mention the fact that frying splattered my stovetop with oil and required almost 40 minutes of watchful cooking in batches. Frying, I decided, was out. I briefly considered roasting the eggplant, but this method also seemed slow for a weeknight meal. The remaining option was sautéing in a lesser amount of oil. Unfortunately, when I tried this approach, the eggplant was almost always underdone and still required cooking in batches. Hoping to cook the eggplant more deeply, I peeled the skin before cubing and sautéing—but the difference was barely discernible, so the peel stayed on.

Looking for new ideas, I recalled an ingenious method for removing moisture from eggplant developed by a test kitchen colleague working on a recipe for Caponata, another Sicilian eggplant dish (July/August 2008). Instead of salting the eggplant and

then leaving it to drain on paper towels on the countertop, he zapped the salted cubes in the microwave for 10 minutes. The salt draws out moisture that microwaving turns into steam, all the while causing the eggplant to collapse and compress its air pockets. The collapsed air pockets, in turn, soak up less oil in the pan. Put into practice for pasta alla Norma, this method was a resounding success. It was much faster than traditional salting and achieved even better results; the eggplant pieces came out of the microwave quite dry (a good start for browning). Furthermore, microwaving shrank the cubes to a size that could handily be cooked in just one batch in a 12-inch skillet.

Now I could try sautéing again, and this time it worked perfectly, browning the eggplant and adding rich flavor. I cooked a few batches, browning them to various degrees. Not surprisingly, the deeply caramelized eggplant tasted the roundest and fullest, with toasty notes accenting the vegetable's elusive sweetness. It was so flavorful that there really was nothing to be missed about not frying.

Finally, I tried different types of eggplant: portly globe eggplant; smaller, more svelte Italian eggplant; and slender, lavender-colored Chinese eggplant. All worked, but in the end, I preferred globe eggplant, which has a tender yet resilient texture and far fewer seeds than other varieties, including Italian eggplant. Cut into cubes, they retained their shape even after sautéing.

A Savory Surprise

The base for pasta alla Norma is a simple tomato sauce to which the eggplant is added. I was sure that in-season tomatoes would give the dish fresh flavor, but after a couple rounds of testing, I concluded that the trouble of peeling and then salting them (to avoid a stringy, watery sauce) was more effort than I wanted for a midweek meal. It would be far better to develop a simple year-round option.

Diced canned tomatoes yielded a bright-tasting sauce with a coarse texture, but since the eggplant was already cut into cubes, the sauce was too chunky. My tasters preferred a sauce made with canned crushed tomatoes—a full 28-ounce can—for its thick consistency, which added cohesion.

Ricotta Salata's Understudies

Ricotta salata, a firm, tangy Italian sheep's-milk cheese that bears little resemblance to the moist ricotta sold in tubs, is an essential component of traditional pasta alla Norma. If you can't find it, consider these options instead. –D.Y.

FRENCH FETA
Milder but tangy, this is a close cousin to ricotta salata in flavor and texture.

PECORINO ROMANO
Hard and dry, with a slightly more assertive aroma and flavor than ricotta salata.

COTIJA
Made with cow's milk, this Mexican cheese has a firm yet crumbly texture, but is less complex than ricotta salata.

To season the sauce, I started with a modest amount of garlic—two cloves, minced—but ended up using twice that amount to add some pungency. A small measure of red pepper flakes added a suggestion of heat, a generous dose of chopped basil brought fresh flavor, and a tablespoon of extra-virgin olive oil stirred in at the end with the basil gave the sauce rich, round, fruity notes.

The sauce tasted fine tossed with the pasta, especially when sprinkled with a generous dose of ricotta salata cheese, yet something was missing. It seemed to lack backbone. I was considering a break with tradition by adding pancetta or prosciutto when a test kitchen colleague offered a novel suggestion: anchovies. Of course! Cooked in oil with garlic and red pepper flakes, one minced fillet was good, but two were even better, giving the sauce a deep, savory flavor without any trace of fishiness.

A Simmering Finale

So far, I had well-browned eggplant and a flavorful tomato sauce. To determine how best to bring these elements together, I made a couple more batches. For the first, I browned the eggplant, set it aside, made the sauce in the same skillet, and then added the eggplant to the sauce and simmered them together only long enough to heat through, no more than five minutes. For the second, I built the tomato sauce right on top of the browned eggplant so that they simmered together for about 10 minutes. The latter wound up a bit mushy and somewhat muddled, with some of the eggplant soggy and tattered. But the former had crisp, clear qualities—the eggplant's caramelization could

still be tasted, and its tender texture had integrity.

Even with only a few minutes of simmering, the eggplant had a tendency to soak up tomato juices, causing the sauce to become rather thick, so the final adjustment was adding a little reserved pasta cooking water when tossing the sauce with the pasta. Now all the components—the pasta, the tomato sauce, and the eggplant—were perfectly in tune. No longer a tragedy, my pasta alla Norma was on the table in well under an hour, without theatrics but with bold and balanced flavors.

PASTA ALLA NORMA
SERVES 4

NOTE: We call for both regular and extra-virgin olive oil in this recipe. The higher smoke point of regular olive oil makes it best for browning the eggplant; extra-virgin olive oil stirred into the sauce before serving lends fruity flavor. If you don't have regular olive oil, use vegetable oil. We prefer kosher salt in step 1 because it clings best to the eggplant. If using table salt, reduce the amount to ½ teaspoon. Ricotta salata is traditional, but French feta, Pecorino Romano, and Cotija (a firm, crumbly Mexican cheese) are acceptable substitutes; see "Ricotta Salata's Understudies," above. Our preferred brands of crushed tomatoes are Tuttorosso and Muir Glen.

1	large eggplant (1¼ to 1½ pounds), cut into ½-inch cubes
	Kosher salt (see note)
3	tablespoons olive oil (see note)
4	medium garlic cloves, minced or pressed through garlic press (about 4 teaspoons)
2	anchovy fillets, minced (about 1 generous teaspoon)
¼–½	teaspoon red pepper flakes
1	(28-ounce) can crushed tomatoes (see note)
1	pound ziti, rigatoni, or penne
6	tablespoons chopped fresh basil leaves
1	tablespoon extra-virgin olive oil
3	ounces ricotta salata, shredded (about 1 cup) (see note)

1. Toss eggplant with 1 teaspoon salt in medium bowl. Line surface of large microwave-safe plate with double layer of coffee filters and lightly spray with nonstick cooking spray. Spread eggplant in even layer over coffee filters; wipe out and reserve bowl. Microwave eggplant on high power, uncovered, until dry to touch and slightly shriveled, about 10 minutes, tossing once halfway through to ensure that eggplant cooks evenly. Let cool slightly.

2. Transfer eggplant to now-empty bowl, drizzle with 1 tablespoon olive oil, and toss gently to coat; discard coffee filters and reserve plate. Heat 1 tablespoon olive oil in 12-inch nonstick skillet over medium-high heat until shimmering but not smoking. Add eggplant and distribute in even layer. Cook, stirring or tossing every 1½ to 2 minutes (more frequent stirring may cause eggplant pieces to break apart), until well browned and fully tender, about 10 minutes. Remove skillet from heat and transfer eggplant to now-empty plate and set aside.

3. Add remaining 1 tablespoon olive oil, garlic, anchovies, and pepper flakes to now-empty but still-hot skillet and cook using residual heat so garlic doesn't burn, stirring constantly, until fragrant and garlic becomes pale golden, about 1 minute (if skillet is too cool to cook mixture, set it over medium heat). Add tomatoes, return skillet to burner over medium-high heat, and bring to boil. Reduce heat to medium and simmer, stirring occasionally, until slightly thickened, 8 to 10 minutes.

4. Meanwhile, bring 4 quarts water to boil. Add pasta and 2 tablespoons salt and cook until al dente. Reserve ½ cup cooking water; drain pasta and transfer back to cooking pot.

5. While pasta is cooking, return eggplant to skillet with tomatoes and gently stir to incorporate. Bring to simmer over medium heat and cook, stirring gently occasionally, until eggplant is heated through and flavors are blended, 3 to 5 minutes. Stir basil and extra-virgin olive oil into sauce; season to taste with salt. Add sauce to cooked pasta, adjusting consistency with reserved pasta cooking water so that sauce coats pasta. Serve immediately, sprinkled with ricotta salata.

PASTA ALLA NORMA
WITH OLIVES AND CAPERS
SERVES 4

Follow recipe for Pasta alla Norma, substituting chopped fresh flat-leaf parsley leaves for basil and adding ½ cup slivered kalamata olives and 2 tablespoons drained, rinsed capers along with parsley and extra-virgin olive oil to sauce in step 5.

📹 **COOK'S VIDEOS** Original Test Kitchen Videos
www.cooksillustrated.com/aug09
HOW TO MAKE
• Pasta alla Norma
VIDEO TIP
• Why should I microwave eggplant before sautéing?

Chopped Salads, Refined

We wanted complementary flavors and textures in every bite—not a random collection of bland, watery produce from the crisper drawer.

Chopped salads had their heyday in the 1950s as a popular menu item for ladies who lunched. If you encounter a good version, it's easy to see why they're making a comeback. The best are lively, thoughtfully chosen compositions of lettuce, vegetables, and sometimes fruit cut into bite-sized pieces, with supporting players like nuts and cheese contributing hearty flavors and textures. Unfortunately, I've had more experience with the mediocre kind. These are little better than a random collection of cut-up produce from the crisper drawer, exuding moisture that turns the salad watery and bland.

Salting some of the vegetables to remove excess moisture was an obvious first step. I singled out two of the worst offenders: cucumbers and tomatoes. I halved a cucumber and scooped out its watery seeds before dicing it, tossing it with salt, and allowing it to drain over a colander. After 15 minutes, the cukes had shed a full tablespoon of water. As for the tomatoes, I had been experimenting with grape tomatoes in a Mediterranean-inspired salad. Seeding them was out of the question; much of the tomato flavor is concentrated in the seeds and surrounding jelly. But I did cut them into quarters to expose more surface area to the salt, releasing 2 tablespoons of liquid from a pint of tomatoes.

As I tried more recipes, it became clear that the dressings weren't doing anything for the chopped salads. Most recipes called for a ratio of 3 parts oil to 1 part vinegar—the same proportions as for a leafy green salad. A more assertive blend of equal parts oil and vinegar was far better at delivering a bright, acidic kick needed in salads boasting hearty flavors and chunky textures.

But could I use the dressing to even greater advantage? Tossing a green salad just before serving prevents the tender leaves from absorbing too much dressing and turning soggy. But a little flavor absorption by some of the sturdier components of a chopped salad would actually be a good thing. Marinating ingredients such as bell peppers, onions, and fruit in the dressing for just five minutes before adding cheese and other tender components brought a welcome flavor boost.

I was now ready to focus on the composition of the salads. I determined that mild, crisp romaine and firm-tender cucumber were musts in every salad, as was the bite of red onion. I also liked the crunch of nuts along with the softer texture of cheese. For a Mediterranean combo, I added chickpeas, feta, and parsley into the standard mix. Another boasted red pepper with pear, cranberry, blue cheese, and pistachios; a third featured fennel and apple with tarragon, goat cheese, and walnuts. These vibrant, full-flavored salads were so good, they might start a new trend: men who lunch.

MEDITERRANEAN CHOPPED SALAD
SERVES 4 AS A LIGHT ENTRÉE OR 6 AS A SIDE DISH

NOTE: For information on how to prepare the cucumbers, see "Seeding and Chopping Cucumbers" on page 30. For our free recipe for Radish and Orange Chopped Salad, go to www.cooksillustrated.com/aug09.

- 1   medium cucumber, peeled, halved lengthwise, seeded, and cut into ½-inch dice (about 1¼ cups)
- 1   pint grape tomatoes, quartered (about 1½ cups)
     Table salt
- 3   tablespoons extra-virgin olive oil
- 3   tablespoons red wine vinegar
- 1   medium garlic clove, minced or pressed through garlic press (about 1 teaspoon)
- 1   (14-ounce) can chickpeas, drained and rinsed
- ½   cup pitted kalamata olives, chopped
- ½   small red onion, minced (about ¼ cup)
- ½   cup roughly chopped fresh parsley leaves
- 1   romaine heart, cut into ½-inch pieces (about 3 cups)
- 4   ounces feta cheese, crumbled (about 1 cup)
     Ground black pepper

1. Combine cucumber, tomatoes, and 1 teaspoon salt in colander set over bowl and let stand 15 minutes.

2. Whisk oil, vinegar, and garlic together in large bowl. Add drained cucumber and tomatoes, chickpeas, olives, onion, and parsley; toss and let stand at room temperature to blend flavors, 5 minutes.

3. Add romaine and feta; toss to combine. Season with salt and pepper and serve.

PEAR AND CRANBERRY CHOPPED SALAD
SERVES 4 AS A LIGHT ENTRÉE OR 6 AS A SIDE DISH

- 1   medium cucumber, peeled, halved lengthwise, seeded, and cut into ½-inch dice (about 1¼ cups)
     Table salt
- 3   tablespoons extra-virgin olive oil
- 3   tablespoons sherry vinegar
- 1   medium red bell pepper, seeded and cut into ¼-inch pieces (about 1 cup)
- 1   ripe but firm pear cut into ¼-inch pieces (about 1 cup)
- ½   small red onion, minced (about ¼ cup)
- ½   cup dried cranberries
- 1   romaine heart, cut into ½-inch pieces (about 3 cups)
- 4   ounces blue cheese, crumbled (about 1 cup)
- ½   cup pistachios, toasted and coarsely chopped
     Ground black pepper

1. Combine cucumber and ½ teaspoon salt in colander set over bowl and let stand 15 minutes.

2. Whisk oil and vinegar together in large bowl. Add drained cucumber, bell pepper, pear, onion, and cranberries; toss and let stand at room temperature to blend flavors, 5 minutes.

3. Add romaine, blue cheese, and pistachios; toss to combine. Season with salt and pepper and serve.

FENNEL AND APPLE CHOPPED SALAD
SERVES 4 AS A LIGHT ENTRÉE OR 6 AS A SIDE DISH

- 1   medium cucumber, peeled, halved lengthwise, seeded, and cut into ½-inch dice (about 1¼ cups)
     Table salt
- 3   tablespoons extra-virgin olive oil
- 3   tablespoons white wine vinegar
- 1   medium fennel bulb, halved lengthwise, cored, and cut into ¼-inch dice (about 1½ cups)
- 2   Braeburn, Jonagold, or Red Delicious apples, cored and cut into ¼-inch dice (about 2 cups)
- ½   small red onion, minced (about ¼ cup)
- ¼   cup coarsely chopped fresh tarragon leaves
- 1   romaine heart, cut into ½-inch pieces (about 3 cups)
- ½   cup coarsely chopped walnuts, toasted
     Ground black pepper
- 4   ounces crumbled goat cheese (about 1 cup)

1. Combine cucumber and ½ teaspoon salt in colander set over bowl and let stand 15 minutes.

2. Whisk oil and vinegar together in large bowl. Add drained cucumber, fennel, apples, onion, and tarragon; toss and let stand at room temperature to blend flavors, 5 minutes.

3. Add romaine and walnuts; toss to combine. Season with salt and pepper. Divide salad among plates; top each with some goat cheese and serve.

◼ COOK'S VIDEOS Original Test Kitchen Videos
www.cooksillustrated.com/aug09
HOW TO MAKE
• Chopped Salads

COOK'S ILLUSTRATED
14

Introducing Tomato Pesto

Not all pesto is basil, pine nuts, and Parmesan. In Sicily, tomatoes and almonds take center stage.

This side of the Atlantic, "pesto" is synonymous with lots of basil, Parmesan cheese, garlic, pine nuts, and good olive oil blended into a rich concoction originating in Genoa, a city in northern Italy's Liguria region. In Italy, you can find countless variations on this theme, with ingredients ranging from parsley and arugula to almonds, walnuts, pecans, sundried tomatoes—even fennel. I've always been intrigued by a "red" variation that hails from Trapani, a village on the western tip of Sicily. Here almonds replace pine nuts, but the big difference is the inclusion of fresh tomatoes—not as the main ingredient, but just enough to tint the sauce and lend fruity, vibrant sweetness.

The Trapanese pesto recipes I'd found in Italian cookbooks used similar techniques and stuck to a core list of ingredients. But when I mixed up a few, the results were distinctly different. One resembled chunky tomato salsa, another was thin and watery, and another was buried in cheese. Only a creamy, reddish-ocher pesto created by Lidia Bastianich, the renowned Italian-American chef and host of the PBS cooking series *Lidia's Italy* (from her book of the same name), came close to the clean, bright sauce I was after. If I could fine-tune her recipe to work with supermarket tomatoes, I'd have a new quick pasta sauce to add to my repertoire.

Like most pesto recipes, Bastianich's came together in just minutes: Pulse tomatoes, basil leaves, toasted almonds, garlic, coarse salt, and red pepper flakes (more on that later) together in a food processor; add olive oil in a slow, steady stream to emulsify; adjust the seasonings; toss with pasta and cheese and serve. The tomatoes contribute bright flavor, while the ground almonds thicken the sauce and offer their own delicate taste and richness.

In fact, once the oil and cheese came into play, tasters wondered if the sauce was a tad too rich, even when used sparingly on pasta. We needed a better sense of the pesto's origins, so we called Bastianich herself. She explained that in Trapani, fishermen bring smaller, unsold fish home to their families, and everyone eats the leftover catch fried over a bed of pesto-tossed pasta. "It's a way to make a little bit of fish go a long way," she said.

▶ **COOK'S VIDEOS** Original Test Kitchen Videos
www.cooksillustrated.com/aug09
HOW TO MAKE
• Pasta with Tomato and Almond Pesto
VIDEO TIP
• Storing and chopping nuts

Tomatoes brighten this typically rich sauce.

In that scenario—stretching a meal—the richness made sense. But I wanted something a bit lighter and brighter. The tomatoes seemed like a good place to start. Farmers' market tomatoes would surely be best, but I wanted a year-round pesto, which meant relying on year-round tomatoes. I plucked UglyRipes, grape tomatoes, and cherry tomatoes from the produce aisle and gave each a try. The UglyRipes were out—their quality was inconsistent. The cherry and grape tomatoes proved equal contenders, sharing a similar brightness and juiciness that was far more reliable. I settled on a generous 2½ cups.

Almonds, just like pine nuts in the Genovese version, are integral to this pesto because they contribute body while retaining just enough crunch to offset the tomatoes' pulpiness. Toasting was a must to release oils and flavor prior to processing. I found blanched, slivered almonds browned more evenly than whole nuts and avoided the muddy flavor often contributed by papery skins. One-quarter cup, plus a relatively modest ⅓ cup extra-virgin olive oil, added plenty of pleasant grittiness and creamy texture without too much richness.

Basil is the star of Genovese pesto, but its role in the Trapanese version is a supporting one. A half cup allowed just enough of its flavor to work in tandem with the tomatoes. For a variation, I swapped out the almonds for pine nuts and the basil for a slightly heavier dose of peppery arugula.

Save for boiling the pasta, my pesto was all but on the table. But something was missing—something small. Bastianich's recipe offered the option of increasing the pepperoncini, by which she meant the dried red peppers native to Tuscany. But I had another association: hot vinegar peppers. On a whim, I added a scant ½ teaspoon. Presto! This was just the kind of zingy touch the sauce needed.

PASTA WITH TOMATO AND ALMOND PESTO (PESTO ALLA TRAPANESE)
SERVES 4 TO 6

NOTE: A half teaspoon of red wine vinegar and ¼ teaspoon of red pepper flakes can be substituted for the pepperoncini. If you don't have a food processor, a blender may be substituted. In step 2, pulse ingredients until roughly chopped, then proceed with the recipe, reducing processing times by half.

- ¼ cup slivered almonds
- 12 ounces cherry or grape tomatoes (about 2½ cups)
- ½ cup packed fresh basil leaves
- 1 medium garlic clove, minced or pressed through garlic press (about 1 teaspoon)
- 1 small pepperoncini (hot peppers in vinegar), stemmed, seeded, and minced (about ½ teaspoon) (see note)
  Table salt
  Pinch red pepper flakes (optional)
- ⅓ cup extra-virgin olive oil
- 1 pound pasta, preferably linguine or spaghetti
- 1 ounce Parmesan cheese, grated (about ½ cup), plus extra for serving

1. Toast almonds in small skillet over medium heat, stirring frequently, until pale golden and fragrant, 2 to 4 minutes. Cool almonds to room temperature.

2. Process cooled almonds, tomatoes, basil, garlic, pepperoncini, 1 teaspoon salt, and red pepper flakes (if using) in food processor until smooth, about 1 minute. Scrape down sides of bowl with rubber spatula. With machine running, slowly drizzle in oil, about 30 seconds.

3. Meanwhile, bring 4 quarts water to boil in large pot. Add pasta and 1 tablespoon salt and cook until al dente. Reserve ½ cup cooking water; drain pasta and transfer back to cooking pot.

4. Add pesto and ½ cup Parmesan to cooked pasta, adjusting consistency with reserved pasta cooking water so that pesto coats pasta. Serve immediately, passing Parmesan separately.

PASTA WITH TOMATO, PINE NUT, AND ARUGULA PESTO

Follow recipe for Pasta with Tomato and Almond Pesto, substituting pine nuts for almonds and replacing basil with ¾ cup lightly packed arugula leaves. Add 1¼ teaspoons grated lemon zest and 1 teaspoon lemon juice to food processor with other ingredients in step 2.

JULY & AUGUST 2009
15

Essential Kitchen Equipment

The 39 must-haves in our kitchen that we recommend for yours. BY LISA GLAZER

Sixteen years of developing recipes and testing pots, pans, knives, tools, and gadgets have taught us not only which items are essential to any well-equipped kitchen, but also the most durable, high-quality brands to choose.

COOKWARE

① ALL-CLAD Stainless Steel 12-Inch Fry Pan ($134.95) This roomy skillet can cook a family-sized meal. The traditional finish allows food to stick, developing the crusty brown bits of fond that contribute flavor.

② ALL-CLAD Stainless Steel 4-Quart Saucepan (with lid) ($184.95)

③ ALL-CLAD Stainless Steel 2-Quart Saucepan (with lid) ($139.95)
For even cooking, we prefer saucepans made of stainless steel sandwiching an aluminum core in a style of construction known as "tri-ply." A 4-quart saucepan is just the right size for making rice or blanching vegetables; a 2-quart saucepan is good for smaller jobs like heating milk or melting butter. For a cheaper alternative, consider nonstick.
➤ Best Buy: **CALPHALON Contemporary Nonstick 2½-Quart Shallow Saucepan ($39.95)**

④ SIMPLY CALPHALON Nonstick 12-Inch Omelet Pan ($50.00)

⑤ SIMPLY CALPHALON Nonstick 10-Inch Covered Omelet Pan ($39.99)
Nonstick is great for delicate, quick-cooking foods like fish or eggs—but don't spend big bucks, since the coating wears off within a few years. These omelet pans are both skillets in shape, if not in name.

⑥ LODGE LOGIC 12-Inch Cast-Iron Skillet ($33.95) Nothing tops cast iron when it comes to creating a flavorful, deeply browned crust on steaks and other foods.

⑦ LE CREUSET 7¼-Quart Round French Oven (with lid) ($269.95) This incredibly versatile Dutch oven made of enameled cast iron is ideal for soups, stews, stocks, braises—even frying and baking.
➤ Best Buy: **TRAMONTINA 6½-Quart Enameled Cast-Iron Dutch Oven ($44.97)**

⑧ CUISINART Chef's Classic Stainless Steel 12-Quart Stockpot (with lid) ($69.95) Lighter than a Dutch oven, a 12-quart stockpot is used mainly for boiling water for pasta, corn, and lobster. This brand's inexpensive price tag is just right for a pot with limited use.

⑨ CALPHALON Contemporary Stainless Steel Roasting Pan with Rack ($119.95) Don't buy nonstick; the dark finish camouflages the crusty brown bits you need to make gravy for roasted meats. This pan's gently flared shape makes stirring and deglazing easy.
➤ Best Buy: **KITCHENAID Gourmet Distinctions Roasting Pan with Rack ($49.95)**

MEASURING TOOLS

⑩ AMCO Stainless Steel Measuring Cups ($11.50) These durable stainless steel cups boast rims flush with the long handles, making leveling off dry ingredients easy.

⑪ CUISIPRO 4-Cup Deluxe Liquid Measuring Cup ($14.95) A pour spout and handle are musts in liquid measuring cups. Read from above, the plastic Cuisipro measures more accurately—and is more durable—than a glass Pyrex cup.

⑫ CUISIPRO 5-Piece Stainless Steel Oval Measuring Spoons ($13.95) We like that these sturdy, elongated spoons are slim enough to dip into narrow spice jars.

⑬ CDN MOT1 Multi-Mount Oven Thermometer ($7.99) The best insurance against varying oven temperatures. For maximum stability, this model sports a magnet, a hook, and a base stand.

⑭ OXO Food Scale ($49.99) For close to 100 percent accuracy when baking, weigh your ingredients on a scale; digital models with large readout displays like this one are the easiest to read.

⑮ POLDER Dual Timer Stopwatch #893 ($15.12) This compact test kitchen favorite is a two-timer, keeping track of two dishes at once.

⑯ THERMOWORKS Super-Fast Thermapen Instant-Read Thermometer ($89) Forgo guesswork and pinpoint exactly when food is done. We call the Thermapen the Ferrari of thermometers for its fast, accurate readings and long probe.
➤ Best Buy: **MAVERICK Redi-Chek Professional Chef's Digital Thermometer DT-01 ($12.99)**

For sources and a list of 10 additional items for the well-outfitted kitchen, go to www.cooksillustrated.com/aug09. Prices were current at press time but are subject to change.

BAKEWARE

17 PYREX Bakeware 13- by 9-Inch Baking Pan ($8.99) A multitasker for cakes, lasagna, and casseroles. Ovensafe glass browns nicely and is compatible with metal cutting utensils.

18 CHICAGO METALLIC Professional Nonstick 9-Inch Round Cake Pan ($16.49) High, straight sides and a dark nonstick finish deliver better browning; you'll need two for most recipes.
➤ Best Buy: BAKER'S SECRET Basics Nonstick 9-Inch Round Cake Pan ($4.99)

19 PYREX 9-Inch Pie Plate ($3.99) Tempered glass, rather than metal, makes it easier to track browning results; plus, glass won't react with acidic fruit to give fillings a tinny flavor.

20 WILTON Ultra-Bake 12-Cup Muffin Tin ($10.99) Choose a sturdy, medium-weight, dark-colored muffin tin like this one for better heat absorption and deeper browning.

21 FRIELING Handle-It 9-Inch Glass Bottom Springform ($33.49) The removable sides make a springform essential for cakes (like cheesecake and ice cream cake) that would be impossible to unmold from a standard cake pan.

22 LINCOLN FOODSERVICE 13-Gauge Half-Size Heavy Duty Sheet Pan ($15.99)

23 CIA Bakeware 17- by 12-Inch Cooling Rack ($15.95) A multitasking duo with duties beyond baking—keep two of each on hand. Our rimmed baking sheet is on call for cookies, but we also use it for oven fries and veggies. And we place the cooling rack within it to roast meat.
➤ Best Buy Cooling Rack: LIBERTYWARE Cross Wire Cooling Rack Half Sheet Pan Size ($5.25)

24 WILLIAMS-SONOMA Goldtouch Nonstick 8½- by 4½-Inch Loaf Pan ($21) The gold-colored nonstick coating on our favorite loaf pan yields baked goods with an even, lightly browned crust.
➤ Best Buy: PYREX 8½- by 4½-Inch Glass Loaf Pan ($6.95)

UTENSILS

25 BEST MANUFACTURERS 12-Inch Standard French Whisk ($9.49) Our favorite all-purpose French whisk is long and agile, with tines that don't bend and twist with prolonged use.

26 FANTE'S French Rolling Pin with Tapered Ends ($6.99) This long, thin, tapered rolling pin is gentler on delicate dough than standard rolling pins.

27 RUBBERMAID 13½-Inch Commercial High Heat Scraper ($18.99) Not your grandmother's spatula. Besides scraping bowls and icing cakes, this heatproof spatula made of silicone can also stir sauces on the stove.

28 OXO Good Grips Box Grater ($14.95) Razor-sharp grates and a collecting cup make this model a standout.

29 OXO Good Grips 12-Inch Locking Tongs ($10.39) The scalloped edges on these tongs get a better grip on food.

30 KUHN RIKON Easy-Squeeze Garlic Press ($20) This press boasts easy-to-squeeze plastic handles and an efficient plunger.

31 MESSERMEISTER Pro-Touch Swivel Peeler ($5.95) The blade on this peeler is extremely sharp and maneuverable enough to glide across the curves of potatoes, apples, and carrots.

32 MESSERMEISTER Take-Apart Shears ($19.95) The "take-apart" feature on these shears allows for thorough cleaning.

33 ARCHITEC The Gripper Nonslip Cutting Board ($14.99) We like this dishwasher-safe board for its durable surface and skid-free bottom.

34 ENDURANCE 5-Quart Pierced Colander ($29.99) Hundreds of tiny holes allow water to drain quickly without losing so much as a pea.

KNIVES

35 VICTORINOX Forschner Fibrox 8-Inch Chef's Knife ($24.95) While it's easy to blow your budget on a fancy chef's knife, the inexpensive, lightweight Victorinox Fibrox remains the test kitchen favorite. We like its high-carbon stainless steel blade, which stays sharper longer, and its nonslip handle.

36 VICTORINOX Forschner Fibrox 4-Inch Paring Knife ($12.95) This knife's sharp, agile blade and firm, comfortable grip can handle close work like paring fruit and slivering garlic.

37 WÜSTHOF 10-Inch Classic Bread Knife ($89.95) The long, slightly flexible blade and pointed serrations on this knife are good for cutting bread, tomatoes, and even cake.
➤ Best Buy: VICTORINOX Forschner Fibrox 10¼-Inch Curved Blade Bread Knife ($24.95)

38 CHEF'S CHOICE 130 Electric Knife Sharpener ($149.95) A true sharpener serves a different function than a sharpening steel, which merely repositions a knife's cutting edge (from bent to straight) rather than actually sharpening it. Electric is a must for restoring nicked, damaged, or very dull blades.

39 ACCUSHARP Manual Knife and Tool Sharpener ($10.99) For knives that aren't severely dulled or damaged, our favorite manual sharpener is almost as good as the electric option and cheap enough to keep in your drawer as a handy alternative.

The Best Grilled Stuffed Flank Steak

These pinwheels of stuffed steak are in butcher cases everywhere. But juicy, smoky meat with a filling that stays put required making them ourselves.

≳ BY J. KENJI ALT ≲

Stuffed flank steak has roots in Italian-American cooking, where it's long been a means of transforming an inexpensive yet flavorful cut of meat into something more interesting. These days, stuffed flank steak can also be found at most supermarkets. In the "ready-to-grill" section of the butcher's case, pinwheel slices of beef neatly encircle a variety of fillings, from spinach and goat cheese to prosciutto, provolone, and bread crumbs.

I've often been tempted by the idea of these pinwheels, with their promise of delectable bites of filling encased by juicy grilled beef. But I knew from experience that while stuffed meat may look nice and tidy uncooked, the filling has a way of escaping once cooking commences. Indeed, I picked up a few steak pinwheels from the supermarket—some stuffed with cheese and herbs, others with veggies, ham, and bread crumbs—placed them on the grill, and minutes later found cheese oozing onto the grate and spiraled meat beginning to unfurl. The meat itself, however, was tender and juicy, cooked to medium-rare over a modified two-level fire (to ensure even cooking, I seared the steak over the hot side and finished it on the cooler side). With a little work, I was sure I could turn this dish into an easy dinner that wouldn't require much more time than buying preassembled pinwheels.

Say Cheese

To make doubly sure I was starting with the right cut of meat, I made a basic recipe with an inch-thick, rectangular slab of flank steak and other grill-worthy cuts, using a simple herbed bread-crumb stuffing and cutting the rolled, stuffed meat into 1-inch pinwheels. I quickly ruled out tenderloin, which has a buttery-smooth texture but almost no meaty flavor (it's pricey, too). Beefier cuts like rib-eye, sirloin, and strip steak were too thick and irregularly shaped to roll easily, an issue that also excluded cheaper cuts like hanger and blade steak. Thanks to its uniform shape and good beefy taste, flank steak was clearly the best bet.

Next, I investigated ingredients that seemed to hold promise for the stuffing. I eliminated bread crumbs from consideration; after grilling, they contributed

To keep our cheese-stuffed pinwheels intact, we used twine plus skewers.

a taste of burnt toast. The classic Italian-American combo of prosciutto and provolone won raves for its salty savor and the way the dry cheese both melted inside the pinwheel and turned crisp where exposed to the grill. Crunchy raw vegetables like asparagus and red pepper were appealing in theory; unfortunately, they were too bulky, making the meat awkward to roll. Chopped spinach, which I first steamed in the microwave until tender, fared better, especially when paired with the complementary flavors of pine nuts and shredded Asiago, another dry Italian cheese. Keeping with the Italian-American theme, I came up with another winning combo of sun-dried tomatoes and capers. All three options benefited from the addition of minced shallots, garlic, and herbs, which I mixed with a couple tablespoons of olive oil and spread directly on the meat to distribute their flavors throughout the roll.

Fit to Be Tied

Now the tricky part: how to hold the stuffing in place. Working with a typical flank steak—about 8 inches long by 6 inches wide—I set the long edge

of the steak parallel to the edge of my cutting board, with the grain of the meat also running parallel. I rubbed the meat with herb oil and placed a layer of prosciutto on top, then followed with a layer of provolone before rolling up the steak. (I rolled it facing away from me.) I knew it would be important to roll it along the shorter dimension: That way, when I sliced it into pinwheels, I'd be cutting against the grain, minimizing toughness. But rolling the steak taught me that even a 1-inch-thick flank steak is too thick to roll tightly; it looked more folded than stuffed.

I needed to start with a flatter, wider piece of meat. Simply pounding the steak didn't work; to flatten even a 1-inch-thick cut I had to really pound away, shredding the meat. Although it would require a little more effort, I decided to try butterflying: By splitting the steak in half horizontally and then opening it up like a book, I could halve its thickness. After butterflying the meat and pounding it briefly, I layered on my stuffing and then rolled the steak, tying twine at 1-inch intervals and slicing between them to produce pinwheels. Now my steak was easier to roll, which meant the stuffing was more evenly distributed, providing a mix of flavors in every bite.

One last issue remained: The meat shrank as it cooked, squeezing the centers of the pinwheels and causing buckling. What if I switched from twine to skewers? I rolled up another flank steak and skewered it at 1-inch intervals before slicing and grilling. Now the buckling was gone, but the unraveling had resumed. I decided to try using both. The tied and skewered pinwheels looked a little odd, but when I took them off the grill and discarded the skewers, the stuffing was cooked through and firmly in place. Finally, I had stuffing that stayed stuffed, with each bite delivering a swirl of crisp prosciutto and melted provolone along with rich, smoky beef.

🎥 **COOK'S VIDEOS** Original Test Kitchen Videos
www.cooksillustrated.com/aug09
HOW TO MAKE
• Grilled Stuffed Flank Steak
VIDEO TIPS
• Using butcher's twine: two different knots
• How do I butterfly a flank steak?

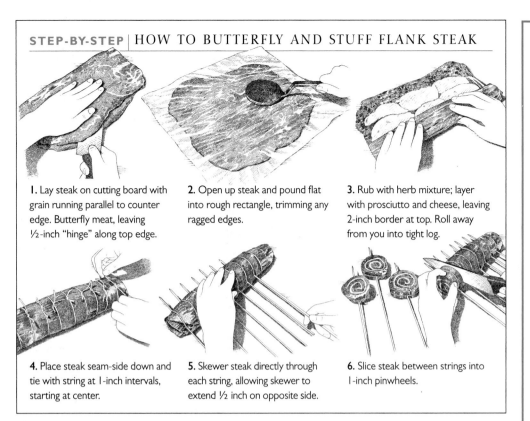

1. Lay steak on cutting board with grain running parallel to counter edge. Butterfly meat, leaving ½-inch "hinge" along top edge.

2. Open up steak and pound flat into rough rectangle, trimming any ragged edges.

3. Rub with herb mixture; layer with prosciutto and cheese, leaving 2-inch border at top. Roll away from you into tight log.

4. Place steak seam-side down and tie with string at 1-inch intervals, starting at center.

5. Skewer steak directly through each string, allowing skewer to extend ½ inch on opposite side.

6. Slice steak between strings into 1-inch pinwheels.

CHARCOAL-GRILLED STUFFED FLANK STEAK
SERVES 4 TO 6

NOTE: Depending on the steak's size, you may have between 8 and 12 pinwheels of stuffed meat at the end of step 2. Freezing the steak for 30 minutes will make butterflying easier. You will need both wooden skewers and twine for this recipe. For our free recipe for Grilled Stuffed Flank Steak with Sun-Dried Tomatoes and Capers, go to www.cooksillustrated.com/aug09.

- 2 medium garlic cloves, minced or pressed through garlic press (about 2 teaspoons)
- 1 small shallot, minced (about 2 tablespoons)
- 2 tablespoons finely minced fresh parsley leaves
- 1 teaspoon finely minced fresh sage leaves
- 2 tablespoons olive oil, plus extra for oiling grate
- 1 (2- to 2½-pound) flank steak (see note)
- 4 ounces thinly sliced prosciutto
- 4 ounces thinly sliced provolone cheese
- 8–12 skewers soaked in water for 30 minutes
  Kosher salt and ground black pepper

1. Combine garlic, shallot, parsley, sage, and olive oil in small bowl. Following illustrations above, butterfly and pound flank steak into rough rectangle. With steak positioned so that grain runs parallel to edge of counter and opened side faces up, spread herb mixture evenly over surface of steak. Lay prosciutto evenly over steak, leaving 2-inch border along top edge. Cover prosciutto with even layer of cheese, leaving 2-inch border along top edge. Starting from bottom edge and rolling away from you, roll beef into tight log and place on cutting board seam-side down.

2. Starting ½ inch from end of rolled steak, evenly space 8 to twelve 14-inch pieces of butcher's twine at 1-inch intervals underneath steak. Tie middle string first; then working from outermost strings toward center, tightly tie roll and turn tied steak 90 degrees so seam is facing you. Skewer beef directly through outermost flap of steak near seam through each piece of string, allowing skewer to extend ½ inch on opposite side. Using chef's knife, slice roll between pieces of twine into 1-inch-thick pinwheels. Season pinwheels lightly with kosher salt and black pepper.

3. Light large chimney starter nearly full with charcoal (5 quarts, about 80 briquettes); allow to burn until coals are fully ignited and partially covered with thin layer of ash, about 20 minutes. Build modified two-level fire by arranging all coals over half of grill, leaving other half empty. Position cooking grate over coals, cover grill, and heat rack until hot, about 5 minutes; scrape grate clean with grill brush. Dip wad of paper towels in oil; holding wad with tongs, wipe cooking grate. Grill is ready when side with coals is hot (you can hold your hand 5 inches above grate for 2 to 3 seconds).

4. Grill pinwheels directly over hot side of grill until well browned, 3 to 6 minutes. Using tongs, flip pinwheels; grill until second side is well browned, 3 to 5 minutes longer. Transfer pinwheels to cooler side of grill, cover, and continue to cook until center of pinwheels registers 125 degrees on instant-read thermometer, 1 to 4 minutes (slightly thinner pinwheels may not need time on cooler side of grill). Transfer pinwheels to large plate, tent loosely with foil, and let rest 5 minutes. Remove and discard skewers and twine and serve immediately.

GAS-GRILLED STUFFED FLANK STEAK

Follow recipe for Charcoal-Grilled Stuffed Flank Steak through step 2. Turn all burners to high and heat with lid down until very hot, about 15 minutes. Scrape grate clean with grill brush. Dip wad of paper towels in oil; holding wad with tongs, wipe cooking grate. Leave primary burner on high and turn off other burner(s). Follow directions from step 4.

GRILLED STUFFED FLANK STEAK WITH SPINACH AND PINE NUTS

Place 4 ounces washed, chopped spinach, ½ teaspoon ground black pepper, ½ teaspoon table salt, and 1 tablespoon water in medium microwave-safe bowl. Cover bowl with large dinner plate (plate should completely cover bowl). Microwave on high power until spinach is wilted and decreased in volume by half, 3 to 4 minutes. Allow to cool completely, then squeeze dry in triple layer of paper towels and stir in ¼ cup toasted pine nuts. Follow recipe for Charcoal-Grilled Stuffed Flank Steak, replacing prosciutto with cooled spinach mixture.

Easier French Fries

Classic crisp French fries with half the oil and no double-frying? We burned through 50-odd pounds of potatoes to land on an uncommonly easy approach.

⇒ BY MATTHEW CARD ⇐

While everyone loves crisp, salt-flecked French fries, few of us like to cook them. Sure, the ingredient list is simple—nothing more than potatoes, oil, and salt—but success depends on precision. The traditional method requires rinsing the sliced spuds to remove excess surface starch that can cause sticking, soaking them in ice water to encourage more even cooking, and then deep-frying them in a vat of oil—not once but twice—at incrementally hotter temperatures. Finally, the fries must be drained, blotted, and salted. This process is time-consuming and potentially hazardous, not to mention messy—oil will splatter near and far. When the craving strikes, it's simpler to head out to a local bistro (or, dare I say, McDonald's) than into the kitchen.

If only an "easier" French fry were possible. Over the years, many cooks have sought to achieve this ideal, and many have failed, producing fries that were either limp and soggy or leathery and mealy. But I didn't let this dismal track record stop me. I was determined to find a way to make crisp, slender fries with a tender interior and earthy potato flavor, and without the rigmarole.

Out of the Pot, Into the Oven

I began by doing some research to make sure I understood the science behind deep-fried potatoes. Spuds are composed mainly of starch and water. When they hit hot oil, moisture on the surface turns to steam, and oil gradually takes the place of escaping water. As the potato surface becomes hotter, the starch at these outermost layers forms a crust, and the browning reactions that create greater depth of flavor and crispness begin to occur. You typically need very hot oil to ensure a good crisp crust (near 350 degrees), but unless you precook the fries in moderately hot oil first (no more than 325 degrees), the fries crisp long before they can cook through and expel sufficient moisture from their centers. The result: Fries that quickly turn limp and soggy once out of the fryer.

This quandary explains double-frying, a method first popularized by Parisian street vendors in the

Our crispy fries are not only less work, they absorb less oil than fries cooked the classic way.

mid–19th century: The potatoes are submerged in moderately hot oil to cook through, then quickly finished in hotter oil to render them golden and crisp.

So-called oven-frying—the potatoes are tossed in a small amount of oil and roasted at a high temperature—is a route cooks often take to avoid the mess and bother of deep-frying. But this approach usually calls for thicker wedges of potato that never achieve the crispness of thinner, deep-fried batons. Simply cutting the spuds (I used russets, our favorite for both French fries and oven fries) into thin lengths and roasting them like thicker wedges yielded tough, desiccated, spottily browned results. With enough testing, I could surely achieve a better outcome. But would it be worth it? The dry heat of an oven and a vessel of hot oil are two very different cooking environments (and one can never entirely replicate the other). Even the best oven fry was sure to have a heartier texture than the shatteringly crisp crust of the true fry that I was after. I decided to move on.

Uncommon Cold Start

I was pondering what to do next when a colleague passed along an impossibly simple-sounding fry recipe from food writer Jeffrey Steingarten. Based on a method attributed to Michelin-starred French über-chef Joël Robuchon, it skips the rinsing and soaking steps, then calls for something even more heretical: The spuds are submerged in a few cups of room-temperature (or "cold") oil, rather than quarts of hot grease, and fried over high heat until browned. I had to try it.

I combined 2½ pounds of ½-inch-thick, peeled russet batons with just enough peanut oil to cover them (6 cups) in a Dutch oven, our preferred vessel for deep-frying. I cranked up the heat and about 25 minutes later pulled out golden fries that looked identical to classic fries and tasted pretty darn good, albeit a little tough in texture.

Intrigued, I approached our science editor for more information. He surmised that by starting with cold oil, I gave the potato interior an opportunity to soften and cook through before the exterior started to crisp. And despite the fact that the temperature of the oil never got as hot as in the classic method (I found it maxed out at around 280 degrees), it was still high enough to trigger the same reactions that led to a golden, nicely crisped crust.

As for the slight toughness, he thought the russet's starchiness might be the culprit. Starchiness is an asset for the typical double-fry method—the starch granules from the outermost layers of the potato swell, burst, and form a gluelike substance that solidifies into a crisp crust. However, with a longer cooking time, too many starch granules were bursting, leading to an overly thick crust that was more leathery than crisp.

If starchy potatoes were the problem, why not start with a less starchy spud? I sliced up a couple pounds of Yukon Golds, which also have more water than russets, and proceeded with my working recipe.

◼ COOK'S VIDEOS Original Test Kitchen Videos
www.cooksillustrated.com/aug09
HOW TO MAKE
• Easier French Fries
VIDEO TIP
• How to cut French fries

AT-A-GLANCE | KEYS TO EASIER CRISP FRENCH FRIES

The classic technique for French fries involves four steps: rinsing the cut potatoes, soaking them in ice water, and then deep-frying—twice—in quarts of hot oil. Our method calls for just one round of frying and a lot less oil.

1. LESS OIL Our fries cook in just 6 cups of oil instead of 2 or 3 quarts.

2. COLD START Beginning with room-temperature oil gives fries time to cook through before their exteriors crisp.

3. ONE FRY Potatoes are fried only once, for about 25 minutes, rather than twice.

They worked well, really well. The exterior was crisp—well within the ballpark of a double-fry fry—with none of the toughness of russets, and the interior creamy. Clearly, the moister, less starchy composition of the Yukon Golds could better withstand the long cooking time of this approach. Plus, Yukon Golds have such a thin skin that they could be used unpeeled, making the recipe even easier.

I was nearly done, but still wanted to consider the oil. The test kitchen has long favored peanut oil over vegetable and canola oil for French fries and, after a couple of tests, so did I.

Type of oil aside, I also wondered: If my cold-start fries were spending longer in oil than the classic method, why didn't they seem greasier? After cooking fries by each method, we sent the results to a lab—and found that our fries contained about a third less oil. (To learn why, see "Giving Fat the Cold Shoulder," right.)

Inspired by fries that were not only far easier to make but also lower in fat, I moved on to resolve the one remaining predicament: fries sticking to the bottom of the pot (and each other). Rinsing or soaking the potato batons before they went into the pot with the cold oil seemed to have no effect. In the conventional deep-fry approach, sticking can be addressed by stirring the potatoes throughout cooking, but with our method, the Yukons (which soften significantly during the early part of cooking) were so fragile that any disturbance caused them to break apart. I found that if I didn't touch the spuds for 20 minutes after putting them in the pot, enough of a crust had formed so that I could stir them with no ill effect. I also determined that thinner ¼-inch fries were less likely to stick (and we liked their greater ratio of crispy crust to creamy interior).

For a final touch, I took a moment to stir together two creamy dipping sauces as alternatives to ketchup. Finally, I had perfect French fries that were remarkably easy to cook in a minimal amount of oil. The only hard part was restraining myself from devouring an entire batch on my own.

EASIER FRENCH FRIES
SERVES 3 TO 4

NOTE: Flavoring the oil with bacon fat (optional) gives the fries a mild meaty flavor. We prefer peanut oil for frying, but vegetable or canola oil can be substituted. This recipe will not work with sweet potatoes or russets. Serve with dipping sauces (recipes follow), if desired. See "Cutting Potatoes for French Fries" on page 31 for help on cutting even batons.

2½ pounds Yukon Gold potatoes (about 6 medium), scrubbed, dried, sides squared off, and cut lengthwise into ¼-inch by ¼-inch batons (see note)
6 cups peanut oil (see note)
¼ cup bacon fat, strained (optional) (see note)
Kosher salt

1. Combine potatoes, oil, and bacon fat (if using) in large Dutch oven. Cook over high heat until oil has reached rolling boil, about 5 minutes. Continue to cook, without stirring, until potatoes are limp but exteriors are beginning to firm, about 15 minutes.

2. Using tongs, stir potatoes, gently scraping up any that stick, and continue to cook, stirring occasionally, until golden and crisp, 5 to 10 minutes longer. Using skimmer or slotted spoon, transfer fries to thick paper bag or paper towels. Season with salt and serve immediately.

CHIVE AND BLACK PEPPER DIPPING SAUCE
MAKES ABOUT ½ CUP

5 tablespoons mayonnaise
3 tablespoons sour cream
2 tablespoons chopped fresh chives
1½ teaspoons juice from 1 lemon
¼ teaspoon table salt
¼ teaspoon ground black pepper

Whisk all ingredients together in small bowl.

SCIENCE EXPERIMENT
Giving Fat the Cold Shoulder

Our easier approach to cooking French fries does not preheat the oil and calls for one prolonged frying instead of the quicker double-dip in hot oil used in the classic method. But does the lengthy exposure to oil lead to a greasier fry?

EXPERIMENT
We prepared two batches of fries using Yukon Gold potatoes, our preferred spud for the cold-start method. We cooked one batch the conventional way, heating 3 quarts of peanut oil to 325 degrees and frying 2½ pounds of potatoes until just beginning to color, removing them, increasing the oil temperature to 350 degrees, then returning the potatoes to the pot to fry until golden brown. Total exposure to oil: less than 10 minutes. The second batch we cooked according to our working method, submerging 2½ pounds of spuds in 6 cups of cold oil and cooking over high heat for about 25 minutes, with the oil temperature never rising above 280 degrees. We then sent samples from each batch to an independent lab to analyze the fat content.

RESULTS
Our cold-start spuds contained about one third less fat than spuds deep-fried twice the conventional way: 13 versus 20 percent.

COLD OIL 13% FAT

EXPLANATION
Fries absorb oil two ways. As the potatoes cook, they lose moisture near their surface, which is replaced by oil. Then, as they cool

DOUBLE FRY 20% FAT

after being removed from the hot grease, oil from their exterior gets pulled in. Because our cold-start method cooks the fries more gently, less moisture is lost (but enough so the fries stay crisp) and less oil is absorbed during frying. Plus, this approach exposes the spuds to just one cool-down, versus the two cooling-off periods of the classic method, so less oil gets absorbed after cooking as well. –M.C.

BELGIAN-STYLE DIPPING SAUCE
MAKES ABOUT ½ CUP

5 tablespoons mayonnaise
3 tablespoons ketchup
1 medium garlic clove, minced or pressed through garlic press (about 1 teaspoon)
½–¾ teaspoon Tabasco sauce
¼ teaspoon table salt

Whisk all ingredients together in small bowl.

Best Buttermilk Pancakes

Most buttermilk pancakes come out tasting the way they look: flat. We cooked over a thousand pancakes to get them full-flavored and fluffy.

∋ BY MARCUS WALSER ∈

When our forebears set out to make pancakes enriched with the sweet tang of buttermilk, they had a built-in advantage: real buttermilk. Instead of the thinly flavored liquid processed from skim milk and cultured bacteria that passes for buttermilk today, these earlier Americans turned to the fat-flecked byproduct of churning cream into butter. This rich, flavorful buttermilk thickened and increased in tanginess the longer it was stored.

The switch from churned buttermilk to cultured buttermilk would account for the lack of true tang in most modern-day buttermilk pancakes—but not for flaws in texture. The ideal flapjack boasts a slightly crisp, golden crust surrounding a fluffy, tender center that has just enough structure to withstand a good dousing of maple syrup. Unfortunately, my attempts to create such perfection gave me a tall stack of pancake pitfalls. Some were thick and cottony; others were dense and gummy or oddly crêpelike. This short-order cook had a long way to go.

No (Pan)cake Walk

Straightforward as it may seem, pancake-making is fickle work, more akin to unleashing a series of volatile chemical reactions in a pan than mixing up a quick batter of flour, sugar, salt, milk, buttermilk, leavening agents, eggs, and melted butter. Here are just some of the dynamics at work: The proteins in flour combine with the water in the milk and buttermilk to form gluten, the network of proteins that give pancakes their basic structure. Eggs add more structure-reinforcing protein, along with moisture that evaporates as the pancake cooks, creating bubbles that help it rise. Baking soda responds to the acid in the buttermilk, producing carbon dioxide gas that further aerates the pancake; baking powder reacts to the heat of the pan to release more carbon dioxide.

The problem is that changing any one of these ingredients sets off a chain reaction that affects the others, with dramatic consequences for the final flapjack. And buttermilk, it turns out, is one of the most potent triggers for such a domino effect.

Case in point: A recipe I tried early on called for

We found the secret to buttermilk pancakes that cook up fluffy from batch to batch.

2 cups of flour, 2 tablespoons of sugar, 1½ teaspoons of baking powder, 1 teaspoon of baking soda, ½ teaspoon of salt, 1 cup of milk, 1 cup of buttermilk, 4 tablespoons of melted butter, and 2 eggs. I mixed the wet and dry ingredients in separate bowls, then gently combined them with a few quick whisks to form a batter (as with all pancake recipes, less is more when it comes to whisking; see "Ensuring Tender Texture" on page 23), which I cooked on a hot, oiled griddle, flipping once during the process. Though the pancakes weren't terrible, they needed to be lighter and, as I'd come to expect, they had only weak buttermilk flavor.

Swapping out regular milk for just the tangy stuff seemed like an obvious solution—until that plan deflated. Literally. More buttermilk means a greater concentration of acid in the mix, which in turn causes the baking soda to bubble too rapidly. The result: pancakes that overinflate when they first cook, then collapse like popped balloons, becoming dense and wet by the time they hit the plate. OK, simple enough—just cut back on the baking soda, right? Wrong. Baking soda promotes browning. Reducing

it leads to pale pancakes completely missing their flavorful, golden brown crust. (To learn why, see "Baking Soda's Browning Boost" on page 23.)

More Tang for the Buck

Just a few tests in, and I was already in a jam. The batter needed more acid for flavor, but upping the acid content meant overinflated, dense pancakes. My only hope was to concentrate on getting the buttermilk flavor just right, then keep my fingers crossed that I could backtrack and fix what would almost certainly be a ruined texture.

Next I tried increasing the amount of buttermilk from 2 to 2½ cups. Not surprisingly, more made the pancakes spread out too thin. They had no real interior—just two crusts smashed together. What about dehydrated buttermilk powder? Technically, it should consist of pure buttermilk with just the liquid component removed. But tasters complained that these pancakes tasted soapy. Maybe a more concentrated acid would help boost flavor. I tried adding a few teaspoons of lemon juice to the batter, but tasters objected to its distinct citrus flavor and aroma. Similarly, vinegar added a sour odor that tasters detected immediately. What about other dairy ingredients? Yogurt has an acidity comparable to that of buttermilk, but is thicker. I figured I could add at least ¼ cup of it without throwing off the consistency of the batter too much. No such luck. Once whisked into the batter, yogurt turned as loose as buttermilk.

Sour cream was my last hope. Since it's cultured with the same bacteria as buttermilk, it has many of the same flavor compounds, but in much higher concentration, yielding more acid per cup. It also boasts far less moisture. Just ¼ cup gave my pancakes the rich tang I was after, without diluting the batter. Tasters didn't even know there was a buttermilk impostor in the mix.

Is the Pan Ready?

Here's a test to make sure your griddle is hot enough: Drop a tablespoon of batter in its center. If, after one minute, the pancake is golden brown on the bottom, the pan is ready. If it remains blond—or is close to burning—adjust the heat accordingly.

ENSURING TENDER TEXTURE

Too much gluten development in pancake batter is the enemy of tender texture. Here's how to keep it in check.

KEEP IT LUMPY, THEN LET IT REST
Mixing encourages gluten to form. For best results, whisk the batter briefly and don't smooth out the lumps. Then, let the batter rest for 10 minutes—this allows the gluten to relax, yielding more tender pancakes.

Inflation Negation

I still had some work to do on texture. As expected, the added acid from the sour cream exacerbated the leavening problem; plus the pancakes had an extremely wet, gummy crumb. As I thought about it, I realized why: A quarter-cup of sour cream has the same amount of fat as a tablespoon of butter. Too much fat can stunt gluten formation by coating the flour proteins so they don't bond with water. Backing off to 3 tablespoons of butter reduced gumminess significantly. Once I fixed the problem of overinflation, it should rid the cakes of gumminess entirely.

I knew that my hyperactive leaveners had to be cut down. Due to its critical role in flavorful browning, removing baking soda was out of the question. What if I removed the baking powder instead? "Double-acting" baking powder is called so for a reason. It has a dual impact, reacting with its own built-in acid (usually cream of tartar) to create carbon dioxide as soon as it encounters moisture; then it reacts again to a second built-in acid (sodium aluminum sulfate) to create more gas when exposed to heat above 120 degrees. Eliminating baking powder would cut out both these reactions.

As I pulled my first batch of tender, fluffy, perfectly risen pancakes off the griddle, I thought I had solved my problem. But over the course of a few batches from this batter, the quality of my pancakes slowly declined. By the time I got to my fourth batch, the cakes were so dense and under-risen as to be nearly inedible. The problem is that baking soda reacts as soon as it gets wet, instantly enlarging the tiny bubbles of gas created by whisking. The first batch gets the full benefit of these bubbles, but subsequent batches are shortchanged as the bubbles dissipate. Without the compensating effect of baking powder creating more gas when the cakes hit the pan, dense texture is the inevitable result.

Eliminating either of these leaveners wasn't an option, but what about cutting back on each of them? I reduced both by ½ teaspoon and instantly proved my earlier assertion that with pancakes, even the smallest change can make the biggest difference. Thankfully, this time the change was for the better. My pancakes had gone from collapsed, flat, and unpalatably dense, to light, fluffy, and full of their trademark tang. Finally, I had buttermilk pancakes that lived up to their name. Pass the syrup, please.

BEST BUTTERMILK PANCAKES
MAKES SIXTEEN 4-INCH PANCAKES
SERVES 4 TO 6

NOTE: The pancakes can be cooked on an electric griddle. Set the griddle temperature to 350 degrees and cook as directed. The test kitchen prefers a lower-protein all-purpose flour like Gold Medal or Pillsbury. If you use an all-purpose flour with a higher protein content, like King Arthur, you will need to add an extra tablespoon or two of buttermilk.

2	cups (10 ounces) unbleached all-purpose flour (see note)
2	tablespoons sugar
½	teaspoon table salt
1	teaspoon baking powder
½	teaspoon baking soda
2	cups buttermilk
¼	cup sour cream
2	large eggs
3	tablespoons unsalted butter, melted and cooled slightly
1–2	teaspoons vegetable oil

1. Adjust oven rack to middle position and heat oven to 200 degrees. Spray wire rack set inside baking sheet with nonstick cooking spray; place in oven. Whisk flour, sugar, salt, baking powder, and baking soda together in medium bowl. In second medium bowl, whisk together buttermilk, sour cream, eggs, and melted butter. Make well in center of dry ingredients and pour in wet ingredients; gently stir until just combined (batter should remain lumpy with few streaks of flour). Do not overmix. Allow batter to sit 10 minutes before cooking.

2. Heat 1 teaspoon oil in 12-inch nonstick skillet over medium heat until shimmering. Using paper towels, carefully wipe out oil, leaving thin film of oil on bottom and sides of pan. Using ¼ cup measure, portion batter into pan in 4 places. Cook until edges are set, first side is golden brown, and bubbles on surface are just beginning to break, 2 to 3 minutes. Using thin, wide spatula, flip pancakes and continue to cook until second side is golden brown, 1 to 2 minutes longer. Serve pancakes immediately, or transfer to wire rack in preheated oven. Repeat with remaining batter, using remaining oil as necessary.

COOK'S VIDEOS Original Test Kitchen Videos
www.cooksillustrated.com/aug09
HOW TO MAKE
• Best Buttermilk Pancakes
VIDEO TIPS
• What's the best substitute for buttermilk?
• What's the difference between baking powder and baking soda?
• Perfectly browned pancakes

Fresh Berry Gratin

Baking berries and custard into a gratin should yield firm but juicy fruit, a creamy topping, and a crisp crust—if the heat doesn't ruin the plan.

⇒ BY YVONNE RUPERTI ⇐

Picked at the peak of ripeness, fresh berries are good enough to eat plain or with a dollop of whipped cream. But when the occasion demands a more dressed-up dessert, my thoughts turn to berry gratin. This dessert is made by spreading fruit in a shallow vessel, covering it with a topping, and baking until the fruit releases its juices and the topping turns crisp and browned. Possibilities range from pastry cream to croissant crumbs to ground almonds to—my favorite—the ethereally light and foamy Italian custard called *zabaglione*.

Zabaglione (also known in French as *sabayon*) is so satisfying it's sometimes served as a dessert on its own. The custard is whisked together from just three ingredients: egg yolks, sugar, and alcohol. It sounds simple, but the whisking is done over heat, so you have to be careful not to overcook the mixture and to whisk for just long enough to transform the egg yolks to the ideal thick, creamy, and foamy texture.

From past experience, I knew heat would also prove a little tricky for the berries—too much and they turn soupy and lose fresh flavor; too little and they barely warm through. I wanted juicy, firm berries covered in frothy zabaglione and topped with a lightly browned crust.

Sweetened wine and a little whipped cream helped ensure the right degree of creaminess in this custard.

Bake or Broil?

Starting with a traditional zabaglione recipe of three egg yolks, 2 tablespoons of sugar, and 3 tablespoons of sweet Marsala wine, I set out to finesse the gratin assembly and baking steps before tweaking the zabaglione preparation and flavor. I knew I wanted to make individual gratins for entertaining and to use a variety of fruit. Raspberries, strawberries, blueberries, and blackberries were the obvious, most widely available choices. I divided 3 cups of berries (the right amount for four servings) among four small heatproof dishes, spooned the zabaglione over the berries, and baked the gratins in a 400-degree oven until the custard developed a golden-brown crust. Unfortunately, just beneath the beautiful custard lurked mushy, overcooked berries.

Thinking that increasing the heat might help the zabaglione brown fast enough that the berries would warm through without overcooking, I ran a series of tests, slowly increasing the oven temperature in 25-degree increments until it was maxed out. But even at 500 degrees, the berries were still turning mushy by the time the topping browned. Only when I added the radiant heat of the broiler was I able to produce a lightly browned crust and gently warmed berries. Two minutes under the heating element was just enough time to develop good caramelization, but now I had the opposite problem: The berries weren't sufficiently juicy.

I decided to try tossing the berries with sugar to draw out their juices. I sprinkled 2 teaspoons of granulated sugar and a pinch of flavor-enhancing salt over the berries and let the mixture sit for 30 minutes, until some of the flavorful liquid began to seep out. Then I topped the juicy berries with the custard and broiled the gratins for two minutes. Success: The custard was golden brown, and the berries were warmed through, with just the right succulent texture.

Zabaglione 101

With the broiling technique nailed down, I could now concentrate on the zabaglione. Up to this point, I had been whisking the yolks, sugar, and Marsala in a makeshift double boiler. I combined the ingredients in a large bowl, placed the bowl over a pot of simmering water, and whisked constantly. When everything went well, the liquid mixture gradually transformed into a soft, creamy foam. But the custard proved finicky: Sometimes it cooked too quickly, and small bits of congealed yolk destroyed its texture. At other times, it seemed underdone: Traditional recipes call for whisking just until soft peaks form, but this was insufficient. Cooked only to the soft-peak stage, the zabaglione ended up thin and frothy. To understand exactly what was happening in that bowl, I consulted our science editor.

I learned that as the custard is slowly heated and whisked, the proteins in the yolks cross-link and form a matrix that supports the thousands of tiny air- and steam-filled bubbles. Yet caution is essential: If the temperature of the foam rises too high, the proteins will begin to coagulate and tighten, an irreversible process that leaves the cook with sweet, scrambled yolks. As for the whisking conundrum, too little whisking forms too few bubbles, which results in a liquid-y zabaglione. More whisking forms more bubbles, creating a thicker sauce.

Using this knowledge, I made three small but significant tweaks to foolproof the technique. First,

I warded off scrambled yolks by turning the heat down slightly, keeping the water beneath the custard bowl to barely a simmer. Second, I compared zabagliones made in metal and glass bowls: The metal bowl conducted heat more quickly, making the custard likely to overcook. Keeping my goal of a no-fail recipe in mind, I chose a thick glass bowl for even, gentle cooking. Finally, to get the right texture, I didn't stop whisking when soft peaks formed; instead, I waited until the custard became slightly thicker, the texture of hollandaise sauce.

Wine Tasting

The next factor to address was flavor. Tasters told me the zabaglione made with Marsala was a bit sweet and cloying on top of the berries. No worries—I had an entire liquor cabinet at my disposal.

Whisking away, I experimented with Grand Marnier (too orangey), Muscat (too intense), and Sauternes (exceedingly sweet). Then I changed course, trying a crisp, dry Sauvignon Blanc. Its clean flavor allowed the berries to shine, but now, no matter how long I whisked, my zabaglione was so frothy, it verged on runny. What had gone wrong?

A close examination of the labels revealed that the key difference was sugar: Marsala, Grand Marnier, and dessert wines like Sauternes all have much more dissolved sugar than Sauvignon Blanc and are therefore more viscous. More viscous alcohol leads to a thicker zabaglione. My choices were to add sugar to the white wine or to find another way of supporting those bubbles.

Sure enough, taking the sugar all the way up to ¼ cup helped to keep my zabaglione stable, but now it was achingly sweet. Even 3 tablespoons was too much for my tasters. Next, I tried swapping out the sugar for equal amounts of viscous corn syrup and honey, but the end results were still somewhat runny.

It was time to introduce another thickening element. Cornstarch increased the viscosity of the custard, but it also made it taste starchy and chalky—no good. I also tried gelatin, but it made the mixture somewhat jellylike. What about whipped cream? I was concerned that it would mute the clear flavor of the wine, but since I was short on options, I gave it a shot. I carefully folded a few tablespoons of whipped cream into my cooked and slightly cooled zabaglione base and then spooned it over the berries. Finally, I had a light, smooth, and creamy concoction cut with a touch of dry wine. The only missing element? A slight crunch. Sprinkling the custard with a mixture of brown and white sugar before broiling created a crackly, caramelized crust.

My arm was sore from hours of whisking, but I had finally achieved my goal: a foolproof zabaglione that pairs perfectly with berries for a refreshing, elegant dessert.

🎥 **COOK'S VIDEOS** Original Test Kitchen Videos
www.cooksillustrated.com/aug09
HOW TO MAKE
• Individual Fresh Berry Gratins

AT-A-GLANCE | STAGES OF ZABAGLIONE

As it cooks, zabaglione gradually transforms from liquid and thin to creamy and thick. Here's what to expect.

1. LIQUID BEGINNING
Mixture starts out fluid and loose. Whisking develops foamy air bubbles, which lighten mixture as it heats.

2. DEVELOPING VOLUME
With further whisking and cooking, mixture expands, thickens, and begins to turn creamy.

3. SHINY AND THICK
Zabaglione is ready when glossy and creamy, with consistency resembling hollandaise sauce.

INDIVIDUAL FRESH BERRY GRATINS
SERVES 4

NOTE: When making the zabaglione, make sure to cook the egg mixture in a glass bowl over water that is barely simmering. Glass conducts heat more evenly and gently than metal. If the heat is too high, the yolks around the edges of the bowl will start to scramble. Constant whisking is required. Although we prefer to make this recipe with a mixture of raspberries, blackberries, blueberries, and strawberries, you can use 3 cups of just one type of berry. Do not use frozen berries. A broilerproof pie plate or gratin dish can be used in place of the individual gratin dishes. To prevent scorching, pay close attention to the gratins when broiling.

Berry Mixture
- 3 cups mixed berries (raspberries, blueberries, blackberries, and strawberries; strawberries stemmed and halved lengthwise if small, quartered if large), room temperature (see note)
- 2 teaspoons granulated sugar
  Pinch table salt

Zabaglione Topping
- 3 large egg yolks
- 3 tablespoons granulated sugar
- 3 tablespoons dry white wine such as Sauvignon Blanc
- 2 teaspoons light brown sugar
- 3 tablespoons heavy cream, chilled

1. **FOR THE BERRY MIXTURE:** Toss berries, sugar, and salt together in medium nonreactive bowl. Divide berry mixture evenly among 4 shallow 6-ounce gratin dishes set on rimmed baking sheet. Set berries aside to release juices while preparing zabaglione.

2. **FOR THE ZABAGLIONE:** Whisk egg yolks, 2 tablespoons plus 1 teaspoon granulated sugar, and wine in medium glass bowl until sugar is dissolved, about 1 minute. Set bowl over saucepan of barely simmering water (water should not touch bottom of bowl) and cook, whisking constantly, until mixture is frothy. Following photos above, continue to cook, whisking constantly, until mixture is slightly thickened, creamy, and glossy, 5 to 10 minutes (mixture will resemble hollandaise and form loose mounds when dripped from whisk). Remove bowl from saucepan and whisk constantly for 30 seconds to cool slightly. Transfer bowl to refrigerator and chill until egg mixture is completely cool, about 10 minutes.

3. Meanwhile, adjust oven rack 6 to 7 inches from heating element and heat broiler. Combine light brown sugar and remaining 2 teaspoons granulated sugar in small bowl.

4. In large bowl, whisk heavy cream until it holds soft peaks, 30 to 90 seconds. Using rubber spatula, gently fold whipped cream into cooled egg mixture. Spoon zabaglione over berries and sprinkle sugar mixture evenly over zabaglione; let stand at room temperature for 10 minutes, until sugar dissolves into zabaglione.

5. Broil until sugar is bubbly and caramelized, 1 to 4 minutes. Serve immediately.

INDIVIDUAL FRESH BERRY GRATINS WITH LEMON ZABAGLIONE

Follow recipe for Individual Fresh Berry Gratins, replacing 1 tablespoon wine with 1 tablespoon fresh lemon juice and adding 1 teaspoon finely grated lemon zest to yolk mixture in step 2.

INDIVIDUAL FRESH BERRY GRATINS WITH HONEY-LAVENDER ZABAGLIONE

Heat 2 teaspoons dried lavender and ¼ cup dry white wine in small saucepan over medium heat until barely simmering; remove from heat and let stand 10 minutes. Strain wine through fine-mesh strainer and discard lavender (you should have 3 tablespoons wine). Follow recipe for Individual Fresh Berry Gratins, replacing white wine with lavender-infused wine and replacing 1 teaspoon granulated sugar with 2 teaspoons honey in step 2.

Sorting Out Oats

Judging from the brands and styles cramming supermarket shelves, there's an oat for almost every taste. Are any better for breakfast or for baking?

≥ BY LISA McMANUS ≤

Often described as "humble" or "wholesome"—euphemisms for "boring"—oatmeal has rarely won much regard. In a legendary quip, Samuel Johnson's dictionary defined oats as a grain "which in England is generally given to horses, but which in Scotland supports the people." Even today, less than 5 percent of the oats grown commercially is for human consumption. Still, breakfast menus at upscale hotels increasingly treat oatmeal with a reverence customarily reserved for risotto, while cookbooks and magazines abound with ways to gussy it up.

To be sure, not all oatmeal is created equal—or even created in the same way. The cereal was originally made by simmering hulled whole oats. Quicker-cooking slivered or ground oats eventually replaced the whole grain and, by the late 19th century, oats were steamed and pressed flat with rollers, creating cereal that could be on the table in five minutes. In 1922, Quaker introduced oats that embodied all three processes (slicing, steaming, rolling), taking just one minute to cook. The company picked up the speed in 1966 with "instant" oatmeal, little packets of powdery flakes that need only a splash of boiling water.

Know Your Oats

Whole, hulled oats are also known as groats. After being heated to inhibit rancidity, they are further processed, according to the particular style.

➤ **STEEL-CUT OATS** Groats sliced into three or four pieces by steel blades. Also called Irish or "pinhead" oats.
Cooking time: 10–20 minutes.

➤ **STONE-GROUND OATS** Groats coarsely stone ground. Also called Scottish or "porridge" oats.
Cooking time: 10 minutes.

➤ **OLD-FASHIONED OR ROLLED OATS** Groats steamed and rolled flat (or "flaked").
Cooking time: 5–20 minutes.

➤ **QUICK OATS** Steel-cut oats steamed and rolled to one third (or less) the thickness of regular rolled oats.
Cooking time: 1 minute.

➤ **INSTANT OATS** Very finely cut groats rapidly cooked and rolled flat.
Cooking time: Instant

Interest has swung back lately toward slower-cooking traditional oats, with stores offering Irish-style steel-cut, Scottish-style stone-ground, and organic varieties in addition to instant, quick, and five-minute "old-fashioned" rolled oats. (For help understanding these categories, see "Know Your Oats," below.) And while Quaker used to be virtually the only brand, the number of companies selling oatmeal has proliferated. Is one style better as a hot cereal or for baking? Do any of the newcomers offer a better oatmeal than Quaker?

Determined to find out, we gathered and tasted more than a dozen top-selling oats. We deliberately passed over instant oats (even in the name of convenience, who can abide their pasty texture?) and eliminated quick oats from serious consideration after preliminary tasting revealed them to be only marginally better (see "Quick Oats" on page 27). That left us with three main styles as contenders: rolled, stone-ground, and steel-cut. After choosing winners in each category for hot cereal, we moved on to the next challenge: figuring out which style worked best in baking (see "Baking with Oats," at right).

Nutty or Not
Tasters began by sampling the oats as plain hot cereal and rating them for flavor, texture, and overall appeal. With each variety, whether slightly firm rolled oats or chewier stone-ground or steel-cut oats, oat flavor was an important factor in separating winners from losers. Tasters favored brands that tasted fresh and nutty, toasty and sweet, even buttery. Middle-ranked oats were bland and flavorless, while a few brands slid to the bottom with sour, grassy notes.

What accounts for these differences? One factor is the way the oats are processed. Oats begin deteriorating as soon as the hull is removed. To stop the oxidation that causes rancidity, oats are usually steamed, then heated in a kiln (or other heat source) to dry them out—a step that (in theory, at least) can create those nutty "browned" flavors that make good oatmeal so appealing. However, since processing details are proprietary, we couldn't determine the specific impact variables such as time, temperature, and heat source had on different brands. But we do know that simply seeing terms like "oven toasted" on the label is no guarantee of nutty taste.

Freshness counts, too. Despite the initial steaming, oats continue to oxidize gradually, in time becoming stale and rancid. If oats languish a long while at the factory, a supermarket, or in your

Baking with Oats

We baked oatmeal scones and oatmeal cookies using our top-ranking steel-cut, rolled, and quick oats. Our advice? Don't bake with steel-cut oats: The result was like aquarium gravel. Quick oats were acceptable, but their small flakes were too crumbly to provide great texture. Traditional rolled oats in the standard size of

GOOD FOR EATING, GREAT FOR BAKING

our runner-up from Quaker did best. (The "extra-thick" style of our favorite rolled oats, by Bob's Red Mill, could not cook through before the cookies or scones dried out.) –L.M.

cupboard, they won't taste fresh. (All of the oats we tasted were within their expiration dates.) And if moisture creeps in during storage, it can impart moldy, earthy, and dirty flavors—another problem that didn't escape our notice in a few brands.

Texture was also key in the rankings. In fact, the two variables were so inextricably intertwined that a brand's good flavor in one style could go unnoticed (or even be panned as bland) in another if the texture was deemed unappealing. Irrespective of style, tasters decried mushy, slimy, "mucilaginous" oats, while firm, chewy, resilient grains earned high marks. Although cooking time can affect texture, some oat varieties (and there are hundreds) are more prone to "swelling, pasting, and gelatinization" (in other words, breaking down into mush), according to Nancy Ames, a research scientist at Agriculture and AgriFoods Canada. (Though here again, how this factor impacted our rankings, we couldn't say, as manufacturers wouldn't disclose which type of oat they use.) Size matters, too. Our top-rated oats were thicker and more substantial than other brands and boasted larger, more intact grains even when cooked (a quality those in the industry call "flake integrity"). The winning rolled oat, in fact, was in a class by itself as the only "extra thick" oat in the lineup.

Palates of Steel
After serving up more than 1,000 bowls of oatmeal, we declared our winners. For breakfast, steel-cut oatmeal won the day, rating higher overall than rolled and stone-ground. This style of oatmeal offers firm, chewy texture and exceptionally full oat flavor. Surprisingly, the most familiar name in oatmeal (Quaker) and the most expensive one (McCann's), came in last in this category.

TASTING OATS

Twenty-one *Cook's Illustrated* staff members sampled 12 brands of steel-cut, old-fashioned rolled, and stone-ground oats as plain oatmeal, following package cooking directions, in three tastings of each style. Brands were selected from top-selling supermarket oats, as compiled by the Chicago-based market research firm Information Resources, Inc. Tasters rated each oatmeal on its oat flavor, texture, and overall appeal. Scores were averaged, and the oats appear, grouped by style, in order of preference.

STEEL-CUT OATS

RECOMMENDED

Bob's Red Mill Organic Steel-Cut Oats
Price: $3.45 for 24 ounces (14 cents per ounce)
Comments: Tasters praised these steel-cut oats for "buttery goodness," and "great oat flavor," that is "earthy" and "nutty," "whole grain-y in a good way," "rich and complex," with "a happy crunch—nibble-y, almost like popcorn." "Creamy yet toothsome" texture with a "nice chew, moist but not sticky," "like tapioca pearls popping in my mouth." "All the good things you want." In sum: "A winner."

Arrowhead Mills Organic Steel-Cut Oats Hot Cereal
Price: $2.99 for 24 ounces (12 cents per ounce)
Comments: "Substantial oats," that were "chewy," "almost crunchy," and "very unconventional." Its texture appealed to many tasters, and its "toasty," "nutty," "brown-rice" or "barley" flavor was "complex" and "hearty." "Like a warm granola bar," one taster raved.

Country Choice Steel-Cut Oats, Organic
Price: $4.79 for 30 ounces (16 cents per ounce)
Comments: "Good texture, like that popping, bursting" feel you get from caviar, said one taster. "Good oat flavor, slightly sweet." "A very nice balance of creaminess and crunch," "toasty and substantial," and "earthy." However, a few tasters found it "a bit horsey."

Hodgson's Mill Premium Steel-Cut Oats
Price: $1.95 for 18 ounces (11 cents per ounce)
Comments: "Good all-around earthy, sweet oat flavor," said tasters, who praised its "natural-tasting" "full-flavored, hearty" and "grainy," "nice, fresh, grassy," "strong" oat flavor. They also enjoyed its "good balance" of creaminess to graininess, though several tasters found it slightly "slimy" or "mucilaginous."

RECOMMENDED WITH RESERVATIONS

Quaker Steel-Cut Oats
Price: $4.69 for 24 ounces (20 cents per ounce)
Comments: Tasters were split on this oatmeal, with some calling it "mild," with "very plain oat flavor, a good canvas," and a "flavor that's pure and clean." Others called it "bland," "middle-of-the-road," and "a bit mushy" and "gooey."

McCann's Steel-Cut Irish Oatmeal
Price: $7.49 for 28 ounces (27 cents per ounce)
Comments: Though some tasters thought this pricey imported oatmeal had "a good chew" and "very earthy flavor," others said it was "too mild, almost timid," "like cardboard or paper pulp," with an "odd aftertaste," that was slightly "bitter" and "vegetal," like "raw seeds" or "grass."

ROLLED OATS

RECOMMENDED

Bob's Red Mill Organic Extra Thick Rolled Oats
Price: $2.40 for 16 ounces (15 cents per ounce)
Comments: "Nice, rich," "good oat flavor—seems real," like "sweet semolina," with "nutty, barley" "browned" overtones and a "good texture" that is "nice and plump," with a "decent chew," while being "creamy and cohesive."

Quaker Old-Fashioned Rolled Oats
Price: $4.99 for 42 ounces (12 cents per ounce)
Comments: Offering a "slight chew," and "subtle sweetness," Quaker's most well known style of oatmeal "felt and tasted very natural," with a texture that tasters deemed "good—plump and crunchy," "hearty," and "with a tiny bit of snap." Its flavor had "good oat-y, toasty notes."

NOT RECOMMENDED

Arrowhead Mills Organic Old-Fashioned Oatmeal Hot Cereal
Price: $3.99 for 16 ounces (25 cents per ounce)
Comments: Tasters decried this oatmeal as "gooey," "like textured thick water." "Awful. I was afraid to swallow." Its flavor was mild to the point of "no flavor at all." In sum: "Starchy, cardboard-y, and one-dimensional."

Bob's Red Mill Old-Fashioned Rolled Oats
Price: $4.49 for 32 ounces (14 cents per ounce)
Comments: While tasters really liked this company's "Extra Thick" rolled oats, they disliked these thinner oat flakes, which became "too mushy," "gluey," and "sticky" and lacked the thicker flakes' appeal. Tasters called them "bland" with "no flavor."

Country Choice Organic Old-Fashioned Oats
Price: $3.39 for 18 ounces (19 cents per ounce)
Comments: "Very mushy and no flavor," or "earthy flavor but bad texture, like slurry," "mushy and viscous and raggedy—take it away!" complained tasters, who found "nothing good here. Bland, like cardboard." "Tastes like grass, with a slight chemical aftertaste."

STONE-GROUND OATS

RECOMMENDED WITH RESERVATIONS

Bob's Red Mill Scottish Oats
Price: $2.99 for 20 ounces (15 cents per ounce)
Comments: Tasters found stone-ground oatmeal "unusual" with "very small oats," "like couscous." Some enjoyed its "nutty flavor," describing it as "almost roasted," and "Cream of Wheat-like." Despite some fans of its "buttery flavor and fabulous texture," several found its texture unappealing, "weird," and "bad."

Quick Oats: Only for Emergencies

In a preliminary tasting, we found quick oats far inferior to chewier, more flavorful rolled or steel-cut oats in oatmeal, so we took them out of our main lineup. Of the four brands we tasted, Quaker Quick Oats fared best but was recommended only with reservations—overall, tasters agreed that it was "Bland City." Country Choice and Bob's Red Mill quick oats were a step down from Quaker, while pricey McCann's Quick Oats lagged far behind, with tasters likening its mushy texture to "nursing home food." With comments like these, who cares if quick oats cook in a minute? For complete tasting results, go to www.cooksillustrated.com/aug09. –L.M.

In the end, tasters declared Bob's Red Mill Organic Steel-Cut Oats their favorite breakfast oatmeal, praising it for outstanding buttery, nutty oat flavor and "creamy yet toothsome" texture. Because oat style is a matter of individual preference, we also chose a favorite rolled oat. Our tasters preferred a substantial, chewy texture and gave top marks to another offering from Bob's Red Mill: Organic Extra Thick Rolled Oats, which were praised for having "nice and plump" flakes with a "decent chew." (By contrast, Bob's Red Mill Scottish Oats, which are stone-ground into couscous-size pieces, did not fare as well with tasters, some of whom found its "Cream of Wheat-like" texture "weird" and unappealing.)

Both of these options take time to cook—about 10 minutes for chewy oatmeal, 20 minutes for softer cereal. We think it's time well spent, but for a faster option, we recommend our second-ranked Quaker Old-Fashioned Rolled Oats, which came in just a hair behind Bob's Red Mill and takes just five minutes to prepare. Quaker's rolled oats also aced our baking tests. If you want to buy only one brand of oats for both breakfast and baking, this is your best choice.

Do You Need Pans for Your Grill?

Grill cookware promises to make it easier to grill small chunks of food so they don't fall into the fire. But can it give you the same results as grilling directly on the grates?

⇒ BY LISA McMANUS ⇐

Grill grates are designed to be spread out, with space between them providing direct exposure to intense heat so that you get the charred, caramelized, slightly smoky taste of perfectly grilled food. Why, then, would you ever need cookware that stands between you and your grill?

While open grates are fine for steaks, burgers, or bone-in chicken pieces, grilling small or delicate items such as seafood or vegetables can require acrobatics to prevent them from falling into the fire. Whether you're cutting zucchini into planks, wrapping fish in foil, or skewering chunks of boneless meat, a new category of cookware promises an easier option. Shaped like indoor cookware but perforated to allow exposure to the fire, grill cookware is designed to contain and cook smaller, more fragile foods without special preparation—and without sacrificing grill flavor, good browning, or even some charring.

That said, there's no consensus among manufacturers as to what form this style of cookware should take—or which material is best. Grill cookware comes in three starkly different designs (woks, skillets with handles, and rectangular sheet pans) and in materials that run the gamut from wire mesh, aluminum, and stainless steel to enameled cast iron and porcelain- or nonstick-coated steel. To determine for ourselves which design and material (if any) worked best, we rounded up models priced from $5.97 to $49.99 in all three styles and a range of materials. We also threw in an adjustable pan that allows the user to manipulate the size from large to small and a disposable aluminum model that could be cut, bent, and shaped.

The Hole Story

Because recent tryouts of other grill accessories (presses and baskets) taught us that most of this equipment isn't worth buying, we approached testing with skepticism. As we grilled flaky cod fillets, medium shrimp with chopped vegetables, and batches of quartered potatoes over a gas grill, our caution proved sound: More than half the grill cookware performed poorly.

The worst were the grill woks. This style of grill pan features a narrow bottom and high sides that kept ingredients crammed together and made food steam

📹 **COOK'S VIDEOS** Original Test Kitchen Videos
www.cooksillustrated.com/aug09
BEHIND THE SCENES
• Testing Grill Cookware

rather than brown for results so lousy we eliminated such pans from consideration. Also on the cutting block: any grill pans (irrespective of design) with nonstick coatings. High temperatures made this type of cookware emit fumes the first few times we used them, tainting food with a chemical smell and taste.

But some pans did impress us, especially as we learned how best to use them. Across the board, we found that preheating the pans on the grill helped our food cook faster, with much better browning and flavor. We also learned which features matter most:

Go for Broad and Low. The broad cooking surface and low sides on grill skillets minimized steaming and promoted browning; sheet pans (also known as "grill toppers") were even more spacious, allowing us to stir food less often and thus maximize caramelization. They also accommodated much larger portions (say, a half-dozen fish fillets at once).

More Holes Are Better. Cookware covered in holes performed best, while pans featuring solid, unperforated edges (a design akin to wrapping food in foil) trapped heat and steamed food. But not just any holes will do. Too-large openings limited the pan's usefulness, allowing pieces of food to fall through and into the grates. Better pans had holes no more than ¼ inch in diameter.

Sturdy Construction Is Critical. Several pans were so flimsy they warped like potato chips on the hot grill, cooking unevenly as we struggled to stir food uphill and down. The adjustable model was one of the worst. Tightening a knob locked its two sliding half-trays into the desired size, but the overlapping half warped upward, trapping food in a metal sandwich.

Material Matters. Grill pans coated with porcelain, a nonstick alternative, were less than ideal, accumulating a sticky residue after several uses that was hard to scrub away. Heavier stainless steel without a coating was a top performer and did not warp on the hot grates like pans made of other materials. Because steel is dense and less conductive than other metals, preheating it gave us the right combination of retaining and then conducting heat slowly and steadily to brown delicate foods without burning. One cast-iron model would also have been outstanding if it had smaller holes—and wasn't so heavy and pricey.

Edges Are Essential. Grill toppers designed as flat sheets with no raised rims were difficult to manage: Chunks of potatoes, shrimp, and vegetables tossed over their surfaces scooted off. A few pans had three raised sides and a single flat one, but we preferred models with four raised edges, which kept everything in place.

Skillets had the advantage of higher sides all around (but not too high to trap heat and cause steaming).

Winner Shares Well

When the smoke cleared, we found two models worth adding to our grilling arsenal. The Weber Professional-Grade Grill Pan ($19.99) is made of sturdy stainless steel that retains enough heat for excellent browning. Its surface is covered with narrow ⅛-inch slits that let in grill flavor and discourage steaming without letting food fall through; its four rimmed sides also contain food nicely, and the raised handles are easy to grasp with grill mitts. It offers a generous cooking surface yet fits easily on our recommended gas and charcoal grills. You can even rotate the pan 90 degrees and push it to one side of a gas grill if you want to share the space with chicken or steak. As an added bonus, the pan's notched corners allow the edges of the grill lid to slide into them and close smoothly.

A grill skillet nearly tied for the top spot. The Williams-Sonoma Mesh Grill-Top Fry Pan ($29.95) is made of steel mesh that allows maximum grill exposure and flavor and ensures minimum food loss. Lightweight and easy to use, it produced moist fish fillets with a crisp surface that didn't break or stick to the mesh. Two minor gripes: It offers less surface area for cooking than our winner, and because the skillet's handle (which is not removable) protrudes just like on an ordinary pan, we kept absentmindedly grabbing it with our bare hands, forgetting that the 600-plus-degree heat had turned it searingly hot.

The bottom line: If you choose a good design and the right material, grill pans can be a definite improvement over futzing around to prevent food from falling through the grates. We're sold.

Greater Than Grates

With its raised edges and small slits, our winning grill topper keeps small chunks of food like potatoes out of the fire—but still allows for browning.

RATING GRILL COOKWARE

After preliminary testing, we eliminated grill woks and any cookware with a nonstick coating, which narrowed our lineup to nine pans: seven rectangular "grill toppers" and two skillets. We used them to cook shrimp, vegetables, potatoes, and cod fillets on our favorite gas grill, the Weber Spirit E-210, and tested them for size on our recommended charcoal grill, the Weber One-Touch Gold. Pans were purchased in Boston-area retail stores or online and are listed in order of preference. Sources for the winning models are on page 32.

SIZE/DIAMETER: We measured the cooking surface of each pan, not the outer dimensions.

COOKING: We preferred pans that produced good grill flavor and tender, browned whole medium shrimp and chopped vegetables; nicely browned, moist cod fillets that remained intact; and crisp-skinned potato quarters with moist interiors.

DESIGN: We preferred abundant small holes, heat-retaining materials, a broad cooking surface, and sturdy no-warp construction.

USER-FRIENDLINESS: We considered pan weight, handle placement, and other factors that increased comfort and ease while manipulating the pan.

CLEANUP: We favored pans that were easy to clean but did not downgrade pans for the slight blackening expected from use on the grill.

HIGHLY RECOMMENDED	PERFORMANCE	TESTERS' COMMENTS

WEBER Professional-Grade Grill Pan
Model: 6435
Price: $19.99
Size: 14 x 11 inches
Material: Stainless steel

Cooking: ★★★
Design: ★★★
User-friendliness: ★★★
Cleanup: ★★★

This sturdy pan was well designed, with ⅛-inch slits rather than holes, so that even chopped onion pieces didn't fall through. Its four raised sides kept food on the pan when we stirred; raised handles helped us lift it off the grill easily with heavy mitts. Good heat retention meant good browning.

WILLIAMS-SONOMA Mesh Grill-Top Fry Pan
Model: 9684432
Price: $29.95
Diameter: 9 inches
Material: Stainless steel mesh

Cooking: ★★★
Design: ★★★
User-friendliness: ★★★
Cleanup: ★★★

Lightweight and easily maneuverable, this skillet of steel mesh with a lattice of ¼-inch spaces caramelized and gave excellent grill flavor to shrimp, vegetables, potatoes, and fish. Though it blackened, the mesh did not trap food or become difficult to clean. The cooking surface is larger than it appears because of gently flared sides. One gripe: We wish the metal handle were removable, so we couldn't accidentally touch it with bare hands.

RECOMMENDED	PERFORMANCE	TESTERS' COMMENTS

BARBECUE GENIUS Stainless Steel Gourmet Grill Topper
Model: 19401
Price: $25
Size: 13¾ x 10½ inches
Material: Stainless steel

Cooking: ★★★
Design: ★★
User-friendliness: ★★
Cleanup: ★★★

We liked this pan's heat-retaining stainless steel and moderately raised handles. At ⅝ inch wide, the holes were small enough to keep food from falling out. However, a wide strip of unperforated metal around each edge allowed food to steam, and the rim only extended to three sides. The pan also warped slightly during cooking.

CHARCOAL COMPANION Large Porcelain-Coated Griddle
Model: CC 3080
Price: $16.99
Size: 16 x 10½ inches
Material: Porcelain-coated steel

Cooking: ★★
Design: ★★★
User-friendliness: ★★★
Cleanup: ★★

A solid performer, thanks to four raised sides, easy-to-grip handles, a generous cooking surface, and square ¼-inch holes. On the other hand, it warped slightly when cooking fish, and over time the porcelain coating acquired a gunky film that was hard to scrub away.

RECOMMENDED WITH RESERVATIONS	PERFORMANCE	TESTERS' COMMENTS

CHARCOAL COMPANION Enamel Cast-Iron Griddle
Model: CC 3515
Price: $49.99
Size: 15½ x 12 inches
Material: Enameled cast iron

Cooking: ★★
Design: ★★
User-friendliness: ★★
Cleanup: ★★

This heavy pan, the priciest in our lineup, had large oval and medium-sized round holes that let smaller onions and potatoes drop into the fire. But it excelled at caramelizing any vegetables that stayed in the pan as well as grilling delicate fish; plus, it retained heat beautifully on cold days. Winter grillers, take note.

NOT RECOMMENDED	PERFORMANCE	TESTERS' COMMENTS

GRILL PRO Porcelain-Coated Grill Topper
Model: 97121
Price: $19
Size: 13¾ x 10½ inches
Material: Porcelain-coated steel

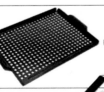

Cooking: ★★
Design: ★
User-friendliness: ★★
Cleanup: ★★

Completely covered with ⅜-inch round holes and featuring three raised sides, this porcelain-coated topper provided good grill exposure. Yet it warped badly, and the porcelain coating became gunky after repeated use.

MR. BAR B Q Deluxe Stainless Steel Skillet
Model: 06058P
Price: $20.50
Diameter: 9⅞ inches
Material: Stainless steel with wood handle

Cooking: ★★
Design: ★
User-friendliness: ★
Cleanup: ★★

The folding (but not removable) wood handle was for storage rather than cooking: It snapped down into our food when we attempted to position it vertically to close the charcoal grill lid, and its metal trim got red-hot.

CUISINART Stainless Steel Grilling Platter with Removable Handle
Model: CGT-111
Price: $39.99
Size: 15 x 11 inches
Material: Stainless steel with plastic handle

Cooking: ★★
Design: ★
User-friendliness: ★
Cleanup: ★★

Big holes on this pricey pan were made worse by a large cutout "Cuisinart" across the middle that allowed small foods to escape. This pan warped, and the removable handle was so poorly designed that we stopped using it, leaving us with a flat and hard-to-maneuver sheet.

GRILL-O-SHEET Reusable Barbecue Sheets
Model: 10102
Price: $5.97 for pack of 2
Size: 17¾ x 11¾ inches
Material: Aluminum alloy

Cooking: ★
Design: ★
User-friendliness: ★
Cleanup: ★

You can snip, bend, and customize these disposable grill sheets, which start out flat. However, they warp dramatically over heat and lose food off the sides and through the ½-inch holes. Once bent, the sheets are impossible to flatten, so when reusing them—which you can do a few times—you are starting with a warped surface.

≥ BY J. KENJI ALT ≤

TECHNIQUE

SEEDING AND CHOPPING CUCUMBERS

Here is an easy way to remove the watery seeds from cucumbers, so they don't dilute the flavors of a recipe, and cut their cylindrical shape into even dice.

1. Peel cucumber, cut in half lengthwise, and scoop out seeds with spoon.

2. Cut each half crosswise into 2- to 3-inch pieces.

3. Place each piece cut-side up on cutting board; slice lengthwise into even batons.

4. Cut batons crosswise into even dice.

TEST KITCHEN TIP Blemish-Free Pancakes

We've all experienced the annoying phenomenon of having the first batch of pancakes turn out splotched with brown spots, while subsequent batches come out evenly golden. Here's why: When fresh oil hits a hot pan, the surface tension of the oil causes it to bead together into little droplets, leaving some of the pan bottom without a coating. Since bare metal conducts heat better than oil, when you ladle your batter into the pan, the spots directly in contact with uncoated metal will cook faster than those touching oil. By the time you get to your second batch of pancakes, the oil has undergone chemical changes that make the molecules less prone to clustering. What's more, the first batch of pancakes has absorbed much of the oil, leaving only a thin film that's more likely to be evenly distributed across the pan.

For spot-free pancakes from the get-go, start by applying oil to an unheated pan or griddle. Allow the oil to heat up over medium heat for at least one minute, then use a paper towel to wipe away all but a thin, barely visible layer to prevent sticking. The pancakes should cook up golden brown from the first batch to the last.

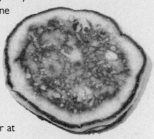

SEEING SPOTS
Tiny droplets of oil that cluster together rather than spread out cause light patches on the first batch of pancakes.

EQUIPMENT TESTING Lettuce Knives

You've seen them on TV and in kitchen stores: serrated plastic knives that supposedly help prevent your lettuce from turning brown after cutting. But do they work better than tearing or using an ordinary kitchen knife? We chopped a head of romaine lettuce and a head of iceberg lettuce using three different knives: one with a stainless steel blade, one with a super-thin high-carbon steel blade, and the Zyliss Fresh Cut Salad Knife ($2.95). We also tore the leaves by hand. After chopping and tearing, we refrigerated the lettuces in plastic zipper-lock bags and waited for them to brown. Though all lettuce began showing some browning on the ribs after 10 days, none showed any signs of browning on the cut or torn surfaces. After 12 days, the heads cut with metal knives showed faint signs of browning on these surfaces, and the lettuce cut with the plastic knife followed a day later. The torn lettuce was last to brown on its ruptured edges, starting to turn at 2 weeks.

Our verdict? The plastic lettuce knife might stave off browning slightly longer than metal knives, but it's not worth the money or the extra drawer space. To prolong the life of lettuce by a day or two, stick to tearing by hand. Tearing allows leaves to break along their natural fault lines, rupturing fewer cells and reducing premature browning.

SAVE YOUR DRAWER SPACE
This plastic lettuce knife from Zyliss is an unnecessary tool.

Oil Change for Baking

Many cakes call for a small amount of vegetable oil. Would it harm the recipe to substitute a different type of oil? To find out, we baked yellow, chiffon, and carrot cakes with vegetable oil (derived from soybeans and corn), corn oil, canola oil, and light olive oil (we avoided extra-virgin olive oil due to its strong taste). Tasters discerned no difference in taste or texture among cakes made with vegetable, corn, or canola oil. But the light olive oil imparted an unwanted savory taste to the yellow and chiffon cakes and made for a slightly denser texture. It worked fine in the coarser carrot cake, where spices obscured its flavor. Lesson learned: Unless the recipe calls for olive oil, stick with neutral-flavored oils like vegetable, canola, or corn in delicate baked goods.

TEST KITCHEN TIP
Taming Raw Onion Flavor

Can the way you cut an onion affect its flavor? We took eight onions and cut each two different ways: pole to pole (with the grain) and parallel to the equator (against the grain). We then smelled and tasted pieces from each onion cut each way. The onions sliced pole to pole were clearly less pungent in taste and odor than those cut along the equator. Here's why: The intense flavor and acrid odor of onions are caused by substances called thiosulfinates, created when enzymes known as alliinases contained in the onion's cells interact with proteins that are also present in the vegetable. These reactions take place only when the onion's cells are ruptured and release the strong-smelling enzymes. Cutting with the grain ruptures fewer cells than cutting against the grain, leading to the release of fewer alliinases and the creation of fewer thiosulfinates.

CUT WITH GRAIN= LESS PUNGENT

CUT AGAINST GRAIN= MORE PUNGENT

A butcher's knot is the best way to take an awkwardly shaped roast and compress it into a compact shape for more even cooking. We prefer this knot to a "granny" or double knot because it's easy to adjust and the knot won't loosen.

1. Wrap a piece of butcher's twine around your roast. Hold the bottom piece (colored gray above) in your right hand and the top piece in your left.

2. With the forefinger of your left hand, pull a loop from the bottom twine to the left, underneath the top piece.

3. Twist this loop once toward you to form a circle.

4. Pass the end of the bottom twine over the top piece and through the loop. Pull tightly on bottom twine (see arrows above) to secure the knot.

5. Pull up and down on the top twine to tighten the string around the roast.

TASTING Eggplants

Four of the most common varieties of eggplant found in the supermarket are large globe, small Italian, slender Chinese, and apple-shaped Thai. Can they all be used interchangeably in recipes? To find out, we prepared each type in five dishes calling for different cooking methods: roasted and pureed in baba ghanoush, sautéed in Pasta alla Norma (page 13), baked in eggplant Parmesan, stewed in Thai curry, and stir-fried with sweet chili-garlic sauce. Only the generously sized globe eggplant was a true multitasker, suitable for all dishes and responding well to all cooking methods. The smaller varieties were prevented by their size from being good choices in eggplant Parmesan, and their excessive amount of seeds made for overly coarse baba ghanoush. The Thai eggplant, with its crisp, applelike texture, was notable for tasting bright, grassy, and appealing simply eaten raw.

Type		Texture	Flavor	Best Uses
BEST ALL-AROUND Globe		Very tender; watery	Mild	Roasting, pureeing, baking, sautéing, stewing, stir-frying
SPICY BUT SEEDY Italian		Moderately moist; lots of seeds	Spicy	Sautéing, stewing, stir-frying
SWEET AND DRY Chinese		Somewhat dry, firm interior; lots of seeds	Intense, slightly sweet	Sautéing, stewing, stir-frying
ODD ONE OUT Thai		Crisp and relatively dry; lots of seeds	Bright and grassy, with hints of spice	Sautéing, stewing, stir-frying, raw

Storing Sliced Onions

Old wives' tales claim that storing sliced or chopped onions in water will help keep their pungency from intensifying, but we found the exact opposite to be the case. We stored sliced onions for two days submerged in water as well as placed directly in zipper-lock bags, and then compared their odor and flavor to freshly sliced onions. The onions submerged in water were unanimously deemed to be most odorous with the sharpest flavor. It turns out that over time, water facilitates the distribution of enzymes known as alliinases across the cut surfaces of the onion, which in turn leads to an increase in the creation of thiosulfinates that produce an onion's pungent odor and flavor. (See "Taming Raw Onion Flavor" on page 30.) Your best bet is to simply slice or chop onions as you need them, but if you find yourself with an excess, store them in the fridge in a zipper-lock bag and give them a quick rinse to remove any thiosulfinates on their surface right before using.

The Problem with Meat Probes

A meat-probe thermometer is left in the meat as it cooks, transmitting readings to a digital console and, in theory, avoiding the need to continually open the oven to check on a roast's temperature with an instant-read thermometer. The problem is, before a roast starts cooking, it's nearly impossible to predict which part of the meat is going to cook the slowest. To illustrate, we roasted four pork loins (two boneless and two bone-in), inserting the probe of our winning meat-probe thermometer, the ThermoWorks Original Cooking Thermometer/Timer ($19), into the center of each. We cooked the roasts in a 350-degree oven until the probes registered 135 degrees. We then removed the roasts from the oven and double-checked their temperatures with our favorite instant-read thermometer, the ThermoWorks Original Super-Fast Thermapen ($89). While the area near the tip of each probe registered 135 degrees, other parts of the loins registered temperatures off between 5 and 15 degrees.

The bottom line: A meat probe is best used to track a roast's general progress without the need for opening the oven door repeatedly. For perfect accuracy, it should be used in conjunction with an instant-read thermometer. When the probe indicates the roast is done, double-check with the instant-read model in the thickest parts of the meat to be sure the whole roast has reached the desired temperature.

CUTTING POTATOES FOR FRENCH FRIES

Cutting potatoes into even pieces, as for our Easier French Fries, page 21, is the first step to a perfect batch.

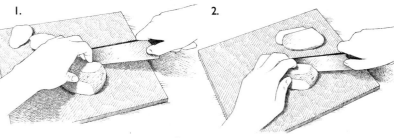

1. Square off potato by cutting a ¼-inch-thick slice from each of its 4 long sides.

2. Cut potato lengthwise into ⅜-inch planks.

3. Stack 3 to 4 planks and cut into ⅜-inch batons. Repeat with remaining planks.

⇒ BY MEREDITH BUTCHER & PEGGY CHUNG COLLIER ⇐

NEW PRODUCT Wine Aerators

If you don't want to wait the standard 10 to 30 minutes for your red wine to "breathe," devices called wine aerators promise instant gratification. Held above a wine glass or inserted into a bottle, an aerator exposes the wine to air while you pour, a process designed to instantly reduce volatile chemicals (like sulfur compounds and free acetaldehyde) that can impart a harsh or flat flavor. We poured a 2005 Bordeaux through five models priced from $29.95 to $39.95, comparing each with wine poured straight from the bottle. Wine poured through all the aerators had a smoother taste than wine poured straight from the bottle, but one had markedly improved flavor and aroma. The Nuance Wine Finer ($39.95), which looks like a perforated cigarette holder, slips firmly into the neck of the bottle to aerate wine as it's poured.

WINE BREATH-A-LYZER
The Nuance Wine Finer helps wine "breathe" in an instant.

EQUIPMENT TESTING Corn Strippers

Corn strippers help you remove the kernels from the hard, fibrous cob. But are they any more effective than a chef's knife? Our lineup of five included models by Kuhn Rikon, Norpro, and OXO, with prices ranging from $2.53 to $14. Most were a disaster, jamming or making a mess by spraying cut kernels. One by Norpro, a metal ring with teeth that you drag down a cob, broke as we attempted our fourth ear. Only the OXO Good Grips Corn Stripper ($12.99), which resembles a computer mouse, cut corn with ease. You grip the oval stripper and scrape the sharp blade along the corn to remove several rows of kernels at a time, which fall neatly into the attached cup. While it's no faster than a chef's knife and

KERNEL CONTROL
The OXO Good Grips Corn Stripper reduces mess by catching loose kernels in a cup.

doesn't cut more deeply, this corn stripper is safer and mess-free for such dishes as fritters and chowder, which call for corn off the cob.

NEW EQUIPMENT Grill Grate Cleaners

We love the Grill Wizard BBQ Brush ($11.98) for removing baked-on food from grill grates. Now, two new scrapers, the Grill Floss and the Grill Daddy, promise to do an even better job. The Grill Floss ($18.95) is a stainless steel rod topped with a wrench-shaped head that wraps around the grates

to scrape them clean from all sides, like dental floss. The tool removed hard-to-reach food underneath the rounded grates of our charcoal grill, but we missed the ease of brush cleaning, and the device wasn't designed to work on the flat grates of our favorite gas grill. The Grill Daddy ($19.99) works like a watering can, forcing water through the sharp bristles on the nozzle to steam and loosen grit. Unfortunately, water merely trickled out, minimizing steam cleaning. The bottom line: The Grill Wizard BBQ Brush still cleans up the competition.

BEST BBQ BRUSH
The Grill Wizard BBQ Brush remains our favorite for removing gunk from grills.

NEW EQUIPMENT FlameDisk

Tired of lugging heavy bags of charcoal, we were thrilled to discover a small, lightweight charcoal replacement. Made of solid ethanol, the uGo FlameDisk ($6.94) is a flat, aluminum-covered, Frisbee-sized disk that sits in the bottom of any kettle grill. The manufacturer claims it releases about 90 percent fewer pollutants than charcoal. Our FlameDisk burned for 40 minutes and left no ash or mess, but it produced near-constant flare-ups instead of even, radiant heat. Flames danced frenetically, charring some of our boneless chicken breasts, while others remained raw. Steaks fared better, but every time fat dripped,

UP IN SMOKE
High flames dashed high hopes for this "green" charcoal replacement.

the flames rushed back up. Because the grill lid must stay off, the FlameDisk limited the types of foods we could cook. Another drawback: A two-level fire, with hotter and cooler sections, was obviously impossible. We're sticking with charcoal.

EQUIPMENT TESTING
Eco-Friendly Sponge Cloths

Do thin, "eco-friendly" sponge cloths made from cotton and wood pulp work as well as a heavy-duty kitchen sponge? We tested two biodegradable cloths, the Skoy Earth-Friendly Cloth (four for $5.99) and the Twist European Sponge Cloth #20 (three for $3.25) against a leading household sponge, the S.O.S All Surface Scrubber Sponge (three for $3), made of synthetic cellulose and nylon. Both eco sponges were far more absorbent than the S.O.S, soaking up much more spilled water, and were better at sweeping up thick barbecue sauce. Another

plus: Hot, soapy water erased all traces of barbecue sauce on the eco sponges, while smells and stains lingered on the traditional sponge. After multiple cycles in the dishwasher, both the Skoy and the Twist surfaced unscathed. Our top pick is the super-absorbent Skoy Earth-Friendly Cloth.

For complete testing results on each item, go to www.cooksillustrated.com/aug09.

GREEN & CLEAN
The Skoy Earth-Friendly Cloth is more absorbent than a kitchen sponge—and it's biodegradable.

Sources

The following are mail-order sources for items recommended in this issue. Prices were current at press time and do not include shipping. Contact companies to confirm or visit www.cooksillustrated.com for updates.

Page 7: BONING KNIFE
- Victorinox Forschner Fibrox 6-Inch Straight Boning Knife: $15.95, item #40511, Cutlery and More (800-650-9866, www.cutleryandmore.com).

Page 11: GRILL LIGHT
- Camp Chef Chef's Grill Light: $25, item #CCH1138, Cookware.com (888-478-4606, www.cookware.com).

Page 24: MINI GRATIN DISH
- Le Creuset Petite Au Gratin Dish, 6-Ounce: $9.95, item #108904, Cooking.com (800-663-8810, www.cooking.com).

Page 27: OATS
- Bob's Red Mill Organic Steel-Cut Oats: $3.45 for 24 ounces, item #6053C24, Bob's Red Mill (800-349-2173, www.bobsredmill.com).
- Bob's Red Mill Organic Extra Thick Rolled Oats: $2.40 for 16 ounces, item #6050C16, Bob's Red Mill.

PAGE 29: GRILL PANS
- Weber Professional-Grade Grill Pan: $19.99, item #458331, Home Depot (800-430-3376, www.homedepot.com).
- Williams-Sonoma Mesh Grill-Top Fry Pan: $29.95, item #9684432, Williams-Sonoma (877-812-6235, www.williams-sonoma.com).

PAGE 32: WINE AERATOR
- Nuance Wine Finer: $39.95, item #1171, WineVine Imports (919-341-4279, www.winevine-imports.com).

Page 32: CORN STRIPPER
- OXO Good Grips Corn Stripper: $12.99, item #1128000, OXO (800-545-4411, www.oxo.com).

Page 32: GRILL BRUSH
- Grill Wizard BBQ Brush: $11.98, item #GRILLWIZ, Barr Brothers Company (800-630-8665, www.thetoolwizard.com).

PAGE 32: ECO-FRIENDLY SPONGE CLOTH
- Skoy Earth-Friendly Cloth: $5.99 for 4 cloths, item #4-pack, SkoyCloth.com (800-990-4757, www.skoycloth.com).

INDEX
July & August 2009

📹 **COOK'S VIDEOS** Original Test Kitchen Videos **www.cooksillustrated.com**

AMERICA'S TEST KITCHEN
Public television's most popular cooking show

Join the millions of home cooks who watch our show, *America's Test Kitchen*, on public television every week. For more information, including recipes and program times, visit www.americastestkitchen.com.

Grill-Smoked Pork Chops, 11

Buttermilk Pancakes, 23

Berry Gratins, 25

Grill-Roasted Boneless Turkey Breast, 7

French Fries, 21

Mediterranean Chopped Salad, 14

Pasta alla Norma, 13

Spanish Tortilla, 9

Grilled Stuffed Flank Steak, 19

Pasta with Tomato and Almond Pesto, 15

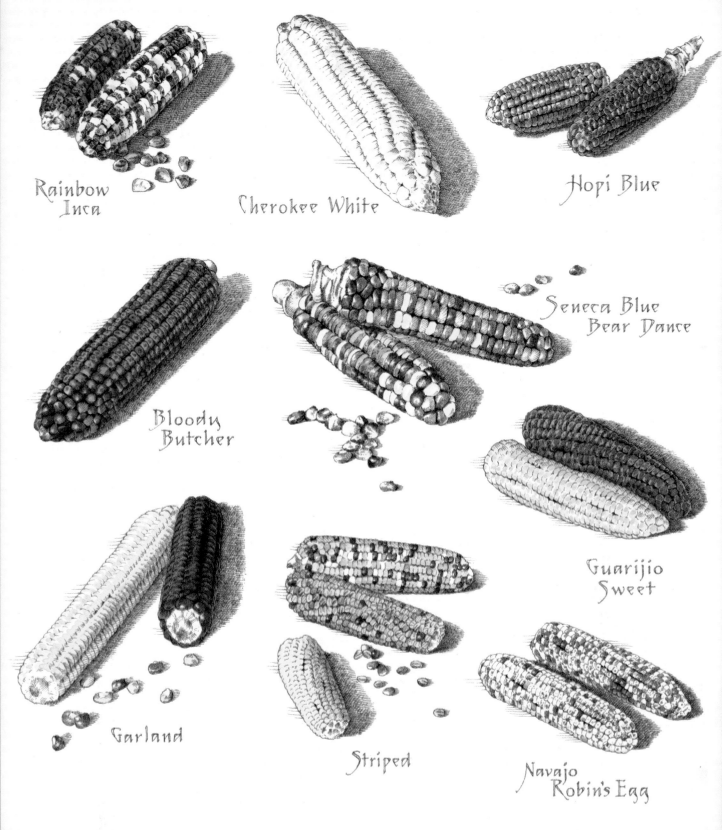

Rainbow
Inca

Cherokee White

Hopi Blue

Seneca Blue
Bear Dance

Bloody
Butcher

Guarijio
Sweet

Garland

Striped

Navajo
Robin's Egg

HEIRLOOM CORN

NUMBER ONE HUNDRED

SEPTEMBER & OCTOBER 2009

COOK'S
ILLUSTRATED

Steak Tips with Gravy

Modern Chicken
& Dumplings

California Olive Oils
Can the New World Compete?

Best Italian
Meat Sauce

"Green" Nonstick
Skillets
Don't Waste Your Money!

How to Brew
Perfect Coffee

Goof-Proof Lemon Soufflé
Vinaigrette Dos and Don'ts
Apple Upside-Down Cake
Austrian Potato Salad
Pasta with Roasted Vegetables
Grilled Corn, Mexican-Style
Thai Pork Lettuce Wraps

www.cooksillustrated.com
$5.95 U.S./$6.95 CANADA

0 74470 62805 7

1 0>

CONTENTS

September & October 2009

COOK'S
ILLUSTRATED

www.cooksillustrated.com

Founder and Editor — Christopher Kimball
Editorial Director — Jack Bishop
Executive Editor — Amanda Agee
Test Kitchen Director — Erin McMurrer
Managing Editor — Rebecca Hays
Senior Editors — Keith Dresser
Lisa McManus
Features Editor — Lisa Glazer
Copy Editor — Amy Graves
Associate Editors — J. Kenji Alt
Bryan Roof
Test Cooks — Andrea Geary
Francisco J. Robert
Yvonne Ruperti
Assistant Test Kitchen Director — Matthew Herron
Assistant Editors — Meredith Butcher
Peggy Chung Collier
Assistant Test Cook — Marcus Walser
Executive Assistant — Meredith Smith
Editorial Assistant — Abbey Becker
Senior Kitchen Assistant — Nadia Domeq
Kitchen Assistants — Maria Elena Delgado
Ena Gudiel
Edward Tundidor
Producer — Melissa Baldino
Contributing Editors — Matthew Card
Dawn Yanagihara
Consulting Editor — Scott Brueggeman
Science Editor — Guy Crosby, Ph.D.
Proofreader — Jean Rogers

Managing Editor, Special Issues — Todd Meier
Production Editor, Special Issues — Elizabeth Bomze

Online Managing Editor — David Tytell
Online Editor — Kate Mason
Online Media Producer — Peter Tannenbaum
Online Editorial Assistant — Mari Levine

Design Director — Amy Klee
Art Director, Magazines — Julie Bozzo
Designers — Jay Layman
Lindsey Timko
Deputy Art Director, Marketing/Web — Christine Vo
Staff Photographer — Daniel J. van Ackere

Vice President Marketing — David Mack
Circulation Director — Doug Wicinski
Circulation & Fulfillment Manager — Carrie Horan
Marketing Assistant — Megan DeFilippo
Partnership Marketing Manager — Pamela Putprush
Direct Mail Director — Adam Perry
Senior Database Analyst — Marina Sakharova
Product Operations Director — Steven Browall
Product Promotions Director — Randi Lawrence
E-Commerce Marketing Director — Hugh Buchan
E-Commerce Marketing Manager — Laurel Zeidman
E-Commerce Search Manager — Elizabeth Dillon
E-Commerce Marketing Coordinator — Tia Freeman
Marketing Copywriter — David Goldberg
Customer Service Manager — Jacqueline Valerio
Customer Service Representatives — Jillian Nannicelli
Kate Sokol
Marketing Intern — Ian Halpern

Sponsorship Sales Director — Marcy McCreary
Retail Sales & Marketing Manager — Emily Logan
Corporate Marketing Associate — Bailey Vatalaro

Production Director — Guy Rochford
Senior Project Manager — Alice Carpenter
Production & Traffic Coordinator — Laura Collins
Senior Production Manager — Jessica L. Quirk
Production & Imaging Specialists — Judy Blomquist
Lauren Pettapiece
Imaging & Color Specialist — Andrew Mannone

Technology Director — Rocco Lombardo
Systems Administrator — S. Paddi McHugh
Web Production Coordinator — Evan Davis
Web Developer — Robert Martinez
Support Technician — Brandon Lynch

Chief Financial Officer — Sharyn Chabot
Human Resources Director — Adele Shapiro
Controller — Mandy Shito
Senior Accountant — Aaron Goranson
Staff Accountant — Connie Forbes
Accounts Payable Specialist — Steven Kasha
Office Manager — Tasha Bere
Receptionist — Henrietta Murray
Publicity — Deborah Broide

For list rental information, contact: Specialists Marketing Services, Inc., 777 Terrace Ave., 4th Floor, Hasbrouck Heights, NJ 07604; 201-865-5800.

Editorial Office: 17 Station St., Brookline, MA 02445; 617-232-1000; fax 617-232-1572. Subscription inquiries, visit www.americas testkitchen.com/customerservice or call 800-526-8442.

Postmaster: Send all new orders, subscription inquiries, and change-of-address notices to Cook's Illustrated, P.O. Box 7446, Red Oak, IA 51591-0446. PRINTED IN THE USA

PUMPKINS Long a staple of Native American diets, pumpkins now serve as both food and decoration. Pik-a-Pies are prized for baking; their rich flesh has classic pumpkin flavor. The red-orange Cinderella is named for the fairy tale princess's carriage. Miniature pumpkins take playful names, like Bumpkins, Lil' Ironsides, Munchkins, and Hooligans, and turn up in autumn arrangements. Jarrahdale pumpkins sport a blue-gray outer shell; their smooth, salmon-colored flesh is used in soups and baked goods. Khaki pumpkins feature orange and green stripes; their seeds are ideal for roasting. The Long Island Cheese, a pumpkin pie favorite, has the same tan coloring as butternut squash. Though edible, Lumina pumpkins are mainly prized for their color: pale yellow to a glowing white. For Halloween décor, the Knuckle Head, or Goosebumps, has bumps that look like warts. The Peanut has a coating that resembles peanut shells.
COVER (*Swiss Chard*): Robert Papp, BACK COVER (*Pumpkins*): John Burgoyne

America's TEST KITCHEN *America's Test Kitchen* is a very real 2,500-square-foot kitchen located just outside of Boston. It is the home of *Cook's Illustrated* and *Cook's Country* magazines and is the workday destination for more than three dozen test cooks, editors, and cookware specialists. Our mission is to test recipes over and over again until we understand how and why they work and until we arrive at the best version. We also test kitchen equipment and supermarket ingredients in search of brands that offer the best value and performance. You can watch us work by tuning in to *America's Test Kitchen* (www.americastestkitchen.com) on public television.

VOTER NUMBER 33

Bunny and Lothar moved to our Vermont town in 1963, becoming the 33rd and 34th voters. They spent $10,000 for a shingled farmhouse built in the 1830s by the Heards just off a grassy track, with no indoor plumbing, heating system, or fireplace, but as Bunny told me, "The house was just waiting for us to arrive." It soon became a true Vermont homestead, made from bits and pieces of other buildings. It was a meeting place of sorts; folks came and went in different configurations, like spare parts that are artfully reassembled. Bunny knew that where you wake up in the morning is not a trifling matter.

They installed a Franklin stove but they didn't split enough wood for the winter, running out by early December. Every week until late spring, Lothar had to chop down a tree on Monday, drag it to the house, and then cut and split it. The wood was so green that the logs stacked in the kitchen ran sap onto the floor, and the creosote buildup in the stovepipe was so thick that every morning, there was a heart-pounding "whoosh" as the accumulated creosote ignited.

Both had lost their parents as young children. Lothar had grown up in an orphanage and Bunny was sent to foster parents after she and her sister almost burned to death, locked inside their house while her mother was busy perched on a barstool at the local watering hole. In the 1950s they lived for a spell in a $5-per-month rental in Mexico, and were pictured in a 1957 issue of *Life* magazine for an article entitled, "Yanks Who Don't Go Home." Lothar was a painter turned sculptor, and their house contained two life-sized pieces featuring his wife as the model: A "Mother and Child" carved out of basswood shows Bunny seated with her son Hasso standing like a naked angel on her thighs, and "Sleeping Woman," fashioned out of mahogany, with Bunny stretched languidly on a bench in the kitchen.

When the well ran dry, they had to fill leaky barrels from the nearby stream, drive hell for leather back to the house, and dump what was still left into the well. Lothar finally dug a hole in the swamp, placed a wooden barrel in it with sand at the bottom through which the water percolated, built a platform and derrick on top, ran a pipe up from the barrel to a sap bucket with a pump to prime the system, and then ran a pipe down to the driveway that filled up an old enameled refrigerator. Then Bunny had to carry pails of water from the makeshift holding tank to the kitchen.

I once asked her if it was a tough life, and she responded, "It wasn't tough; it was just the way it was. It was life." Bunny learned to eat everything from daylilies, butternuts, milkweed (blanch it three times; the first bite tastes like asparagus), to locust tree flowers (add them to pancake batter), and made wine out of daisies, rhubarb, tomatoes, and roses. Her favorite meal, the one she fed weekend guests, was Compost Soup. You start with lentil or pea soup and then just keep adding leftovers — it all just went into the soup pot. When asked for the recipe, she always laughed since it never came out the same way twice.

As for meat, Lothar hunted and finally bagged a buck, field-dressed it, and then dumped it on the kitchen table, expecting Bunny to do the butchering. She said, nonchalantly, that it was just like cutting up a chicken, although she had to borrow a library book to teach herself how to do it. One year they found a raccoon in the basement, drunk on dandelion wine; another time they saw a bear moseying down their hill, curious about Bunny who was busy flying a kite.

When Bunny first moved to town she thought everyone was friendly since they always waved. What she soon learned is that you were not taken seriously until you had made it through at least one hard winter. This was a town where generations of Lombergs, Skidmores, Bentleys, Tudors, Wilcoxes, and Woodcocks had been born and raised, and it took years for her to understand the respect she owed those who had deeper roots. Although the old-timers didn't much like to give advice (Vermonters are wary of being blamed if something goes wrong), they were almost always right. Bunny and Lothar were told never to prune an old pear tree. When they did, it bloomed magnificently the next spring, but, as predicted, it fell over dead a few weeks later. They were

Christopher Kimball

also the butt of practical jokes. One day, Ken Wilcox invited Bunny and Lothar over to see the magnificent view through his telescope. Turns out that the "view" was a naked woman painted on the far end.

The last time I saw Bunny, we sat on her back porch in early spring. The birds had returned and their music was still freshly sung. She pointed out the stone walls that she and Lothar had built over the decades. We both knew that she was dying, and yet Bunny, who had never been scared of life, had no fear of death, either. In our small town, some circles of neighbors rarely overlap, so the two of us had crossed paths only occasionally, rendering our conversation bittersweet. I had, at the very end of her days, come to a stranger's house, one that should have been as familiar as my own back porch.

Two weeks after my spring visit, Bunny was gone, having taken to her bed without food or drink, knowing that her life was now behind her. I have seen many at life's end, but none of them conquered death as well as Bunny. Her sparkling eyes, her lust for life, her nonchalant discussion of where she was to be buried—under a rock above the orchard, next to her beloved Lothar—had lifted a tremendous burden from my middle-aged shoulders. But perhaps that was Bunny's magic all along: to feed others, to make her house a home for visitors, to laugh aloud naked in a hot sauna at midnight, or to serve Compost Soup, making something special out of nothing.

A few days ago, I tracked down a copy of the *Life* magazine article and turned to a full-page photo of Lothar and Bunny in Mexico, bathing in Lake Chapala, hair wet and tangled, surrounded by a vast sea of lily pads. Bunny was young and beautiful, and Lothar, turned to her and smiling, looked every bit the handsome Beat generation artist he was. Today, across the continent and half a century later, our two neighbors are still with us, happy, I suspect, with a damn good view of their children and grandchildren, on a hill above the house that is their eternal home.

FOR INQUIRIES, ORDERS, OR MORE INFORMATION

www.cooksillustrated.com

At www.cooksillustrated.com, you can order books and subscriptions, sign up for our free e-newsletter, or renew your magazine subscription. Join the website and gain access to 16 years of *Cook's Illustrated* recipes, equipment tests, and ingredient tastings, as well as companion videos for every recipe in this issue.

Cookbooks

We sell more than 50 cookbooks by the editors of *Cook's Illustrated*. To order, visit our bookstore at www.cooksillustrated.com.

COOK'S ILLUSTRATED Magazine

Cook's Illustrated magazine (ISSN 1068-2821), number 100, is published bimonthly by Boston Common Press Limited Partnership, 17 Station St., Brookline, MA 02445. Copyright 2009 Boston Common Press Limited Partnership. Periodicals postage paid at Boston, Mass., and additional mailing offices USPS #012487. Publications Mail Agreement No. 40020778. Return undeliverable Canadian addresses to P.O. Box 875, Station A, Windsor, ON N9A 6P2. POSTMASTER: Send address changes to Cook's Illustrated, P.O. Box 7446, Red Oak, IA 51591-0446. For subscription and gift subscription orders, subscription inquiries, or change-of-address notices, visit us at www.americastestkitchen.com/customerservice or write to us at Cook's Illustrated, P.O. Box 7446, Red Oak, IA 51591-0446.

Introducing White Soy

I've recently seen white soy sauce in my grocery store. How does it differ from regular soy sauce, and can it be used in its place?

CAROLE R. HANNA
MEMPHIS, TENN.

➤ Regular soy sauce is typically made from equal amounts of soybeans and wheat, while white soy sauce (which is actually golden) is produced with more wheat than soybeans. To see if the two could be used interchangeably, we purchased our top-ranked soy sauces (Lee Kum Kee Tabletop Soy Sauce for cooked applications and Ohsawa Nama Shoyu Organic Unpasteurized Soy Sauce if used as a condiment) and compared them to white tamari ($6.20 for 300 ml) from the White Soy Sauce Food Company in California. Served over rice, they each had fans among tasters. Some preferred the "sweeter" and more "subtle" flavor of the white sauce and noticed similarities to rice wine, while others favored "richer" regular soy. In a stir-fry (where soy sauce is one ingredient among many) the balance shifted to white soy, while in chicken teriyaki (where soy dominates) tasters overwhelmingly chose the "deep, caramel" flavor of the regular stuff. We contacted the White Soy Sauce Food Company and learned that while regular soy is made by roasting wheat and steaming soybeans prior to fermentation, in white soy it's the reverse: The wheat is steamed and the soybeans are roasted. Then, during fermentation, the starch in the wheat turns to sugar, which explains white soy's sweetness and alcoholic edge.

The bottom line: While we don't recommend using white soy interchangeably with regular soy, it's definitely worth trying as a condiment (a dipping sauce for sushi, for example) and in dishes where soy isn't the primary flavor. It also comes in handy if you want to add soy sauce to a dish without changing its color.

Pricey Oil Pressing

I noticed that expeller-pressed canola oil is more expensive than regular canola oil. What is expeller pressing and is it worth the added expense?

LISA HARTANOV
SPOKANE, WASH.

➤ To understand expeller pressing, it helps to first understand the standard extraction process for canola oil. Manufacturers typically use a chemical called hexane to extract oil from a hybrid version of rapeseed, then remove the chemical with further processing, refine the oil, and bleach it to lighten its color and reduce odors. Expeller pressing, on the other hand, involves a mechanical screw-type press that uses friction and pressure to squeeze the oil out of the seeds. While it isn't as efficient as standard extraction (hence its higher price), the oil undergoes fewer chemical changes. The result, some manufacturers claim, is more natural flavor and less damage to the oil's nutrients.

To see if we could tell these types of oil apart, we bought a bottle of Spectrum's organic expeller-pressed canola oil ($9.99 for 32 ounces) and Wesson canola oil ($3.50 for the same quantity) and used the oils to make stir-fried beef and simple lemon vinaigrette. Both oils produced equally well-browned crusts in the beef with no difference in taste. The expeller-pressed vinaigrette was cloudier than the vinaigrette made with regular canola oil, but again, tasters found they had exactly the same flavor.

Our advice: If you are buying for taste alone, it's not worth spending more for expeller-pressed canola. But if you want to avoid chemical processing, expeller-pressed oil is worth the extra cost.

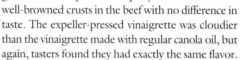

HIGHER PRICE, LESS PROCESSING

"Blooming" Mustard Powder

I've heard that the flavor of mustard powder is improved by mixing it with water and allowing it to sit for a while. Is that correct?

ROBERT VANDERVOORT
PINEHURST, N.C.

➤ Brands of dry mustard powder, including McCormick and Colman's, recommend mixing the powder with water and allowing it to sit for 10 minutes to develop the fullest sharp, tangy flavor. To test this recommendation, we stirred together mustard and water, sampling the mix immediately and at the 10-minute mark. Tasters compared the just-mixed mustard to "cardboard" and "rancid walnuts." But after sitting 10 minutes, it developed heat and well-balanced mustard flavor. Here's why: When mustard seeds are ground into powder, their cells are broken down and the enzymes that contribute to flavor are deactivated, but introducing moisture revives the enzymes and allows them to release pungent aromatic compounds.

We then wondered if we could improve our Classic Macaroni and Cheese (which calls for 1½ teaspoons of mustard powder) by first "blooming" the flavor of the powder in cold water for 10 minutes. The answer was a flat no—in a blind side-by-side tasting, tasters didn't notice any difference between the two batches.

The takeaway: If you're turning your mustard powder into a condiment, mix it with water and wait for the flavor to bloom. In recipes where mustard powder is combined with other ingredients, it's not necessary.

Whole-Wheat Swap

To help make baked goods like muffins and cookies a little healthier, I'm often tempted to swap some of the white flour in the recipes with whole wheat. Is there a rule of thumb for how much whole-wheat flour you can substitute before the texture is affected?

KEVIN ANDERSON
NEW YORK, N.Y.

➤ To answer your question, we made blueberry, bran, and corn muffins with all-purpose flour and compared them to muffins in which we substituted whole-wheat flour in increments of 25 percent, 50 percent, and 75 percent. We also baked chocolate chip, peanut butter, and brown sugar cookies, comparing them to cookies in which we subbed in the same percentages of whole-wheat flour. In every application, most tasters found anything beyond 25 percent whole-wheat flour unappealing. Any more and the muffins and cookies become so tough, dense, and chewy that only the most die-hard whole-wheat enthusiasts gave them a thumbs-up.

Here's what accounts for the textural differences: Whole-wheat flour is ground from the whole berry—the outer bran layer, the germ, and the endosperm (the heart of the wheat berry)—whereas all-purpose flour is ground from just the endosperm. While the germ layer gives whole-wheat flour more protein than all-purpose flour gets from just the endosperm, it does not form gluten. Gluten provides lift and structure to baked goods, so less of it means a denser crumb. Additionally, the germ and bran particles in whole-wheat flour contribute to greater chewiness.

Our conclusion: In recipes calling for all-purpose flour only, don't substitute with more than 25 percent whole-wheat flour or texture will suffer. If you want to bake with more whole-wheat flour, you will need recipes specifically designed for this goal.

LESS WHOLE WHEAT, AIRY CRUMB   **MORE WHOLE WHEAT, DENSE CRUMB**

Rewashing Prewashed Lettuce?

Should bagged prewashed lettuce be washed again before eating?

CHRISTOPHER HUNT
STOUGHTON, MASS.

➤ To kill off bacteria, packagers of prewashed organic and conventional lettuce first rinse the greens with water and then typically spray them with a diluted chlorine solution. Despite these measures, E. coli outbreaks associated with prewashed bagged lettuce and spinach have been reported. Nonetheless, the U.S. Food and Drug Administration and many other food safety experts take the position that prewashed lettuce can be used without further washing. Here's why: Prewashed produce is likely to have fewer bacteria (or none at all) than your kitchen sink or counter, and washing the greens may actually introduce bacteria. (We found this to be the case when we took swabs from prewashed lettuce straight from the bag and swabs from lettuce we "rewashed" in the test kitchen. The rewashed lettuce grew bacteria in a petri dish, while the untouched prewashed greens did not.) Furthermore, according to Trevor Suslow, a microbiologist specializing in food safety research at the University of California, Davis, if pathogens such as E. coli or Salmonella are actually present, rewashing removes very few cells and may actually spread contamination.

CLEAN GREENS

The bottom line: We agree with the experts who say additional washing of ready-to-eat greens is not likely to enhance safety.

Bubbly Beverage Substitution

What is the difference among club soda, seltzer, and sparkling mineral water? Can they be used interchangeably?

KATIE BOOMS
DENVER, COLO.

➤ Club soda and seltzer are both made from water charged with carbon dioxide to give them bubbles. Club soda often contains sodium bicarbonate. In contrast, mineral water gets its more delicate effervescence from naturally occurring springs and, as the name suggests, contains more minerals than the other water types.

To find out whether these three effervescent waters could be used interchangeably, we tasted Polar seltzer, Schweppes club soda, and Perrier mineral water straight up and in our Shrimp Tempura, a dish where the fizz of seltzer plays an important role in the development of an ethereally light batter.

Sipped from the bottle, the seltzer had a neutral taste, the club soda had a slightly acrid bite, and the mineral water had a subtle salty earthiness that tasters preferred for drinking. In the tempura, club soda

and seltzer both made a crisp, perfectly light crust that evenly coated shrimp. Mineral water, however, produced a thin, weakly adhering batter that fried up soggy. We attributed this to the fact that mineral water contains less gas than club soda and seltzer. The higher carbonation in club soda and seltzer makes the batter light and more aerated. It also does a better job inhibiting gluten development—in tempura batter, weaker gluten means a lighter, less bready crust.

Our conclusion: Club soda and seltzer can be used interchangeably in recipes, while sparkling mineral water is better for drinking.

Best Climate for Bread Dough

I've never understood why some bread recipes call for proofing dough at room temperature, while others suggest a warm environment, and still others specify a cold environment like the fridge. Is one approach better than another?

NONA GRACE
REHOBOTH BEACH, DEL.

➤ The surrounding temperature influences the speed at which dough undergoes its final rise before baking, a step known as proofing. To speed the process, many bread recipes (including some of our own) recommend keeping the dough in a warm place. But what effect does proofing temperature have on the quality of the finished bread? To find out, we proofed three batches of rustic Italian bread in three different temperature zones: an oven preheated to 200 degrees and then shut off, a cool spot outside of the kitchen, and the fridge. Proofing at a cool

room temperature (below 72 degrees Fahrenheit) took 2½ hours for the bread to double in size and yielded loaves with a decent brown crust and an even rise. Proofing in the oven took half as long but resulted in loaves with alcoholic aromas, less-browned crusts, and a less-even rise. Proofing in the fridge took nearly 24 hours but produced the best results: loaves with a good rise, complex flavor, darker brown crusts, and chewier, more airy crumbs.

Here's why: As dough proofs, yeast slowly digests sugars present in the flour and produces alcohol and carbon dioxide gas, causing the dough to rise. However, at higher temperatures, enzymes break down gluten (the protein network that gives bread structure), which forces the yeast to work harder and faster to make the bread rise. In this situation, the yeast must digest much more sugar to create enough carbon dioxide to achieve a decent rise, but this also means more alcohol production. These actions affect the final results in rustic loaves composed of just yeast, flour, salt, and water: Less sugar leads to less surface browning, the additional alcohol production creates boozy tang, and the yeast's exertions can result in an uneven rise.

To summarize: Unless speed is of the essence, we recommend proofing at a cool room temperature or—if time permits—in the fridge.

SEND US YOUR QUESTIONS We will provide a complimentary one-year subscription for each letter we print. Send your inquiry, name, address, and daytime telephone number to Notes from Readers, Cook's Illustrated, P.O. Box 470589, Brookline, MA 02447, or to notesfromreaders@americastestkitchen.com.

WHAT IS IT?

I was recently cleaning out my kitchen and discovered this gadget at the back of my utensil drawer. I have no idea what it is. Do you have any insights?

SANDY STEIN
BROOKLYN, N.Y.

➤ It took quite a bit of research, but we eventually discovered that the item you own is a tenderizer for corn on the cob. Patented in 1966 by John Majeske, the plastic utensil has a handle and a spool-shaped roller with small, triangular teeth. According to the patent application, the tenderizer is meant to be rolled along the surface of an ear of cooked corn to break open the skin of the kernels, "thereby rendering the corn not only more flavorful but also more digestible." When we tried out your device (boiling corn, tenderizing it, then slathering it with butter), we immediately spotted a problem: Breaking open the kernels allows flavorful corn milk to escape. The second problem: Tasters didn't care for the slightly mushy texture of the "tenderized" corn. However, they did say it tasted more buttery than ordinary boiled, buttered corn, probably because piercing the kernels created lots of nooks and crannies to soak up the fat. Our conclusion: This device might come in handy to make bland, out-of-season corn taste more buttery—but it isn't necessary for sweet, tender corn that's in season.

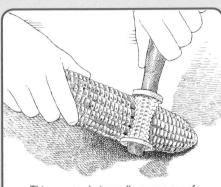

This corn tenderizer rolls over an ear of cooked corn on the cob, piercing the kernels and allowing corn milk to escape.

Quick Tips

⇒ COMPILED BY YVONNE RUPERTI & FRANCISCO J. ROBERT ⇐

An Extra Utensil Rack

Looking for extra space to hang ladles and whisks, Michelle Whalen of Poughkeepsie, N.Y., fastened a cooling rack to the wall. Attaching S-hooks to the rack allows utensils (and cookware) of any size to hang easily.

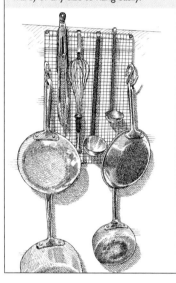

No More Nonstick Scrapes

Julie Jenkins of New York, N.Y., used to grab a metal knife to loosen cakes or muffins from her nonstick pans. However, over time she noticed that the knife was marring the nonstick surface. To prevent scratches, she now uses a plastic "takeout" knife. She stores it in her utensil drawer within easy reach, so she's not tempted to grab something sharp.

Undiluted Fruit Punch

Chilling fruit punch or sangria with ice cubes can water it down. Gloria Saenz of Seguin, Texas, has a clever alternative.

1. Freeze assorted chunks of fruit, such as apple, orange, pineapple, pear, peach, and grapes, on a baking sheet for 1 to 2 hours (depending on the size of the fruit).
2. Add the frozen fruit to the drink. Not only does the fruit help keep the drink cold, it can be eaten at the end.

Easier Fat-Skimming

Skimming fat from a simmering pot of soup or stock often means chasing it around a bubbling surface. To make this task easier, Tom Dube of Somerville, Mass., moves the pot to one side of the burner so that only half has contact with the heat. The simmering bubbles on the heated side push the fat to the cooler side, making it easier to skim.

Avoiding Soggy Fruit

Fresh-cut fruit, especially watermelon, can exude a lot of juice. Left in a bowl, the fruit at the bottom inevitably turns mushy. Rachel Perrone of Washington, D.C., avoids this problem by storing chopped fruit in a salad spinner, where the juice can drain from the spinner's basket into the surrounding bowl. (A strainer set in a bowl also works well.)

Steamed Corn for a Crowd

Kelly McKinney of Broken Arrow, Okla., wanted to steam a large amount of corn but didn't have a big enough pot. Here's the solution she devised.

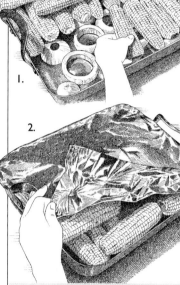

1. Cut 2 medium onions into 1-inch-thick slices, separate them into rings, and arrange them on the bottom of a large roasting pan. Fill the pan with 1 inch of water and place ears of shucked corn on top of the onions. Cover the pan with aluminum foil and seal tightly.
2. Set the pan over two burners and steam over high heat until tender, about 10 minutes.

Safer Skewer Storage

The sharp ends of skewers can be dangerous if left loose in a drawer. Roxanne Tizravesh of Brooklyn, N.Y., found a safe storage solution. She sticks the pointed ends of the skewers into the end of a wine cork (real cork, not plastic), then secures the opposite ends with a twist tie and stores the bundle in the drawer. After use, the skewers easily slip back into the holes.

Sponge on a Rope
Janet Favrot of New Orleans, La., has a handy way to keep track of sponges dedicated to surface cleaning.

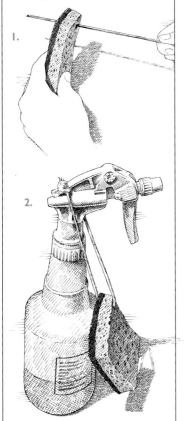

1. Poke a small hole in the sponge.
2. Thread a string through the hole and loop the sponge over the neck of a spray bottle filled with vinegar and water or any cleaning solution.

When a Nip Is All You Need
Some recipes call for just a small amount of alcohol. Rather than buying large bottles of liquor, which can be expensive and take up storage space, Joe Wirtz of Traverse City, Mich., buys nip-sized bottles. They usually contain 50 ml, about 3.38 tablespoons each.

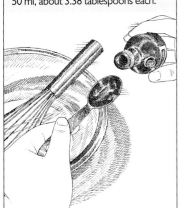

Make Your Own Kitchen Scrapers
A flexible plastic scraper is useful for scraping dough from bowls or scooping chopped vegetables for transfer from cutting board to pan. Sandy Nason of Logansport, Ind., found that many scrapers were not as flexible as she wanted and decided to make her own.

1. Draw a line along the edge of a plastic lid, such as one from a cottage cheese container, and cut along the line, leaving one-third of the edge intact for stability.
2. Use this homemade tool as you would a store-bought plastic scraper.

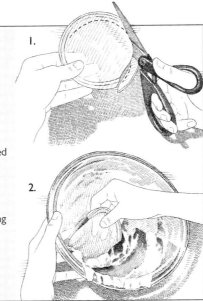

Cookbook Page Protectors
To protect her cookbooks from cooking splatter, Bonnie McKinlay of Portland, Ore., shields open pages with heavy-duty clear protector sheets, which are available at any office store. Two taped-together sheets fit neatly over an open cookbook. This cover can be wiped clean with a damp cloth and reused.

Parchment Paper Substitute
Leaya Chang of New York, N.Y., was about to bake a cake when she realized that she didn't have any parchment paper to line the bottom of the pan. After a quick look around her kitchen, she decided to try using a large (8- to 10-cup) basket-style paper coffee filter. She greased an 8-inch cake pan, placed the flattened filter in the bottom of the pan, sprayed it with nonstick cooking spray, and poured in the cake batter. It worked perfectly, without any special trimming to make the coffee filter fit inside the pan.

Warming Coffee Mugs
When you pour hot coffee into a cold mug, the mug absorbs heat, making the coffee cool down faster. To keep his coffee hot longer, Philip Carey of Nashville, Tenn., preheats the mug by filling it with hot tap water and letting it sit while the coffee brews. When the coffee is ready, he pours out the hot water.

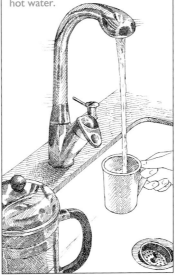

Another Way to Peel Beets
Kassandra Calderon of Peach City, Ga., loves eating beets but hates the stains they leave behind. To keep her hands stain-free, she grasps the cooked (and slightly cooled) beets with a plastic bag, such as one used for produce. Then, working from the outside of the bag, she rubs the skins right off.

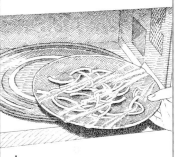

Sweeter Onions
Diane Farrell of Mount Carroll, Ill., enjoys onions in her salads but finds their flavor harsh when raw. She tempers them with the following method.

1. Place the onion slices on a microwave-safe plate, cover with plastic wrap, and microwave on high power for 15 to 30 seconds.
2. Once they're cool, toss the mellowed onions into your salad.

Steak Tips with Mushroom Gravy

To rescue this typically sorry combination of chewy meat and flavorless gravy, we chose a beefy cut and stopped washing the pan.

⇒ BY KEITH DRESSER ⇐

Steak tips smothered in mushroom and onion gravy is a classic combination, appearing on menus at pubs and family-style restaurants across the country. This dish always beckons with its promise of juicy meat and hearty, satisfying flavors—but often it's nothing more than chewy, overcooked beef swimming in either a thin, generic brown sauce or a thick sludge of bland gravy. When I researched recipes for the dish, I quickly realized why this meal is often disappointing. It usually calls for small, easily overcooked strips of beef and flavor-sacrificing shortcuts like canned cream of mushroom soup, dried onion soup mix, or ketchup. It wasn't hard to envision a much better rendition, one that featured tender, meaty pieces of steak covered in a sauce enriched by the essence of fresh mushrooms and onions. If I could figure out an efficient way to coax full flavor from these simple ingredients— ideally using only one pan—I'd have a great addition to my weeknight repertoire.

For best results, cut 1½-inch chunks from a whole steak.

One-Skillet Method

Before I got into specific ingredients, I needed to develop a basic framework for the recipe. After some initial tests, I found it was indeed possible to cook the entire dish in one skillet, first searing the beef and setting it aside, then building the gravy, and finally adding the meat back to the gravy to cook through. Besides convenience, this method offered two key advantages: First, the initial sear left my skillet full of the crusty browned bits known as *fond*, which provided a flavorful base for the sauce. Second, adding the partially cooked beef to the gravy and simmering until it cooked through allowed the flavors to mingle and build depth.

The next task was finding the right beef for the job. Though you occasionally find the dish made with tender, richly flavored, expensive cuts like strip steak, rib-eye steak, and tenderloin, I didn't want to pay top dollar for a midweek meal—and why drown prime beef in sauce? I turned instead to cheaper cuts: flank steak, round steak, and, of course, the most common choice, sirloin steak tips (also known as flap meat), cut from the sirloin area between the cow's short loin and back legs. This beefy cut has a wealth of internal marbling that melted into the coarse muscle fibers of the steak, adding tenderness when the meat was cooked to medium-rare. Flank steak made a suitable substitute if steak tips were unavailable but wasn't nearly as meaty-tasting, while round steak lacked intramuscular fat, easily turning bland, dry, and chalky after simmering in the gravy. Steak tips were ideal for this dish after all.

When it came time to prepare the steak, I wanted to develop a flavorful, well-seared crust yet leave the interior slightly underdone, so it wouldn't turn chewy and tough when I returned it to the pan to simmer with the gravy. I experimented with cutting the meat into various sizes to see which pieces cooked best and eventually settled on 1½-inch chunks. These gave me plenty of surface area to brown in a reasonable amount of time (six to eight minutes) and were large enough that they didn't overcook in the sauce. To promote browning and a good, flavorful crust on the meat, I sprinkled the pieces with a little sugar before searing. These steak tips tasted pretty darn good, but could I get them even juicier?

One of the test kitchen's proven methods for beefing up steak flavor and juiciness is a quick soak in soy sauce. (The salty soy draws juices out of the steak, and then the reverse happens as the soy, along with the moisture, flows back in, bringing deep flavor into the meat.) Adding the sugar to the soy sauce instead of sprinkling it on separately bolstered flavor even more. After its 30-minute soak in the sugar-soy mixture and a quick sear, I produced the beefiest steak yet, with a substantial crust and plenty of fond left behind. With a rich flavor base now encrusting the pan, I figured the rest would be gravy.

Triple Fond, Triple Flavor

Up to this point, I had been adding a little vegetable oil to the pan and starting my sauce with half a pound of sliced white mushrooms. The flavor proved more mild than meaty, so I tried increasing the amount of mushrooms. Although I found I could cook up to a pound in one batch, the flavor was still lacking. Costlier creminis and portobellos were incrementally more earthy, but unfortunately tasters also found the portobellos leathery. Plus, unless

I scooped out their black gills (a tedious process), the portobellos left the gravy unappealingly gray and murky. Looking beyond fresh mushrooms, I tried adding ¼ ounce of dried porcinis (hydrated in some beef broth) to the pan along with the white mushrooms. While their texture was only subtly perceptible, the porcinis contributed the intense mushroom flavor I was looking for.

My next consideration was the liquid component of the sauce. Homemade stock was out of the question; this was a weeknight meal, after all. Instead, I was making do with canned beef broth—a beefy but mild alternative—so I decided to try adding some of the usual suspects to boost flavor: Worcestershire sauce, tomato paste, red wine, and more soy sauce. Tasters felt lukewarm about each addition, telling me that instead of enhancing meatiness, these ingredients actually overpowered it.

Then I stumbled upon a better way to boost the gravy's flavor. To cook the mushrooms in the same pan that I used to cook the beef, I needed to make sure they released moisture quickly enough to dissolve the flavorful fond before it burned. Lightly salting the sliced mushrooms immediately after placing them in the pan helped break down their cell walls and set their juices flowing more quickly than heat alone. Once the mushrooms had "deglazed" the pan and started to brown, I added a thinly sliced onion and more salt to the skillet (to expedite the onion's release of moisture) and waited until the vegetables were deeply browned, their liquid had cooked off, and even more browned bits clung to the pan. I now had a triple-header for flavor: a classic meat fond compounded by two layers of vegetable fond.

Stirring cornstarch into the skillet seemed like an easy way to thicken the broth into gravy, but it created a gelatinous sauce that reminded tasters of a bad beef stir-fry. Sprinkling flour over the mushrooms as they sautéed was equally simple but much more effective in creating a rich, lump-free gravy. As a finishing touch, I added a minced garlic clove and ½ teaspoon of chopped thyme, which accented the woodsy flavor of the mushrooms nicely.

After making a final batch and gently simmering the meat and gravy together for five minutes to meld their flavors without overcooking the beef, tasters told me I was done. I took a few bites and agreed: My homemade steak tips were better—far better—than anything I'd ever been served in a pub.

STEAK TIPS WITH MUSHROOM-ONION GRAVY
SERVES 4 TO 6

NOTE: Steak tips, also known as flap meat, are sold as whole steak, cubes, and strips. To ensure evenly sized chunks, we prefer to purchase whole steak tips and cut them ourselves. If you can only find cubes or strips, reduce the cooking time slightly to avoid overcooking any smaller or thinner pieces. Cremini mushrooms can be used in place of the white mushrooms. Our preferred brand of beef broth is Pacific. Serve over rice or egg noodles.

- 1 tablespoon soy sauce
- 1 teaspoon sugar
- 1½ pounds sirloin steak tips, trimmed of excess fat and cut into 1½-inch chunks (see note)
- ¼ ounce dried porcini mushrooms, rinsed well
- 1¾ cups low-sodium beef broth (see note)
  Table salt and ground black pepper
- 2 tablespoons vegetable oil
- 1 pound white mushrooms, stems trimmed, caps wiped clean and cut into ¼-inch slices (see note)
- 1 large onion, halved and sliced thin (about 1½ cups)
- 1 medium garlic clove, minced or pressed through garlic press (about 1 teaspoon)
- ½ teaspoon minced fresh thyme leaves
- 4 teaspoons unbleached all-purpose flour
- 1 tablespoon chopped fresh parsley leaves

1. Combine soy sauce and sugar in medium bowl. Add beef, toss well, and marinate at least 30 minutes or up to 1 hour, tossing once.

2. Meanwhile, cover porcini mushrooms with ¼ cup broth in small microwave-safe bowl; cover with plastic wrap, cut several steam vents in plastic with paring knife, and microwave on high power 30 seconds. Let stand until mushrooms soften, about 5 minutes. Lift mushrooms from liquid with fork and mince (you should have about 1½ tablespoons). Strain liquid through fine-mesh strainer lined with paper towel into medium bowl. Set mushrooms and liquid aside.

3. Sprinkle meat with ½ teaspoon pepper. Heat 1 tablespoon oil in 12-inch skillet over medium-high heat until smoking. Add meat and cook until well browned on all sides, 6 to 8 minutes. Transfer to large plate and set aside.

4. Return skillet to medium-high heat and add remaining tablespoon oil, white mushrooms, minced porcinis, and ¼ teaspoon salt; cook, stirring frequently, until all liquid has evaporated and mushrooms start to brown, 7 to 9 minutes. Scrape pan to loosen fond. Add onion and ¼ teaspoon salt; continue to cook, stirring frequently, until onion begins to brown and dark bits form on pan bottom, 6 to 8 minutes longer. Add garlic, thyme, and flour; cook, stirring constantly, until vegetables are coated with flour, about 1 minute. Stir in remaining 1½ cups beef broth and porcini soaking liquid, scraping bottom of pan with wooden spoon to loosen browned bits, and bring to boil.

5. Nestle steak pieces into mushroom and onion mixture and add any accumulated juices to skillet. Reduce heat to medium-low and simmer until steak registers 130 degrees on instant-read thermometer, 3 to 5 minutes, turning beef over several times. Season with salt and pepper, sprinkle with parsley, and serve.

🎥 **COOK'S VIDEOS** Original Test Kitchen Videos
www.cooksillustrated.com/oct09
HOW TO MAKE
• Steak Tips with Mushroom-Onion Gravy
VIDEO TIPS
• Supermarket Mushrooms 101
• What are steak tips?

RECIPE DIAGNOSIS **Steak Mistakes**

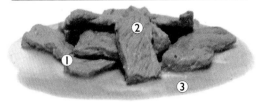

1. PETITE PIECES
Beef cut into thin, too-small pieces results in dry, tough meat drowning in sauce.

2. LEAN MEAT
Lean cuts, such as round steak, turn leathery instead of tender.

3. BLAND GRAVY
Sauce made from processed ingredients such as canned cream of mushroom soup or ketchup has muffled meaty flavor with a bland, one-dimensional taste.

AT-A-GLANCE | KEYS TO RICH, HEARTY STEAK TIPS WITH GRAVY

1. MARINATE MEAT
Soaking steak tips in soy sauce and sugar boosts meaty flavor and browning.

2. CREATE MEAT FOND
Searing steak tips creates flavorful browned bits (fond) that serve as base for rich gravy.

3. BUILD MORE FOND
Cooking mushrooms, then onions, until deeply caramelized in unwashed pan allows each to form extra layer of flavorful fond.

Introducing Austrian Potato Salad

For potato salad that's both creamy and light, do as the Austrians do: Ditch the mayo and look to the soup pot.

≩ BY J. KENJI ALT ≨

Wiener schnitzel (veal cutlets pounded thin, breaded, and fried) is undoubtedly Austria's greatest claim to culinary fame. But another dish deserves to share this status: *erdäpfelsalat*, or potato salad. In Austria, schnitzel is almost never without this creamy but light accompaniment. Unlike mayonnaise-based American or bacon-studded German renditions, Austrian potato salad (served warm or at room temperature) uses comparatively little fat. Instead, it calls on the help of the starch from the potatoes along with an unexpected ingredient—broth—to create a luxuriously thick, velvety dressing. The broth (usually chicken or veal) lends complexity without adding too much richness or a meaty presence. Meanwhile, the potatoes are sturdy enough that they maintain their shape, yet soft enough that they practically melt in your mouth.

Most of the recipes I found went something like this: Boil whole potatoes (typically a somewhat starchy Austrian fingerling variety known as crescent) in their jackets, then peel and slice them. Toss in a dressing made of white wine vinegar, vegetable oil (preferred over olive oil for its more neutral flavor), chicken stock, onions, pickles, herbs, and a little sugar and salt until the starch from the potato turns the dressing creamy.

But the proper luxurious consistency for both potatoes and sauce was not so easy to achieve, as my first few attempts demonstrated. If I cooked the potatoes for too long, they disintegrated when I added the dressing, turning the mix into a kind of loose mash. Undercooking them meant the spuds couldn't work their thickening magic on the sauce, leaving it soupy instead of creamy. And then there was the issue of stirring: Too much can turn the potatoes gluey. Was there a reliable way to defeat these problems?

Proper Potato Treatment

First, I would need to find a more widely available potato than the crescent fingerling. Earthy-flavored russets were out; their low moisture and abundant starch made it all too easy for the salad to devolve into a mash. Waxy reds didn't

Starch from the potatoes—instead of mayonnaise—is the key to this potato salad's creamy dressing.

have enough starch and left the sauce thin. Buttery Yukon Golds were my best bet: They had just enough starch to contribute creaminess to the salad without breaking up too readily.

Though many recipes called for cooking the potatoes in their skins to improve flavor, I found it made very little difference—and definitely not enough to warrant burning our fingers by peeling two pounds

of them hot. Boiled whole, small fingerling potatoes cook quickly and evenly, but Yukon Golds are a different story. By the time their centers are tender, the exteriors are irretrievably overcooked. Cutting them into pieces before cooking was the only way to go. Now, what to do about getting them to just the right degree of tenderness every time?

Here's a potato under a microscope: Individual plant cells are filled with starch and glued together with pectin. As a potato cooks, two things happen. The pectin weakens and cells begin to burst, releasing their starch. What I needed was a way to release enough starch to thicken the sauce, but at the same time prevent the pectin from weakening so much that the potatoes fall apart. I knew that pectin breakdown is inhibited in acidic environments. (For example, we've found that naturally acidic apples such as Granny Smiths are more likely than other varieties to hold their shape when cooked.) Perhaps adding acid in the form of vinegar to the cooking water would help keep the potatoes' structure intact? Once I got the amount right, vinegar worked beautifully (see "Spuds Gone Sour" on page 9), allowing the potatoes to stay firm for several minutes after they softened and making it far easier to avoid overcooking.

Adding vinegar to the cooking water had another effect: It penetrated the potatoes as they cooked, deepening the tanginess of the finished dish. This gave me an idea: Since my dressing was primarily liquid, why not use it instead of plain water to cook the potatoes to allow more flavors to be absorbed?

AT-A-GLANCE | SECRETS TO LIGHT, CREAMY POTATO SALAD

1. COOK IN BROTH
Chicken broth adds more flavor than boiling water.

2. REDUCE LIQUID
Concentrated cooking liquid forms base for dressing.

3. MASH SOME SPUDS
Small amount of mashed potatoes thickens dressing.

4. STIR INTO REMAINDER
Mashed and intact potatoes create unique consistency.

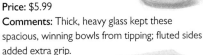

Rather than submerging the potatoes in a large pot of water, I put 2 pounds of peeled, chopped potatoes in a 12-inch skillet and simmered them in 1 cup each chicken stock and water (so that the reduced liquid would not taste overly chicken-y), 2 tablespoons of vinegar, and a little sugar and salt. To prevent the tops of the potatoes from drying out, I covered the skillet. After 15 minutes, when the potatoes started turning tender, I removed the lid and turned up the heat to high to reduce the cooking liquid and intensify its flavors. Once the potatoes were cooked, I drained the liquid, reserving a half cup to mix in with the remaining dressing ingredients.

I'd struck gold: This new method allowed the potatoes to absorb the flavor of the chicken broth, vinegar, and sugar for a much more deeply flavored salad. Not only that, cooking the potatoes in a shallow pan at a bare simmer made them extremely easy to monitor, further ensuring that overcooking was a thing of the past.

COOK'S VIDEOS Original Test Kitchen Videos
www.cooksillustrated.com/oct09
HOW TO MAKE
• Austrian-Style Potato Salad
VIDEO TIP
• How to mince chives

Mash Up

With this new cooking method, I was almost there, but there was still one area of inconsistency: the amount of starch released by stirring. Even with perfectly cooked potatoes, if I stirred too much, an excess of starch made it into the mix, turning the potatoes from creamy to gluey. For foolproof results, I needed to ensure that the same amount of starch was released from the spuds each time. But how, exactly? Then it struck me: Instead of trying to control how much starch I released from a whole batch of potatoes, why not just home in on a few of them? I cooked up a new batch of potatoes and removed ½ cup of them, which I mashed into the ½ cup of reserved cooking liquid until the mixture turned thick and creamy. I then gently folded in the remaining potatoes. Bingo! This allowed me to create a sauce that was virtually identical from batch to batch.

All that was left was to finesse the flavorings. Austrian cooks incorporate a style of lightly pickled cucumber known as *sauergurken* that requires a trip to a specialty store—if they're available at all. I tried a range of pickles from the supermarket, finding that bread and butter, sweet gherkins, and relish added a cloying sweetness to the salad that tasters didn't like. Kosher dills were an acceptable substitute, but the best replacement was cornichons. This small French variety can be a little tough to track down, but its sharp, salty flavor made the effort worthwhile. Mild sweetness and crunch gave red onion the edge over yellow onion or shallots, Dijon mustard added pungency, and a few tablespoons of chopped chives finished the dish.

With such light, flavorful, foolproof results, this potato salad was definitely a winner. I might make a batch especially to serve with schnitzel—but in the meantime, it's also a perfect accompaniment to grilled meats and fish.

AUSTRIAN-STYLE POTATO SALAD
SERVES 4 TO 6

NOTE: The finished salad should be creamy and loose, with chunks of potato that keep their shape but are very tender. If you can't find cornichons, chopped kosher dill pickles can be used in their place. To maintain its consistency, don't refrigerate the salad; it should be served within 4 hours of preparation.

2	pounds Yukon Gold potatoes (about 4 large), peeled, quartered lengthwise, and cut into ½-inch-thick slices
1	cup low-sodium chicken broth
1	cup water
	Table salt
1	tablespoon sugar
2	tablespoons white wine vinegar
1	tablespoon Dijon mustard
¼	cup vegetable oil
1	small red onion, chopped fine (about ¾ cup)
6	cornichons, minced (about 2 tablespoons) (see note)
2	tablespoons minced fresh chives
	Ground black pepper

1. Bring potatoes, broth, water, 1 teaspoon salt, sugar, and 1 tablespoon vinegar to boil in 12-inch heavy-bottomed skillet over high heat. Reduce heat to medium-low, cover, and cook until potatoes offer no resistance when pierced with paring knife, 15 to 17 minutes. Remove cover, increase heat to high (so cooking liquid will reduce), and cook 2 minutes.

2. Drain potatoes in colander set over large bowl, reserving cooking liquid. Set drained potatoes aside. Pour off and discard all but ½ cup cooking liquid (if ½ cup liquid does not remain, add water to make ½ cup). Whisk remaining tablespoon vinegar, mustard, and oil into cooking liquid.

3. Add ½ cup cooked potatoes to bowl with cooking liquid mixture and mash with potato masher or fork until thick sauce forms (mixture will be slightly chunky). Add remaining potatoes, onion, cornichons, and chives, folding gently with rubber spatula to combine. Season to taste with salt and black pepper. Serve warm or at room temperature.

Rethinking Sunday Gravy

This over-the-top Italian-American tomato sauce typically calls for six cuts of meat and a day at the stove. We wanted the same flavor with a lot less work.

⋟ BY BRYAN ROOF ⋞

The Italian-American classic known as Sunday gravy is not just a dish, it's a feast. Bowls of lightly sauced pasta and slow-cooked tomato sauce are served alongside platters of meat that have been braised for hours in this gravy. These can include ribs, meatballs, pork shoulder, hot and sweet sausages, and the dish's typical crowning glory: *braciole*, the stuffed, rolled Italian beef that's a meal on its own. Why such extravagance? Italians who immigrated to the United States in the late 19th and early 20th centuries found meat far more abundant and affordable here than in their home country. Sunday gravy became a weekly celebration of this good fortune.

Even today, Italian grandmothers famously spend the better part of a day preparing Sunday gravy. After trying a handful of these all-day cooking productions, I couldn't help but be impressed by the sheer plenitude of the dish and the richness of the long-simmered sauce. But I also had to wonder: Was so much time and effort—and meat—really necessary? My goal: A full-flavored meal on the table in less than four hours (with no more than an hour of hands-on cooking).

Meat of the Matter

In the classic, no-holds-barred recipes, you first mix and shape the meatballs and make the beef braciole. Then you brown these and the sausages, ribs, and pork shoulder in separate batches, removing each when they're done. Next, you sauté flavorings like onions, oregano, and garlic in the same pan, scraping off the crusty, browned bits of meat on the bottom (the fond) to add flavor to the sauce. Tomatoes go in, and the meats return to simmer until tender—sometimes for a few hours, often for much longer. Just before serving, the meats get transferred to a platter and a little sauce is stirred into the pasta, with the remaining sauce passed separately.

With six types of meat, the browning alone took 40 minutes. As my first step toward making the dish more manageable, I decided to limit myself to just one kind of sausage and one cut of pork. The sausage decision was easy: Tasters preferred the mild kick that hot Italian links gave to the sauce over the predominantly fennel taste of the sweet sausage. As for pork, I tried neck bones, butt, pork chops, and all manner of ribs—country-style ribs, spareribs, and baby back ribs. Baby back ribs were our favorite;

We kept our sauce to just three meats: pork ribs, sausage, and meatballs.

unlike other cuts, they weren't too fatty and turned moist and tender in just a few hours. Even better, the bones added richness to the sauce.

Next, I turned my attention to the braciole. After making several versions, all following the same laborious approach (pound lean steaks cut from a top round roast; fill with a stuffing of Pecorino Romano, prosciutto, and herbs; roll and tie with twine; brown and simmer), the same issue kept cropping up.

Tasters loved the beefy flavor it brought to the sauce and the sharp, salty taste of the filling, but the lean cut always turned out a little dry, even when I took care not to cook it too long in the sauce. With a little tinkering, I was sure I could fix the problem. But did I really need to?

If I could nail down an approach to truly standout meatballs, maybe they could serve as the meal's centerpiece, instead of the fussier braciole. I had a head start with a proven technique from the test kitchen: Instead of plain ground beef, we like to use a mixture of ground beef and pork. Meatloaf mix, a combination of ground beef, pork, and veal, produced even juicier results. Following our approach, I then incorporated a panade (or binder) made of bread and buttermilk to ensure tenderness and add subtle tangy flavor. Minced garlic, parsley, and red pepper flakes, plus an egg yolk for richness, boosted flavor even further. There was just one problem: The meatballs became lopsided from sticking to the bottom of the Dutch oven and so tender that they broke apart at the end of the long simmer. I easily solved this by browning them separately in a nonstick skillet, then adding them to the sauce in the last 15 minutes of cooking.

With such moist, richly flavored meatballs, tasters weren't clamoring for the braciole to go back in—but what they did miss were the distinctive flavors of its filling. A new thought occurred to me: Why not simply incorporate some of those same ingredients into my meatballs? When I added a couple of ounces of finely

---

Not Your Nonna's Gravy

By choosing our ingredients carefully, we created a sauce with almost the same flavor as the more time-consuming traditional approach.

RIGHT RIB
These baby back pork ribs turn tender after just 2½ hours of cooking; the bones enrich the sauce.

MISSING LINK
Who needs sweet Italian sausage when you've got the mild kick of these spicy links?

MORE THAN A MEATBALL
Prosciutto and Pecorino Romano give our meatballs authentic flavor.

BEEFY BOOSTER
Though unconventional, a touch of beef broth reinforces the meatiness of the sauce.

chopped prosciutto and a half cup of Pecorino Romano to the ground meat along with the other flavorings, it led to a sauce that tasted surprisingly close to the gravy made with bona fide stuffed beef—with far less work.

Beefing Up the Sauce

With my meats settled, I could now move on to perfecting the sauce. As a benchmark, I compared a sauce simmered for four hours with the full spectrum of Sunday gravy meats to my pared-down working recipe (simmered for just 2½ hours—the time it took for the ribs to become tender). While the difference wasn't huge, tasters found that the classic sauce did have deeper, meatier flavor.

Before finessing flavor, I first had some streamlining to do. Up to this point, I had been using whole canned tomatoes and pureeing them in a blender before adding them to the pan with tomato paste, as called for in the better recipes I found in my research. To get around this step, substituting tomato puree wasn't an option; it added an unwelcome cooked flavor to the sauce. As we found in our recent recipe for Quick Tomato Sauce (May/June 2009), crushed tomatoes were a winner, producing a sauce with nice thickness and body. Our favorite brands, Tuttorosso and Muir Glen, boast bright tomato flavor, thanks in part to minimal processing.

As an easy first step toward building more complexity, I sautéed the onions until they were just beginning to brown. I also experimented with a technique that a colleague recommended for intensifying the flavor of tomato paste: Instead of merely browning the tomato paste for 30 seconds, I cooked it until it nearly blackened, which concentrated its sweetness. Though in Italy meat sauces aren't known for assertive garlic flavor, tasters appreciated the added intensity brought on by four cloves of minced garlic.

So far, so good, but what could I do to inject more meaty flavor? Without braciole—and the meatballs added at the end—my sauce was benefiting only from the juices of the sausages and ribs. I experimented with some of the usual suspects, including soy sauce and Marmite, a flavor enhancer made from yeast extract. The best booster turned out to be the simple, straightforward addition of an ingredient rarely found in tomato sauce: beef broth. Just ⅔ cup added a rich depth that the sauce had lacked.

One last tweak: Instead of simmering the meat and the sauce together on the stovetop, which requires constant monitoring, I covered the Dutch oven and transferred it to the even heat of a 325-degree oven, where I could leave it unattended for most of the cooking time.

Three and a half hours after first setting foot in the kitchen, I had a sauce to rival any Italian

🎥 **COOK'S VIDEOS** Original Test Kitchen Videos
www.cooksillustrated.com/oct09
HOW TO MAKE
• Hearty Italian Meat Sauce (Sunday Gravy)
VIDEO TIP
• Which pork ribs should I use?

grandmother's Sunday gravy, and a feast I'd be proud to invite family and friends to share.

HEARTY ITALIAN MEAT SAUCE (SUNDAY GRAVY)
SERVES 8 TO 10

NOTE: We prefer meatloaf mix (a combination of ground beef, pork, and veal) for the meatballs in this recipe. Ground beef may be substituted, but the meatballs won't be as flavorful. Six tablespoons of plain yogurt thinned with 2 tablespoons of milk can be substituted for the buttermilk. This recipe makes enough to sauce 1½ pounds of pasta. Our preferred brands of crushed tomatoes are Tuttorosso and Muir Glen. The sauce can be prepared through step 4 and then cooled and refrigerated in the Dutch oven for up to 2 days. To reheat, drizzle ½ cup of water over the sauce (do not stir in) and warm on the lower-middle rack of a preheated 325-degree oven for 1 hour before proceeding with the recipe.

Sauce
- 2 tablespoons olive oil
- 1 rack (about 2¼ pounds) baby back ribs, cut into 2-rib sections
  Table salt and ground black pepper
- 1 pound hot Italian sausage links
- 2 medium onions, chopped fine (about 2 cups)
- 1¼ teaspoons dried oregano
- 3 tablespoons tomato paste
- 4 medium garlic cloves, minced or pressed through garlic press (about 4 teaspoons)
- 2 (28-ounce) cans crushed tomatoes (see note)
- ⅔ cup beef broth
- ¼ cup chopped fresh basil leaves

Meatballs
- 2 slices hearty white sandwich bread, crusts removed and bread cut into ½-inch cubes
- ½ cup buttermilk (see note)
- ¼ cup chopped fresh parsley leaves
- 2 medium garlic cloves, minced or pressed through garlic press (about 2 teaspoons)
- 1 large egg yolk
- ½ teaspoon table salt
- ¼ teaspoon crushed red pepper flakes
- 1 pound meatloaf mix (see note)
- 2 ounces thinly sliced prosciutto, chopped fine
- 1 ounce Pecorino Romano cheese, grated (about ½ cup)
- ½ cup olive oil

- 1½ pounds spaghetti or linguine
- 2 tablespoons table salt
  Grated Parmesan cheese for serving

1. **FOR THE SAUCE:** Adjust oven rack to lower-middle position and heat oven to 325 degrees. Heat oil in large Dutch oven over medium-high heat until just smoking. Pat ribs dry with paper towels and

Cooking the tomato paste until nearly blackened concentrates its sweetness and adds complexity to the sauce.

season with salt and pepper. Add half of ribs to pot and brown on both sides, 5 to 7 minutes total. Transfer ribs to large plate and brown remaining ribs. After transferring second batch of ribs to plate, brown sausages on all sides, 5 to 7 minutes total. Transfer sausages to plate with ribs.

2. Reduce heat to medium, add onions and oregano; cook, stirring occasionally, until beginning to brown, about 5 minutes. Add tomato paste and cook, stirring constantly, until very dark, about 3 minutes. Stir in garlic and cook until fragrant, about 30 seconds. Add crushed tomatoes and broth, scraping up any browned bits. Return ribs and sausage to pot; bring to simmer, cover, and transfer to oven. Cook until ribs are tender, about 2½ hours.

3. **FOR THE MEATBALLS:** Meanwhile, combine bread cubes, buttermilk, parsley, garlic, egg yolk, salt, and red pepper flakes in medium bowl and mash with fork until no bread chunks remain. Add meatloaf mix, prosciutto, and cheese to bread mixture; mix with hands until thoroughly combined. Divide mixture into 12 pieces; roll into balls, transfer to plate, cover with plastic, and refrigerate until ready to use.

4. When sauce is 30 minutes from being done, heat oil in large nonstick skillet over medium-high heat until shimmering. Add meatballs and cook until well browned all over, 5 to 7 minutes. Transfer meatballs to paper towel–lined plate to drain briefly. Remove sauce from oven and skim fat from top with large spoon. Transfer browned meatballs to sauce and gently submerge. Cover, return pot to oven, and continue cooking until meatballs are just cooked through, about 15 minutes.

5. Meanwhile, bring 6 quarts water to boil in large pot. Add pasta and salt and cook until al dente. Reserve ½ cup cooking water; drain pasta and transfer back to cooking pot.

6. **TO SERVE:** Using tongs, transfer meatballs, ribs, and sausage to serving platter and cut sausages in half. Stir basil into sauce and adjust seasoning with salt and pepper. Toss pasta with 1 cup sauce and reserved pasta cooking water so that sauce lightly coats pasta. Serve pasta, passing remaining sauce and meat platter separately.

Updating Chicken and Dumplings

A stew as thick and heavy as pot-pie filling was fine for our forebears. Our goal:
a lighter broth and dumplings that wouldn't sink to the bottom of the pot.

⇒ BY FRANCISCO J. ROBERT ⇐

Chicken and dumplings is as classic as American food gets: Cooks in this country have been making the dish since the colonists arrived at Jamestown in the early 17th century. Over time, the dish has taken on distinct regional differences: Northerners typically like their broth thick and their dumplings fluffy, while down South the broth is usually more soup-like, with flat, square dumplings. Regional variances aside, a general rule applies to the chicken: The more mature the bird, the better the flavor. Generations ago, an egg hen or rooster several years old would be simmered for four or even six hours until falling off the bone, producing a rich broth. The simple addition of dumplings turned the broth into a flavorful, thrifty meal.

Chickens sold in supermarkets today are usually no more than seven weeks old. By comparing these young fowl in traditional recipes calling for hours of stewing with modern ones that simmer the birds for under an hour, I proved conventional wisdom right: No matter how long you cook them, whole young chickens yield unimpressive broth. To coax old-fashioned, full flavor from supermarket birds—and create dumplings that would please both northern and southern palates—it was time for some modern adjustments.

Our stew boasts dumplings as airy as drop biscuits in a broth full of clean, concentrated chicken flavor.

INGREDIENTS Best Parts for Broth

NATURAL THICKENER
The multiple joints in chicken wings contain lots of collagen that converts into gelatin during cooking—a better broth thickener than flour, which masks chicken flavor.

WINGS

FULL O' FLAVOR
Pound for pound, chicken thighs impart richer flavor to broth than any other part of the bird. Plus, they require far less cooking time than eking the flavor out of a whole bird or carcass.

THIGHS

Stock Answers

Great chicken broth needs two things: flavor and body. Without a mature chicken for my broth, my first task was figuring out if a particular part of a younger bird would produce a flavorful broth. To this end, I made a series of broths with thighs, drumsticks, and breasts, both skin-on and skin-off, simmering a pound of each in a quart of water for 45 minutes. With or without skin, the stock made with just white meat was thin and flavorless, the meat dry and bland. Drumsticks produced richer broth with meat that was less dried out, but the skin-on thighs were a clear winner, with the most deeply flavored broth of the lot and meat that stayed tender.

To further boost flavor, I implemented a few tricks the test kitchen has used with success. First trick: Replace water with canned broth. Though canned broth can taste thin and metallic on its own, when cooked with real chicken parts, it turns decidedly richer, and its tinny flavor is no longer detectable. Second trick: Brown the meat before adding the liquid. As the skin crisps, the Maillard

reaction kicks in, creating hundreds of new, complex flavors. Finally, trick three: Finesse the flavor by browning aromatic vegetables in the browned bits from the seared chicken and adding alcohol. Browning chopped carrots, celery, and onions until caramelized introduces sweetness, while ¼ cup of dry sherry—preferred by tasters over white wine and vermouth—adds acidity and depth.

I had the flavor of the broth where I wanted it, but I still had to resolve the North-South debate about body. Northerners turn to flour as a thickener, while southerners tend to leave well enough alone. I prepared two versions: The first batch I left plain, the other I thickened with ½ cup of flour (the amount typical in many Yankee versions of the dish) just before deglazing with the sherry. Tasters rejected the sludgy consistency of this broth outright as "heavy" and akin to "chicken pot pie filling." Knocking the flour down to ¼ cup produced broth with just the right amount of body (my colleagues deemed the straight broth too thin), but all agreed it muted the chicken flavor. Cutting the flour to 2 tablespoons still masked chicken essence. Switching to cornstarch had the same effect.

Looking for an alternative, I recalled that extended boiling (at least a couple of hours) converts the connective tissue in a chicken carcass to gelatin and thickens the broth. I didn't want my broth cooking for hours, but then I realized I'd left something out of my initial broth testing: wings. Because of their multiple joints, wings contain far more connective tissue than legs or breasts. If I added plenty of wings (a package of six seemed right) with the thighs, could I extract enough gelatin to thicken the broth? This turned out to be just what I needed to create a full-bodied liquid with potent chicken flavor that was rich without being in any way heavy. Time to move on to the dumplings.

Dumpling Divide

In the South, dumplings are made of dough rolled out to about ¼ inch thickness and cut into squares that are then added to the pot. It's a tedious and messy process that yields dense, doughy dumplings. The Yankee approach is far simpler, resulting in fluffier dumplings made just like drop biscuits. Here you simply mix flour and leavener in one bowl and fat and a liquid in another, combine the two mixtures rapidly, and scoop out biscuit-sized balls that you drop into the broth.

Given the differences in technique, I wasn't disappointed when (except for two holdouts from Kentucky and Alabama) my colleagues preferred the lighter Yankee dumplings. The problem was, they weren't actually all that light.

Since the Yankee dumplings are so closely related to oven-baked drop biscuits, I tried using our standard drop biscuit recipe (flour, salt, sugar, baking powder and soda, butter, and buttermilk) in the soup to see if it would produce more pillowy results. These dumplings had great tangy buttermilk flavor. And because they had more leavener and butter than the earlier recipes I had tried, they were far from leaden. In fact, they had the opposite problem: They were so fragile, they disintegrated into the broth as they cooked.

The ideal dumpling should have all the lightness of our drop biscuits, but enough structure to hold together in the broth. Knowing that fat coats flour and weakens its structure, I tried gradually cutting down on the 8 tablespoons of butter in the recipe. At 4 tablespoons, their structure improved somewhat; removing any more compromised flavor. Since I was cooking my dumplings in a moist environment instead of a dry oven, my next thought was cutting back the liquid. Reducing the amount of buttermilk from a full cup to ¾ cup was another improvement—but the dumplings were still far too delicate.

Perhaps the problem was too much leavener, which can lead to over-rising and poor structure. Completely eliminating the baking powder (only baking soda remained) gave them just the right density in the center, but they were still mushy around the edges. While eggs are not traditional biscuit ingredients, I tried adding one, hoping that the extra protein would help the dumpling hold together. A whole egg was too much: Tasters didn't like the eggy flavor. A single egg white whisked into the buttermilk added just the right amount of structure without affecting flavor. Another useful tweak was waiting to add the dumplings until the broth was simmering, reducing their time in the broth to help keep them whole.

One last problem remained: Steam was condensing on the inside of the lid of the Dutch oven and dripping onto the dumplings, turning their tops soggy. Could I somehow catch the moisture before it dripped back down? I tried wrapping a kitchen towel around the lid of the Dutch oven. It worked like a charm, trapping the moisture before it had a chance to drip down and saturate my light-as-air dumplings and flavor-packed broth.

🎥 **COOK'S VIDEOS** Original Test Kitchen Videos
www.cooksillustrated.com/oct09
HOW TO MAKE
• Lighter Chicken and Dumplings
VIDEO TIP
• Buying and using portion scoops

LIGHTER CHICKEN AND DUMPLINGS
SERVES 6

NOTE: We strongly recommend buttermilk for the dumplings, but it's acceptable to substitute ½ cup plain yogurt thinned with ¼ cup milk. If you want to include white meat (and don't mind losing a bit of flavor in the process), replace 2 chicken thighs with 2 boneless, skinless chicken breast halves (about 8 ounces each). Brown the chicken breasts along with the thighs and remove them from the stew once they reach an internal temperature of 160 degrees, 20 to 30 minutes. The collagen in the wings helps thicken the stew; do not omit or substitute. Since the wings yield only about 1 cup of meat, using their meat is optional. The stew can be prepared through step 3 up to 2 days in advance; bring the stew back to a simmer before proceeding with the recipe.

Stew

- 6 bone-in, skin-on chicken thighs (about 2½ pounds), trimmed of excess fat (see note)
  Table salt and ground black pepper
- 2 teaspoons vegetable oil
- 2 small onions, chopped fine (about 1½ cups)
- 2 medium carrots, peeled and cut into ¾-inch pieces (about 2 cups)
- 1 medium celery rib, chopped fine (about ½ cup)
- ¼ cup dry sherry
- 6 cups low-sodium chicken broth
- 1 teaspoon minced fresh thyme leaves
- 1 pound chicken wings (see note)
- ¼ cup chopped fresh parsley leaves

Dumplings

- 2 cups (10 ounces) unbleached all-purpose flour
- ½ teaspoon baking soda
- 1 teaspoon sugar
- 1 teaspoon table salt
- ¾ cup cold buttermilk (see note)
- 4 tablespoons (½ stick) unsalted butter, melted and cooled about 5 minutes
- 1 large egg white

1. FOR THE STEW: Pat chicken thighs dry with paper towels and season with 1 teaspoon salt and ¼ teaspoon pepper. Heat oil in large Dutch oven over medium-high heat until shimmering. Add chicken thighs, skin-side down, and cook until skin is crisp and well browned, 5 to 7 minutes. Using tongs, turn chicken pieces and brown on second side, 5 to 7 minutes longer; transfer to large plate. Discard all but 1 teaspoon fat from pot.

2. Add onions, carrots, and celery to now-empty pot; cook, stirring occasionally, until caramelized, 7 to 9 minutes. Stir in sherry, scraping up any browned bits. Stir in broth and thyme. Return chicken thighs, with any accumulated juices, to pot and add chicken wings. Bring to simmer, cover, and cook until thigh meat offers no resistance when poked with tip of paring knife but still clings to bones, 45 to 55 minutes.

3. Remove pot from heat and transfer chicken to cutting board. Allow broth to settle 5 minutes, then skim fat from surface using wide spoon or ladle. When cool enough to handle, remove and discard skin from chicken. Using fingers or fork, pull meat from chicken thighs (and wings, if desired) and cut into 1-inch pieces. Return meat to pot.

4. FOR THE DUMPLINGS: Whisk flour, baking soda, sugar, and salt in large bowl. Combine buttermilk and melted butter in medium bowl, stirring until butter forms small clumps; whisk in egg white. Add buttermilk mixture to dry ingredients and stir with rubber spatula until just incorporated and batter pulls away from sides of bowl.

5. Return stew to simmer; stir in parsley and season with salt and pepper to taste. Using greased tablespoon measure (or #60 portion scoop), scoop level amount of batter and drop over top of stew, spacing about ¼ inch apart (you should have about 24 dumplings). Wrap lid of Dutch oven with clean kitchen towel (keeping towel away from heat source) and cover pot. Simmer gently until dumplings have doubled in size and toothpick inserted into center comes out clean, 13 to 16 minutes. Serve immediately.

AT-A-GLANCE | NO MORE BROKEN SINKERS

Here's how we lightened up our dumplings and kept them intact.

ADD AN EGG WHITE
Adding an egg white helps develop light-as-air dumplings that don't disintegrate.

LET LIQUID SIMMER
Waiting to add the dumplings until the broth is simmering sets their bottoms and keeps them whole.

CATCH CONDENSATION
Wrapping the lid with a towel absorbs excess moisture that can turn dumplings soggy.

Introducing Thai Pork Lettuce Wraps

Making this light but bold-flavored Thai specialty isn't a matter of rounding up a lot of exotic ingredients. The problem is as familiar as it gets: ensuring tender, juicy pork.

⇒ BY KEITH DRESSER ⇐

As much as I like ordering a rich, spicy curry when I'm in a Thai restaurant, sometimes I long for the same complexity of flavor in a lighter incarnation. That's when I order a salad of boldly flavored minced pork (or sometimes beef or chicken) known as *larb*. Served slightly warm or at room temperature, this Thai classic is made with finely chopped, cooked meat tossed with fresh herbs and a light dressing that embodies the cuisine's signature balance of sweet, sour, hot, and salty flavors. My favorite way to eat the moist, tangy pork is to scoop it up with lettuce leaves.

When I reviewed a few recipes for the dish, I discovered it has yet another thing going for it: This pungently flavored, light meal is not only incredibly simple to make, it also calls for ingredients I could easily find in the supermarket. Along with the ground pork, shallots, and limes, it takes the salty, fermented Asian condiment known as fish sauce, which these days is found in grocery stores everywhere. Even the raw rice that's toasted, ground, and sprinkled over the dish wouldn't be hard to replicate. As for the palm sugar and Thai bird chiles that are occasionally listed, I was confident that my pantry could provide worthy substitutes.

It's a Grind

Nearly every recipe I found, whether in traditional Thai cookbooks or aimed at an American audience, treats the meat in a similar way: It's cooked briefly in a large pot of boiling water, then drained, cooled, and tossed with a dressing made from lime juice, fish sauce, chiles, mint, cilantro, shallots, and some form of sugar. The difference is that traditional recipes call for hand-chopping pieces of pork (usually from the rib), while those aimed at American cooks typically call for supermarket ground pork.

How does preground pork from the meat section affect the recipe? Not positively, I soon found out. The meat was sometimes grainy and dry, sometimes greasy; rarely was it tender, flavorful, and juicy. It didn't matter what brand of pork I used or where I bought it; the results

We like the fresh crispness of a lettuce wrap, but this pork can also be served on its own with rice.

were equally inconsistent. Closer inspection of the raw meat in samplings from different packages helped explain why: Some were ground almost to a paste; others had visible chunks of meat and fat. Furthermore, unlike ground beef, the fat percentage in ground pork

is never listed and, judging from my testing, seems to vary from package to package. Conversations with supermarket butchers confirmed that most grind whatever scraps are on hand—making ground pork akin to packaged stew meat, where any number of different cuts may be included.

To get a consistent result, I would have to chop the meat myself. In Thailand, cooks mince meat using two cleavers. In my kitchen, a food processor would do just fine. I bought the most commonly available boneless pieces of pork—tenderloin, boneless rib chops, and boneless country-style ribs—cleaned them of visible fat, put them in the freezer long enough for them to harden around the edges (so they would process more uniformly), chopped them coarsely in the food processor, and made a batch of the recipe from each sample. Tasters unanimously favored the ground tenderloin for being the leanest and most tender. Though tenderloin is a slightly less flavorful cut than chops and ribs, once the other ingredients were added, this didn't matter much. What did matter was dryness—a problem tasters had with even the fattiest cuts of pork.

Main Squeeze

How can meat cooked in liquid turn out dry? The problem is that when pork is heated above 165 degrees, its protein fibers shrink, wringing out liquid like a wet towel and making the meat chewy and dry,

even if it's surrounded by broth or water. Water is an excellent conductor of heat (even better than the air in an oven), so that pork cooked in boiling water quickly rises above the crucial 165-degree mark. And any flavor that leaches into the boiling water eventually gets dumped down the drain.

Many of our pork recipes, whether for stir-fries or grilled chops, call for marinating the meat in a salty liquid (either soy sauce or a saltwater brine) before cooking. This precooking soak alters the structure of the meat, allowing it to retain more moisture. I didn't want to add soy sauce or a brine to my recipe, but since I was already using salty fish sauce in the dressing, I tried adding a tablespoon to the chopped meat. For ground meat, just 15 minutes was sufficient for the sauce to penetrate the pork, adding depth of flavor without tasting fishy. Now the meat was more moist and tender, but could I do even better?

I tried stir-frying. It helped the meat cook evenly (provided I stirred constantly) but required me to add oil to the pan, making the final salad a little greasy—exactly what I was trying to avoid by using tenderloin—and detracting from the lightness that defines the dish. Next, I tried cooking the pork with much less water—just 1 cup. When I added the cold pork to this smaller volume of hot water, its temperature dropped enough to allow the pork to cook much more gently. I cooked it just until its pink color faded, keeping its overall temperature below 165 degrees, and the results were even better, tender and juicy. This inspired me to try reducing the liquid even more. Using a mere ¼ cup and exchanging the water for flavorful chicken broth killed two birds with one stone: This pork was perfectly cooked and the most flavorful yet.

"Thai-ing" Up the Flavors

With the cooking method set, my next task was refining the flavors. Fish sauce is essential in Thai cuisine, much like soy sauce in Chinese cuisine. Although many traditional recipes call for equal amounts of fish sauce and lime juice, my tasters preferred a ratio of 3 tablespoons of lime juice to 2½ tablespoons of the salty stuff. As for heat, this salad should have only a hint. Dried chiles are nearly as common in traditional recipes as fresh chiles. While the two don't taste the same, in such small doses only the heat comes through anyway. I found that ¼ teaspoon was the perfect amount. Finally, Thai food invariably has some sweetener to balance the tart, salty, and hot flavors. The most traditional choice is palm sugar. Since white sugar is often used even in Thailand, I went for that.

As for the aromatic components, recipes varied. Many simply added a handful of familiar fresh herbs like cilantro and mint; others used harder-to-find ingredients like galangal, lemon grass, and kaffir lime leaves. In due diligence, I took a trip to several Asian markets to round up these items. The salads made with them were good, but they didn't justify the extra trouble. The slight pungency of thinly sliced shallots and the bright flavor of roughly chopped mint and cilantro yielded a very flavorful salad without a trip to a specialty store.

I also had to address *kao kua*, which is an integral but less familiar element of this dish: the raw rice toasted until golden brown, ground in a mortar and pestle, and sprinkled over the meat. Tasters found just a tablespoon of toasted, ground white rice (any size grain will do) made for a good hit of nutty flavor and subtly pleasing textural contrast. Some cooks claim this rice also helps absorb excess moisture from the meat, but I didn't find this to be true. I did find that if I sprinkled a teaspoon of toasted rice over the cooked pork, it blended with the juices released by the meat and added satisfying body to the dressing.

The lettuce cups were my final consideration. Although most any lettuce leaves could be used to eat the pork, I prefer the crisp spine, tender leaf, and mild taste of Bibb lettuce. It's a perfect complement to this full-flavored salad.

THAI PORK LETTUCE WRAPS
SERVES 6 AS AN APPETIZER OR 4 AS A MAIN COURSE

NOTE: We prefer natural pork in this recipe. If using enhanced pork, skip the marinating in step 2 and reduce the amount of fish sauce to 2 tablespoons, adding it all in step 5. Don't skip the toasted rice; it's integral to the texture and flavor of the dish. Any style of white rice can be used. Toasted rice powder (kao kua) can also be found in many Asian markets. This dish can be served with sticky rice and steamed vegetables as an entrée. To save time, prepare the other ingredients while the pork is in the freezer.

1	pork tenderloin (about 1 pound), trimmed of silver skin and fat, cut into 1-inch chunks (see note)
2½	tablespoons fish sauce
1	tablespoon white rice (see note)
¼	cup low-sodium chicken broth
2	medium shallots, peeled and sliced into thin rings (about ½ cup)
3	tablespoons juice from 2 limes
2	teaspoons sugar
¼	teaspoon red pepper flakes
3	tablespoons roughly chopped fresh mint leaves
3	tablespoons roughly chopped fresh cilantro leaves
1	head Bibb lettuce, washed and dried, leaves separated and left whole

1. Place pork chunks on large plate in single layer. Freeze meat until firm and starting to harden around edges but still pliable, 15 to 20 minutes.

2. Place half of meat in food processor and pulse until coarsely chopped, 5 to six 1-second pulses. Transfer ground meat to medium bowl and repeat with remaining chunks. Stir 1 tablespoon fish sauce into ground meat and marinate, refrigerated, 15 minutes.

3. Heat rice in small skillet over medium-high heat; cook, stirring constantly, until deep golden brown, about 5 minutes. Transfer to small bowl and cool 5 minutes. Grind rice with spice grinder, mini food processor, or mortar and pestle until it resembles fine meal, 10 to 30 seconds (you should have about 1 tablespoon rice powder).

4. Bring broth to simmer in 12-inch nonstick skillet over medium-high heat. Add pork and cook, stirring frequently, until about half of pork is no longer pink, about 2 minutes. Sprinkle 1 teaspoon rice powder over pork; continue to cook, stirring constantly, until remaining pork is no longer pink, 1 to 1½ minutes longer. Transfer pork to large bowl; let cool 10 minutes.

5. Add remaining 1½ tablespoons fish sauce, remaining 2 teaspoons rice powder, shallots, lime juice, sugar, red pepper flakes, mint, and cilantro to pork; toss to combine. Serve with lettuce leaves.

■ **COOK'S VIDEOS** Original Test Kitchen Videos
www.cooksillustrated.com/oct09
HOW TO MAKE
• Thai Pork Lettuce Wraps
VIDEO TIPS
• How do I use a mortar and pestle?
• What's the best way to store lettuce?

Secrets to a Perfect Cup of Coffee

You can spend $20 a pound for premium coffee, but unless it's fresh and you're using proper brewing techniques, it's a waste of money. Here's what you need to know to make the perfect cup. BY KEITH DRESSER

BUYING AND STORING TIPS

➤ **DO** buy loose beans in small quantities no more than a few days from the roasting date (ask before you buy); our testing has shown that roasted beans are ready for the compost pile after just 10 to 12 days (see "Flavor Countdown" at right). Buy from a local roaster or a store that sells a high volume, upping your chances of buying beans from a recently roasted batch.

➤ **DO** buy prebagged coffee in a heat-sealed, aluminized Mylar bag with a one-way degassing valve. This valve (sometimes no more than a bump) releases carbon dioxide to stop the bag from inflating while keeping out oxygen, which turns coffee stale. Unopened, these bags keep beans as fresh as the day they were roasted for up to 90 days (the outer limit for beans in such packaging cited by roasters including George Howell Terroir Coffee Company, in Acton, Mass., and national retailer Peet's Coffee & Tea). Of course, as soon as you open the bag, the clock starts ticking on freshness.

➤ **DON'T** rely on expiration dates. We've found some supermarket brands of coffee with expiration dates as far as two years out from the roasting date.

➤ **DON'T** buy preground coffee. Grinding speeds oxidation and the deterioration of flavor. When we compared coffee brewed from just-ground beans with coffee brewed from beans ground 24 hours earlier, tasters overwhelmingly preferred the coffee brewed from freshly ground beans. Grinding the night before is also not optimal: Studies show the exposed coffee cells begin to break down within the hour.

Flavor Countdown

To determine how long coffee maintains ideal flavor after roasting, we bought 30 bags of beans (all from the same batch, packaged within hours of roasting in one-way valve bags). Over two weeks, we used our haul to prepare two pots of coffee daily: one made with beans from a just-opened bag, the other using beans stored on the counter in a sealed zipper-lock bag with the air pressed out. A few very discriminating tasters noticed a change in taste after just a few days of storage; many tasters noticed a deterioration after 10 days; most tasters agreed the coffee tasted markedly less fresh after 12 days. Bottom line: Opened beans stored in an airtight container should be used within 10 to 12 days.

Where to Store Beans: Counter, Fridge, or Freezer?

If you finish a bag of beans in less than 10 to 12 days (see "Flavor Countdown," above), store them either in the original bag or in a zipper-lock bag away from heat and light. If you plan to keep beans longer than this time frame, store them in the freezer to limit contact with air and moisture. (Never store coffee in the fridge, where it will pick up off-flavors.) For the best results, portion beans (whether storing on the counter or in the freezer) in small zipper-lock bags in one-day allotments to keep air and moisture exposure to the barest minimum.

BEST BREWING PRACTICES

For perfect coffee, the goal is to extract 18 to 22 percent of the soluble solids—coffee brewed below this range tastes sour and weak; above this range, it tastes harsh. Here are tips to ensure ideal extraction and flavor.

1. USE FILTERED WATER A cup of coffee is about 98 percent water, so if your tap water tastes bad or has strong mineral flavors, your coffee will too. We found that the test kitchen's tap water masked some of the coffee's complexity, compared to coffee made with filtered water. Don't bother buying bottled water—just use a filtration pitcher.

2. HEAT WATER TO THE PROPER TEMPERATURE The most desirable flavor compounds in coffee are released in water between 195 and 205 degrees. A panel of our tasters judged coffee brewed at 200 degrees as having the fullest, roundest flavor. Once water has boiled (212 degrees), let it rest 10 to 15 seconds to bring it down to this temperature.

3. USE THE RIGHT GRIND, BREW FOR THE RIGHT TIME These two components go hand in hand. Brewing time will dictate how you grind the coffee. In general, the longer the brewing time, the coarser the grounds should be (see "Recommended Brewing Methods" on page 17). As a rule, brewing should take 4 to 6 minutes. Don't try to adjust strength by changing the grind; grounds that are too fine for your brewing method will result in overextraction, while grounds that are too coarse will be underextracted.

4. ADD THE RIGHT AMOUNT The norm is 2 tablespoons of ground beans for every 6 ounces of water. If you prefer stronger or weaker coffee, adjust the amount of grounds per cup; changing the amount of water can easily lead to over- or underextraction, because the less water you use, the shorter the brewing time and vice versa.

5. KEEP THE POT CLEAN Since coffee beans contain oils, every time you brew a pot, some oil is left behind. Over time, that oil will make your coffee taste rancid. Rinse your pot with hot water after each use and scrub all brewing apparatus with hot soapy water at least once a week.

Freshness Test

To check if your beans are fresh, scoop ½ cup into a zipper-lock bag and press out all the air, then seal the bag and leave it overnight. If the beans are within seven to 10 days of roasting, they will make the bag puff up from the carbon dioxide that they release. If the bag remains flat, then the beans are not producing gas—a sign they've passed the point of peak freshness.

PUFFED = STILL FRESH

FLAT = PAST THEIR PRIME

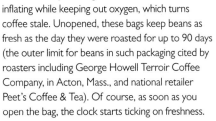

RECOMMENDED BREWING METHODS

While we can't dispute the convenience of an automatic drip coffee maker, we've learned that most models brew crummy coffee—they don't heat the water to the ideal temperature, and the brewing times are too long or too short. Unless you're willing to splurge on the one coffee maker we really like (See "A Cup Above" at right), we recommend a French press or manual drip.

French Press

How It Works: A French press (or plunger pot) directly infuses ground coffee in just-boiled water. Once properly extracted, the grounds are pressed to the bottom of the carafe.

Why We Like It: Because the coffee's oils are not filtered out, this method yields coffee nearly as full-bodied as espresso. It also allows you to control water temperature and brew time.

Downside: Cleaning requires taking apart the pieces.

The Right Grind: Medium-coarse (a little coarser than couscous).

1. Add 2 tablespoons coffee for every 6 ounces water (preheat pot first with hot tap water).

2. Add just-boiled water steadily, saturating all the grounds.

3. Using long spoon or chopstick, stir coffee to aid extraction.

4. Add lid and steep coffee for about five minutes (four minutes for smaller pots).

5. With even pressure, steadily press down filter.

Manual Drip

How It Works: Place ground coffee in a wedge-shaped filter holder and pour water over it into a container below.

Why We Like It: The manual drip allows the natural acidity of coffee to shine through, yielding bright, flavorful coffee. As with the French press, you control water temperature and brew time.

Downside: Since you have to add water in batches, you can't leave the kitchen during brewing.

The Right Grind: Medium (like coarse cornmeal) for paper filters; medium-fine (like fine cornmeal) for metal filters.

1. Add 2 tablespoons coffee for every 6 ounces water to filter (warm thermos with hot tap water).

2. Pour ½ cup just-boiled water over grounds, saturating thoroughly; let stand 30 seconds.

3. Pour remaining hot water over grounds, in batches if necessary, stirring gently after each addition.

A Cup Above

The following pieces of equipment are test kitchen favorites for a more enjoyable cup.

FRENCH PRESS

BODUM CHAMBORD
8-cup French Press
Price: $39.95
Comments: Coffee connoisseurs willing to overlook the precise calibration and multiple steps required by the French press rave about the complex flavors of its brew. And few high-quality drip coffee makers can beat its price.

COFFEE GRINDER

CAPRESSO Cool Grind
Price: $19.95
Comments: Like many blade grinders, this one struggles to grind evenly. But we like two other features: a large capacity and a deep cup that holds grounds without spilling.

THERMAL CARAFE

THERMOS NISSAN
Stainless Steel Carafe
Price: $50.99
Comments: Besides its excellent temperature retention, we liked this carafe's lever-action stopper, which allows for one-handed pouring without dripping. Both the carafe and lid are dishwasher-safe (most others aren't).

DRIP COFFEE MAKER

TECHNIVORM
Moccamaster Coffee Maker
Price: $265
Comments: If you must buy an automatic drip machine, this is the one. Though pricey, it's the only drip coffee maker that hit optimal temperatures for brewing and serving in our tests. It's also fast and very simple to operate, and pieces disassemble easily for cleaning.

🎥 **COOK'S VIDEOS**
Original Test Kitchen Videos
www.cooksillustrated.com/oct09
VIDEO TIPS
• How to buy and store coffee
• How to brew coffee

Foolproof Vinaigrette

Basic vinaigrette has a fundamental problem: It doesn't stay together. We sought a way to make oil and vinegar form a long-term bond.

⇒ BY DAWN YANAGIHARA ⇐

A vinaigrette is one of the simplest preparations in the sauce lexicon. At its most basic, it requires only two ingredients: oil and vinegar. However, as many accomplished cooks can attest, turning these ingredients into a dressing that transforms unadorned greens into a finished, well-balanced salad isn't simple at all. Vinaigrettes can sometimes seem a little slipshod—harsh and bristling in one bite, dull and oily in the next. The best ones do the job quietly, complementing the greens without dominating them or engaging in combat. I was determined to nail down a formula for the perfect vinaigrette, one that would consistently yield a homogeneous, harmonious blend of bright vinegar and rich oil in every forkful.

Vinegar and Other Variables

I began by brushing up on form—unearthing texts from culinary school, perusing classic French culinary tomes, even contacting noted French chefs like Eric Ripert and Jacques Pépin. The books and the experts agreed on one thing: Ingredient selection and the ratio of oil to vinegar depend on what's being dressed.

To my chagrin, that was it. What method, which oil or vinegar to use, whether shallots are advised over garlic, and even what herbs and other seasonings to add were all in dispute. In fact, what I thought of as the "classic" method of mixing, the one I learned in culinary school (combine the vinegar and seasonings, then gradually whisk in oil to create a temporary emulsion), didn't seem so widespread after all. Neither *Larousse Gastronomique* nor Escoffier's *Guide Culinaire* even mention this approach (and Pépin, for one, often resorts to simply shaking the ingredients in a jar).

I wanted two styles: a vinaigrette for tender, mild greens (such as butter lettuce and mesclun) and another for assertive, spicy greens (such as arugula, radicchio, and escarole). I would have to test ingredients, proportions, and techniques until

🎥 **COOK'S VIDEOS** Original Test Kitchen Videos

www.cooksillustrated.com/oct09

HOW TO MAKE
• Foolproof Vinaigrette

VIDEO TIP
• Science Experiment: Which emulsifier works best?

A secret ingredient keeps our vinaigrette thoroughly emulsified, for salads that taste well balanced in every bite.

I figured out on my own what worked best.

I began by examining ingredients. With only two starring components, quality would be critical, so I tried the test kitchen's favorite white wine, red wine, and balsamic vinegars, each mixed with our top-rated extra-virgin olive oil as a placeholder. I also threw champagne vinegar into the mix. Tasters did not prefer one kind of vinegar to another, though balsamic tended to overpower mild lettuce and would only serve for more assertive greens. As for oil, tasters strongly preferred fruity extra-virgin olive oil to plain olive, vegetable, peanut, and grapeseed oils as an all-purpose option, and walnut oil won fans as an alternative for nuttier vinaigrettes. For due diligence, I then tested lower-end vinegars and olive oils. Not surprisingly, the results were inferior. High-quality ingredients were clearly a must.

As for ratio, Escoffier recommends 3 parts oil to 1 part vinegar in his *Guide Culinaire* (first published in 1903), yet many modern recipes employ a ratio of 4 to 1. Have palates changed, I wondered, or have vinaigrette ingredients? It also occurred to me that mixing methods have grown a little slack. Recipes these days routinely dump and stir, with all the ingredients added to a bowl and whisked until more or less combined; others do as Pépin does and simply shake the ingredients in a sealed jar. Since most of

the dump-and-stir and dump-and-shake recipes I had collected use a 4:1 ratio, could these be related?

After mixing oil and vinegar with each method and ratio, I found out what mixing can do to flavor. The quicker, less thorough methods yielded vinaigrettes that began to separate even before they could be tossed with greens. This gave me salads with overly acidic bites in spots where the vinegar had settled. For vinaigrettes made with the quick methods, tasters preferred 4 parts oil to 1 part vinegar, which subdued the acidity more than the 3:1 ratio.

Overall, these easy vinaigrettes couldn't compete with those I made following culinary school protocol, whisking so gradually that my arm ached. These "classic" vinaigrettes were more stable and separated more slowly (after five to 10 minutes), pouring onto the greens intact. Tasters now switched their preference: 3 parts oil to 1 part vinegar had a pleasantly vibrant flavor, while a 4:1 ratio tasted dull. In general, the slow-whisked vinaigrette was smoother and more even in flavor. Yet I wasn't satisfied. I wanted a more forgiving vinaigrette that could sit for a while.

Mix Mastery

Some quick research revealed what was going on. Oil and vinegar don't typically mix, since vinegar is 95 percent water. Vigorous action (whisking) creates an emulsion that combines them more smoothly, though almost as soon as the action stops, the vinegar droplets cluster back together, and the vinaigrette breaks apart.

Using the classic whisking method, the vinegar droplets become exceedingly small, creating a vinaigrette that is even in flavor and remains stable until this profusion of tiny droplets starts to come together. I needed to introduce an emulsifying agent that would keep the vinegar and oil combined. All emulsifiers function the same way: They have molecules that include both a fat-compatible region and a water-compatible region. These regions latch onto oil and water alike, serving as a liaison that keeps those two ingredients from parting ways.

Mustard is a common emulsifier in salad dressing, so I tried it. A half teaspoon of Dijon contributed a nice tang but didn't help to stabilize the sauce. Although a whole teaspoon worked better, it turned my standard wine vinaigrette into a mustard dressing. I decided to keep a little mustard for flavor and continue searching for the right emulsifier.

Considering my options, I recalled something that Pépin had mentioned in passing: a type of vinaigrette that uses raw egg yolk to create a mayonnaise-like sauce. I wasn't wild about incorporating raw egg into what I hoped would be my staple dressing, but what about trying a little mayo, which contains egg yolk but isn't overtly eggy? I added store-bought mayo in ¼-teaspoon increments and found that ½ teaspoon mayonnaise combined with ½ teaspoon mustard created a stable vinaigrette with pleasant acidity. How long could it sit without separating? As it turned out, more than an hour.

Our science editor explained why: The egg yolk in mayonnaise contains lecithin, a fatty substance that emulsifies brilliantly. Thanks to lecithin, I needed only a small amount of mayo to keep my dressing stable (for more information on emulsifiers, see "Emulsification Magic" at right). The lecithin also allowed the vinaigrette to emulsify with slightly more flexibility: I could add the oil a bit more quickly, and all was not lost if a little extra spilled in. After testing three dozen vinaigrettes, I finally had one that was foolproof. Now I could make a dressing with a 3:1 ratio that would reliably produce smooth, satisfying results.

Finessing the Dressing

All that remained was fine-tuning the flavor. I added salt to the vinegar to ensure it dissolved fully (salt won't dissolve in oil). Then I experimented with shallots and garlic, both typical additions. (Shallots are milder than onions.) Tasters favored 1½ teaspoons of very finely minced shallot and just a hint of garlic—instead of adding it to the vinaigrette, I rubbed a clove inside a salad bowl before adding the lettuce.

With the master recipe settled, I whisked together a few variations. Mustard and balsamic vinegar matched assertive greens, while the version for mild greens omitted the shallots and used lemon juice in place of vinegar. I also created an option with rich walnut oil and another with fresh herbs. Mayonnaise was a constant, and regular and light products worked equally well to keep the mixture together.

FOOLPROOF VINAIGRETTE
MAKES ABOUT ¼ CUP, ENOUGH TO DRESS 8 TO 10 CUPS LIGHTLY PACKED GREENS

NOTE: Red wine, white wine, or champagne vinegar will work in this recipe; however, it is important to use high-quality ingredients (see "Winning Ingredients," page 18). This vinaigrette works with nearly any type of green (as do the walnut and herb variations). For a hint of garlic flavor, rub the inside of the salad bowl with a clove of garlic before adding the lettuce.

- 1 tablespoon wine vinegar (see note)
- 1½ teaspoons very finely minced shallot
- ½ teaspoon regular or light mayonnaise
- ½ teaspoon Dijon mustard
- ⅛ teaspoon table salt
  Ground black pepper
- 3 tablespoons extra-virgin olive oil

1. Combine vinegar, shallot, mayonnaise, mustard, salt, and pepper to taste in small nonreactive bowl. Whisk until mixture is milky in appearance and no lumps of mayonnaise remain.

2. Place oil in small measuring cup so that it is easy to pour. Whisking constantly, very slowly drizzle oil into vinegar mixture. If pools of oil are gathering on surface as you whisk, stop addition of oil and whisk mixture well to combine, then resume whisking in oil in slow stream. Vinaigrette should be glossy and lightly thickened, with no pools of oil on its surface.

LEMON VINAIGRETTE

NOTE: This is best for dressing mild greens.

Follow recipe for Foolproof Vinaigrette, substituting lemon juice for vinegar, omitting shallot, and adding ¼ teaspoon finely grated lemon zest and pinch of sugar along with salt and pepper.

BALSAMIC-MUSTARD VINAIGRETTE

NOTE: This is best for dressing assertive greens.

Follow recipe for Foolproof Vinaigrette, substituting balsamic vinegar for wine vinegar, increasing mustard to 2 teaspoons, and adding ½ teaspoon chopped fresh thyme along with salt and pepper.

WALNUT VINAIGRETTE

Follow recipe for Foolproof Vinaigrette, substituting 1½ tablespoons roasted walnut oil and 1½ tablespoons regular olive oil for extra-virgin olive oil.

HERB VINAIGRETTE

Follow recipe for Foolproof Vinaigrette, adding 1 tablespoon minced fresh parsley or chives and ½ teaspoon minced fresh thyme, tarragon, marjoram, or oregano to vinaigrette just before use.

Pasta with Roasted Vegetables

The problem with this dish isn't the vegetables or the pasta. It's the sauce.

⇒ BY MARCUS WALSER ⇐

Combining perfectly caramelized roasted vegetables with pasta should be a winning proposition. Anyone who's tried this, however, knows that the idea doesn't necessarily translate. The catch isn't so much the vegetables (which are sweet and complex if properly roasted) as the lack of a true sauce—most recipes attempt to unify the vegetables and pasta with nothing more than olive oil and a little cheese. Although oil helps make the dish more cohesive, it also makes it greasy; using less oil solves that problem, of course, but is likely to leave you with a dry and uninspiring mix. Could I create a simple sauce that would succeed in uniting the components of this dish?

At the outset, I decided to develop a few different dishes, each focused on getting the best from a single vegetable. I settled on cauliflower (sweet and nutty when roasted), broccoli (which browns nicely), and portobello mushrooms (for their intense, meaty taste). I used the test kitchen's proven method for roasting vegetables: cutting them into slices or wedges to maximize the surface area available for browning, then tossing them with oil, salt, pepper, and a little sugar to jump-start caramelization, and finally roasting them on a preheated baking sheet. (Preheating cuts the cooking time nearly in half and boosts browning dramatically.)

Now I was ready to face my central dilemma—the sauce. My options included cream sauces, vegetable-based sauces, and vinaigrettes. First I tried an array of cream-based sauces, which added moisture to the pasta but muted the vegetable flavor. Vegetable-based sauces weren't much better: A puree of roasted red peppers overwhelmed my veggies, while a puree of roasted onions turned the pasta an unappetizing gray. Only a garlicky vinaigrette was a step in the right direction—I liked the way the garlic bumped up the overall flavor of the dish—but the vinegar was harsh. Cutting back on vinegar meant upping the oil, and then I was back where I started.

What I needed was an ingredient that could replace some of the oil, adding body and complementary flavor without overt richness. I found a solution right in front of me: garlic. When roasted, garlic turns sweet and buttery-soft, making it perfect for spreading on bread or adding depth to sauces. I wrapped two whole garlic heads in foil and roasted them along with the veggies, then squeezed the roasted cloves from their skins and mashed them with extra-virgin olive oil and a little lemon juice. This creamy puree worked beautifully as a sauce, adding an earthy sweetness that complemented all three vegetables.

I was almost there, but still wanted a bit more flavor and contrasting texture in each dish. The answer was to add herbs, nuts, and cheese. I matched the cauliflower with parsley, walnuts, and sharp Parmesan; the broccoli with basil, almonds, and nutty Manchego; and the mushrooms with rosemary, pine nuts, and tangy Pecorino Romano.

PASTA WITH ROASTED CAULIFLOWER, GARLIC, AND WALNUTS
SERVES 4

NOTE: This dish is best with short molded pasta, such as fusilli, campanelle, or orecchiette. Prepare the cauliflower for roasting after you put the garlic in the oven; this way, both should finish roasting at about the same time.

- 2 heads garlic, papery skins removed, top quarter of heads cut off and discarded
- 6 tablespoons plus 1 teaspoon extra-virgin olive oil
- 1 head cauliflower (about 1½ pounds) (see note) Table salt and ground black pepper
- ¼ teaspoon sugar
- 1 pound pasta (see note)
- ¼ teaspoon red pepper flakes
- 2–3 tablespoons juice from 1 lemon
- 1 tablespoon chopped fresh parsley leaves
- 2 ounces Parmesan cheese, grated (about 1 cup)
- ¼ cup chopped walnuts, toasted

1. Adjust oven rack to middle position, place large rimmed baking sheet on rack, and heat oven to 500 degrees.

2. Cut one 12-inch sheet of foil and spread flat on counter. Place garlic heads, cut-side up, in center of foil. Drizzle ½ teaspoon oil over each head and seal packet. Place packet on oven rack and roast until garlic is very tender, about 40 minutes. Open packet and set aside to cool.

3. While garlic is roasting, trim outer leaves of cauliflower and cut stem flush with bottom. Cut head from pole to pole into 8 equal wedges. Place cauliflower in large bowl; toss with 2 tablespoons oil, 1 teaspoon salt, pepper to taste, and sugar.

4. Remove baking sheet from oven. Carefully transfer cauliflower to baking sheet and spread into even layer, placing cut sides down. Return baking sheet to oven and roast until cauliflower is well browned and tender, 20 to 25 minutes. Transfer cauliflower to cutting board. When cool enough to handle, chop into rough ½-inch pieces.

5. While cauliflower roasts, bring 4 quarts water to boil in large pot. Add 1 tablespoon salt and pasta; cook until al dente. Squeeze roasted garlic cloves from their skins into small bowl. Using fork, mash garlic to smooth paste, then stir in red pepper flakes and 2 tablespoons lemon juice. Slowly whisk in remaining ¼ cup oil.

6. Drain pasta, reserving 1 cup cooking water, and return pasta to pot. Add chopped cauliflower to pasta; stir in garlic sauce, ¼ cup cooking water, parsley, and ½ cup cheese. Adjust consistency with additional cooking water and season with salt, pepper, and additional lemon juice to taste. Serve immediately, sprinkling with remaining ½ cup cheese and toasted nuts.

PASTA WITH ROASTED BROCCOLI, GARLIC, AND ALMONDS

Cut 1½ pounds broccoli at juncture of crowns and stems; remove outer peel from stems. Cut stems into 2- to 3-inch lengths and each length into ½-inch-thick pieces. Cut crowns into 4 wedges if 3 to 4 inches in diameter or 6 wedges if 4 to 5 inches in diameter. Follow recipe for Pasta with Roasted Cauliflower, Garlic, and Walnuts, substituting prepared broccoli for cauliflower and reducing roasting time in step 4 to 10 to 15 minutes. Proceed with recipe as directed, substituting ¼ cup chopped fresh basil for parsley, grated Manchego cheese for Parmesan, and toasted slivered almonds for walnuts.

PASTA WITH ROASTED MUSHROOMS, GARLIC, AND PINE NUTS

Remove and discard stems of 8 portobello mushrooms (each 3 to 4 inches in diameter). Wipe caps clean and cut into ¾-inch slices. Follow recipe for Pasta with Roasted Cauliflower, Garlic, and Walnuts, substituting prepared mushrooms for cauliflower and flipping mushrooms once halfway through cooking in step 4. Proceed with recipe as directed, substituting chopped fresh rosemary for parsley, grated Pecorino Romano cheese for Parmesan, and toasted pine nuts for walnuts.

◧ COOK'S VIDEOS Original Test Kitchen Videos
www.cooksillustrated.com/oct09
HOW TO MAKE
• Pasta with Roasted Vegetables
VIDEO TIP
• How do I prep vegetables for roasting?

Introducing Mexican Grilled Corn

Mexican street vendors add kick to grilled corn by slathering it with a creamy, spicy sauce.
Could we deliver authentic south-of-the-border flavor from our own backyard?

≥ BY FRANCISCO J. ROBERT ≤

One of Mexico's most popular street foods is *elote asado*: corn on the cob grilled until it's intensely sweet, smoky, and charred, then slathered with a cheesy sauce spiked with lime juice and chili powder. This spicy corn has such potent flavor that I'll go out of my way for it, not only when I'm visiting Mexico but whenever I'm in a Mexican neighborhood in the States. This summer, I decided it was time to develop my own rendition. After experimenting with numerous batches, I came up with three goals. First, achieve maximum charring without drying out the corn. Second, deliver authentic flavor without relying on hard-to-find ingredients. Finally, thicken the sauce just enough to keep it from sliding off the corn.

Grilling can be a great alternative to boiling corn—the dry heat and smoke intensify its flavor—but the juicy kernels are prone to overcooking. To resolve this dilemma, the test kitchen's usual approach is to remove all but the innermost layer of husk, then grill the corn over a medium-hot fire. The husk allows smoke to pass through to the kernels, at the same time trapping moisture and providing protection from the hot coals. While this method delivered juicy, smoky corn, it didn't give me enough charring.

I decided to ditch the husk and grill directly on top of the grates, brushing the ears with oil first to prevent sticking. After about 10 minutes, the corn was still not as charred as I wanted—but any longer and the kernels dried out and shriveled. Why not apply the same principles we use when pan-searing thin cuts of steak: Cook them fast in a blazing-hot pan to achieve good browning without drying out the meat? I mounded the coals on one side of the grill (they needed the grill wall for support) and placed the corn on top of the grate. Thanks to the greater heat of coals piled up closer to the grate, in seven to 12 minutes I had corn charred to a burnished black-brown that was still pretty juicy.

Next: the sauce. Since authentic recipes typically call for *crema* (soured Mexican cream) as the base, I knew I would need to find a more widely available replacement. Some recipes skip the crema and call for

COOK'S VIDEOS Original Test Kitchen Videos
www.cooksillustrated.com/oct09
HOW TO MAKE
• Mexican-Style Charcoal-Grilled Corn
VIDEO TIP
• What's the best way to store corn?

Grilling over high heat delivers the best char without drying out the kernels.

mayonnaise. When I tried this, tasters liked the richness of the sauce but missed the crema's tanginess. My remedy: Swap out some mayonnaise for regular sour cream. Because the American stuff is thicker than crema, I now had a thicker sauce that clung more readily to the corn.

Besides the crema, most recipes also call for either *queso fresco* (a fresh, mild cheese) or *Cotija* (a drier, saltier, more pungent aged cheese). Since these cheeses have such distinct flavor profiles and textures, I needed to cast a wide net for substitutes, eventually singling out dry, tangy Pecorino Romano as the best choice. As for seasonings, tasters appreciated the liveliness of the usual additions of cilantro, lime, and garlic but complained that the other key flavoring, chili powder, didn't offer enough depth. If I bumped up the spice to more than ¾ teaspoon, tasters found it turned the sauce gritty. I knew toasting brings out the essential oils and aromas of spices, enhancing their flavor. But who needs to toast if you're already grilling? By adding ½ teaspoon chili powder to the oil I was using to coat the corn before it went on the grates (I reserved ¼ teaspoon for the sauce), I was able to bloom the spice over the hot coals. For final touches, I added a dash of cayenne to the sauce and tinkered with the lime juice, landing on a generous 4 teaspoons as the right amount for bright punch.

After grilling 200 ears of corn, I had my ideal Mexican version, without searching for street carts.

MEXICAN-STYLE CHARCOAL-GRILLED CORN
SERVES 6

NOTE: If you can find queso fresco or Cotija, use either in place of the Pecorino Romano.

	Vegetable oil for cooking grate
¼	cup regular or light mayonnaise
3	tablespoons sour cream
3	tablespoons minced fresh cilantro leaves
1	medium garlic clove, minced or pressed through garlic press (about 1 teaspoon)
¾	teaspoon chili powder
¼	teaspoon ground black pepper
¼	teaspoon cayenne pepper (optional)
4	teaspoons juice from 1 lime
1	ounce Pecorino Romano cheese, grated (about ½ cup) (see note)
4	teaspoons vegetable oil
½	teaspoon kosher salt or ¼ teaspoon table salt
6	large ears corn, husks and silk removed

1. Light large chimney starter filled with charcoal (6 quarts, about 100 briquettes) and allow to burn until coals are fully ignited and partially covered with thin layer of ash, about 20 minutes. Arrange all coals in even layer over half of grill, leaving other half empty. Position cooking grate over coals, cover grill, and heat grate until hot, about 5 minutes; scrape grate clean with grill brush. Dip wad of paper towels in vegetable oil; holding wad with tongs, wipe cooking grate.

2. While grill is heating, combine mayonnaise, sour cream, cilantro, garlic, ¼ teaspoon chili powder, black pepper, cayenne (if using), lime juice, and cheese in large bowl; set aside. In second large bowl, combine oil, salt, and remaining ½ teaspoon chili powder; add corn and toss until coated evenly.

3. Grill corn over coals, turning occasionally, until lightly charred on all sides, 7 to 12 minutes total. Remove from grill and place in bowl with mayonnaise mixture; toss to coat evenly. Serve immediately.

MEXICAN-STYLE GAS-GRILLED CORN

Follow recipe for Mexican-Style Charcoal-Grilled Corn, turning all burners to high and heating grill with lid down until very hot, about 15 minutes. Scrape and oil grate. Proceed with recipe from step 2, leaving burners on high and cooking corn with lid down.

Apple Upside-Down Cake

Ever since pineapple came to town, apple upside-down cake has been a bit player.
A successful comeback would require a flavorful topping and just the right kind of cake.

≥ BY YVONNE RUPERTI ≤

Pineapple and upside-down cake are practically synonymous. But long before the introduction of canned pineapple in the early 1900s sparked a craze for pineapple in baked goods, upside-down cakes were made with seasonal fruit such as apples. The technique was straightforward: Pour melted butter and brown sugar into a pan or skillet, add sliced apples, spread cake batter over them, and bake. The apples caramelize on the bottom of the pan, revealing a layer of burnished amber fruit when the cake is upturned.

After testing a few recipes, however, I understood why sweet, juicy pineapple had overshadowed the humble apple. Rather than a luscious topping full of deeply fruity, caramelized flavor, the apple slices tasted bland and watery and seemed more garnish than topping. To restore apple-pie order to this upside-down cake, I would need to start from the top down—or, rather, from the bottom up.

Grappling with Apples

Tinkering with the apple topping seemed like a good place to start. I tried several good baking varieties: sweeter Golden Delicious and Braeburns as well as more tart Cortlands and Granny Smiths. Cortlands in particular boasted that fresh-from-the-orchard flavor and complexity, but their flesh broke down and turned mushy. Braeburns were too sweet after being caramelized in sugar. Golden Delicious worked reasonably well, but the notably crisp texture and sharper acidity of Granny Smiths worked best.

With that choice made, I turned my attention to the rest of the topping. The ingredients and method were roughly the same in most recipes: Melt about four tablespoons of butter and ⅔ cup light brown sugar in a saucepan, pour the mixture into a 9-inch round cake pan, fan two sliced apples across the top, spread cake batter over them, and slide the pan into the oven. But when I inverted the cake onto a plate and cut a slice, I found that the two apples had cooked down to a shriveled layer, with patches of cake peeking through.

The obvious solution? Add more apples. When three apples didn't provide enough apple heft, I sliced up a fourth. I expected a substantial topping steeped with fruit flavor but instead got a cake jammed with unevenly cooked apples—some slices made contact

To accommodate 2 pounds of apples, we precook half of the fruit.

with the pan and caramelized; the rest just steamed and their surplus moisture left the cake gummy.

Then I recalled that we'd faced a similar dilemma with our Deep-Dish Apple Pie (September/October 2005): how to cram in lots of apples without flooding the dessert with juice. In that case, our solution was to precook the apples to draw out excess moisture before baking. Following suit, I sautéed four sliced apples in a few tablespoons of butter until they just softened slightly and developed a deep golden color, then added the brown sugar, waited for the crystals to dissolve, and poured the topping into the cake pan, followed by the batter. Voilà! Not only did precooking the fruit release excess moisture, it allowed me to fit all four apples into the pan if I pressed them down gently. What's more, all of the fruit was infused with caramelized flavor, even if it didn't touch the pan.

There was just one problem: Precooking meant sacrificing fresh apple flavor. Hoping to strike a compromise, I tried cooking half of the apples, then folding in the remainder before turning the topping into the pan. This was an improvement. A few more tests revealed that slicing the uncooked apples thinner (¼ inch) let them bake evenly with the apples that had been sliced ½ inch thick and sautéed. All this full-flavored topping needed was a squirt of fresh lemon juice to add brightness and balance.

Correcting the Cake

There was still the cake to contend with. I had been using the standard butter cake called for in the typical pineapple version. While its tender texture worked fine for pineapple upside-down cake, which needed less fruit, it was buckling under the weight of the 2 pounds of apples in my recipe. The creaming method for this cake—wherein you beat the butter with the sugar, beat in the eggs, and then alternately fold in the dry and liquid ingredients (in this case, just milk)—was to blame. Creaming creates lots of air bubbles that produce lightness, volume, and delicate texture. For a coarser crumb, I would need to use the so-called quick-bread method, in which the butter is melted and the liquid and dry ingredients are mixed separately before being combined together. The melted butter introduces less air into the batter than creamed butter, for a sturdier crumb. Sure enough, the cake made with this approach was moist with a more substantial crumb that held up under the topping.

That said, compared to the intense apple topping, the cake tasted a little lackluster. Trading the milk for either yogurt or buttermilk improved matters, but sour cream was a standout. Its subtle tang balanced the sweetness of the cake and complemented the caramelized apple. For another dimension to the sweetness, I swapped ¼ cup of white sugar for light brown sugar, which offered a hint of molasses. Sprinkling a tablespoon of cornmeal into the dry ingredients added earthy flavor and pleasantly coarse texture.

Cooling It

This apple cake was perfect—until the upside-down part came in. Most recipes call for a stay of five or 10 minutes in the pan before inverting the cake onto a serving plate, but this caused the bottom of the cake to steam, resulting in a gummy base. In addition, the apples slid off, while the piping-hot caramel dripped down the sides of the cake like sauce over ice cream. By mustering a little more patience, I found a remedy: letting the cake rest in the pan for a good 20 minutes, which allowed the apple topping to set. Afterward, turning the cake out onto a rack to finish cooling let the bottom of

◄ COOK'S VIDEOS Original Test Kitchen Videos
www.cooksillustrated.com/oct09
HOW TO MAKE
• Apple Upside-Down Cake
VIDEO TIP
• What's the best way to store flour?

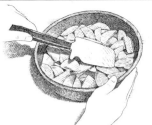

1. PRECOOK APPLES
Precook half of apples in butter to deepen their flavor and reduce their volume, allowing more to be added.

2. ADD FRESH APPLES Add raw apples, brown sugar, and lemon juice to pan, then cook briefly to preserve fresh flavor.

3. PRESS INTO PAN
Transfer apple topping to cake pan and gently press into even layer.

4. ADD BATTER AND BAKE Spread batter over apple topping and bake.

5. SET AND COOL
Let cake cool in pan for 20 minutes to help set apple topping, then transfer to cooling rack to keep cake bottom dry.

the cake breathe, avoiding sogginess. How 'bout them apples? Move over, pineapple, because this fall-fruit rendition takes the cake.

APPLE UPSIDE-DOWN CAKE
SERVES 8

NOTE: You will need a 9-inch nonstick cake pan with sides that are at least 2 inches high for this cake. Alternatively, use a 10-inch ovenproof stainless steel skillet (don't use cast iron) to both cook the apples and bake the cake, with the following modifications: Cook the apples in the skillet and set them aside while mixing the batter (it's OK if the skillet is still warm when the batter is added) and increase the baking time by 7 to 9 minutes. If you don't have either a 2-inch high cake pan or an ovenproof skillet, use an 8-inch square pan.

Topping
- 4 tablespoons (½ stick) unsalted butter, cut into 4 pieces, plus extra for pan
- 4 Granny Smith or Golden Delicious apples (about 2 pounds), peeled and cored
- ⅔ cup packed (4⅔ ounces) light brown sugar
- 2 teaspoons juice from 1 lemon

Cake
- 1 cup (5 ounces) unbleached all-purpose flour
- 1 tablespoon cornmeal (optional)
- 1 teaspoon baking powder
- ½ teaspoon table salt
- ¾ cup (5¼ ounces) granulated sugar
- ¼ cup packed (1¾ ounces) light brown sugar
- 2 large eggs
- 6 tablespoons (¾ stick) unsalted butter, melted and cooled slightly
- ½ cup sour cream
- 1 teaspoon vanilla extract

1. **FOR THE TOPPING:** Butter bottom and sides of 9-inch round, 2-inch-deep nonstick cake pan; set aside. Adjust oven rack to lowest position and heat oven to 350 degrees.

2. Halve apples from pole to pole. Cut 2 apples into ¼-inch-thick slices; set aside. Cut remaining 2 apples into ½-inch-thick slices. Heat butter in 12-inch skillet over medium-high heat. When foaming subsides, add ½-inch-thick apple slices and cook, stirring 2 or 3 times, until apples begin to caramelize, 4 to 6 minutes. (Do not fully cook apples.) Add ¼-inch-thick apple slices, brown sugar, and lemon juice; continue cooking, stirring constantly, until sugar dissolves and apples are coated, about 1 minute longer. Transfer apple mixture to prepared pan and lightly press into even layer. Set aside while preparing cake.

3. **FOR THE CAKE:** Whisk flour, cornmeal (if using), baking powder, and salt together in medium bowl; set aside. Whisk granulated sugar, brown sugar, and eggs together in large bowl until thick and homogeneous, about 45 seconds. Slowly whisk in butter until combined. Add sour cream and vanilla; whisk until combined. Add flour mixture and whisk until just combined. Pour batter into pan and spread evenly over fruit. Bake until cake is golden brown and toothpick inserted into center comes out clean, 35 to 40 minutes.

4. Cool pan on wire rack 20 minutes. Run paring knife around sides of cake to loosen. Place wire rack over cake pan. Holding rack tightly, invert cake pan and wire rack together; lift off cake pan. Place wire rack over baking sheet or large plate to catch any drips. If any fruit sticks to pan bottom, remove and position it on top of cake. Let cake cool 20 minutes (or longer to cool it completely), then transfer to serving platter, cut into pieces, and serve.

APPLE UPSIDE-DOWN CAKE
WITH ALMONDS

Follow recipe for Apple Upside-Down Cake, combining ⅓ cup finely ground toasted almonds with flour and adding 1 teaspoon almond extract with sour cream and vanilla in step 3.

APPLE UPSIDE-DOWN CAKE
WITH LEMON AND THYME

Follow recipe for Apple Upside-Down Cake, adding 1 teaspoon finely grated lemon zest and 1 teaspoon finely chopped fresh thyme leaves with sour cream and vanilla in step 3.

Everyday Lemon Soufflé

Swapping the ramekin for a skillet took some of the fuss out of this finicky French dessert. But for brighter lemon flavor, we had to fudge another French technique.

≥ BY MEGAN WYCOFF ≤

I've always believed that part of a soufflé's ability to inspire fear among cooks is in the presentation. Towering like chefs' toques over the fluted rims of porcelain ramekins, they seem too daunting for a casual weeknight menu. Recipes that propose baking a soufflé in a 10-inch skillet aim to introduce it to the company of cobblers and crisps. The problem is, I haven't found a skillet recipe for a lemon soufflé (my favorite flavor) that comes close to the lightness we're looking for—it inevitably ends up wet and under-risen. And like most lemon soufflés (skillet or traditional), they don't have a truly bright taste. Plus, these recipes still have too many steps.

The most time-consuming part of any soufflé is making the base: a cooked mixture of flour, milk, butter, sugar, and egg yolks, to which whipped egg whites are added before baking. The base provides stability, while the whipped whites offer lift.

Not willing to take anything for granted (particularly stodgy French tradition), I attempted a soufflé without a true béchamel base. I whisked together five egg yolks and ⅔ cup of sugar and, reasoning that the dairy elements might be dulling the lemon flavor, omitted the butter and replaced a full cup of milk with ⅓ cup lemon juice. A typical soufflé contains about 1 tablespoon of flour per egg. But with far less liquid in the mix, I settled on just 2 tablespoons of flour altogether. With such a small amount, adding raw flour to the base (versus cooked in a true béchamel) wasn't likely to be a problem. I folded the meringue into the base and poured the mixture into a skillet to bake at 375 degrees.

It worked, sort of. Tasters couldn't detect the presence of raw flour and found the lemon flavor far brighter without the muting effect of dairy. Plus, the soufflé rose dramatically above the rim of the skillet. But, as with all the skillet soufflé recipes I tested in my research, the bottom of this one was also undercooked. Clearly the thick metal of the pan was protecting its underside, preventing it from cooking properly.

Dropping the oven temperature to 300 degrees in an effort to promote more even cooking between the top and the bottom was a bust. A soufflé needs high heat to cause the air inside it to expand quickly and create its signature rise; otherwise, it turns out more like a lemon pancake. Then my thoughts shifted to another one of France's great desserts (also cooked in a skillet): tarte Tatin. In this rustic dish, apples are first caramelized in the skillet, topped with a layer of pastry, and placed in the oven. The double whammy

of heat from below and then from above ensures that the fruit is fully cooked through. It sounded crazy, but could we use this method on our soufflé?

I gently heated a tablespoon of butter in a 10-inch skillet (just enough to prevent sticking) and poured the batter directly into the pan. It immediately started to set, and after about two minutes was lightly puffed and gently bubbling on the edges. I quickly transferred the skillet to the oven and kept a careful watch. Not 10 minutes later, a golden brown, perfectly puffed soufflé emerged from the oven. Cutting into it with a spoon revealed that the light, moist, and creamy interior went all the way from top to bottom. Once out of the oven, every soufflé will eventually fall—but in this case, tasters made sure it never had a chance to.

SKILLET LEMON SOUFFLÉ
SERVES 6

NOTE: Don't open the oven door during the first seven minutes of baking, but do check the soufflé regularly for doneness during the final few minutes in the oven. Be ready to serve the soufflé immediately after removing it from the oven. A 10-inch skillet is essential to getting the right texture and height.

5	large eggs, separated
¼	teaspoon cream of tartar
⅔	cup (4¾ ounces) granulated sugar
⅛	teaspoon table salt
⅓	cup juice and 1 teaspoon grated zest from 2 to 3 lemons
2	tablespoons unbleached all-purpose flour
1	tablespoon unsalted butter
	Confectioners' sugar, for dusting

1. Adjust oven rack to middle position and heat oven to 375 degrees. Using stand mixer, whip egg whites and cream of tartar together on medium-low speed until foamy, about 1 minute. Slowly add ⅓ cup sugar and salt, then increase speed to medium-high and continue to whip until stiff peaks form, 3 to 5 minutes. Gently transfer whites to clean bowl and set aside.

2. Using stand mixer (no need to wash mixing bowl), whip yolks and remaining ⅓ cup sugar together on medium-high speed until pale and thick, about 1 minute. Whip in lemon juice, zest, and flour until incorporated, about 30 seconds.

3. Whisk ¼ of whipped egg whites into yolk mixture until almost no white streaks remain. Gently

Our soufflé gets a jump-start on the stove before finishing in the oven.

fold in remaining egg whites until just incorporated.

4. Melt butter in 10-inch ovenproof skillet over medium-low heat. Swirl pan to coat evenly with melted butter, then gently scrape soufflé batter into skillet and cook until edges begin to set and bubble slightly, about 2 minutes.

5. Transfer skillet to oven and bake soufflé until puffed, center jiggles slightly when shaken, and surface is golden, 7 to 11 minutes. Using potholder (skillet handle will be hot), remove skillet from oven. Dust soufflé with confectioners' sugar and serve immediately.

SKILLET CHOCOLATE-ORANGE SOUFFLÉ

NOTE: Grating the chocolate fine is key here; use either a Microplane grater or the fine holes of a box grater.

Follow recipe for Skillet Lemon Soufflé, substituting ⅓ cup orange juice for lemon juice and 1 tablespoon grated zest from 1 orange for lemon zest. Gently fold 1 ounce finely grated bittersweet chocolate (about ½ cup) into soufflé batter after incorporating whites in step 3.

■ **COOK'S VIDEOS** Original Test Kitchen Videos
www.cooksillustrated.com/oct09
HOW TO MAKE
• Skillet Lemon Soufflé

Has California Olive Oil Come of Age?

California growers have spent the last two decades developing extra-virgin olive oils that might rival the best of Europe. Is it time to stop importing foreign oil?

⋛ BY LISA McMANUS ⋚

In 1976, the world was stunned when California wines trumped French contenders in a blind tasting by French wine experts, an event now known as the Judgment of Paris. These days, it's California's olive growers who are working to make a product that could compete with Europe. Over the past 20 years or so, growers around the state, guided by experts at the University of California, Davis, have been planting olive trees, learning the best practices for harvesting and blending, and experimenting with a variety of olive presses, all in an effort to create great domestic extra-virgin olive oil. Last year, U.C. Davis opened the Olive Center, with 30 faculty researchers, acres of olive groves, and a new olive press—all with a focus on oil.

Olives are not new to California. Franciscan monks planted olive trees as they established Catholic missions throughout the area in the 1700s. But until recently, most California olives were canned for eating rather than pressed for oil. Today, California produces less than 1 percent of the 70 million gallons of olive oil consumed each year in the United States—a mere toehold that industry proponents hope to expand. Since the key to extra-virgin olive oil is freshness—its flavor degrades over time, even when sealed in a bottle—the potential benefits of buying domestic oil that doesn't have to be imported and waylaid by customs are built in. Wondering if California already sells olive oils as good as our favorite imports, we anonymously purchased 10 extra-virgin oils from the state's largest and most established producers and tasted them blind.

For comparison, we included a bottle of our favorite imported oil, Columela, an extra-virgin olive oil from Spain that sells for about $19 per half liter. The California oils in our lineup range from $12 to $37.33 per half liter, plus shipping, though a few producers ship for free. (Some California growers are working on driving prices even lower so that they can compete in supermarkets against mass-market imported oils. Since harvesting the olives is the biggest production cost, these growers are experimenting with a new trend that is revolutionizing the industry worldwide, so-called super-high-density planting—see "Faster, Cheaper—and Fresher" at right—which also entails mechanical harvesting.) Tasters sampled the oils plain, with green apples to cleanse the palate, and on a crusty baguette with sea salt. We don't generally cook with extra-virgin oil because its unique flavors and aromas dissipate with heat.

The Best Olive Oil?

As to the single "best" flavor profile for extra-virgin olive oil, experts disagree—it would be like choosing the single best type of wine. While many olive oil novices shy away from bitter oils, tasting experts consider bitterness one of the three main positive attributes of extra-virgin oil, along with fruitiness and pungency. Olive oils earn high scores from international tasting panels for having a harmonious balance of these three qualities. They can be marked down for moldy, musty, fermented, or rotting-olive notes or flatness, among other possible flaws.

There are hundreds of varieties of olives. Each contributes a different typical flavor, but even the same olive can produce very different oils depending on the soil and climate where it was grown, the weather during the growing season, and its ripeness when picked. Deciding when to harvest is a critical skill for olive oil makers. Earlier-harvested olives tend to yield a greener, more bitter oil that is rich in polyphenols (a group of antioxidant compounds that lend color and flavor to plants). Later-harvested, riper olives usually create mild, buttery oil, with much lower polyphenol levels. In California, harvest can begin as early as late September and run through January.

The best olive oil is pressed soon after harvesting. Scrupulous oil makers use tree fruit (rather than overripe olives that fell off the tree onto the ground) that is picked carefully and pressed quickly (ideally within 24 hours), before the olives begin to rot and ferment. Pressing and storage equipment must be kept very clean, or olive oil will pick up off-flavors. In other words, if the olives are not handled correctly and pressed quickly under pristine conditions, there will be flavor defects, and the oil will not qualify as true extra-virgin.

The oil maker can bring out certain characteristics depending on the choice of press. For example, olives may be stone-crushed or fed into a hammer mill or a metal-toothed blade mill. Oil makers can gently boost the bitterness in a too-mild olive by using metal-toothed blades that cut into the skin, releasing polyphenols. Or they can produce a milder oil by selecting a stone mill; its crushing motion

Faster, Cheaper—and Fresher

To increase production, drive down costs—and make fresher oil—some California olive growers are implementing a revolutionary new way of growing and harvesting olives known as "super-high-density planting." This approach, which relies on irrigation, was pioneered by Spanish growers in the mid-1990s and allows for up to 10 times as many trees to be planted per acre than in traditional groves (in the past, the number was limited to what groves in dry Mediterranean climates could sustain without irrigation). Equally important: It allows for machine harvesting—a faster, cheaper way of getting olives to the press. Machines can harvest an entire crop in a matter of hours, not days that hand harvesting takes, for supremely fresh-tasting oil. Thanks to super-high-density planting and machine harvesting, the olives of our winning brand, California Olive Press, can be sent to the press in as little as 90 minutes. –L.M.

TRADITIONAL GROVE

HIGH-DENSITY PLANTING

extracts fewer polyphenols. Some growers even use a combination of presses.

Whether to blend the oil is another key choice. Like wine, olive oil can be made from a single varietal or a mix. Blends can be created in the field, with olive trees that are planted and harvested and their olives pressed together, or in the mill, where an expert mixes batches of oils to create a particular flavor profile. European olive oils are often blends; the types of olive are listed in small print on the label, if at all. By contrast, California oil producers often focus on a specific type of olive and may sell multiple oils each year highlighting different types (for example, a choice of an Ascolano, an Arbequina, or a Miller's Blend).

The producer must also decide whether to filter the oil or leave it unfiltered. Unfiltered oil contains more flavorful olive particles, but these shorten the shelf life of the oil, as they are prone to spoilage.

Finally, the storage method makes a significant difference. Olive oil stays freshest when protected from air, light, and heat in nonreactive stainless steel tanks, topped with an odorless and inert gas to prevent oxygen exposure and bottled only on demand. (Many of the oils we tasted were bottled on demand or in very small batches, making them far fresher than the olive oil sold in the typical supermarket or gourmet store.) The shelf life of bottled olive oil depends on how well the oil was protected from air, heat, and light and can range from as few as three months up to 18 months after the bottle is opened. Why? Different oils age differently even when stored properly. Some olives naturally contain more antioxidants, which resist the oxidation that causes rancidity.

No "California" Flavor

Far from having one typical flavor profile, the California oils we tasted featured a range of styles. Although the state's first olive oil producers favored Tuscan olive varieties and picked them early in the season for a green, bitter profile that mimicked Tuscan oils, California oils today run the gamut from buttery and mild to pungent and robust. With many different microclimates in the state, California olive producers have experimented with olives that grow well in parts of Europe that have similar climates. (Experimentation and collaboration are hallmarks of the California olive oil industry.)

What did our tasters conclude? The top-ranked oil across the board was still Columela, the Spanish oil that our tasters praised for its full, fruity, well-balanced flavor and low bitterness. But the real surprise was that a domestic challenger ranked just below it. California Olive Ranch's extra-virgin oil, made from Arbequina olives, won raves for its fresh, sweet, fruity flavor and pleasing hint of bitterness.

Based in the northern California city of Oroville, California Olive Ranch is the largest North American producer of olive oil and one of the pioneers in cheaper growing and harvesting methods. In addition to lowering production costs, California Olive Ranch's high-density planting and all-mechanical harvesting helps capture fresh flavor, since olives can be picked and sent to the press in just 90 minutes. Most olives around the world are still harvested by hand. Traditionally, nets are spread under the trees, and laborers use wooden rakes to pull off the olives or employ a machine that shakes the trunks so that olives fall onto the nets, which are then loaded into bins for travel to the press. This process is time-consuming, labor-intensive, and costly. When acres of olives ripen at once, as they tend to do in hot climates like in Spain or Tunisia, olives may sit around fermenting as they wait to be pressed. This is the source of one of the chief flavor defects in olive oil, an attribute experts term "fustiness."

Fresh olive flavor is one of the qualities our tasters found most appealing in our highest-ranked oils. The oils we bought were harvested no earlier than fall 2007, but most of our top-ranked oils were from the more recent harvest of 2008, pressed a scant few months before we tasted them in March 2009. (Olive oil usually is placed in a holding tank for a month or two before bottling; it takes that long for most of the olive sediment to settle to the bottom of the tank for removal and for the flavors to meld and mellow.) We didn't intentionally set out to buy olive oil from two different harvest years; when you place an order, you get the oil available for sale at that time. If stored properly, the previous year's harvest will still be in its prime.

Our tasters also preferred unfiltered oils. Filtering removes fine, suspended olive particles and clarifies the oil but also removes some of the fresh olive flavor tasters enjoyed.

As for specific olive preferences, our tasters liked the flavor of the Arbequina olives in the California Olive Ranch oil—which happens to be one of the four olive varieties blended in Columela oil. Common in Spain, Arbequina has recently become one of the most-planted olive varieties in California, both for its fruity, well-balanced flavor and because it is suited to super-high-density planting. Oils made with typical Tuscan varieties (Frantoio, Leccino, Maurino, Pendolino) scored less favorably with our panel, possibly because they have a more bitter, pungent profile, which is an acquired taste. Sevillano olives, used in the high-ranking Sciabica oil, are traditionally canned as eating olives, but when pressed create exceptionally fruity oil.

Columela Extra-Virgin Olive Oil is still the test kitchen favorite. Like many of the California oils we tested, it is made by a family-run business (Anfora Quality Products of Cordoba, Spain) that maintains quality by owning and controlling every aspect of production. The company picks and presses its olives within 24 hours, hand-picking as well as using tree-shaking machinery. After processing the premium oil as Columela, the company re-presses those olives and sells the remaining oil at a lower price, under a different brand name. Finally, Columela is bottled only when distributors place an order, and once the new harvest is in, any oil from the previous year's

Fresh Off the Press

Every year at harvest time, Italians look forward to the *olio nuovo*, or "new oil." It's the first extra-virgin olive oil off the press—full of fine olive particles suspended in brilliant green oil. (Ordinarily, fresh-pressed extra-virgin olive oil is stored in steel tanks for about two months before bottling to give sediment time to settle to the bottom and let the oil's flavor mellow and stabilize.) Italians use olio nuovo lavishly, relishing its fresh, intense flavor, because within several weeks that olive sediment begins to ferment into off-flavors, and it's all over until next year's harvest.

Unless you're lucky enough to have Old World relatives with an olive press, olio nuovo can be hard to come by. It wasn't until last December, when I visited California olive oil makers in the middle of harvest season, that I had the opportunity to taste olio nuovo.

At the Olive Press in Sonoma, managing partner Deborah Rogers filled a small glass bottle right from the stream of oil trickling out of the press, and we sat down to sample it. The full, vivid, fresh flavor proved addictive. Back at home, I tried olio nuovo from McEvoy Ranch in Marin County and California Olive Ranch in Oroville, enjoying them daily until they ran out.

Many California oil producers sell olio nuovo on their websites, and I'm planning to make ordering it a winter tradition. Who needs European connections? –L.M.

FIRST OIL OF THE SEASON
Once exclusively an Old World pleasure, olio nuovo is now available from California.

harvest remaining in storage is sold off under its lower-priced label.

For now, we're convinced that Europe still maintains a stronghold in this intercontinental oil battle, but the California growers—particularly the folks behind our favorite, relatively affordable California Olive Ranch Extra Virgin Oil ($13.97 per half liter plus shipping)—have clearly struck something promising. As they further refine their products, we'll look for the day when we can pick up California olive oil in the supermarket, right next to the imported oils.

TASTING CALIFORNIA EXTRA-VIRGIN OLIVE OILS

Twenty-one members of the *Cook's Illustrated* staff tasted 10 California extra-virgin olive oils, comparing them to our favorite imported olive oil, Columela, a Spanish product that has beaten nearly two dozen oils in previous tastings. We tasted them both plain and on French bread and rated them on fruitiness, bitterness, balance of flavor, and overall appeal. Results were averaged, and Columela came in first by a mere half point on a scale of 0–10. The California oils are listed in order of preference. Prices were paid online and are calculated by the half liter to assist in price comparison; bottles may not be sold in that size. Prices for mail-order oils do not include shipping (though two producers offer free shipping). The source for the top-ranked oil appears on page 32.

RECOMMENDED

CALIFORNIA OLIVE RANCH Arbequina
Price: $13.97 per half liter
Olive: Arbequina, unfiltered
Harvest: Fall/Winter 2008
Comments: This oil by North America's largest olive oil producer came in just a fraction of a point behind our imported favorite (Columela), winning out over other California oils with a similar profile: full, fruity olive flavor and little bitterness or pungency. "Lovely, nutty, and fruity," with notes of "lemon," "vanilla," and "honey." "Quite buttery and round and almost sweet," tasters raved. "The aftertaste is fresh, pure olive."

SCIABICA'S Sevillano Variety Fall 2008 Harvest
Price: $26.60 per half liter
Olive: Sevillano, unfiltered
Harvest: Fall 2008
Comments: "Green, pungent, and moderately bitter," agreed tasters. "Tastes like it's fresh," with a "spicy, peppery aroma and a buttery aftertaste" and notes of "fennel/licorice," "green apple," and "green grass"; flavors are "harmonious" and "balanced," "surprisingly sweet," "like fresh peas." "Smells like sun-warmed hay, very clean and soft." One taster simply wrote: "Olive-y goodness."

PACIFIC SUN Tehama County Blend
Price: $12 per half liter
Olives: Mission and Ascolano, unfiltered
Harvest: December 2008
Comments: A blend of mild, late-harvest Mission olives with peppery, early-harvest Ascolano olives, this oil impressed tasters as "buttery, not bitter at all," "not pungent" but "mild," "smooth," "floral," like "roses," with a "fruity aroma" and notes of "passion fruit, pineapple," and "melon" with a "nutty" finish, "like walnuts." "Nice flavor, more complex than most."

LUCERO Ascolano
Price: $28 per half liter, free shipping for orders $50 and up
Olive: Ascolano, unfiltered
Harvest: Fall/Winter 2008
Comments: "Unusually fruity," this olive oil "tastes like olives in a fruity, rounded way." Tasters found it "apple-y and fresh, with a peppery kick" and "strong," with "cut-grass," "clover," or "grapefruit" notes. "Tastes like it smells." One summed it up as "slightly too bitter, but perfectly balanced potency."

RECOMMENDED WITH RESERVATIONS

DaVERO Dry Creek Estate
Price: $37.33 per half liter
Olives: Field blend of Leccino, Frantoio, Maurino, and Pendolino, planted at a ratio of 50%, 25%, 15%, and 10%, unfiltered
Harvest: Fall/Winter 2007
Comments: "Wow, it sure does taste like fresh olive oil. Reminiscent of green herbs and artichokes. I like it," wrote one happy taster. "Complex and almost zesty," agreed another. Others found this blend of Italian olives too "harsh" and "bitter" in a way that "overpowered the fruitiness" and was "very peppery, sharp, and pungent," though one taster noted, "It grows on you. Bitter at first, but mellows nicely."

RECOMMENDED WITH RESERVATIONS (CONT.)

McEVOY RANCH Traditional Blend
Price: $28 per half liter
Olives: Frantoio, Leccino, Pendolino, Maurino, Coratina, and Leccio del Corno, organic and unfiltered
Harvest: Fall 2008
Comments: "Yikes!" "Quite pungent, very bitter flavor, like olive leaves and pits," "like swallowing an M-80 of cayenne," "horseradish strong!" "like fresh ground peppercorns," or "rosemary grass." "Tastes quite young," wrote one taster; "like a peppered apple," "full bodied," and "almost too potent," said others. In sum: "The bitter taste is bullying the fruity one."

STELLA CADENTE L'Autunno Blend
Price: $25 per half liter
Olives: Leccino, Frantoio, Pendolino, Coratina, and Mission, unfiltered
Harvest: Fall/Winter 2007
Comments: "Light and fruity," this oil started out tasting "subtle" and "buttery." "Really tame," said one taster, while others remarked on "citrusy" or "lemony" notes. Several were turned off by a "viscous," "greasy" texture and a slightly "musty" smell, as well as a "harsh," almost "sour" aftertaste that was "sharp" and "stays with you." One taster concluded, "Everything in balance but meek and mild."

APOLLO Mistral Blend
Price: $26.60 per half liter
Olives: Picholine, French Columella, Groussane, and Ascolano, organic and filtered
Harvest: December 2007
Comments: "Extreme peppery kick with a lot of bitterness," "super-green," "very pungent," "robust," and "not for the faint of heart," this "complex" oil had "big fruit and spice," with tasters describing "unripe flavors" and notes of "artichokes," "lemon," "grass," "hay," and "olive leaves." Some tasters picked up off-notes, including a hint of "copper penny" or "gasoline." "Astringent" and (to some) "overwhelming," it was also "vaguely nutty," "like cashews."

LODESTAR Traditional Late Harvest Mission
Price: $17.95 per half liter, free shipping
Olive: Mission, filtered
Harvest: January 2008
Comments: "Spicy yet smooth," this mellow oil was described as either "mild" or "dull," depending on the taster. While some called it "floral" and "delicate," "buttery, almond-y, and nutty," others deemed it "nothing special" or "bland," "like canola oil," "somewhat flat," with "little body, hardly any flavor" and "slight vanilla/cherry notes." "Very surprising that this is extra-virgin," said one taster.

THE OLIVE PRESS Arbequina
Price: $26 per half liter
Olive: Arbequina, unfiltered
Harvest: 2007
Comments: Tasters described this oil as having "fruity flavor that was mild and fleeting," with a "really sharp and bitter" finish that was "strong and lasting" and "overpowered the fruity, vegetal" flavors; "just too bitter," "almost inedibly so." One taster summed it up as offering "too little flavor, a lot of bite," though another noted, "too strong by itself, but I love the taste of this oil with bread."

Are "Green" Skillets Really Green?

Eco-friendly nonstick skillets promise to help the planet while they cook your dinner. But do any actually measure up?

⊰ BY MEREDITH BUTCHER ⊱

With every product from the shopping bag to the SUV undergoing an environmentally friendly makeover, it's no surprise that the nonstick skillet is getting its turn. Cookware makers have launched a variety of nonstick pans touted as "eco-friendly," some also promising that their new coatings will last longer, work at higher temperatures, and resist scratches. But as our testing revealed, it's not easy being both green and a solid performer. Furthermore, whether some of these pans are really any greener than the old nonstick is a big open question.

Two of the new coatings (ceramic and silicone) are entirely free of the chemicals identified in traditional, Teflon-style nonstick. But a third type merely eliminates the most notorious chemical, PFOA. (For a rundown on concerns about the chemicals in traditional nonstick coatings, see "What's Wrong with Regular Nonstick?," below.)

We rounded up all the "green" skillets available as open stock items in a 12-inch size (or the closest to it) in each of the three types. We took these eight pans and compared them to our previous Best Buy nonstick skillet with a traditional Teflon-style coating from WearEver (it has since been discontinued).

In each pan, we cooked several of the dishes that nonstick skillets do so well—scrambled eggs, fish fillets, and frittatas, along with steak and stir-fries—and rated the pans on how evenly they cooked the foods and how easily they released them. We used metal utensils on the pans to test manufacturers' claims about scratch resistance; we also monitored their tendency to stain or discolor and the durability of their coatings. Since we don't recommend spending a lot of money on nonstick pans because the coating gradually wears off, this was a particular concern. A well-designed pan was another requirement, so we also rated them on balance, weight, and shape.

Underachievers

Not a single one of these "green" pans was without flaws. In some, delicate eggs burned, thin fish fillets stuck, and steak charred on the outside while remaining raw within. Others stained or transferred heat inconsistently. Some pans started to build the browned bits known as *fond* as we seared steak, indicating an unwanted sticking power. Stir-fries were more forgiving, but a few pans steamed the meat and left vegetables pallid and rubbery.

To test claims made by some manufacturers that the pans could withstand metal utensils, we made frittatas and sliced them directly in the skillets with a chef's knife, then used a metal pie server to remove each slice (a test we have conducted on regular nonstick skillets). While some models sustained shallower scratches than others, all showed marks and scrapes, just as the traditional nonstick pan did. (Despite manufacturers' claims, we recommend treating "green" skillets as carefully as you would any regular nonstick pan; do not use metal utensils.)

Overall, the performance of the new skillets was subpar compared with our traditional nonstick skillet. A pan's strengths and shortcomings depended mostly on the type of nonstick coating.

Surface and Performance

Ceramic coatings are made by slowly baking a mixture of ceramic powder and water or solvent onto a base of stainless steel or aluminum. Because ceramics are extremely brittle, expanding and contracting at a different rate than the metal base they are bonded to, we expected that such coatings might prove less durable. Testing confirmed our suspicions; when we were done, the surface of one ceramic pan was even covered with what looked like burst bubbles.

Ceramic-coated aluminum pans had another flaw: Because aluminum is a rapid conductor of heat, these pans quickly became extremely hot. But due to the thinness of the ceramic coating, the pans could not retain heat once food was added, resulting in overly slow cooking and steaming rather than browning.

Silicone copolymer coatings, in which a fine layer of a silicone copolymer is sprayed over a metal pan, proved more resilient than ceramic coatings, but still wore off within a few days as we cooked and washed them repeatedly. While these pans reacted more predictably to temperature adjustment, steak did not release easily and left fond; eventually food stuck even when we added oil, leaving a blackened mess. Despite this flaw, their low marks on durability, and their tendency to discolor and become scratched, these pans still outperformed the ceramic contenders.

The final category of skillets, whose coatings are PFOA-free but contain the moisture-repellent PTFE, performed much as we expected, maintaining their nonstick properties well compared to other models. These pans easily released food and browned evenly during every test. Eggs cooked perfectly. Fish did not stick, nor did it leave an imprint. However, like traditional nonstick, these pans can emit dangerous fumes from the PTFE if left empty over high heat.

Not Ready for Prime Time

As we conducted cooking tests, we realized we don't really care how good the nonstick coating is if the pan is uncomfortable to use. None of the skillets had a flawless design—if it was the right size, it was too heavy; if it was lightweight and maneuverable, the cooking surface was too small for many recipes. We had to conclude that while the engineers focused on new nonstick coatings, they forgot about the basic requirement of a comfortable, well-designed pan.

In addition, most of these pans are also just not as durable as traditional nonstick. Hugh Rushing of the Cookware Manufacturers Association (a trade association) concurred with our assessment. Based on testing the CMA has done in its own test kitchens, the ceramic-coated models are simply "not as well-performing," Rushing said.

Experts like Rushing are also not convinced that these pans are really "green." Because of their newer technology, ceramic- and silicone-coated skillets require more resources to manufacture than traditional nonstick pans. And how "green" can a pan really be that still contains at least one potentially harmful chemical, PTFE? Rushing's answer: "Not very." Until "green" skillet technology improves, we're sticking with traditional nonstick or a well-seasoned cast-iron pan.

What's Wrong with Regular Nonstick?

Traditional nonstick coatings use two controversial chemicals: PFOA and PTFE. While some "green" skillets have eliminated both chemicals from their coatings, others still contain PTFE. A few facts to consider about each:

- PFOA, or perfluorooctanoic acid, is a processing agent widely used in manufacturing that has been detected in water, food, wildlife, and human blood samples. The Environmental Protection Agency cites it for causing birth defects in laboratory animals and has urged that companies eliminate it by 2015.

- PTFE is polytetrafluoroethylene. Though inert, when heated above 660 degrees (a range easily reached if the pan is left empty over high heat), PTFE breaks down and releases toxic fumes that can kill birds and cause flulike symptoms in people. –M.B.

TESTING "GREEN" SKILLETS

We tested eight "green" skillets ranging in price from $32.24 to $139.99, comparing them to our previous favorite traditional nonstick pan from WearEver (since discontinued). Prices were paid in Boston-area retail stores or online. Skillets are listed in order of preference.

NONSTICK PERFORMANCE: We scrambled eggs, fried fish fillets, seared steaks, and stir-fried beef and vegetables. High marks were given to pans that released food evenly, browned well while avoiding fond development, and cleaned up easily.

DESIGN: We considered features such as handles, weight, and shape.

DURABILITY/ SCRATCHING: To assess durability, we used the pans repeatedly for three 8-hour days, hand-washing the pans between tests. To test scratch resistance, we sliced a frittata with a chef's knife in each skillet and removed slices with a metal pie server.

The Original Green Skillet

It's heavy, and it needs to be seasoned—but a cast-iron skillet is chemical-free, inexpensive (our favorite 12-inch model, from Lodge, costs $33.95), with great nonstick performance that will last you a lifetime. You can't get any greener than that.

LODGE LOGIC CAST-IRON SKILLET

RECOMMENDED WITH RESERVATIONS

	PERFORMANCE	TESTERS' COMMENTS

SCANPAN Professional 12.25" Fry Pan
Model: 60003200
Price: $129.95
Coating: Contains PTFE, no PFOA
Base Material: Compressed aluminum with ceramic titanium
Cooking Surface: 10.75" Weight: 3.3 lbs

Nonstick Performance: ★★★
Design: ★★
Durability/Scratching: ★★

Steaks seared well and browned evenly on this pan's generous surface area, which was gentle enough to cook fish and scramble eggs without sticking. Metal utensils left slight scratches, but overall this pan had the most durable surface of all the models and performed closest to traditional nonstick. Still, the pan was unbalanced, too heavy, and slightly oversized: At 12.25 inches, a standard 12-inch lid will not fit it.

EARTH PAN 12" Hard Anodized Skillet
Model: 19495EPR
Price: $39.95
Coating: Silicone copolymer
Base Material: Hard anodized aluminum
Cooking Surface: 9.62" Weight: 2.18 lbs

Nonstick Performance: ★★
Design: ★★
Durability/Scratching: ★★

At first this pan easily released food, but after days of testing, we noticed deterioration of the nonstick surface, fond that began to build up when we cooked, and light but visible scratches. However, the skillet felt comfortable, and sautéing was quick and easy, though a few testers felt the handle was a little low and awkward.

DEMEYERE-RESTO 12.6" Ecoglide Frying Pan without Lid
Model: 85632
Price: $139.99
Coating: Contains PTFE, no PFOA
Base Material: Stainless steel
Cooking Surface: 10.75" Weight: 3.9 lbs

Nonstick Performance: ★★★
Design: ★
Durability/Scratching: ★

Far too heavy and cumbersome, but the nonstick quality was excellent. It took noticeably longer to heat than other skillets, but once the pan was at temperature, food browned evenly. Scrambled eggs turned out light and fluffy, though the coating became severely scratched when we used metal utensils.

NOT RECOMMENDED

	PERFORMANCE	TESTERS' COMMENTS

GREENPAN Frypan 12.5"
Model: 355051
Price: $84.95
Coating: Ceramic
Base Material: Hard anodized aluminum
Cooking Surface: 9" Weight: 2.55 lbs

Nonstick Performance: ★★
Design: ★★
Durability/Scratching: ★

This ceramic-coated aluminum pan performed extremely well starting out but slipped as testing went on. Eggs and fish released easily, but we struggled to cook steak evenly. The higher, more vertical sides and small cooking surface cramped food; it also discolored and became severely scratched. The comfortable, heat-resistant handle was one of the few bright spots.

CUISINART GreenGourmet 12" Skillet with Helper Handle
Model: GG22-30H
Price: $69.95
Coating: Ceramic
Base Material: Hard anodized aluminum
Cooking Surface: 9" Weight: 3.4 lbs

Nonstick Performance: ★
Design: ★
Durability/Scratching: ★★

The extra handle came in handy on this heavy pan, but that feature couldn't outweigh its generally subpar performance. Scrambled eggs stuck to the sides and rivets. The vertical sides and smaller cooking surface crowded steaks, which burned on the outside before they were cooked through. However, stir-fry results were good and scratches and other wear and tear were minimal.

STARFRIT Alternative Eco Pan 11" Fry Pan
Model: 30432-003-0000
Price: $33.60
Coating: Ceramic
Base Material: Cast aluminum
Cooking Surface: 9.62" Weight: 2.25 lbs

Nonstick Performance: ★
Design: ★
Durability/Scratching: ★

The handle on this flimsy pan started to loosen after the first few tests, and because it is not heat-resistant, the pan couldn't go in the oven. Temperature was hard to control; eggs stuck. Steaks were crowded and steamed. Fish stuck and ripped when we tried to remove it from the skillet. The pan sustained deep scratches.

CLASSICOR Go Green Nonstick 11.5" Skillet
Model: 29352
Price: $32.24
Coating: Ceramic
Base Material: Stainless steel
Cooking Surface: 8.75" Weight: 2.1 lbs

Nonstick Performance: ★
Design: ★
Durability/Scratching: ★

During the first test, the interior deteriorated and chipped (after making scrambled eggs!). The results headed south from there. The small surface area made things cramped, food steamed, and the pan became terribly scratched.

XTREMA 10" Open Skillet
Model: 99359
Price: $99.99
Material: Solid ceramic
Cooking Surface: 8.75" Weight: 2.1 lbs

Nonstick Performance: ★
Design: ★
Durability/Scratching: ★

This clunky, pottery-like skillet—made of 100 percent ceramic—barely functioned. Food consistently stuck or, worse, burned. The coating was destroyed after one test. Scrambled eggs became so encrusted we had to soak the pan overnight. Steaks burned on the outside before cooking through.

TASTING **Dried Mushrooms**

Our recipes often call for dried porcini mushrooms to add an intense, earthy flavor to stews and sauces. But what about other dried mushroom offerings at the supermarket? We bought packages of dried morel, chanterelle, and black trumpet mushrooms and then followed our typical method for reconstituting them—covering them in water, microwaving on high for 30 seconds, and allowing them to steep for five minutes. We then used each one in place of dried porcini in recipes for mushroom risotto and porcini-Marsala pan sauce. With some adjustments, all proved acceptable substitutes. Our changes were straightforward: bumping up the proportion of mild morels, increasing the soaking time for chewy chanterelles, and reducing the amount of smoky-flavored black trumpets.

DRIED MUSHROOMS	FLAVOR/TEXTURE	HOW TO SUBSTITUTE
Morel 	Milder than porcini. Woodsy, with a meatlike flavor. Ridged texture is good for catching sauce.	For each ounce of dried porcini, use 1 ½ ounces dried morels.
Chanterelle 	Bright, fresh, slightly sour flavor, with a perfumelike aroma.	Use the same amount of dried chanterelles as dried porcini. Steep for 35 minutes after microwaving to fully soften. Discard any stems that do not soften.
Black Trumpet 	Smoky and peppery, with an aroma of moist earth.	For every ounce of dried porcini, use ½ ounce dried trumpets. Because trumpets hold lots of grit and pine needles, rinse with extra care.

TECHNIQUE

HOW TO USE A MORTAR AND PESTLE

The key to using a mortar and pestle effectively is circular grinding, not up-and-down pounding. (Pounding is less efficient and scatters ingredients.) Here's how to effectively grind spices to a fine powder.

Place the spices in the mortar. Steady it in your left hand and press the pestle's rounded base against the inside of the mortar with your right hand (reverse for lefties). Rotate the pestle, without lifting the head and maintaining downward pressure at all times, until your spices are ground to the desired consistency.

Lighter Béchamel

A béchamel is a basic French white sauce made by stirring milk into a butter-flour roux. It is the base for numerous dishes such as lasagna and creamed spinach. To find out whether skim milk can be substituted for whole milk in a béchamel without sacrificing flavor, we cooked up both kinds using 4 tablespoons butter, ¼ cup flour, 4 cups milk, and ¾ teaspoon salt. Tasted on its own, the skim version lacked the rich flavor of the sauce made with whole milk and was noticeably less viscous. Flavor differences faded away once we tasted the sauces baked in spinach lasagna and lasagna Bolognese, but the skim milk sauce's thinness was still evident. To add body, we experimented with increasing the amounts of both butter and flour. Ultimately, we found that just an extra teaspoon of flour per cup of milk was enough to turn this lighter sauce into a perfectly acceptable substitute for whole-milk béchamel when cooked into recipes.

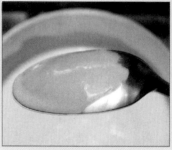 

SWIMMING IN SKIM
Substituting skim milk for whole milk results in watery béchamel.

FLOUR FIX
An extra teaspoon of flour per cup of skim milk helps thicken it to the right consistency.

The Rundown on Coffee Roasts

As any coffee hound knows, roasting is the process that transforms the green beans into far more complex-tasting entities, and the degree to which they are roasted has as much of an impact on their final profile as their intrinsic flavors. While coffee roasters use a variety of names to categorize the darkness of their roasts (Italian, French, Viennese, or Full City, to name a few), there are no industry standards regulating this nomenclature. At best, these terms offer only general clues as to coffee flavor. We've found it's more useful to categorize roasts by color. At one end of the spectrum are light roasts, characterized by their pale brown color and the bright, fruity, more acidic flavors that emerge in the early stages of roasting. As the beans continue to be roasted and their color deepens, the acids are broken down, and sweeter, more caramelized flavors begin to surface.

Choosing your roast is a matter of preference, but how you take your coffee is also a consideration. In taste tests, we preferred lighter roasts for black coffee, but when milk was added, our preference switched to darker roasts. That's because the proteins in milk and cream bind some of the bitter-tasting phenolic compounds in these more deeply roasted beans, reducing both bitterness and intensity of coffee flavor.

ROAST	COLOR/TEXTURE	FLAVOR
Light	Pale brown with dry surface	Light body and bright, fruity, acidic flavor
Medium	Medium brown with dry surface	Less acidity and the beginnings of richer, sweeter notes
Medium-Dark	Dark mahogany with slight oily sheen	Intense, caramelized flavors with subtle bittersweet aftertaste
Dark	Shiny black with oily surface	Pronounced bitterness with few nuances

A Better Brand of Vanilla Extract: Your Own

Most of vanilla's flavor compounds are soluble in either water or alcohol, so the most shelf-stable form of vanilla is vanilla extract, produced by soaking vanilla beans in a solution of 65 percent water and at least 35 percent alcohol. We wondered if we could make our own vanilla extract by soaking a split vanilla bean in heated vodka (which would contribute very little of its own flavor). After testing several ratios of vanilla beans to vodka, we arrived at 1 bean per ¾ cup of vodka as the proportion most closely resembling the potency of our recommended store-bought brand, McCormick Pure Vanilla Extract. We then tested our homemade extract against this supermarket product in sugar cookies, crème brûlée, and vanilla buttercream frosting. In each case, our extract outperformed the commercial version, boasting cleaner, more intense vanilla flavor.

To make vanilla extract, split a fresh bean lengthwise and scrape out the seeds. Place the seeds and split pod in a 1-cup sealable container. Add ¾ cup hot vodka (we used Smirnoff—a premium brand is not necessary) and let the mixture cool to room temperature. Seal the container and store at room temperature for one week, shaking gently every day. Strain the extract, if desired, and store in a cool, dark place. The extract should keep indefinitely.

BETTER FLAVOR, BETTER PRICE
This store-bought extract costs about $4 per ounce; our homemade version costs half that.

TEST KITCHEN TIP Lettuce Storage

Here's the best way to store the most common types of lettuce when you get home from the supermarket:

LETTUCE TYPE	HOW TO STORE
Crisp heads, such as iceberg or romaine	Core lettuce, wrap in moist paper towels, and refrigerate in plastic produce bag or zipper-lock bag left slightly open. 
Leafy greens, such as arugula, baby spinach, or mesclun	Store in original plastic container or wash and dry thoroughly in salad spinner and store directly in spinner. 
Tender heads, such as Boston (or Bibb or butterhead) lettuce	If lettuce comes with root attached, leave lettuce portion attached to root and store in original plastic container, plastic produce bag, or zipper-lock bag left slightly open. If lettuce is without root, wrap in moist paper towels and refrigerate in plastic produce bag or zipper-lock bag left slightly open.

TEST KITCHEN TIP Do-It-Yourself Ricotta

We find most supermarket ricotta to be gummy and grainy, lacking the rich, milky-sweet flavor and moist texture of ricotta handmade without stabilizers. Fortunately, making your own is very simple: Heat 1 gallon whole milk and 1 teaspoon salt to 185 degrees over medium-high heat in a Dutch oven; remove from the heat and slowly stir in ⅓ cup lemon juice. Allow the mixture to stand, undisturbed, for 5 minutes. If the milk hasn't separated into solid white

SUPERIOR TO STORE-BOUGHT
Ricotta made from scratch has a sweet, milky flavor and pillowy texture.

curds and translucent liquid whey, gently stir in 1 more tablespoon of lemon juice and let stand again, repeating the process if necessary. Spoon the curds into a colander lined with cheesecloth and drain, without pressing or disturbing, overnight in refrigerator. This technique will yield 3½ cups of a superior-tasting ricotta facsimile (true ricotta is made from the whey created as a byproduct of cheese-making) that can be used in recipes from lasagna and manicotti to cheesecake and ricotta pie. To view our free video, "How to Make Ricotta," visit www. cooksillustrated.com/oct09.

TECHNIQUE | STABILIZING THE WHISKING BOWL

Many recipes, like vinaigrette or mayonnaise, call for slowly drizzling an ingredient into a bowl with one hand while simultaneously whisking the mixture with the other, leaving you with no free hands to keep the bowl stable. Here's how to keep things steady.

1. Line a heavy pot slightly smaller than your mixing bowl with a dampened kitchen towel, tucking one corner of the towel under another to secure it.

2. Place the mixing bowl inside the towel-lined pot. Your bowl will now be held securely as you whisk.

The Final Word on Coffee Filters

When it comes to which filter is better for manual and automatic drip coffee makers—paper or metal—the experts are divided. Some say brewing through paper filters can impart papery off-flavors and trap some of the delicate aromatic oils that enrich coffee flavor. Others insist that metal filters produce a weaker brew and that their larger openings allow too many grounds to pass through. To see for ourselves, we ground enough beans for two batches of coffee, brewing one batch in a manual-drip coffee maker using a paper filter and the other in a second manual-drip using a metal filter. Our in-house panel of experts found the two brews virtually identical in flavor, with no unwanted tastes or lack of complexity in the paper-filtered coffee. The coffee made with a metal filter clearly had more body from the presence of fine particles and tasted ever so slightly weaker than the paper brew. Our recommendation? Use paper if you like your coffee without any particles in the mix. Metal is fine if you prefer coffee with body, but since water passes through this kind of filter faster than paper, grind the coffee a little finer to achieve the proper extraction.

PARTICLE-FREE BREW

COFFEE WITH BODY

EQUIPMENT CORNER

⇒ BY MEREDITH BUTCHER & PEGGY CHUNG COLLIER ⇐

EQUIPMENT TESTING

Upscale Blenders

Does a blender that costs three times as much as a good mid-priced model really do that much better of a job? We pitted our favorite moderately priced blender, the KitchenAid 5-Speed Blender ($149.99), against two new upscale appliances, the Blendtec Total Blender ($399.95) and the Vita-Mix 5200 ($449). After putting the three machines through their paces, we found the Blendtec absurdly turbo-charged, turning a smoothie into thin juice. Worse, it couldn't perform the main function required of a blender (crushing ice),

MILLIONAIRES' MODEL
The Vita-Mix 5200 offers ultimate blending—at a steep price.

as its extreme speed and power made no difference when ice got trapped out of reach. As for the Vita-Mix 5200 (an update of a model we recommended in 2002), it aced our crushing, blending, and mixing tests. A low setting on the dial transformed chickpeas into creamy hummus in seconds; with a quick turn, it burst full speed ahead, pulverizing frozen fruit into perfect, lump-free smoothies. If your blender is in constant use, the Vita-Mix is a great investment. But for most of us, the $149.99 KitchenAid 5-Speed Blender will do just fine.

DO YOU REALLY NEED THIS?

French Fry Pans

Special "French fry pans" claim to improve crispness when you bake frozen fries (and other frozen foods where a crisp exterior is desirable) by allowing hot air to circulate through perforations in the pan. We baked frozen fries on three models, by Kaiser Bakeware ($24), KitchenAid ($19.99), and Hampton ($8.99)—all made of dark, nonstick metal—and compared them to fries cooked on a regular rimmed baking sheet. The results were not pretty: Fries baked on these specialty pans were either pale and soggy or dehydrated, and in all cases less crisp than the baking-sheet batch. Here's why: Perforations allow moisture from the potatoes to release and evaporate, lowering the temperature of the pan. We'll stick with a baking sheet for frozen fries.

THE HOLE TRUTH
Perforations in this Kaiser French fry pan fall short on their promise to make oven-baked frozen fries crisp.

EQUIPMENT TESTING

Barbecue Basting Bottles

Plastic basting bottles with brush heads eliminate messy dripping between your bowl of barbecue sauce and the grill. Just fill the bottle, screw on the brush head, and squeeze to release sauce onto the brush. We tried out four bottles, basting grilled chicken. Brushes with soft silicone bristles gently distributed sauce, while stiffer bristles tore and even removed delicate chicken skin. We also preferred long-necked bottles, which kept our hands far from the heat. The winner: Grilling Enthusiast Mr. Bar-B-Q Silicone Brush Basting Bottle with Storage Cap ($4.77).

BETTER THAN A BOWL
Grilling Enthusiast Mr. Bar-B-Q Silicone Brush Basting Bottle is a tidy alternative to basting brushes.

EQUIPMENT TESTING The IceOrb

The IceOrb by Fusionbrands ($13.99) has two functions: ice bucket and ice tray. Instead of lying flat (like an ice tray), its soft silicone is bent into a circular wall, creating a small bucket with protruding pockets you fill with water for ice. To use it, fill the bucket with an inch of water, push in a plastic liner to force the water up and into the mold, place its lid on top, and freeze. Once the orb is frozen, wine or ice cream can be inserted in its center and kept cold for transport or serving. To free the ice, you squeeze out the cubes, producing about two cups of ice that can be stored in the bucket (which successfully kept cubes frozen at room temperature for more than an hour). We have two quibbles: The fill line is nearly invisible, and freeing the ice was a little tricky (we advise letting the orb thaw for a few minutes before removing the cubes). All in all, we like the IceOrb, especially for serving ice cream or other cold foods at summer parties and picnics.

ICY INNOVATION
The IceOrb by Fusionbrands makes ice cubes, chills water, and keeps ice cream cold.

EQUIPMENT TESTING

Soap-Filled Scrub Brushes

Soap-filled dish brushes eliminate the need to keep grabbing the soap bottle. We tested three that use replaceable nylon bristles. One by OXO fits in your palm; the two others (by OXO and Casabella) were attached to a handle. All dispensed soap easily, but the Casabella brush soon began to leak. Widely spaced bristles on all models removed most of the oatmeal encrusted in a pot but struggled to

clean away cooked-on strawberry jam. The OXO Steel Soap-Squirting Dish Brush ($11.99) scrubbed best, thanks to a built-in scraper, plus its handle kept our hands dry. Still, for heavy-duty jobs, we'll reach for a scouring pad.

SQUIRT & SCRUB
The OXO Steel Soap-Squirting Dish Brush makes constantly reaching for dish detergent unnecessary.

Sources

The following are mail-order sources for items recommended in this issue. Prices were current at press time and do not include shipping. Contact companies to confirm or visit www.cooksillustrated.com for updates.

Page 9: MINI PREP BOWLS
• Pyrex 4-piece 6-ounce Dessert Dish Set: $5.99, item #6001142, Pyrexware (800-999-3436, www.pyrexware.com).

Page 15: MORTAR AND PESTLE
• Fox Run Kitchens Iron Mortar and Pestle: $29.99, item #6417, Fante's Kitchen Wares Shop (800-443-2683, www.fantes.com).

Page 17: COFFEE BREWING EQUIPMENT
• Bodum Chambord 8-cup French Press: $39.95, item #1928-16US6, Bodum (800-232-6386, www.bodumusa.com).
• Capresso Cool Grind: $19.95, item #591768, Sur la Table (800-243-0852, www.surlatable.com).
• Thermos Nissan Stainless Steel Carafe: $50.99, item #TGS1500P, Thermos Store (877-419-8272, www.shopthermos.com).
• Technivorm Moccamaster KBT-741 Coffee Maker with Thermal Carafe: $265, item #KBT-741, Boyd Coffee Company (800-223-8211, www.boydscoffeestore.com).

Page 23: APPLE SLICER
• Williams-Sonoma Dial-A-Slice Apple Divider: $19.95, item #5266705, Williams-Sonoma (877-812-6235, www.williams-sonoma.com).

Page 27: CALIFORNIA OLIVE OIL
• California Olive Ranch Arbequina Extra Virgin Olive Oil: $13.97 for half liter plus shipping, item #B500QX09, California Olive Ranch (916-239-2999, www.californiaoliveranch.com).

Page 32: BLENDERS
• KitchenAid 5-Speed Blender: $149.99, item #23244, Chef's Catalog (800-338-3232, www.chefscatalog.com).
• Vita-Mix 5200: $449, item #00, Vita Mix (800-848-2649, www.vita-mix.com).

Page 32: BASTING BOTTLE
• Grilling Enthusiast Mr. Bar-B-Q Silicone Brush Basting Bottle with Storage Cap: $4.77, item #06383, Le Gourmet Chef (888-548-2651, www.legourmetchef.com).

Page 32: ICE ORB
• Fusionbrands IceOrb: $13.99, item #HK-8014, La Prima Shops (www.laprimashops.com).

Page 32: SOAP-FILLED SCRUB BRUSH
• OXO Steel Soap-Squirting Dish Brush: $11.99, item #1068584, OXO (800-545-4411, www.oxo.com).

INDEX

📹 **COOK'S VIDEOS** Original Test Kitchen Videos www.cooksillustrated.com

MAIN DISHES

- **How to Make Hearty Italian Meat Sauce (Sunday Gravy)**
- Which pork ribs should I use?

- **How to Make Lighter Chicken and Dumplings**
- Buying and using portion scoops

- **How to Make Pasta with Roasted Vegetables**
- How do I prep vegetables for roasting?

- **How to Make Steak Tips with Mushroom-Onion Gravy**
- Supermarket Mushrooms 101
- What are steak tips?

- **How to Make Thai Pork Lettuce Wraps**
- How do I use a mortar and pestle?
- What's the best way to store lettuce?

SALAD AND SIDE DISH

- **How to Make Austrian-Style Potato Salad**
- How to mince chives

- **How to Make Mexican-Style Charcoal-Grilled Corn**
- What's the best way to store corn?

SALAD DRESSINGS

- **How to Make Foolproof Vinaigrette**
- Science Experiment: Which emulsifier works best?

DESSERTS

- **How to Make Apple Upside-Down Cake**
- What's the best way to store flour?

- **How to Make Skillet Lemon Soufflé**

TECHNIQUES

- How to Buy and Store Coffee
- How to Brew Coffee
- How to Make Ricotta Cheese

AMERICA'S TEST KITCHEN

Public television's most popular cooking show

Join the millions of home cooks who watch our show, *America's Test Kitchen*, on public television every week. For more information, including recipes and program times, visit www.americastestkitchen.com.

Skillet Lemon Soufflé, 24

Mexican-Style Grilled Corn, 21

Hearty Italian Meat Sauce, 11

Apple Upside-Down Cake, 23

Lighter Chicken and Dumplings, 13

Thai Pork Lettuce Wraps, 15

Steak Tips with Mushroom Gravy, 7

Austrian-Style Potato Salad, 9

Pasta with Roasted Cauliflower, 20

Foolproof Vinaigrette, 19

PHOTOGRAPHY: CARL TREMBLAY, STYLING: MARIE PIRAINO

Hooligan

Long Island
Cheese

Jarrahdale

Cinderella

Knuckle
Head

Khaki

Lumina

Bumpkin

Lil' Ironsides

Munchkin

Peanut

Pik-a-Pie

P U M P K I N S

COOK'S
ILLUSTRATED

Old-Fashioned Stuffed Turkey
Lost Technique Adds Big Flavor

Holiday Beef Tenderloin
Potato-Horseradish Crust

Crispiest Roasted Potatoes

Triple-Chocolate Mousse Cake

Ultimate Chef's Knife

Best Small Appliances
17 Winners You Should Own

Cinnamon Taste Test

Great Holiday Gadgets
Chicken Bouillabaisse
Best Shortbread
Perfect Pan-Seared Scallops
Rethinking Cassoulet

www.cooksillustrated.com
$5.95 U.S./$6.95 CANADA

0 74470 62805 7

1 2>

CONTENTS

November & December 2009

COOK'S
ILLUSTRATED

Founder and Editor	Christopher Kimball
Editorial Director	Jack Bishop
Executive Editor	Amanda Agee
Test Kitchen Director	Erin McMurrer
Managing Editor	Rebecca Hays
Senior Editors	Keith Dresser
	Lisa McManus
Features Editor	Lisa Glazer
Copy Editor	Amy Graves
Associate Editors	J. Kenji Lopez-Alt
	Bryan Roof
Test Cooks	Andrea Geary
	Francisco J. Robert
	Yvonne Ruperti
Assistant Test Kitchen Director	Matthew Herron
Assistant Editors	Meredith Butcher
	Peggy Chung Collier
Assistant Test Cook	Marcus Walser
Executive Assistant	Meredith Smith
Editorial Assistant	Abbey Becker
Senior Kitchen Assistant	Nadia Domeq
Kitchen Assistants	Maria Elena Delgado
	Ena Gudiel
	Edward Tundidor
Producer	Melissa Baldino
Contributing Editors	Matthew Card
	Dawn Yanagihara
Consulting Editor	Scott Brueggeman
Science Editor	Guy Crosby, Ph.D.
Proofreader	Jean Rogers
Managing Editor, Special Issues	Todd Meier
Production Editor, Special Issues	Elizabeth Bomze
Online Managing Editor	David Tytell
Online Editor	Kate Mason
Online Media Producer	Peter Tannenbaum
Online Editorial Assistants	Eric Grzymkowski
	Mari Levine
Design Director	Amy Klee
Art Director, Magazines	Julie Bozzo
Designers, Magazines	Jay Layman
	Lindsey Timko
Deputy Art Director, Marketing/Web	Christine Vo
Designer, Marketing/Web	Beatrice Keng
Staff Photographer	Daniel J. van Ackere
Vice President Marketing	David Mack
Circulation Director	Doug Wicinski
Circulation & Fulfillment Manager	Carrie Horan
Marketing Assistant	Megan DeFilippo
Partnership Marketing Manager	Pamela Putprush
Database & Direct Mail Director	Adam Perry
Senior Database Analyst	Marina Sakharova
Product Operations Director	Steven Browall
Product Promotions Director	Tom Conway
E-Commerce Marketing Director	Hugh Buchan
E-Commerce Marketing Manager	Laurel Zeidman
E-Commerce Search Manager	Elizabeth Dillon
E-Commerce Marketing Coordinator	Tia Freeman
Marketing Copywriter	David Goldberg
Customer Service Manager	Jacqueline Valerio
Customer Service Representatives	Jillian Nannicelli
	Kate Sokol
Sponsorship Sales Director	Marcy McCreary
Retail Sales & Marketing Manager	Emily Logan
Corporate Marketing Associate	Bailey Vatalaro
Production Director	Guy Rochford
Senior Project Manager	Alice Carpenter
Production & Traffic Coordinator	Laura Collins
Senior Production Manager	Jessica L. Quirk
Production & Imaging Specialists	Judy Blomquist
	Lauren Pettapiece
Imaging & Color Specialist	Andrew Mannone
Technology Director	Rocco Lombardo
Lead Developer	Scott Thompson
Web Developer	Robert Martinez
Web Production Coordinator	Evan Davis
Web Production Assistant	Jennifer Millet
Systems Administrator	S. Paddi McHugh
Support Technician	Brandon Lynch
Chief Financial Officer	Sharyn Chabot
Human Resources Director	Adele Shapiro
Controller	Mandy Shito
Senior Accountant	Aaron Goranson
Staff Accountant	Connie Forbes
Accounts Payable Specialist	Steven Kasha
Office Manager	Tasha Bere
Receptionist	Henrietta Murray
Publicity	Deborah Broide

For list rental information, contact: Specialists Marketing Services, Inc., 777 Terrace Ave., 4th Floor, Hasbrouck Heights, NJ 07604; 201-865-5800.

Editorial Office: 17 Station St., Brookline, MA 02445; 617-232-1000; fax 617-232-1572. Subscription inquiries, visit www.americastestkitchen.com/customerservice or call 800-526-8442.

Postmaster: Send all new orders, subscription inquiries, and change-of-address notices to Cook's Illustrated, P.O. Box 7446, Red Oak, IA 51591-0446. PRINTED IN THE USA

HOLIDAY CAKES In France, the Christmas table may feature pain d'épices, a loaf traditionally made with rye flour, honey, and spices, or bûche de Noël ("yule log"), a chocolate-frosted, rolled sponge cake. Christmas pudding, a British staple with raisins, nuts, spices, and molasses, is either steamed or boiled. Fruitcakes are laced with nuts, spices, and candied and dried fruit. Eastern European makowiec, an oblong cake filled with poppy seeds, raisins, orange peel, and nuts, is served at Christmas and Easter. Many Rosh Hashanah dinners include a thick honey cake that symbolizes the wish for a sweet new year. Small, dense mooncakes, eaten in China during the Mid-Autumn Festival, contain sweet bean or lotus seed paste. King cakes, a Mardi Gras tradition, are twisted rings of yeast bread topped with a glaze and festive purple, green, and yellow sugar.

COVER (*Pomegranates*): Robert Papp, BACK COVER (*Holiday Cakes*): John Burgoyne

America's
TEST KITCHEN

America's Test Kitchen is a very real 2,500-square-foot kitchen located just outside of Boston. It is the home of *Cook's Illustrated* and *Cook's Country* magazines and is the workday destination for more than three dozen test cooks, editors, and cookware specialists. Our mission is to test recipes over and over again until we understand how and why they work and until we arrive at the best version. We also test kitchen equipment and supermarket ingredients in search of brands that offer the best value and performance. You can watch us work by tuning in to *America's Test Kitchen* (www.americastestkitchen.com) on public television.

BITS AND PIECES

At the annual Ox Roast last August, I was watching two steamship rounds of beef move herky-jerky on the makeshift sheep-fence rotisserie. John Wayne, who helps me carve up and slice the beast, told me about his bear problems. Early one morning, he heard a scratching on the side of his house. He opened the door a crack, and there was a 220-pound black bear, trying to get in. He gave John a nasty "Where's breakfast?" look, turned and walked away. A week later, he came back, and this time headed for the bird feeder. He sniffed, realized that it was empty, and then gave John, who was once again watching, another nasty, "I can't believe you didn't fill it" look, and slowly departed. John got mad, spent 6 hours building a sturdy gate to protect his front porch, and then strung a bunch of copper wire on it hooked up to a 120-volt system. One day, John came home from work, found the gate torn apart, the wire all balled up, and tracks on his porch. Guess the bear was mad about the new fence too.

Another neighbor at the Ox Roast announced that he was building a fish and chips restaurant right on his property. It will be called the Crashing Boar, a pun on uninvited guests who, over the years, have preyed on his hospitality. The punch line? It will be "by invitation only." Doug Wright recently reminded me of the time he had a gorgeous young model from NYC pumping gas; he had done some work on her car, she didn't have enough money to pay, and so she worked it off. Soon enough, the gas station was lined up with pickups, every red-blooded male in the county getting their tank topped off—a dollar, fifty cents—even if they had just filled up. As she commented, "Vermonters sure are cheap!"

As a law student, Calvin Coolidge ate at a boardinghouse where hash was frequently served. The lady proprietor had a dog and cat, so when the hash was set on the table, Coolidge looked gravely concerned and would ask, "Where's the dog?" The dog would be brought out from the kitchen and presented. Then he would ask, "Where's the cat?" The cat would be

found and brought down for a viewing. Only then would a look of relief appear on his face and he would tuck into supper.

On a recent trip to the Coolidge homestead in central Vermont, Adrienne and I ran into John who worked at the same store that Coolidge's father used to run a hundred years ago. In fact, John remembers when it was still a going concern, not a tourist shop. He also remembered a story from his father. It was 1910 and his dad came running home yelling, "I've seen the antichrist!" John's grandfather followed the boy out to the road and, sure enough, there it was: a brand-new Model T Ford, the first car ever in that part of Vermont. Another neighbor liked to have fun with the party line. Just before going to bed he would ring his own number and then hang up the phone. After three or four rings he would pick it up and then listen until he heard a few clicks on the line. Then he shouted out, "Goodnight, neighbors!"

Years ago, a young man and his uncle set out from Beartown, the northern part of our village, hiking over the mountain to attend a country fair. On the trek back, the uncle lay down in a field to take a nap. The young man, seizing the opportunity, put a good-sized helping of "pasture patty" in the uncle's outstretched right hand and then tickled his nose with a length of timothy. He got the desired effect but had to run hard all the way home—his uncle moved as fast as a man half his age.

Speaking of Beartown, a hundred years ago a new family in town was renting a farmhouse and they were disturbing the peace and tranquility of their neighbors. Late one night, one of the young farmers tacked up a length of fiddle string to the house and ran the other end into the bushes where he was hiding. Then, using a fiddler's bow, he scratched out a high, haunting noise. After a couple of weeks, the family was so spooked that they moved away.

Christopher Kimball

Two years ago, a drunk turkey showed up at Sherman's store (fermented apples, we think) and had a public face-off with the owner's small dog. Some say the turkey won. Meanwhile—this was hunting season—a couple of hunters helped themselves to a few illegal deer right in the game warden's backyard; they figured that was the last place he would look. A dim-witted hunter showed up last year at Sherman's to brag about it and weigh in the spike horn he had just shot. Vermont had changed the law the year before (now only three-pointers are legal). Someone called the game warden and the young man was hauled off.

Vermonters have a habit of living across the street from their ex-wives, just to keep an eye on them. The famous cartoonist Don Trachte built a house high on a hill looking down on his Betty, who had remarried. Darryl Brown, our local plumber, did the same thing. Our town gave up outhouses reluctantly. Not too long ago, our neighbor John used to give the early morning weather report while sitting in his. (His outhouse had only one modern convenience: phone service.)

My favorite local story, one I heard repeatedly in the 1960s, was about Chester and Clark Hayes who, one night, decided to jack a deer up at the Bartlett Lot. They hitched up a cart to a workhorse and set off hunting. They got lucky, shot a large doe and, on their way back, Chester said to Clark in a worried voice, "We're coming up to Charlie Randall's place. He'll peek out the window and catch us red-handed." Clark suggested that they prop the doe up between them on the buckboard and commented, "Charlie can't see too good anyhow." Sure enough, they rode by and saw Charlie's round face peeking through the window. The next day, Chester saw Charlie, who crabbed right up to him and says, "Who was that comin' down with you last night?" Chester shot back, "Oh, just a local girl." Charlie grinned and said, "Well, kinda ugly ain't she?"

FOR INQUIRIES, ORDERS, OR MORE INFORMATION

www.cooksillustrated.com

At www.cooksillustrated.com, you can order books and subscriptions, sign up for our free e-newsletter, or renew your magazine subscription. Join the website and gain access to 17 years of Cook's Illustrated recipes, equipment tests, and ingredient tastings, as well as companion videos for every recipe in this issue.

Cookbooks

We sell more than 50 cookbooks by the editors of Cook's Illustrated. To order, visit our bookstore at www.cooksillustrated.com.

Cook's Illustrated Magazine

Cook's Illustrated magazine (ISSN 1068-2821), number 101, is published bimonthly by Boston Common Press Limited Partnership, 17 Station St., Brookline, MA 02445. Copyright 2010 Boston Common Press Limited Partnership. Periodicals postage paid at Boston, Mass., and additional mailing offices USPS #012487. Publications Mail Agreement No. 40020778. Return undeliverable Canadian addresses to P.O. Box 875, Station A, Windsor, ON N9A 6P2. POSTMASTER: Send address changes to Cook's Illustrated, P.O. Box 7446, Red Oak, IA 51591-0446. For subscription and gift subscription orders, subscription inquiries, or change-of-address notices, visit us at www.americastestkitchen.com/customerservice or write us at Cook's Illustrated, P.O. Box 7446, Red Oak, IA 51591-0446.

Getting to the Root of Wasabi

I have noticed that wasabi is available as powder or paste. Which form do you recommend?

MARK COOL
DULUTH, MINN.

➤ True wasabi is a species of horseradish (*Wasabia japonica*) indigenous to Japan that grows in the loose, gravelly soil of mountain streams. It is also cultivated by a handful of growers in other parts of Asia and in North America. The spicy, nasal-clearing rhizome is most commonly used as a condiment for sushi and sashimi, but is also added to recipes when a fiery kick is desired. Because wasabi is difficult to farm even in ideal conditions, it fetches an exorbitant price.

When we purchased several brands of wasabi powders and pastes from a local Asian specialty market, we were surprised to find that none contained any Japanese horseradish at all. Instead, these products were derived from the root of the same garden-variety horseradish (*Armoracia rusticana*) found in jars of prepared horseradish, along with additives like cornstarch, mustard, and artificial colorants. We searched harder and tracked down a real wasabi paste (we had no luck finding a powder) from a mail-order purveyor in Oregon, Pacific Farms. We then tasted the real and faux products side by side, along with some freshly grated wasabi root we threw in for good measure.

The good news: The real wasabi paste (about $3 per ounce) rated identically with the far more expensive freshly grated root (about $8 per ounce), with heat that most tasters agreed "grew in intensity" and then "dissipated quickly," ending with a "sweet," "grassy," "watercress" flavor. The bad news: The impostor products (made from powder) were consistently described as "boring," "stale," and "metallic."

Though we suspect these more readily available fakes are generally what you're served in all but the most high-end sushi restaurants, you'll have a totally different experience if you seek out real wasabi, whether in paste form or the fresh root.

WASABI:
FRESH CUT...   ...AND PASTED
Many wasabi products don't contain any real wasabi at all.

Caramelizing vs. Browning

Most of my favorite meat and vegetable recipes include a step where the ingredients are either caramelized or browned. But aren't caramelizing and browning the same thing?

EDEN CASTEEL
HILLSDALE, MICH.

➤ In a word, no. Lots of people—even professional chefs—use "caramelize" and "brown" interchangeably, but if you look at the science behind these flavor-boosting techniques, they're actually quite different. (Though both, of course, lead to a literal "browning" of the food.)

Caramelization describes the chemical reactions that take place when any sugar is heated to the point that its molecules begin to break apart and generate hundreds of new flavor, color, and aroma compounds. Consider crème brûlée—after being exposed to high heat, the sugar atop the custard turns golden brown with rich, complex caramelized flavors. (A similar process takes place when you cook onions, carrots, apples, or any other high-sugar fruit or vegetable—the food's sugars caramelize once most of the moisture has evaporated.)

As for browning, here the process involves the interaction of not just sugar molecules and heat but also proteins and their breakdown products, amino acids. Some of the foods that benefit from browning are grilled and roasted meats and bread. Like caramelizing, browning creates a tremendous number of flavors and colors, but they're not the same as those created by caramelization because protein is involved. In case you're wondering, another name for browning is the Maillard reaction, after Louis Camille Maillard, the French chemist who first described it in the 1900s.

Preheating a Pizza Stone

Why do your recipes for thin-crust pizza call for preheating the pizza stone in the oven for a full hour?

MATT AND JEN HOGAN
WEST CHESTER, PA.

➤ Generally, the hotter the pizza stone, the better the browning and expansion of the dough. Since a pizza stone can match an oven's highest temperature and store that heat, a stone preheated for an hour should make a better crust than one preheated for less time, or not at all.

To demonstrate the point, we cooked thin-crust pizzas on stones that had been preheated for 60 and 30 minutes and compared them to pizzas prepared on an unheated stone. The 60-minute stone produced the best pizza by far, with a tender, airy, well-browned crust. The 30-minute stone produced

decent but not stellar results. As we expected, the unheated stone yielded a blond, dense crust, even after spending twice as long in the oven. Lastly, we baked pizza on an overturned baking sheet preheated for 30 minutes (ample time for the baking sheet's lesser mass), our recommended substitute for a pizza stone. It performed reasonably well, but still not quite as well as a pizza stone.

Follow these guidelines: To achieve the best possible thin-crust pizza, preheat a pizza stone for a full hour. If you don't have a pizza stone, preheat an inverted baking sheet for 30 minutes.

HOT STONE   STONE COLD
Sixty minutes of preheating produces a crisp, golden crust.

Figuring Out Folding

Can you explain the mechanics of folding? I'm never sure if I'm doing it right.

GABRIEL STEIN
BROOKLYN, N.Y.

➤ The goal of folding is to incorporate delicate, airy ingredients such as whipped cream or beaten egg whites into heavy, dense ingredients such as egg yolks, custard, or chocolate without causing deflation. The tools required for folding are a balloon whisk and a large, flexible rubber spatula.

In the test kitchen, we like to start the process by lightening the heavier ingredients with one-quarter or one-third of the whipped mixture. A balloon whisk is ideal for the task: Its tines cut into and loosen the heavier mixture, allowing the whipped mixture to be integrated more readily. Next, the remaining whipped mixture can be easily incorporated into the lightened mixture. For this round of folding, we preserve the airiness of the dessert by using a rubber spatula, which is gentler than a whisk.

To demonstrate the importance of folding, we made two kinds of lemon soufflés and our Triple-Chocolate Mousse Cake using three methods: incorporating the whipped ingredients in two additions as specified in the recipes; folding the whipped ingredients in all at once; and finally, vigorously stirring in the whipped ingredients in one addition. The results were not surprising. When the beaten egg whites or whipped cream was incorporated in two batches, the soufflés and mousse were perfectly smooth and light.

When we ignored the two-step process and folded everything together at once, the desserts were not quite as ethereal. Finally, strong-armed stirring produced a lumpy, dense end-product.

Our recommendation: Don't cut corners when it comes to folding. Take your time and use a light hand to gradually incorporate whipped cream or beaten egg whites into heavier ingredients.

Pancetta Substitute

I often keep bacon on hand, but rarely have pancetta in my refrigerator. Can bacon be substituted for pancetta?

KAREN FIERROS
WEST ROXBURY, MASS.

➤ Bacon and pancetta are both cut from the belly of the pig, but the products are not identical. Bacon is cured with salt, then smoked and sliced. Pancetta (sometimes called Italian bacon) is cured with salt, black pepper, and spices and rolled into a cylinder. It is never smoked.

Replacing pancetta with bacon won't ruin a dish, but because bacon is overtly smoky, many recipes recommend blanching it before swapping it for pancetta. To test the validity of this practice, we made our recipes for Hearty Tuscan Bean Stew and Pasta with Greens and Beans, first blanching bacon in boiling water, then proceeding with the recipe, subbing the blanched bacon for pancetta.

As we prepared the recipes, we noticed that blanching had removed a considerable amount of the fat from the bacon. In fact, for the stew recipe, we had to supplement the bacon with a small amount of oil to properly sauté the aromatics. And when we tasted the finished dishes, we noticed that despite the blanching, subtle hints of smokiness remained. Even so, tasters deemed the substitution acceptable.

Our conclusion: If you want to eliminate most of its smoky flavor, blanch bacon in boiling water for two minutes before swapping it for pancetta. Because blanched bacon is not as fatty as pancetta, you may need to add extra oil to the recipe.

Sweetening with Agave

I've recently seen a sweetener called agave nectar at my supermarket. Is it a good substitute for sugar?

JEAN LINDENBAUM
ATLANTIC BEACH, N.Y.

➤ Agave nectar comes from the sap of the thorny, thick-leaved agave plant native to Mexico. The nectar ranges in color from pale gold to amber, depending on the amount of filtration during processing. Lighter nectar has a relatively neutral flavor, while darker nectar has a caramel-like taste. Agave contains 2.9 calories per gram compared to sugar's 4 calories per gram. Agave is also sweeter than sugar, so less of it is needed, further reducing the caloric intake.

We purchased several bottles of nationally available light Madhava Agave Nectar ($6.99 for 23.5 ounces) and used it to replace granulated sugar in

oatmeal cookies, yellow cake, sweet iced tea, and margaritas, following the proportions recommended on the Madhava website: 2/3 cup agave nectar for every cup of sugar. Madhava also advises reducing the liquid content of recipes by 1 ounce per 2/3 cup of agave used, dropping the oven temperature by 25 degrees, and upping the baking time by 6 percent. Even with these measures, the cookies were marred by a soft, bready texture, while the cake had a layer of tough, chewy agave that settled on the bottom of the pan. On the bright side, there were no off-flavors.

When we used agave in beverages, the results were more to our liking. In the sweet tea, tasters found the agave a perfectly acceptable substitute, despite the slightly bitter aftertaste some of the more discerning tasters detected. The agave margaritas were hugely popular, which makes sense given that tequila is derived from the agave plant. Another bonus: Because it is a liquid, the nectar dissolves better in drinks than granulated sugar.

In sum: Agave is great for sweetening drinks, but don't use it for baking.

Juice of Many Colors

Why does freshly squeezed orange juice appear lighter in color at different times of the year while the appearance of the carton juice is consistent?

JEFF BIELZEKIAN
WATERTOWN, MASS.

➤ The color of orange juice depends on the variety of orange used and when in the season it was harvested. The earliest juice is virtually clear, while late-harvest juice has that familiar deep-orange color of carton juice. Though color doesn't necessarily have anything to do with taste or sweetness, manufacturers of carton juice (like Tropicana) try to ensure their juice always looks the same. They squeeze and store

juice from the early, mid-, and late-season harvests in super-chilled vats that preserve flavor, then mix the juices together to make them consistent from carton to carton. To further enhance color, manufacturers add up to 10 percent vividly colored mandarin orange juice as well as pigment from orange peels.

When you buy freshly squeezed orange juice, you're getting the juice direct from harvesting, with no mixing and matching, so the color may change as the season goes on. You may notice another difference with freshly squeezed juice: It tends to separate, while carton juice doesn't. Carton juice is pasteurized at a high temperature (over 190 degrees) to extend shelf life and to deactivate an enzyme called pectinesterase that causes the juice to separate upon standing. Freshly squeezed juice is "flash pasteurized" at a lower temperature that doesn't impact this enzyme.

In a nutshell: Any variance in a natural, minimally processed product like freshly squeezed orange juice is, well, natural.

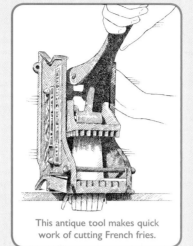

CARTON   FRESH

Unlike carton juice, freshly squeezed orange juice has natural variations in color.

SEND US YOUR QUESTIONS

We will provide a complimentary one-year subscription for each letter we print. Send your inquiry, name, address, and daytime telephone number to Notes from Readers, Cook's Illustrated, P.O. Box 470589, Brookline, MA 02447, or to notesfromreaders@americastestkitchen.com.

Quick Tips

COMPILED BY YVONNE RUPERTI & FRANCISCO J. ROBERT

Impromptu Strainer

After using her rasp-style grater to zest lemons, Isabell Berger of Williamsville, N.Y., found that if she turned the grater over, she could also use it to strain the pits and pulp from the juice.

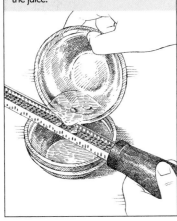

Draining a Water Bath

Recipes for crème brûlée, cheesecake, and soufflé often call for a water bath, a technique where the ramekins or baking dish is placed in a large, shallow pan of warm water to ensure gentle, even baking. If you find that you've overfilled the pan with water, Mary Flack of Schulenburg, Texas, offers this simple, splash-free remedy: Use a turkey baster to siphon off the excess.

Croutons in a Crunch

Homemade croutons are a great way to recycle stale bread. Sandra Weiswasser of Washington, D.C., came up with a quick method that doesn't even require an oven.

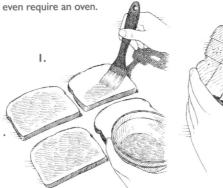

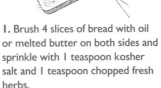

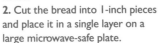

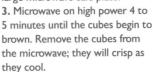

1. Brush 4 slices of bread with oil or melted butter on both sides and sprinkle with 1 teaspoon kosher salt and 1 teaspoon chopped fresh herbs.
2. Cut the bread into 1-inch pieces and place it in a single layer on a large microwave-safe plate.
3. Microwave on high power 4 to 5 minutes until the cubes begin to brown. Remove the cubes from the microwave; they will crisp as they cool.

Pliable Tortillas

Some tortillas have an annoying tendency to crack and break when you fold them into wraps or burritos. To make them more pliable, Michael Hsieh of Somerville, Mass., briefly warms them in the microwave.

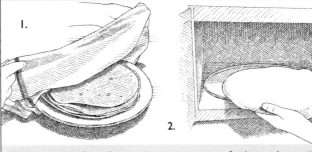

1. Place a stack of tortillas on a large microwave-safe plate and cover it with a damp kitchen towel.
2. Microwave on high power for 15 to 30 seconds. Carefully remove the towel and use the tortillas immediately.

Grating Bread Crumbs

Since he doesn't have a food processor, Adam Iser of Brooklyn, N.Y., uses his box grater to grate fresh bread into crumbs. But sometimes even firm bread can be difficult to grate into uniformly fine crumbs. Here is his solution:

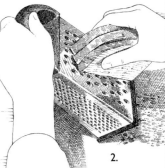

1. Place the bread in a bag in the freezer until frozen.
2. Gripping 2 or 3 slices at a time, grate the frozen bread on the large holes of a box grater.

Labeling Leftover Cheese

If leftover cheese hunks aren't returned to their original packaging, it can be hard to remember what type of cheese you're storing. To keep track, B.J. Ray of Jamaica Plain, Mass., snips the label from the original packaging and stores it with his leftovers.

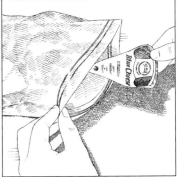

Send Us Your Tip We will provide a complimentary one-year subscription for each tip we print. Send your tip, name, and address to Quick Tips, Cook's Illustrated, P.O. Box 470589, Brookline, MA 02447, or to quicktips@americastestkitchen.com.

Packet o' Spice

Spices and herbs are a must in soups and stews, but some (like bay leaves, whole peppercorns, and cloves) have to be fished out before serving. To make removal easy, Jenny Hattori of Salinas, Calif., creates individualized spice packets.

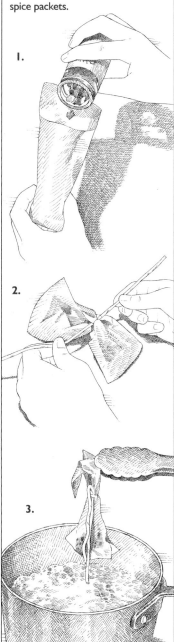

1. Fill a tea filter bag made for loose tea with spices.
2. Tightly tie the packet closed with kitchen twine and add it to the pot.
3. When your dish is ready, simply remove the packet.

Spices, Stay Put

Kevin Flynn of Saskatoon, Saskatchewan, Canada, likes to grind his own spices with a mortar and pestle, but he finds that some spices, like peppercorns, tend to fly out of the mortar in the process. His tip:

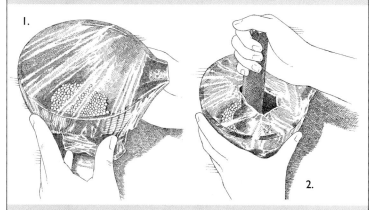

1. Put the spices in the mortar and cover it tightly with plastic wrap.
2. Make a tiny slit in the wrap and poke the pestle through. Even though the slit will end up stretching as you grind, as long as the wrap seals the edges, the spices will stay put.

Rescuing Hard-to-Peel Eggs

It's easy to peel freshly boiled eggs, but after they sit in the refrigerator for a day or two, the task becomes more difficult. Cheryl Kremkow of New York, N.Y., uses this method to make the shell release more easily.

1. Submerge the hard-cooked eggs in hot water for 1 minute.
2. Transfer the eggs to ice water and submerge for 1 minute more. The shell will now peel off more easily.

Crushing Fresh Tomatoes

Sweet and juicy crushed fresh tomatoes are perfect for a quick sauce when in season. This method from Molly Hawkins of Chelsea, Mass., delivers all the pulp while leaving the skins behind.

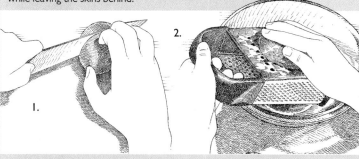

1. Slice the tomato across its equator.
2. Grate the cut side of each tomato half on the large holes of a box grater until all the flesh has been pressed through and only the skin remains.

Easy Olive Slicing

If you're making nachos or another dish that requires lots of sliced olives, individually cutting each olive can be tedious. James C. Eakes of Ketchikan, Alaska, found that his egg slicer speeds up the process.

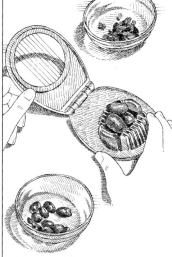

1. Depending on the size of the olives, set two or three in the egg slicer and push down to slice.
2. If a coarse chop is desired, turn the olives 90 degrees and slice again.

Deveining Shrimp

Deveining usually creates a large, unsightly slit on the outer curve of shrimp. Fred Hill of Tucson, Ariz., developed a technique for more attractive results.

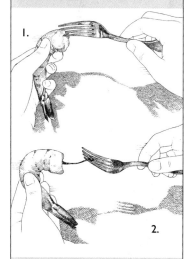

1. Insert one tine of a dinner fork into the shrimp, pass the tine beneath the vein, and hook it under.
2. Draw the vein out through the very small hole you've created, leaving the shrimp looking virtually untouched.

Old-Fashioned Stuffed Turkey

We read up on American cookery to rescue a rare bird from the brink of extinction—namely, the holiday turkey that has it all.

⋛ BY MARCUS WALSER ⋚

Nothing has immortalized the Thanksgiving feast quite like Norman Rockwell's iconic painting of a perfectly bronzed turkey glistening on a serving platter. Originally splayed across the cover of *The Saturday Evening Post* as a wartime call to action, it's had the unintentional effect of raising the bar for holiday tables ever since.

But the skeptic in me has always wanted a peek beneath the surface of that mahogany-hued bird. Like anyone who's ever roasted a turkey, I know even the best recipes involve compromise. Cook a turkey long enough to get the skin immaculately burnished and the white meat is usually dry as sawdust. Brining adds moisture to the meat, but it can turn skin soggy. Salting (dry-brining) solves the crisping woes, but the drippings get too seasoned to make a proper gravy. Stuffing the cavity compounds the headaches, slowing the roasting time to a crawl and upping the chance for uneven cooking.

Still, I couldn't help but wonder: Could an old-fashioned secret to a turkey with everything in one package—juicy meat, crisply burnished skin, rich-flavored stuffing that cooked inside the bird, and drippings suitable for gravy—actually exist? I went into the test kitchen to find out, once and for all.

Roastin' to the Oldies

If the key to compromise-free turkey was lost somewhere in time, I had a good idea where to find it: the old-school cookbooks in our library. But as I surveyed bygone wisdom, my heart sank. The oldest recipes were barely recipes at all! "Stuff the craw…, spit it, and lay it down a good distance from the fire, which should be clear and brisk," advised *The Virginia Housewife* (1838). One by one, I discarded recipes for being too vague, too live-fire–specific, or too close to the basic (and unreliable) roast-and-baste method popular to this day. Only one technique, from the classic *Boston Cooking School Cook Book* (1896) by Fannie Farmer, which promised crispier skin on roast chicken, piqued my interest enough to convince me to give it a whirl: rubbing the entire bird with a flour-butter paste. Alas, it was a bust on turkey; the skin was tough, not crisp.

The Tried and True

It was time to return to proven techniques. First decision: salting or brining? Unwilling to compromise on skin, I opted for salting, which initially draws moisture out of the meat, but after a 24-hour rest in the fridge, all this moisture gets slowly drawn back

For uncommonly rich flavor, we roasted this turkey with strips of salt pork draped over its back.

in, seasoning the meat and helping it retain moisture. In the past we've used as many as 5 tablespoons of salt on the bird—a nonstarter for making gravy from drippings. Reducing to 3 tablespoons allowed for gravy that didn't make tasters wince, but the meat was not quite as juicy and tender.

Maybe I needed to reconsider the roasting method. I'd been using a test-kitchen favorite developed in 1994, where you start the turkey in a blazing hot oven breast-side down, flip it once, and finish at a lower, gentler pace. Since then, we've proved that, across the board, meats from pork chops to roast beef cook more evenly when you reverse the order and start out at a lower oven temperature. Why not whole turkey? I cooked the bird in a gentle 325-degree oven for a couple of hours, then cranked up the temperature to 450 to give it a final blast of skin-crisping heat and to bring the center up to temperature. It worked beautifully, yielding breast meat that was as moist and tender as I could hope for.

As for the skin, some might call it crisp—but I wanted it brittle enough to crunch. I brought out a secret weapon we developed recently for chicken: massaging the skin with a baking powder and salt rub. The baking powder has a twofold effect: It helps skin dehydrate more readily and raises its pH, making it more conducive to browning. At the same time, we poke holes in the skin to help rendering fat escape. This technique was just the ticket, producing skin as crackling-crisp as pork rinds.

The Stuff of Dreams

All that was left was the stuffing. I made a basic recipe (toasted cubes of sandwich bread mixed with sautéed celery, onions, herbs, broth, and eggs) and shoehorned as much of it into the turkey as I could, placing the remainder in a baking dish to be cooked separately. For due diligence, I kept the bird in the oven until the stuffing was cooked to a safe 165 degrees—at which point the breast had reached a bone-dry 180 degrees.

To get around this, some recipes have you preheat the stuffing in the microwave before it goes into the bird, so it cooks more or less in tandem with the white meat. I had a different idea. Since my turkey needed to rest a good 30 minutes after roasting anyway, why not remove the undercooked stuffing and finish cooking it on its own as the bird rested? As I took the stuffing out of the bird for my next go-round, I remembered the bland "poor relation" batch waiting to go in the oven. I had a new brainstorm: The parcooked stuffing was saturated with turkey juices, with plenty to spare. If I combined this with the uncooked batch, all the stuffing would get a flavor boost. But with eggs in the mix, the cooked stuffing had firmed up and wouldn't blend easily into the uncooked portion. The solution? I moistened the batch that went in the turkey with broth alone, then waited to add the eggs until I took it out of the bird and combined it with the uncooked portion.

In theory, I now had it all: moist breast meat, crisp skin, and rich stuffing in every bite. Still, today's turkeys are milder in flavor, and I couldn't get rid of the nagging feeling that the meat was bland. But short of mail-ordering a heritage bird, what could I do? For inspiration, I went back to our library. This time I grabbed a more contemporary classic: *James Beard's American Cookery* (1972). A variation on the once-popular technique of barding—wrapping lean meat with fattier meat—caught my eye. I salted another turkey, applied the baking powder–salt rub, added the stuffing, and then draped the bird with meaty salt pork. The barded bird smoked heavily in the oven, but its flavor was unbelievably intense. Not unlike the way adding a ham bone to a pot of beans can impart a meaty flavor without making them taste outright porky, the salt pork enhanced the turkey without making its presence too clear. To fix the smoking problem, I removed the salt pork and drained the drippings from the roasting pan before cranking up the heat and returning the bird to the oven.

The resulting meal was perfect—stuffing with crisp edges and a savory flavor from the turkey; tender, juicy breast meat with unparalleled richness; and crackling, golden-brown skin. I even had gravy! I'm not sure if a stuffed Thanksgiving turkey was ever this good in the past, but I know it'll be part of my future.

AT-A-GLANCE | SECRETS TO OLD-FASHIONED STUFFED TURKEY

1. DRY BRINE Salting turkey 24 to 48 hours seasons meat and keeps moisture inside.

2. STAB THE FAT Poking holes in fatty deposits speeds up fat-rendering process.

3. DRY RUB Rubbing skin with baking powder and salt just before roasting encourages browning.

  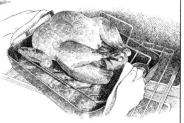

4. BARD Draping strips of salt pork on turkey as it roasts enriches it with deep flavor.

5. INSIDE/OUTSIDE Combining stuffing cooked inside bird with uncooked stuffing, then baking, yields best flavor.

6. HIGH-HEAT FINISH Blasting bird with intense heat for last 45 minutes of roasting helps crisp skin.

OLD-FASHIONED STUFFED TURKEY
SERVES 10 TO 12

NOTE: Table salt is not recommended for this recipe because it is too fine. To roast a kosher or self-basting turkey (such as a frozen Butterball), do not salt it in step 1. Look for salt pork that is roughly equal parts fat and lean meat. The bread can be toasted up to 1 day in advance. For our free recipes for Best Turkey Gravy, Sausage and Fennel Stuffing, and Dried Fruit and Nut Stuffing, go to www.cooksillustrated.com/dec09.

Turkey
1 turkey (12 to 15 pounds), giblets and neck reserved for gravy, if making (see note)
3 tablespoons plus 2 teaspoons kosher salt (see note)
2 teaspoons baking powder
12 ounces salt pork, cut into ¼-inch-thick slices and rinsed (see note)

Stuffing
1½ pounds (about 15 slices) white sandwich bread, cut into ½-inch cubes (about 12 cups)
4 tablespoons unsalted butter, plus extra for baking dish
1 medium onion, chopped fine (about 1 cup)
2 celery ribs, chopped fine (about 1 cup)
   Kosher salt and ground black pepper
2 tablespoons minced fresh thyme leaves
1 tablespoon minced fresh marjoram leaves
1 tablespoon minced fresh sage leaves
1½ cups low-sodium chicken broth
1 36-inch square cheesecloth, folded in quarters
2 large eggs

1. **FOR THE TURKEY:** Using fingers or handle of wooden spoon, separate turkey skin from meat on breast, legs, thighs, and back; avoid breaking skin. Rub 1 tablespoon salt evenly inside cavity of turkey, 1½ teaspoons salt under skin of each breast, and 1½ teaspoons salt under skin of each leg. Wrap turkey tightly with plastic wrap; refrigerate 24 to 48 hours.

2. **FOR THE STUFFING:** Adjust oven rack to lowest position and heat oven to 250 degrees. Spread bread cubes in single layer on baking sheet; bake until edges have dried but centers are slightly moist (cubes should yield to pressure), about 45 minutes, stirring several times during baking. Transfer to large bowl and increase oven temperature to 325 degrees.

3. While bread dries, heat 4 tablespoons butter in 12-inch skillet over medium-high heat; when foaming subsides, add onion, celery, 2 teaspoons salt, and 1 teaspoon pepper; cook, stirring occasionally, until vegetables begin to soften and brown slightly, 7 to 10 minutes. Stir in herbs; cook until fragrant, about 1 minute. Add vegetables to bowl with dried bread; add 1 cup broth and toss until evenly moistened.

4. **TO ROAST THE TURKEY:** Combine remaining 2 teaspoons kosher salt and baking powder in small bowl. Remove turkey from refrigerator and unwrap. Thoroughly dry inside and out with paper towels. Using skewer, poke 15 to 20 holes in fat deposits on top of breast halves and thighs, 4 to 5 holes in each deposit. Sprinkle surface of turkey with salt–baking powder mixture and rub in mixture with hands, coating skin evenly. Tuck wings underneath turkey. Line turkey cavity with cheesecloth, pack with 4 to 5 cups stuffing, tie ends of cheesecloth together. Cover remaining stuffing with plastic wrap

and refrigerate. Using twine, loosely tie turkey legs together. Place turkey breast-side down in V-rack set in roasting pan and drape salt pork slices over back.

5. Roast turkey breast-side down until thickest part of breast registers 130 degrees on instant-read thermometer, 2 to 2½ hours. Remove roasting pan from oven (close oven door) and increase oven temperature to 450 degrees. Transfer turkey in V-rack to rimmed baking sheet. Remove and discard salt pork. Using clean potholders or kitchen towels, rotate turkey breast-side up. Cut twine binding legs and remove stuffing bag; empty into reserved stuffing in bowl. Pour drippings from roasting pan into fat separator and reserve for gravy, if making.

6. Once oven has come to temperature, return turkey in V-rack to roasting pan and roast until skin is golden brown and crisp, thickest part of breast registers 160 degrees, and thickest part of thigh registers 175 degrees, about 45 minutes, rotating pan halfway through. Transfer turkey to carving board and let rest, uncovered, 30 minutes.

7. While turkey rests, reduce oven temperature to 400 degrees. Whisk eggs and remaining ½ cup broth together in small bowl. Pour egg mixture over stuffing and toss to combine, breaking up any large chunks; spread in buttered 13- by 9-inch baking dish. Bake until stuffing registers 165 degrees and top is golden brown, about 15 minutes. Carve turkey and serve with stuffing.

◼ COOK'S VIDEOS Original Test Kitchen Videos

www.cooksillustrated.com
HOW TO MAKE
• Old-Fashioned Stuffed Turkey

Horseradish-Crusted Beef Tenderloin

We wanted to jazz up bland tenderloin with a crisp, pungently flavored horseradish crust.
What would it take to make our plan stick?

⇒ BY BRYAN ROOF ⇐

Cooks go to all kinds of crazy lengths to beef up the taste of bland, buttery-smooth tenderloin. The most famous example is beef Wellington, in which the meat is coated in foie gras and minced mushrooms, then encrusted in pastry. More recent innovations try everything from encasing the beef in a double-truffle crust (bread crumbs, sliced truffles, and truffle oil) to saucing it with concoctions that include specialty vinegar, black cherries, and bittersweet chocolate. By comparison, simply serving tenderloin with pungent horseradish sauce, a fine but standard accompaniment, seems a little uninspired for the special dinners at which this pricey cut is typically served. But if I could combine the bracing flavor of horseradish with a crisp, golden crust that would also add textural contrast to rosy, medium-rare meat—now, that would be a different story.

When I did some research, I discovered that I wasn't the only one to have this idea. But the recipes I found were disastrous. Most did nothing more than add the horseradish to a basic bread-crumb mixture before spreading it over the beef and roasting it in the oven. The crust absorbed the meat's juices, causing most of it to turn mushy and fall off, while what "shell" still remained had only a trace of horseradish flavor.

TASTING Horseradish

"Prepared horseradish" can taste strikingly different depending on where in the store you buy it. Shelf-stable products are full of additives and had such weak flavor that we eliminated them from consideration, sticking with four brands from the refrigerator aisle. Tasters gave high marks to brands with fine, versus coarse, texture and sinus-clearing heat. For complete testing results, go to www.cooksillustrated.com/dec09. –Peggy Chung Collier

HOT TO TROT
BOAR'S HEAD All-Natural Horseradish
Price: $2.49 for 9 ounces
Comments: The kick of this winner reminded tasters of "straight wasabi."

MILD MANNERED
GOLD'S Prepared Horseradish
Price: $2.99 for 6 ounces
Comments: A "sweet, relish-y" taste put this horseradish in third place.

To intensify beefy flavor, we seared the tenderloin in a hot pan before applying the coating.

Meat and Potato

My starting point was choosing the right cut of meat and the key ingredients for my crust. A center-cut roast—also known as Châteaubriand—was a must, because its uniform shape cooks evenly. For the crust, I figured I'd work with Japanese panko crumbs (for their ultra-crisp texture) and try a common breading technique: lightly flouring the meat, applying a thin wash of egg white, and then rolling the roast in crumbs flavored with horseradish, minced shallot, garlic, and herbs.

As for the horseradish, it seemed likely that the fresh stuff would have more pungency than the bottled variety, so I grated a couple of tablespoons of the gnarly-looking root and added it to my panko mix before breading and roasting the tenderloin. To my disappointment, the fresh horseradish turned unpleasantly bitter when cooked, and the crumb coating failed to crisp. Bottled prepared horseradish, made with grated horseradish and vinegar, proved a better choice. A good brand (see "Horseradish" at left) boasts a bright—not bitter—bite, even after exposure to heat. Pressing the horseradish in a strainer removed the excess moisture, but since weight for weight prepared horseradish is less potent than freshly

grated, I needed to use a full quarter cup to get the flavor I wanted. But even after pressing it, this amount of wet horseradish was still dampening the crust.

Perhaps I needed to reevaluate my choice of breading. Crackers and Melba toast were OK but added too much of their own flavor. On a whim, I tried crushed potato chips. These were mostly a hit, keeping their crunch and contributing a salty potato flavor that tasters loved. The only problem was their slightly processed taste. With a cut this expensive, I wanted only the best—so why not whip up my own potato crumbles? I shredded a small potato on a box grater, rinsed the shreds to remove surface starch, and then cooked them in oil until browned and crisp. A test run proved that combining them with the panko (which I pretoasted) was the best option: The panko coated the nooks in the meat that the potatoes couldn't reach, while the potato shreds jutted out, making for a craggy, golden crust full of savory flavor.

Still, my results weren't ideal. In order to keep the crust truly crisp, the most horseradish I could add to the crumb mixture was 2 tablespoons. I'd have to find another way of upping horseradish flavor.

Hold Your Horseradish!

If I couldn't add more horseradish to the crust, why not just add some to the egg wash? Unfortunately, the wash (which was just egg white, for minimal egg flavor) was too thin to hold the horseradish, which dripped down the meat. Perhaps the answer was adding mayonnaise to create a paste, another approach we've used successfully to make breading stick. This worked well; by combining 1 beaten egg white, 1½ teaspoons mayonnaise, and 2 tablespoons horseradish, I was able to make a pungently flavored paste that clung firmly to the tenderloin. Adding a bit of mustard to this mix enhanced the spiciness of the horseradish. Everything seemed to be going well until I roasted the tenderloin and tried to slice it, at which point the beef came out of its shell—literally. The crust cracked into pieces that fell straight onto the cutting board.

🎬 **COOK'S VIDEOS** Original Test Kitchen Videos
www.cooksillustrated.com
HOW TO MAKE
• Horseradish-Crusted Beef Tenderloin

Stumped, I consulted our science editor. He came up with a novel idea: Replace the egg white with gelatin (see "Stick-to-It Solution," below). I added just ½ teaspoon to the horseradish mixture, applied it to the tenderloin, and roasted the meat. Unlike the crackly egg-based paste, the gelatin mixture bound the bread crumbs firmly to the meat yet yielded slightly as I cut it. At long last, each slice delivered rosy beef topped by a cohesive horseradish crust.

Only one problem remained: Given time, the crust still became slightly soggy from meat juices released during cooking. Three final tweaks fixed this problem. First, I adjusted the oven temperature to 400 degrees (up until now, I'd been using a more moderate 300), which helped keep the crust a little crisper. Second, I seared the meat in a hot skillet, then let it rest on a wire rack set in a baking sheet so that its juices could drain off before applying the paste and the crumbs. Finally, I coated only the top and sides of the tenderloin, leaving an "opening" on the bottom for meat juices to escape as it roasted.

Served with a horseradish cream sauce, this beef tenderloin was a standout, combining succulent meat with a crisp, salty, pungent crust. Who needs beef Wellington?

HORSERADISH-CRUSTED BEEF TENDERLOIN
SERVES 6

NOTE: If using table salt, reduce the amount in step 1 to 1½ teaspoons. Add the gelatin to the horseradish paste at the last moment, or the mixture will become unspreadable. If desired, serve the roast with Horseradish Cream Sauce (recipe follows; you will need 2 jars of prepared horseradish for both the roast and sauce). If you choose to salt the tenderloin in advance, remove it from the refrigerator 1 hour before cooking. To make this recipe 1 day in advance, prepare it through step 3, but in step 2 do not toss the bread crumbs with the other ingredients until you are ready to sear the meat.

1	beef tenderloin center-cut Châteaubriand (about 2 pounds), trimmed of fat and silver skin Kosher salt (see note)
3	tablespoons panko bread crumbs
1	cup plus 2 teaspoons vegetable oil
1¼	teaspoons ground black pepper
1	small shallot, minced (about 1½ tablespoons)
2	medium garlic cloves, minced or pressed through garlic press (about 2 teaspoons)
¼	cup well-drained prepared horseradish (see note)
2	tablespoons minced fresh parsley leaves
½	teaspoon minced fresh thyme leaves
1	small russet potato (about 6 ounces), peeled and grated on large holes of box grater
1½	teaspoons mayonnaise
1½	teaspoons Dijon mustard
½	teaspoon powdered gelatin (see note)

TECHNIQUE | THREE STEPS TO A CRISPER COATING

Fried potato shreds made for a far crisper—and more flavorful—crust than the typical bread-crumb coating.

1. GRATE potato on large holes of box grater for thin slivers that will crisp up quickly.

2. RINSE shreds to remove surface starch, then squeeze dry in kitchen towel.

3. FRY potatoes in oil to create savory crumbles that keep their crunch.

1. Sprinkle roast with 1 tablespoon salt, cover with plastic wrap, and let stand at room temperature 1 hour or refrigerate for up to 24 hours. Adjust oven rack to middle position and heat oven to 400 degrees.

2. Toss bread crumbs with 2 teaspoons oil, ¼ teaspoon salt, and ¼ teaspoon pepper in 10-inch nonstick skillet. Cook over medium heat, stirring frequently, until deep golden brown, 3 to 5 minutes. Transfer to rimmed baking sheet and cool to room temperature (wipe out skillet). Once cool, toss bread crumbs with shallot, garlic, 2 tablespoons horseradish, parsley, and thyme.

3. Rinse grated potato under cold water, then squeeze dry in kitchen towel. Transfer potatoes and remaining cup oil to 10-inch nonstick skillet. Cook over high heat, stirring frequently, until potatoes are golden brown and crisp, 6 to 8 minutes. Using slotted spoon, transfer potatoes to paper towel–lined plate and season lightly with salt; let cool for 5 minutes. Reserve 1 tablespoon oil from skillet and discard remainder. Once potatoes are cool, transfer to quart-sized zipper-lock bag and crush until coarsely ground. Transfer potatoes to baking sheet with bread-crumb mixture and toss to combine.

4. Pat exterior of tenderloin dry with paper towels and sprinkle evenly with remaining teaspoon pepper. Heat reserved tablespoon oil in 12-inch nonstick skillet over medium-high heat until just smoking. Sear tenderloin until well browned on all sides, 5 to 7 minutes. Transfer to wire rack set in rimmed baking sheet and let rest 10 minutes.

5. Combine remaining 2 tablespoons horseradish, mayonnaise, and mustard in small bowl. Just before coating tenderloin, add gelatin and stir to combine. Spread horseradish paste on top and sides of meat, leaving bottom and ends bare. Roll coated sides of tenderloin in bread-crumb mixture, pressing gently so crumbs adhere in even layer that just covers horseradish paste; pat off any excess.

6. Return tenderloin to wire rack. Roast until instant-read thermometer inserted into center of roast registers 120 to 125 degrees for medium-rare, 25 to 30 minutes.

7. Transfer roast to carving board and let rest 20 minutes. Carefully cut meat crosswise into ½-inch-thick slices and serve.

HORSERADISH CREAM SAUCE
MAKES ABOUT 1 CUP

½	cup heavy cream
½	cup prepared horseradish
1	teaspoon table salt
⅛	teaspoon ground black pepper

Whisk cream in medium bowl until thickened but not yet holding soft peaks, 1 to 2 minutes. Gently fold in horseradish, salt, and pepper. Transfer to serving bowl and refrigerate at least 30 minutes or up to 1 hour before serving.

SCIENCE EXPERIMENT
Stick-to-It Solution
A simple egg wash is the usual choice for binding a bread-crumb coating to meat, but it didn't work for our slippery horseradish–bread-crumb mixture. Could we do better by replacing the egg white with gelatin?

THE EXPERIMENT
We prepared two pastes, one made with egg white, horseradish, mayonnaise, and mustard and a second where we substituted ½ teaspoon of gelatin for the egg white. We applied each paste to a beef tenderloin and then cooked the roasts according to our recipe.

THE RESULTS
The gelatin paste kept the bread crumbs attached to the meat much better than the egg version. It also had a slight elasticity that allowed it to remain firmly stuck to the meat as we sliced it.

THE EXPLANATION
Meat and gelatin have a natural affinity. Both are made up of linear proteins that are able to form tight bonds with each other. The proteins in egg whites, on the other hand, are globular (wound up like balls of yarn). Although egg whites do eventually stretch into more linear shapes when heated, they still form a weaker bond with meat than gelatin. –B.R.

Introducing Chicken Bouillabaisse

Could we take the garlicky fennel and saffron flavors of France's most famous fish stew and adapt them to a chicken dinner?

⋛ BY J. KENJI LOPEZ-ALT ⋚

I love the intense garlicky fennel, orange, and saffron flavors of *bouillabaisse*, the traditional Provençal fish hodgepodge. Served with crusty bread and a hefty dollop of *rouille* (a spicy, garlicky, bread-thickened mayonnaise), it's one of the world's greatest stews. But even in a fish town like Boston, buying and boning a half dozen varieties of fresh seafood, making a stock from the bones, and then cooking each type of seafood to the right degree of doneness is a task best left to restaurant chefs. Enter chicken bouillabaisse. A classic Provençal stew in its own right (even Eric Ripert, chef at New York's Le Bernardin, arguably the best seafood restaurant in the country, sees its virtues), it offers home cooks the promise of potent bouillabaisse flavor in a 45-minute chicken dinner. I had to try it.

Stock and Rouille

Most of the recipes I found followed a similar process: Cook thinly sliced onions, leeks, fennel, and lots of garlic over a gentle flame until soft and sweet. Add chicken pieces to the pot (browned or left raw) along with saffron, cayenne pepper, tomatoes, and chicken stock and cook until the chicken is tender. Stir in a shot of *pastis* (an anise-flavored liqueur) and orange zest and simmer briefly. The dish is served with boiled potatoes (cooked separately) along with the requisite rouille-slathered bread.

With such all-star ingredients in the pot, none of the recipes I tried was

The garlicky, saffron-scented mayonnaise (rouille) adds robust flavor to the stew.

A Taste of Provence

ANISE ACCENTS
Fennel and a liqueur such as pastis or Pernod bring the licorice-like flavors common in southern French cooking to our chicken stew.

awful, but even the best needed tweaking. Most of the rouilles (made from egg yolk, bread, olive and vegetable oils, garlic, and saffron) were heavy and dull. And while searing the chicken flavored the broth (through the crusty brown bits, or *fond*, left behind), it seemed a shame to then take my nicely crisped chicken and submerge it. I wanted to find a way to get the chicken infused with the flavor of the broth but still keep some crisp skin.

Garlic: Less Is More

My stew base started with a fennel bulb, one leek, an onion, and a whole head of garlic sweated in olive oil. But since all of these aromatics turn sweet as they sweat, my tasters found the end result rather cloying. I knew I couldn't touch the fennel: It provides the anise backbone. Garlic was a better candidate. A whole head (20 cloves), cooked long enough to lose its sharpness, contributed mainly a caramel-like sweetness to the mix. By cutting the amount down to a mere four cloves—sautéed briefly only after the other vegetables had softened—I was able to retain garlicky flavor while dialing back on sweetness. To tone it down even more, I experimented with eliminating the onion and

found that tasters actually preferred the broth made with milder, less-sweet leeks alone.

A traditional bouillabaisse is only as good as its short-simmered yet concentrated fish stock (also known as a *fumet*). Happily, with all the other flavorings contributing complexity to the stew, I found canned chicken broth worked almost as well as homemade stock in the chicken rendition. But to give the broth more body and a long-simmered flavor, I added a tablespoon each of flour and tomato paste to the pan with the saffron and cayenne before adding the broth. And instead of stirring in the orange zest late in the cooking, as most recipes instructed, I found it worked best to add it at the same time as the broth to allow it to give up more of its flavor. Tasters also preferred the pastis added at the start of the simmer, which burned off more of its alcoholic taste, leaving only the essence of licorice. As for the other ingredients, wine and tomatoes were givens. A half-cup of white wine brought just the right brightness, while drained diced canned tomatoes were the best way to ensure consistently good tomato flavor year-round.

With my broth in order, I moved on to the rouille. With a full cup of oil and an egg yolk, it definitely needed brightening, despite the presence of saffron and cayenne. Four teaspoons of lemon juice helped, but Dijon mustard (a nontraditional ingredient) brought even more tangy depth. To maximize saffron flavor, I steeped the threads in hot water before adding them (see "Making the Most of Saffron" on page 31).

Stovetop-to-Oven Switch

The only problem remaining was the chicken: The meat itself was tender and well flavored, but the skin was flabby. Many recipes call for browning the chicken with the skin on (to contribute flavor and protect the meat from drying out), then stripping it off before adding the chicken back to the pot. This solves the flabby skin problem, but I just couldn't get comfortable throwing out that nice crisped skin.

Then I realized a potential solution was right in front of me: the potatoes I was planning to boil separately. If I cooked them right in the broth, they'd stick up above the liquid, creating a sort of "raft" on which I could rest the chicken. When I tried this, the prognosis looked good, as I ladled some of the finished stew into a bowl and placed a golden-brown piece of chicken on top. But to my frustration, when I bit in, the skin was still flabby.

TECHNIQUE

CRISP BRAISED SKIN

HIGH AND DRY

Crisp skin on stewed chicken? It sounds like an oxymoron. But by resting the chicken on the potatoes as the bouillabaisse cooks in the oven, the skin stays out of the liquid and becomes crisp. A quick blast of broiler heat before serving further enhances crispness.

I took a closer look at my next batch and understood the problem: Steam rising from the simmering liquid was soaking the skin. Maybe the fix was a switch from the stovetop to the oven, where the heat from above could keep moisture from condensing on the chicken. This was a giant step forward, but I still wasn't there. What if I placed the pot under the broiler just before serving? That did it: The intense blast of heat recrisped the skin in no time. With croutons and tangy rouille complementing the appealing chicken meat and skin, my stew made the most of its Provençal roots, and it didn't give tasters a chance to even think about fish.

CHICKEN BOUILLABAISSE
SERVES 4 TO 6

NOTE: The rouille and croutons (steps 4 and 5) can be prepared either as the chicken cooks or up to 2 days in advance. Leftover rouille will keep refrigerated for up to 1 week and can be used in sandwiches or as a sauce for vegetables and fish. For information on anise-flavored liqueur options, see page 31.

Bouillabaisse
- 3 pounds bone-in, skin-on chicken parts (breasts, thighs, and drumsticks, with breasts cut in half), trimmed of excess fat
  Table salt and ground black pepper
- 2 tablespoons olive oil
- 1 large leek (white and light green parts only), halved lengthwise, rinsed, and sliced thin (about 1 cup)
- 1 small fennel bulb, halved lengthwise, cored, and sliced thin (about 2 cups)
- ¼ teaspoon saffron threads
- ¼ teaspoon cayenne pepper
- 1 tablespoon unbleached all-purpose flour
- 4 medium garlic cloves, minced or pressed through garlic press (about 4 teaspoons)
- 1 tablespoon tomato paste
- 1 (14.5-ounce) can diced tomatoes, drained
- ½ cup dry white wine
- 3 cups low-sodium chicken broth
- 1 strip orange zest (from 1 orange), removed with vegetable peeler, about 3 inches long, cleaned of white pith
- ¼ cup pastis or Pernod (see note)
- ¾ pound Yukon Gold potatoes (1 large or 2 small), cut into ¾-inch cubes
- 1 tablespoon chopped fresh tarragon or parsley leaves

Rouille and Croutons
- 3 tablespoons water
- ¼ teaspoon saffron threads
- 1 baguette
- 4 teaspoons juice from 1 lemon
- 2 teaspoons Dijon mustard
- 1 large egg yolk
- ¼ teaspoon cayenne pepper
- 2 small garlic cloves, minced or pressed through garlic press (about 1½ teaspoons)
- ½ cup vegetable oil
- ½ cup plus 2 tablespoons extra-virgin olive oil
  Table salt and ground black pepper

1. **FOR THE BOUILLABAISSE:** Adjust oven racks to middle and lower positions and heat oven to 375 degrees. Pat chicken dry with paper towels and season with salt and pepper. Heat oil in large Dutch oven over medium-high heat until just smoking. Add chicken pieces, skin-side down, and cook without moving until well browned, 5 to 8 minutes. Using tongs, flip chicken and brown other side, about 3 minutes. Transfer chicken to large plate.

2. Add leek and fennel; cook, stirring often, until vegetables begin to soften and turn translucent, about 4 minutes. Add saffron, cayenne, flour, garlic, and tomato paste and cook until fragrant, about 30 seconds. Add tomatoes, wine, broth, orange zest, pastis, and potatoes; bring to simmer. Reduce heat to medium-low and simmer 10 minutes.

3. Nestle chicken thighs and drumsticks into simmering liquid with skin above surface of liquid; cook, uncovered, 5 minutes. Nestle breast pieces into simmering liquid, adjusting pieces as necessary to ensure skin stays above surface of liquid. Bake on middle rack, uncovered, until instant-read thermometer inserted into thickest part of chicken registers 145 degrees for breasts and 160 for drumsticks and thighs, 10 to 20 minutes.

4. **FOR THE ROUILLE:** While chicken cooks, microwave water and saffron in medium microwave-safe bowl on high power until water is steaming, 10 to 20 seconds. Allow to sit 5 minutes. Cut 3-inch piece off of baguette; remove and discard crust. Tear crustless bread into 1-inch chunks (you should have about 1 cup). Stir bread pieces and lemon juice into saffron-infused water; soak 5 minutes. Using whisk, mash soaked bread mixture until uniform paste forms, 1 to 2 minutes. Whisk in mustard, egg yolk, cayenne, and garlic until smooth, about 15 seconds. Whisking constantly, slowly drizzle in vegetable oil in steady stream until smooth mayonnaise-like consistency is reached, scraping down bowl as necessary. Slowly whisk in ½ cup olive oil in steady stream until smooth. Season to taste with salt and pepper.

5. **FOR THE CROUTONS:** Cut remaining baguette into ¾-inch-thick slices. Arrange slices in single layer on rimmed baking sheet. Drizzle with remaining 2 tablespoons olive oil and season with salt and pepper. Bake on lower rack until light golden brown (can be toasted while bouillabaisse is in oven), 10 to 15 minutes.

6. Remove bouillabaisse and croutons from oven and set oven to broil. Once heated, return bouillabaisse to oven and cook until chicken skin is crisp and instant-read thermometer inserted into thickest part of chicken registers 160 degrees for breasts and 175 for drumsticks and thighs, 5 to 10 minutes (smaller pieces may cook faster than larger pieces; remove individual pieces as they reach temperature).

7. Transfer chicken pieces to large plate. Skim excess fat from broth. Stir tarragon into broth and season with salt and pepper. Transfer broth and potatoes to large shallow serving bowls and top with chicken pieces. Drizzle 1 tablespoon rouille over each portion and spread 1 teaspoon rouille on each crouton. Serve, floating 2 croutons in each bowl and passing remaining croutons and rouille separately.

🎥 **COOK'S VIDEOS** Original Test Kitchen Videos

www.cooksillustrated.com
HOW TO MAKE
• Chicken Bouillabaisse
VIDEO TIP
• Maximizing the flavor of saffron

Really Crisp Roasted Potatoes

After weeks of testing, we discovered the secrets to the crispiest, creamiest roasted potatoes ever: the right spud, the right shape, and—surprisingly—a not-so-delicate touch.

⇒ BY FRANCISCO J. ROBERT ⇐

Most of the time, roasted potatoes aren't made using a recipe at all. Instead, they get the generic treatment: chopped medium, drizzled with oil, tossed into the oven at some high-ish temperature, and pulled out when they've got some color.

This one-size-fits-all approach is seldom disastrous. (Indeed, almost any veggie roasted with plenty of oil and salt comes out edible, if not tasty.) The problem is consistency. For every batch of golden-crisped wedges with perfectly velvety interiors, there's a surfeit of dud spuds sporting mealy innards, leathery crusts, and—unless you've been diligent about giving every surface adequate facedown time on the baking sheet—uneven browning.

A survey of roasted-potato recipes revealed that foolproof techniques are few and far between. Most employed very hot ovens and long roasting times (one took a whopping hour and a half!) to get a well-browned exterior but at the expense of a velvety interior, and often that beautifully browned crust was actually less crisp than tough and chewy. The recipes that produced the creamy interior I was after ended up pale-golden and not the least bit crisp. Undeterred, I set out to achieve the perfect balance of these textures: crisp on the outside, silky-smooth on the inside.

Par for the Course
Flawed as they were, this initial gambit of recipes wasn't devoid of lessons. An unmistakable pattern had emerged: The best exterior texture, hands down, came from recipes that parcooked the spuds by either boiling or simmering before moving them to the oven. As these recipes also called for shorter roasting times, the results seemed counterintuitive. What would cause better crisping with less time in the oven? Surely, they weren't getting crisp in the water.

Puzzled, I dusted off some of the food-science tomes in our library and boned up on potato cookery. Turns out, I was only half right. Indeed, no actual crisping was occurring during parcooking, but an important step in the process was getting a serious jump-start.

Cutting the potatoes into thick rounds, not chunks, contributed to much more even browning.

For a potato to brown and crisp, two things need to happen, both of which depend on moisture. First, starch granules in the potatoes must absorb water and swell, releasing some of their amylose, a water-soluble type of starch. Second, some of the amylose must break down into glucose (i.e., sugar). Once the moisture evaporates on the surface of the potato, the amylose hardens into a shell, yielding crispness, and the glucose darkens, yielding an appealing brown color. In the dry heat of the oven, this is a lengthy process because the starch granules swell slowly, releasing little amylose. In contrast, parboiled potatoes are swimming in the requisite moist heat, releasing lots of amylose on the surface of the potato. By the time parcooked spuds get transferred to the oven, they are ready to begin browning and crisping almost immediately.

A lot of science for a side dish—but would it stand up to kitchen tests? To find out, I cut up two batches of potatoes (I opted for standard russets) into 1½-inch chunks. I parboiled the first batch until tender (about 10 minutes), spread the chunks on a baking

sheet drizzled with ¼ cup olive oil, and roasted them at 450 degrees, flipping them partway through cooking with tongs. The second batch skipped the parcooking step altogether and went straight into the oven. After about 45 minutes, the parcooked spuds were nicely browned and fairly crisp, with relatively creamy interiors. The oven-only batch, on the other hand, took an hour to reach the same level of browning and crispness—at which point the potato interiors were far more dried out.

So parcooking was key. But was boiling the right method? Surely, some of that great exterior starch was getting washed off in all the commotion. On a hunch, I prepped another batch, this time using a gentler form of moist heat: steaming. When I pulled this batch out of the oven, yes, the color was a deep, dark brown, but the texture was all out of whack—tacky and chewy, almost like taffy. The diagnosis: too much starch and sugar, which had formed a gluey residue. The magic formula, then, was to draw out the starch and sugar quickly, but to wash away the excess. I found that the small but significant step of using a slightly more gentle parsimmering (bringing to a boil, then immediately reducing the heat so that the vigorous action of boiling wouldn't wash away too much starch) produced the best texture yet.

Roughing It Up
I was on the right track, but there was room for improvement. Although I was achieving a modicum of crispness and browning, the browning was uneven. Also, tasters still wanted creamier interiors and—by the way—could the exteriors be crisper still, please? The uneven browning wasn't hard to solve. I identified two culprits: First, the chunky cubes I was using, which demanded several turns with the tongs to give every surface time against the baking sheet and were hard to keep track of. Two, the parsimmered potatoes were so delicate that it was hard to transfer them to the oven without a few breaking apart into smaller pieces that cooked at a different rate.

Experimenting with simmering times, I found that reducing the parcooking time to just 5 minutes was long enough to get the starch breakdown going but short enough that the potatoes could be handled without breaking. As for the shape,

📹 **COOK'S VIDEOS** Original Test Kitchen Videos

www.cooksillustrated.com
HOW TO MAKE
• Crisp Roasted Potatoes

I simplified matters considerably by cutting the potatoes into rounds—with only two surfaces, I only had to flip them once. A few tests later, I arrived at ½-inch rounds as the optimal thickness for providing the right ratio of crisp exterior to creamy interior.

Now for the tricky part: upping the crispness and the creaminess. I seemed to be at an impasse. Creaminess depended on interior moisture, which escapes as the potatoes cook, yet crispness depended on adequate roasting time. One was the enemy of the other. Although jump-starting the starch-breakdown process had cut down the roasting time, I still needed to allow enough time for the surface moisture to evaporate. (Until that happens, the temperature at the potato's surface can't rise beyond 212 degrees—the boiling point of water—far below the temperature needed for crisping.)

The big breakthrough came courtesy of our science editor, who observed that the parcooking step was doing more than just jump-starting the surface starch. It was also speeding up the evaporation process by creating a rough surface. A rougher surface, he explained, offers more escape routes for moisture than the flat surface of a raw potato, and the damaged exterior cells surrender their moisture more readily than intact cells. So why not try roughing up the surface even more?

Easy enough. Using a fork to gently scrape the surfaces of the parcooked potatoes, I roasted another batch. Sure enough, I achieved the best results yet,

but assiduously scraping individual potato slices seemed absurd. There had to be an easier way. For my next experiment, I tried tossing the potatoes—vigorously—with olive oil and salt, hoping the salt would mimic the friction of the fork. In the process, a thick layer resembling mashed potatoes formed on the exterior. Success! Once roasted, the spuds were crisper than ever—and nicely seasoned, to boot.

Yukon Territory

At this point, I'd reduced the roasting time to less than an hour. By preheating the baking sheet along with the oven, I shaved off a few more minutes. The abbreviated session in the dry heat had a noticeable effect on the interior; allowing more retention of moisture and thus a creamier texture. The only way to up the creaminess would be to reduce the roasting time further, but I wasn't willing to sacrifice the incredible exterior texture I had worked so hard to achieve.

That's when it dawned on me to revisit potato choice. I had been using regular old russets, which have a high starch content and low moisture. With the parcooking and surface-roughing steps, I had starch in spades. But moisture I could use. Substituting Red Bliss potatoes (high moisture, low starch) gave me creamy interiors, but at the expense of too much crispness. It's when I substituted Yukon Golds (medium starch, medium moisture) that I reached the finish line. These yellow-hued beauties crisped up just as perfectly as the russets, yet the extra moisture kept the interiors far creamier. Tasting a final batch, colleagues marveled at the results: crisp as a chip and creamy as a bowl of mashed potatoes—the best of both worlds.

AT-A-GLANCE | KEYS TO CRISP, EVENLY BROWNED SPUDS

1. DISKS, NOT CHUNKS
Half-inch rounds require only one flip, making it far easier to ensure each side gets equal time facedown on the pan.

2. PARCOOK
Simmering the potatoes brings the starch to the surface, jump-starting the crisping process.

3. PREHEAT SHEET
Preheating a rimmed baking sheet also gives cooking a head start, for crisper results.

4. TOSS VIGOROUSLY
Roughing up the parboiled potatoes with salt and oil damages the surface cells, which speeds up evaporation.

SCIENCE Just Scratching the Surface

While developing our recipe for Crisp Roasted Potatoes, we discovered that parcooked potato slices browned faster in the oven than raw slices. When we subsequently "roughed up" the parcooked slices by tossing them vigorously with salt and oil, they browned faster still. The explanation? It's all a matter of surface area. Browning or crisping can't begin until the surface moisture evaporates. The parcooked, roughed-up slices—riddled with tiny dips and mounds—have more exposed surface area than the smooth raw slices and thus more escape routes for moisture. If you have trouble getting your head around two potato slices

ROUGHED-UP SURFACE = FAST EVAPORATION

SMOOTH SURFACE = SLOW EVAPORATION

of identical width having vastly different surface areas, think of it this way: Five square miles of Colorado's mountain region will have far more exposed surface area than 5 square miles of the Kansas plains. (Just try walking them both.) –F.R.

CRISP ROASTED POTATOES
SERVES 4 TO 6

NOTE: The steps of parcooking the potatoes before roasting and tossing the potatoes with salt and oil until they are coated with starch are the keys to developing a crisp exterior and creamy interior. The potatoes should be just undercooked when they are removed from the boiling water.

2½ pounds Yukon Gold potatoes, rinsed and cut into ½-inch-thick slices
Table salt
5 tablespoons olive oil
Ground black pepper

1. Adjust oven rack to lowest position, place rimmed baking sheet on rack, and heat oven to 450 degrees. Place potatoes and 1 tablespoon salt in Dutch oven; add cold water to cover by 1 inch. Bring to boil over high heat; reduce heat and gently simmer until exteriors of potatoes have softened but centers offer resistance when pierced with paring knife, about 5 minutes. Drain potatoes well and transfer to large bowl. Drizzle with 2 tablespoons oil and sprinkle with ½ teaspoon salt; using rubber spatula, toss to combine. Drizzle with another 2 tablespoons oil and ½ teaspoon salt; continue to toss until exteriors of potato slices are coated with starchy paste, 1 to 2 minutes.

2. Working quickly, remove baking sheet from oven and drizzle remaining tablespoon oil over surface. Carefully transfer potatoes to baking sheet and spread into even layer (skin-side up if end piece). Bake until bottoms of potatoes are golden brown and crisp, 15 to 25 minutes, rotating baking sheet after 10 minutes.

3. Remove baking sheet from oven and, using metal spatula and tongs, loosen potatoes from pan, carefully flipping each slice. Continue to roast until second side is golden and crisp, 10 to 20 minutes longer, rotating pan as needed to ensure potatoes brown evenly. Season with salt and pepper to taste and serve immediately.

Great Pan-Seared Scallops

Juicy, crisp-crusted perfection means overcoming two obstacles: chemically treated scallops and weak stovetops.

⫸ BY BRYAN ROOF ⫷

For a restaurant chef, pan-seared scallops are as easy as it gets: Slick a super-hot pan with oil, add the shellfish, flip them once, and serve. The whole process takes no more than a couple of minutes and produces golden-crusted beauties with tender, medium-rare interiors. But try the same technique at home and you're likely to run into trouble. The problem is that most home stovetops don't get nearly as hot as professional ranges, so it's difficult to properly brown the scallops without overcooking them. Moreover, restaurant chefs pay top dollar for scallops without chemical additives, which are known in the industry as "dry." The remainder, called "wet" scallops—the type available in most supermarkets—are treated with a solution of water and sodium tripolyphosphate (STP) to increase shelf life and retain moisture. Unfortunately, STP lends a soapy, off-flavor to the scallops, and the extra water only compounds the problem of poor browning.

To achieve superior pan-seared scallops, I had to find a solution to the browning conundrum. I also had to get rid of the chemical taste of STP.

Watershed Moments

My first stop was the supermarket fish counter. Scallops are available in a range of sizes: A pound of the hard-to-find large sea variety contains eight to 10 scallops, while a pound of the petite bay variety may have as many as 100 pencil eraser–sized scallops. Since small scallops are more prone to overcooking than large, I opted for the biggest commonly available size: 10 to 20 per pound. I decided to work with wet scallops first. After all, if I could develop a good recipe for finicky wet scallops, it would surely work with premium dry scallops.

I started by seasoning 1½ pounds (the right amount for four people) with salt and pepper. I heated 1 tablespoon of vegetable oil in a 12-inch stainless-steel skillet, then added the scallops in a single layer and waited for them to brown. After three minutes, they were steaming away in a ¼-inch-deep pool of liquid. At the five-minute mark, the moisture in the

▣ **COOK'S VIDEOS** Original Test Kitchen Videos
www.cooksillustrated.com
HOW TO MAKE
• Pan-Seared Scallops
VIDEO TIPS
• Dry versus wet scallops
• Preparing scallops for cooking

For ultra-crisp crusts, we baste the scallops with butter.

skillet evaporated and the flesh began to turn golden. But at this point it was too late: The scallops were already overcooked and tough, and I hadn't even flipped them.

To dry out the scallops, I tried pressing them between kitchen towels. When 10 minutes didn't work, I tried a full hour—even leaving a third batch overnight in the refrigerator. The results were disheartening. While slightly drier than unblotted scallops, the pressed batches still exuded copious amounts of liquid in the skillet (and they still tasted soapy; I'd focus on that later). My conclusion: Beyond a 10-minute blot, there's no point in trying to remove moisture from wet scallops before cooking.

It was becoming clear that to dry out the waterlogged scallops for good browning, I'd have to get the pan as hot as possible. Without a high-output range, it was important to pay careful attention to technique. I started by waiting to add the scallops to the skillet until the oil was beginning to smoke, a clear indication of heat. I also cooked the scallops in two batches instead of one, since crowding would cool down the pan. Finally, switching to a nonstick

skillet ensured that as the scallops cooked, the browned bits formed a crust on the meat instead of sticking to the skillet. These were steps in right direction, but the scallops were still overcooked and rubbery by the time they were fully browned.

Butter Up

Would switching from oil to butter help my cause? Butter contains milk proteins and sugars that brown rapidly when heated, so I hoped that it would help the scallops turn golden before they overcooked. But my hopes were dashed when in my next batch, the butter that I'd swapped for oil actually made matters worse: It burned before the scallops were cooked through.

Then I recalled a method I'd used when cooking steaks and chops in restaurants: butter-basting. I gave it a try with my scallops, searing them in oil on one side and adding a tablespoon of butter to the skillet after flipping them. I tilted the skillet to allow the butter to pool, then used a large spoon to ladle the foaming butter over the scallops. Waiting to add the butter ensured that it had just enough time to work its browning magic on the shellfish, but not enough time to burn. The scallops now achieved a deep golden brown crust in record time, and their moist interiors were preserved. They weren't quite as tender and juicy as dry scallops, but they were darn close.

Lemon Aid

Only one problem remained, and it was a big one: the soapy flavor of STP. I already knew from earlier tests that blotting removes neither excess water nor STP, but what about the opposite approach: soaking in water to wash out the STP? It was a flop. No matter how long or carefully I rinsed the scallops, the STP still remained (see "Going for a Soak" on page 15).

I thought things over and decided that if I couldn't remove the STP, I would try to mask it. I thought maybe a saltwater brine was the answer because it would penetrate the scallops deeply. The brine did provide even seasoning, but not enough to mask the chemical flavor. I noted that the phosphate in STP is alkaline. What if I covered it up by putting acidic lemon juice in the brine? Problem solved. Only the most sensitive tasters now picked up on a hint of chemical off-flavors; most tasted only the sweet shellfish complemented by the bright flavor of citrus.

With my wet-scallop approach established, it was finally time to test my recipe on dry scallops. I skipped the soaking step, which was unnecessary in the absence of STP, and proceeded with the recipe. The result? Scallops that rivaled those made on a powerful restaurant range, golden brown on the exterior and juicy and tender on the interior. I was happy to serve them with just a squeeze of lemon, but fancier occasions call for a sauce. For those instances, I developed a few recipes based on a classic accompaniment: browned butter.

PAN-SEARED SCALLOPS
SERVES 4

NOTE: We strongly recommend purchasing "dry" scallops (those without chemical additives). If you can only find "wet" scallops, soak them in a solution of 1 quart cold water, ¼ cup lemon juice, and 2 tablespoons table salt for 30 minutes before proceeding with step 1. In step 2, season the scallops with pepper only. If you are unsure whether your scallops are wet or dry, conduct this quick test: Place 1 scallop on a paper towel–lined, microwave-safe plate and microwave on high power for 15 seconds. If the scallop is "dry," it will exude very little water. If it is "wet," there will be a sizable ring of moisture on the paper towel. (The microwaved scallop can be cooked as is.) Prepare the sauce (if serving) while the scallops dry (between steps 1 and 2) and keep it warm while cooking them. For our free recipes for Orange-Lime Vinaigrette, Ginger Butter Sauce, and Caper-Mustard Sauce, go to www.cooksillustrated.com/dec09.

1½	pounds dry sea scallops, 10 to 20 per pound, small side muscles removed (see note)
	Table salt and ground black pepper
2	tablespoons vegetable oil
2	tablespoons unsalted butter
	Lemon wedges or sauce (recipes follow) for serving

1. Place scallops on rimmed baking sheet lined with clean kitchen towel. Place second clean kitchen towel on top of scallops and press gently on towel to blot liquid. Let scallops sit at room temperature 10 minutes while towels absorb moisture.

2. Sprinkle scallops on both sides with salt and pepper. Heat 1 tablespoon oil in 12-inch nonstick skillet over high heat until just smoking. Add half of scallops in single layer, flat-side down, and cook, without moving, until well browned, 1½ to 2 minutes.

3. Add 1 tablespoon butter to skillet. Using tongs, flip scallops; continue to cook, using large spoon to baste scallops with melted butter (tilt skillet so butter runs to one side) until sides of scallops are firm and centers are opaque, 30 to 90 seconds longer (remove smaller scallops as they finish cooking). Transfer scallops to large plate and

SCIENCE **Going for a Soak**

So-called wet scallops have been treated with sodium tripolyphosphate (STP), which lends a disagreeable flavor. Could we get rid of the STP by soaking the scallops in water?

THE EXPERIMENT
We prepared three batches of "wet" scallops, soaking the first in a quart of water for 30 minutes, soaking the second for an hour, and leaving the third untreated. We then cooked each batch according to our recipe and sent them to a lab to be analyzed for STP content.

THE RESULTS
The scallops soaked for 30 minutes only had about 10 percent less STP than the untreated batch, and soaking for a full hour wasn't much better: Only about 11 percent of the STP was removed. Tasters were still able to clearly identify an unpleasant chemical flavor in both soaked samples.

THE EXPLANATION
The phosphates in STP form a chemical bond with the proteins in scallops. The bonds are so strong that they prevent the STP from being washed away, no matter how long the scallops are soaked.

THE SOLUTION
Rather than try to remove the chemical taste from STP-treated scallops, we masked it by soaking them in a solution of lemon juice, water, and salt.

CHEMICAL COVERUP
A lemon-flavored brine camouflages the off-taste of "wet" scallops.

tent loosely with foil. Wipe out skillet with wad of paper towels and repeat cooking with remaining oil, scallops, and butter. Serve immediately with lemon wedges or sauce.

LEMON BROWN BUTTER
MAKES ABOUT ¼ CUP

4	tablespoons (½ stick) unsalted butter, cut into 4 pieces
1	small shallot, minced (about 1½ tablespoons)
1	tablespoon minced fresh parsley leaves
½	teaspoon minced fresh thyme leaves
2	teaspoons juice from 1 lemon
	Table salt and ground black pepper

Heat butter in small heavy-bottomed saucepan over medium heat; cook, swirling pan constantly, until butter turns dark golden brown and has nutty aroma, 4 to 5 minutes. Add shallot and cook until fragrant, about 30 seconds. Remove pan from heat and stir in parsley, thyme, and lemon juice. Season to taste with salt and pepper. Cover to keep warm.

TOMATO-GINGER SAUCE
MAKES ABOUT ½ CUP

6	tablespoons (¾ stick) unsalted butter
1	medium plum tomato, cored, seeded, and chopped small
1	tablespoon grated fresh ginger
1	tablespoon juice from 1 lemon
¼	teaspoon red pepper flakes
	Table salt

Heat butter in small heavy-bottomed saucepan over medium heat; cook, swirling pan constantly, until butter turns dark golden brown and has nutty aroma, 4 to 5 minutes. Add tomato, ginger, lemon juice, and pepper flakes; cook, stirring constantly, until fragrant, about 1 minute. Season to taste with salt. Cover to keep warm.

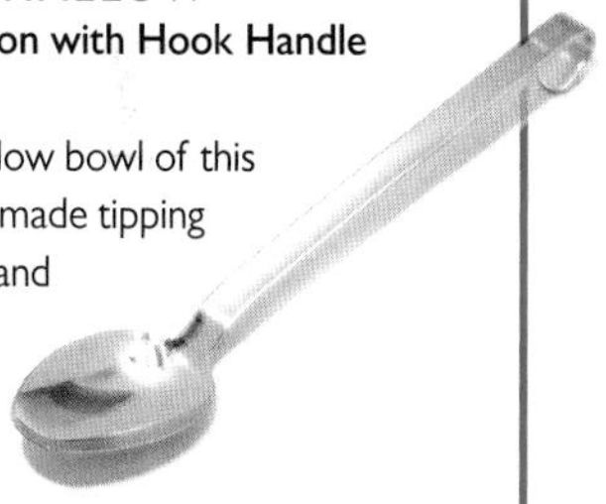

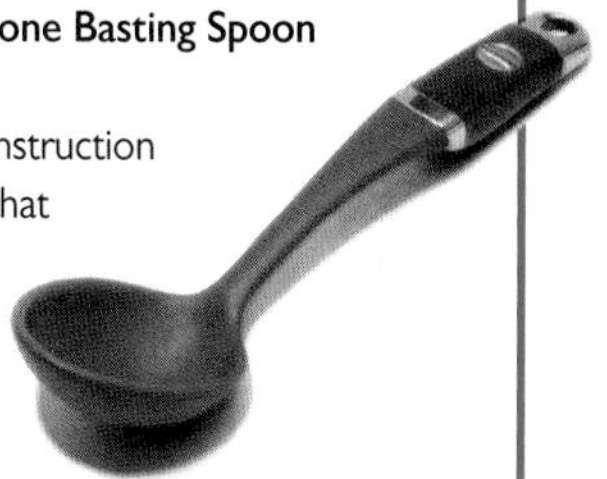

The Best Small Appliances

Small appliances promise convenience—but the wrong ones can wind up as clutter. Here's our guide to top-quality workhorses and test-kitchen champs. BY LISA GLAZER

After nearly two decades testing small appliances, we know how to identify keepers—the most useful, durable, and high-quality equipment and brands. (Don't look for an electric wok on this list.) While a few items are not inexpensive, they're worth the investment for better cooking and baking.

FOOD PROCESSOR

➤ **KITCHENAID 12-Cup KFP750 Food Processor, $199.95**

This peak performer aced all our vegetable prep tests, chopping and slicing as evenly and cleanly as an expertly wielded knife—but a lot faster. It went on to win perfect scores pureeing steamed broccoli into soup and cutting fats into flour for pastry. The 12-cup bowl is spacious enough for an extra-large batch of pizza dough, but you can also attach a 4-cup mini bowl and blade for smaller chores like chopping a handful of parsley.

Best Buy
➤ **CUISINART Pro Custom 11, $169**
For $30 less, the Cuisinart is also a stellar performer. Its only downside? It's less of a chopping champ than the KitchenAid.

BLENDER

➤ **KITCHENAID 5-Speed KSB580 Blender, $149.99**

When frozen cocktails beckon, only a blender offers impeccable ice-crushing power. Because food processors can leak, a blender is also a better bet for swirling smoothies, soups, and purees. Our favorite boasts a tapered, V-shaped jar and four blades (each positioned at a different angle, the better to catch and pulverize foods) that left nary a lump or trace of pulp in smoothies made with rock-hard frozen berries and fibrous mango.

Best Buy
➤ **KALORIK BL Blender, $47.95**
If you're fine with a slower pace, look to the far-cheaper Kalorik, which excelled at core tasks, despite taking a longer time to get the job done.

STAND MIXERS

➤ **KITCHENAID Professional 600 Series 6-Quart Stand Mixer, $399.99**
➤ **CUISINART 5.5-Quart Stand Mixer, $299**

These two stand mixers ranked neck and neck in our testing. Both are pricey—but they're powerhouse performers, masters at whipping egg whites, creaming butter and sugar, kneading basic bread dough, and mixing even the stiffest cookie dough. The KitchenAid 600 Series 6-Quart has a slightly larger capacity; newer models feature a spiral dough hook attachment that makes kneading a cinch. (See "Attachment Issue" on page 30 for our views on its paddle attachment.) The Cuisinart 5.5-Quart Stand Mixer includes not only an efficient dough hook but modern updates such as a digital timer with automatic shut-off and a splashguard attachment.

Best Buy
➤ **KITCHENAID Classic Plus Stand Mixer, 4.5-Quart, $199.99**
This stand mixer (reviewed in a separate testing of inexpensive stand mixers) has a smaller capacity and less brute force than our winners, but still performed remarkably well in our tests.

IMMERSION BLENDER

➤ **KITCHENAID Immersion Blender, $49.99**

If you already own a blender or food processor (or both), why bother with a smaller appliance with the same blending function? Because with this tool, there's no need to blend in batches, and it's easy to rinse off and toss back into the drawer. Our top choice has a stainless-steel shaft, which can be plunged into pans even as they sit over a direct flame.

HANDHELD MIXER

➤ **CUISINART Power Advantage 7-Speed Hand Mixer, $49.95**

Not big on baking? A handheld mixer isn't as powerful as a stand mixer, but a good model still does a decent job whipping, creaming, and mixing. Even with thick cookie dough, the metal beaters on our winner offer smooth, steady, controlled mixing action.

ELECTRIC KNIFE SHARPENER

➤ **CHEF'S CHOICE 130 Professional Sharpening Station 130, $149.95**

An electric sharpener has the edge, so to speak, over manual options because it doesn't just sharpen, it also removes nicks and notches. Our favorite includes spring-loaded blade guides that hold the blade against the sharpening wheels at the proper angle, ensuring a fine, polished edge every time. If you have both European and Asian-style knives, the **Chef's Choice AngleSelect Knife Sharpener, Model 1520 ($169.95)**, can restore both a 15-degree angle on your Asian knives and a 20-degree angle on your European cutlery.

WAFFLE MAKER

➤ **BLACK & DECKER Grill and Waffle Baker, $49.99**

We prefer the convenience of large, square waffle makers, which cook four waffles at once. Our favorite delivers good height and even browning and also doubles as a griddle.

ICE CREAM MAKER

➤ CUISINART Automatic Ice Cream, Frozen Yogurt, and Sorbet Maker ICE-20, $49.95

Our winner relies on a prefrozen revolving canister and prepares ice cream in only 20 minutes. Competing models (with revolving beaters) initially produced lighter, airier desserts, but after two days in the freezer the results shifted—the ice cream made with revolving beaters was more likely to have ice crystals, while the results from our winner remained smooth and creamy.

ELECTRIC GRIDDLE

➤ BROILKING Professional Griddle, $99.99

Our winner is roomy enough for eight pieces of French toast, and it's made of heavy-duty cast aluminum, which evenly distributes heat for perfectly browned pancakes and crisp bacon. The removable backsplash stops grease from splattering.

Best Buy
➤ WEST BEND Cool-Touch Nonstick Electric Griddle, $51.95

This has a smaller surface area but cooks equally well.

TOASTER

➤ HAMILTON BEACH Michael Graves Design 4-Slice Toaster, $37.99

A toaster is a one-trick appliance, so it shouldn't break the bank—but it should produce toast that's evenly browned on both sides. Our top choice has a similar number of heating elements on each side of the toasting slots to help ensure even cooking; browning overall was more consistent from batch to batch than in other models we tested. Extra-wide slots accommodate bagels.

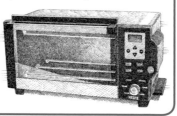

SLOW COOKER

➤ ALL-CLAD Stainless Steel Slow Cooker with Ceramic Insert, $179.95

A slow cooker (or crockpot) cooks pot roasts, beans, and stews with slow, steady heat. Turn it on, leave the house, and return hours later to a finished dish. The All-Clad offers user-friendly handles on the ceramic insert, a see-through lid, and a timer that automatically shifts to a "keep warm" setting at the end of cooking.

Best Buy
➤ HAMILTON BEACH Programmable Slow Cooker with Temperature Probe, $62.99

This model performed nearly as well as the winner, but its insert doesn't have handles.

RICE COOKER

➤ SANYO 5.5-Cup Electric Rice Cooker and Steamer, $54.95

A rice cooker isn't a timesaver—it's a foolproof way to avoid gummy or dried-out grains. Many high-end models can be preset in the morning and left until evening, but since rice isn't on our daily menu (as it is in Japan), we prefer a more basic, affordable model. Our winner delivers consistently excellent white, brown, or sushi rice with a reliable "keep warm" option.

Don't Get Burned: Toaster Ovens

Should you buy a toaster oven? Traditionally, toaster ovens have been known for making lousy toast, brown on top and white on the bottom—plus their small size and typically inconsistent heating elements make them inadequate as ovens. We found these problems persist, even in a new generation of super-sized models tricked out with fancy features like convection capability, digital displays, and custom cookware. Our one recommended model, the Krups 6-Slice Digital Convection Toaster Oven FBC2 ($249.99) cooked food more evenly (including roasted chicken) than the other models we tested, offering reliable cooking, user-friendly controls, solid construction—and even decent toast. But since it is expensive, we only recommend it if you want to invest in a higher-end toaster oven for small cooking projects. You can do equally well (and save a lot of money) with an ordinary toaster and your full-size oven.

COFFEE GRINDER/SPICE GRINDER

➤ CAPRESSO Cool Grind 501, $19.95

Like many blade grinders, this one can struggle to grind evenly. But it has two features we value highly: a large capacity and a deep cup that contains grinds without spilling. It also works well as a spice grinder—buy two, one for coffee and another for spices (unless you don't mind coffee with a hint of spice, or vice versa).

ELECTRIC KETTLE

➤ CAPRESSO H20 Plus Glass Kettle, $59.95

This sleek appliance shaves minutes off the wait for boiling water, sits on a separate base to conserve stovetop space, and includes automatic shut-off/boil-dry safeguards. The 6-cup glass carafe is easy to pour and clean—plus we like the view of rising bubbles as water boils.

AUTOMATIC DRIP COFFEE MAKER

➤ TECHNIVORM Moccamaster Coffee Maker KBT-741, $265

The only automatic coffee maker we like achieves perfect temperatures for brewing and keeps the coffee hot in a thermal carafe (instead of turning acrid in a glass carafe on a hot plate). It's easy to use and brews exceptionally smooth, balanced coffee. Sure, it's expensive—but not compared to a year's worth of Starbucks. (Still have sticker shock? Try a manual drip filter or French press.)

ELECTRIC CITRUS JUICER

➤ BREVILLE Citrus Press, $169.95

Pressing on the handle squeezes the fruit, which starts the powerful motorized reamer of this Rolls-Royce of juicers. Made from heavy stainless steel, it extracts every last drop of juice quickly and smoothly.

Best Buy
➤ BLACK & DECKER CitrusMate Plus Citrus Juicer, $21.49

Here's the good news: The CitrusMate may not purr like a Rolls—but it's almost as efficient at a fraction of the price.

For sources, go to www.cooksillustrated.com/dec09. Prices were current at press time but are subject to change.

Rethinking Cassoulet

In France, this 700-year-old pork-and-bean casserole is a three-day production. Could we turn it into an afternoon's work?

⇒ BY J. KENJI LOPEZ-ALT ⇐

Though it may look like just a humble peasant stew of white beans and meat, no dish defines French country cooking better—or drums up more controversy—than cassoulet. Debates over whether mutton is mandatory or heretical or the number of times bread crumbs should be stirred into the pot during cooking (if included at all) have raged for centuries. Even the Académie Universelle du Cassoulet, an organization dedicated to maintaining the integrity of this casserole around the world, hasn't been able to put such questions to rest. Still, two things are certain: This stew yields the most deeply flavorful pork and beans imaginable—and, however you make it, count on setting aside at least a couple of days. You'll need that time to first grind and stuff your own sausage and to preserve duck (or goose) in fat until meltingly supple for confit. Only then can you get down to the business of cooking: Brown the sausage and some form of pork stew meat (like belly or shoulder), then simmer these in white wine and stock with aromatics until tender. Add the confit and stir the stewed meat together with the beans (parcooked separately) in a wide-rimmed earthenware vessel called a *cassole*. When bread crumbs are involved, they're sprinkled over the top. Finally, the casserole gently bakes until the beans have reached a luxuriously creamy texture and a golden brown crust forms on top.

While I'm not one to shy away from a weekend of cooking, if I hoped to make cassoulet more than once every few years, I had to find a streamlined approach.

We add crumbs twice to create a crust that's truly crisp.

Meat and Beans

The first place to streamline was obviously the confit. Store-bought confit wasn't a good option, as it's expensive and inconsistent. While many variations (restaurant versions in particular) do include this deeply flavorful preserved meat, it's by no means essential. I decided to look for other ways to bring some richness into the dish.

For starters, I'd need another source of animal fat. Bacon seemed like a good idea, but imparted too much of a sweet-smoky flavor. Salt pork proved best, contributing richness without overpowering the dish, as long as I blanched it first to remove excess salt. As for the stewing pork, I needed a cut with plenty of connective tissue that wouldn't dry out during prolonged cooking. Pork shoulder fit the bill, preferred over spare ribs, belly, and country-style ribs. A replacement for the sausage was a little trickier. Since the Toulouse sausage often used in cassoulet tastes mainly of pork with a hint of garlic and spices, typical supermarket options like Italian (too much fennel) or kielbasa (too smoky) were out. Instead, tasters deemed mild Irish bangers or German bratwurst the best substitutes. To help the sausages keep their shape, I blanched them whole with the salt pork before slicing.

Following standard flavor-building procedure, I browned the sausages and the pork shoulder in a few tablespoons of oil in a Dutch oven. Many traditional recipes have you tie all the aromatics (carrots, onions, celery, bay leaf, and thyme) in a cheesecloth sachet, along with the salt pork. But it was much easier and just as flavorful to finely dice the carrots and onions, and leave them in the finished dish. This left me with the celery and herbs, which I tied together to facilitate easy removal later on. Though they're not on the list of ingredients sanctioned by the Académie Universelle du Cassoulet, I found tomato paste and canned diced tomatoes worked better than white wine alone in balancing out the richness of the meat. Broth made from poultry or pork is the most traditional cooking liquid, and store-bought chicken broth worked just fine.

All cassoulets use some form of white bean, the most celebrated being the *tarbais*, a half-inch-long

STEP-BY-STEP | COOKING TENDER, FLAVORFUL FRENCH PORK AND BEANS

1. BRINE Soak beans overnight in salt solution for tender texture.

2. BLANCH Blanch salt pork (to remove excess salt) and sausage (to help firm up).

3. BROWN Brown sausage, remove; brown pork shoulder, carrots, and onion.

4. FLAVOR Return sausage and add wine. Stir in tomatoes, aromatics, salt pork, broth, and beans.

5. BAKE Bake, covered, 1½ hours, until beans are creamy and full of meaty flavor.

ACHIEVING A CRISP CRUST

After baking the casserole for 1½ hours to perfect flavor and bean texture, here's how to create just the right crisp crust.

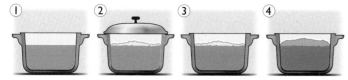

I. BAKE UNCOVERED Remove celery bundle and salt pork; return pot to oven, uncovered. **2. ADD CRUMBS; COVER** Bake, covered, 15 minutes to allow crumbs to form cohesive "raft." **3. BAKE UNCOVERED** Uncover and bake 15 minutes more to dry raft so it can support more crumbs. **4. ADD MORE CRUMBS; CRISP** Add remaining crumbs and bake until crisp.

---

kidney-shaped bean with a very thin skin and a supremely creamy texture. Unfortunately, these handpicked beans from the south of France cost around $20 a pound. Widely available dried cannellini provided a similar tender creaminess.

Soaking the beans overnight, parcooking them for two hours in a separate pot before combining them with the braised meat, and simmering in the oven for another couple of hours, as many traditional recipes call for, seemed fussy. Why not cook beans and meat together from the get-go? I added the soaked beans directly to the browned meat, flavorings, and broth and simmered everything in the oven for three hours. The beans had great meaty flavor but lacked the smooth creaminess of the parcooked ones. Increasing the cooking time to a full four hours gave me better beans, but now my meat was dried out and stringy. I had to figure out a way to get my beans more tender in less time.

Most recipes strictly advise against salting beans before they finish cooking, claiming that salt prevents softening. However, we've proven that beans soaked overnight in salt water are vastly superior in texture and flavor to those soaked in regular water. During brining, the sodium ions in salt replace magnesium and calcium in the beans—two minerals responsible for toughness. When I went ahead and cooked the brined beans, I discovered another boon to the approach: It allowed my beans to achieve the ideal creamy, velvety texture in just three hours—at which point the meat was perfectly cooked.

The Upper Crust

One element now stood between me and flawless cassoulet: a crisp crust to contrast with the creamy beans and tender meat. Ideally, as the cassoulet cooks, a dry skin should form on its surface so that when bread crumbs are added, they stay afloat and crisp up. This works in a traditional wide-rimmed cassole. But in the Dutch oven I was using for cooking, moisture trapped by the tall sides keeps the surface moist. When it came time to apply the crumbs, they inevitably failed to get crisp and sank, thickening the broth until it resembled bread pudding.

I needed a more intense heat from above to dry out the surface. I cooked my beans at a gentle pace until they were nearly done, then uncovered the pot and raised the oven temperature to 350 degrees for 20 minutes, in the hopes of drying the surface. This time I had the opposite problem: My bread crumbs stayed perfectly afloat, but because they were so dry, they remained crumbly and sandy as they cooked, instead of forming the kind of uniform brown crust that you can crack with a spoon. I learned that the optimal crust requires a perfect balance of moisture and heat. What if I split the task, purposely getting half of them a little moist to form a coherent raft before adding the remaining crumbs on top? I applied half of the bread crumbs to my casserole and baked the pot covered for 15 minutes, allowing the crumbs to slightly moisten and bind together. Then I removed the cover, baked the mixture for a few more minutes, added the remaining crumbs, and let them cook until crisp.

Finally, with the perfect crusty top covering tender, flavorful beans, I bet my streamlined casserole would even pass muster with the Académie Universelle du Cassoulet.

FRENCH PORK AND WHITE BEAN CASSEROLE
SERVES 8 TO 10

NOTE: Instead of an overnight soak, you can "quick brine" the beans: In step 1, combine the salt, water, and beans in a large Dutch oven and bring to a boil over high heat. Remove the pot from the heat, cover, and let stand 1 hour. Drain and rinse the beans and proceed with the recipe. If you can't find fresh French garlic sausage, Irish bangers or bratwurst may be substituted. To make a more authentic version of the dish, see our free recipe for French Pork and White Bean Casserole with Homemade Duck Confit at www.cooksillustrated.com/dec09.

Table salt
1 pound dried cannellini beans (about 2 cups), rinsed and picked over
2 medium celery ribs
1 bay leaf
4 sprigs fresh thyme
1½ pounds fresh French garlic sausage (see note)
4 ounces salt pork, rinsed of excess salt
4 tablespoons vegetable oil
1½ pounds pork shoulder, cut into 1-inch chunks
1 large onion, chopped fine (about 1½ cups)
2 medium carrots, peeled and cut into ¼-inch dice (about 1 cup)
4 medium garlic cloves, minced or pressed through garlic press (about 4 teaspoons)
1 tablespoon tomato paste
½ cup dry white wine
1 (14.5-ounce) can diced tomatoes
4 cups low-sodium chicken broth
Ground black pepper
4 large slices high-quality white sandwich bread, torn into rough pieces
½ cup chopped fresh parsley leaves

1. Dissolve 2 tablespoons salt in 3 quarts cold water in large bowl or container. Add beans and soak at room temperature, 8 to 24 hours. Drain and rinse well.

2. Adjust oven rack to lower-middle position and heat oven to 300 degrees. Using kitchen twine, tie together celery, bay leaf, and thyme. Place sausage and salt pork in medium saucepan and add cold water to cover by 1 inch; bring to boil over high heat. Reduce heat to simmer and cook 5 minutes. Transfer sausages to cutting board, allow to cool slightly, then cut into 1-inch pieces. Remove salt pork from water; set aside.

3. Heat 2 tablespoons oil in large Dutch oven over medium-high heat until beginning to smoke. Add sausage pieces and brown on all sides, 8 to 12 minutes total. Transfer to medium bowl. Add pork shoulder and brown on all sides, 8 to 12 minutes total. Add onion and carrots; cook, stirring constantly, until onion is translucent, about 2 minutes. Add garlic and tomato paste and cook, stirring constantly, until fragrant, 30 seconds. Return sausage to Dutch oven; add white wine, using wooden spoon to scrape browned bits from bottom of pan. Cook until slightly reduced, about 30 seconds. Stir in tomatoes, celery bundle, and reserved salt pork.

4. Stir in broth and beans, pressing beans into even layer. If any beans are completely exposed, add up to 1 cup water to submerge (beans may still break surface of liquid). Increase heat to high and bring to simmer. Cover pot, transfer to oven, and cook until beans are tender, about 1½ hours. Remove celery bundle and salt pork and discard. (Alternatively, dice salt pork and return to casserole.) Using large spoon, skim fat from surface and discard. Season with salt and pepper. Increase oven temperature to 350 degrees and bake, uncovered, 20 minutes.

5. Meanwhile, pulse bread and remaining 2 tablespoons oil in food processor until crumbs are no larger than ⅛ inch, 8 to ten 1-second pulses. Transfer to medium bowl, add parsley, and toss to combine. Season with salt and pepper.

6. Sprinkle ½ cup bread-crumb mixture evenly over casserole; bake, covered, 15 minutes. Remove lid and bake 15 minutes longer. Sprinkle remaining bread-crumb mixture over top of casserole and bake until topping is golden brown, about 30 minutes. Let rest 15 minutes before serving.

◀ COOK'S VIDEOS Original Test Kitchen Videos
www.cooksillustrated.com
HOW TO MAKE
• French Pork and White Bean Casserole
• Duck Confit

Perfecting Triple-Chocolate Mousse Cake

To rate a perfect 10, this triple-decker confection would need to lighten up and lose its one-note texture.

> BY YVONNE RUPERTI

Triple-chocolate mousse cake comes in many forms, but the two most common are a triple-chocolate layer cake with mousse filling covered in a dark, shiny glaze or a cocoa-charged tower of dark, milk, and white chocolate mousse. I prefer the latter concept (given the choice, who wouldn't want more mousse and less cake?), but time and again I've sliced into this triumvirate only to be let down. Most times the mousse texture is exactly the same from one layer to the next, and the flavor is so overpoweringly rich that I can't finish more than a few forkfuls. To be worth the effort, this showy confection needed some tweaking. By finessing one layer at a time, starting with the dark chocolate base and building to the top white chocolate tier, I aimed to create a triple-decker that was incrementally lighter in texture—and richness—with each layer.

Base Plan

"Mousse," French for froth or foam, is a simple concoction, often nothing more than melted chocolate combined with sugar, whipped cream, or egg whites (though many also enrich the mixture with egg yolks and even butter). Once incorporated, tiny air bubbles from the whipped cream or beaten egg whites (or both) help develop its signature billowy texture, while chilling crystallizes the cocoa butter in the chocolate and firms the fat in the cream, enabling it to remain solid even at room temperature.

For simplicity's sake, I decided to build all three mousse layers, tier by tier, in the same springform pan. I would need a bottom layer that wasn't just solid but had the heft to support the upper two tiers. Starting with a typical recipe, I gently cooked four egg yolks and a few tablespoons of sugar until thick and custardy, whisked the mixture into 7 ounces of melted bittersweet chocolate, and folded in 2 cups of whipped heavy cream. As I might have predicted, even after hours of chilling, the resulting mousse was a little too soft and airy. Adding extra chocolate turned the dessert into a slab of truffle—way too rich, even for the bottom. Rather than tinkering endlessly, I decided to reconsider the foundation and use a cake for my base. Both chocolate sponge cake and devil's food cake turned gummy and chewy in the fridge (where any base layer would necessarily sit for hours as the two mousse layers chilled).

Why not try flourless chocolate cake—which shares the same ingredients as mousse (butter,

The bottom layer of our dessert is baked, while the top two layers are firmed up with whipped cream and gelatin.

chocolate, eggs, and sugar)—but gets cooked in the oven instead of on the stove, for a dense yet velvety texture? Just out of the oven, the cake fit the bill. But once again chilling interfered, rendering this layer overly heavy and sludgy. Somehow the batter needed to be airier from the start.

The solution proved simple: Instead of using whole eggs, I separated the whites, whipped them to soft peaks, then gently fold them into the batter. Fifteen minutes in the oven yielded a decadent (but not fudgelike) baked mousse base that collapsed slightly as it cooled but still remained sturdy. Espresso powder added complexity to the chocolate without announcing its presence, as did swapping out the white sugar for light brown sugar's hint of smoky molasses.

Lightening Up

It was time to construct the second layer. My worst fear here was middle-child syndrome—a sandwiched component that neither blended harmoniously with the other two nor showed any distinct personality of its own. My starting point was the test kitchen's

dark chocolate mousse recipe (January/February 2006), which relies on bittersweet chocolate, cocoa powder, and a splash of water for a mousse that's a standout by itself: silky and chock-full of chocolate flavor. Texture-wise, this recipe was perfect, but its deep chocolate flavor was almost indistinguishable from the bottom layer. I tried substituting milk chocolate for the bittersweet chocolate. Bad call: The latter has fewer cocoa solids, which made the mousse too soft to slice. Next, I tried reducing the chocolate, starting with the bittersweet bar. A minimal cutback—from 8 ounces to just 7—moderated richness without sacrificing structure. The eggs—a rich fat source—would have to go, too, but at the expense of the texture; now the mousse was too dense. To compensate, I upped the whipped cream from 1 cup to 1½ cups. Voilà! My second tier was now light, chocolaty, and creamy—noticeably different from the über-rich base.

Cream Rises to the Top

Finally, I made it to the top—and met another challenge. Ideally, this crowning mousse would be ethereally silky, with a sweet, milky, buttery white chocolate flavor, but keeping it light while maintaining structural integrity wasn't easy, since the chocolate was completely cocoa solid–free. After melting 6 ounces of white chocolate, I folded in whipped cream and layered it on top of the dark chocolate mousse. The texture was light and creamy, but even after chilling

TASTING White Chocolate

Guittard Choc-Au-Lait White Chips ($3.29 for 12 ounces) lack a high enough concentration of cocoa butter to qualify as true white chocolate but impressed tasters with smooth texture, strong vanilla flavor, and mild sweetness, beating out four real white chocolates. As it turns out, a lesser amount of cocoa butter has its advantages: Fake whites boast a longer shelf life and are less finicky in cooking. For complete results on the nine brands we sampled, go to www.cooksillustrated.com/dec09. –Peggy Chung Collier

GREAT WHITE FAKE

it had a tendency to ooze during slicing. I tried increasing the chilling time, to no avail. Instead, I turned to gelatin. One teaspoon stiffened the topping to a fault, but ¾ teaspoon was just right. The only accessory this crown needed was a few wispy curls of chocolate. My tasting panel agreed: This triple-decker rated a 10.

TRIPLE-CHOCOLATE MOUSSE CAKE
SERVES 12 TO 16

NOTE: This recipe requires a springform pan at least 3 inches high. It is imperative that each layer is made in sequential order. Cool the base completely before topping it with the middle layer. We recommend Ghirardelli Bittersweet Chocolate Baking Bar for the base and middle layers; our other recommended brand of chocolate, Callebaut Intense Dark L-60-40NV, may be used, but it will produce drier, slightly less sweet results. Our preferred brand of white chocolate is Guittard Choc-Au-Lait White Chips. For the best results, chill the mixer bowl before whipping the heavy cream. The entire cake can be made through step 7 and refrigerated up to a day in advance; leave it out at room temperature for up to 45 minutes before releasing it from the cake pan and serving. For neater slices, use a cheese wire (see page 30 for tips on using a cheese wire and page 32 for our recommended brand) or dip your knife in hot water before cutting each slice. For instructions on how to shave chocolate, see page 31.

Bottom Layer
- 6 tablespoons (¾ stick) unsalted butter, cut into 6 pieces, plus extra for greasing pan
- 7 ounces bittersweet chocolate, chopped fine (see note)
- ¾ teaspoon instant espresso powder
- 1½ teaspoons vanilla extract
- 4 large eggs, separated
    Pinch table salt
- ⅓ cup packed (about 2½ ounces) light brown sugar, crumbled with fingers to remove lumps

Middle Layer
- 2 tablespoons cocoa powder, preferably Dutch-processed
- 5 tablespoons hot water
- 7 ounces bittersweet chocolate, chopped fine (see note)
- 1½ cups cold heavy cream
- 1 tablespoon granulated sugar
- ⅛ teaspoon table salt

Top Layer
- ¾ teaspoon powdered gelatin
- 1 tablespoon water
- 6 ounces white chocolate chips (see note)
- 1½ cups cold heavy cream

    Shaved chocolate or cocoa powder for serving, optional (see note)

AT-A-GLANCE | TRIPLE-DECKER CONSTRUCTION

Our Triple-Chocolate Mousse Cake is assembled in one pan and features progressively lighter layers.

BOTTOM LAYER
A modified flourless chocolate cake made with whipped egg whites, egg yolks, butter, dark chocolate, and sugar provides a sturdy—but not dense—base. The cake collapses as it cools.

MIDDLE LAYER
This layer's silky yet sliceable consistency is similar to regular mousse in texture, with flavor from dark chocolate and cocoa powder.

TOP LAYER
Made with whipped cream and white chocolate, this layer is the lightest in flavor and texture. The addition of a little gelatin helps to make the topping sliceable.

1. **FOR THE BOTTOM LAYER:** Adjust oven rack to middle position and heat oven to 325 degrees. Butter bottom and sides of 9½-inch springform pan. Melt butter, chocolate, and espresso powder in large heatproof bowl set over saucepan filled with 1 inch of barely simmering water, stirring occasionally until smooth. Remove from heat and cool mixture slightly, about 5 minutes. Whisk in vanilla and egg yolks; set aside.

2. In stand mixer fitted with whisk attachment, beat egg whites and salt at medium speed until frothy, about 30 seconds. Add half of brown sugar and beat until combined, about 15 seconds. Add remaining brown sugar and beat at high speed until soft peaks form when whisk is lifted, about 1 minute longer, scraping down sides halfway through. Using whisk, fold one-third of beaten egg whites into chocolate mixture to lighten. Using rubber spatula, fold in remaining egg whites until no white streaks remain. Carefully transfer batter to prepared springform pan, gently smoothing top with offset spatula.

3. Bake until cake has risen, is firm around edges, and center has just set but is still soft (center of cake will spring back after pressing gently with finger), 13 to 18 minutes. Transfer cake to wire rack to cool completely, about 1 hour. (Cake will collapse as it cools.) Do not remove cake from pan.

4. **FOR THE MIDDLE LAYER:** Combine cocoa powder and hot water in small bowl; set aside. Melt chocolate in large heatproof bowl set over saucepan filled with 1 inch of barely simmering water, stirring occasionally until smooth. Remove from heat and cool slightly, 2 to 5 minutes.

5. In clean bowl of stand mixer fitted with whisk attachment, whip cream, granulated sugar, and salt at medium speed until mixture begins to thicken, about 30 seconds. Increase speed to high and whip until soft peaks form when whisk is lifted, 15 to 60 seconds.

6. Whisk cocoa powder mixture into melted chocolate until smooth. Using whisk, fold one-third of whipped cream into chocolate mixture to lighten. Using rubber spatula, fold in remaining whipped cream

until no white streaks remain. Spoon mousse into springform pan over cooled cake and gently tap pan on counter 3 times to remove any large air bubbles; gently smooth top with offset spatula. Wipe inside edge of pan with damp cloth to remove any drips. Refrigerate cake at least 15 minutes while preparing top layer.

7. **FOR THE TOP LAYER:** In small bowl, sprinkle gelatin over water; let stand at least 5 minutes. Place white chocolate in medium bowl. Bring ½ cup cream to simmer in small saucepan over medium-high heat. Remove from heat; add gelatin mixture and stir until fully dissolved. Pour cream mixture over white chocolate and whisk until chocolate is melted and mixture is smooth, about 30 seconds. Cool to room temperature, stirring occasionally, 5 to 8 minutes (mixture will thicken slightly).

8. In clean bowl of stand mixer fitted with whisk attachment, whip remaining cup cream at medium speed until it begins to thicken, about 30 seconds. Increase speed to high and whip until soft peaks form when whisk is lifted, 15 to 60 seconds. Using whisk, fold one-third of whipped cream into white chocolate mixture to lighten. Using rubber spatula, fold remaining whipped cream into white chocolate mixture until no white streaks remain. Spoon white chocolate mousse into pan over middle layer. Smooth top with offset spatula. Return cake to refrigerator and chill until set, at least 2½ hours.

9. **TO SERVE:** If using, garnish top of cake with chocolate curls or dust with cocoa. Run thin knife between cake and side of springform pan; remove side of pan. Run cleaned knife along outside of cake to smooth sides. Cut into slices and serve.

◼ COOK'S VIDEOS Original Test Kitchen Videos
www.cooksillustrated.com
HOW TO MAKE
• Triple-Chocolate Mousse Cake
VIDEO TIPS
• How to slice a soft cake
• Making chocolate curls

The Best Shortbread

Achieving rich, buttery taste in this simple cookie is easy. But for the optimal crumbly, evenly browned texture, we needed to take a step back in time.

≥ BY J. KENJI LOPEZ-ALT ≤

If your experience with shortbread is limited to bland, chalky specimens from a tin, you might wonder how this plain-looking bar (which dates back to at least 12th-century Scotland) came to be one of the British Isles' most famous teacakes. But when shortbread is made well, it's easy to understand why it earned a reputation as a favorite of high-ranking palates from Mary, Queen of Scots to Elizabeth II. The best versions are an alluring tawny brown and crumble in the mouth with a pure, buttery richness. Shortbread's distinctive sandy texture distinguishes it from the simple crispness of its cousin, the American butter cookie, while its moderate sweetness makes it easy to go back for another helping—and another.

Shortbread originated as a way to turn leftover oat bread into something more special: The scraps were sprinkled with sugar and left to harden overnight in an oven still hot from the day's baking. By the 16th century, wheat flour had replaced oat bread in the recipe, and this biscuit morphed from a foodstuff of commoners into the more refined confection prized by nobility.

And yet, its venerable history left surprisingly few clues to reproducing a worthwhile version. The basics haven't changed much over the past five centuries: Combine flour, sugar, butter, and salt, then pat the dough into a round and bake. But the recipes I unearthed varied in their proportions. Some called for equal parts butter and flour, and some for only half this ratio; several included unlikely ingredients like rice flour or cornstarch. Results were also all over the map. While some cookies crumbled in my hand before I could even take a bite, others were sturdy and crisp to a fault, and still others turned out either greasy or overly airy and cakelike. Moreover, nearly every version suffered from some degree of uneven cooking and overbrowning.

In the Mix

To get my bearings, I decided to limit my ingredients to the basic four before tinkering with anything extra. As for proportions, I ruled out a 1–1 ratio of butter to flour after preliminary tests proved this was just too greasy. I settled on a more moderate 4–5 ratio, with two sticks of butter, 2 cups all-purpose flour, ⅔ cup sugar, and ¼ teaspoon salt.

For shortbread with an ultra-fine, sandy texture, we swapped out white sugar for powdery confectioners' sugar.

And what mixing method would work best? I would need to test the most traditional approach, which is akin to making pie crust: Cut the butter and dry ingredients together until they form wet crumbs, then pack the crumbs together into a dough. I also made two batches using more modern methods. In one, I creamed the butter and sugar in a stand mixer before adding the flour; in the other, I employed reverse creaming, mixing the flour and sugar before adding the butter.

Next, I formed cookies from my three doughs. Shortbread traditionally takes one of three shapes: one large circle with a hole cut in the center and then scored into wedges, or "petticoat tails," so called because the uncut cookie resembles a dressmaker's pattern; individual round cookies; or rectangular "fingers." Pursuing the petticoat shape (for no reason except that it was reportedly the shape favored by Mary, Queen of Scots), I pressed the dough into a 9-inch disk, used a biscuit cutter to remove a hole from the center, and placed the shortbread in a 450-degree oven for a few minutes. Following the usual high-low baking protocol called for in shortbread recipes, I then reduced the oven to 300 degrees and continued to bake the cookies for an hour before scoring and cooling them.

I evaluated the results. The traditional, packed-crumb method produced cookies that were crumbly in some spots and brittle in others. Regular creaming was also out. This method incorporated too much air into the dough, making for soft, airy, cakelike cookies. Reverse creaming, which creates less aeration, yielded the most reliable results and was clearly the way to go. Tweaking the recipe, I reduced the butter even further, from 16 to 14 tablespoons, which resulted in a dough that was pliable and had plenty of buttery flavor but did not exude grease during baking. I also swapped the white sugar for confectioners' sugar to smooth out an objectionable granular texture. Although my basic ingredients and mixing technique now seemed to be in order, the shortbread cookies were somewhat tough, and they were not as crisp as I wanted.

Tough Cookie

Two factors played into my texture problem: gluten and moisture. Gluten, the protein matrix that lends baked goods structure and chew, forms naturally when liquid and all-purpose flour are combined, even without kneading. The liquid in my recipe was coming from the butter, which contains 20 percent water—just enough to make my cookies tough. In addition, cookies can only become truly crisp and crumbly if they are perfectly dry. My goals, then, were to limit gluten development and to help the cookies dry out completely.

Intuition told me that a higher oven temperature would drive moisture from the cookies. I baked a batch entirely at 450 degrees, but the edges started overbrowning after just 10 minutes, while the inner portion remained wet. When I thought about it, I realized that baking shortbread is analogous to cooking a roast: The higher the oven temperature, the less even the cooking, and the more prone to overcooking the edges will be. I tried again, baking a second batch at

Gothic Grain

The earliest 12th-century versions of shortbread were made with oats. We included this ingredient because oats form much less gluten than wheat, leading to cookies that are crisp without being tough.

NO TOUGH COOKIES

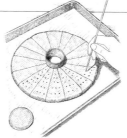

1. PRESS AND SMOOTH
Press dough into closed upside-down springform pan collar; smooth with back of spoon.

2. CUT HOLE
Cut hole in center of dough with 2-inch biscuit cutter; replace cutter in hole.

3. OPEN PAN COLLAR
Open collar. Bake 5 minutes at 450 degrees, then 10 to 15 minutes at 250 degrees.

4. SCORE AND POKE
Score partially baked shortbread into wedges, then poke 8 to 10 holes in each wedge.

5. TURN OFF OVEN
Return shortbread to turned-off oven to dry; prop open door with wooden spoon or stick.

---

450 degrees for 5 minutes (to help set the dough) and then lowering the temperature to 250 degrees. This was better, but still not perfect.

Early shortbread was made by leaving the dough in a still-warm oven heated only by dying embers. What if I briefly baked the shortbread, shut off the oven, and left it inside until it was completely dry? With just 15 minutes or so of "real" baking in a hot oven—and an hour with the oven turned off—the results were striking: This batch was dry through and through, with an even, golden brown exterior.

With the moisture issue resolved, I shifted my focus to the toughness caused by excess gluten development. Various 21st-century recipes have tried to solve this problem by substituting low-protein, gluten-free rice flour for some of the all-purpose flour. I gave it a try. As I broke apart the rice-flour shortbread in my hands, its crumbly texture looked promising. But when I took a bite, I realized that reducing the all-purpose flour had also reduced the flavor; these cookies were woefully bland. Cornstarch (another gluten-free ingredient used in some modern recipes) yielded equally insipid results.

I needed to curb gluten development without compromising flavor. Scanning the test kitchen's pantry shelves, I spotted a possible solution: old-fashioned oats. Oats have a nice, nutty flavor and contain few of the proteins necessary for gluten development; on top of that, they're traditional to early shortbread recipes. I ground some oats to a powder in a spice grinder and substituted ¾ cup of this home-milled oat flour for some of the all-purpose flour in my recipe, keeping my fingers crossed that this historic ingredient would offer a tidy fix. The resulting cookies had a promising crisp and crumbly texture, but the oats muted the buttery flavor. Still, I knew I was on the right track. For my next batch, I used less oat flour and supplemented it with a modest amount of cornstarch. This worked handsomely. The cookies were now perfectly crisp and flavorful, with an appealing hint of oat flavor.

So Long, Spreading

I had one last problem to solve: spreading. As buttery shortbread bakes, it expands, losing its shape as the edges flatten out. I tried baking the dough in a traditional shortbread mold with ½-inch-high sides, but it still widened into an amorphous mass. Clearly, the dough needed a substantial barrier to keep its edges corralled. My solution? A springform pan collar. I set the closed collar on a parchment-lined baking sheet, patted the dough into it, and then opened the collar to give the cookie about half an inch to spread out.

With my baking method perfected, I put together a gussied-up variation, dipping a pistachio-studded version in melted chocolate. History had repeated itself, and I now had the finest shortbread of its time.

BEST SHORTBREAD
MAKES 16 WEDGES

NOTE: Use the collar of a springform pan to form the shortbread into an even round. Mold the shortbread with the collar in the closed position, then open the collar, but leave it in place. This allows the shortbread to expand slightly but keeps it from spreading too far. Wrapped well and stored at room temperature, shortbread will keep for up to 7 days. For our free recipes for Ginger Shortbread and Toasted Oat Shortbread, go to www.cooksillustrated.com/dec09.

½	cup old-fashioned rolled oats
1½	cups (7½ ounces) unbleached all-purpose flour
¼	cup cornstarch
⅔	cup (2⅔ ounces) confectioners' sugar
½	teaspoon table salt
14	tablespoons (1¾ sticks) unsalted butter, cold, cut into ⅛-inch-thick slices

1. Adjust oven rack to middle position and heat oven to 450 degrees. Pulse oats in spice grinder or blender until reduced to fine powder, about ten 5-second pulses (you should have ¼ to ⅓ cup oat flour). In bowl of stand mixer fitted with paddle attachment, mix oat flour, all-purpose flour, cornstarch, sugar, and salt on low speed until combined, about 5 seconds. Add butter to dry ingredients and continue to mix on low speed until dough just forms and pulls away from sides of bowl, 5 to 10 minutes.

2. Place upside-down (grooved edge should be at top) collar of 9- or 9½-inch springform pan on parchment-lined rimmed baking sheet (do not use springform pan bottom). Press dough into collar in even ½-inch-thick layer, smoothing top of dough with back of spoon. Place 2-inch biscuit cutter in center of dough and cut out center. Place extracted round alongside springform collar on baking sheet and replace cutter in center of dough. Open springform collar, but leave it in place.

3. Bake shortbread 5 minutes, then reduce oven temperature to 250 degrees. Continue to bake until edges turn pale golden, 10 to 15 minutes longer. Remove baking sheet from oven; turn off oven. Remove springform pan collar; use chef's knife to score surface of shortbread into 16 even wedges, cutting halfway through shortbread. Using wooden skewer, poke 8 to 10 holes in each wedge. Return shortbread to oven and prop door open with handle of wooden spoon, leaving 1-inch gap at top. Allow shortbread to dry in turned-off oven until pale golden in center (shortbread should be firm but giving to touch), about 1 hour.

4. Transfer baking sheet to wire rack; cool shortbread to room temperature, at least 2 hours. Cut shortbread at scored marks to separate and serve.

CHOCOLATE-DIPPED PISTACHIO SHORTBREAD

Follow recipe for Best Shortbread, adding ½ cup finely chopped toasted pistachios to dry ingredients in step 1. Bake and cool shortbread as directed. Once shortbread is cool, melt 8 ounces finely chopped bittersweet chocolate in small heatproof bowl set over pan of almost-simmering water, stirring once or twice, until smooth. Remove from heat; stir in additional 2 ounces finely chopped bittersweet chocolate until smooth. Carefully dip base of each wedge in chocolate, allowing chocolate to come halfway up cookie. Scrape off excess with finger and place on parchment-lined rimmed baking sheet. Refrigerate until chocolate sets, about 15 minutes.

COOK'S VIDEOS Original Test Kitchen Videos

www.cooksillustrated.com
HOW TO MAKE
• Best Shortbread

Easy Peas, Updated

To play up this legume's sweet, delicate flavors, we began by skipping the heavy sauce.

⇒ BY FRANCISCO J. ROBERT ⇐

You wouldn't catch me reaching into my freezer for a bag of broccoli florets or precut carrots, but when charged with the task of preparing the holiday meal—or even just a quick weeknight dinner—there's nothing I'm more thankful for than a bag of frozen peas. They're convenient, ready in minutes, and, barring any access to just-picked pods (almost impossible at this time of year), sweeter and more tender than fresh peas, which turn starchy and bland within 24 hours of harvest. What's more, the clean sweetness of frozen peas is enhanced with any number of flavorful embellishments: classic cream- and butter-based sauces and also lighter, fresher add-ins like herbs, aromatics, and quick-sautéed vegetables. For a rich holiday dinner, a flavorful but still light side dish was definitely the ticket.

I started by taking a look at the typical back-of-the-bag recipe for petits pois, or baby peas, which we've found are even more sweet and tender than regular frozen peas. Since frozen peas have already been blanched, the key here is not overdoing it: Five minutes of simmering to heat them through is all they need.

To build up their sweet, grassy taste, I sweated minced shallot and garlic with oil in a saucepan before adding the peas with a little water. This helped—until I realized that a good bit of flavor was being poured down the sink when I drained the peas. For my next go-round, I served the cooking liquid spooned over the peas, but tasters told me it was too thin and bland to act as a sauce. Swapping the water for chicken broth was a step in the right direction, adding depth without overwhelming the peas.

A pat of butter stirred in after the peas finished simmering (not too much—tasters wanted a little richness without drowning the peas in fat) contributed body, while a generous dose of chopped fresh mint provided a nice aromatic complement. Still, something was missing. A smidge of sugar added to the broth and a healthy squirt of lemon juice stirred into the peas just before serving were all it took to bring everything into balance. My final tweak: switching from a saucepan to a skillet to ensure the peas heated a tad more quickly and evenly across its larger surface area.

With my recipe established, I set to work on variations. Peas paired nicely with leeks and a modest amount of cream in one option, while another with ham and chives successfully straddled sweet and salty. Other favorite combinations included earthy thyme and mushrooms; fresh, aromatic fennel; and a Thai-inspired version with coconut milk and cilantro. These peas were as easy as ever—and so flavorful, no one would ever know that they weren't fresh from the garden.

SAUTÉED PEAS WITH SHALLOT AND MINT
SERVES 4

NOTE: Do not thaw the peas before cooking. Regular frozen peas can be used in place of baby peas; increase the cooking time in step 2 by 1 to 2 minutes. Add the lemon juice right before serving, otherwise the peas will turn brown.

- 2 teaspoons olive oil
- 1 small shallot, minced (about 1½ tablespoons)
- 1 medium garlic clove, minced or pressed through garlic press (about 1 teaspoon)
- 1 pound frozen baby peas (3 cups) (see note)
- ¼ cup low-sodium chicken broth
- ¼ teaspoon sugar
- ¼ cup minced fresh mint leaves
- 1 tablespoon unsalted butter
- 2 teaspoons juice from 1 lemon
  Table salt and ground black pepper

1. Heat oil in 12-inch skillet over medium-high heat until shimmering. Add shallot and cook, stirring frequently, until softened, about 2 minutes. Add garlic and cook, stirring frequently, until fragrant, about 30 seconds.

2. Stir in peas, broth, and sugar. Cover and cook until peas are bright green and just heated through, 3 to 5 minutes. Add mint and butter and toss until incorporated. Remove pan from heat; stir in lemon juice. Season with salt and pepper; serve immediately.

SAUTÉED PEAS WITH LEEKS AND TARRAGON

Follow recipe for Sautéed Peas with Shallot and Mint, substituting 1 small leek, white and light green parts cut into ¼-inch dice (about ½ cup), for shallot and increasing cooking time in step 1 to 3 to 5 minutes (leek should be softened). Continue with recipe as directed, substituting heavy cream for chicken broth, 2 tablespoons minced tarragon for mint, and white wine vinegar for lemon juice.

SAUTÉED PEAS WITH HAM AND CHIVES

Follow recipe for Sautéed Peas with Shallot and Mint, substituting 3 ounces deli-style baked ham, cut into ¼-inch cubes (about ½ cup), for shallot and decreasing cooking time in step 1 to 1 minute. Continue with recipe as directed, substituting 2 tablespoons minced fresh chives for mint.

For the best flavor, our peas cook in broth, not water.

SAUTÉED PEAS WITH FENNEL

Follow recipe for Sautéed Peas with Shallot and Mint, substituting ½ small fennel bulb, cored and cut into ¼-inch dice (about ½ cup), for shallot and increasing cooking time in step 1 to 3 to 5 minutes (fennel should be softened). Continue with recipe as directed, substituting 2 tablespoons minced fennel fronds for mint.

SAUTÉED PEAS WITH MUSHROOMS AND THYME

Follow recipe for Sautéed Peas with Shallot and Mint, substituting 6 ounces cleaned and quartered cremini mushrooms for shallot and increasing cooking time in step 1 to 3 to 5 minutes (mushrooms should be light golden brown). Continue with recipe as directed, substituting 2 tablespoons minced fresh thyme for mint.

SAUTÉED PEAS WITH COCONUT MILK AND CILANTRO

Follow recipe for Sautéed Peas with Shallot and Mint, substituting 2 tablespoons grated fresh ginger for shallot and decreasing cooking time in step 1 to 1 minute. Continue with recipe as directed, substituting coconut milk for chicken broth, cilantro for mint, and lime juice for lemon juice.

▶ COOK'S VIDEOS Original Test Kitchen Videos
www.cooksillustrated.com
HOW TO MAKE
• Sautéed Peas with Shallot and Mint

The New Chef's Knife: East Meets West

In Europe, the chef's knife is a sturdy tool that can chop and slice anything. In Japan, it's a thin, light precision instrument. What happens when East meets West?

⇒ BY LISA McMANUS ⇐

A good chef's knife is the single most essential piece of kitchen equipment—at least in the European-American tradition. It serves as an all-purpose tool for cutting, slicing, mincing, and chopping everything from herbs to vegetables to meat. The Western chef's knife is 8 to 10 inches long, with a pointed tip for precision work, a thick spine for strength to push through tough foods, and a curved edge that helps rhythmically rock the blade to chop a pile of carrots, dice an onion, or slice a cucumber. The cutting edge won't easily chip or break and is simple to resharpen; it also works like a wedge, pushing food apart with a 20-degree angle to each side.

By contrast, in Japan, there is no such thing as one all-purpose chef's knife. Since cutting technique is paramount in this cuisine—in some ways more important than actual cooking—Japanese chefs have always used at least three different knives. The *yanagi* has a long, slim blade for slicing raw, boneless fish. The *deba* is a thick-spined, heavy little knife for butchering meat and filleting fish. The *usuba* has a slim, rectangular blade for cutting vegetables.

Japanese chefs believe that cutting food without any crushing is essential to retaining its natural flavor. As a result, their knives (even the chunky deba) have extremely thin, sharp cutting edges honed on just one side to a 15-degree angle (see "East–West Blade Geometry," above). To support this thinness, the knives must be made of very hard steel. The downside? Such blades are both more brittle and harder to resharpen than the softer steel of a Western-made knife. But brittleness is unimportant in a knife that is drawn along the board to slice (or held in the hands in a paring action), as opposed to pounded up and down, Western-style.

For centuries, these two culinary traditions have remained distinct. Now, top Japanese knife makers (including the famous "three Ms": Masamoto, Masahiro, and Misono)—and even venerable German manufacturers Henckels and Messermeister—have merged East and West in an entirely new breed of knife. Called the gyutou (ghee-YOU-toe) in Japan, this hybrid tool fuses Japanese knifemaking (harder steel, a straighter edge for slicing rather than rocking, and slimmer, sharper 15-degree cutting angle) with Western knife design (the Western chef's knife shape,

and a blade sharpened on both sides). The result is feather-light, lethally sharp, wonderfully precise—and nothing like the heavy German-style knives many of us are accustomed to using. For me, taking up one of these knives for the first time was like removing heavy ski boots after a day on the slopes. You're expecting a heaviness that's no longer there.

But no matter how gloriously light, sharp, and deft these knives might be, would any work better than the traditional chef's knife for the typical American home cook? To find out, we chose eight fusion knives, six by Japanese companies and two from European manufacturers, setting a price cap of $200. For comparison, we also tested our favorite inexpensive chef's knife, the Victorinox Forschner Fibrox 8-Inch ($24.95). Since the Forschner is very inexpensive, this new style of knife would have to be pretty special to justify spending north of $100 to add it to our arsenal.

We chose testers of varying hand sizes and knife skills to perform a range of tasks in the test kitchen: dicing onion, mincing fresh parsley, cutting up a whole raw chicken, quartering butternut squash. Because how well a blade holds its edge is another critical part of the equation, we mailed off a set of the knives to Sheffield, England, where the Cutlery and Allied Trades Research Association (CATRA) machine-tested the durability of their sharpness. Finally, we chose the two knives that scored highest in our kitchen tests and sent them home with a couple of staff members to see how they held up in day-to-day cooking.

Divergent Traditions

In the West, the chef's knife is the tool we turn to for virtually every type of cutting task, from precision work like mincing garlic and herbs to heavy-duty jobs like hacking apart chicken bones. In Japan, each different cutting job calls for a different type of knife. The three most important are the usuba (for vegetables), the deba (for meat), and the yanagi (for raw fish).

East–West Blade Geometry

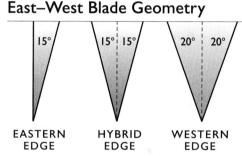

| EASTERN EDGE | HYBRID EDGE | WESTERN EDGE |

Traditional Japanese knives (left) have a single-sided, 15-degree cutting edge for precision slicing. Hybrid knives (center) borrow that narrow angle, but use it on both sides like a Western knife (right).

The Eastern Edge

In test after test, the best knives stunned us with their ability to make precise, effortless slices. Taking apart a whole chicken at the joints and boning the breasts was a breeze with their narrow tips and maneuverable blades, and the rubbery skin practically opened up on its own. These precision instruments truly minced—rather than crushed—delicate herbs, leaving minuscule pieces of parsley unbruised, fluffy, and separate, rather than dark, oozing, and stuck together. For me, the difference stood out most when I cut through crisp onion. In contrast to clunky Western blades that tend to crush their way through the layers, my feeling of control—and the lack of irritating tears—was absolute as the thin, sharp blades glided through the onion with the barest pressure.

Usuba

Deba

Yanagi

EUROPEAN
One all-purpose chef's knife.

JAPANESE
Different knives for different uses.

That said, not all of the knives were stellar performers. When mincing parsley, some test cooks found the straighter blades on a number of models took some getting used to. They missed the familiar curved blade of a Western knife, which encourages a rhythmic rocking motion, and favored any with a little more curve. Low handles on certain Japanese blades made larger-handed cooks' knuckles strike the board as they worked. Some knives lost points for quirky design features, such as the metal handle on the slimmest, lightest knife in the lineup, which felt dangerously slippery to a few testers. Furthermore, while none failed at the task, some Japanese blades felt too delicate when confronted with hard, dense butternut squash.

Curiously, the two German hybrids were veritable flops. One, the Messermeister, was universally disliked by testers for its "heavy," "clunky" feel and rated the poorest in edge retention—something corroborated by our testers, who actually noticed it dulling as they worked. While the Henckels-made knife boasted a "beautiful" blade that was "sharp and fairly maneuverable," its long-necked Japanese-style handle felt awkward, keeping testers' hands too far from the blade. The only test where these two knives excelled was hacking through squash—a task that's not very common, even in an American kitchen.

Keeping the Edge
Conventional wisdom holds that the harder the steel, the longer a knife will stay sharp—an impression only fueled by knife companies bragging about the high "Rockwell hardness" of their blades, an industry scale where higher numbers indicate harder metal. But this supposed truism wasn't borne out by our testing. We sent all of the knives in our lineup to the CATRA lab in England to evaluate durability. There, a machine sliced them through stacked sheets of sandpaper, then rated them according to how many sheets they cut before becoming dull. We compared these results to the Rockwell number for each blade—and found only a weak correlation. The Messermeister, for example, did a far worse job of holding its edge than knives sharing the same Rockwell rating (or even those with a lower number, indicating softer metal).

It turns out that how well a blade's edge will hold up is far more complicated than just its Rockwell rating. The properties of the blade depend on the exact steel alloy used to manufacture the knife (there are dozens of different types) as well as the makers' secret formulas for heating, cooling, and hammering. Each of these factors affects the grain of the metal, the alignment of its molecules—and how long the knife will remain sharp.

📹 **COOK'S VIDEOS** Original Test Kitchen Videos
www.cooksillustrated.com
BEHIND THE SCENES
• Testing hybrid chef's knives
VIDEO TIP
• Using an Asian knife sharpener

Since Asian knives boast a 15-degree angle versus the 20-degree angle of Western knives, you can't just use your usual sharpener on them and expect to get back that perfect, effortless slicing you enjoyed when the knife was new. Or can you?

We sharpened our favorite Japanese hybrid chef's knife, the Masamoto VG-10 Gyutou, on five sharpeners designed for Japanese knives as well as on our favorite Chef's Choice 130 electric sharpener ($149.99), which hones blades to a 20-degree angle. Testers then compared each sharpened knife side by side with a brand-new version of the knife as they sliced ripe tomatoes.

The good news: Most testers found both the 15- and 20-degree edges sharp enough to slice tomatoes. Our test cooks noticed some drag on the tomato with the 20-degree angle that wasn't there when the angle was 15 degrees. So in a pinch, you could just use a good Western knife sharpener—it's preferable to a dull knife.

Even better news: We found one compact, low-cost, easy-to-use manual sharpener, the Chef's Choice Asian Knife Sharpener, Model 463 ($39.99), that did a great job restoring the hybrid knives to the proper 15-degree angle. In addition, Chef's Choice offers two electric options: the Diamond Sharpener for Asian Knives, Model 315S ($99.99) and the AngleSelect Knife Sharpener, Model 1520 ($169.99), which handles both Eastern and Western knives—a great choice if you don't already own an electric sharpener. (For full testing results, see www.cooksillustrated.com/dec09.) –L.M.

SHARP CHOICE
CHEF'S CHOICE Model 463
Price: $39.99
Comments: This compact manual sharpener uses diamond abrasives to put the proper 15-degree angle on Japanese knives.

Honda versus a Maserati?
In the end, we fell in love with two knives: the Masamoto VG-10 ($136.50) and the Misono UX-10 ($156). Both weigh 6 ounces and had among the slimmest spines in our lineup, tapering dramatically to their cutting edges, giving them the narrowest profile for precision slicing. Cooks with a range of hand sizes and knife skills found each equally comfortable.

The interesting thing is, despite sharing what seemed to be a very similar blade design, each of these knives had a very distinct personality in the hand. Here's why: Knifemakers can craft the way a blade feels and performs by making subtle changes in its blade geometry. For example, manufacturers can adjust the mass and balance of the blade not only by manipulating how much it tapers vertically from spine to cutting edge and horizontally from handle to tip, but where the horizontal taper begins—near the handle, midway down the knife, or even near the tip. The Masamoto seems lighter and thinner because of a more extreme taper, both from handle to tip and vertically from spine to cutting edge. Testers who like German knives preferred the Misono for being stiffer and more solid. Scores were tied—until lab results revealed the final advantage: The Masamoto's steel was much better at staying sharp. (Another finding that disproved any notion that hardness alone helps a knife keep its edge. The Masamoto had a lower Rockwell rating than the Misono.)

And what about our cheap champ, the $24.95 Forschner? Even faced with a sleek new breed of competition, this steady performer beat all but our top two contenders. It is comfortable, efficient, very affordable, and interestingly similar in design to Japanese blades (see "Forschner Fibrox: Still a Breed Apart," right). But as much as we admire this knife, it's still a Honda. The best of the fusion knives are like trading up to a Maserati. In our opinion, the sheer pleasure of using their sleek, well-designed blades makes them a worthy addition to any cook's knife block.

Forschner Fibrox: Still a Breed Apart

As it has done time and time again, the Victorinox Forschner Fibrox 8-Inch Chef's Knife ($24.95) defeated a majority of far more costly knives. Interestingly, it boasts some of the characteristics of the new mixed-breed style featured in this most recent testing: It's lightweight (just ⅜ ounce heavier than the top-rated hybrid), relatively thin (three of the hybrid knives were actually thicker at the spine), and shares the same percentage of distal taper (the progressive narrowing of the spine from handle to tip) as our winner. While it lacks the extreme precision that makes cutting with the hybrids so much fun, at $25, it's hard to argue that you need more knife than this for everyday cooking. –L.M.

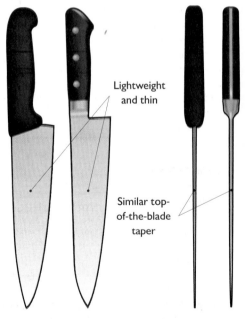

Lightweight and thin

Similar top-of-the-blade taper

FRATERNAL TWINS?
Our inexpensive traditional chef's knife, the Forschner (left), shares similarities in blade design with our pricier winning hybrid knife, the Masamoto (right).

TESTING "HYBRID" CHEF'S KNIVES

We tested nine chef's knives (eight hybrids and our winning traditional chef's knife), priced under $200, with a range of tasks and sent them to a lab to test edge retention. In addition, we sent the top two knives home with staff members for routine use for several weeks. Knives are listed in order of preference. Prices were paid at online retailers. Sources for top-rated knives are on page 32.

STEEL HARDNESS

Hardness of the blade according to the Rockwell scale, a metal industry standard in which higher numbers indicate greater hardness.

SPINE

Width at the top of the blade near the handle.

CUTTING

The average score from evaluations carried out in the test kitchen (butchering chicken, dicing onion, mincing parsley, quartering butternut squash) and home testers' scores, where applicable.

DESIGN

User-friendliness, including shape and comfort of both blade and handle.

EDGE RETENTION

Results from the Cutlery and Allied Trades Research Association (CATRA) in Sheffield, England, which machine-tested the knives, slicing each through sheets of sandpaper, rating durability by the number of sheets cut before dulling. Ratings were on a scale of Poor, Average, Good, Very good, Excellent.

HIGHLY RECOMMENDED · PERFORMANCE · TESTERS' COMMENTS

MASAMOTO VG-10 Gyutou, 8.2"
Price: $136.50 Model: VG-10 Origin: Japanese
Material: High-carbon stainless steel, wood composite handle
Steel Hardness: 58–59
Weight: 6 ounces Spine: 2 mm
Edge Retention: Very good

Cutting: ★★★
Design: ★★★

"Feels fantastic when you pick it up: comfortable, light, ready." "A dream" for cutting up chicken and dicing onion, with its "very slim, sharp tip" and an acutely tapered blade that made it feel especially light as well as slightly flexible. With a blade more curved than most of the Japanese knives, it assisted a rocking motion that effortlessly "pulverized parsley into dust."

MISONO UX-10 Chef's Knife, 8.2"
Price: $156 Model: UX-10 Origin: Japanese
Material: Swedish stain-resistant steel, wood composite handle
Steel Hardness: 59–60
Weight: 6 ounces Spine: 2 mm
Edge Retention: Average

Cutting: ★★★
Design: ★★★

"Exceptional slicing, with no effort," "excellent balance," "the best-feeling knife in my hand," raved some testers, though others disliked its squared-off collar. Rigid enough for squash, it sliced raw chicken skin without catching, but its straight blade was not conducive to rocking. As light as the Masamoto but less tapered, it has a stiffer, substantial feel that appealed to German-knife users.

VICTORINOX Forschner Fibrox 8" Chef's Knife
Price: $24.95 Model: 40520 Origin: European
Material: X50 CrMoV stainless steel, Fibrox handle
Steel Hardness: 55–56
Weight: 6⅜ ounces Spine: 2.2 mm
Edge Retention: Average

BEST IN THE WEST

Cutting: ★★★
Design: ★★

Our favorite inexpensive chef's knife rivaled fancier, pricier knives yet again. Though "clearly not as amazing," it had "no trouble going through anything," with a "good curve" for rocking. While its profile is slim, the blade is stiff enough to cut squash easily. Rounded, textured plastic handle is "grippy, very comfortable." "This knife even looks friendly."

RECOMMENDED · PERFORMANCE · TESTERS' COMMENTS

TOGIHARU Inox Gyutou, 8.2"
Price: $85 Model: HKR-INOX-G Origin: Japanese
Material: Inox stain-resistant steel, wood composite handle
Steel Hardness: 57–58
Weight: 5⅞ ounces Spine: 2.3 mm
Edge Retention: Average

Cutting: ★★★
Design: ★★

"Lovely, sharp, precise, light, and slim. Gets down to business." However, its straight blade won't rock, and some deemed its balance blade-heavy. Large hands found the grip too small, and knuckles knocked. Struggled with squash, but "effective" in butchering chicken, where it was "good at getting into little corners and tight angles."

MAC PROFESSIONAL 8" Chef's Knife with Dimples
Price: $109.95 Model: MTH-80 Origin: Japanese
Material: High-carbon stain-resistant molybdenum alloy, Pakkawood handle (resin-impregnated)
Steel Hardness: 59–60
Weight: 6½ ounces Spine: 2.1 mm
Edge Retention: Average

Cutting: ★★★
Design: ★★

This "santoku-like" knife had less taper from the spine, adding solidity, but subtracting agility. "Blade feels a little fat; it catches on the onion, wedging it apart," said testers; "not as precise or as nimble as I'd like." While most found it comfortable, it "bottomed out" in a "jarring" way, banging the board rather than rocking. But it cut squash "like a hot knife through butter," with "perfect control."

GLOBAL G-2, 8" Chef's Knife
Price: $99.95 Model: G-2 Origin: Japanese
Material: CROMOVA 18 stainless (proprietary chromium, molybdenum, vanadium blend)
Steel Hardness: 56–58
Weight: 5⅞ ounces Spine: 1.8 mm
Edge Retention: Very good

Cutting: ★★★
Design: ★★

Its extreme design—the lightest, thinnest, most dramatic taper—was loved or hated. In greasy hands, the metal grip felt slippery, a deal-breaker to some. Others found it "nicer than expected." "I was really surprised by how much I liked working with this"; "it leapt to my hand." "Very easy to make thin, even slices," "exceptionally well balanced." Tackling squash, "it didn't hesitate."

AKIFUSA Gyutou, 8.2"
Price: $168.95 Origin: Japanese
Material: Powdered metallurgical stainless steel blade, "san mai" soft steel layered over harder core, Pakkawood handle
Steel Hardness: 64
Weight: 5¾ ounces Spine: 2.3 mm
Edge Retention: Very good

Cutting: ★★
Design: ★★

"Very nice, sharp, light. Overall, a good knife." Slightly rough edges made the grip less comfortable. Stiffness made the blade seem substantial, but while it "went through chicken and skin very easily," it struggled with squash, cutting irregularly. Being the "straightest knife of the bunch" made rocking awkward; larger hands' knuckles hit the board. In sum: "Not quite as super-sleek as others."

NOT RECOMMENDED · PERFORMANCE · TESTERS' COMMENTS

MIYABI 7000 MC Series 8" Gyutou (by Zwilling J.A. Henckels)
Price: $199.95 Model: 34583-203 Origin: European, made in Japan
Material: Micro-carbide powder steel; Micarta handle (resin-impregnated fiber)
Steel Hardness: 66
Weight: 8⅛ ounces Spine: 2.1 mm
Edge Retention: Excellent

Cutting: ★★
Design: ★

"Beautiful, obviously well-made," "sharp and fairly maneuverable" (and top-rated in edge retention), but we hated its long handle, finding hands "too far from the blade" and the knife "too heavy," "the least balanced." "It's weird, like they took a Japanese handle and stuck it on a Western knife. If this is fusion, they got a little too much of both and not enough of either."

MESSERMEISTER Meridian Elite 8" Stealth Chef's Knife
Price: $133 Model: E/3686-8S Origin: European
Material: X50 CrMoV 15 stainless; molded plastic POM handle
Steel Hardness: 56–58
Weight: 9 ounces Spine: 2.6 mm
Edge Retention: Poor

Cutting: ★
Design: ★

Named "Stealth" because it is more than 8.5 percent lighter and 20 percent thinner than the company's regular chef's knife, it still outweighed the rest of the lineup. Universally disliked and rated "poor" for edge retention, its heavy, wedgelike blade did wonders with squash—its only virtue. It was "too heavy," "too awkward," and "clunky," "like a toy."

Sleuthing Cinnamon

Cinnamon used to be the most basic spice in your cupboard. Now it's gone upscale. So will a fancy brand from Vietnam costing $8 an ounce actually make baked goods taste better?

⇉ BY PEGGY CHUNG COLLIER ⇇

One taster declared flatly, "cinnamon is cinnamon," at the start of our marathon tasting of 10 different supermarket and mail-order brands. Not too long ago, that may have been the case. These days, it's anything but a standardized commodity. Labels tout origin and claim distinctions such as "extra fancy" or "gourmet," with prices to match. Processing has advanced to include cryogenic—yes, cryogenic—grinding to preserve more of the three key volatile oils responsible for cinnamon's unmistakable aroma and hot, spicy flavor. Texture, moreover, can vary from uniformly fine to dusty or gritty. And the spice most of us Americans regard as cinnamon? Turns out it's different from what the rest of the world calls cinnamon.

In virtually every other part of the globe, "cinnamon" means Ceylon cinnamon; in the United States, we are accustomed to the bolder, spicier flavor of a species known as *cassia* (also called bastard cinnamon). Both types derive from the bark of tropical evergreens in the *Cinnamomum* genus. Ceylon (*Cinnamomum verum*) is grown primarily in Sri Lanka, while cassia (*Cinnamomum cassia*, among others) may be grown in Indonesia, China, and Vietnam. American traders turned to importing cassia in the early 20th century following a rise in the price of the Ceylon spice, and it continues to be the main variety sold in supermarkets in this country.

Harvesting cinnamon entails stripping the exterior bark and then scraping its interior into strips, or quills, which are sun-dried and ground. Older trees contain the most oils and presumably yield the sharpest spice. "Saigon" cassia cinnamon from Vietnam is usually harvested from 20- to 25-year-old trees of a species containing the most volatile oil of any cinnamon on the market—often more than 3 percent of the total weight of the quill. Indonesian, or Korintji, cinnamon and Chinese cinnamon are harvested from trees younger than 10 years and contain less volatile oil. In cassia trees, the oldest bark, near the base of the trunk, is considered best; bark from the middle of the trunk is of moderate worth, and bark from the top and the branches is regarded as the lowest in quality.

But here's the question: Once the spice is processed and packaged and sprinkled into your food, how much does all this stuff really matter?

Flavor Sources

To find out, we gathered 10 supermarket and mail-order brands. Some jars specifying "Saigon" were more than twice as expensive as containers simply labeled "cinnamon." (In fact, one Saigon brand was a whopping eight times the cost of the cheapest spice in the lineup.) Our tasters then evaluated the spices mixed into applesauce and rice pudding and baked into cinnamon swirl cookies and cinnamon buns.

In every application, tasters declared that three factors mattered most: heat, complexity of flavor, and texture. Our top-ranked cinnamons had a spicy heat that built gradually, complex and balanced clove and floral flavors and aromas, and a fine texture that could not be detected when mixed into food. Lower-ranked cinnamons tasted like Red Hots candy and not much else—their heat hit hard and faded quickly. Some cinnamons were ground finely enough to incorporate smoothly, while others were slightly gritty in both applesauce and rice pudding. Our tasters described low-ranking cinnamons as having no complexity and a conspicuous (and therefore objectionable) texture. Baking—the chief reason most of us buy cinnamon—only brought out the differences: The taste of the lowest-ranked brand was barely discernible in cinnamon cookies, for example, while the two highest-ranked cinnamons retained their heat and complexity.

Chemical Trials

The volatile oils that give cinnamon its distinctive flavor are made up of several chemical compounds. The most dominant of the oils is cinnamaldehyde, which gives cinnamon its heat. Eugenol adds the flavor and aroma of cloves, while linalool adds a floral aroma. We surmised that a good ratio of all three oils is necessary to create strong, complex, well-balanced cinnamon flavor.

To test our theory, we sent cinnamon samples to a laboratory to measure their levels of volatile oils. The results were revealing: Our winning cinnamon, Penzeys Extra Fancy Vietnamese Cassia Cinnamon, had the highest percentage of volatile oils, at nearly 7 percent. Another favorite, Smith and Truslow Freshly Ground Organic Cinnamon (also from Vietnam), was the second highest, at 4.5 percent. Their high levels of volatile oils offered substantial flavor. McCormick Ground Cinnamon, our lowest-ranked contender, had just 2.5 percent volatile oils.

But then came a stealth champ from the supermarket: Durkee Ground Cinnamon, from Indonesia, tied for second place with only 2.9 percent volatile oils. It possessed a complex flavor profile like its Vietnamese counterparts, but contained only slightly more volatile oils than lower-ranked cinnamons. How could this be?

It's a Grind

We learned that much of the volatile oil in *Cinnamomum* bark can be lost during grinding, dissipating under the heat generated by whirring blades, and that eugenol and linalool (responsible for complex aromas) dissipate faster than cinnamaldehyde (source of spicy heat). Lower-ranked cinnamons possessed a higher percentage of cinnamaldehyde because most of the eugenol and linalool burned off during grinding. No wonder they tasted as one-dimensional as Red Hots candy—which, in fact, is flavored with 100 percent cinnamaldehyde.

To avoid this, some spice companies use a cold process called cryogenic grinding, which makes the most of all three types of volatile oils. Cryogenic grinding is a more costly process than ordinary grinding, and Durkee confirmed that its company does, in fact, use this method, preserving more of the potency of the eugenol and linalool and giving its cinnamon a complexity on a par with high-end cinnamons.

Will the Real Cinnamon Please Stand Up?

Curious why much of the world prizes Ceylon cinnamon over cassia cinnamon, the main variety sold in supermarkets in this country, we staged a taste-off. We pitted a pricey Ceylon cinnamon ($3.38 per ounce) from spice purveyor Penzeys against the 10 brands of cassia cinnamon (grown in Vietnam, Indonesia, and China) in our tasting. Sampled in applesauce, the Ceylon cinnamon came in dead last, trounced by far cheaper cassia brands that received lukewarm ratings in the main tasting. What could account for Ceylon's weak showing? To our American taste buds, it just didn't taste like cinnamon. Although it possessed complex clove, citrus, and floral aromas, it lacked the spicy heat tasters expected. Ceylon cinnamon is harvested from the tender young shoots of evergreen trees native to Sri Lanka, from the thinnest inner layer of bark, which contains little volatile oil. As a result, Ceylon cinnamon has delicate flavor and scant heat. The rest of the world may consider this mild-mannered spice the real deal, but we're standing by the more vibrant complexity of cassia cinnamon. –P.C.C.

TASTING CINNAMON

Twenty-one *Cook's Illustrated* staff members tasted 10 brands of cinnamon (two mail-order and eight top-selling supermarket brands, as compiled by the Chicago-based market research firm Information Resources, Inc.), stirred into applesauce and rice pudding and baked into cinnamon swirl cookies and cinnamon buns. The cinnamons appear below in order of preference. Prices were paid in Boston-area supermarkets and online. A source for the winner appears on page 32.

RECOMMENDED

PENZEYS Extra Fancy Vietnamese Cassia Cinnamon
- **Price:** $5.45 for 1.7 ounces ($3.21 per ounce)
- **Origin:** Vietnam
- **Comments:** "Slightly smoky" and filled with complex "warm clove" and "fruity" flavors, its spiciness was "strong, yet not overpowering"; it "started mellow, then built to a spicy finish." "I'm taken to the Far East!" raved one taster of the "warm and fragrant" flavor and aroma. When it was baked into cookies and cinnamon buns, tasters could detect "toasty" flavors and "clove and floral" aromas. It had the most volatile oil of all the cinnamons, at about 7 percent of its total weight.

BEST BUY

DURKEE Ground Cinnamon
- **Price:** $3.50 for 1.75 ounces ($2 per ounce)
- **Origin:** Indonesia
- **Comments:** Nearly tied with the winner, this grocery store cinnamon was "unique," "complex," "woodsy," and "floral." Tasters perceived a "finely ground texture" that "incorporated wonderfully" into food. It reminded tasters of "cloves," "allspice," and "nutmeg." "Very present, but not too pungent," its "warmth lingered in the mouth." Its "fruity, floral" flavors were evident in the cookies and cinnamon buns.

SMITH AND TRUSLOW Freshly Ground Organic Cinnamon
- **Price:** $26 for 3.2 ounces—four 0.8-ounce jars ($8.13 per ounce)
- **Origin:** Vietnam
- **Comments:** Freshly ground to order, this mail-order brand is the most expensive cinnamon in our lineup. Described as "woodsy," "citrusy," and "floral," it was a favorite for a "remarkably sweet" flavor that "gradually gets hotter."

ADAMS Ground Cinnamon
- **Price:** $3.99 for 2.33 ounces ($1.71 per ounce)
- **Origin:** Indonesia and China
- **Comments:** The "sweet," "complex" flavor of this cinnamon from a Texas spice company tasted of "cardamom" and "cloves." Described as "rather fruity," this cinnamon was a little too "floral-tasting" for some. Others sensed a faint flavor of "Red Hots candy."

MORTON & BASSETT Ground Cinnamon
- **Price:** $5.19 for 2.2 ounces ($2.36 per ounce)
- **Origin:** Indonesia
- **Comments:** This "warm" cinnamon had "fruity" and "honey" flavors that made it "easy on the palate." But the "mild cinnamon taste" seemed to "wash out at the end," leaving tasters wanting more spiciness.

RECOMMENDED WITH RESERVATIONS

SAUER'S Ground Cinnamon
- **Price:** $3.50 for 2.25 ounces ($1.56 per ounce)
- **Origin:** Indonesia
- **Comments:** This cinnamon possessed a "peppery," "fragrant" profile, but was "somewhat weak" with "very little heat" and tasted "more floral than spicy." "Reminds me of my grandma's potpourri," commented one taster. Another asked, "Is this true cinnamon?" In sum: "Underwhelming."

SPICE ISLANDS Ground Saigon Cinnamon
- **Price:** $4.75 for 1.9 ounces ($2.50 per ounce)
- **Origin:** Vietnam
- **Comments:** This "sweet and warm" cinnamon with "clove" notes was "pleasant" and "slightly smoky" with "moderate heat" and a "pronounced Red Hots candy flavor" that started strong but "faded quickly." Some tasters noticed a "rather gritty" texture and likened it to "sawdust." Others complained about a "medicinal flavor" and an "artificial" aftertaste.

McCORMICK Gourmet Collection Saigon Cinnamon
- **Price:** $4.69 for 1.87 ounces ($2.51 per ounce)
- **Origin:** Vietnam
- **Comments:** This cinnamon was called "quite strong" and "earthy" by some, but many tasters found it "flat," "one-dimensional," "ho-hum" and "generic," like "Hot Tamales candy" that "doesn't blow my head off." Other tasters felt it was "harsh and bitter," evoking "soap" or even "furniture polish."

TONE'S Ground Cinnamon
- **Price:** $6 for 8 ounces (75 cents per ounce)
- **Origin:** Indonesia
- **Comments:** This "average" cinnamon was described as "muted," "meek," and "dull"—"simply not hot." It initially tasted like "Big Red chewing gum" but then "really mellowed out at the finish." Some tasters noticed a "dusty" quality. Overall, it was "run-of-the-mill" with "very little depth."

McCORMICK Ground Cinnamon
- **Price:** $2.99 for 2.37 ounces ($1.26 per ounce)
- **Origin:** Indonesia
- **Comments:** This cinnamon had a "peppery finish" and possessed a "very assertive," "Red Hots candy" taste, but its "big cinnamon flavor" had "little complexity" that faded when baked in cookies and cinnamon buns. Some tasters detected a "gritty, dusty" texture; others found it "musty" and "stale" with a "chemical flavor and metallic finish."

Eugenol has another interesting attribute: It's a natural anesthetic. In a complex-tasting cinnamon, eugenol briefly acts this way on your palate by slightly numbing the ability to perceive the initial spicy heat of cinnamaldehyde, thus letting other flavors and aromas come through. It then wears off, allowing the heat to arrive as a pleasing aftertaste.

Finally, texture plays a part in flavor perception. Fine grinding exposes more surface area, leaving the spice susceptible to quicker loss of volatile oils as the cinnamon sits in your cupboard. Some manufacturers may choose a coarser grind to increase their cinnamon's shelf life. Durkee's grinding method results in a fine texture that earned it high marks for blending seamlessly into food while still retaining complexity of flavor.

The Bottom Line

Although our tasters had their favorites, most brands of cinnamon rated reasonably well as long as they were fresh (see "Don't Let Your Cinnamon Live On [and On]" at right). Though you may choose to buy our mail-order favorite, Penzeys Extra Fancy Vietnamese Cassia Cinnamon, we'll go for our supermarket Best Buy, Durkee Ground Cinnamon; at more than a dollar less per ounce, it scored only a hair below Penzeys.

Don't Let Your Cinnamon Live On (and On)

Cinnamon is one of those spices that tends to live in your cupboard well beyond the typical 12-month expiration date cited on the label. When we rummaged up a jar predating the 2004 Red Sox comeback, it smelled fine—fragrant and spicy. Then we opened a fresh bottle of the same brand and mixed each into applesauce. The old cinnamon tasted flat and faded. Our advice: If you can't remember when you bought your cinnamon, it's probably time for a new jar. –P.C.C.

EQUIPMENT TESTING | Attachment Issue

In our January/February 2009 issue, we recommended the SideSwipe Spatula Mixer Blade ($24.95), an innovative stand mixer paddle attachment with silicone fins that's a whiz at swiping the sides of the bowl. Without the need to constantly stop the mixer to scrape the bowl, mixing goes much faster. SideSwipe designed the attachment to fit KitchenAid mixers and other brands—but KitchenAid recently declared that the blade strains its motor due to friction from the fins. (To our knowledge, no other mixer manufacturers have stated a similar finding.) If the machine becomes damaged as a result, KitchenAid will void the mixer's warranty.

We hadn't noticed any motor strain when we tested the SideSwipe. But to find out for sure, we turned on two KitchenAid mixers, one with the brand's regular paddle attachment and one with the SideSwipe, and beat identical batches of soft cookie dough for an extended period. After 2½ hours on medium speed, the mixer with the SideSwipe was significantly hotter (by 55 degrees) than the KitchenAid fitted with its own paddle attachment, and the motor was slowing down. But since most times you're not mixing for more than a few minutes, is motor strain really an issue? To find out, we made spritz cookies and proved, once again, that the SideSwipe is more efficient than the KitchenAid paddle—the SideSwipe only took 46 seconds to cream butter and sugar, while the KitchenAid paddle took over three minutes. And when we checked the motor temperatures, the mixer with the KitchenAid paddle was actually 2 degrees hotter than the SideSwipe mixer, since it took longer to cream.

Our conclusion: If you steer clear of stiff bread dough or any recipe requiring extended mixing, the risk of using the SideSwipe appears minimal.

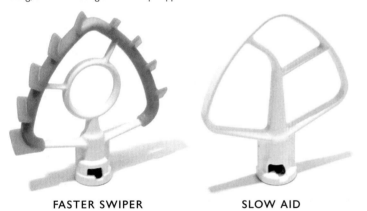

FASTER SWIPER   **SLOW AID**

The fins on the SideSwipe paddle swipe the sides of the bowl clean, speeding up mixing time. (But save it for quickie mixing jobs so you don't risk straining the motor of your KitchenAid.) The KitchenAid paddle is slower at mixing and not as effective at scraping.

TEST KITCHEN TIP | When to Rinse Rice

Do you always need to rinse rice? In the test kitchen, we recommend rinsing long-grain white rice when we want separate, distinct grains. That's because rinsing flushes away excess starch that would otherwise absorb water and swell, causing grains to stick together. To see if this was also true for other types of white rice, we gathered up three of the most common kinds called for in our recipes and cooked them, rinsed and unrinsed, in a few typical applications: We cooked medium-grain, high-starch Arborio rice in risotto, medium-grain rice in rice pudding, and steamed long-grain, low-starch basmati plain. After side-by-side tastings, we confirmed that for steamed rice, where individual grains are the desired result, rinsing improves texture. But for creamy dishes like risotto or rice pudding, rinsing compromises the texture of the finished dish. The bottom line: Unless you want a sticky, creamy texture, rinse your rice.

TECHNIQUE | A BETTER WAY TO SLICE SOFT CAKE

To create perfectly smooth slices of soft desserts such as our Triple-Chocolate Mousse Cake (page 21), the best tool is not a knife. It's a cheese wire—the minimal surface area produces less drag for cleaner, neater slices. (For our recommended brand, see page 32.) If you don't have a cheese wire, dental floss will work almost as well.

1. Hold the handles and pull the wire taut. Using your thumbs to apply even pressure, slice down through the cake. Wipe the wire clean with a dry towel.

2. Make a second cut, perpendicular to the first. Continue to make cuts around the circumference.

TASTING | Dried White Beans

The average supermarket offers a half-dozen varieties of dried white beans. So which should you choose if the recipe doesn't specify? We cooked six varieties in a white bean casserole, a hearty white bean soup, and a simple white bean puree. Our favorites: cannellini and regular white limas. While their flavor differences proved subtle, both share a lush, creamy texture and a large size that translates to a high ratio of interior to skin, so that even skins that cook up slightly tough are less noticeable. Though none of the beans were bad, tasters singled out two types as the lesser whites of the lot: Great Northern, for its slightly chalky texture, and small white, which tasters found bland and starchy. Whenever possible, we'll seek out cannellini and regular white limas.

DRIED BEAN TYPE		FLAVOR	TEXTURE
Cannellini		Buttery with a subtle mushroomlike character	Meaty and lush
Lima		Rich, buttery, with a distinct sweetness and earthiness	Very creamy
Baby lima		Same as regular limas	Very creamy
Navy		Nutty and sweet	Very creamy
Small white		Mild, bland	Starchy
Great Northern		Strong mineral notes	Slightly chalky and mealy

Anise-Flavored Liqueurs

The anise-flavored liqueurs Pernod and pastis are often sipped in cafés in the south of France as well as used interchangeably in many classic recipes for Provençal soups and stews. But unless you do a lot of southern French cooking, a whole bottle of either one could spend years in your liquor cabinet. Would other, slightly more common anise-flavored liqueurs such as Schnapps, sambuca, and ouzo (which you might already have on hand) work just as well? We tried each in our Chicken Bouillabaisse (page 11) as well as a tomato-herb pan sauce to see if any could be swapped in as a suitable substitute. Tasters consistently condemned the sambuca and Schnapps for being far too sweet, but the ouzo proved itself an admirable stand-in, fooling tasters in both dishes. It can be used interchangeably with Pernod and pastis.

LICORICE LIKENESS
Pastis and ouzo share a strong anise flavor and can be used interchangeably in recipes.

Grass-Fed vs. Grain-Fed Beef

Picking out a steak is no longer as simple as choosing the cut, the grade, and whether or not the beef has been aged. Another consideration: the cow's diet. While most American beef is grain-fed, many supermarkets are starting to carry grass-fed options as well.

Grain-fed beef has long been promoted as richer and fattier, while grass-fed beef has gotten a bad rap as lean and chewy with an overly gamey taste. To judge for ourselves, we went to the supermarket and bought 16 grass-fed and 16 grain-fed rib-eye and strip steaks. Because the grass-fed steaks were dry-aged 21 days, we bought the same in the grain-fed meat. When we seared the steaks to medium-rare and tasted them side by side, the results surprised us: With strip steaks, our tasters could not distinguish between grass-fed and grain-fed meat. Tasters did, however, notice a difference in the fattier rib-eyes, but their preferences were split: Some preferred the "mild" flavor of grain-fed beef; others favored the stronger, more complex, "nutty" undertones of grass-fed steaks. None of the tasters noticed problems with texture in either cut.

What accounts for the apparent turnaround in meat that's often maligned? The answer may lie in new measures introduced in recent years that have made grass-fed beef taste more appealing, including "finishing" the beef on forage like clover that imparts a sweeter profile. Perhaps even more significant is that an increasing number of producers have decided to dry-age. This process concentrates beefy flavor and dramatically increases tenderness.

Our conclusion: For non-dry-aged grass-fed beef, the jury is still out over whether it tastes any better (or worse) than grain-fed. But if your grass-fed beef is dry-aged—and if you're okay with fattier cuts like rib-eye that taste a little gamey—you'll likely find the meat as buttery and richly flavored as regular grain-fed dry-aged beef.

TECHNIQUE | MAKING CHOCOLATE CURLS

Wispy chocolate curls are an easy way to decorate desserts like our Triple-Chocolate Mousse Cake (page 21).

Use a vegetable peeler to peel curls off of a large block of milk or dark chocolate. (Large blocks of chocolate make nicer shavings than thin bars of chocolate.)

The Average Egg

Recipes that call for separated eggs can leave you with extra yolks or whites. You can save these leftovers in the fridge, but since yolks are hard to separate from one another (and the whites are impossible), their use is often limited to inexact recipes like scrambled eggs. To solve this dilemma, we weighed dozens of eggs in the four most commonly available sizes and averaged their weights whole as well as separated into yolks and whites. The chart below (and a digital scale) will enable you to use your eggy spare parts even in finicky baking recipes requiring the utmost accuracy.

EGG SIZE	AVERAGE TOTAL WEIGHT	AVERAGE YOLK WEIGHT	AVERAGE WHITE WEIGHT
Medium	1.57 ounces	0.51 ounce	1.06 ounces
Large	1.73 ounces	0.54 ounce	1.19 ounces
X-Large	1.90 ounces	0.57 ounce	1.33 ounces
Jumbo	2.08 ounces	0.63 ounce	1.45 ounces

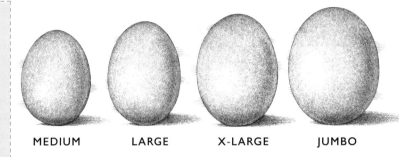

| MEDIUM | LARGE | X-LARGE | JUMBO |

Making the Most of Saffron

Saffron is one of the most expensive spices on the market; one ounce can fetch upward of $150. To that end, we wondered if there are other, more cost-effective ways to extract maximum flavor from pricey threads of saffron, rather than simply crumbling them directly into your dish.

THE EXPERIMENT

We made three batches of *rouille*, a garlicky, saffron-accented sauce that gets stirred into our Chicken Bouillabaisse (page 11), three ways:

Batch 1: All ingredients (saffron, bread crumbs, water, lemon juice, mustard, egg yolk, cayenne pepper, garlic, and oil) combined and rested overnight.
Batch 2: Saffron steeped in 3 tablespoons hot water for 5 minutes before being added to remaining ingredients.
Batch 3: Saffron and remaining ingredients simply stirred together.

THE RESULTS

Batch 3 had a pale yellow color that matched its muted saffron flavor, while both the rested and the steeped batches boasted a deep orange-yellow color and markedly stronger saffron flavor.

THE EXPLANATION

Saffron's flavor compounds are soluble in water, which means it needs the presence of liquid to realize its full aromatic potential. In a rouille, most of the water molecules (from the added water as well as lemon juice and egg yolks) are bound in an emulsion, slowing down the time it takes for the flavor compounds to dissolve fully. Resting the sauce overnight allows this to happen—but steeping the saffron in hot water first achieves the same goal more efficiently. Molecules move faster in hot water than in room-temperature liquid, so they bump into the saffron with greater frequency and force, pulling the soluble flavor compounds into the solution more quickly.

⇒ BY MEREDITH BUTCHER AND PEGGY CHUNG COLLIER ⇐

EQUIPMENT TESTING
Stovetop Waffle Irons

How do manual waffle irons compare to electric waffle makers? We made dozens of waffles on both gas and electric stoves to test six manual stovetop models. We quickly discovered that material matters: Models made of light-colored, shiny metal yielded pale, dry waffles that stuck, while cast-iron wafflers produced waffles with ideal golden color but had sticking issues even after repeated seasoning and oiling. Dark, nonstick metal was king, producing evenly crisp, golden brown waffles that released easily. The top performers were the Nordic Ware Nonstick Stovetop Belgian Waffler ($49.95) and the Coleman Waffle Iron ($19.99), but the Nordic Ware has an edge over the Coleman for its four-waffle capacity versus the Coleman's two. Compared to electric wafflers (which preheat automatically, then cook waffles to a preset degree of doneness), handheld models are less of a no-brainer (the cook has to gauge when the waffler is preheated, manually flip the waffles, then judge when they're done). Still, both produce equally crisp, golden results, and both can be submerged in water for easy cleaning.

STOVETOP WAFFLES
The handheld Nordic Ware Nonstick Stovetop Belgian Waffler produces great results but requires more guesswork than electric models.

NEW PRODUCT
DoneRight Kitchen Timer

If you're cooking for a crowd, with a pot topping each burner and food in the oven, it's hard to keep track of when each dish is done. The 5 in 1 DoneRight Timer ($24.95) offers a clever solution: a stove-shaped device with four individual timers in the position of each burner as well as one for the oven. The timers only clock up to 99 minutes, but we found them easy to use and readable at a glance. While we're not ready to throw away our old favorite, the Polder Dual Timer Stopwatch 893-90 (which is small, portable, and times up to 20 hours), the DoneRight is a useful gadget, especially during the holidays.

GOOD TIMING
The 5 in 1 DoneRight Timer offers five timers to keep track of dishes on the stove and in the oven.

NEW PRODUCT
Jamie Oliver Flavour Shaker

Developed by British celebrity chef Jamie Oliver to crush, grind, and mix an array of ingredients, the dishwasher-safe Flavour Shaker ($29.95) is akin to an enclosed mortar and pestle: You open up the plastic cup, put in whole garlic cloves or spices, close it tight, and shake. Thanks to a heavy Ping-Pong–sized ceramic ball rolling around inside, the ingredients quickly break down. Without much effort, we were able to grind cumin and mustard seeds, crack lots of pepper, and create ¼ cup of salad dressing (first pulverizing garlic, then adding oil and vinegar). We recommend this tool for easy spice crushing and quick dressings.

CELEBRITY CRUSH
Jamie Oliver's Flavour Shaker quickly crushes spices and garlic.

EQUIPMENT TESTING
Baker's Cooling Rack

When you need to cool multiple sheets of cookies, finding enough counter space can be a problem. We tested the Linden Sweden Baker's Mate Cooling Rack ($19.99), which vertically stacks cooling baking sheets. We put hot trays of heavy chocolate chunk oatmeal cookies on the rack and removed them randomly to see if different stacking combinations would cause it to tip. It barely wobbled. Then we stacked four sheet cakes in heavy 13- by 9-inch Pyrex baking dishes. No problems. Shelves are spaced 3¼ inches apart and collapse to fit tall items. The entire unit folds down to a height of 1 inch, making it easy to store. One quibble—each "shelf" is a single metal rod shaped as a 9½-inch rectangle, so it can't hold a pan of brownies baked in an 8-inch square baking pan, because the pan would fall through. But the next time we go on a baking spree, we'll reach for this handy rack.

SPACE SAVER
Linden Sweden Baker's Mate Cooling Rack handily stacks baked goods, plus it folds down for easy storage.

EQUIPMENT TESTING Cheese Wire
A cheese wire is an invaluable tool for cutting through semifirm or soft cheeses. Lately, we've given it a new job: cutting smooth slices of creamy cheesecake and chocolate mousse cake. The Handled Cheese Wire ($2.99) from Fante's eliminates the need to dip your knife in hot water before every slice—a method that's far from foolproof. You simply hold the handles and pull the wire taut, then press down through the cake.

TAKES THE CAKE
Designed to cut cheese wheels, the Handled Cheese Wire from Fante's also excels as a cake cutter.

For complete testing results, go to www.cooksillustrated.com/dec09.

Sources

The following are mail-order sources for items recommended in this issue. Prices were current at press time and do not include shipping. Contact companies to confirm or visit www.cooksillustrated.com for updates.

PAGE 2: WASABI PASTE
- Real Wasabi Paste: $19.95 for six 1.53-ounce tubes, Pacific Farms (800-927-2248, www.freshwasabi.com).

PAGE 15: BASTING SPOON
- Rösle Basting Spoon with Hook Handle: $28.95, item #10062, Chef's Resource (866-765-2433, www.chefsresource.com).

PAGE 27: CHEF'S KNIVES
- Masamoto VG-10 Gyutou 8.2": $136.50, item #HMA-CG50, Korin (800-626-2172, www.korin.com).
- Misono UX-10 Gyutou 8.2": $156, item #HMI-71G, Korin.
- Victorinox Forschner Fibrox 8" Chef's Knife: $24.95, item #40520, Chef's Resource (www.chefsresource.com, 800-765-2433).

PAGE 29: CINNAMON
- Penzeys Extra Fancy Vietnamese Cassia Cinnamon: $5.45 for 1.7 ounces, item #43258, Penzeys Spices (800-741-7787, www.penzeys.com).

PAGE 30: SPATULA MIXER BLADE
- SideSwipe Spatula Mixer Blade: $24.95, item #KTH-1, Frut LLC (www.sideswipeblade.com).

PAGE 32: WAFFLE IRONS
- Nordic Ware Nonstick Stovetop Belgian Waffler: $49.95, item #164023, Cooking.com (800-663-8810, www.cooking.com).
- Coleman Waffle Iron: $19.99, item #807-804T, Coleman (800-835-3278, www.coleman.com).

PAGE 32: TIMER
- Tuscan Concepts 5 in 1 DoneRight Timer: $24.95, item #692043, Cooking.com.

PAGE 32: SHAKER
- Jamie Oliver Flavour Shaker: $29.95, item #J21100EXP, Cutlery and More (800-650-9866, www.cutleryandmore.com).

PAGE 32: BAKER'S COOLING RACK
- Linden Sweden Baker's Mate Cooling Rack: $19.99, item #24453, Chef's Catalog (800-338-3232, www.chefscatalog.com).

PAGE 32: CHEESE WIRE
- Handled Cheese Wire: $2.99, item #97959, Fante's Kitchen Wares Shop (800-443-2683, www.fantes.com).

INDEX
November & December 2009

RECIPES

Triple-Chocolate Mousse Cake, 21

Horseradish-Crusted Beef Tenderloin, 9

Pan-Seared Scallops, 15

French Pork and White Bean Casserole, 19

📷 **COOK'S VIDEOS** Original Test Kitchen Videos www.cooksillustrated.com

MAIN DISHES
- How to Make Chicken
  Bouillabaisse
- Maximizing the flavor of saffron

- How to Make Duck Confit

- How to Make French Pork and
  White Bean Casserole

- How to Make Horseradish-
  Crusted Beef Tenderloin

- How to Make Old-Fashioned
  Stuffed Turkey

- How to Make Pan-Seared Scallops
- Dry versus wet scallops
- Preparing scallops for cooking

SIDE DISHES
- How to Make Crisp Roasted
  Potatoes

- How to Make Sautéed Peas with
  Shallot and Mint

DESSERTS
- How to Make Best Shortbread

- How to Make Triple-Chocolate
  Mousse Cake
- How to slice a soft cake
- Making chocolate curls

TESTING
- Behind the Scenes: Testing Hybrid
  Chef's Knives
- Using an Asian knife sharpener

Old-Fashioned Stuffed Turkey, 7

Crisp Roasted Potatoes, 13

Sautéed Peas with Shallot and Mint, 24

AMERICA'S TEST KITCHEN
Public television's most popular cooking show

Join the millions of home cooks who watch
our show, *America's Test Kitchen*, on public
television every week. For more information,
including recipes and program times, visit
www.americastestkitchen.com.

Chicken Bouillabaisse, 11

Best Shortbread, 23

Christmas Pudding

Bûche de Noël

King Cake

Mooncake

Honey Cake

Fruitcake

Makowiec

Pain d'épices

HOLIDAY CAKES